Cambridge Studies in Biological and Evolutionary
Evolving Human Nutrition

While most of us live our lives according to time schedules of the working week, we did not evolve to be bound by industrial schedules, nor did the food we eat. Despite this, we eat the products of industrialization, and often suffer as a consequence. This book considers different aspects of changing human nutrition from both evolutionary and social perspectives. It considers what a 'natural' human diet might be, how it may have been shaped across evolutionary time, and how we have adapted to respond to changing food availability.

The transition from hunting and gathering and the rise of agriculture through to the industrialization and globalization of diet are explored. Far from being adapted to a 'Stone Age' diet, humans can consume a vast range of foodstuffs. However, being able to eat anything doesn't mean that we should eat everything, and engagement with the evolutionary underpinnings of diet and factors influencing it is key to better public health practice.

STANLEY ULIJASZEK is Professor of Human Ecology and Director of the Unit for Biocultural Variation and Obesity, both at the University of Oxford, and Vice-Master, St Cross College, Oxford. His work on nutritional ecology and anthropology has involved fieldwork and research in Papua New Guinea, the Cook Islands and South Asia, while his interests in dietary transitions have led him to examine the evolutionary basis of obesity.

NEIL MANN is Professor of Nutritional Biochemistry and head of the Food Science department at RMIT University in Melbourne, Australia. He has worked extensively on the nutritional biochemistry of fatty acids and has led several nutritional clinical trials investigating the role of altered macronutrient dietary balance in diseases related to western lifestyle, including acne and diabetes.

SARAH ELTON is Reader in Anatomy at the Hull York Medical School. She works on the ecological context for human evolution, with a focus on primate morphology, biogeography, ecology and evolution. Alongside her research into primates, she has written on evolutionary approaches to human diet, reproduction and medical education.

Cambridge Studies in Biological and Evolutionary Anthropology

Series editors

HUMAN ECOLOGY
C. G. Nicholas Mascie-Taylor, University of Cambridge
Michael A. Little, State University of New York, Binghamton
GENETICS
Kenneth M. Weiss, Pennsylvania State University
HUMAN EVOLUTION
Robert A. Foley, University of Cambridge
Nina G. Jablonski, Penn State University
PRIMATOLOGY
Karen B. Strier, University of Wisconsin, Madison

Evolving Human Nutrition

Implications for Public Health

STANLEY J. ULIJASZEK

Institute of Social and Cultural Anthropology
University of Oxford, UK

NEIL MANN

Discipline of Food Science
School of Applied Sciences
RMIT University, Melbourne, Australia

SARAH ELTON

Hull York Medical School
University of Hull, UK

CAMBRIDGE
UNIVERSITY PRESS

CAMBRIDGE UNIVERSITY PRESS
Cambridge, New York, Melbourne, Madrid, Cape Town,
Singapore, São Paulo, Delhi, Mexico City

Cambridge University Press
The Edinburgh Building, Cambridge CB2 8RU, UK

Published in the United States of America by Cambridge University Press, New York

www.cambridge.org
Information on this title: www.cambridge.org/9781107692664

First published 2012
First paperback edition 2013

A catalogue record for this publication is available from the British Library

Library of Congress Cataloguing in Publication Data
Ulijaszek, Stanley J.
Evolving human nutrition : implications for public health / Stanley Ulijaszek, Neil Mann,
Sarah Elton.
 p. cm. – (Cambridge studies in biological and evolutionary anthropology ; 64)
 ISBN 978-0-521-86916-4 (Hardback)
 1. Human evolution. 2. Prehistoric peoples–Food. 3. Human behavior–Nutritional
aspects. 4. Food habits–History. 5. Diet–History. 6. Nutrition–History. I. Mann,
Neil. II. Elton, Sarah. III. Title.
 GN281.U55 2012
 599.93´8–dc23

 2012008941

ISBN 978-0-521-86916-4 Hardback
ISBN 978-1-107-69266-4 Paperback

Contents

The authors

Stanley Ulijaszek is Professor of Human Ecology at the University of Oxford and Director of the Unit for Biocultural Variation and Obesity. His work on nutritional ecology and anthropology has involved fieldwork and research in Papua New Guinea, the Cook Islands and South Asia, while his interests in dietary transitions have led him to examine the evolutionary basis and cultural drivers of obesity.

Neil Mann is Professor of Nutritional Biochemistry at RMIT University in Melbourne, Australia. He has worked extensively on the nutritional biochemistry of fatty acids and has written extensively on evolution and human nutrition, with many of the other leaders in this field.

Sarah Elton is Reader in Anatomy at the Hull York Medical School. She works on the ecological context for human evolution, with a focus on primate morphology, biogeography, ecology and evolution. She teaches evolutionary anatomy, anthropology and evolutionary medicine to medical students. Alongside her research into primates, she has written on evolutionary approaches to human diet, reproduction, medical education and medicine more broadly.

Acknowledgements

The ideas that led to this book came from many sources, and we thank Robert Attenborough, Barry Bogin, Claude Fischler, Colin Groves, Maciej Henneberg, Jeya Henry, John Krebs, Tony McMichael, Randolph Nesse, Ryutaro Ohtsuka, Stephen Oppenheimer, Nellie Phoca-Cosmetatou, Kate Pickett, Andrew Prentice, David Raubenheimer, Steve Simpson and Andrew Whiten for comments and suggestions at various stages of the project. We thank Robin Dunbar, Wolfgang Enard, Keith Frayn, Michael Goran, Karen Hardy, Francis Johnston, Julia Lee-Thorp, Staffan Lindeberg, Barry Popkin, Caroline Potter, Tom Saunders, Andy Sinclair, Nicolas Timpson and Peter Ungar for their critical reviews of various chapters. We also thank all the behind-the-scenes workers at Cambridge University Press, and especially Lynn Davy, for helping make this book happen.

1 *Introduction*

Is another book on evolution and the human diet needed? We think so, largely because we know a lot more about the subject than we did just over a quarter of a century ago, when Eaton and Konner (1985) put forward their idea of the 'Stone Age diet'. By collating and quantifying nutrient intakes of contemporary hunter-gatherer groups and showing how similar they were to dietary recommendations for the prevention of chronic diseases, they identified dietary ideals for good health that deviated from the practice of developing dietary norms from foods that are currently available (but not necessarily ideal). While the imposition of a 'Stone Age' ascription to contemporary hunter-gatherer diets is a problematic aspect of their argument, their work was an important deviation from usual nutrition practice. It freed nutritional theorists to think beyond the ecology of food within their particular locale or nation. Public health nutritionists now think broadly about the challenges faced by populations in a rapidly transforming and globalizing world, from trying to construct good nutrition from what the food system delivers, to thinking about what type of food system would deliver the best nutrition. Food production, supply, consumption and education is highly political, and contemporary approaches to public health nutrition may also stress this: various food guide pyramids for the United States (US) have been deconstructed, for example, as representing political, rather than health, interests (Nestle 2002).

Various reformulations of the 'Stone Age diet' theme (Eaton *et al.* 1988; 2002; Milton 2000a; Cordain *et al.* 2000a) have been made across the years that followed Eaton and Konner's (1985) original work. Methods and the ideas they inform move on, however, and recent developments in palaeoanthropology, population genetics and epidemiology mean increasing certainty about evolutionary processes related to diet, the time-frames in which they took place, and how they inform our knowledge of contemporary human diet. The 'Stone Age' (often taken to be synonymous with the archaeological Palaeolithic period and the geological Pleistocene epoch) is broadly the period

1

in human prehistory from the first appearance of stone tools around 2.6 million years ago to the origins of agriculture (around 10 000 years ago), when people lived in foraging (hunting and gathering) societies. But the diets and subsistence strategies of the hominin and primate ancestors of *Homo sapiens* had already been shaped across the millions of years before then. While much of human nutrition is clearly biological, explanations in this domain usually stop at proximal levels, such as the biochemistry of nutrient requirements and the physiology of energy balance. Up-stream, or more distal, answers to questions such as 'why do humans have a requirement for vitamin C, while most other mammals do not?', and 'why are human protein requirements much lower than those of non-human primates?' are rarely addressed. These are more fundamental questions which can help frame expectations of human physiological responses to diet and dietary change, especially in contemporary societies that are undergoing rapid transformations in the quality and quantity of foods available.

The field of evolutionary medicine frames human illness, disorder and pathology in a distinct evolutionary framework. It emphasizes that diseases arise from the inevitable compromises of an evolved body interacting with novel environments (Nesse 2008). Many advocates of evolutionary medicine view present-day environments as changing faster than human physiology can (Eaton *et al.* 2002). Since human form and function change but slowly and must respond to rapidly altering dietary circumstances, it is important to understand both the evolutionary baggage that humans carry, and the nutritional changes created by the social and economic transformations that they undergo.

Human societies have undergone many transformations, most of which have seen changes in dietary and nutritional circumstances. The Neolithic transformation, for example, was characterized by radical economic, societal and technological change that eventually saw agriculture become the dominant subsistence practice for the majority of the world's populations. European exploration and political expansion from the fifteenth century onwards saw New World plants like tomato, capsicum and potato enter European diets, and European cereal-based crops and livestock such as cattle and sheep enter the Americas. Seventeenth century globalization saw cosmopolitan diets emerge in all places affected by colonialism. With the industrial revolution, urbanization saw dietary transformation on a scale previously unknown, including the emergence of fast foods and convenience foods. Globalization in the late twentieth century has seen the amplification of earlier cosmopolitanization of diets and the rapid spread of fast and convenience foods.

Human genomes, which have been shaped over hundreds of thousands of generations, interact with the new food environments created by these processes on a daily basis. Any discussion of dietary evolution and dissonance between the human genome and contemporary diet is only half-informed if the creation of new food environments is not considered. Thus we engage with a range of theoretical perspectives, including theories of class, capital, globalization, networks and inequality, as well as human and hominin evolution, biochemistry and nutrition. Disciplinary boundaries make the combined study of these aspects of diet and nutritional health very difficult. We therefore resist any claim of a seamless account of diet and nutrition in human evolutionary and social context. Rather, we have striven to identify disciplinary intersections that are susceptible to collaborative investigation and understanding.

This book considers different aspects of changing human nutrition from evolutionary and social perspectives, and identifies the importance of up-to-date knowledge of human evolution and social theory to public health nutrition practice. The book is framed in three parts: *The Animal Within*; *A Brave New World*; and *Once Upon a Time in the West*. In the first part, we consider what a 'natural' human diet might be and how it may have been shaped across evolutionary time (Chapters 2 and 3), and the extent to which human plasticity in response to changing food availability is a baseline adaptation, especially in relation to climatic seasonality (Chapter 4). We also examine the transition in subsistence from hunter-gatherer to agricultural forms of economic life (Chapter 5). In the second part, we discuss the problems of nutritional ill-health created by the dietary change associated with this transition (Chapter 6). We also examine the new nutritional challenges that came with the emergence of new infectious diseases and the increased intensity of infection of existing pathogens (Chapter 7), and the social and economic inequality (Chapter 8) that came after the emergence of agriculture. In the third part, we discuss the modern intensification of food production and its consequences for nutritional health among contemporary nation states. Nutrition transition (Chapter 9) and the high levels of consumption of fats (Chapter 10) and refined carbohydrates (Chapter 11) are all associated with the high prevalence of the relatively recently emerged disorders of cardiovascular disease (CVD) and Type 2 diabetes, as well as a number of cancers. The three parts that form this book are more usually considered separately. However, there is enough understanding of diet and nutrition from a wide range of perspectives to bring these fields together, and this is what we try to do. Before giving a brief outline of the various chapters, it is useful to consider human nutrition within a biological framework that incorporates genetics, physical plasticity and epigenetic change as interactive adaptations to dietary circumstances.

Nutrition, genetics, physical plasticity and epigenetics

Subsistence provides food; food provides nutrition. Nutrients variously supply energy, promote growth and repair of bodily tissues and regulate bodily processes. The requirement for nutrients varies across species, between populations and from individual to individual. All mammals, humans and other primates among them, need a mix of macronutrients and micronutrients (Figure 1.1). Macronutrients include the energy-containing substances carbohydrates, lipids and proteins as well as water and fibre; micronutrients comprise vitamins and minerals. In public health nutrition, the nutritional adequacy of a diet is determined by the extent to which it matches or surpasses the recommended daily allowance (RDA) for various nutrients. This is a population-based statistical estimate of nutrient requirements, based on the premise that, for most nutrients apart from energy, it is sufficient to meet the needs of 98% of healthy individuals in a given population (Kennedy and Meyers 2005). The RDA is set at two standard deviations above the mean for normally distributed nutrient requirements because this takes account of biological variability in individual physiological requirements for different nutrients.

A large proportion of biological variability in nutrient requirement is due to genetic variation that controls the production of enzymes that in turn control the absorption, distribution, retention and utilization of different nutrients (Molloy 2004). Furthermore, genes and gene products act on, or are acted upon, by nutrients, and shape the optimal nutrient intakes of any individual (Stover and Caudill 2008). Individuals with different polymorphisms in genes coding for the metabolism of any nutrient (via hormones and enzymes) can have different physiological outcomes at equal levels of intake of a particular

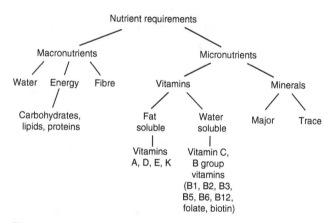

Figure 1.1. Generalized nutrient typology for mammals.

nutrient. Some of these outcomes may be associated with disease. For example, polymorphisms in genes encoding enzymes involved in folate metabolism influence physiological processes that can lead to aging, cancers and CVD, largely because of the involvement of folate in DNA methylation (Friso and Choi 2002; Ulrich 2005). Alternatively, different apolipoprotein E (ApoE) isoforms (different forms of the same lipoprotein molecule) that are variously involved in fat transport and metabolism are associated with different levels of risk of developing atherosclerosis. Individuals with at least one allele for ApoE4 have an increased chance of developing this condition relative to those with either E2 or E3 isoforms (Greenow *et al.* 2005), as the former predisposes individuals to serum cholesterol elevation on high fat diets (Tikkanen *et al.* 1990). Those with the ApoE4 isoform also have greater reductions in LDL cholesterol with reduced intake of saturated fat and cholesterol than individuals with either the E2 or E3 isoform (Krauss 2001).

Another type of human variability is due to phenotypic plasticity that permits exploitation of changing and changeable environments. For example, human children can undergo growth faltering due to poor food availability and exposure to infection, and show catch-up growth when these stresses are removed. This was probably an adaptation acquired in human evolutionary history in response to seasonal environments, by tuning body size and proportion to food available within any ecosystem (Chapter 4). This remains a fundamental phenotypic response to poor food security across the less developed world in the present-day. However, it may have become maladaptive in parts of the contemporary world experiencing epidemiological and nutrition transition where plastic responses to poor early life environments have left individuals and populations at greater risk of chronic disease later in life. Epidemiological studies and animal dietary interventions show that maternal nutritional imbalance and metabolic disturbances during critical time windows of development have a persistent effect on the health of the offspring and are likely to be transmitted to the next generation (Gallou-Kabani and Junien 2005). The 'developmental origins of health and disease' concept hypothesizes that chronic diseases that develop later in life originate *in utero* by environmental fetal programming (Barker *et al.* 1992, 2002). Otherwise known as the 'thrifty phenotype' hypothesis, it proposes that during development *in utero*, a child's physiology responds to nutritional shortages with metabolic adaptations that will maximize its later survival in an environment of chronic food shortage. Such individuals will have smaller body size and lowered metabolic rate. However, if such children go on to live and grow in an environment of ample food energy, they will be more likely to develop metabolic disorders, such as obesity, Type 2 diabetes and the metabolic syndrome (Robinson *et al.* 2007).

Stoeger (2008) suggests that the mechanism for the developmental origins of health and disease model is an epigenetic one during early development. As a new synthesis of the thrifty genotype (Neel 1962) and thifty phenotype (Hales and Barker 1992) hypotheses for explaining the rapid emergence of obesity and diabetes among the world's populations, he put forward the 'thrifty epigenotype' hypothesis. In this formulation, metabolic thrift (the capacity for efficient acquisition, storage and use of energy) is seen as an ancient, complex genetic trait, which is encoded by a gene network that is canalized or channelled in a specific direction, such that it is robust against individual mutations and is able to produce the same phenotype in a population regardless of variability in environment and genotype. DNA sequence polymorphisms are seen to play a minor role in the aetiology of obesity and Type 2 diabetes; rather, susceptibilities to these two disorders are seen as being predominantly due to inherited changes in the phenotype or gene expression during the early development of bodily tissues and organs. Epigenetic changes also increase susceptibility to CVD (Waterland 2009) and play a major role in cancer formation (Esteller 2008). Epigenetic changes related to chromatin remodelling and regulation of gene expression have been identified as likely factors involved in the developmental programming of metabolic syndrome (Gallou-Kabani and Junien 2005), as characterized by disturbances in glucose and insulin metabolism, excess abdominal fat mass, dyslipidemia (abnormal amounts of cholesterol and other fats in the blood) and hypertension. Fetal under-nutrition (often manifested as low birth weight) and maternal over-nutrition (in the case of a diabetic mother) increase the future risk of Type 2 diabetes (Yajnik and Deshmukh 2008).

Across recent decades, clinical signs of obesity, Type 2 diabetes and metabolic syndrome have started to appear in childhood, have become more severe from generation to generation, and have come to affect increasing numbers of pregnant women across time. Thus, on top of direct factors like inadequate maternal nutrition, individuals with metabolic syndrome may display trans-generational effects by way of incomplete erasure of epigenetic factors carried by parents and grandparents (Gallou-Kabani and Junien 2005). Epigenetic regulation during fetal programming of the individual in preparation for the environment they expect to enter is likely to be a response to seasonal energy imbalance; changes that favour metabolic efficiency are likely to be adaptive in such circumstances. Removal of seasonal energy stress, as has taken place in contemporary industrialized societies, may turn this efficiency towards pathology. Humans thus have an evolved animal model that can respond genetically (through natural selection), phenotypically (through developmental plasticity) and epigenetically (by a balance of both) to changing dietary and nutritional circumstances. Given this baseline set of adaptations, we can explore how they evolved among the primates (including hominins and humans) and how they may have predisposed (and may continue to predispose) to nutritional ill-health or related pathologies past and present.

The animal within

'Stone Age' diets have captured the public imagination because they instruct us in how we might have deviated from a supposed natural diet that we are adapted to eat. In times of rapid change and uncertainty, as with the rapid emergence of chronic disease in the late twentieth century, it is comfortable to hark to a past age when things are thought to have been ideal. But such an ideal past is very unlikely to have existed: there is no 'Garden of Eden' diet. Rather, humans, and ancestral hominins before them, are more likely to have muddled through with their diets and adaptations to them. It is precisely this muddle that we attempt to understand better in writing this book.

   To understand the type of diets that contemporary humans may be adapted to biologically, we need to dig deeper than the 'Stone Age', since many of the attributes of our hominin ancestors, including their diets and behaviours associated with foraging and feeding, were established well before then (Elton 2008a). New methods and perspectives, especially in genetics, epigenetics, archaeological science, network analysis and anthropology, permit this in a way that was not possible 25 years ago. In digging deeper in this book, we use an evolutionary ecology framework (Ulijaszek 2002) to examine relationships between mammals, primates, and extinct hominins with respect to their various subsistence environments and adaptations – morphological, physiological and genetic – to them (Chapters 2 and 3). Biologically, humans are primates. The understanding of what natural human diets might be is therefore helped by comparison with modern primates and the types of dietary constraints they live with, including seasonal ones (Chapter 4).

   Great species diversity is evident in the human family tree over time (Figure 1.3). The profound morphological differences in hominin skulls, teeth and skeletons hint at considerable interspecific dietary diversity (Chapter 3). As well as diversity between species, the human propensity for intra-specific, and even intra-individual, dietary flexibility probably also has relatively deep evolutionary roots (Chapter 3). Environments change from moment to moment, across the day, across the year, and across decades, centuries and millennia. Humans (and other mammals) are adapted to cope with environmental change and variation. Diet reflects environmental change in its seasonality and year-on-year variation (Chapter 4). Dietary diversity and flexibility were important prerequisites for hominin dispersals out of the tropics, and for

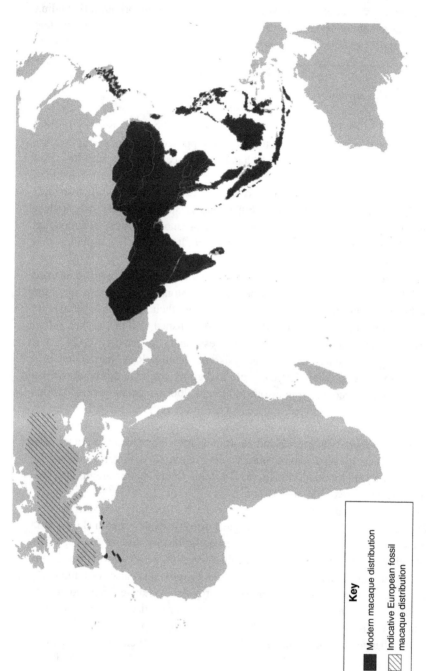

Figure 1.2. Global distribution of macaques.

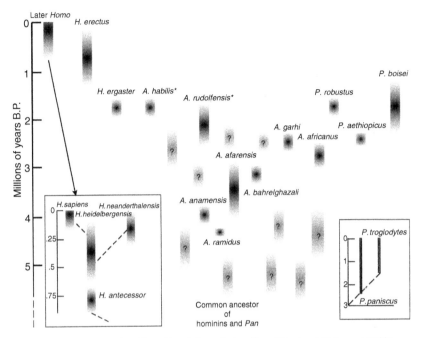

Figure 1.3. Time-line of hominin evolution (from Wood and Richmond 2000). Horizontal axis separates species according to the relative size of brain and chewing teeth. Taxa with large molar and premolar crowns are to the right, while those with smaller postcanine teeth are to the left. The hypothetical taxa marked with a question mark indicate that in the less explored period of between 2 and 6 million years ago, the number of taxa are likely to increase. Although the two taxa marked with asterisks are, or have been, conventionally assigned to *Homo*, it is likely that they are more closely related to *Australopithecus* species.

their exploitation of all the major biomes. Human dispersal across the world far surpasses the colonizing abilities seen even in that most tenacious of primates, the macaque (Figure 1.4). Members of the papionin genus *Macaca*, macaques are the only living non-human wild primates to be found in temperate as well as tropical latitudes. Figure 1.2 gives the geographical distribution of different living and extinct macaque species, showing them to range from North Africa into south, east and north Asia as far as Taiwan and Japan, and in the past to have lived in many parts of Europe. Considering what macaques eat and how they obtain this food, as discussed in Chapter 2 alongside data for other non-human primates, allows human dietary adaptation to be viewed through a broader comparative lens.

Whereas most primates are tropical animals, humans are cosmopolitan, inhabiting not only the tropics but also much higher latitudes, including above

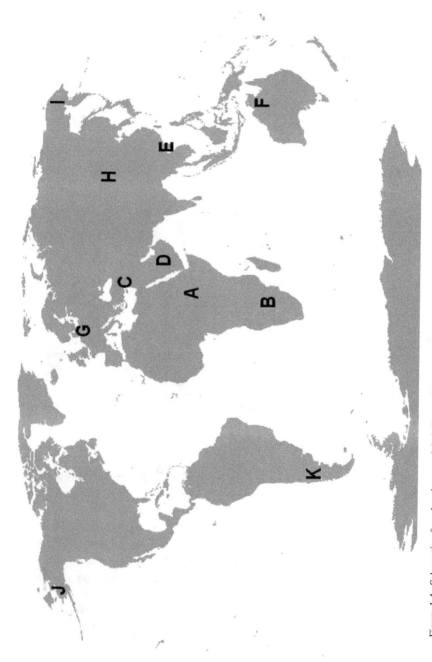

Figure 1.4. Schematic of modern human global dispersal. Data taken from Dillehay *et al.* 2008; Goebel 1999; Moodley *et al.* 2009; Oppenheimer 2009; Beyin 2011.

A	Modern humans originated in Africa between 200 000 and 150 000 years ago, with the earliest human remains recovered from East Africa. The evolution and dispersals of modern humans were complex, with DNA evidence for inbreeding with earlier, archaic humans including European Neanderthals and the Denisovans from northern Asia.
B	Archaeological and palaeontological evidence indicates that modern humans were present in southern Africa prior to 100 000 years ago. Some molecular data suggest that modern humans originated in southern Africa, but this is yet to be demonstrated unequivocally.
C	One of the earliest dispersals of modern humans occurred via the Levant around 90 000 to 130 000 years ago, as indicated by the fossils from Skhul and Qafzeh. These populations do not appear to have left a signal in the contemporary human gene pool.
D	One probable dispersal route for modern humans out of Africa was via the Bab al Mandab Strait on a landbridge at times of low sea level, into Arabia. The populations that eventually colonized southeast Asia may have left Africa by this route around 85 000 years ago.
E	Molecular data indicate that modern humans spread rapidly into southeast Asia, with populations arriving possibly as early as 75 000 years ago.
F	Australia was probably colonized around 60 000 years ago, based on genetic estimates, with the first fossils, from southern Australia, dated to about 50 000 years ago.
G	Modern humans entered Europe from Asia around 46 000–50 000 years ago, based on molecular, archaeological and palaeontological evidence.
H	Molecular data suggest that modern humans spread into the Asian interior around 40 000 years ago. The possible modern human mandible from Zhirendong in China, dated to 100 000 years ago, may represent an earlier wave of modern human dispersal that did not contribute to the contemporary human gene pool.
I	Based on archaeological evidence, modern humans had occupied western Beringia (the landmass linking Asia and America at low sea level) by 32 000 years ago, soon after they moved into high subarctic and arctic Siberia and Russia.
J	The earliest unequivocal archaeological evidence for human occupation of eastern Beringia is dated to 14 000 years ago, with human coprolites dated to a little earlier, and molecular data indicating a rapid human migration into the Americas around 15 000 years ago, after the contraction of glacial ice sheets that had previously been a barrier.
K	Human artifacts from Chile, dated to around 14 000 years ago, indicate that the spread of humans into continental North America and South America was rapid.
L	Molecular analysis of the bacteria *Helicobacter pylori*, a parasite of humans, indicates that humans colonized the islands of Polynesia from southeast Asia around 5000 years ago, although the less distant islands of Melanesia were colonized much earlier, 30 000–40 000 years ago.

Figure 1.4. (*cont.*)

the Arctic Circle, a geographic range unknown in any other modern or extinct primate. Humans have used their technological abilities to harvest, process and consume a very wide range of foods, including meat, to help inhabit this very wide range of environments (Elton 2008b). Dietary eclecticism has been profound in shaping human evolutionary history and has allowed humans to exploit varied and variable environments, just as it does now in many Old World monkey species, including macaques. Dietary flexibility is enabled genetically, and it has been critical to human evolutionary success. Gut anatomy is one phylogenetically determined trait essential to feeding success (Chapter 2). The human gut largely follows the general primate plan, but the larger small intestine and the smaller large intestine suggest adaptation to a higher-quality, or higher-energy-density, diet. Meat-eating may have been a selective pressure for this change, starting around the time of *Homo erectus* (Figure 1.3).

Although humans can eat most things, they vary greatly in their food preferences between and within societies. In Chapter 5 we examine how human food choices and diets have evolved, and how eating behaviours that favour consumption of foods that are either sweet or fatty now emerge as being detrimental to human well-being. Primates, humans included, select food by using vision, smell and taste to discriminate palatable from less palatable potential food items (Ulijaszek 2002). The ability of all mammals to enjoy and want sweetness is separate from Pavlovian learning to consume sweet things (Smith *et al.* 2011) and is likely to have evolved in response to the emergence of fruit and honey as food sources at the time of angiosperm (flowering plant) diversification between 275 and 65 million years ago (Friis *et al.* 2010; Magallón 2010). Their consumption would have been driven physiologically by the need for dietary energy. This drive is common to all mammals, but humans have the most highly developed neocortical regulation of appetite and food intake. Hominin encephalization (increased brain to body size, across evolutionary time) mostly involved increases in the size of the neocortex, and later hominins (humans among them) were able to apply aspects of sensory perception, thought and language to the production of associative pleasure with food in ways not possible by other mammals.

Without a large neocortex, humans could not have elaborated cuisines, not only because cooking can be a complex process involving a range of technologies, but also because the neurophysiology for discerning different qualities among foods and appreciating them in an associative manner would not exist. However, the human neocortex allows much more than associative pleasure in food (and other things); it allows complex sociality, intelligence and enskilled engagement with the world and other people through objects (Ingold and Vergunst 2007). Through sociality and kinship, humans have formed societies which undergo change and transformation. Foods and their use also undergo change, whether for nutrition, social or symbolic reasons. These usages result in the production of nutritional health, or nutritional ill-health, often as a side product of social transactions and consumptions.

Our brave new world

For most of human evolutionary history, people have been foragers, subsisting on plants and animals gathered and hunted in the wild. It is only in the past 10 000 years or so that human populations have produced food themselves, growing and rearing domesticated plants and animals in or near to permanent settlements. The eating and foraging behaviours of humans, as one of several primates with the ability and inclination to exploit a wide range of food resources (Chapter 2), were important pre-requisites for the move to food production. Theories to explain the origins of agriculture range from abrupt climate change (Childe 1936) to feasting and social display (Hayden 2009). Regardless of its motivating force, the origin of agriculture was the key evolutionary transformation in the history of our species (Winterhalder and Kennett 2009), with broad-reaching dietary change. Within the evolutionary medicine literature, the origin of agriculture tends to be seen as the primary point at which dietary 'adaptation' switches to 'maladaptation' within humans (Eaton *et al.* 1998; Eaton and Eaton 1999).

Agriculture originated independently in several parts of the world, with the best-known early agricultural sites, dated to around 10 000 years ago, being found in the Fertile Crescent in the Near East. Here, the founder crops were einkorn and emmer wheat, barley, lentils, peas, flax, bitter vetch, chickpea and possibly fava (broad) beans (Brown *et al.* 2009). In eastern China, the origin of rice cultivation in paddy fields, and domestication of pigs, dates to around 8000 years ago (Zong *et al.* 2007). Bananas and taro formed major parts of diets in New Guinea by 10 000 years ago, with domestication of the banana having taken place by around 7000 years ago (Sandweiss 2007). In Mesoamerica, the cultivation of squash and maize originated over 8000 years ago (Piperno *et al.* 2009). In South America, potato, peanut and manioc were early domesticated crops (Brown *et al.* 2009), with manioc cultivation possibly having been undertaken around 8000 years ago (Price 2009). In many of these regions, animal domestication also occurred at similar times. The dog, not usually a source of food for humans, was likely to have been the first large animal to live routinely alongside them, with estimates for dog domestication varying widely but probably first occurring between around 12 000 and 14 000 years ago (reviewed in Dobney and Larson 2006). Sheep, pigs and cattle were other species that were domesticated early, with the best estimates of sheep and pig domestication in the near east being around 12 000 and 9000 years ago respectively, with cattle following at about 8000 years ago (Dobney and Larson 2006).

The process of domestication took many generations and was very probably a gradual process rather than a rapid, dramatic event. Humans are pragmatic, adaptable and behaviourally flexible. In modern populations, the boundary between foraging and cultivation is often blurred (Ellen 1991), and there is no good reason to dismiss similar flexibility in past populations. Well before the earliest evidence of 'true' agriculture, human populations exhibited behaviours, including dog domestication, seed processing, fine control of fire, division of labour and food sharing, that formed important precursors of an agrarian existence (Belfer-Cohen and Goring-Morris 2009; Pearsall 2009). Storage of food is often viewed as a Neolithic innovation and a key element in the development of agrarian economies, but the earliest evidence for pots significantly pre-dates the Neolithic (Boaretto *et al.* 2009). The earliest fired ceramic storage vessels come from China, dated to around 18 000 years ago (Boaretto *et al.* 2009), while pots dated to around 16 000 years ago have been found in Japan and the far east of Russia (Kuzmin 2006).

Since the process of domestication itself takes time, populations would have shifted their subsistence methods relatively slowly. Initially, domesticated animals would have differed little in size and shape from their wild ancestors, and the earliest changes in their characteristics would have been subtle (Dobney and Larson 2006). Numerous human modifications that pre-dated agriculture included selection of plant species and morphologies (such as larger grain in non-shattering ears), land preparation, and refinement of cultivation practices (Brown *et al.* 2009). Once established in the Fertile Crescent, agriculture spread through Europe, very probably through the movement of people rather than cultural adoption (Pinhasi *et al.* 2005; Balaresque *et al.* 2010). This diffusion took 3000 to 4000 years to reach northwest Europe (Balaresque *et al.* 2010). A long period of transition to agriculture is also seen in the tropical area of Latin America (Pearsall 2009). Foraging persisted in many cultivating populations across the world, with domesticated crops and animals often supplementing wild-gathered and -caught foods (*sensu* Zong *et al.* 2007).

A great deal has been written about the decline in health in early agricultural populations (reviewed in Lambert 2009) but often small numbers of case studies are used and extrapolated to all emerging agricultural societies, with few contemporaneous foraging populations being examined (Elton 2008a). It may well be that many populations experienced health challenges, but these were accompanied by increases in fertility rates and population growth (Lambert 2009) which created a Neolithic demographic transition (see Gage and DeWitte 2009 for a circumspect review). Similar phenomena are evident today in developing economies, where poverty, poor health and food insecurity often go hand-in-hand with high reproductive rates (Lambert 2009). This may be one reason why humans are so successful, as they are able to reproduce rapidly in unstable environments (Wells 2010; and Chapter 4). The net evolutionary result of the adoption of agriculture could be therefore an increase in evolutionary fitness (Lambert 2009) rather than 'maladaptation', despite some negative effects on individual health. Invoking the emergence of agrarian economies as the start of a slide towards obesity and chronic disease in the contemporary world seems misleading in this context, especially as these are not highly prevalent in present-day populations that are dependent on traditional subsistence practices. It is much more likely that obesity and chronic disease are to some extent products of the industrialization of food production (Strassmann and Dunbar 1998) (Chapters 10 and 11), although the emergence and success of agriculture made grains the obvious source materials for much industrially produced food (Chapter 9).

In Chapter 6, we contrast foraging and contemporary industrial diets in their nutritional properties, and put into sharp relief how far we have come from nature. Contemporary industrial diets exert their effects in part through level of consumption. For example, Figure 1.5 shows the prevalence of obesity and diabetes in a number of nations between the years 2000 and 2010, according to daily dietary energy availability. Although dietary availability does not equate directly with consumption since it does not take account of food wastage and non-food uses, it is a close proxy. Unsurprisingly, there is a relationship between how much dietary energy people have available to them and the prevalence of obesity; below around 3000 kcal per day, national obesity rates are low. However, both Italy and South Korea have lower levels of obesity than might be expected at their levels of energy availability, while Japan has higher levels than expected, although Japanese food intakes are low relative to income. This indicates that other factors are also important in the causation of obesity, and the diseases of civilization associated with it. In Figure 1.5, diabetes rates show little variation according to availability of dietary energy alone. For the US, Gross *et al.* (2004) have identified relationships between diabetes prevalence and intakes of carbohydrate and high-fructose corn syrup, in addition to intakes of fat and total energy (Gross *et al.* 2004) (Chapter 10).

Globalization and industrialization have resulted in decreased diversity of fresh plant foods in many populations (Milton 1999a). Human diets constituting a broad range of animal and plant foods in the Pleistocene have been largely displaced by ones based increasingly on processed foods rich in refined grains, sugars and oils. Thus, dietary energy capture has become more efficient than ever before, but micronutrient capture has declined. In 2001, over one

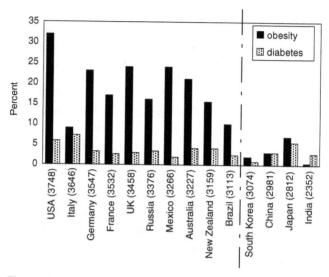

Figure 1.5. Proportion of populations obese and diabetic, according to daily dietary energy availability (in brackets). Data from World Health Organization 2011a; Food and Agriculture Organization 2011.

third of the world's population was estimated to have suffered from micronutrient deficiency (Tontisirin *et al.* 2002), while less than half this number suffered from chronic energy deficiency (Food and Agriculture Organization 2010a). Well in excess of a billion people currently suffer iron deficiency and its attendant anaemia, while iodine deficiency disorders persist. Cost and availability inhibit many of the world's poorest people from consuming meat, even though they may prize it as food. Cost and availability also preclude them from obtaining micronutrients from dietary sources. One answer to this problem in recent decades has been the medicalization of nutrition, and the administration of nutrient supplements in non-food forms.

While agriculture emerged as a solution to population problems in different parts of the world at quite similar times, infectious disease added new complexity to an already changed nutritional ecology. That is, agricultural practice changed patterns of human behaviour and organization, concentrating population densities around intensified subsistence. This process aided the spread of pathogens present among humans at low intensity of infection prior to the emergence of agriculture and increased the rate at which pathogens infecting animals could cross the species barrier into humans. Whenever humans change how they do things, responses to existing stressors often allow the emergence of new stressors. The origins of agriculture, industrialization and globalization are all associated with changes that saw the emergence of new infections or increased vigour of infection. Nutrition (with its powerful impacts on immune function) would have been a major environmental mediator of disease susceptibility, exposure and outcome, and of natural selection against infectious agents. The nutritional stresses that followed agricultural intensification would have increased immunological susceptibility to infection, while many diseases would have raised nutritional requirements during the course of infection. In Chapter 7, comparisons are made between the emergence of undernutrition and infectious disease in prehistory and present-day patterns of undernutrition and infection in the modern less economically developed world.

Food security is undermined by poverty, contributing to the interactions between nutritional state and infection that impact on child growth and survivorship. Human populations have differential genetic resistance and susceptibility to past infections, and varied types and levels of nutritional adaptation. Some evolutionary adaptations influence susceptibility to modern diseases. For example, the CCR5 delta 32 deletion which confers resistance to HIV infection is likely to have arisen as a single mutation among a European population around 2000 years ago, and increased in frequency as a result of exposure to a disease that persisted since its origin, perhaps smallpox, but not the plague (Galvani and Novembre 2005). Because of such genetic diversity and its implications for disease susceptibility (an understanding of which is still unfolding), future public health solutions to nutrition–infection interactions will need to be more complex than presently conceived.

Global inequality in nutritional health in the present day is clear to see, with around 13% of the world's population being undernourished and around 5% of it obese. Variation in food consumption patterns and nutritional health across nations reflects differences in history, ideology, and power relationships, which become expressed in differences in economic development. In Chapter 8, we add anthropological and evolutionary ecological perspectives to the understanding of the emergence of social inequality in humans. We examine how population size is fundamental to the ways in which societies can be structured, and how unequal nutritional health appears to be epiphenomenal to the larger economic project that drives the success or failure of all societies. We argue that social and economic inequalities are likely to have conditioned nutritional health from the origins of agriculture to the present day, and that social inequality and nutritional inequalities are linked through the attribution of symbolic value to goods, including (and sometimes especially) food. Food is the most elementary of symbolic goods because it is used to mark status in all societies. It has been elaborated to a high degree across human prehistory and history, a process that now continues at break-neck pace, with the development of global food cultures and the diversity of shops and restaurants that deliver them. Food preferences and consumption are used to define social class differences, and play out in the production of differential nutritional health. We argue that the deep social embeddedness of food as a symbolic good is something that is actively exploited by food manufacturers and marketers, and can have profound effects on the nutritional health of populations.

Once upon a time in the West

In the contemporary world, intensification of food production and the commodification of fats and carbohydrates have allowed growing urban populations in industrialized and industrializing nations to be fed cheaply and generally stably, free of many of the major fluctuations associated with food seasonality. This should be a good thing, except that the consumption of food products developed for mass use has been linked to a number of chronic diseases. Across the twentieth century and especially during the latter half of it, dietary change as an outcome of modernization and globalization has led to the emergence of epidemics of obesity, CVD and Type 2 diabetes. A subset of epidemiological transition theory (Omran 1971), nutrition transition theory has been developed by Popkin (2002a) as an explanatory framework for changes in nutritional health according to stages of dietary consumption types and physical activity patterns, from prehistory to the present. Nutrition transition theory places societal changes towards industrialized diets and sedentary ways of life centrally to the emergence and propagation of chronic disease across the world in recent decades. In Chapter 9, nutrition transition theory is described, and its relationship to broader transformative processes discussed.

Mexico is currently an economically emerging nation affected by globalization and beset with increasing levels of obesity and related chronic diseases. By examining recent nutrition transition in Mexico in relation to inequality, colonialism and globalization, an extension to nutrition transition theory is proposed in which prehistories and histories shape the responses of populations to changing nutritional circumstances. In this chapter we also locate changes in nutritional health in Mexico within a framework of dependency, initially with Spain, as its earliest colonizer, and then with the US. In places like Mexico, the industrialized food system is perhaps an unwitting accomplice of nutritional structural violence. Most broadly, its achievements have transformed human quality of life across the world by delivering predictable, safe and clean food to the billions of people that do not engage in subsistence agriculture. However, its central ethos of profit maximization often promotes consumption in ways that do not promote nutritional health. As an agent of dietary change, the history of the industrialized food system is an important part of the nutrition transition narrative, although one that is not currently widespread.

In Chapter 10, one component of dietary energy intake implicated in nutrition transition is considered. This is the consumption of fat, which has increased in quantity and changed in type in most populations across the past 50 years or so. From an evolutionary perspective, consumption of dietary fat is important because it provides greater energy density than any other macronutrient. It allowed the dietary energy budgets of hominins and early humans to be met more easily than with other foods. Only in recent times in industrialized societies, where food availability has been secured and physical work schedules have declined to very low levels, has its importance been questioned. Increased overall consumption of fat with recent nutrition transition has led to increased dietary energy intake, alleviating the problems of undernutrition for some, and creating the new problem of obesity for others. Fat is not just fat: there are many types of fat, varying by carbon chain-length, numbers and types of double bond, and influencing human physiology and health outcomes differently. Saturated fat consumption is associated with CVD, as is that of the industrially-produced trans-fats. Consumption of long chain n-3 polyunsaturated fatty acids (PUFA) is associated with better health outcomes than any other type of fat, as they are protective of many of the chronic diseases that emerged as significant public health problems in the past 50 years or so. However, grain-based n-6 PUFA are less healthy than n-3 PUFA, and they form a dominant part of total fat availability in most industrialized nations. In Chapter 10, we show the importance of the types of dietary fat available for consumption when investigating diet quality in public health.

In Chapter 11 we examine another output of the industrialized food system, that of refined carbohydrates, and how their consumption relates to the production of chronic diseases (Trowell and Burkitt 1981) including Type 2 diabetes and CVD, as well as the predisposing conditions of obesity and insulin resistance. Links between the consumption of refined carbohydrates and the common disorders of gout, acne and myopia are also considered. We link these three conditions as carbohydrate transition disorders, and see them as a subset of nutrition transition. We show that carbohydrate transition is most advanced in the US, where high-fructose corn syrup (HFCS) has become a major source of dietary carbohydrate and sweetness for the population. Human genetics and physiology have evolved in ways that can enhance survivorship through improving fat deposition from the consumption of sugars, especially fructose. These biochemical mechanisms have very deep ancestry, and have been recruited for new tasks, particularly in relation to the digestion of HFCS, often with negative health consequences.

An integrated view

The diversity and flexibility of the human diet is fundamental to our success as a species. However, our taste for food novelty and for creating social signifiers with types of food may be central to our nutritional short-comings. We hope that this book shows that, far from being adapted to a 'Stone Age' diet and maladapted to post-agricultural subsistence, humans are suited to consuming a vast range of foodstuffs (Elton 2008a). The fact that novelty is created from a very limited range of food commodities and chemicals by industrialized food systems, and that as a whole, humans respond by buying and eating new food products, places considerable responsibility on the systems of production for maintaining nutritional health. At the time of writing, global food security is in question, while the economic system for delivering adequate nutrition (in both quantity and quality) is in a precarious state. There is no better time to evaluate how food is produced, manufactured, distributed and consumed. This book presents an evolutionary evaluation of how and what we eat. We link nutrition with human form and function as an evolving work in progress, and with the social and political systems that shape human populations and their food systems. It is far from being a complete account, but by showing how prehistoric and historic processes inform and shape present-day nutritional health, we hope to have created a framework for examining other nutritional phenomena in similar ways.

Part I

The Animal Within

2 *Locating human diet in a mammalian framework*

Humans carry evolutionary baggage. Most, but not all, is useful for present-day populations. Without understanding evolutionary heritage, we cannot make sense of what human populations can and should eat. Imagine an X-ray screening device at the airport check-in, which hopefully identifies objects that are potentially dangerous to the community of air travellers. The objects that some of us carry in our evolutionary baggage are no less deadly than bombs and missiles, but there is no equivalent to the X-ray device to scan it. The closest instrument we have is genome scanning, but this does not yet reveal anywhere close to the full extent of health-related gene–gene and gene–environment interactions that may exist. Genes have evolved within communities of living individuals, whose metabolomes – the full set of metabolites within an organism, a metabolic analogue of the genome – are shaped by day-to-day behaviours and decisions that influence the food-getting, reproductive and child-rearing strategies that pattern survivorship. There is thus the possibility that other emergent instruments, using approaches that focus on complex interactions within biological systems, may complement genome scanning to provide profiles of how individual metabolomes relate to health (Panagiotou and Nielsen 2009).

Influences on diet and nutrition are multifaceted, having not only phylogenetic but also ecological, social, cultural and behavioural components, and a mammalian perspective is needed to locate the evolution of human diet in a broader framework. From this, general trends in feeding behaviour and food preferences can be better understood, as can the functional and dietary constraints imposed by our anatomy and physiology. Examining diet within a mammalian context helps understanding of the 'hows' and 'whys' of human nutrition rather than simply recording the 'whats'. Public health nutrition often uses knowledge of nutritional requirements in a strictly functional way, since the implications of specific deficiencies (or sometimes excesses) can be physiological inefficiencies, pathologies, and ultimately death. With an evolutionary framework, we aim to locate human nutrition more firmly in biology, the primary aim of this chapter.

Many articles have been written about diets in the context of human evolutionary history (Eaton and Eaton 1998; Eaton *et al.* 1999; Cordain *et al.* 2000; Elton 2008a). These, which mainly focus on 'Stone Age' diets, are discussed in Chapters 3, 5 and 6. There is also interest in situating human diets in a broader mammalian, particularly primate, context (Milton 2000b; Fitch and Stanford 2004), although such approaches have not captured the public imagination in the same way as 'Stone Age' diets; possible reasons why such diets have resonance for many people are given in Chapter 1. Mammalian comparisons may be more useful than 'Stone Age' perspectives, as many of the attributes of hominin diets and the behaviours associated with obtaining them were probably established well before the Pleistocene, the time stone-agers were around (Foley 1995; Ulijaszek 2002; Elton 2008a). Evolutionary ecology approaches, in which the relationships between organisms and their environments are examined alongside the processes that lead to adaptation, can help us understand these dietary trends (Ulijaszek 2002).

Locating human diet within a meaningful mammalian context requires understanding of evolutionary history and phylogeny as well as ecology. Humans have diverse diets, but then so do brown bears. Comparing the diets of the two gives important background about dietary ecology and the advantages or disadvantages of adopting particular dietary strategies. However, unless the traits compared have a deep prehistory, or are highly conserved, such comparisons do not necessarily yield useful information about the evolutionary underpinnings of human diet and dietary adaptation. Since humans are primates, primate data will form the basis of comparison in this chapter, with data from other mammals used when appropriate to do so.

The comparison with primate diet is made complex by the hierarchy of comparison within the primates. The Order Primates (Figure 2.1) is subdivided into the Strepsirhini (lemurs and lorises) and Haplorhini (tarsiers, monkeys and apes). Humans are haplorhines and are further included in the Catarrhini ('narrow nosed' primates), comprising Old World monkeys and apes. At a lower taxonomic level, humans are members of the Hominidae, the ape family that also includes the gorillas, chimpanzees and orangutans. Many dietary comparisons are therefore made among the apes, but as different species of the living apes are ecologically specialized, it is often appropriate to make comparisons of human diet and dietary behaviour with other catarrhines, the Old World monkeys, that tend to be more generalized (Aiello *et al.* 2000; Elton 2006; Codron *et al.* 2008). In this chapter, we explore human diets by focusing first on general dietary patterns and adaptations within the primates. Since two prominent characteristics of human diets are meat-eating and eclectic feeding

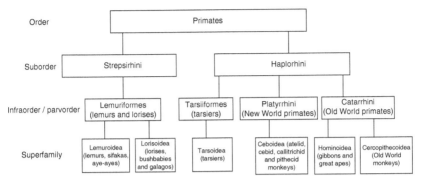

Figure 2.1. A classification of the Order Primates (adapted from Szalay and Delson 1979).

('omnivory'), we then contextualize these behaviours in more detail. We also discuss the many sources of variation in primate diets, foraging behaviours and nutrition, and finally discuss what an understanding of mammalian, specifically primate, diets brings to the study of human nutrition.

Human and non-human primate diets: patterns and adaptations

What is a primate?

Primates are difficult to define. The anatomist Le Gros Clark (1959) was one of the first to draw up a list capturing the main features and trends of primates, which was subsequently augmented by the primatologists and anatomists Napier and Napier (1967). This list is still used widely today. According to these authors, primates are characterized by: a skeleton that is relatively unspecialized (allowing movement in trees and on the ground); stereoscopic, binocular vision (facilitating depth perception); high dependence on sight and less dependence on smell; having nails rather than claws; large brains; sociality, flexible behaviour, and an advanced ability to learn; a good placental blood supply; small litter sizes; high investment in offspring; long interbirth intervals; and long lives (Le Gros Clark 1959; Napier and Napier 1967). Many of these features are also seen in other animals, but together they form a useful working definition of the Order to which humans belong. Unsurprisingly, many of the defining traits of primates relate to their large brains. A big brain is linked to sociality, learning and behavioural flexibility. Animals with larger brains, including primates, are 'K-selected' and live life in the slow lane. In animal ecology, r/K selection theory considers the traits species need for maximizing either the quantity or quality of offspring. *K*-selected taxa (such as primates) have long lives, are very competitive, and usually have only a small number of offspring that they actively care for, often for a considerable period after birth. Although humans are generally *K*-selected, reproductive rates are high relative to other primates, and they recover from population crashes fairly easily. However, humans continue many of the morphological and life-history trends observed in primates, taking some, like large brains, to extremes. Even human bipedalism, which seems very different from the locomotion used by other primates, is rooted in the upright or orthograde posture seen in apes.

Why flowering plants are important

Primate-like mammals are first found in the fossil record of the early Paleocene (around 65 million years ago), although a recent statistical estimate (which used a speciation model that can to some extent accommodate extinct primate species not retained in the fossil record) pushes primate origins to before 80 million years ago (Tavaré *et al.* 2002). The first 'true' primates (the euprimates) probably originated in the early Eocene (around 55 million years ago), with the adapoids and omomyoids (two ancestral primate genera) being the earliest well-known euprimate radiations (Covert 2003). The origins and radiation of the primates are commonly linked to the diversification and radiation of flowering plants, or angiosperms, in the Paleocene, 65–56 million years ago (Sussmann 1991). Fossil evidence places the origin of angiosperms in the Cretaceous period, between 145 and 65 million years ago (Friis *et al.* 2010), although some molecular phylogenetic analyses place their origins at between 216 and 275 million years ago (Magallon 2010). Phylogenetic analyses of insects and plants suggest that biotic pollination in seed plants evolved at least three times: in the cycads, *Gnetales* and angiosperms. Although it is not clear whether this symbiosis facilitated the spread and diversification of the latter (Herrera and Pellmyr 2002), the majority of living (and very probably extinct) primates are (and were) heavily ecologically dependent on them.

Primates feed on most surface parts of flowering plants, both the structural (leaves) and reproductive (fruits, seeds and flowers) parts, as well as the gums and exudates they might produce. Some, like the baboon, also exploit underground storage organs such as tubers, corms and rhizomes. Humans follow this general primate trend in exploiting angiosperms. Table 2.1 gives a phylogeny of angiosperms and the common names of plants and plant products that are commonly used by primates and humans. It shows that angiosperms are fundamental to both primate and human diets. Indeed, flowering plant foods

Table 2.1 *Phylogeny of edible angiosperms*

Angiosperm subclass	Genus, family or order	Examples of food plants eaten now
Magnolids	*Persea*	Avocado
Monocots	Poaceae	Wheat, maize, rice
	Musa	Bananas
	Asparagus	Asparagus
	Allium	Onion
Eudicots	Rosids	Cucumber, melon, soy bean, apple, orange, lemon, grapefruit
	Saxifragales	Currants (including red and blackcurrants), gooseberry
	Asterids	Tomato, potato, lettuce, sunflower, blueberry
	Caryophyllales	Beet

Adapted from The Angiosperm Phylogeny Group 2009

form the dietary 'bedrock' of many human populations (Chapter 6), the species as a whole consuming significant quantities of them from a wide range of plant families (Peters *et al.* 1992; Proches *et al.* 2008).

While humans may consume a large variety of angiosperms, these are limited to the magnolid, eudicot and monocot groups. Of the edible magnolids, the avocado is the most prominent in contemporary diets, while the eudicots furnish modern diets with a range of plant foods including apples, cabbages, tomatoes, lettuce, macadamia and blueberries. These two groups are often included in the dicots, traditionally one of the major angiosperm subdivisions, now known to be a paraphyletic group, in which some but not all of the descendents of a common ancestor are represented. The third angiosperm radiation exploited by humans, the monocots, is a monophyletic group (where all the members share a common ancestor) descended from a dicot ancestor. The monocots have been called most heavily into the dietary service of humanity in recent evolutionary times. The major staples wheat, rice and maize are monocots, as are banana, sugarcane, taro, coconuts and pineapple. Humans thus live in a monocot world, with the grasses and palms being of particular economic and dietary importance. At some point in human evolution, these plants, along with many other monocot species, came to dominate the human diet. Monocots form part of the diets of several modern primates, either as a fallback or as a staple. For example, wild ginger (the monocot family Zingiberaceae) is a staple for western gorillas (Harcourt and Stewart 2007), while grasses are important seasonal fallback foods for macaques (O'Regan *et al.* 2008) and baboons (Codron *et al.* 2006). The dependence on monocots seen in contemporary humans is not common to primates as a whole, however. The types of fruits that chimpanzees, baboons and capuchin monkeys eat and disperse as seeds are primarily eudicots (including figs of various types) and magnolids (including types of acacia and tamarind fruit). Their role in environmental enrichment of fruit sources probably helped selection for eudicots and magnolids, but is much less important for monocots. In humans, the move towards increasing exploitation of monocots is a mark of dietary niche expansion (Chapter 5), and the widespread adoption of agriculture is an obvious point of transition to a 'monocot world'.

Despite the dominance of monocots in the human diet, there is a great deal of inter- and intrapopulation and seasonal variation in human plant consumption. In foraging populations, the proportion of plants in the diet is partly related to primary production, which is the capture of chemical energy in organic compounds by plants, most usually from atmospheric carbon dioxide by photosynthesis. In areas of low productivity, such as polar regions, it is difficult for humans to subsist on plants. As an example, polar Inuit inhabit land with productivity of around 45 g of biomass/m^2/year, and when employing traditional subsistence practices, spend only around 10% of their time gathering plant foods directly (Kelly 1995). To realise how low this productivity is, imagine a small back-yard in England of 5 m × 5 m moved above the Arctic Circle. Across the course of a year, it would generate just over a kilogram of biomass in total; this is a mere fraction of the biomass that needs to be cleared to keep this English yard looking neat during a wet and warm summer. In contrast to Inuit, the land of the !Kung and G/wi people of the Kalahari desert is much more productive biologically and as a consequence they have a high dependence on plant food (more than 80% of total energy intake) (Kelly 1995).

Some foraging populations use an enormous range of plant foods: the Seri of northern California reportedly exploit foods from around 35 plant families, a similar number to those taken by the north Australian Bardi (Cotton 1996) and the Wopkaimin hunter-horticulturalists of Papua New Guinea (Hyndman 1982), who use foods from 36 plant families. The Seri consume mostly cacti and desert plants, and there is no documentary evidence of them consuming monocot plants. The only monocots the Bardi consume are wild yams, while about half of the wild foods consumed by the Wopkaimin are monocots. The Chippewa (Minnesota, USA) consumed 39 species of plants, at least two of which were monocots, wild rice and cultivated maize (Densmore 1974). The Ayoreo of Paraguay consume 33 species of plant, including at least one monocot, cultivated maize (Schmeda-Hirschmann 1994).

Even though primates as a whole include a high proportion of angiosperms in their diets, humans do consume non-angiosperm plants. For example, pine nuts are a non-angiosperm food well known to Western consumers. Non-angiosperm plant foods form a larger part of forager diets than agrarian ones.

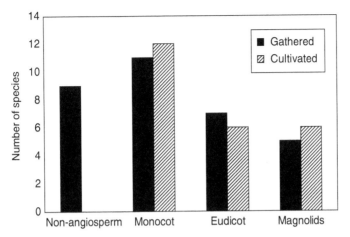

Figure 2.2. Wopkaimin (Papua New Guinea) gathered and cultivated plant foods according to angiosperm group (data from Hyndman 1979).

This is illustrated in Figure 2.2 for the Wopkaimin of Papua New Guinea (Hyndman 1979), who engage in both gathering and cultivation of plant foods. Angiosperms (monocots in particular) dominate both gathering and cultivation practice, and non-angiosperms are gathered but not cultivated for food. This is a pattern replicated throughout the world: for example, the sister taxa of the angiosperms, the gymnosperms, are cultivated heavily for timber but much less for other products including pine nuts (viewed as a delicacy in many parts of Europe, Asia and north America) and ginkgo leaves, used as a tea and food supplement.

Foraging peoples today make up only a fraction of the world's population. Most people live in agrarian economies, some of which employ practices and use plant foods that have a deep history. Many of these (and indeed archaeological and historical populations) depend heavily on a single plant food, often a grain or root, usually a monocot (wheat, rice, maize, millet, banana, taro, sago), but sometimes a eudicot (manioc). Cultivation of crops is often viewed as a move away from dietary diversity, towards a monoculture that has ecosystemic fragility. A dramatic example of such fragility is the Great Famine of Ireland, which took place between 1845 and 1852 and resulted in significant population decline. While potato blight (*Phytophthora infestans*) had infested potato crops across Europe from the 1840s after being introduced from the Americas (Donnelly 2002), the Irish poor were particularly vulnerable to famine because of their near-total dependence on the potato staple. However, not all groups practising cultivation experience such fragility. In some cases, a single plant food may be the dietary staple but the total number of taxa exploited may be large (Cotton 1996). For example, the Waimiri Atroari of Amazonia, swidden agriculturalists and hunters who cultivate manioc as their main staple, exploit 30 plant families for food (Cotton 1996). Other populations may not have a particularly varied diet from day-to-day but retain traditional ethnobotanical knowledge of many foods that are eaten in times of food insecurity (Cotton 1996). Nonetheless, globalization, modernization and industrialization (Chapters 9 and 11) have resulted in decreased diversity of fresh plant foods in many populations, even in tropical regions where diversity is highest.

Frugivory is central to primate diets

Although dependent on angiosperm plant foods, primates show diverse diets and feeding behaviours. The three major dietary strategies seen in primates are fruit-eating (frugivory), leaf-eating (folivory) and insectivory (Figure 2.3). The majority of primates are frugivorous (at least to an extent), supplementing their diets with insects, leaves or gums. In many tropical forests, primates are the dominant and most abundant frugivores, their roles as seed dispersers making them integral to the complex ecology of tropical forests (Chapman 1995). Palaeontological data indicate that the earliest primates, once thought to be insectivores, incorporated fruits and seeds into their diets (Rasmussen 2003), and it is likely that frugivory has been a fundamental primate adaptation since the origins of the order Primates.

Fruits are not a homogeneous resource. Along with the numerous varieties and attendant variations by season, region, year, location, position in the canopy and required processing, fruits can also be harvested at different points in their developmental schedule, from unripe to ripe. This adds extra complexity not only to the digestive adaptations needed to process fruits at different degrees of ripeness but also to foraging behaviour, including interspecific competition and access to resources. Once a single fruit, ripe or unripe, is picked, it is not available to other animals. Thus, getting to the resource first, and being able to eat unripe fruit, gives consumers an adaptive advantage over animals that specialize in ripe fruit. It has been proposed that the ability to eat unripe fruits is one reason why living Old World monkeys have been more successful, as judged by their geographic range and population size, than non-human apes (Andrews 1981). However, this suggestion is not entirely watertight. Although one radiation of Old World monkeys, the colobines, are able to digest unripe fruit very effectively, several apes, including gorillas, siamangs and orangutans, also eat unripe fruits even though apes as a whole tend to favour ripe fruits (Wheatley 1987).

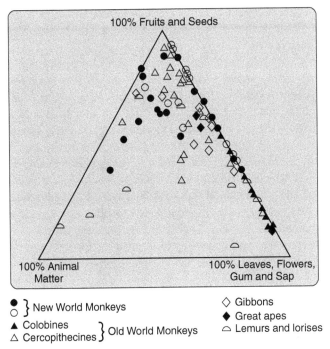

Diets can be represented in the form of a triangular diagram, with 100% faunivory, 100% folivory and 100% frugivory at the three corners. Here, the average diets of 80 primates are shown with fauni-frugivores to the left and foli-frugivores to the right; strepsirhine species [a suborder that includes lemurs and lorises] are particularly variable in their diets.

Figure 2.3. Primate diets according to proportion of frugivory, folivory and insectivory (Chivers 1992).

In general, frugivorous primates have larger brain sizes relative to body mass than do folivorous ones. One explanation has been the 'maternal energy hypothesis' (Martin 1996), which postulates that the lower basal metabolic rate of folivorous primates may influence the amount of energy a mother is able to supply its fetus, which may, for a given gestation period, have a knock-on effect on physical growth, and of the brain especially, *in utero*. The suggestion is that since primates experience much greater brain growth during gestation than do most other mammals (Martin 1996), if maternal energy constraints play a part in limiting growth, there may be a disproportionate effect on the size of the primate brain. Since folivores are more energy-constrained than frugivores, this may inhibit brain growth of the former more than the latter. Other, less contentious, explanations for the larger brain sizes of frugivorous primates include the greater mental capacities needed to engage in extractive foraging (Gibson 1986) and exploit patchily distributed resources (Clutton-Brock and Harvey 1980).

Edible parts of plants, particularly fruits and seeds, are often embedded within a hard outer casing and require extractive foraging. Vertebrate consumption might also need extractive foraging. Extractive foraging may need greater cognitive ability and having to get food in this way may have been a selection pressure for the evolution of increased brain size relative to the size of the body (encephalization) (Gibson 1986). Humans have taken extractive foraging to extremes. Whether butchering meat, processing sago or producing a Big Mac, human populations have developed extensive technological responses to food procurement and preparation. It is possible that tool use and extractive foraging, particularly of animal carcasses, contributed to brain size increases in Plio-Pleistocene hominins, between 3 and 1 million years ago (Elton *et al.* 2001).

Frugivores need to exploit patchily distributed resources (Clutton-Brock and Harvey 1980) and thus often have larger home ranges than folivores. Frugivory may therefore require more cognitive processing power to locate patches of fruiting trees (which will vary by season), and to communicate the availability and distribution of resources to other individuals. In short, mental maps, sets of information whereby activities in time and space can be planned and varied according to circumstance, are required for successful navigation (Milton 1988). The concept of mental mapping has been developed in relation to foraging among grey-cheeked mangabey monkeys, who take weather patterns into account when making foraging decisions (Janmaat *et al.* 2006). Temperature and hours of sunlight affect fruit ripening as well as the maturation of other foodstuffs such as insect larvae, and monkeys make these links and retain episodic memories of the quality, energy density and yield of fruiting patches (Janmaat *et al.* 2006).

Humans evolved from a frugivorous ancestor, and fruit was an important part of the diets of many early hominins. In many ways, humans are the perfect 'patchy foragers', and the links between human feeding behaviour and cognition are obvious. Their natural predisposition to patchy foraging is linked not only to the cognitive ability to exploit a complex environment but also to the origins and evolution of the unique mode of locomotion that is human bipedalism (Isbell *et al.* 1998). The 'prime mover' for the emergence of bipedalism is unknown, although a dominant argument is that it emerged as a means for large arboreal apes to move on large flexible branches, facilitating foraging (Thorpe *et al.* 2007). For example, orangutans can move on flexible branches, like humans running on springy tracks, by increasing knee and hip extension. In this scheme, human bipedalism is less an innovation than an exploitation of a locomotor behaviour retained from the common great ape ancestor (Thorpe *et al.* 2007). Orangutans can move along branches quadru-pedally, bipedally or by orthograde suspension (hanging below branches, using hands or hands and feet, with the trunk of the body in an upright, vertical position). Although bipedalism is the least favoured of these, it is practised as often as quadrupedalism when orangutans must negotiate thin branches.

It is possible that selection for bipedal locomotion was reinforced by the need to exploit highly dispersed food patches on the ground (Foley and Elton 1998), where bipedalism could have been used to travel long distances more easily. It would have been a boon to the earliest hominins, who lived in wooded environments (Elton 2008b), but may have been even more important for members of our own genus, *Homo*, evolving in environments that were becoming increasingly arid (Reed 1997; Elton 2008b). Forest and woodland may have become less widespread, food supplies more unpredictable, and ranging area would have increased (Pennycuick 1979). Analogy with the living patas monkey, which inhabits grassland environments, suggests that *Homo erectus* foraging in open environments would have required a large home range (Isbell *et al.* 1998). The ability to move efficiently between feeding patches that were spread over a wide area would therefore have been essential. Mammals with a large range tend to have good locomotor economy (Pennycuick 1979), and when compared with chimpanzee locomotion, modern human bipedalism is exceptionally energetically efficient (Rodman and McHenry 1980; Sockol *et al.* 2007).

An evolutionary heritage of fruit eating may also explain a common char-acteristic of many human diets, that of alcohol consumption. The 'drunken monkey hypothesis' of Dudley (2004) posits that the human ancestry of ripe fruit-eating provides the basis of the widespread attraction among humans to ethanol consumption. Primates with an ability to detect ethanol have a com-petitive advantage in foraging, and hominins (including humans) could have had a predisposition to seek out alcohol as a marker of energy-rich food resources (Dudley 2004). Against this, Milton (2004) suggests that ethanol consumption is not restricted to ripe fruit eaters, that over-ripe fruit is often less favoured, that many volatile aromatic substances are encountered in the wild and that intoxication is rarely if ever observed among wild primates.

Nutritional qualities of fruits, leaves and insects

Like humans and other mammals, other primates require a mix of macronutri-ents as well as micronutrients (Figure 1.1 shows the relationships among the nutrients). To gain adequate nutrition, most primates ingest a mix of food-stuffs, although these vary not only by species but also by population and individual. Fruit, the primate staple, has different dietary characteristics depending on whether it is ripe or unripe. Wild ripe fruit usually contains high levels of sugar, particularly glucose but also fructose, both of which are monosaccharides (Milton 1999a). Cultivated ripe fruit, of the type eaten by the majority of humans, bred in the contemporary world to taste sweeter and thus be more palatable, is much higher in the disaccharide sucrose (Milton 1999a). Wild fruit also differs from cultivated fruit in that it contains much more fibre, pectin, protein and micronutrients (Milton 1999a), but is still easy to digest and metabolize because of its high levels of simple carbohydrates (Lambert 1998). Although many primates reject novel foods, they are more likely to eat them if they contain high levels of sugar; this could be a mechanism by which preferential consumption of high-energy resources is ensured (Johnson 2007). Unripe fruits, whether wild or cultivated, have much less sugar than when ripe, may contain more tannins and other substances that deter insects (antifeedants), are harder to digest, and potentially less palatable for many animals. Primates that specialize in unripe fruit consumption, like the colobine monkeys, have morphological and physiological adaptations that help digestion. Although wild fruits are higher in protein than cultivated species, they tend to be much lower in protein than leaves, which are also high in fibre and low in energy (Milton 1999a).

The fibre in leaves comes from complex structural carbohydrates that form cell walls, primarily cellulose. Fermentation releases energy from glucose molecules that make up cellulose (Lambert 1998). The palatability and digestibility of leaves usually decreases as they mature. Many frugivorous primates that supplement their diet with leaves choose young rather than mature ones. Seed coatings are also made up of structural carbohydrates and, like leaves, can be high in protein (Lambert 1998). Although often grouped in a dietary category with fruits, seeds are structurally and nutritionally very different and hence are processed differently, often through fermentation, in a similar way to leaves. It is possible that seed eating was a transitional step between frugivory (the ancestral and most common state) and folivory (Bodmer 1989).

Underground storage organs and tubers, eaten by some primates, including many papionin monkeys, contain high quantities of polysaccharide starches. These are complex carbohydrates, which need to be reduced during digestion to forms that can be metabolized (Lambert 1998). Similarly, gums, although not starchy, are high in complex carbohydrates (although saps are not) (Nash 1986). Structural, complex carbohydrates are found even in insects, the exoskeletons of which are made of chitin, a carbohydrate similar to cellulose (Committee on Animal Nutrition 2003). In some cases, the exoskeleton is discarded before eating, although some primates can digest chitin. Other than the exoskeleton, insects tend to be relatively easy to digest (Schmidt-Nielsen 1997), and are a good source of protein and fats, with some larvae being particularly lipid-rich (Committee on Animal Nutrition 2003).

Along with macronutrients, foodstuffs contain micronutrients and secondary compounds (Chapters 1 and 4). All animals require micronutrients, but their exact needs are less well understood than those of humans (Milton 2000b; Committee on Animal Nutrition 2003). It is very likely that wild primates ingest much higher quantities of vitamins and minerals than do humans, because wild plant foods tend to be more micronutrient-rich than cultivated ones (Milton 2000b). Primates also ingest micronutrients from faunal matter, including insects, and in some cases from geophagy (Committee on Animal Nutrition 2003). One well known example of geophagy in wild animals is the exploitation of naturally occurring mineral (or 'salt') licks, which can provide a variety of trace elements including zinc, potassium, chloride, sodium, cobalt, selenium and manganese (Mills and Milewski 2007). Geophagy can also help to neutralize ingested secondary plant compounds, and it is likely that several primate species ingest clays, soils or other materials, like charcoal, for this purpose.

Antifeedants produced by plants as chemical deterrents against being consumed by insects and other animals include: tannins, which give the dry or bitter taste to over-brewed tea, for example; nicotine; caffeine; and steroids that mimic mammalian sex hormones (Glander 1982; Wynne-Edwards 2001). Defensive antifeedants are found in all plant parts (seeds, tubers, young leaves, mature leaves) but relative concentrations are ecologically determined and hence may vary within a plant as well as across species (Jackson 1991). For animals that rely on plant foods, it is important to overcome secondary compounds in one way or another, although a plant that is toxic to one species may be edible by another (Glander 1982). Since the activity of enzymes, including those of the detoxification system cytochrome P450, scales negatively with body size, smaller monkeys may cope better with relatively higher amounts of secondary toxins (Lambert 2002). Thus, although a larger body may be advantageous in buffering against fluctuating or seasonal resource availability, it may also preclude the consumption of certain foods that are laden with toxins. One possibility for the extinction in the Pleistocene of very large baboons could have been that their large size precluded their consumption of foods high in antifeedants, such as unripe fruits and certain types of leaf. Some primates minimize the effects of secondary compounds through behaviour, for example by varying their foodstuffs to avoid over-consumption from a single plant species (Strier 2000). They may preferentially choose young or rare leaves, containing fewer tannins, as has been observed in black and white colobus monkeys at Kibale (Oates 1977). Primates may not always act to minimize tannin consumption, however. Humans often mask the bitter taste of tannins in tea with sugar. There are few data on whether similar behaviours occur in wild primates, although captive gorillas will consume solutions with higher concentrations of tannins than is habitual, as long as the solutions also have a high sugar content (Remis and Kerr 2002). This suggests that the potential costs of tannin consumption may be outweighed by the benefits of sugar consumption (Remis and Kerr 2002).

Humans, like other mammals, have physiological defences against antifeedants, most commonly through cytochrome P450-enzyme linked activity (Teel and Huynh 1998), but have extended the range of edible plants available to them through processing and cooking, which can denature secondary compounds by altering their chemical structure (Johns 1999; Wynne-Edwards 2001), by washing them out or diluting them. Manioc is a well-known example of a staple food that cannot be eaten without processing (Berlin and Berlin 1977). It contains cyano-glucosides such as linamarin, which can release cyanide in the body under enzymic degradation. Konzo is a paralytic disease associated with almost exclusive consumption of manioc which, because of food and water shortages, is poorly processed (Tylleskär *et al.* 1993). Domestication of various plants has also reduced their toxicity and increased their palatability, and humans actively exploit some antifeedants for medicines, recreation and industry. Humans show great variation in susceptibility to certain secondary plant compounds; for example, some people with glucose-6-phosphate dehydrogenase deficiency are unable to metabolize the glycosides in broad (fava) beans (Jackson 1991), leading to haemolytic anaemia among many, but resistance to malaria, if it is endemic (Chapter 7).

Digestive adaptations

Teeth, guts and the microbiota of the gut co-evolve with diet. The type of dentition a species has influences what can be consumed, according to the physical properties of a potential food. For example, molars are useful for grinding seeds, while incisors are useful for biting fruit and pulling flesh from bones. Gut morphology influences what can and can't be digested. For example, the chimpanzee has a much bigger large intestine relative to body size than its equivalent in humans. This permits chimpanzees to partly digest herbaceous piths that are high in the insoluble fibres hemicelluloses and cellulose (Wrangham *et al.* 1991) that are much less digestible for humans. The gut microbiota influence the energy availability of foods, both through salvage from otherwise indigestible polysaccharides, and increased glucose uptake and lipid storage (Backhed *et al.* 2005).

To release the energy and nutrients in food, both mechanical and chemical processing are usually needed. In the vast majority of mammals, mechanical processing is performed by the dentition, breaking up foodstuffs into quantities small enough to form a bolus that can then be swallowed. Mechanical processing is also needed to increase the surface area of particles and allow for efficient action of digestive chemicals. Among mammalian species, the links between diet and mechanical properties of foods, and gross morphological adaptations of teeth are well known (Lucas 2004; Ungar 2010). Any child, for example, can describe the carnassials found in many carnivores. In primates, dental adaptations tend to track the three major dietary strategies of insectivory, folivory and frugivory. The posterior dentition (molar and premolar teeth) of insectivores have sharp, pointed cusps to pierce insect exoskeletons and help to chop them into very small pieces, optimizing the effectiveness of digestive enzymes. This pointed cusp morphology also requires less force for mastication (Kay 1975), which may conserve energy and time spent in chewing. Folivores tend to have thin dental enamel on their posterior dentition which wears into numerous shearing crests, to slice through leaves and other tough foodstuffs. Frugivores have thicker molar tooth enamel with more rounded cusps, to crush fruit pulp; although modern human teeth are relatively small, they have a generalized frugivore morphology. Mechanical processing is also helped by the overall morphology of the cranium and mandible (Chapter 3), which is both evolutionarily and developmentally determined. In humans and tool-using primates (the best known of which are chimpanzees and cebus monkeys), mechanical processing begins prior to ingestion. For both humans and primates, this includes the removal of seed husks. Humans also practise peeling, scraping and cutting of foods during preparation and prior to consumption. Using a knife and fork is another example of human mechanical processing.

The digestive system starts at the mouth, where chemical processing also begins. In humans, the enzyme salivary amylase reduces polysaccharide starches to disaccharides which are then metabolized further to monosaccharides in the small intestine. Starch is not a feature of all primate diets, and New World monkeys, and possibly bonobos, do not produce salivary amylase, while expression in common chimpanzees is relatively low (Perry *et al.* 2007). Human salivary amylase is less effective than that found in cercopithecine monkeys (Lambert 1998), and it may be that the high levels of starch found in unripe fruits were the selective impetus for increasing the efficiency of salivary amylase in cercopithecine cheek pouches (*sensu* Lambert 2005). Selection may have acted rapidly when humans were faced with starch as a novel dietary component after the origins of agriculture, with increased copy number variation of the salivary amylase *AMY1* gene, related to starch

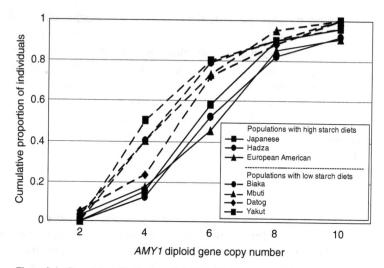

Figure 2.4. Cumulative distribution of diploid AMY1 copy number for populations traditionally consuming high- and low-starch diets, respectively (adapted from Perry *et al.* 2007).

dependence within different populations (Perry *et al.* 2007) (Figure 2.4). This represents positive selection in response to the consumption of starchy diets after the origins of agriculture, through improved digestibility of starchy foods (Perry *et al.* 2007).

After the mouth, chemical processing continues through enzymatic and bacterial activity in the stomach (proteins, carbohydrates) and intestine (lipids, carbohydrates), and detoxification in the liver. Bacteria in the gut are crucial to digestion, and the diversity of gut microbiota is itself an outcome of strong host selection and coevolution. The *Cytophaga*, Flavobacteria, *Bacteroides* (of the phylum Bacteroidetes) and bacteria of the Firmicute phylum that are predominantly associated with the mammalian gut are the most derived, or furthest from their common ancestor, in their clade of micro-organisms, suggesting that they underwent rapid evolution once they adapted to mutualism with mammals (Backhed *et al.* 2005). The absorption, storage and energy harvest from the diet by microbiota is a true symbiosis, since it takes place through systemic modulation of bile acid conjugation, fat emulsification and absorption (Martin *et al.* 2007). Furthermore, the relative proportion of *Bacteroides* to Firmicutes is important in energy balance. Among humans, obese individuals have lower ratios of the latter to the former than do lean people, the ratio increasing with weight loss among the obese. Activation and elevation of the endocannabinoid system in the intestine by Firmicutes increases gut permeability, fatty acid synthesis and fat mass development

(Muccioli *et al.* 2010). What is eaten and how much is eaten both influence gut microbiota and the physiological energy derived from food (Ley *et al.* 2005). Thus the energy densities of foods are not fixed, as portrayed in food composition tables, but vary between individuals according to transit time through the gut and the make-up of the microbiota (Backhed *et al.* 2005). This is true for mice and men (Ley *et al.* 2005), and therefore also likely to be true for mammals more generally. Differences in gut microflora occur between very closely related primates (Bruorton *et al.* 1991) and within individual primates across time (Wireman *et al.* 2006). Macaques have over five times more bacterial species of *Bacteroidales* than Firmicutes relative to humans, estimated as taxonomic operational units based on 16*S* rRNA gene sequencing of gut contents (McKenna *et al.* 2008). This indicates that the macaque microbiome is less efficient at energy harvest, absorption and storage than is the human microbiome.

Leaves, insects and fruit pose different digestive challenges. Leaves, whether young or mature, contain large amounts of structural carbohydrates that must be broken down. The gut microbiota of folivorous mammals can ferment and degrade cellulose and other structural carbohydrates into short-chain (volatile) fatty acids that are sources of energy (Lambert 1998). Fermentation can occur in the forestomach, as in domestic cows and colobine monkeys, or in an enlarged caecum and colon (caeco-colic fermentation), as in most of the primates including baboons, macaques, apes and humans (Chivers 1994). Caeco-colic fermentation is an efficient mechanism for the digestion of diets low in structural carbohydrates (Alexander 1993), and primates that feed eclectically (omnivores) are largely caeco-colic fermenters. Table 2.2 gives the relative gut volume proportions for a number of primate species, showing humans to have a proportionately smaller colon and larger small intestine. Mammals that depend on foods high in structural carbohydrates can digest them more efficiently by forestomach fermentation (Alexander 1993). This requires a large, complex, multichambered stomach in which microbes start to break down food prior to enzymatic breakdown and absorption (Lambert 1998). In addition to fermentation, low-quality foods such as leaves usually require a longer gut passage or retention time for maximal extraction of nutrients in mammals. Thus, folivores generally have slower passage time than frugivores, although there is considerable inter- and intraspecific variation (Lambert 1998).

Insectivory requires digestive adaptations that in many ways are similar to folivory, since chitin, like cellulose, is a carbohydrate that requires special processing. Alongside the efficient mechanical processing necessary for successful digestion of insect matter, the microbiota of the caecum produce enzymes that digest chitin (Lambert 1998). Such chitinolytic enzymes are widespread in nature, and are synthesized by bacteria, fungi, nematodes, plants, insects and fish (Gianfrancesco and Musameci 2004). Among mammals, they

Table 2.2 *Relative gut volume proportions for some primate species (% of total volume)*

Species	Stomach	Small intestine	Caecum	Colon
Gibbon	24	29	2	45
Orangutan	17	28	3	54
Gorilla	25	14	7	53
Chimpanzee	20	23	5	52
Human	17	67	0	16

Adapted from Milton 1987.

are found in mice, chimpanzees, humans (Gianfrancesco and Musameci 2004), pottos and galagos (Kay and Sheine 1979). Without the exoskeleton, insects are easily digested, with the small intestine being the main site of absorption (Lambert 1998). Thus, the small intestine is relatively longer in insectivores, compared to the relatively larger colon found in primates that eat more plant material (Chivers and Hladik 1980).

Foraging on a dispersed and limited resource such as fruit requires a different suite of digestive adaptations. Primates do not store or cache food, so when a patch of food is found, they must eat to satiety or to the exhaustion of the resource. Chimpanzees maximize their intakes of fruit by having a large yet morphologically simple stomach. Cercopithecines, such as baboons and macaques, on the other hand, use cheek pouches for food storage, foraging for multiple items and then moving from the food patch to eat them (Lambert 2005). Cercopithecine use of cheek pouches may help to minimize competition or exposure to predators by allowing individuals to retreat to lower-risk areas to consume what they have foraged and stored in them. Since the pulp of ripe fruit comprises non-structural carbohydrate, it is easier to digest than leaves or seeds, and frugivorous primates usually have relatively unspecialized guts (Lambert 1998). Differences in frugivore gut morphology follow the supplemental food of choice, whether leaves or insects (Lambert 1998).

The role of body size in primate diets

Body size is a fundamental aspect of an animal's biology that influences dietary patterns, energetics, home range size and life history (Damuth and McFadden 1990). Smaller mammals are more likely to be insectivorous, while larger ones are more likely to be folivorous. Insectivorous primates usually weigh less than 500 g as adults whereas folivores are likely to weigh more than this (Kay 1984; Fleagle 1999). This boundary has been formalized as Kay's threshold. Insectivory is particularly common in strepsirhines (which tend to be smaller than haplorhines) and some of the very small-bodied haplorhines, particularly the tarsier, some callitrichids (marmosets and tamarins) and the talapoin monkey. To gain adequate nourishment, animals must be able to extract and absorb nutrients and process enough food to meet their daily energy needs (Lambert 1998). Smaller animals expend more energy per unit of body mass than larger ones, and therefore require a proportionally higher energy intake to maintain energy balance (Kleiber 1961). One way in which a small primate can meet such energy needs is by concentrating on high-quality foods, such as insects, which tend to be nutrient-rich and easily digested. Small primates have faster transit times than larger ones, perhaps because they have absolutely shorter guts. Since smaller animals also need absolutely less food, they can rely on a diet comprising non-ubiquitous and small food sources like invertebrates.

Larger primates can be folivorous because their lower dietary energy requirement per unit of body mass relative to smaller primates means that they can eat food of lower quality and energy density. This relationship has been formalized in the Jarman/Bell principle, derived from studies of antelopes (Bell 1971; Jarman 1974), but shown to be applicable to primates (Gaulin 1979) (Figure 2.5). Notable outliers to this simple principle include some small mammals that are folivorous, including primates. One highly folivorous small primate, *Lepilemur*, has been reported to process leaves by using coprophagy, eating faeces that contain high proportions of undigested plant materials (Hladik 1978). It has also been argued that because enzyme activity scales negatively with body size, smaller animals can process secondary plant compounds (found at high concentrations in some leaves and unripe fruits) more effectively (Lambert 2002).

It pays for larger animals to be folivorous, if such foods are abundant. Although their relative energy intake is lower compared with small-bodied animals, they must still consume absolutely more food. Large-bodied animals would struggle to meet their daily energy needs if they favoured rare or highly dispersed foods, regardless of how energy-rich they were, given that time is an important additional constraint on energy intake (Dunbar 1988). Humans and their closest relatives, the great apes, have the largest body sizes of all living primates, ranging in mass from 33 kg (female bonobos) to 175 kg (male gorillas) (Smith and Jungers 1997). In general, they conform to the rule that larger-bodied animals can eat a lower-quality fruit- and foliage-based diet, although they can be generalized as ripe fruit eaters. Like many other primates, however, the apes differ in their diets and foraging behaviours. Mountain gorillas eat a high proportion of leaves, although when fruit is available they, like the lowland gorillas, will seek it preferentially (Morgan and Sanz 2006). Gorillas will also forage opportunistically on insects (Morgan and Sanz 2006).

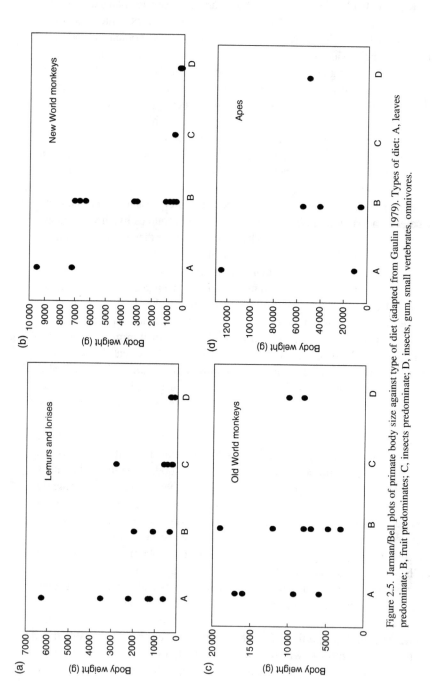

Figure 2.5. Jarman/Bell plots of primate body size against type of diet (adapted from Gaulin 1979). Types of diet: A, leaves predominate; B, fruit predominate; C, insects predominate; D, insects, gum, small vertebrates, omnivores.

Orangutans eat a range of foods, favouring ripe fruits but also consuming insects, seeds, leaves and bark (Fox *et al.* 2004).

The smaller great apes (common chimpanzees and bonobos) are among the most eclectic in their feeding strategies and food preferences, although some lowland gorilla populations are also highly eclectic feeders (Rogers *et al.* 1990). Chimpanzee diets vary greatly within populations as well as across Africa. This is related to individually determined age and sex behaviour, local ecologies and traditions. In large part, chimpanzees have a preference for ripe fruits and seem particularly dependent on figs (Morgan and Sanz 2006). Even though the termite-fishing and monkey-hunting of common chimpanzees is well documented, these foodstuffs make up only a small proportion of their diets. Mainly confined to tropical forest habitats, chimpanzees sometimes inhabit forest fringes, with some populations being known as savannah dwellers. However, unlike other African primates such as baboons that also exploit forest fringes, chimpanzees rarely ingest tropical grasses or sedges (Sponheimer *et al.* 2006a).

Superficially, human (or hominin) diets may appear continuous with those of chimpanzees: humans consume faunal matter (including, in some populations, significant quantities of insects (DeFoliart 1992)) as well as ripe fruits and leafy foods. There are several important differences, however. Humans tend to have discrete meals (Chapter 5), rather than browsing and eating opportunistically throughout the day. Although humans are large-bodied primates, their overall dietary quality and energy density tends to be much higher than of other apes, mainly as a result of their meat-eating but also because they employ technologies to process foods prior to ingestion to make them more digestible. Humans have a relatively unspecialized gut, with a colon that is shorter relative to overall size than in other apes; this is often attributed to the greater reliance on faunivory in humans (Chivers and Langer 1994). Overall gut passage time for humans is around 31 hours compared with 37 hours in gorillas and orangutans (Milton 1984), and 23 hours in chimpanzees (Lambert 1997, cited in Lambert 1998). Unlike the other apes, humans are not confined to 'browse' vegetation (discussed further in Chapter 3) like fruits and leaves, and make extensive use of tropical grasses and their animal consumers, a behaviour perhaps established early in hominin evolution (Lee-Thorp *et al.* 2003; Peters and Vogel 2005). Humans also show remarkable dietary flexibility and adaptability.

Human dietary diversity and flexibility in context

Human diets are as diverse as the people that eat them. Compared with other primates (even those with great dietary flexibility such as chimpanzees and baboons), modern humans have extraordinarily varied and variable diets.

Some of this variability is driven by ecology and environment, but cultural and social behaviours are powerful influences. The processes of agriculture, urbanization, globalization and industrialization also alter diets. It is difficult to pinpoint what the human diet actually is, especially as some populations have diets that comprise a wide variety of foods, whereas others rely on a small number of staples. Nonetheless, humans are frequently described as omnivores.

In ecological terms, omnivores feed at more than one trophic level (Pimm and Lawton 1978), although some prefer to define omnivory specifically as feeding on both plants and animals (Arim and Marquet 2004). Omnivory is now known to be common in both vertebrates and invertebrates (Arim and Marquet 2004). Within terrestrial mammals, omnivores include small canids such as the red fox, brown and black bears, pigs and many rodents. However, 'omnivory' is a continuum rather than a straightforward, discrete category. Some omnivorous animals eat foodstuffs in more or less equal measure from several trophic levels (Williams and Martinez 2004). Humans clearly fall into this group, eating primary producers (plants), primary consumers (herbivores) and even some secondary ones (carnivores, such as fish like mackerel), although human omnivory may only be possible because of technological processing (Chivers and Langer 1994). Other animals described as 'omnivores' focus mainly on foods from a single trophic level and supplement with food from an adjacent level (Williams and Martinez 2004).

Animals with broad or diverse diets that generally feed at a single trophic level may be better described as 'eclectic feeders' rather than true omnivores. Many primate species lie at this end of the continuum, reflecting the morphological constraints on eating a highly mixed diet (Chivers and Langer 1994): the short, simple guts seen in faunivorous primates, for example, are unsuited to eating a highly folivorous diet. Several modern primate species are eclectic feeders, showing considerable dietary breadth and flexibility. This is particularly so for the Old World monkeys, and is one of the main reasons for their success in terms of range and population size. Many Old World monkeys, including baboons, vervets and several macaque species (all from the cercopithecine subfamily), can tolerate a wide range of environments (sensu Vrba 1980): baboons and vervets are found across huge swathes of sub-Saharan Africa, while macaques have a geographic distribution that discontinuously stretches from Morocco to Japan (Chapter 1). Along with their diverse diets, they are able to exploit a wide range of habitats and respond relatively easily to changing environments, including those that are disturbed by human activity. Even among the colobines (the Old World monkey subfamily deemed to be more specialized) some species, such as the black and white colobus monkey and the common langur, have eclectic diets, comprising fruits and seeds as well as leaves, and wide habitat tolerances, with black and white colobus exploiting many different forest types across central and east sub-Saharan Africa, and the common langur, as well as inhabiting varied forest types, also being at home in towns and cities.

Baboon (*Papio hamadryas* subspecies) diets have been particularly well described, as the relative ease in observing them has resulted in over 40 years' worth of systematic field studies. They therefore offer a good illustration of primate dietary eclecticism. Baboon diets vary seasonally and geographically, as well as across the life of an individual (Altmann 1998). Although baboons are highly selective in their choice of foods (Barton *et al.* 1992), their behavioural flexibility allows them to vary their diets according to availability and need. Hill and Dunbar (2002) found that baboon diets from populations across Africa were dominated by fruits, seeds and subterranean resources, with the latter, requiring increased foraging time, being used as a fallback when fruit was not available. This accords with stable isotope data from southern African baboons, indicating use of C_4 resources that varied across the year (Codron *et al.* 2008). The majority of plants follow either the C_3 or the C_4 photosynthetic pathway, although some arid environment specialists follow an alternative pathway, that of Crassulacean Acid Metabolism (CAM). Plants following the C_3 pathway fix atmospheric carbon dioxide as a three carbon molecule before entering photosynthesis, and include shrubs, trees (and hence their fruits and leaves) and non-tropical grasses. Tropical grasses and sedges are C_4 plants; these fix atmospheric carbon dioxide as a four carbon molecule before entering photosynthesis. Analysis of carbon isotopes can give information about dietary components in animals both living and extinct (Lee-Thorp *et al.* 2003; Codron *et al.* 2008); for example, the ratio of C_3 to C_4 isotopes can give an estimate of the proportion of non-grass to grass plant material consumed by humans, and largely also the cereal consumption. In the southern African baboons studied by Codron and colleagues (2008), the C_4 component in most populations comes from grasses (and potentially from their rhizomes), although at least one population consumes a significant proportion of CAM-photosynthesizing succulents that also contributes to the C_4 signal.

Human dietary eclecticism and omnivory appear to have relatively deep evolutionary roots, and can be traced back within the Hominini (the phylogenetic tribe comprising humans and their closest extinct relatives) to the australopiths (Chapter 3). Stable isotope studies (see Lee-Thorp *et al.* 2003; Codron *et al.* 2008; Cerling *et al.* 2011) show that C_4 resources were important components of early hominin diets. This contrasts with data from modern savanna chimpanzees, indicating that they rarely consume such foods (Sponheimer *et al.* 2006a). This suggests that hominin diets, even in the Plio-Pleistocene, had shifted away from the ripe fruit and browse vegetation that extant great apes consume (Sponheimer and Lee-Thorp 2003) and that has been reconstructed for Miocene apes. There are very few isotope data on the Miocene apes, but one of the few studies indicates that *Sivapithecus*, an orangutan-like species from Asia, lived in and therefore subsisted in an environment rich in C_3 plants (Nelson 2007). Why and how hominins shifted their dietary strategies to converge with those of the papionins (baboons and their close relatives), which exploited tropical grassland resources even in the Pliocene and Pleistocene (Lee-Thorp *et al.* 1989), remains a major question, addressed in Chapter 3.

Most primates are tropical animals, whereas humans are cosmopolitan, inhabiting not only the tropics but also much higher latitudes. Contextualization of human diets is therefore enriched through comparison with the diets of the few modern primates found in temperate regions. Members of the papionin genus *Macaca,* macaque monkeys, are the only living primate other than humans to be found in temperate as well as tropical latitudes (Figure 1.2). The extensive geographic range of macaques and the relative abundance of several species among them are often attributed to the ability to feed eclectically (Jablonski 2002), with obvious parallels to *Homo*. Modern macaques consume a wide range of foods including ripe fruit, flowers, mature and immature leaves, seeds and bark, invertebrates and occasionally vertebrates (Hill 1997; Hanya *et al.* 2003). Macaque diets change markedly according to habitat (Hanya *et al.* 2003), with those found in tropical regions consuming more fruit than those in temperate or more marginal zones, which tend to be more folivorous (Hill 1997). Stable isotope analysis of rhesus macaque hair has demonstrated that individuals that lived at relatively high latitudes (greater than 29° N) seasonally supplemented their largely C_3-plant based diets with C_4 plants (O'Regan *et al.* 2008). The catholic use of plant resources seen in temperate macaques suggests that eclectic feeding is a fundamental macaque adaptation to life in temperate, harsh or marginal environments. It also suggests that human – or hominin – dietary flexibility was an important prerequisite of dispersal out of the tropics and exploitation of all the major biomes of the world.

Among the non-human apes, chimpanzees are the most eclectic feeders but their dietary – and indeed ecological – flexibility is less than that seen in cercopithecines, which is why some have argued that Old World monkeys may be better ecological comparators for hominins (Aiello *et al.* 2000; Elton 2006; Codron *et al.* 2008). Cercopithecines (papionins and their sister taxon, the guenons) may be able to increase dietary breadth and exploit a range of foods that are of low quality and are difficult to digest, alongside their preferred resources, because of their slow gut passage rates and their ability to deal with phytochemical toxins (Lambert 2002). The slow passage rate evident in cercopithecines is determined not by body size but by muscular contraction of the gut, which may have been selected for within the clade (Lambert 2002). Why hominins and their dietary adaptations appear to correspond more to baboons than chimpanzees is not yet resolved, but there are some potentially fruitful lines of enquiry. For example, relatively small functional changes in digestive physiology, such as expression of the *AMY1* gene or changing peristaltic movement, may significantly alter dietary breadth in animals with a similar bauplan, or morphological blueprint. Thus, unfortunately for palae-ontologists, some of the most significant dietary adaptations in the early hominins may not have been in the bones and teeth preserved in the fossil record but in saliva and soft tissue.

Fully understanding primate and hence hominin foraging behaviour requires a knowledge of the whole ecosystem, including plants, their predators and defences, and gut microbiota. However, when examining human diet in a mammalian context, we must not lose sight of the fact that humans and non-human primates are different. The dietary eclecticism of humans varies from that of non-human primates in a number of important ways. Most fundamen-tally, humans have access to a wider range of resources through technology, including tool use and cooking. As a species, humans also depend much more on meat. In addition, food may be accepted or rejected on the basis of symbolic or cultural value, rather than simply due to its palatability or nutritional qualities (Ulijaszek 2002). This is an extension of the 'social facilitation' of eating behaviour observed in some primates, including capuchin monkeys, whereby 'encouragement' by conspecifics can over-ride learned or innate caution when faced with novel foodstuffs (Visalberghi and Fragaszy 1995).

Human meat-eating contextualized

Meat-eating, although not universal across modern populations, is an import-ant feature of the diets of many humans, and is a highly prized resource in many societies. Meat-eating, as part of a general propensity to dietary eclecti-cism and omnivory, is at the root of human cosmopolitanism (being found across the world). Many members of the order Carnivora are also cosmopolitan (Turner 1992), because sources of meat are available in most places across the world, while leaves and fruits are not necessarily so available. Subsistence foragers at the highest northerly latitudes view marine resources and herbi-vores adapted to digest low quality plant foods (secondary consumers) as essential dietary components (Kelly 1995), since it is not possible for humans to consume and digest high latitude plants in sufficient quantities.

Additionally, unlike many edible parts of plants (young leaves, fruits, seeds), meat is not a highly seasonal resource in temperate zones (Chapter 4).

The human ability to eat significant quantities of meat and fish is a significant departure from the dietary norm of the haplorhine primates, especially for animals in the larger size classes. Insects and other invertebrates are often important components of the diets of smaller primates (usually those weighing less than 1 kg), and some small primates also take vertebrates opportunistically: callitrichid monkeys from South America, for example, will kill and eat snakes. However, many medium-sized (1–10 kg) and large primates (>10 kg) opportunistically supplement their diets with invertebrates and sometimes vertebrates, but tend not to rely on such foods. Several primate species exploit aquatic or marine resources, but unlike humans, only do so opportunistically (Kempf 2009). Humans share many features of their gut morphology with other primates, particularly great apes, and have a gut structure that reflects their evolutionary heritage as plant, specifically ripe fruit, eaters (Milton 1999b). The pronounced sacculations ('bags') seen in the colons of humans and apes are particularly linked to plant-eating (Milton 1999b). However, human small intestines are longer than would be predicted for an ape of that body mass and the colon is relatively short, indicating adaptation to meat-eating at some point in the human evolutionary lineage (Milton 1999b).

The chimpanzee cooperative 'monkey hunt' and subsequent sharing of food is the most dramatic example of meat-eating within the non-human primates, and one which resonates with human food procurement experiences (e.g. Stanford 1995, 1998). Nonetheless, it differs from human hunting behaviours in that it is opportunistic rather than planned, and it has been suggested that chimpanzee hunting yields more social than nutritional benefits (Stanford 1998). For example, female chimpanzees are more likely to have sex with males who have shared meat with them over an extended period of time than with those that have not (Gomes and Boesch 2009). Despite the high profile given to chimpanzee meat-eating and hunting (Stanford 1998; Preutz and Bertolani 2007), there have been no attendant shifts in their gut proportions (Milton 1999b).

The view that chimpanzees are not physiologically adapted to meat-eating is reinforced by observations that some captive chimpanzees are at high risk of developing hypercholesterolaemia and vascular disease, despite being fed controlled diets (Finch and Stanford 2004). Chimpanzees may be more susceptible than humans to the atherogenic effects of saturated and trans fats and cholesterol in the diet, as humans appear to have acquired genes that offer some protection from the hypercholesterolemic effects of dietary lipids (Kaplan *et al.* 2000). The *apoE* gene involved with lipid metabolism and transport in lipoprotein particles in the blood is a prime candidate for such a gene. Chimps have only one *apoE* genotype, considered the ancestral primate form, which is similar to human *apoE4* (Hanlon and Rubinsztein, 1995). However, in humans the main isoform is *apoE3*, which has a 65%–85% prevalence (Sandholzer *et al.* 1995). It seems to have arisen around 200 000 years ago (Fullerton *et al.* 2000). Humans with *E4/E4* genotypes respond to dietary saturated fat and cholesterol with a fourfold increased serum cholesterol compared to those with *E3/E3* genotypes (Sarkinen *et al.* 1998).

Discussion

Understanding mammalian, specifically primate, diets and foraging behaviours gives a template for understanding human action in relation to food and its consumption. First, flowers are important, since without flowering plants, mammalian, primate and human diets could not be what they are. Flowers can be beautiful, but they are also signalling devices for the seasonally future emergence and abundance of fruits and seeds. Hunter-gatherers and subsistence agriculturalists know this, and perhaps primates and other mammals do too. However, industrialized human society has largely severed the link between the beauty of flowers and the functionality of flowering plants as foods.

So what does comparative analysis of mammalian form reveal about human dietary and nutritional needs? The human digestive system follows the general primate plan in many ways, but the larger small intestine and the smaller large intestine suggest adaptation to a higher quality, or higher energy density, diet. Milton (1999b) argues strongly for the role of meat-eating as a selective pressure for these changes, starting around the time of *Homo erectus* (around 1.8 million years ago) but it is possible that increasingly processed, including cooked, food was an important contributor (Wrangham *et al.* 1999). It is difficult, if not impossible, to estimate accurately whether earlier hominins shared the gut morphology of modern humans, but it has been suggested that *Homo erectus,* the first hominin to have an unequivocally human-like post-cranial skeleton, may have had a reduced gut size overall (Aiello and Wheeler 1995). This fits with the hypothesis that meat-eating was an important pressure in the reduction of gut size but also does not preclude a role for food processing: *H. erectus* is associated with increasingly complex tool technology and controlled use of fire, both of which could increase the digestibility of food and hence promote gut size reduction. This is explored further in Chapter 5.

Gut proportions can be highly variable within species, although the intra-individual plasticity evident in birds – where proportions can alter rapidly under different dietary regimens – has not been observed in mammals (see

O'Regan and Kitchener 2005 for a review). It is likely that there is a strong phylogenetic component to digestive morphology in humans and other apes (Milton 2003). This is especially true for the dentition, the gross morphology of which is determined prior to eruption and hence before being used for feeding. It is clear that humans have not converged on the dental morphology of the Carnivora, and retain many features in common with other primates. This emphasizes the importance of a mixed diet with a significant plant component for humans (Milton 1999a). Although some populations, particularly in Arctic regions, have traditionally subsisted on a diet dominated by meat, this is a cultural response to extreme environments, facilitated by technology, which has arisen since the origin of modern humans (Elton 2008a). Such subsistence could only be possible with the availability of fatty animal tissue, especially organs, rather than lean meat, since the former can provide adequate nutrition for humans and the latter cannot. Evidence for this is provided by the 'rabbit starvation' observed in people attempting to subsist off lean game (Chapter 5) (Cordain *et al.* 2000b). It is therefore unlikely that humans could be true carnivores in the way that felids are.

The eclectic and omnivorous diet that humans consume is phylogenetically determined through gut form, as caeco-colic fermenters are better adapted to digest a wide range of foodstuffs than are forestomach fermenters. Although some human groups have relatively homogeneous diets, due in part to social and political circumstance (Chapter 8), our nutritional history is one of dietary diversity (Milton 1999a). This supports public health approaches that promote increased consumption of fruit and vegetables, even if the plant foods available now are very different in nutrient composition to those in the Pleistocene and before (Elton 2008a). The role of dietary eclecticism in shaping human evolutionary history is profound. It allows humans to exploit varied and variable environments, just as it does in many Old World monkey species. It may also moderate the effects of intra- and interspecific competition, which in some circumstances could make humans a more egalitarian primate species than most: the 'affluent and egalitarian' foraging populations described by Sahlins (1974) may be a case in point. Chapter 8 considers the emergence of inequality in human societies and how this has shaped diets.

Although large body size may also help buffer humans during periods of seasonal stress, dietary flexibility may be particularly crucial in seasonal environments where resource availability changes throughout the year (Chapter 4). Dietary diversity and flexibility was an important prerequisite of hominin dispersal out of the tropics and exploitation of all the major biomes of the world. It has also been a key element in human dispersal across the globe, which far surpasses the colonizing abilities seen even in that most tenacious of primates, the macaque (Chapter 1). Meat-eating has allowed humans to colonize high latitudes and very open landscapes. However, bearing in mind the phylogenetic constraints that prevent humans from being true carnivores, such expansion was probably not accomplished through meat-eating alone. Instead, humans have used their ability to technologically harvest, process and consume a very wide range of foods to help exploit all major biomes (Elton 2008b).

Humans have a major advantage over other primates in that technology has helped them overcome some of the time limitations faced by foragers in patchy or seasonal environments. Since primates must devote a significant portion of their day to socializing in order to maintain group cohesion, this limits the time available for foraging. Thus, environmental quality and day length not only affect group sizes but also the latitudinal extent of their ranges (Dunbar 1988; Hill *et al.* 2003). This is illustrated well by the forestomach fermenting colobines that need enforced resting time for digestion, and as a result tend to have more restricted latitudinal ranges than the cercopithecines (Korstjens and Dunbar 2007). Outside the tropics, primates may 'run out of time' during winter days with short daylight periods, making them unable to balance their commitments to socializing, foraging, resting and travelling, regardless of how flexible their diets and behaviour are. Under current climatic conditions, this restricts the geographic regions that non-human primates can inhabit. Although human populations also face time pressures, cultural solutions have to a great extent solved the time budget problems experienced by other primates. Such solutions include the use of fire for cooking (which increases the energy availability of many foods) and artificial light, which allows extension of the waking day and time available for socializing.

Human foraging can be viewed as a logical extension of primate ecology and behaviour in several ways. Co-operative food procurement is a feature not only of humans and chimpanzees engaged in hunting, but also of other primates. These include those that predate upon insects, as well as frugivores where group living allows sharing of information about food patches. Among primates, group living may increase overall access to resources through more effective competition for food with other groups and increased vigilance against predation (Janson 1992). One disadvantage of living in groups is an increase in competition for resources within a restricted area (Isbell 1994); primates therefore engage in a delicate cost–benefit balancing act. Humans face similar group living costs, exacerbated by social stratification and inequality (Chapter 8), again modifying a trend already present within primates. Another 'modified trend' is the human ability, found in frugivores, to exploit patches of food rather than relying on more ubiquitous resources. Humans have taken this to extremes and it is highly likely that bipedalism, which originated at least 4 million years ago, altered the way in which humans and their closest ancestors used their environments and procured food.

Examining the evolutionary heritage of humans as primates enables us to identify major points of similarity, and to determine where the human path splits from that of our closest relatives. Humans are strikingly similar to other primates in many aspects of their feeding biology and behaviour, from their general digestive morphology to the costs and benefits of group living. Of course, all primate species diverge from the norm in one way or another – that is, after all, what makes them unique, and a distinct taxonomic unit. However, humans have diverged more than most and exploit their environments in ways unfamiliar to other primates. In terms of diet and nutrition, the major points of difference are in dietary quality (including significant meat-eating) and their extreme dietary flexibility. Identifying when, why and how these changes occurred in humans is the subject of later chapters.

3 *Diet and hominin evolution*

Introduction

The human fossil record holds many clues about when, why and how human diets and feeding behaviour diverged from primate norms. The links between human and primate diets are clear and undeniable (Chapter 2). However, human diets have shifted in a number of important ways. One of the most significant of these is increased dietary quality (usually synonymous with higher energy density), including the extent to which meat was incorporated into the diet (Chapter 5). Another is the degree to which humans can exploit an incredibly wide range of resources, eating foods from almost every trophic level and varying their diets to exploit numerous environments (Chapter 4). In this chapter, we outline the main ways of reconstructing palaeodiets. We discuss the major trends in hominin diets, including how hominin dietary niches varied between species and shifted over time. In doing so, we provide general information about the diets of several hominins, but it is not our intention to provide an exhaustive review of the diets of all species. Instead we aim to show the patterns that resulted in modern human diet and feeding behaviour and when, why and how the extreme dietary flexibility of humans evolved.

Humans do not live in isolation, either from each other or from other organisms in their ecological communities. The diets and behaviours of community members often impact on others. Predation is one good example of this, where one member of a community can end up as lunch for another, and which influences the group sizes, reproductive output, habitat exploitation and body mass of prey species (Isbell 1994; Cowlishaw 1997; Hill and Dunbar 1998; Willems and Hill 2009; Creel *et al.* 2009). At the same trophic level, animals often compete for resources, and this has helped to shape human feeding behaviour, sociality and dietary choices. Competition occurs between individuals, between groups or populations (intraspecific) and between species (interspecific). Competition for food is rarely uniform. Among primates, for example, higher-ranking individuals may have better access to resources (Nakagawa 2008), although this is not universally observed (Brosnan and de Waal 2003), partly because the ways in which food resources are distributed can themselves alter the dynamics of group hierarchies (Nakagawa 2008). In some monkeys, when food is evenly distributed or highly abundant, a despotic or hierarchical structure is less likely than when resources are patchily distributed or scarce (Nakagawa 2008). These 'monkey politics' resonate with the human condition: for humans, access to food and water is highly politicized, and socioeconomic status is a key determinant of diet and consequently health (Chapter 8). Hominins are very likely to have competed for resources, and competition and differential access to resources have deep evolutionary roots. However, this is no excuse for deterministic attitudes about the inevitability of nutritional and health inequalities within present-day humans (Chapter 8).

Within primates, and by analogy hominins, resource competition and eating behaviour alter across the life course and by sex: infant food differs from adult food, and male diet may differ from female diet. This is partly attributable to different processing abilities – in some capuchin monkeys, for instance, skull morphology in males and females indicates sexual differences in diets and foraging strategies, partially facilitated by the larger size of males, who are able to bite larger food items (Masterson 1997). Behavioural differences also occur because of different social roles within groups that sometimes divide by sex. For example, male chimpanzees trade meat they opportunistically hunt for social favours (Gomes and Boesch 2009; and Chapter 2). If early hominins did the same, this could have had a direct impact on individual reproductive success, even if the net nutritional benefit had been marginal. What is observed in primates and inferred for hominins bears marked similarity to familiar scenarios in modern humans, where diets of adults and children, males and females, and their respective foraging and sharing behaviours within a group, are often different (Lee and DeVore 1968; Bird and Bliege Bird 2000; Elton 2008b). The interactions between diet and social behaviour in primates are taken to extremes in modern humans, for whom food procurement and consumption is not simply driven by the need for nutrition but also moulded and mediated socioculturally (Chapters 5 and 8).

Dietary choices may alter according to competition for a specific resource as well as food availability. Considerable intraspecific variation in diet, biology and behaviour can therefore be caused by localized differences in food resources and competition, as seen, for example, in many widespread primates (e.g. vervets: Fedigan and Fedigan 1988; baboons: Barton *et al.* 1993; red colobus: Struhsaker 2010). There is no reason why this would be different for hominins, and thus may have contributed to human dietary evolution. It is likely that many hominins, at least from the origins of the genus *Homo* but probably several earlier hominins, were generalist and opportunistic in their feeding and habitat choices. The effects of intra- and interspecific competition for food alongside the variation expected for such a mammalian generalist may have heightened the need for flexibility and could have contributed to 'variability selection', argued to have been a major factor in the evolution of brain size and bipedalism (Potts 1998; Chapter 5). However, accurately quantifying variation within a species is not straightforward for modern animals that can be observed directly (O'Regan *et al.* 2008) and is even more challenging when considering the diets and ecologies of extinct animals.

When investigating intra- and interspecific variation in hominin diets, a number of assumptions must be made that are rarely testable in an empirical way. It must be assumed, for example, that the small number of hominin specimens recovered represent the norm for a particular species. Shifts in diet, unless they are extreme, may not be well reflected in the fossil and archaeological records. Morphology may not vary predictably with dietary change as there are numerous influences on form, including dietary adaptation but also sexual selection, phylogeny, geography and genetic drift, which are often hard to tease apart. Similarly, the behavioural traces of diet and foraging contained in the archaeological record are affected by taphonomy; preservation, if material exists at all, will differ from site to site. Accurately accounting for variation over time and in different areas can also be a problem given the small and patchily distributed fossil samples available. Nonetheless, identifying the ecological and biological differences, including diet, between hominin species is necessary to investigate human evolutionary history and to understand the adaptive radiation of hominins. It is therefore essential when making comparisons to ensure they are appropriate, to account for the limitations in reconstructing the diets of extinct animals and to assess the resolution of the data.

Reconstructing palaeodiets

The data available from fossils, stone tools and occupation sites are the primary sources of evidence when judging intra- and interspecific differences in hominin diet. Diets of most extinct animals, including hominins, can be studied by using a wide range of methods that are crudely subdivided into indirect and direct approaches. Indirect approaches such as the study of fossil morphology or archaeological remains either give important general information about dietary adaptation (but not actual diets) for individuals, or provide contextual information that may not be easily attributable to individuals or even species. Direct approaches, including isotope and dental microwear analyses, give information about the actual diet of an individual through study of chemical composition of teeth, parts of the skeleton and other bodily tissues, or microscopic tooth wear. Direct and indirect evidence of individual diet or dietary adaptation are often extrapolated to the species, although this must be done with caution, bearing in mind individual variability.

Morphology and material properties of fossilized teeth and bones

The gross morphology of the face, teeth and mandible provides important information about general dietary adaptations (Chapter 2). Such 'hard tissues' give vital clues about species-level dietary adaptations, and broad interspecific variations in diet can be identified by examining dental, facial and mandibular form among species (Taylor 2006). However, the face, jaw and teeth reflect more than dietary adaptation. There can be a strong phylogenetic component to craniofacial and dental form, and closely related species with different diets may have very similar morphologies. This is exemplified by members of the Plio-Pleistocene African hominin genus *Paranthropus*: *Paranthropus robustus* is a generalist whereas *Paranthropus boisei* is a grass or sedge specialist (Cerling *et al.* 2011), although the two nonetheless share a robust skull form with pronounced keels for muscle attachments, flaring cheekbones, and enormous molar teeth. The face and dentition have an important role in signalling to mates and potential competitors for those mates, leading to sexually dimorphic features (Plavcan and Carel 1997; Weston *et al.* 2004). Facial form can also alter according to allometry (size-related changes in size) and dental development (Taylor 2002), while stochastic processes such as genetic drift have also been shown to influence facial morphology in hominins (Ackermann and Cheverud 2004). All these factors must be considered when using craniofacial and dental morphology as lines of evidence in dietary reconstruction.

The material properties of foods (how hard, soft, brittle or tough they are) cause varying stresses and strains on teeth and bone. The external morphology and internal architecture of hard tissues are adapted to withstand the demands of mastication, given a diet that is 'normal' for a given organism (bearing in mind that 'normal' does not necessarily mean 'most common'). Bone is a dynamic structure. Specialist cells, osteoblasts, osteocytes and osteoclasts, respectively form, maintain and remove bone tissue over an extended period of time. Bone therefore responds or 'remodels' to the conditions experienced by the organism during its life, even after the initial growth phase. It can thus be 'adaptively plastic' (Gotthard and Nylin 1995), the stresses and strains of mastication remodelling the internal architecture and external morphology of bone (Ravosa *et al.* 2007). Thus inter-individual variation in facial and mandibular form occurs. Such changes also occur within individuals over the life course (Ravosa *et al.* 2007): all mammals start life on a diet of milk and so the foods they consume, along with the associated alteration in stresses and strains on the masticatory system, shift dramatically at weaning. Age- and load-related degeneration of bone can also occur (Ravosa *et al.* 2007), which may influence masticatory efficiency and food choices.

Controlled *in vivo* experiments (e.g. Ravosa *et al.* 2007) allow the stresses and strains of mastication and any resulting remodelling to be quantified in living organisms. However, this is not an option for extinct animals, including hominins. In these cases, sophisticated '*in silico*' (computer-based) models in combination with advanced imaging methods such as micro computed tomography (μCT) are used to investigate masticatory stresses and strains and their possible effects on the internal architecture and external morphology of bones (Kupczik 2008). Dental adaptation can also be studied in a similar way. Finite elements analysis (FEA) is one technique that is used to examine dietary adaptation in hominins. It highlights where strains are expressed under specific loads and thus helps to indicate the function of specific morphological traits (Kupczik 2008). For example, a study of the *Australopithecus africanus* skull and dentition indicated that the pillars of bone in the maxillary and nasal regions were very important functionally and that within its varied diet, *A. africanus* may have used its premolars to break the outer shells of nuts and seeds (Strait *et al.* 2009). However, these results are not necessarily supported by other lines of evidence including tooth wear (Grine *et al.* 2010). In another study using data from gross morphology and FEA, Macho and colleagues (Macho *et al.* 2005; Macho and Shimizu 2010) suggested that the teeth of the Pliocene hominin *Australopithecus anamensis* were adapted to the consumption of hard and tough foods, although this is apparently not supported by microwear evidence (Grine *et al.* 2006). Both sets of conclusions may be consistent with repetitive heavy loading of the teeth, however. One major strength of FEA and other *in silico* modelling approaches is that they can be used to explore the functional and adaptive limits of a structure. This in turn helps to generate hypotheses that should then be tested by using other established methods available to palaeobiologists for dietary reconstruction (Grine *et al.* 2010).

The morphological adaptations of the skull (or indeed dentition) may not indicate preferred foods or even those most commonly eaten. Instead, it has been argued (Lambert *et al.* 2004; Marshall and Wrangham 2007) that the adaptive significance of differences in masticatory form relates to foods eaten during times of scarcity of preferred resources. These so-called 'fallback foods', although abundant, may be more difficult to eat and require more mechanical processing to extract nutrients, having higher proportions of roughage and lower energy content. Some Asian colobine monkeys provide a good example of a 'mismatch' between dental adaptation and preferred foods, with gross dental morphology showing adaptations to folivory but observational studies indicating that leaves are not a primary part of the diet (Marshall *et al.* 2009). In this case, leaves may act as fallback foods, and because they are more difficult to process mechanically and chemically than fruits, require specialist adaptations to exploit them efficiently (Marshall and Wrangham 2007). The ability to do this could improve survival and hence fitness. The facial buttressing of *A. africanus*, which may have allowed high premolar loadings to crack nut and seed casings, could be an adaptation to fallback foods (Strait *et al.* 2009). It has also been suggested that the very large molar teeth, molarized premolars and large masticatory muscles of *Paranthropus* are an adaptation to consuming underground storage organs as fallback foods (Laden and Wrangham 2005). However, recent isotope data (Cerling *et al.* 2011) indicate that *P. boisei* ate large quantities of grasses and sedges, possibly utilizing the whole of the plant including underground storage organs, but as a main food source across the year rather than as a fallback (Lee-Thorp 2011).

Dental microwear

In many studies based on gross morphology, teeth and bones are treated as part of the same functional complex. However, teeth and bones are not identical tissues and give different information about diet. In contrast to bone, teeth are formed before exposure to the external environment and are not plastically remodelled during life: bones when broken can heal but teeth do not. Thus, because tooth gross morphology (including overall shape, cusp formation and enamel thickness) does not respond to environmental influences in the same way as bone, teeth may give a 'cleaner' signal of genetic adaptations. Nonetheless, although there is no remodelling, external tooth form does not remain static: the exterior surfaces of teeth wear down to give important clues to the diets of individuals. Some tooth wear is easily visible to the naked eye, often becoming increasingly obvious as individuals age, especially if the diet contains abrasives, as found for example in traditionally milled stone-ground flour. In severe form this can affect the normal functioning of the teeth and alter feeding behaviour. However, it is the microscopic tooth wear that does not impair function (microwear) that is most powerful in revealing dietary components.

Dental microwear studies have contributed enormously to the understanding of hominin diets (Teaford and Ungar 2000; Scott *et al.* 2005). When foods are eaten, both the occlusal (chewing) and non-occlusal surfaces of teeth are abraded. The wear patterns that remain, usually revealed by using high-resolution micro-scopy, give information about what is being consumed, as different food types leave characteristic signatures on the teeth (Teaford and Walker 1984). 'Scratches' or striations are left by tough leaves and other vegetation, whereas hard and brittle objects leave pits (Teaford and Walker 1984). By quantifying the relative proportions of pits and scratches or undertaking texture analysis of the tooth surface (whereby a large number of pits creates a complex texture and a large number of scratches an anisotropic or directionally textured surface (Scott *et al.* 2005)), it is possible to reconstruct what the animal was eating just prior to its death (or loss of the tooth). Comparative samples of microwear from modern species of known diet are vital to ensure that the inferences made about the diets of fossil animals are as accurate as possible, albeit with the proviso that modern animals may not provide a direct analogue for those that are extinct.

Tooth wear arises through a destructive process, so new wear obliterates the old. Dental microwear thus gives a direct insight into the 'last meal': a snapshot in time rather than a long-term picture of diet (Teaford and Oyen 1989). This contrasts with the more general picture of an animal's diet provided by gross morphological features, and can be used to 'fine tune' or refine reconstructions of palaeodiets. 'Last meal' data from microwear studies can be highly variable: individuals within a species exhibit dietary variation, because of individual tastes, geography, seasonality and life stage. Combining microwear data from different individuals without thought to the effects of these factors may give a misleading view of dietary variation and variability across individuals, geographic ranges and species. This underlines the import-ance of accounting for the potential sources of variation and using as large or as representative a sample as possible when reconstructing palaeodiet, what-ever the data.

Stable light isotope analysis

The foods eaten by an organism are reflected in the chemical composition of its bodily tissues: in that sense we are truly what we eat. Stable light isotope analysis of these tissues can help to reveal diet. The most commonly studied tissues in ecological and archaeological research are faeces, hair, bone, and bioapatite from dental enamel, with nitrogen and carbon isotope ratios fre-quently analysed. Nitrogen can be examined only when skeletal, hair or other tissues from specimens retain collagen. Nitrogen data can thus be recovered, at least sometimes, from Late Pleistocene Neanderthal and early modern human subfossils, but dietary information for true fossils (which do not contain collagen), including hominins, is taken only from carbon data. Tooth enamel is highly resistant to structural change after death and deposition in the ground for a prolonged period, so is the source of analytic material for most palaeontological studies (Lee-Thorp and van der Merwe 1987). Since isotope data reflect the tissues from which they are derived, they reflect diet during their formation times, and tissue turnover rates can influence the dietary signal obtained (O'Connell and Hedges 1999). For example, as bone collagen and bioapatite are formed and experience turnover (replacement through the actions of osteoclasts and osteoblasts, as with the remodelling described above) across a relatively long period, a time-averaged signal of several years' diet will be given (Ambrose 1993). This is in contrast to hair, which forms more quickly and therefore reflects more recent diet, potentially including seasonal shifts (O'Regan *et al.* 2008). These factors must be considered when interpreting isotope data. Biochemical components of foods also change in their isotope concentrations when they become part of bodily tissues, a process commonly known as 'fractionation' (Hobson and Clark 1992). Corrections to stable isotope data, appropriate to the tissues being used, are thus necessary before dietary inferences can be drawn (O'Connell and Hedges 1999; Sponheimer *et al.* 2003b; Cerling *et al.* 2006).

The ratio of nitrogen 15 (^{15}N) to nitrogen 14 (^{14}N) gives an indication of trophic level. Carnivores generally have higher $^{15}N/^{14}N$ ratios than herbivores living in the same ecosystem (Schoeninger and DeNiro 1984). Since marine food chains tend to be longer than terrestrial ones, consumers of marine foods often have higher $^{15}N/^{14}N$ ratios than individuals that eat primarily terrestrial resources (Schoeninger and DeNiro 1984). Infants prior to weaning also usually have higher $^{15}N/^{14}N$ ratios as they are effectively 'eating' their mothers when they breastfeed (Jenkins *et al.* 2001). However, interpretation of nitrogen isotope signals is far from straightforward, with soil (and hence plant and animal) nitrogen varying markedly by region and according to climate (Handley *et al.* 1999). The nitrogen signature of an individual also alters depending on consumption of certain plants. These include legumes, involved in nitrogen fixation (making nitrogen biologically useable), with leguminous plant consumers generally having lower $^{15}N/^{14}N$ ratios (Delwiche *et al.* 1979). These environmental factors can make it difficult to relate $^{15}N/^{14}N$ ratios to diet.

The ratio of carbon 13 (^{13}C) to carbon 12 (^{12}C) gives information about the plant groups eaten (either directly or through secondary consumption) but does not reveal trophic level. Plants can be divided into three groups, C_3 plants, C_4 plants and CAM (crassulacean acid metabolism) plants, according to their photosynthetic pathway. C_4 plants are adapted to environments with strong sunlight and mainly comprise savanna grasses and sedges (O'Leary 1988), particularly in tropical regions of the world. Outside the tropics, the vast majority of plants follow the C_3 pathway, which can vary biochemically from environment to environment, leading to a range of $\delta^{13}C$ values. C_3 plants, which have a near-global distribution, include most trees, shrubs and forbs (O'Leary 1988). Plants of the CAM group, mostly succulents, are relatively uncommon, especially in temperate regions, and have an isotope range that overlaps those of both C_3 and C_4 plants (O'Leary 1988). There is a predictable relationship between the photosynthetic pathways of the plant foods consumed (either as primary sources or secondarily through eating the meat of plant-eating animals), the external environment and the ratio of $^{13}C/^{12}C$ in tissues (Sponheimer *et al.* 2003a). This allows aspects of the diet of modern and extinct animals to be elucidated, especially for those living in the tropics, where both C_4 and C_3 plants are common. It is possible to distinguish, for example, between modern tropical animals that subsist almost exclusively on grass (grazers) and those that mainly eat leaves and shoots (browsers), as well as those that eat both (Sponheimer and Lee-Thorp 2003). There is also a difference between atmospheric and oceanic carbon, reflected in organisms that live on land as against the sea (Chisholm *et al.* 1982). In animals from C_3 ecosystems with a marine component to their diets, $\delta^{13}C$ (differential uptake of ^{13}C) values are higher than those that subsist on terrestrial foodstuffs (Chisholm *et al.* 1982). Since most of Europe, especially after the middle Pleistocene, is a C_3 ecosystem, differences in $^{13}C/^{12}C$ ratios observed in late Pleistocene hominins from Europe are attributed to differential consumption of marine food resources (Richards *et al.* 2001). Just as with nitrogen analysis, environmental factors must be considered in interpretations of diet based on carbon isotope signatures. Increased shade and moisture as well as lower temperatures can reduce plant $^{13}C/^{12}C$ ratios (Heaton 1999). Forest cover also alters $^{13}C/^{12}C$ ratio (the canopy effect) with forest floor plants being between 0.2% and 0.5% lower in $\delta^{12}C$ than open habitat or upper canopy plants (Heaton 1999). Altitude can also affect $^{13}C/^{12}C$ ratios, due to changes in partial pressure of CO_2: $\delta^{13}C$ is higher at higher altitude (Heaton 1999).

Stable carbon isotope analysis has been used to provide information about palaeodiet in hominins for over two decades (e.g. Lee-Thorp and van der Merwe 1987). It has transformed the ways in which hominin diets and feeding behaviour are perceived. In particular, it was isotope evidence that drew attention to the likelihood that *P. robustus* and *A. africanus* were eclectic feeders, consuming a mix of C_3- and C_4-derived foods (Lee-Thorp *et al.* 1994; Sponheimer and Lee-Thorp 1999). Since hominins lack the specialist dentition (and most probably the gut adaptations) required to process and digest grasses efficiently, a parsimonious interpretation of the C_4 component of their diets is that they ate vertebrates (including small animals such as lizards) or insects that themselves consumed C_4 plants (Lee-Thorp *et al.* 1994; Sponheimer and Lee-Thorp 1999; Peters and Vogel 2005). Another possibility is that they exploited C_4 wetland plants, including papyrus rootstocks (Peters and Vogel 2005). Whatever the interpretation, isotope data clearly suggest that several early hominins studied had broad dietary niches, possibly feeding across a number of trophic levels.

Like any other method of diet reconstruction, stable light isotope analysis is not a 'magic bullet', but has a number of limitations. Animals consume what is in their ecosystem. Since the vast majority of plants use C_3 photosynthesis, even in the tropics (Peters and Vogel 2005), carbon isotope analysis only provides limited information: if an animal lives in a C_3 ecosystem it will eat C_3 plants, although differences in isotope signal, between plants from environments of different temperatures, altitudes or tree cover for example, will occur. Carbon isotope analysis has proven to be so useful in palaeoanthropology because the initial radiation of hominins, in the late Miocene through to the early Pleistocene, occurred in tropical and subtropical Africa in ecosystems with C_4 plants. These plants were therefore available for consumption, as were the animals that themselves ate them. Outside C_4 regions (in more northerly latitudes, for example, including much of Europe), the value of stable carbon isotope analysis, used in isolation, diminishes for palaeodiet reconstruction of hominins. Thus, for Pleistocene hominins dispersing out of the C_4 ecosystems of Asia and Africa (Chapter 5), carbon isotope analysis does not reveal much dietary information. However, carbon isotope data combined with those from oxygen isotope analysis can provide information about palaeoenvironment. In younger subfossil material from relatively cold regions (primarily Europe), where there is preserved collagen, carbon isotope data in combination with nitrogen data are useful indicators of diet, since they can discriminate between the exploitation of marine and terrestrial foods (Schoeninger and DeNiro 1984). Even in ecosystems with a C_4 component, nearly all fruit and leaves are derived from C_3 plants, so isotope analysis itself cannot distinguish between frugivory and folivory. However, isotope analysis can be used to identify dietary supplementation with C_4 plants in animals that generally prefer C_3 foods (Codron *et al.* 2008; O'Regan *et al.* 2008) (Chapter 2), although if a significant component of C_4 is identified and ascribed to dietary factors, it is not always easy (especially if nitrogen data are lacking) to determine whether this is because of direct plant consumption or meat eating.

Archaeology as 'fossilized' behaviour

The study of hominin bones and teeth alone, whether based on morphology, microwear or chemical composition, does not necessarily allow a rounded reconstruction of diet. Many inferences about diet and feeding behaviour come from archaeological, palaeoenvironmental and palaeoecological research. These are indirect ways of investigating diets that provide hugely informative contextual data. The extent and resolution of archaeological data differ according to region and time period. Theoretically, the prehistoric archaeological record should become richer as time moves towards the present day, because of the increased likelihood of preservation and the increased complexity and abundance of hominin material culture. In practice, however, the record is patchy, and preservation differs according to region as well as time period. Stone tools are the first unequivocal archaeological material. The earliest known stone tools come from Gona, Ethiopia, and are dated to 2.6 million years ago (Semaw *et al.* 1997). Other archaeological remains found in the Plio-Pleistocene and later periods include animal bone showing evidence of hominin modification, such as percussion and cut marks (Bunn and Kroll 1986). The earliest such bones come from Dikika in Ethiopia, and are dated to around 3.4 million years ago, some 800 000 years before direct evidence of stone tools in the archaeological record (McPherron *et al.* 2010).

There is widespread consensus that the earliest tools were used to process animal carcasses, although whether the animals were first hunted by hominins or secondarily scavenged is yet to be resolved (see, for example, Blumenschine *et al.* 2007). Hominins lack the specialized dentition found in carnivorans (the group of animals that includes the cat and dog families) and other habitual meat and bone eaters, so must have needed to have pre-processed at least some of the meat in their diet (Chapter 2). Observations of modern chimpanzee hunting behaviour show that it is possible to hunt, kill and eat animals without using tools (chimpanzees pull colobus monkeys apart, for example). However, exploiting larger carcasses in this way would be much more difficult. The use of stone tools thus appears to be requisite for more extensive processing and consumption of meat, as cooking may also have been. The products of this processing – animal bone – along with occasional fish bones and bird eggshells themselves provide important evidence about diet, especially if they are modified. The types of bony elements (for example, long bones), the species of animal and their relative abundance all help to piece together aspects of hominin diet. At some well-preserved sites, often those from the later parts of human evolutionary history, it is possible to quantify favoured prey animals and compare patterns of accumulation (and hence probably consumption) between regions (e.g. Weniger 1989).

The presence of bone in an archaeological assemblage does not indicate that meat was the principal dietary component; as in all of archaeology and palaeontology, only the material that is preserved can be recovered and studied, even though it represents only a fraction of the original evidence. Understanding the 'lifecycle' of material that forms the archaeological and palaeontological records and the processes that influence its preservation is part of a discipline known as taphonomy, or the 'laws of burial' (Efremov 1940). Just as Sherlock Holmes found the dog that didn't bark to be crucial to one of his investigations, 'absence of evidence' in the fossil and archaeological records does not imply 'evidence of absence'. Thus, presence of animal bone without plants does not indicate that plants were not included in or were a less significant part of the diet, especially as plants themselves are not well represented in the Pliocene and Pleistocene fossil records. Teasing out which objects found together in the record were preserved or lived together, and determining the actions of external agencies on archaeological and fossil material, are important aspects of taphonomy. For example, the concentrations of bones and stone tools at some Plio-Pleistocene archaeological sites were initially interpreted as occupation sites or 'home bases', where hominins prepared meat and discarded both bones and tools (Isaac 1983). In fact, these deposition patterns are more likely to have come about because of non-hominin factors (Bunn and Kroll 1986), such as fast-flowing water redistributing in a concentrated way what were initially more broadly distributed discarded bones and stones.

Diet may be inferred from the cut and percussion marks that tools leave on animal bones, the animal species butchered or scavenged, and in some cases material that adheres to the tool itself. Microscopic plant remnants from the edges of stone tools indicate that tools from many time-periods were used to process plants as well as animals (Dominguez-Rodrigo *et al.* 2001; Mercader *et al.* 2008). In some cases, stone tools were used for woodworking rather than for preparation of plant foods (Dominguez-Rodrigo *et al.* 2001), as suggested by the identification of phytoliths, or 'plant stones', tiny particles of silica deposited by plants in soil. However, stone tools have variously yielded starch grains (Mercader *et al.* 2008) and fibres from tubers (reported in Gibbons 2009), both of which are likely to be food traces. The first tools, the Oldowan industry (2.6 to 1.7 million years ago), were relatively simple choppers, scrapers and hammerstones. As time progressed, tools became more sophisticated. By the late Pleistocene, there was extensive differentiation in the hominin toolkit, which helps to reveal dietary content and variation. The presence of harpoons, for instance, strongly indicates fishing and hence fish-eating. But as harpoons are not found in all early modern human archaeological assemblages (Schmider 1982), their use probably varied geographically and culturally.

The archaeological record is a valuable source of information about hominin diets and feeding behaviour, but like every other source, has limitations. Not all hominins are associated with stone tools. In some cases this is because the species in question did not make or use them. However, this does not imply that they did not use any sort of tool or failed to engage in any technological processing of foodstuffs before ingestion. Stone is durable whereas other materials that can be used to make tools (such as wood and bamboo) are not. The earliest hominins may have used tools made of non-durable materials (wooden termite fishing rods and digging sticks, for example) to procure food. Analogy with modern animals and birds (for example, chimpanzees, capuchin monkeys, elephants and New Caledonian crows) suggests that basic tool use by the earliest hominins during foraging cannot be discounted. Even after stone tools appear in the archaeological record, they are not ubiquitous. In some regions, suitable materials for stone tool manufacture are not available. Just as modern human groups have different environments and cultural practices that favour some tools, toolmaking methods and materials over others, hominins also may have had geographic and cultural differences. The paucity of stone tools in south-east Asian early Pleistocene assemblages, for example, has been attributed to the use of abundant bamboo (Boriskovskii 1968), although this is heavily debated (West and Louys 2007). Such tools may not leave definite traces on bone (West and Louys 2007), concealing some aspects of diet and feeding behaviour. Other archaeological evidence of diet, including that of animal bone, may not be preserved in the record: the actions of animals and microbes often completely obliterate surface markings and indeed destroy the bone itself. Furthermore, bones and stones can be transported after deposition so although archaeology indicates hominin activity, it is not guaranteed to have occurred in the area in which the material was recovered. Thus, it is not always easy to associate bones, stones and other archaeological material with particular hominin fossils, species or even local areas.

Similar limitations pertain to palaeoenvironmental reconstruction, which can be local, regional, continental or global in scale. Although it is not always possible to link fossil, population or species with a palaeoenvironment precisely, such data, especially at the local and regional levels, provide the context for diet and feeding behaviour. Food provides a direct link between organism and environment, since organisms can only eat what is available. Being able to reconstruct hominin environments to discover, for example, how productive habitats were, what their vegetation types and fauna were, and whether hominins were most likely to have inhabited woodland, open areas or forest, gives clues to diet and associated behaviour. On a larger scale, continental and global reconstructions of climate change can also contextualize hominin dietary strategy. For instance, the abrupt climate fluctuations in Europe during the Pleistocene, with cycles of glacials and interglacials, may have affected diet, with Neanderthals in northerly latitudes in cold periods, for example, having a meat-dominated diet (Fiorenza *et al.* 2008).

Integrative approaches

Palaeodiet reconstruction is rarely accomplished on the basis of a single line of evidence. This notwithstanding, caution must be exercised when combining different reconstruction methods. Many lines of evidence are not directly comparable. Gross morphology of teeth indicates genetic and species-level functional adaptation, as does bone, with the added 'noise' – or evidence – provided by plastic changes during the whole life of a fossilized individual. Isotope data from tooth enamel reflect the diet during the formation of that tooth, and depending on how it is sampled, may reflect the whole tooth formation period or a part of it. Whereas morphology provides indirect evidence of diet, isotope analysis gives more direct data. However, it is not truly direct, owing to fractionation effects. Both morphology and isotope analysis give evidence at totally different temporal scales and resolution to dental microwear. Obvious problems when combining contextual evidence with fossil material include confidently associating archaeological traces with species or individuals and understanding the scale at which climatic changes may have a direct bearing on the diets of individuals, groups and species. However, judicious use of multiple lines of evidence, if available, can be incredibly powerful. Data that at first glance seem contradictory may in fact hint at dietary and adaptive complexity and variability. Trying to understand dietary evidence at different scales can nonetheless give a more rounded picture of the relationships between functional adaptation and individual variability or how behaviour shifts over the life course. Understanding the limits and limitations of the data used to reconstruct palaeodiets is therefore crucial.

A brief history of hominin diets and niche differentiation

It is highly likely that the majority of hominin species and populations ate a relatively diverse diet based on a variety of plant foods (centred on fleshy fruits, nuts and seeds rather than leaves, but also including stems and underground storage organs), and variably supplemented with fauna, both vertebrate and invertebrate. Diets would have varied geographically and over time within the same species. There would also have been differences in dietary strategy across hominin species, allowing co-existence in the same geographic area. At the east African Plio-Pleistocene site of Koobi Fora, for example, as many as four hominin species may have existed contemporaneously (at the same time) or sympatrically (in the same place). There and elsewhere, as in modern ecosystems, competition between sympatric species or populations may well have been reduced through niche differentiation (Elton 2006), which often happens by resource partitioning, feeding on different foods or exploiting similar resources in different ways. Such niche partitioning may have been crucial to hominin survival and success.

Over the course of human evolutionary history hominins would have increasingly constructed and actively shaped their niches (Chapter 5). Occupying an ecological niche is not passive nor determined by natural selection. Organisms partially construct their own niches, either through making choices about diet or habitat or by actively building parts of their environments (Day *et al.* 2003). Humans provide the most extreme example of this, with much niche differentiation taking place through cultural means. Human groups living side by side often exploit the same geographic region in markedly different ways. In Tanzania, for example, several groups with distinct languages, religions and traditions employ different subsistence strategies: foraging with no domesticated animals and a basic toolkit (Hadza); pastoralism with domesticated animals (Datoga); and crop cultivation (Iraqw and Isanzu). These groups have co-existed in largely the same geographical region for several centuries, interacting with each other to varying degrees (Marlowe 2002). The possession of different political ecologies, and speaking languages of four distinct phyla, have been important to this partitioning. Understanding niche differentiation among hominins gives important context for the evolution and diversification of modern human diets. A focus on resource partitioning emphasizes that humans do not live in isolation from their environments, even when they are part of industrialized economies. Humans must compete for food, not only with each other but also with other organisms, including mammals, birds and insects. For example, foraging populations may compete with carnivores for meat and birds for fruit, and the crops cultivated by agriculturalists may be favoured by insects or primates. Resource partitioning can help mitigate these competitive interactions, although in modern economies based on monocultures that have a restricted number of dietary components, there may be few opportunities to use this effectively.

Little research has been undertaken on hominin niche partitioning, competition and interaction (Codron *et al.* 2008; Lee-Thorp *et al.* 2003), even though this is an essential part of understanding dietary ecology. One problem with attempting a detailed examination of hominin ecology from the perspective of interspecific interaction and competition is establishing sympatry from the fossil record. Any two (or more) fossil species identified from a region are not guaranteed to have lived alongside one another, because of the effects of time and space averaging, where materials from different time periods and areas are brought together. Nonetheless, sympatry is common in modern primates so it is fair to assume that it also occurred in the past, especially when fossils of different species are found geographically close together over long periods of geological time, even if this cannot be proved conclusively.

Miocene hominins

The last common ancestor of the chimpanzee/bonobo–human clade existed between 6 and 8 million years ago (Steiper and Young 2006), in the Miocene epoch (Figure 3.1). Although genetic data indicate that there may have been a complex history of speciation in the human and chimpanzee lineages (Patterson *et al.* 2006), the first fossil candidates for the earliest hominins, assigned to the taxa *Sahelanthropus tchadensis, Orrorin tugenensis* and *Ardipithecus kadabba*, are found in the palaeontological record of the late Miocene in Africa (both East and central) around 6–7 million years ago (Senut *et al.* 2001; Haile-Selassie 2001; Brunet *et al.* 2002, 2005). Determining 'stem' species (those that lie at the base of an evolutionary radiation) is hugely challenging (Wood and Richmond 2000; Andrews and Harrison 2005; Cobb 2008). It is thus yet to be shown unequivocally that *Sahelanthropus, Orrorin* and *Ardipithecus* are more closely related to humans than to other African apes. However, there is enormous value in considering their dietary adaptations: they lie so close to the base of the hominin family tree that they provide vital contextual information about when hominin diets shifted to the pattern seen in modern humans.

A small canine tooth, honed only at the tip rather than, as seen in chimpanzees, along the edge of the tooth, is one of the few features used to identify fossils as being early hominins (Wood 2002). Sexual selection exerts a powerful influence on morphology, with canine form across the primates heavily influenced by mating system (Plavcan 2000), so it is unlikely that changes in the hominin canine represent a majory dietary shift. Unfortunately, detailed evidence about diets in the putative earliest hominins is slim. The diets of many apes, both extant and extinct, include a significant proportion of fruit (Chapter 2). However, as might be expected given their extensive adaptive radiation, the Miocene apes (some of which were not directly related to the modern ape lineage that includes gorillas, chimpanzees and humans) had varied dietary strategies, including folivory (Teaford and Ungar 2000). Both *Sahelanthropus tchadensis* and *Orrorin tugenensis* have relatively small molar teeth with fairly thick enamel; based on the palaeo-biologies of other Miocene ape species with similar dental morphology, it has been suggested that their diets included soft fruits (Andrews and Harrison 2005). Palaeoenvironmental reconstructions indicate that the earliest hominins evolved in woodland habitats (see review in Elton 2008b), which is

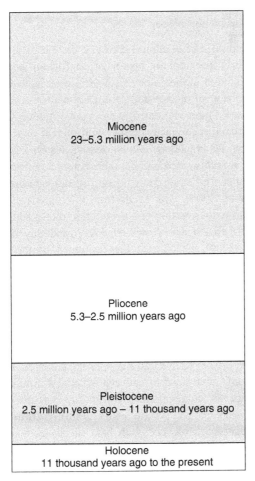

Figure 3.1. Schematic of geological epochs relevant to human evolution.

consistent with dietary dependence on fruits. However, more recent research on the occurrence of thick tooth enamel in Miocene apes indicates adaptation to hard-object feeding (such as seeds with a protective outer coating), possibly as a fallback strategy (Alba *et al.* 2010). Thick enamel may help to prolong tooth life in hard-object feeders as it is better able to withstand radial stress fractures (Lucas 2004). Thus, some of the earliest hominins, in the Miocene, may have been adapted to consume hard objects, which are argued to have been a dietary component of Plio-Pleistocene hominins such as *Australopithecus africanus* (Strait *et al.* 2009) and *A. anamensis* (Macho *et al.* 2005; Macho and Shimizu 2010).

Pliocene hominins

Compared to the large number of hominin species of the later Pliocene and early Pleistocene, relatively few hominin taxa have been identified from the earliest Pliocene (around 5.4–4 million years ago). Nonetheless, it seems that early hominins occupied several dietary and ecological niches. *Ardipithecus ramidus*, found at sites in Ethiopia and dated to around 4.4 million years ago, has smaller molar teeth than many australopiths, with thinner dental enamel that is nonetheless thicker than in modern chimpanzees (Suwa *et al.* 2009). The reconstruction of the *Ar. ramidus* palaeodiet has them eating an eclectic mix of foods without great dependence on ripe fruits, tough vegetation or hard objects such as seeds (Suwa *et al.* 2009), with foods from C_3 sources dominating (White *et al.* 2009b). This reconstruction of a generalized diet is supported by data from microwear analysis, which shows relatively randomly distributed scratches (Suwa *et al.* 2009). Given that the dentitions of the Miocene *Ardipithecus kadabba* and Pliocene *Ar. ramidus* are so similar that they were initially placed within the same species (Haile-Selassie 2001), it is possible that their diets could also have been fairly similar.

Australopithecus anamensis, from East Africa, is the only other hominin apart from *Ar. ramidus* securely known between 4 and 4.5 million years ago, although *A. afarensis* may also be present (Macchiarelli *et al.* 2004). The *A. anamensis* range extends from Kenya into Ethiopia and although it has been found in deposits at Aramis and dated to between 4.1 and 4.2 million years ago, there is no evidence for contemporaneity with *Ar. ramidus*, which is found some 200 000 years earlier (White *et al.* 2006). *Australopithecus anamensis* has dental features associated with hard object-feeding (Macho *et al.* 2005; Macho and Shimizu 2010), which is consistent with its exploitation of a more open, wooded environment (White *et al.* 2006). It has been argued that the difference between the dietary strategies of *Ar. ramidus* and *A. anamensis* represents an 'ecological breakout' and niche expansion with the emergence of *Australopithecus* (White *et al.* 1994, 2006). This is uncertain. First, as seen in the earlier radiation of Miocene apes, hard-object feeding is one of several dietary 'options' available to large-bodied primates and does not necessarily represent a significant ecological shift exclusive to hominins. In addition, microwear data indicate (at least in the few individuals studied) limited hard-object feeding in *A. anamensis*, which had a diet that overlapped with that of *A. afarensis*: dental microwear patterns from *A. afarensis* specimens (ranging from 3.6–3.2 million years ago) appear similar to patterns resulting from gorilla and chimpanzee diets, dominated by soft and tough foods such as ripe fruits and leaves (Grine *et al.* 2006). This suggests that it favoured soft or tough foods over hard or brittle ones, with morphology indicating that fine abrasives rather than tough foods created the observed microwear patterns (Grine *et al.* 2006). Since the realized niche of an organism is often narrower than its potential niche, it is not surprising that direct 'last meal' data point to different dietary components than do data from functional morphology, including dental enamel thickness.

Plio-Pleistocene hominins

The ability to eat a range of foods would have helped hominins to partition resources successfully in the face of competitors, and may have allowed them to move into new niches in novel environments more easily. Both resource partitioning and rapid adaptation to novelty are no more evident than in the Plio-Pleistocene. An extensive hominin radiation occurred at this time in Africa and Asia, with more than ten species identified. There was likely to have been significant dietary variation within and between species, with the facial shape changes and marked decrease in molar tooth size that emerged in *Homo erectus* just after 2 million years ago indicating a move towards the modern human condition (Wood and Collard 1999), including a dietary niche characterized by high-quality foods.

Australopithecus africanus (found around 3 to 2.4 million years ago), from southern Africa, had a highly varied diet incorporating a wide range of resources that probably included meat and insects (Sponheimer and Lee-Thorp 1999). *A. africanus* was not contemporaneous with *P. robustus* (found in southern Africa around 2–1.2 million years ago), which also had a varied diet (Lee-Thorp *et al.* 1994), so would not have competed for resources. *A. africanus* has relatively large teeth and thick tooth enamel, albeit thinner than that of *P. robustus* (Olejniczak *et al.* 2008). This difference points to interspecific dietary variation, with *P. robustus* probably being adapted, possibly as a fallback strategy, to eating more hard, brittle foods than *A. africanus* (Scott *et al.* 2005; Olejniczak *et al.* 2008). Nonetheless, microwear data indicate that their diets, although highly variable across species, overlapped to some extent (Scott *et al.* 2005). It is possible that the extinction of *A. africanus* allowed *P. robustus* to fill in part the niche that the older hominin vacated. Species diversity increased in southern Africa in the very early Pleistocene: *P. robustus* is found at the same localities and in the same deposits as *Homo* (Brain 1981). The recent discovery of *Australopithecus sediba*, a gracile hominin found at Malapa (about 15 km from the major fossil sites that yielded *P. robustus*) and dated to around 1.95 million years ago, also increases early Pleistocene hominin diversity in southern Africa (Berger *et al.* 2010). Currently there are no data on its dietary adaptations and little on its palaeoecology but its discovery nonetheless highlights that Plio-Pleistocene hominins from southern as well as East Africa, where up to four species co-occurred, may have faced significant competition from other hominin species as well as many other organisms.

By the Plio-Pleistocene, hominins were widely distributed across Africa, found not only in southern and East Africa but also, albeit less abundantly, in central Africa (Brunet *et al.* 1995). By the end of this period, hominins had dispersed out of Africa into Asia (Gabunia *et al.* 2000). Diet is fundamental to exploiting the environmental diversity that is inevitable with such a wide geographic range. Plio-Pleistocene hominins appear to have used at least two distinct strategies. The first, discussed more extensively below, is to be an eclectic feeder, a behaviour apparent in many hominins including *Ar. ramidus* (Suwa *et al.* 2009), *A. africanus* (Sponheimer and Lee-Thorp 1999), *P. robustus* (Lee-Thorp *et al.* 1994) and early *Homo* (Ungar *et al.* 2006). The second, seen in *P. boisei* and in contrast to previous reconstructions (Wood and Strait 2004; Ungar *et al.* 2008), is to be a specialist feeder focusing on a ubiquitous resource, tropical grasses and sedges (Cerling *et al.* 2011). Exploiting C_4 foods distinguishes hominins from the other apes.

It is not only the morphological diversity evident in the Plio-Pleistocene that facilitated niche differentiation. Tools, which have important roles in food procurement and processing, would have also contributed to this. Even simple instruments that require very little modification from their original form, like sticks for termite fishing and digging, can bring a vast range of otherwise unavailable resources into dietary reach. At Swartkrans, early hominins very probably used modified bones to fish for termites (Backwell and d'Errico 2001). For animals living on the edge of negative energy balance or with pressured time budgets, tools can also aid survival through increasing the efficiency of collecting and processing food. However, if the technologies used were digging or fishing sticks, made from perishable materials, it is likely that they left no trace in the archaeological record.

Although several animal species use tools, extensive modification of stone to create tools in the wild is associated uniquely with the hominins, and emerged during the Plio-Pleistocene. Manufacture and use of the earliest stone tools is commonly linked to meat processing (Bunn and Kroll 1986). Cut and percussion marks, indications of butchery and marrow extraction with tools, have been found on fossil bones of ungulates and other prey species from archaeological and palaeontological sites in East and southern Africa (Shipman *et al.* 1981; Bunn and Kroll 1986; Pickering *et al.* 2004; McPherron *et al.* 2010). However, stone tool manufacture and use were probably not part of the repertoires of all hominins. There is no direct evidence that the earliest hominins, including *A. afarensis* and *A. africanus*, made stone tools, as they pre-date the first tools at 2.6 million years ago (Semaw *et al.* 1997), although this is subject to constant review, especially with the emerging evidence from Dikika for bone modification prior to 3 million years ago (McPherron *et al.* 2010).

There is widespread acceptance that all members of the genus *Homo* were tool makers and users (Wood and Collard 1999). It is uncontroversial that *Homo ergaster* and *Homo erectus* (the first hominins that are undeniably members of *Homo* (Wood and Collard 1999)) manufactured Acheulean tools, the tool technology characterized by bifacial, teardrop-shaped handaxes that first appeared in the archaeological record around 1.8 million years ago in Africa. It is also highly likely that 'early *Homo*', particularly *Homo habilis* but also *Homo rudolfensis*, made and used Oldowan tools (Plummer 2004). However, it is unclear whether other hominin species made or even used the stone tools produced by other species. The close association in space and time between the earliest stone tools, tool-modified bone and the Ethiopian fossils attributed to the relatively megadont *Australopithecus garhi* and dated to 2.5 million years ago (de Heinzelin *et al.* 1999) may mean that this species made tools. Thus, the making and use of stone tools may not have been confined to *Homo*, especially as the first known *Homo* fossils are around 300 000 years younger than the date of the oldest stone tools (Plummer 2004). It is unhelpful to think that only members of the genus *Homo* can be toolmakers, especially making the assumption that if a hominin appears to be a toolmaker (associated with tools in the archaeological record) it must be *Homo*. Instead, it is better to consider the anatomical adaptations probably required for toolmaking and assess the degree to which they are evident in different species. Such adaptations include manual dexterity and a degree of cognitive sophistication that may be inferred from brain size. This approach is not without problems, however: given that most species are defined on the basis of craniodental features it may be difficult to assign postcranial material to a particular taxon. Estimating brain size from fragmentary remains can be challenging, and there is no straightforward relationship between cognitive ability and endocranial volume. In addition, the earliest putative members of the genus *Homo* may be more australopith than *Homo*-like, and it has been argued that the first true member of *Homo* was *H. erectus/H. ergaster* rather than the older *H. habilis* (Wood and Collard 1999). If this is the case, the link between *Homo* and Oldowan toolmaking is severed.

Members of the genus *Paranthropus* (the robust australopiths) are commonly found at Plio-Pleistocene stone-tool-bearing sites. In southern Africa, Oldowan material has been recovered at sites, including geological Member 5 at Sterkfontein, southern Africa, where the predominant hominin is *P. robustus* (Kuman and Clarke 2000). The possibility that *Paranthropus* manufactured and used Oldowan tools cannot be discounted, especially as associations between *P. boisei* skeletal remains and stone tools have been found in East Africa. Research on hand bones from one individual at Swartkrans attributed to *P. robustus* (but not definitely assigned as such) suggests the required anatomical adaptations were present for relatively precise manipulation and hence tool manufacture (Susman 1994). Brain size may have increased in *P. boisei* over the million years or so of its tenure in the east African fossil record with no evidence of a corresponding increase in body mass (Elton *et al.* 2001). More recently it has been suggested that *Paranthropus* would have been an unlikely stone tool maker, not least because there was no obvious change in the archaeological record when it went extinct (Plummer 2004). Its need for tools may have been lessened by its anatomical adaptations (Plummer 2004; Wood and Strait 2004). It is also possible that even if *Paranthropus* individuals did not make tools, they could have used tools discarded by other hominins (Elton 2006).

Hominin manufacture and use of stone tools to assist food procurement and processing was an important shift from the foraging behaviours of ancestral primates, as well as the behaviours of other animals. Tools would have assisted niche differentiation, especially if some but not all of the contemporaneous and sympatric hominins in southern and East Africa made and used them. Observations of modern chimpanzees and baboons show that tool use is not an essential pre-requisite for meat eating but would undoubtedly have made carcass processing much more efficient. Along with opening an expansive meat-eating niche formerly only occupied by the carnivorans, tool-use would have allowed plants to be exploited more efficiently, either by expanding the range of plant parts (such as tubers) in the diet or by reducing the need for extensive chewing. Later advances in tool technology, that ultimately resulted in the sophisticated and highly differentiated toolkits characteristic of modern humans, would have further altered, expanded and elaborated food-processing potential.

Pleistocene hominins

Homo was the dominant hominin genus of the Pleistocene, although *Paranthropus* survived until around 0.9 million years ago. By the Middle Pleistocene (around 500 000 years ago), *Homo* (the one remaining hominin genus) had dispersed out of Africa into Asia and Europe and was firmly embedded within an eclectic-feeding dietary niche that probably included significant meat-eating, or at least a diet of higher quality and energy density with less bulk. This may have been helped by cooking (Chapter 5), even in the earlier part of the Pleistocene. Members of the genus *Homo* would have needed to respond to ecological pressures and constraints, but also would have shaped their niches actively. Such niche construction is found across nature but the genus *Homo* takes it to extremes. Tool use and controlled fire, part of this dietary niche construction, were the first steps in the extra-somatic food processing that led eventually to the industrialization of food production that is integral to contemporary industrial diets. By modifying foodstuffs so extensively, digestive anatomy and physiology in *Homo* altered: teeth became smaller and guts simpler, two changes that are evident from the emergence of 'true' *Homo* at 1.8 million years ago (Wood and Collard 1999). These alterations point to the consumption of a diet of higher quality that required less processing, both mechanical (in the mouth) and chemical (in the gut) (Aiello and Wheeler 1995; Chapter 5). However, it is wrong to assume that Pleistocene *Homo* moved from a plant-based diet to one dominated by meat. Increasingly sophisticated methods of studying residual food traces in the archaeological record have revealed starch grains from a range of plant parts (including seeds, piths and tubers) from diverse botanical families on African stone tools from the middle to late Pleistocene periods (Mercader *et al.* 2008). Plants thus remained important to the diets of most if not all Pleistocene hominins, with traces on tools indicating that they were processed prior to ingestion, just as meat was.

Pleistocene *Homo* lacks the morphological diversity of the Plio-Pleistocene hominin radiation: although different species have been identified in the fossil record, the majority (with the exception of *H. floresiensis*, the diminutive hominin from Indonesia with a mosaic of australopith- and *Homo*-like traits (Lieberman 2009)) are similar and closely related to modern humans. This morphological similarity does not imply dietary homogeneity, however. More than any other animal, *Homo* shapes its own dietary niche, and it is likely that Pleistocene populations living in different geographic regions and influenced by cultural preference had diets that varied beyond that usual among widespread mammals. The same would also have been true for different *Homo* species living in the same region, as far as they existed. The best example of Pleistocene *Homo* dietary difference and possible niche partitioning – assuming the two were contemporaneous and sympatric – comes from studies of Neanderthals and anatomically modern humans. Stable isotope analysis of carbon and nitrogen indicate that sampled individuals from the two species had very different diets. Neanderthals have been argued to be 'top level' predators, with diets dominated by meat, whereas early modern human diets included resources from a number of trophic levels as well as terrestrial and marine sources (Richards *et al.* 2001; Richards and Trinkaus 2009). Microwear data partly support these observations but also emphasize geographic variation in Neanderthal diet (el-Zaatari 2007; Fiorenza *et al.* 2008). Those individuals that inhabited northerly regions and who went through significant cold periods (some of which were tens of thousands of years long) had diets in which meat was hugely important, but Neanderthals in southern Europe, especially during warmer periods, had varied diets that contained plant and animal foods (Fiorenza *et al.* 2008). The plant component of Neanderthal diets is also evident from other microwear studies (Perez-Perez *et al.* 2003) and plant traces in dental calculus (Henry *et al.* 2011) as well as extrapolation from what is known about digestive physiology and biochemistry in modern humans (Hardy 2010). Along the Mediterranean coast, Neanderthals exploited marine foods including seals and mussels (Stringer *et al.* 2008).

Given the nutritional limitations of lean meat of the type generally obtained from wild game (Chapters 2 and 5), Neanderthals would have needed to include either fatty meat (for example, from marine mammals) or carbohydrate from plants, possibly from underground storage organs but also from other sources such as berries and nuts, in their diets for at least part of the year (Hardy 2010). Plant traces are much more poorly preserved in the fossil record than animal remains, and the stable isotope analyses used for Neanderthals plus associated faunal assemblages, while good at identifying protein and animal components, do not reflect the complete diet (Hardy 2010). 'Absence of evidence' does not equate to 'evidence of absence', and the meat-eating signals from numerous types of data probably swamp the plant-eating signals for Neanderthals. Their dietary variability across space and time is consistent with the pattern observed within the hominin clade as a whole, and illustrates hominin dietary adaptability. It also mirrors the trends observed in modern foragers, whereby those populations that live in less productive environments have a greater (albeit generally not exclusive) dependence on meat. Differences in Neanderthal and early modern human diet may have resulted from exploitation of different environments: within Europe and Asia, it has been argued that modern humans exploited marginal areas, such as steppe environments, whereas Neanderthals may have preferred more mosaic, Mediterranean-type habitats (Finlayson 2004). Environmental factors influence diet, in that foodstuffs differ across environments, but in order for an organism to be successful in a given environment it must be able to extract resources from it. The modern human ability to survive in marginal environments may have been because of a superior ability to use the resources available, and modern humans may have expanded into a much broader range of environments because they were better able to manipulate their dietary niches.

Examining modern human and Neanderthal diets emphasizes two major themes in the evolution of hominin diets and dietary niche differentiation. The first is a trend towards increasing dietary quality or increased energy density, with high quality resources such as meat and fish becoming increasingly important in the hominin dietary niche from the late Pliocene and early Pleistocene. In some instances, exemplified by the Neanderthals, it resulted in hominins joining the carnivore guild and occupying a top-level predator niche that some human groups still inhabit now. Meat-eating and increasing dietary quality is discussed further in Chapter 5. The second theme that emerges is the importance of dietary eclecticism – 'omnivory' – which seems to be a feature of hominin diets from at least 4.4 million years ago (Suwa *et al.* 2009). Such eclecticism is evident in the diets of individual hominins and within a species among populations separated by space or time. It allows flexible and opportunistic resource partitioning in changing and changeable environments (defined both by climatic fluctuation and shifts in competition both within and across species).

Dietary eclecticism in the hominins

It is likely that some hominin species exploited ecological and dietary niches that have no analogue in modern humans, apes or other primates. Nonetheless, dietary diversity and eclectic feeding are the norm rather than the exception in the hominin clade (Teaford and Ungar 2000). The Olduvai Hominid 5, now assigned to the species *P. boisei* and discovered by the archaeologists Louis and Mary Leakey during their extensive fieldwork in east Africa in 1959, was found associated with remnants of eggshell, lizards and baby pigs. The Leakeys concluded from this that early hominins were opportunistic foragers, with a diet comprising mainly fruits and leaves, but supplemented with some animal food (Leakey 1960). However, it was only with the use of more direct methods of dietary reconstruction, dental microwear and stable isotope analysis, that the full extent of mixed feeding within the hominins was recognized (Lee-Thorp *et al.* 1994; Sponheimer and Lee-Thorp 1999; Teaford and Ungar 2000), even if *P. boisei* has recently been shown to be much more specialist (Cerling *et al.* 2011).

Eclectic feeding has ancient roots within the hominins, with the Pliocene hominin *Ar. ramidus*, dated to around 4.4 million years ago, probably having a diverse diet that nonetheless focused largely on C_3 resources (Suwa *et al.* 2009). However, it is not accurate to assume that all early hominin species had highly diverse diets within populations, across space or over time: *P. boisei* is a case in point. Based on stable isotope data, its diet seemed to stay focused on C_4 resources, probably grasses or sedges, over time and at different sites (Cerling *et al.* 2011). Relying on a stable, ubiquitous resource may have allowed it to 'ride out' environmental fluctuations during the Pleistocene. Based on dental microwear data from 19 individuals from different sites in

East Africa and spanning the period between 3.6 and 3.2 million years ago, the diet of *A. afarensis* also did not appear to change over time or in different environments, implying that it was able to extract its preferred foods from a range of environments over a long period of time (Grine *et al.* 2006). It is also possible that the lack of change in the *A. afarensis* diet is due in part to its existing prior to the onset of the most intense climate fluctuations and the dramatic habitat changes that accompanied them.

By around 2.5 million years ago, there is evidence for dietary eclecticism throughout the hominin radiation, including mixed feeding and intraspecific dietary diversity in *A. africanus* (Sponheimer and Lee-Thorp 1999), *P. robustus* (Sponheimer *et al.* 2006b) and early *Homo* (Ungar *et al.* 2006). Since microwear (and to a lesser extent stable isotope) analyses provide data about actual diets at different temporal scales and on an individual by individual basis, they potentially allow for detailed study of dietary variation and variability, provided suitable fossil specimens exist. Frustratingly, however, the study of *A. afarensis* diet (Grine *et al.* 2006) is one of the only cases where the links between hominin diet, environment and time have been systematically examined. This is partly due to the paucity of suitable specimens for analysis (in a study of *P. boisei* microwear, for example, only seven out of an available 53 specimens had sufficient antemortem microwear preserved for analysis (Ungar *et al.* 2008)). It is also due to the low resolution of dietary data. When pooled, such data can provide a good basis for statistically sound cross-species comparison, but when examined within-species, it is often difficult to differentiate between the 'noise' generated by normal individual variation and the variation that has arisen because of spatial and temporal factors. To date, therefore, most assumptions about the importance of dietary eclecticism for hominin adaptation and adaptability are made on the basis of the ranges of variation observed within a species rather than the correlation of this variation with specific environments or time periods.

Highly detailed reconstructions of dietary variability within individuals and groups of fossils that conceivably made up a population are possible if sampling is undertaken carefully (Sponheimer *et al.* 2006b). For example, serially sampling teeth along enamel growth lines has revealed that the diets of *P. robustus* varied seasonally from year-to-year, and between individuals (Sponheimer *et al.* 2006b). Such within-individual variation could represent seasonal resource exploitation in a single area, or migration between different feeding sites at certain times of the year (Sponheimer *et al.* 2006b). Whatever the explanation, likely in any case to differ from region to region and between species, such dietary flexibility was probably crucial to the hominin ability to adapt to environmental changes caused by global climate fluctuations that intensified in the Pleistocene (Sponheimer *et al.* 2006b). *P. robustus* was one of several hominins to endure for hundreds of thousands of years in the fossil record. At least two hominins, *P. boisei* and *H. erectus*, survived for over a million years, at the time when the Pliocene gave way to the Pleistocene. During this period, these species would have experienced intense climate change (de Menocal 1995), with attendant shifts in local and regional environments, including the foods available to them. Their long tenure (around five times longer than modern humans to date) provides strong evidence for their ability to respond to these changes (Wood and Strait 2004). *P. boisei* is found over a relatively wide geographic area in East Africa, stretching from Ethiopia at the northernmost edge of the Rift Valley (Suwa *et al.* 1997) to Malawi at the far southern edge (Kullmer *et al.* 1999). Distribution of *H. erectus* was even wider, being found outside Africa as well as within it. The widespread dispersal of *H. erectus*-grade hominins was probably helped by it being a generalized, opportunistic feeder, with an increasing focus on high-quality foods including meat (Chapters 4 and 5). For *P. boisei*, it seems likely that exploiting a ubiquitous and increasing resource, C_4 grass, facilitated its long tenure and relatively extensive range.

Despite the onset of the global climate cycles that led to successive glacial and interglacial periods, there was no sudden switch to open, arid environments in the African Plio-Pleistocene, and woodlands and forests remained important habitats for hominins (Elton 2008b). However, C_4 grassland environments became more common by the start of the Pleistocene (around 2 million years ago), with a limited amount of archaeological evidence indicating that such habitats were exploited by toolmaking hominins (Plummer *et al.* 2009). One major line of evidence for dietary eclecticism within the hominins comes from stable isotope analyses that demonstrate that several Plio-Pleistocene species exploited a range of C_3 and C_4 resources (Lee-Thorp *et al.* 1994; Sponheimer and Lee-Thorp 1999; Lee-Thorp *et al.* 2003; Peters and Vogel 2005; Sponheimer *et al.* 2006a, b; Plummer *et al.* 2009), alongside the C_4 specialism apparent in *P. boisei* (Cerling *et al.* 2011). Eating C_4 foods, as well as the adaptive flexibility of their use, parallels the dietary strategies of modern papionins, including the specialist grazing gelada, as well as the more opportunistic C_4 grass-eating baboons (Codron *et al.* 2005, 2006) and macaques (O'Regan *et al.* 2008) but is in contrast to the behaviour of savanna-living chimpanzees (Sponheimer *et al.* 2006b). Although the majority of primates are dependent on C_3 foods ('browse' vegetation such as fruits and leaves), the use of C_4 resources (including tropical grasses and rhizomes as well as fauna that consume tropical grasses) is important to Old World monkey adaptive flexibility (Codron *et al.* 2005, 2006; O'Regan *et al.* 2008). It seems highly likely that this was also true for early hominins (Sponheimer *et al.* 2006b).

Old World monkeys and hominins have a number of similarities (Jolly 1970, 2001; Elton 2006). Both underwent extensive adaptive radiations during the Plio-Pleistocene, with many of the resulting species being extinct today. Most pertinent to dietary evolution, both also radiated into diverse ecological niches, exploiting both C_4 and C_3 environments with corresponding dietary variation (Elton 2006). Both remain widespread and successful, due in no small measure to their ecological flexibility, which surpasses that of modern apes. Although chimpanzees feed opportunistically on a wide range of food-stuffs (Chapter 2), and inhabit forest fringe areas, they do not exploit C_4 resources. This may be a significant constraint on their ability to adapt to environmental change and expand their dietary niches (Sponheimer *et al.* 2006b). One question that may remain unanswered, for the time being at least, is why this is the case. Old World monkey and hominin consumption patterns are analogous rather than homologous. That is, their abilities to exploit a mix of C_3 and C_4 foods are helped by different behavioural, anatomical and physiological mechanisms (specialist adaptations to grass-eating in baboons, for example). Both baboons and modern humans feed on many of the same plant species but often use different parts of them as food (Peters and O'Brien 1994). Both Old World monkeys and hominins moved separately into C_4 niches, probably as a result of similar selective pressures and ecological opportunities (Dunbar 1983). After the divergence of humans and chimpanzees in the late Miocene, the chimpanzee ancestor became a deep-forest, ripe-fruit specialist while hominins exploited more open forest, woodland and grassland, reducing competition. Differences in dental adaptation of hominins and modern chimpanzees support this view (Suwa *et al.* 2009). The more recent move of chimpanzees from the deep forest into more open environments such as forest fringe may be because of ecological pressures (including the late Pleistocene and Holocene exploitation of forest by modern humans). A combination of anatomical and behavioural constraints (such as dental adaptations for soft-object feeding or reticence to try novel foods (Chapter 5)) could have prevented their ancestors from extensively exploiting C_4 resources. Hominin shifts into such niches several million years earlier may have been helped by relatively small functional changes to the digestive system caused by differences in gene expression (see, for example, Perry *et al.* 2007; Somel *et al.* 2008) (Chapter 2).

It has been suggested that hominins experienced a significant dietary transition to mixed C_3 and C_4 feeding at the end of the Pliocene and/or beginning of the Pleistocene, when there was a climatic shift (Sponheimer *et al.* 2006a). Some dietary and environmental reconstructions for earlier hominins, such as *Ar. ramidus* (White *et al.* 2009b), stress the importance of C_3 diets and ecosystems. However, it has also been argued that open, C_4 environments were less important to australopiths than to *Homo*, which may have been better able to exploit a wide range of environments, including grasslands (Plummer *et al.* 2009). It is likely that neither scenario neatly explains the evolution of hominin diets or the foraging choices made by hominins, which would have been influenced not only by abiotic factors but also by the living components of their ecosystems, including competitors. What is plausible, however, is that several hominins from the late Pliocene had the potential to occupy very wide dietary niches. Some, like *A. africanus*, could have achieved this by using morphological solutions such as facial buttressing (Strait *et al.* 2009) to allow consumption of non-preferred, potentially tough or hard foods when necessary, and others (particularly true *Homo*) achieved it largely through behavioural and cultural means. Even if the realized niche was not as wide as the potential niche, many hominins were eclectic feeders, with significant quantities of animal material being consumed within a broadly plant-based diet from the Plio-Pleistocene onwards. This ability would have been essential for *Homo* living in non-tropical regions, where plant productivity and diversity is less, and the need to exploit animal resources is more pressing. It has been argued that early *Homo*, particularly *H. erectus*, helped by behaviour and culture, was able to eat an even broader range of foods than could earlier hominins (Ungar *et al.* 2006) (Chapter 5). Such dietary breadth provided the basis of all later dietary evolution in humans, with different hominin species and populations exploiting all or part of this wide dietary spectrum depending on local ecologies and economies.

Discussion

From the emergence of the hominin clade around 7 million years ago there has been a trend towards increased dietary quality and energy density alongside variability and flexibility in both consumption patterns and foraging behaviour. Stepping back, it is hard to pinpoint when the hominin niche expanded into 'true omnivory' (feeding consistently from a range of trophic levels) as opposed to eclectic feeding on plants with some supplementation with animals. There appears to have been no 'point of no return' for hominins to mark the beginning of the modern human diet. Instead, the pattern that emerges from the late Pliocene onwards is one of adaptation to environments that vary geographically and over short (seasonal) (Chapter 4) and longer timescales. The grade shift that occurred with *H. erectus* was not accompanied by punctuated or dramatic dietary change: by then, a stone toolkit had been established (Plummer 2004), hominins were systematically processing animal carcasses (Bunn and Kroll 1986), may have been working together to forage (Plummer

2004), and had dispersed out of Africa (Gabunia *et al.* 2001). The emergence of 'true' *Homo* does have significance, however, for understanding the evolution of modern human diets. At this point, dietary adaptations in the dentition and skeleton begin to resemble those seen in modern humans very closely (Wood and Collard 1999). These adaptations indicate the consumption of a diet of higher quality and energy density and a committed move from processing within the body with teeth and digestive enzymes to technological processing (both mechanical and chemical), often associated with meat-eating.

Humans consume more meat than other primates, a dietary characteristic established in the late Pliocene/early Pleistocene (explored further in Chapter 5). There have been periodic attempts to downplay the importance of meat in the evolving hominin diet. Meat-eating has been described as a 'high risk, high reward' behaviour that would have benefited hominins only in periods of resource abundance (Wrangham *et al.* 1999). For the majority of hominins, meat, particularly from large vertebrates, would have been only part of a diet that also included a range of plants, insects and other animal products such as eggs and honey. Increased dietary quality would have been partially facilitated by meat-eating but would have also come about because of tool use, cooking and other food-processing techniques. Humans thus inhabit an 'omnivorous' niche, eating a wide range of animal and plant foods, and varying their diets according to environment, competition and tradition. Dietary flexibility and opportunism in hominins can be traced back to the early Pliocene. A message for public health nutrition that emerges from studying the evolution of human diets is that there is not, nor has there ever been, a 'set' human diet. However, the two characteristics that underpin the diets of members of the genus *Homo*, including modern humans, are overall high dietary quality and energy density within an often-varied menu of foodstuffs. This is essential for coping with the stresses of environmental and social perturbation. Where environmental stresses have been minimized, as in the contemporary industrialized world, the drive to consume diets of high energy density has become associated with the emergence of obesity and the chronic diseases that go with it (Chapter 9).

4 *Seasonality of environment and diet*

Humans can live just about anywhere. This ability stems not only from biology but also from sophisticated cultural and behavioural adaptations. Relatively recent innovations, such as ice-breaking ships, allowed Antarctica (the only continent without indigenous human settlement) to be colonized, but even without such modern technology, humans have inhabited or exploited all of the major biomes of the world (freshwater, marine, desert, forest, grassland and tundra) for much of their evolutionary history. In each of these major global biomes, environmental variability in day-length, temperature and rainfall can be measured within timeframes of a day, a year, decades, centuries, millennia and more. Environmental variability is thus the norm, and modern humans are very capable of responding physiologically, behaviourally and culturally to such variability (Elton 2008a, b), better than any other primate species. Humans are a technological species, in many cases relying more on cultural innovation and behavioural responses – including tools, shelters, clothes, fire, social controls and taboos – than genetic and even physiological adaptation to environmental variability. As a consequence, they have expanded the ancestral primate range out of the tropics and into temporal and Arctic regions (Elton 2008b). Moving into temperate regions exposed the earliest modern humans and their ancestors to more extreme seasons of photoperiod, temperature and resource availability than ever before. Even before this dispersal across the globe, hominins in the tropics would have experienced climatic seasonality, especially in rainfall, and consequent shifts in food resources. Since seasonal environments are evident in the African Miocene, much of human evolution is likely to have occurred within a seasonal context (Foley 1993).

Seasonality has continued to influence activity and behaviour, even though humans, particularly in the industrialized world, are buffered against many aspects of environmental seasonality. Figure 4.1 illustrates the seasonality of some fruits and vegetables that are common to widely different societies: local

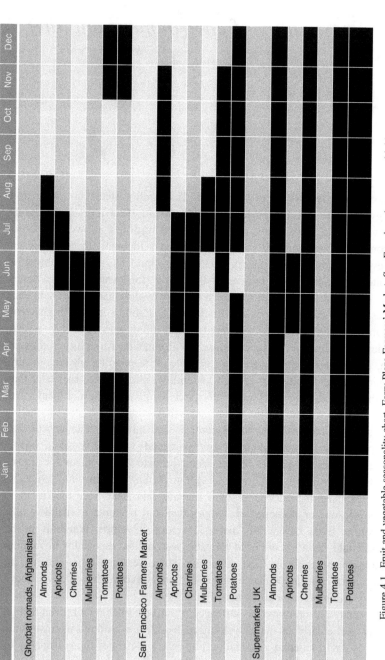

Figure 4.1. Fruit and vegetable seasonality chart, Ferry Plaza Farmers' Market, San Francisco (www.austenblokker.com/sites/farmersmarket/seasonal/charts.html), typical supermarkets in the United Kingdom, and Afghani nomads (Rao and Casimir 1988).

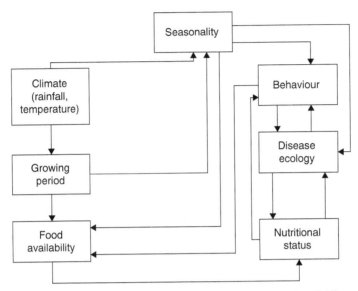

Figure 4.2. Relationships between seasonal changes in climate, food availability, nutrition, disease ecology and human behaviour.

producers on the West Coast of the United States (US) and Afghani nomads. The figure shows differences in the duration and timing of availability, even with similar foods, largely due to differences in absolute and seasonal rainfall and temperature and local varieties of the same foods. Supermarket data from the United Kingdom show that participation in global food markets means that most foods are available year-round. Whether past or present, a complex web of relationships between seasonal changes in climate, food availability, nutrition, disease ecology and human behaviour exists (Figure 4.2). In this chapter, we explore the nutritional aspects of this web, starting with the exposure of our evolutionary ancestors to seasonality and environmental variation and their physiological, behavioural and cultural adaptations to it. We examine the ways in which early humans, both foragers and agriculturalists, dealt with, were affected by, and sometimes shaped seasonality and environmental variability. We consider how contemporary human populations respond to variations in food availability and the implications this has for the setting of nutritional standards and dietary recommendations. We also address the links between seasonality and undernutrition. Where relevant, we consider the effects of other types of environmental perturbation, including climate change, which presents an increasing challenge for public health nutritionists and policymakers.

Seasonality and environmental variation in human evolution

Of the major transitions that anatomically and behaviourally modern humans have experienced, the dispersal of populations out of Africa (assuming a recent single-origin model of evolution) was among the most significant. The earliest fossil evidence for anatomically modern humans is in north-east sub-Saharan Africa, dated to around 160 000 years ago (Rightmire 2009). Modern humans appear to have dispersed rapidly around Africa. Archaeological evidence in southern Africa dating to around 160 000 years ago indicates behavioural modernity, the use of pigments, manufacture of bladelet tools and expansion into coastal, shellfish-eating niches (Marean *et al.* 2007). Both fossil and archaeological evidence show widespread distribution of modern humans across the North African coast around 130 000 years ago (Osborne *et al.* 2008). This distribution alone implies that different populations of humans would have exploited different environments and resources.

Modern humans may have resided in Africa for tens of thousands of years before dispersing into Eurasia (Rightmire 2009). The first fossil and archaeo-logical evidence for modern humans outside Africa is from the Levant, between 130 000 and 90 000 years ago (Rightmire 2009). Genetic data for modern human dispersal suggests rapid dispersal out of Africa around 70 000 years ago (Macaulay *et al.* 2005), although this is yet to be supported unequivocally (Bailey 2009). By 60 000 to 50 000 years ago, modern humans had colonized Australasia (Roberts *et al.* 1994) and much of Eurasia. By around 27 000 years ago, there were human populations above the Arctic Circle (Pitulko *et al.* 2004), pushing expansion far beyond that seen in any other hominin species.

Africa, the Levant and parts of Asia may have shared similar environments in the Pliocene and early Pleistocene (Dennell 2003). Once early modern humans colonized North Africa, possibly moving along riverine corridors (as detected by remotely sensed images of ancient river channels) in the Sahara that connected sub-Saharan Africa with the Mediterranean (Osborne *et al.* 2008), further steps into the Levant may have been relatively straightforward, given the relatively benign environments they would have found. Thus the first stages of dispersal out of Africa may not have imposed significant environmental stress when compared to the variety of environments experienced by modern humans in Africa.

Although dispersal out of Africa into south-east Asia may have occurred preferentially along coastal routes (Macaulay *et al.* 2005), the lack of an unbroken coastal strand between Africa and south-east Asia makes this unlikely: long 'detours' inland would have been necessary (Bailey 2009). It is probable that modern human populations in the Pleistocene spread inland as well as along coasts, pushed along by competition for resources and increasing population sizes in their existing habitats, and pulled towards new ones by relatively attractive resource possibilities elsewhere. These new habitats may have already supported populations of hominins, and so were not necessarily devoid of competition. New environments would have exposed hominins to new stresses, physical, biological and social, which would have varied over time and place. Pleistocene populations, in the tropics as well as temperate regions, may have experienced a double burden of resource fluctuation through seasonality as well as shifts in their environment caused by abrupt climate change (Figure 4.3). In some cases, this climate change would have been appreciable only over many generations. At points in the Pleistocene, however, especially during the short-lived warming events that occurred within glacial periods, climatic transitions that potentially affected food security and resource distribution may have taken place over much shorter time-scales: decades rather than many generations (Dowdeswell and White 1995). With less time to adapt, it is easy to imagine the starvation- and cold-related mortality that resulted, especially among those that pushed the envelope of adaptability at higher latitudes in temperate regions. Figure 4.4 shows seasonal temperature differences at the Boxgrove ancient human site, United Kingdom, around 500 000 years ago. This illustrates the marked seasonality experienced by ancient humans, with greater temperature extremes than seen at the same site today.

Modern humans were the first hominins to colonize very high latitudes, so would have needed to adapt to previously unknown seasonal conditions, not only very low winter and modest summer temperatures but also huge variations in day length. In winter, short days limit the time available for hunting, while snow and ice preclude foraging for plant foods. The first modern humans above the Arctic Circle were faced with these problems, as well as global climate change that may have severely limited foraging possibilities, even in the short summer. The last glacial maximum ('ice age') occurred around 19 000 to 18 000 years ago, several millennia after humans reached Arctic regions (Pitulko *et al.* 2004). One way in which the inhabitants of these very high latitudes responded to climate change was to contract their geographic ranges at the time of global cooling when the ice sheets were at their largest and expand them again when warming resumed and the ice retreated (Goebel 1999).

Humans, past and present, need a large behavioural and cultural armoury to successfully exploit extreme environments. Culture and traditions that promote social integrity and sophisticated material culture are all essential to survival (Fitzhugh 1997). The first humans to inhabit high latitudes needed to control fire, manufacture shelters and make specialist weapons, including harpoons, for hunting large prey in order to exploit these habitats (Fitzhugh 1997). Since

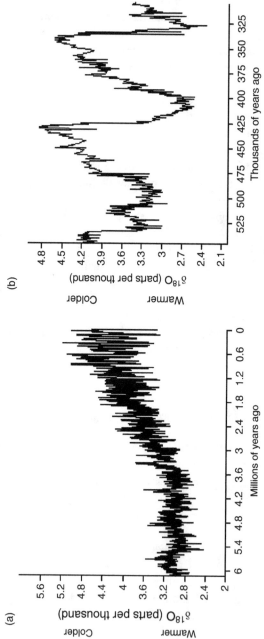

Figure 4.3. Global climate change across the past 5 million years (a) and between around 500 000 and 300 000 years ago (b). Data based on: (a) the V19–30, ODP 677, ODP 846 composite oxygen isotope sequence (composite oxygen isotope data downloaded from http://delphi.esc.cam.ac.uk/coredata/v677846.html, originally derived from Shackleton and Pisias 1985; Shackleton *et al.* 1990; 1995a;b); (b) oxygen isotopic composition of *Cibicidoides wuellerstorfi* from sediment core MD01–2446, downloaded from supplementary material from Voelker *et al.* (2010) doi:10.1594/PANGAEA.742790.

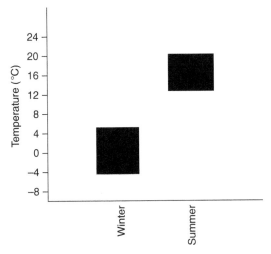

Figure 4.4. Seasonal temperature differences at the Boxgrove ancient human site, United Kingdom, around 500 000 years ago. Range estimates derived from Holmes *et al.* (2010) based on assumptions of environmental tolerances of ostracod species found at the site.

plant productivity and diversity in tundra and boreal environments are low with a short growing season, humans living there (despite their greater dependence on plant foods elsewhere (Chapter 5)) rely heavily on animal resources, both terrestrial and marine. Exploitation of marine resources is likely to have been a key factor in the modern human expansion into Arctic regions (Fitzhugh 1997). In less severe environments, behavioural adaptations to extreme seasonality include nomadism and transhumance. This seasonal relocation of human groups or the animals they rear, respectively, continues to be practised by many rural human populations today. Archaeological evidence indicates that nomadism was practised by Arctic populations between 4000 and 5000 years ago (Powers and Jordan 1990), with seasonal movement potentially having been practised as early as the late Pleistocene (Goebel 1999). Other aspects of human behaviour would also have helped colonization of a wide range of often inhospitable environments. Group cohesion is an important aspect of primate life (Dunbar 1988). Living together offers protection against predation and relatively easy access to mates and allows alloparenting, caregiving by group members who are not the parents of an offspring (Dunbar 1988). Primates also exploit environments in groups, sharing information about food sources and sometimes pooling foraging effort (Dunbar 1988). It is extremely unlikely that humans could have moved into so many varied and variable environments without the benefits of group living.

It is also likely that distinctive aspects of human grouping behaviour, such as social control (evident even in societies deemed to be egalitarian), ritual and taboo, would help to keep groups together and working together towards shared goals, including survival. Such cohesion would enable extreme environments like those above the Arctic Circle to be inhabited.

Behavioural and cultural adaptation to environmental variability is not confined to those living at the highest latitudes, and the relationship between environmental pressures and social responses is not unidirectional. Sociality not only allows people to respond to environmental change, but environmental change may also promote shifts in social organization, culture and behaviour (Minnegal and Dwyer 2007). There are clear links, for example, between the adoption of agriculture, a major shift that had both environmental causes and consequences, and social change, including increasing population density and complexity (Chapters 1 and 8). Catastrophic events that destroy infrastructure and reduce populations (either through death or migration) can result in the reshaping of social structures: on the Greek island of Thera, for example, the departure of the least and most wealthy following an earthquake in the 1950s reduced social inequality and led to a relaxation of marriage rules (Hoffman 1999). Societal changes precipitated by environmental events are shaped by the social organization from which they emerged, so different communities can respond in different ways to similar challenges (Minnegal and Dwyer 2007). For instance, after severe drought and consequent food shortage during the El Niño event of 1997, some Bedamuni communities in Papua New Guinea broke up, partly because individual families relocated within their territories but also because hardship exacerbated existing societal tensions (Minnegal and Dwyer 2007). In contrast, the Kubo people, responding to the same drought, did not experience community fission, relocating en masse to more favourable areas (Minnegal and Dwyer 2007). The two groups varied in social response partly because they had different prior expectations: Bedamuni assume that resources are generally stable, with defined roles and land for individuals living within the community, whereas the Kubo prepare for the worst, having flexible attitudes towards land use, based on current occupation rather than family history, and sharing food widely within the community as necessary (Minnegal and Dwyer 2007).

It seems unlikely that a species with fewer cultural and technological solutions and less potential for behavioural modification could expand into the variety of environments that modern humans are able to exploit. Nevertheless, the geographic range of Pleistocene hominins prior to the evolution of *Homo sapiens* was not trivial. Plio-Pleistocene hominins dispersed out of Africa and into the Caucasus (at a latitude of 40 degrees north) by 1.8 million years ago (Gabunia *et al.* 2000), with an expansion several thousand miles to the east into present-day China by around 1.3 million years ago (Zhu *et al.* 2001). By 700 000 years ago, archaic *Homo* had reached the fringes of Eurasia (52 degrees north), to the region now known as England (Parfitt *et al.* 2005). There was very little further expansion until modern humans dispersed north-wards into the Arctic and Arctic fringes. Neanderthals, despite popular belief that they were cold-habitat specialists (with genetic adaptations to cold inferred primarily from morphology, and behavioural and cultural adaptations recon-structed from the archaeological record), failed to exploit latitudes above around 55° N (equivalent to present-day Denmark and north Germany) and may have confined themselves mostly to relatively warm temperate areas, which in glacial periods would have been quite southerly, such as the Iberian peninsula (Finlayson 2004).

Although isolated fossil and archaeological finds are helpful in showing the far reaches of hominin geographic dispersion, they give no information on the population sizes that lived there. Such information would shed further light on environmental variability and exposure to seasonality of hominins in different locations. A naive 'join the dots' approach suggests that huge tracts of land were used by hominins. However, the effective total hominin population (simplistically, breeding individuals) as estimated from genetic data was small, at around 10 000 (Harpending *et al.* 1998), before expansion out of Africa. Only a fraction of total range would have been habitable due to low resource availability, and the ability of hominins to procure food in marginal areas. Since sociality would have been important for dealing with seasonal stresses, it is likely that the hominin population was clustered in different environmental niches, which would have led to varying adaptive responses to particular climatic stresses in different locations. Modern human population sizes and densities, now and in the past, are greater than those of ancestral hominins, and the niche expansion made possible by modern human culture, behaviour and cognition has allowed them to occupy a larger number of habitats and environments than earlier hominin species. In doing this, humans have been exposed to a larger range of seasonal conditions than other hominins.

Human adaptation and adaptability in a seasonal context

Given that modern humans evolved less than 200 000 years ago and have inhabited extremely seasonal environments such as the Arctic sporadically for only around 30 000 years, human adaptations and responses to seasonality are biologically recent. This is particularly true among agriculturalists, whose subsistence strategies (which magnify seasonal inequity in resources and represent a major transition in human evolution (Chapter 8)) were adopted less than 10 000 years ago. In this context, Pliocene and early Pleistocene hominin adaptation and adaptability to shifting conditions and a fluctuating resource base seems to have little relevance to how modern humans respond to seasonality today. However, some important features (especially larger body size, plasticity and dietary flexibility) that promote survival in changing and marginal habitats are the products of hominin life in the Pliocene and Pleistocene.

Larger-bodied mammals need proportionally less energy (Chapter 2) and have a greater proportion of body weight as fat (Lindstedt and Boyce 1985). Both factors make them more resilient to periods of food shortage. The relationship between larger size and the ability to endure food shortage may be as important within species as between species (Lindstedt and Boyce 1985); although larger individuals need absolutely more energy, there is a fitness advantage in having even modest body size increase. Humans are mid-sized mammals and are reasonably buffered against periods of seasonal stress. The early hominins, like many other primates, were also mid-sized, with similar advantages when faced with scarce resources. At least one trait necessary for survival in seasonal environments was therefore established in the human lineage well before modern humans evolved.

Pliocene and early Pleistocene hominins weighed around 10–15 kg less than the worldwide average for modern humans. The lowest mean mass of a Plio-Pleistocene hominin species (*Homo habilis*) was around 33 kg (Robson and Wood 2008). Modern human-like stature and body proportions were established with *Homo erectus* at least 1.5 million years ago. Estimated body masses for *H. erectus* are above the modern human species mean, and within the modern human overall range (Robson and Wood 2008). Later hominins, *Homo heidelbergensis* and *H. neanderthalensis*, have estimated mean body masses of over 70 kg (Robson and Wood 2008). The reasons for the evolution of increased body size among the hominins may be linked to life history strategy, increased dietary quality and climatic pressures, of which seasonality is one and global cooling another. In colder climates, animals may grow more slowly and attain larger body masses over this longer growth period (Vrba 1994). The trend towards the evolution of greater body size from early to later hominins would have been advantageous in the face of resource unpredictability.

Body fat

Humans are fat primates. Measured in human societies that had not experienced overweight or obesity at the time of study, essential fat (needed for healthy metabolic and physiological function) represents around three per cent of body mass in males and nine per cent in females, and storage fat around 12% of body mass in males and 15% in females (Norgan 1997). This is about an order of magnitude more than the two per cent total body fat observed for baboons (Altmann *et al.* 1993), the only non-human primate for which adiposity has been measured in the wild (Wells 2010). Given the opportunity, all mammals (including primates) can become overweight. This is usually part of the adaptive repertoire. When food is consistently plentiful, such as when baboons have ready access to discarded human food in rubbish dumps, body fat can increase to as much as 23% of body mass (Altmann *et al.* 1993). Similarly, captive primates have a regular food supply and can deposit even greater amounts of fat if their diets are not controlled by availability (Chapter 5). For example, the proportion of body mass as fat (as determined by dissection) of one captive female lowland gorilla was 44% (Zihlman and MacFarland 2000). This level of fatness is likely to be as unhealthy in primates as in humans; Hsing Hsing, an orangutan in Perth Zoo, Australia, developed maturity-onset diabetes at the age of 22 years (orangutans become adult at around 11 years of age), after an early adult life of excessive weight. His diabetes, and weight, have been carefully managed across the 11 years since diagnosis. Humans have been able to generate even higher levels of body fatness. Classified as super-super-obese, the few individuals with body mass index above 60 kg/m^2 (the range of normality is 18.5 to 25 kg/m^2) are estimated (using prediction equations of Deurenberg *et al.* 1991) to have in excess of 63% of body mass as fat. None of these examples of extreme fatness can claim to be the natural biological state, nor to be healthy, but they show the extent of plasticity in body composition in hominoids (Zihlman and MacFarland 2000).

Levels of obesity are rising in modern industrialized and transitional economies across the globe. As discussed in Chapters 8 and 9, it is a complex, multifactorial phenomenon, attributed in part to increasingly energy-dense, processed food and decreased physical labour. However, another contributory factor is steady food supply across the year and the decline in seasonal resource fluctuation. Although on the one hand this is positive rather than negative – few people want to go hungry – the types of foods that tend to be available throughout the year, high in fats and sugars (both preservatives) and processed to ensure their longevity, help to create an obesogenic environment.

At least one ape, the orangutan, gains weight when food is plentiful and then loses it during periods of scarcity (Knott 2005). The high level of usual body fatness relative to other primate species seen in modern humans similarly helps to buffer against fluctuations in food availability. Body mass in modern humans living under seasonal conditions and in traditional subsistence economies fluctuates in a fairly predictable manner, with a decrease in body mass in the hungry season (when lowest food reserves among agriculturalists often coincide with intense physical labour) and restoration of weight and replenishment of fat stores when food is plentiful (as at harvest time among agriculturalists) (Ferro-Luzzi *et al.* 1994). Seasonal shortage of dietary energy can lead to body mass reductions of up to five per cent (Ferro-Luzzi and Branca 1993). Although difficult to quantify, and subject to significant intra- and inter-population variation, the potential speed of weight loss is exemplified by controlled weight loss studies, where BMI can fall by over 2 kg/m^2 over three weeks (Shintani *et al.* 1991; Saris 2001). This is more or less equal to a weight loss of 6 kg in an American adult male of average height with an initial BMI of 25 kg/m^2.

Fossil and archaeological records are unhelpful in determining when hominins became fat primates. Body fat percentages for hominins have been estimated using measures of overall body size combined with human-based ratios of lean mass and adiposity (Wells 2010). These equations yield estimates of 11% and 15% body fat for male and female *Australopithecus afarensis* and around 16% for both male and female *Paranthropus robustus* (Wells 2010). Estimates for *H. erectus* are around 14% for males and 25% for females. However, the lack of good estimates of body fat for wild primates, including apes, thwarts such reconstructions. It was only with the evolution of *Homo erectus*, the first unequivocal member of the genus *Homo*, that hominins truly became more human than ape-like (Wood and Collard 1999). Even though early hominins were not identical to modern apes, they were similar, and it is reasonable to assume that their percentage body fat, at least in the late Miocene and early Pliocene, was more like that of wild non-human primates than modern humans. Equations based on modern human data, therefore, although the best currently available, may over-estimate percentage body fat in hominins prior to *H. erectus*.

It is also difficult to reconstruct the patterns of change in body composition of early hominins and the relative importance of seasonality to them. Body fatness of different hominin species may have increased gradually over the course of the Pliocene and Pleistocene, moving in concert with climate change, increasing quality and energy density of diet, as well as the increased energy needs of an enlarging brain among some species of *Homo* (Wells 2010). Despite several major shifts in African climate, the long-term overlying trend was towards more arid environments (DeMenocal 2004), which in some places may have translated into greater seasonal extremes. Also supporting the idea of a gradual change in essential body fatness is the lack of a stepped increase in diet quality and energy density in the Plio-Pleistocene, at least prior to the emergence of *H. erectus* (Chapter 3). An alternative is that body fatness may have shifted incrementally alongside other evolutionary transitions, including bipedalism. Some Miocene ape species inhabited seasonal woodland (Andrews and Humphrey 1999), and the adoption of bipedalism would have opened new niches. This would have altered seasonal resource pressures and created a selective environment for increasing adiposity as a physiological survival strategy. Another major transition, from the early hominins to *H. erectus* (Wood and Collard 1999), was associated with changes in morphology, brain size, technology and life history, as well as body composition (Wells 2010). It is possible that the body composition we recognize in modern humans only evolved with the major transition that occurred with their emergence as a species.

Human success in varied and variable environments cannot be uncoupled from morphology and physiology. Wells (2010) argues that although seasonality was a key element in promoting energy storage, it is only one of a number of factors that contribute to high levels of body fatness in humans. Others include encephalization, costs of reproduction, and disease burden. Wells (2010) suggests that adiposity contributed to the colonizing ability of hominins, particularly *Homo*, through increasing maternal energy stores (allowing shorter interbirth intervals and increased number of offspring), alongside the buffering against environmental variability afforded by being a fat primate. A feedback loop is likely: seasonality exerted a selective pressure on body size and composition in hominins, which enabled greater tolerance of environmental variability and facilitated population dispersal through shifts in reproduction. Larger body size, a baseline adaptation to seasonality, was already present when *Homo sapiens* evolved. Adiposity, another adaptation to seasonality, may also have been a trait associated with the genus *Homo* in general rather than modern humans in particular.

Plasticity and flexibility

Alongside adaptations such as larger body size and adiposity, phenotypic and behavioural plasticity are important in surviving fluctuations in resource availability. Plasticity is the ability of an individual to change in response to external stimuli. Closely allied to this is the concept of the reaction norm, or phenotypic variation in a species along an environmental gradient. Plastically driven changes can be a response to environmental differences, a type of preparation for future environmental differences, or a combination of the two. Often, phenotypic plasticity takes place during ontogeny (development from the immature to mature form). One classic study of developmental phenotypic plasticity, undertaken by Weaver and Ingram (1969), separated newly weaned pigs from the same litter into two groups, and reared one group in a controlled cold environment (5 °C) and the other in a hot environment (35 °C). On reaching maturity, the cold-reared pigs showed classic features predicted by Bergmann's Rule, including a short, stocky body, morphologically unlike their littermates reared in the hot environment (Weaver and Ingram 1969). Adults can also show plasticity, as with human acclimatization to low oxygen tension at altitude (Frisancho 1993).

Modern human adiposity and body mass fluctuations have been linked to survival in unpredictable environments, including seasonal ones. Hypotheses of thrift (thrifty genotypes and phenotypes) have been discussed and critiqued extensively elsewhere (e.g. Pollard 2008; Wells 2010). In these formulations, the relative importance of genes (as adaptation) and developmental plasticity are currently unresolvable. Over the past couple of decades, increasing attention has been paid to thrifty phenotypes, partly because of a lack of solid genomic data supporting thrifty genotypes (Chapter 10) but also because of mounting interest in developmental programming, the fetal environment, and epigenetics (Chapter 1). Plasticity is at the heart of the thrifty phenotype hypothesis, in that poor maternal nutrition prepares the fetus for similarly poor conditions after birth through invoking a plastic response in metabolic programming (Barker 1999; Kuzawa 2007). An example of neonatal body composition and thrift is the so-called thin-fat baby (Yajnik *et al.* 2002). South Asian infants born to relatively small mothers have a tendency towards low body weight in combination with a high proportion of adipose tissue, often distributed centrally (Yajnik *et al.* 2002). This morphotype, often associated with insulin resistance in later life, may help the survival of offspring emerging into a nutritionally deprived environment (Yajnik *et al.* 2002). Although it is impossible to ascertain whether hominins were developmentally plastic in this way, it is highly likely that they were. Experimental studies on other mammals indicate that maternal size and nutrition has a significant influence on both offspring size and insulin resistance (Martin *et al.* 2000). Developmental plasticity of this type may thus be a conserved trait that enables individuals to cope with resource insecurity, as occurs under seasonal regimens. Strong seasonal changes to the environment might complicate this preconditioning (Kuzawa 2007), however.

Wells (2010) has argued that developmental programming does not prepare offspring for future conditions but is instead 'backward-looking', preparing them on the basis of conditions experienced by their mother. This is much like the discipline of science itself, which can only construct the future (and make predictions about it) based on what has been observed before (Latour 2003). Nature has constructivist features, because in the absence of constraints, biological evolution favours the production of more offspring, and greater body mass and complexity. Developmental programming is a more deeply constructivist mechanism than that of the individual reproductive event, how-ever. According to data on intergenerational experiences of the matriline (reviewed in Kuzawa and Quinn 2009) the fetus picks up longer-term cues which smooth out the effects of seasonality and perhaps longer-term environ-mental fluctuations. The nutrition of the mother when she was *in utero* primes the uterine environment for her own offspring; this mechanism may prevent the offspring responding in too plastic (or drastic) a manner to short term changes (Kuzawa and Quinn 2009). This mechanism does not, however, prepare offspring for extreme transformations, such as those associated with recent globalization, for example (Chapter 10).

Behaviour is more plastic than physical development, and behaviours asso-ciated with diet selection and foraging patterns are key adaptations to season-ality. Dietary flexibility is often crucial to survival, and is practised by all mammals, including primates. Behavioural plasticity, including dietary flexi-bility, is likely to be the product of the interaction between pre-programmed and learned behaviours (Mery and Burns 2010) and is an evolved feature (at least in part), with genetic limits setting an organism's phenotypic and behav-ioural plasticity. Many primates show both types of plasticity in the face of differential access to food. For example, vervet monkeys in Kenya with access to cultivated food are larger and have slightly different body proportions than those with more restricted access to such foods (Turner *et al.* 1997). The plasticity in this case encompasses not only differential growth and ontogen-etic development but also behaviours, in that conspecifics are able to exploit (and indeed may choose to exploit) different foods. Primate behaviour can alter in novel environments and humans have taken this trait to extremes. The significance of such plasticity can go beyond short- to longer-term evolution-ary change. When faced with the challenges imposed by their different envir-onments, individuals in two sister populations, branching from a parent population, could respond plastically to create behavioural differences between the two populations. Such differences, for example, may include exploitation of different resources. Over time, the variation that was initially facilitated by plasticity may be reinforced by selection, as might occur if shifts in diet caused evolution in jaw or tooth morphology. In a theoretically similar way, the intergenerational nutritional environment that programmes the human fetus may bridge the gap between individual plasticity (responding to seasonal shifts as they happen) and selection (that occurs over a much longer term) (Kuzawa and Quinn 2009).

Hominin species such as *H. erectus* that survived for over one million years and had wide geographic ranges with attendant variations in habitat (Chapter 3) could not have exploited these different environments effectively without plasticity. It has been argued that the highly changeable and changing nature of the early hominin environment was responsible for the evolution of some key human characteristics, including bipedality, encephalization and complex sociality. This variability selection hypothesis counters the notion that all selection in hominin evolution was directional and instead stresses that environmental inconsistency favoured traits that promoted flexibility and diversity (Potts 1998). A corollary of this is that hominins have an inbuilt ability to respond to environmental fluctuations, of which seasonality is one. The plasticity, both behavioural and phenotypic, that is evident in modern humans and which allows them to exploit changing and changeable environments, was very probably a feature of earlier hominins and did not emerge initially with *H. sapiens*. However, modern humans have taken behavioural flexibility far beyond that seen in primates and earlier hominins. This has enabled exploitation of extremely seasonal environments with immense shifts in food availability. It has not, however, prevented resource insecurity through seasonality being a major source of nutritional stress in human populations.

Seasonality and subsistence in modern foraging and early human populations

The earliest modern humans were foragers. When considering responses to seasonality, even in contemporary, industrialized populations, it is therefore important to understand how seasonality influences foraging, diet and eating behaviour in contemporary and ancient foraging populations. In modern populations, foraging encompasses a broad spectrum of behaviour and dietary strategies: groups such as the Kalahari G/wi have heavily plant-based diets whereas Inuit populations depend much more on animal-based foods (Kelly 1995). Archaeological evidence indicates that similar diversity in ecology and food preference existed in the past (Elton 2008b). The behavioural ecology of foraging groups does not necessarily vary predictably with geography, environment or their change over time, but seasonality is likely to play (and have played) a key role in the ecology of foraging populations. For example, many such populations are mobile, and this mobility may help to overcome seasonal resource fluctuation, including seasonal changes in animal home ranges (O'Dea 1991a). Just as importantly, being mobile may confer some protection against seasonal resource depletion. The earliest modern humans, in the Late Pleistocene and beginning of the Holocene (around 10 000 years ago), were seasonally mobile in many parts of the world (Bailey 1975; Lieberman 1993; Parkington 2001), although patterns of seasonal movement in the deep past can be difficult to pinpoint with certainty. Seasonality, along with other climatically induced effects on food supply, present challenges for foragers (Yesner

1994), although it must not be uncritically assumed that flexible social organization and mobility are necessary adaptations to seasonal challenges (Sellen
2000). Biological traits and cultural and behavioural responses buffer humans
against the effects of seasonality and help to compensate for resource fluctuations, but if such strategies are incomplete or insufficiently responsive, nutritional stress is an outcome (Yesner 1994). The seasonal challenges faced by
foragers vary from population to population. At high latitudes, the effects of
temperature and photoperiod seasonality are extremely marked, while seasonal
variations in the tropics are greatest in relation to rainfall. Seasonal food supply
does not follow straightforward patterns of presence or absence (or boom or
bust) at different times of the year. Species that might be used as food sources
vary in abundance, diversity and sequential availability according to both their
adaptations and the local ecology. Seasonal shifts in resource availability will
also vary across space and time, the latter tracking short term variations in
climate, such as exceptionally cold or dry seasons. Although most often
associated with seasonal stress in agrarian populations (drought that leads to
failure of crops for example), foraging populations also experience such
temporal unpredictability alongside spatial and temporal variations in resource
availability.

   A distinction should be made between nutritional stress that occurs regularly
versus that which occurs unusually. Seasonal stress is expected to be regular,
tracking seasonal shifts in resource availability, whereas catastrophic events
that lead to famine are more unusual. In archaeological populations, periods of
arrested growth (hypoplasia) leave distinct traces on teeth and bones, which
can be used to identify seasonal stresses in humans and most other mammals.
For example, microscopic study of tooth sections from the extinct monkey
Theropithecus oswaldi has revealed regular hypoplastic events in the enamel,
probably linked to dry-season reductions in food availability (Macho *et al.*
1996). In long bones, hypoplasia results in Harris Lines, detectable through
radiography. Regularly spaced Harris Lines, argued to be related to seasonal
food imbalances, have been identified in bones of archaeological foraging
populations from the Arctic, coastal North America and Australia (reviewed
in Yesner 1994).

   The relationship between seasonal food shifts and seasonal nutritional stress
differs with population and through time, and it cannot be assumed that intense
seasonal stress (leading to some combination of physical growth perturbation,
severe weight loss and changes to birth and death rates) is or was routine
among foragers. Recent study of diets of Ache foragers of Paraguay showed
marked seasonal variation in the plant species they ate but much less variation
in energy intake over the year (Hill *et al.* 1984). This may be due to their high
dependence on meat, consumption of which varied little from season to season

(Hill *et al.* 1984). As with many populations, a small number of foods accounted for the vast majority of Ache energy intake (Chapter 2), even though the overall number of plant species consumed was relatively large (Hill *et al.* 1984). In one quarter of the year, honey was very abundant and copious amounts of it were eaten (Chapter 10) (Hill *et al.* 1984). Similar patterns have been noted among Australian hunter-gatherers (O'Dea 1991a), where foods such as grubs and honey were only available seasonally, with other foods acting as staples during specific seasons (for example, wild yam in the dry season) (O'Dea 1991). As with the Ache, subsistence-level foraging among Australian hunter-gatherers was seasonally interspersed with periods of relative plenty (O'Dea 1991). Despite this, when asked, the Ache said they were hungry (Hill and Hurtado 1996), preferring to consume more food than they could procure and suggesting that they experienced some habitual level of chronic energy deficiency.

Seasonality of food security is often closely tied to water availability, and water stress is an equally important issue for many populations, especially in arid regions. Among the !Kung in the Kalahari Desert, the distribution of waterholes was a major determinant of movement patterns and foraging group size in the dry season (Lee 1968). Because permanent waterholes are relatively uncommon and distributed patchily across the landscape, the !Kung were forced to form larger and more dense groups near these water sources, before switching to smaller and more dispersed groups in the wet season (Lee 1968). Their dependence on a limited number of water sources in the dry season also influenced their day- and home-ranges (the distance travelled or area covered during foraging, either in a single day or in total), with gathering often being restricted to land relatively near water (Lee 1968). Hunting was also affected, because game is more dispersed and therefore the effort of procuring it is much higher than in the wet season, with the rewards less certain (Halperin 1980).

The !Kung, Ache and many Australian aboriginal people live in tropical or subtropical regions, where seasonal stress is often related more to aridity than temperature and photoperiod. In the tropics and subtropics, there is no marked decline in plant productivity and animal activity as there is in the cold seasons of temperate and higher-latitude regions. It is plausible that foragers living at higher latitudes experience more intense seasonal stress, and starvation may have been a significant cause of death there (Dunn 1968). However, historical demographic data from Sami populations of northern Scandinavia and Russia (who are traditionally hunter-gatherers dependent on fishing, reindeer-herding and hunting) indicate that their birth and mortality rates were less strongly affected by climatic variation than were births and deaths among agricultural-ists living in the same place and time (Helle and Helama 2007). This suggests that extreme environmental seasonality, as occurs in the high-latitude regions that the Sami inhabit, does not necessarily result in extreme shifts in overall energy and resource availability. It also implies that mobile hunting and gathering is more compliant than subsistence agriculture in the face of even quite dramatic seasonality. This is reinforced by the observation that archaeological foraging groups that became more sedentary, with larger populations and greater societal complexity, experienced greater seasonal stress than groups that were smaller, more mobile and less stratified (Yesner 1994).

One way to buffer against seasonal fluctuations in resource availability is to store food. Although popularly believed to store little if any food, several foraging populations, such as the Ainu of Japan and several Northwest Coast Native American groups, rely greatly on seasonal storage of food (Testart 1982; Kelly 1995). Some Mesolithic foraging populations, like the Ertebølle of southern Scandinavia, also stored food (Rowley-Conwy 1983). The relative importance of this practice depends to a large extent on whether the foraging population is sedentary (Testart 1982). Binford (1968) argued that the demands placed on resource availability and security by seasonality, especially with increasing latitude, caused major changes in the structure of foraging groups, leading to increased food storage and decreased mobility. However, being mobile does not preclude storage, especially as many groups have well-defined ranges and patterns of movement, revisiting fixed points at intervals (Ingold 1982). In mobile Australian aboriginal foraging groups, home ranges may be determined, at least partly, by seasonal fatness of major prey (Chapter 5), but modest food storage (drying of meat or plants, which are then buried or kept in dry places) helps to offset some variation in resource availability (O'Dea 1991a). To ensure relative stability of food supply throughout the year, foragers who store food need to combine this with daily foraging (Rowley-Conwy 1982) to protect against seasonal failure of a stored resource (Rowley-Conwy 1982). This is especially important as food storage is not always particularly effective, with multiple factors including pest attacks, unfavourable storage conditions such as high humidity and container failure causing significant losses to many stored cereals even in contemporary societies (Payne 2002).

There is a fine line between adequate and inadequate nutrition in seasonal environments. Humans are able to gain weight (as adipose tissue) quickly when in positive energy balance, liberating those energy stores in periods of negative energy balance. Data from the Ache, Australian aboriginal populations (Hill *et al.* 1984; O'Dea 1991a) and other groups (reviewed in Halperin 1980) indicate that many foraging populations have at least one season when bodily fat stores can be built up. The physiological potential of humans to gain weight is a baseline adaptation to fluctuating food supplies. External storage of food can augment this, buffering further against resource fluctuations.

Food storage is beneficial because consumption of seasonal resource gluts can be spread over a longer time period. However, over-reliance on stored food can lead to undernutrition if the harvest fails (Rowley-Conwy 1982) or if storage fails. External environmental conditions and the dynamics of ecological communities (with changes in one part of a food web having consequences elsewhere) can also alter resource availability and have profound effects on nutritional status.

There are many examples of how foragers alter their hunting and gathering practices in the face of seasonality. These changes occur not only because of changing availability of foodstuffs, but also because of other ecological and social constraints, such as increases in population density around limited resources such as water. In some groups, baseline resources are available almost year-round. For example, for the Ona of Tierra del Fuego, shellfish and fish were readily available and were supplemented by seasonal resources such as migratory birds and seals (Halperin 1980). In other groups, key and desirable foodstuffs (such as pine nuts in the Great Basin, United States) were only available seasonally, either because they become gathered-out or because of their seasonal growth cycle. Foragers, depending on their social system and settlement patterns, have a variety of ways of coping with this. The !Kung used supplementary foods, then replacement ones such as roots and bulbs (Lee 1968), whereas the Shoshoni stored nuts but nevertheless often experienced significant food shortage over the winter, as they were highly dependent on plant foods (Steward 1955).

Although foods cannot be hunted or harvested if they are not available, flexibility of resource use is likely to be essential to surviving seasonal shifts. Knowledge of how food sources may be temporally or spatially heterogeneous and the ability to exploit alternative food sources are essential aspects of survival for foragers. This is not just confined to humans: compliant foraging behaviours are key to the success of baboons and several other Old World monkey species (Chapter 2) and are likely to have been hugely important for long-lived and abundant hominins like *H. erectus*. However, over-dependence on a single (or very small range) of staple foods in human groups can lead to profound nutritional insult, not only because of the potential for diets to supply a more restricted nutrient intake, but also because of the lack of adequate fall-back foods.

It has been argued that the transition to agriculture (the use of domesticated crops and animals) in the Neolithic moved humans to dietary maladaptation, partly because of reduced dietary diversity (Eaton and Eaton 1999; Eaton *et al.* 1999). However, many populations have fuzzy boundaries between subsistence strategies, with rapid and short-term switches from cultivation to foraging and back again, as among the Hill Kharia of Bengal (Reddy 1994) and the

Nuaulu of Seram, Indonesia (Ellen 1991), both of whose subsistence is reliant on both foraging and cultivation at the same time, and who trade with other groups for specific resources. Traditional subsistence strategies therefore fall along a continuum rather than exist as discrete entities (Elton 2008a). Over-dependence on a very restricted number of food sources is not an inevitable consequence of cultivation. By extension, subsistence based on agriculture rather than foraging may not necessarily result in greater seasonal energy imbalance.

It is not accurate to extrapolate in an uncritical manner from modern subsistence-level foragers, pastoralists or agriculturalists to those in the past, since within- and between-population dynamics have changed over time just as they alter from group to group. But although exact responses to seasonal shifts in resources cannot be determined simply through analogy with modern groups, many underlying principles are likely to be similar. Bearing in mind the array of different subsistence strategies in modern groups, it is highly likely that similar diversity existed in the past. Hence, the transition to agriculture in the Neolithic was not a straightforward process that resulted simply from the demands of increasingly large populations that became more sedentary and complex, nor was it likely to have been due to a single prime mover such as climate change.

According to McCorriston and Hole (1991), seasonality may have been an important contributing factor in the development of agriculture, within an inter-connecting web of influences that included social and technological innovation. They argue that the intensely seasonal environments present at the beginning of the Holocene caused by changes in the tilt of the earth's axis (which caused an increase in northern hemisphere average summer temperatures and a decrease in average winter temperatures) provided a set of unique conditions that promoted the emergence of agriculture in the Near East. Although seasonal climate was not the sole cause or prime mover for the adoption of agriculture, McCorriston and Hole (1991) argue that arid summers provided the necessary conditions for successful cultivation of annual food crops, providing an impetus for cultivation rather than total dependence on foraging. Thus, dry summers altered seasonal resources and their distribution, which may in turn have made people store more food to buffer against shortage in the height of the dry season, cultivation offering a new solution to the challenges of food procurement in a seasonal environment.

Agriculture emerged in a number of regions of the world at roughly the same time (Chapter 1), and seasonal pressures cannot be implicated strongly in all origin models. After it emerged in a number of centres, agriculture spread to other areas and populations. The complexities of the changing subsistence strategies among populations in the Mesolithic and Neolithic are exemplified by studies of the Ertebølle, settled foragers. With a diet heavy in coastal and marine resources, they were relatively slow to adopt agriculture, despite being sedentary (Rowley-Conwy 1984). Many of their foods, identified from archaeological sources to have included acorns, cod, water birds and seals, would have been available only seasonally and seasonal shifts in resources would have exerted significant pressure on the population. Rather than depend on lean game, with attendant problems in gaining all vital nutrients (Chapters 2 and 5), Rowley-Conwy (1984) argues that oyster consumption helped to bridge the seasonal gap in resources, providing sufficient energy and protein and a wide enough range of micronutrients to offset foraging effort.

Archaeological study of middens indicate that oyster consumption declined sharply at the beginning of the Neolithic, with oyster shells at coastal sites being replaced by cockle and mussel shells. A decline in marine salinity is likely to have been the cause of this change (Rowley-Conwy 1984). With oyster populations in decline, and other shellfish being a poor substitute (partly because of their short seasonal availability), the Ertebølle were less buffered against seasonal shortages of their other preferred foods, with serious undernutrition becoming a distinct possibility in particularly harsh years. Being settled rather than mobile allowed them less scope for exploiting resources flexibly. Given the proximity of agriculturalists, Rowley-Conwy (1984) has argued that adoption of their practices rather than a switch to mobile foraging was the preferred alternative strategy. Thus, for the Ertebølle, seasonal food shortage in combination with ecological changes may have induced a subsistence transition.

The effects of seasonality on nutrition in contemporary agrarian populations

In 1994, Ferro-Luzzi and colleagues estimated that over 400 million adults worldwide were at risk of severe seasonal energy stress (Ferro-Luzzi *et al.* 1994). Children are buffered to varying extents against seasonal food insecurity (Ulijaszek and Strickland 1993), but the scale of seasonal food insecurity and the impact of seasonality on public health nutrition is enormous. Absolute numbers of undernourished people on earth have varied between 800 and 1000 million since the 1990s (Food and Agriculture Organization 2010a), while patterns of climatic seasonality are changing with climate change (McMichael and Githeko 2001). Seasonal stress in human energetics can be caused by increased physical work output with or without reduced energy intake. In subsistence agrarian economies, these are often coincidental, occurring just prior to and during the harvest period, when food is scarce but crop-tending is at its most intense. In addition to energy stress, seasonal shifts in resource availability can cause deficiencies in micronutrients.

The burden of seasonal food scarcity is carried by the economically less developed world, with food availability and eating behaviour in industrialized nations being linked to seasonality primarily through price. In the transitional economies of Eastern Europe, food seasonality may play a greater part in dietary composition than in other industrialized nations. In particular, fresh fruit and vegetables were scarce in the winter months with greater dependence on meat, fat and carbohydrates. However, the magnitude of seasonal food availability is less than it was in the past (Smolkova *et al.* 2004). In a study of rural and urban Slovakians, a twofold seasonal difference in fruit and vegetable consumption made a significant difference to folic acid intake (Smolkova *et al.* 2004). Changing subsistence patterns in non-industrialized and developing economies in Africa, South America and Asia have also resulted in a more seasonally homogeneous diet for some sectors of the population, as traditional diets give way to more industrialized and commoditized ones.

In rapidly urbanizing and industrializing societies, the increased year-round availability of processed energy-dense foods, coupled with decreased physical labour, is a major contributor to rising levels of obesity (Popkin 2001) (Chapter 9). Being overweight or obese does not equate with being healthy, and among those who are malnourished, dietary deficiencies are common. The latter is due, at least in part, to reduced dietary diversity. In forest living foragers in Borneo, south-east Asia, there is a positive relationship between dietary diversity and nutritional status and health (Dounias *et al.* 2007). There is also a strong link between dietary diversity and proximity to urban areas, with groups who live in more remote regions maintaining more diverse diets, and those living closer to towns adopting more urbanized and industrialized diets (Dounias *et al.* 2007). Dietary diversity also helps to offset seasonality of staple resources. Studies in rural Burkina Faso have shown that dietary diversity of women increases during the grain shortage seasons (Savy *et al.* 2006). Children in Benin appear to have a diet that alters in response to seasonal availability, with relative quantities of staple foods and supplementary foods varying throughout the year: fruits and vegetables, for example, are more readily available in the period prior to the main cereal harvest (Mitchikpe *et al.* 2009). Overall energy and nutrient intakes are fairly consistent over the year, indicating that households steward resources in the face of marginal food supplies (Mitchikpe *et al.* 2009). In the very dry Monte region of Patagonia, South America, Mapuche communities who practise seasonal transhumance of cattle supplement their diets with wild-gathered plants. This contributes to dietary diversity and provides a buffer against food shortages (Ladio and Lozada 2009). Foods eaten during times of seasonal stress may not be preferred, but eaten as fall-back foods. Tuber consumption by the Hadza of Tanzania is a classic example of a fall-back food, eaten when berries are scarce (Marlowe and

Berbesque 2009). Fall-back foods, although they contribute to dietary diversity, are usually considered to be of lower status (Marlowe and Berbesque 2009).

Not every population has options that permit significant dietary diversity, and some populations depend very heavily on a small number of staple foods, often including monocot plants (Chapter 2). Increased dietary diversity, one definition of which is 'the number of individual foods or food groups consumed over a reference period' (Hoddinott and Yohannes 2002), is linked to higher birthweight, healthier anthropometric status of children and reduced incidence of chronic disease (reviewed in Hoddinott and Yohannes 2002). Limited dietary diversity is associated with food insecurity (Hoddinott and Yohannes 2002) and can have negative health outcomes. 'Hidden hunger', malnutrition due to inadequate micronutrient intake, occurs frequently in communities where overall energy intake may be adequate (Kennedy *et al.* 2003). In these cases, lack of dietary diversity and dependence on a very limited range of foods can lead to serious health problems including blindness (because of vitamin A deficiency), brain damage (due to iodine deficiency) and neural tube defects (as a consequence of folic acid deficiency) (Kennedy *et al.* 2003). Very common starchy staples, such as rice, wheat and maize, contain relatively few micronutrients but contain anti-nutrients, such as phytates, which inhibit maximal absorption of some micronutrients from other foods eaten with them (Kennedy *et al.* 2003). Tea and coffee also contain absorption inhibitors such as tannins.

Nutrient supplementation, which has helped to address diseases caused by lack of specific micronutrients in industrialized nations, is one public health measure that can be used to address deficiencies; promoting diverse diets may do the same (Kennedy *et al.* 2003), without overly medicalizing the problem. However, this requires knowledge of traditional diets, eating behaviours and local availability of potential foods. Understanding how seasonality can impact on dietary diversity, both positively and negatively, is important in this respect. In some regions, including those with severe food insecurity, encouraging or re-introducing a diverse diet may be difficult for social, political or ecological reasons. In Niger, for example, farmland is scarce, due to a complex web of sociopolitical factors, and households struggle to produce sufficient food to cover their needs for half of the year, with the food that they do produce being relatively homogeneous and deficient in many micronutrients (Baro and Deubel 2006).

Environmental variability, undernutrition and resource security

In non-industrialized economies, seasonal fluctuations in resource availability can cause severe food insecurity and nutritional stress, with those of poorest nutritional status being at most risk (Ferro-Luzzi *et al.* 1994). Among

Lese horticulturalists of the Democratic Republic of Congo, a decade ago around one quarter of the population experienced seasonal energy deficiency (Bentley *et al.* 1999). In Dagota pastoralists of Tanzania, almost half of the women in one study were found to be chronically energy-deficient, and half of the children were stunted due to undernutrition (Sellen 2000). This under-nutrition was magnified in the hungry season (Sellen 2000).

Seasonal resource stress does not affect all individuals in a society equally, and patterns vary from population to population. In a number of African and Andean populations, children were observed to have preferential access to resources (Leonard 1991), but in some south Asian families, birth order determined access to food during periods of seasonal scarcity (Behrman 1988). In one Indian agricultural community, adult female nutrition (including caloric intake) was worse than that of adult males (Edmundson and Edmundson 1988), and among Tanzanian agriculturalists, weight loss in women was significantly higher than in men (Wandel and Holmboe-Ottesen 1992). In some Ethiopian groups, weight loss in males was highly detrimental to their ability to undertake hard physical labour, and males were buffered against food shortage by other members of the community (Ferro-Luzzi *et al.* 2001). These data are in contrast to observations of Andean agriculturalists where male nutritional status was worse (Leonard 1991), and weight loss in elderly Kenyan males, working as smallholders, was greater than that in females (seven per cent of body weight compared with three per cent) (Kigutha *et al.* 1998).

Division of labour and level of physical activity appear to be crucial factors in determining which sectors of a population are most affected by seasonal differences in food availability and work patterns. Throughout the world, women and children often undertake work that is vital to food production, whether it be children herding animals and collecting firewood, or women working in the fields. Under these circumstances, they have increased vulnerability to seasonal undernutrition, which may be reinforced by social factors including preferential provision of foodstuffs to males. However, women may also be better able to supplement their diets in times of food shortage. Their control of household food and responsibility for cooking, for example, may allow them to snack during the day, even if overall food availability is low (Bentley *et al.* 1999). In addition, the activity of one group may directly influence the nutritional status of another, especially within households. During times of less intense agricultural work, for example, women may have more time to cook and feed children, which may help to alleviate their seasonal nutritional stress (Wandel and Holmboe-Ottesen 1992). Parents often employ complex investment strategies in the face of limited resources, including those affected by seasonal shifts in availability. Models of nutrient allocation (including micronutrient as well as energy content of food) among south Asian agricultural families suggest that during times of seasonal food shortage, earlier-born children are favoured, whereas when there is food surplus household food distribution is more even (Behrman 1988). This has potentially important implications for policymakers and public health nutrition practitioners: owing to parental investment choices, increasing the amount of food available to a household during times of seasonal shortage does not automatically improve the nutrition of all children in it (Behrman 1988).

Seasonal declines in body mass are common, but not universal (Ferro-Luzzi and Branca 1993). For example, lean Ethiopian women showed very little seasonal weight loss in the hungry season, but experienced a reduction in basal metabolic rate (BMR), in contrast to heavier Beninese women (Ferro-Luzzi and Branca 1993). Reduction of BMR was also observed in Lese women from the Democratic Republic of Congo (Bentley *et al.* 1999). In contrast, among Nepali agropastoralists, thinner women who lose very little weight seasonally had higher and relatively consistent total energy expenditure throughout the year, whereas heavier people experienced both a rise in energy expenditure and a drop in body mass during periods of heavy seasonal work (Panter-Brick 1996).

In many primates, seasonal food shortages are offset by reductions in non-essential activities, and this adaptive strategy is also found in some human populations, including the Lese (Jenike 1996). Seasonal weight loss may have knock-on influences for future physical work output and therefore productivity in later years among Lese males (Jenike 1996). However, seasonal weight loss may not always have negative consequences, especially in transitional economies (Simondon *et al.* 2008). In rural Senegalese women, BMI decreased in the hungry season but arm circumference increased, at least in the first part, as a function of more intense physical activity levels (Simondon *et al.* 2008). This suggests that these women do not lose muscle mass because of seasonal pressures, and therefore remain relatively healthy. Body masses in rural Senegalese populations are rising, albeit more slowly than among migrants living in urban areas, and it is likely that seasonality, particularly in physical work effort, delays or prevents a trend towards obesity, despite cultural preferences for fatter figures (Simondon *et al.* 2008).

Climatic unpredictability

Seasonal reductions in resource availability, although subject to significant flux, are generally more predictable and of smaller magnitude than those that occur because of extreme climatic events. Climatic unpredictability (including drought, monsoons or monsoonal failure, hurricanes, cyclones and El Niño effects) affects food supply, can result in serious food shortage and famine, and can have a major impact on conception and infant survival (Dyson 1991). All human populations through time have had to cope with the effects of extreme climate on food supply in some way, and there is no reason to suppose that periods of climatic instability in the past were less severe and therefore had less impact on biological fitness and fertility than those observed in recent times. Much of sub-Saharan Africa experiences seasonal resource fluctuations, and is vulnerable to either seasonal extremes (uncharacteristically wet or dry weather, for example) or unexpected environmental perturbation (encompassing events such as insect plagues). However, in recent food crises and famines, climate and ecology seem to have had less influence on food security than social and political factors, with failure of distribution and supply being more important than overall production (Baro and Deubel 2006). For example, two decades of increasing resource depletion, land scarcity in the face of rising populations, low status of women as well as economic and environmental marginalization, all contributed to the 2005 Niger famine (Baro and Deubel 2006). If a population already has large numbers of chronically undernourished individuals, there is no buffer – physiological or otherwise – against seasonal food shortages.

Long-term climate change, in the form of global warming, can change resource security in at least three ways. Through altering general climatic and environmental conditions, crop cycles can change, as can the types of plants grown. Changing plant growth changes what is possible with animal husbandry. Extreme weather events, including droughts, floods and storms, can lead to crop failure, while possible rise in sea levels can reduce the amount of land available for cultivation and livestock. Nicholls and Leatherman (1995) estimate that tens of millions of people in Egypt, Bangladesh and China will be affected directly by global warming, with, for example, a 16% reduction in rice production in Bangladesh if sea levels rise by one metre. Such a rise is predicted to occur within the next 100 years (Rahmstorf 2010). Land losses due to sea-level rise might be borne disproportionately by relatively fertile areas, such as river deltas, which tend to be agriculturally productive because of irrigation and rich sediment deposits, but vulnerable because of their coastal proximity and low-lying nature. The importance of deltaic areas to food production is exemplified in Vietnam, where, according to Gommes *et al.* (1998), the Red River and Mekong deltas between them account for 70% of national rice yields.

Models of anthropogenically induced global warming indicate that equatorial and tropical regions, which contain a large proportion of food insecure households, are likely to feel the effects of climate change more than higher latitude areas (Gommes *et al.* 1998). The impact of global warming on the world's poorest people is likely to be synergistic rather than additive: their vulnerability, whether due to seasonality, social or economic marginalization, would be exacerbated and reinforced. This would increase their exposure and susceptibility to all insults, not just those that are driven by climate (Department for International Development 2004). Climate change is likely to magnify global nutritional inequality (Chapter 8). Humans have experienced abrupt and severe climate change in the past, and it is possible that climate change has precipitated huge subsistence transitions, such as the emergence of agriculture. The circumstances under which contemporary populations live are radically different, however. Population densities are much higher, societies more stratified and inequalities more marked. Furthermore, globalization ensures that actions and decisions in one part of the world often have huge implications for people elsewhere.

Recommended daily allowances and seasonal resource shifts

Humans evolved in seasonal environments (Foley 1993) and human evolutionary history has been characterized by variable and varying environments. Physiological and behavioural plasticity enables humans, as well as many other mammals, to cope with seasonal fluctuation in resources. Seasonal variation in diet is at odds, however, with the notion that individuals require a set array of nutrients on a regular, daily (or at least short-term) basis. Recommended daily (or dietary) allowances (RDAs) were developed in the mid twentieth century, with specific values calculated by the US National Academy of Sciences in the late 1960s and early 1970s. Following 20 years of Expert Group meetings, the FAO/WHO published its *Handbook on Human Nutritional Requirements* in 1974 (Passmore *et al.* 1974). The first daily intake standards were designed for food labels in the US in 1973 (Pennington and Hubbard 1997), with similar standards adopted in the UK in the late 1970s. The estimated average requirement (EAR) is calculated from epidemiological and clinical studies, and is a population-based statistical estimate of nutrient requirements. The recommended daily allowance (RDA) is the EAR plus two standard deviations for all nutrients apart from energy, based on the premise that it is sufficient to meet the needs of 98% of healthy individuals in a given population, often defined by age and sex (Kennedy and Meyers 2005). Energy is not treated in this way, since a two-standard-deviation allowance would be a dietary recommendation for obesity. Periodic revisions of these recommendations (with attendant changes in nomenclature) have occurred, and RDAs are now often replaced by Dietary Reference Values (DRVs) in the UK and Dietary Reference Intakes (DRIs) in the US.

The terminology surrounding recommended intakes, as well as their derivations, are complex and often confusing. According to Pennington and Hubbard (1997), when reviewing the standards for Daily Values, the US Food and Drug Administration distinguished between two different types of reference values, the Reference Daily Intake (RDI), which relates to target intake levels, and Daily Reference Values, reflecting maintenance and upper limits (Pennington and Hubbard 1997). Agencies often also give a Safe Upper Limit (SUL) for micronutrients, because although deficiency can be detrimental to health, excess can also be harmful due to the potential toxicity of various vitamins and minerals if consumed in high doses (Hanekamp and Bast 2007). More recent evaluations of recommended intakes seek to integrate EAR, SUL, RDA and adequate intake into Dietary Reference Intakes to make the distinctions between safe, adequate and target intakes clearer (Kennedy and Meyers 2005).

One reason for the confusion is due to differences and changes across time in the ways in which such reference and standard values are derived, as well as the philosophies underpinning their creation and use. The initial impetus for developing standards was to address undernutrition, and this is still a major focus of public health efforts in non-industrialized and developing economies (Hanekamp and Bast 2007, 2008). In industrialized countries, increasing emphasis is placed on the precautionary use of RDAs, particularly in protection against chronic disease (Hanekamp and Bast 2008). In concert with this, and driven by concepts of acceptable risk and uncertainty, captured by Ulrich Beck (1992) as 'the risk society' (how modern populations are increasingly concerned with notions of safety and how to systematically cope with risk), SULs have been developed to protect consumers from micronutrient levels that might be toxic (Hanekamp and Bast 2008). One major limitation of both RDAs and SULs is the often limited evidence used to generate them. Recommended levels for some nutrients are based on studies with very small sample sizes. For example, the US EAR for Vitamin C was originally based on data from six men (Yates 2006). Also, new findings about the health benefits of certain nutrients may not be reflected in RDAs. For example, vitamin D consumption at levels higher than current RDAs may lower the risk of developing some cancers (Hanekamp and Bast 2008).

Dietary references and standards, particularly RDAs, can be critiqued in other ways. As the RDA is set at two standard deviations above the mean for normally distributed nutrient requirements, it is an overestimate of the required level of intake for many individuals (Kennedy and Meyers 2005). Since they are developed for populations not individuals, they do not give precise measures of need for any given person. Nonetheless, dieticians and other health care professionals, in the absence of individualized measures, often use RDAs to develop nutrition plans for specific patients (Sims 1996). Despite their conceptual inappropriateness, they remain the best tool for doing this, however.

Recommended daily allowances may be unachievable in many populations in seasonal environments. This is most easily considered in relation to energy balance and averaged needs, although the principles apply to other nutrients. In non-industrialized populations engaged in traditional subsistence, resource availability may change across the year, with corresponding impacts on energy intake and expenditure, body mass and percentage body fat. Such variation suggests that RDAs and other references or standards for daily energy intake have limited practical value in traditional subsistence economies. The exact proportions of weight loss and gain differ from population to population. In a Tanzanian farming community, for example, women lost around 3% of their body mass in the hungry season (Wandel and Holmboe-Ottesen 1992). Tanzanian pastoralist women were two per cent (roughly 1 kg) lighter during the late dry season than in the wet season, although there was little decrease in lean mass (Sellen 2000). In Nepali agropastoralist women, there was a weight difference of around four per cent between seasons (Panter-Brick 1996). One of the most marked seasonal changes in body mass has been recorded in Senegalese women agriculturalists, whose weight loss was in the order of 3–4 kg (Simondon *et al.* 2008).

While a minimum daily energy intake is required for maintenance metabolism as well as the demands of physical activity, growth, reproduction and other functions, the plasticity of human physiology is such that if this minimum intake is not met in a given day, the body can liberate available internal energy stores (glycogen and fat) to compensate for the shortfall. In populations subject to seasonality, energy balance is thus best assessed over a longer period, and intakes above or below a RDA on a given day should not be used to make blanket assessments of overall energy balance. Micronutrient intakes also fluctuate by season, and again measured intake over a short period may not be representative of longer-term trends and nutritional status. Fat-soluble vitamins are stored in the liver, and if overall long-term requirements for them are met, seasonal fluctuations are managed physiologically. Most water-soluble vitamins are not stored, and short-term excesses are excreted. A more regular supply of these vitamins is therefore necessary, and one threat of seasonality is that such vitamins, along with other micronutrients, may be in short supply at certain times of the year.

Seasonal variations in micronutrient consumption may have subtle health consequences. For example, decreased folic acid levels in winter, related to lower fruit and vegetable availability and consumption at that time of year, may be associated with increased oxidative damage in bodily lipids, a risk factor for chronic disease (Smolkova *et al.* 2004). Seasonal differences in micronutrient intake have been identified in pregnant women of European origin in New Zealand, and are viewed by some to be linked to a range of conditions that emerge at different life-stages, by way of season of birth, including schizophrenia, multiple sclerosis and Type 1 diabetes (Watson and MacDonald 2007). Just as the uterine environment may influence metabolic changes that persist across postnatal life (developmental programming, Chapter 1), relatively small shifts in micronutrient consumption by the mother may have effects at the cellular level that affect future health (Watson and MacDonald 2007). The challenge for public health nutrition, especially in transitional economies where the resource base and subsistence strategies are in flux (Chapter 9), is to draw up meaningful and useful standards that acknowledge seasonal resource shifts and at the same time encourage at least an acceptable level of nutrition year-round. Such references and standards must take into consideration not only the physiological differences between different groups within a population but also behavioural differences that may influence diet and nutrition. Pregnant and lactating women, for example, may have specific nutrient and energy needs, but may also have differential access to resources or practise food taboos that restrict their diets (Bentley *et al.* 1999). These factors may act in synergy with seasonal resource shifts, and could cause additional pressure in already stressed subpopulations.

Discussion

Understanding how food and its availability shift by season and how people respond to these changes is crucial to understanding nutritional status and the production of undernutrition among the world's population. Although humans evolved in seasonal environments and have a range of adaptations and strategies to cope with resource fluctuations, seasonal nutritional stress is still a reality for millions of people. Apart from the direct consequences of energy- or micronutrient-based undernutrition, seasonality of food availability can interact with infectious disease (Chapter 7). Furthermore, insecurity, of whatever type, is a risk factor for mental health problems such as anxiety and depression (Hadley and Patil 2008). Given that seasonality is a major cause of food insecurity, those living in environments characterized by seasonal resource fluctuations are at greater risk of developing such conditions.

The importance of understanding seasonality and its effects on diet and nutrition do not diminish in transitional economies (Chapter 9). Neither seasonal stresses nor improvements in health due to economic growth are experienced equally by those at different ends of the socioeconomic scale

(Hong 2007). Foods out of season, however necessary to good health or nutrition, are often much more expensive, and as a result, lower income households are more likely to be deprived of them. On a global scale, the demand in industrialized nations for foods that are locally out of season, whatever the cost, distorts food production economies in less industrialized nations, with land previously used for subsistence agriculture turned over, for example, to green beans or snow peas (mange-tout) for overseas consumers. The better off are not only buffered to a greater extent against seasonality than the less well-off, but usually also benefit disproportionately from economic growth. Thus, economic transition can reinforce inequalities already present because of seasonality and marginalization, among other factors. In addition, the dietary changes that occur during urbanization and nutritional transition may reduce resilience to seasonal food shortage among the poor, because of a reduction in dietary diversity and over-dependence on a small number of foods.

Seasonality interacts with a large number of factors that influence public health nutrition, yet drawing up universal policies to mediate the effects of seasonal food stress is difficult. Assessing dietary requirements is complicated by the fact that accepted standards, such as the RDA, do not easily allow for seasonal variation in resource availability and physiological responses to that variation in availability. Seasonal coping mechanisms vary from population to population, even in the same region, depending not only on ecology (for example, whether the primary mode of subsistence is foraging, agriculture or pastoralism) but also on social system and belief framework. The latter is exemplified by neighbouring Karen farming groups in highland Thailand: in a seasonal area, one group, the Sgaw, were found to be better-nourished relative to the other, the Pwo (Omori and Greksa 2002). This was partly attributed to the animistic beliefs of the Pwo, who put the foodstuffs that nutritionally buffer the Sgaw in the hungry season to ritual rather than dietary purposes (Omori and Greksa 2002). The Karen have increasingly adopted Buddhism and Christianity, the Sgaw more so and less recently than the Pwo. Where Buddhism has been adopted by the Pwo, this has been in addition to their animistic beliefs; where Christianity has been adopted, this has displaced animism. Thus it is easy to see how religion, and religious conversion, might influence seasonal nutritional state. In west Africa, taboos against eating wild animals among Lese horticulturalists have been shown to have negative effects on seasonal nutritional status (Bentley *et al.* 1999).

Within agricultural populations, households may respond to the same seasonality differently because of different economic circumstances, whether direct (being able to buy food when it is short) or indirect (having land which is more resilient to forms of seasonality such as flooding or drought). This has implications for formulating public health nutrition policy; in the real world one size does not fit all, even in small communities. Within households, inequality in resource distribution, by age or sex, can also complicate efforts to offset seasonal food stress. Conversely, the level of plasticity in human responses to dietary variability indicates that humans in industrialized societies should not use dietary standards slavishly, but treat them as guidelines that are constructed with a fairly rigid view of how humans should eat – that is, to consume equal amounts of dietary energy daily and to match expenditure closely. This mirrors industrial society, with its 'nine-until five, five days a week' schedule of economic activity that is divorced not only from the behaviour of traditional subsistence humans and ancestral hominins, but also pre-industrial agricultural societies in nations like the US and the United Kingdom.

Alongside the challenges posed by seasonality are issues of climate change and extreme climatic events. Global changes in climate may magnify usual seasonal patterns such that, for example, droughts become more severe, increasing the possibility of consecutive harvest failures. In such cases, there can be a fine line between usual seasonal stress and famine (Longhurst 1986). For the people affected, existing physiological, ecological, behavioural and cultural adaptations to seasonality may not be sufficient to buffer them on a longer basis. For public health and development organizations, judgements must be made about when severe seasonal food shortage becomes long-term and unrelieved undernutrition.

Hominins and humans have been exposed to environmental variability, including both climate change and seasonality, across their entire evolutionary history. This has resulted in an array of adaptations. These have provided imperfect solutions to fluctuating resources, with the result that seasonality and climate change have sometimes profound effects on the nutritional status and food security of populations. This reminds us that humans are not a finished product, but respond variously to the stresses of everyday life, much as the hominins before us did.

5 Evolution of human diet and eating behaviour

Although humans can eat most things, they show great variability in their food preferences. Some of these have become formalized as cuisines, a summation of the ways in which societies and communities frame their collective food likes and dislikes, preferred flavours, textures and patterns of processing (Douglas 1978; Mela and Catt 1996). Traditionally, these have been products of regional food availability (an outcome of climate and biological productivity) as well as historical, social and cultural factors that define aspects of nature as food or otherwise. Food preferences have changed with introductions of new foods, which have both cosmopolitanized diets and given rise to new traditions. Eating behaviour is dependent on qualities internal to foods, such as flavour, smell and texture, and external factors such as the availability and diversity of foodstuffs, and the social context of eating (Eertmans *et al.* 2001). It is impossible to know whether prehistoric foragers had cuisine, but they are certain to have had food preferences, if only on the basis of energy density, sweetness or fattiness of foods (Chapter 2). Even early hominins may have had different cultural traditions that included differences in eating or foraging behaviour. There are local, learned differences in foraging traditions in chimpanzees (Whiten *et al.* 2007), which indicate that humans are not the only animals to show innovation in diet and foraging behaviour. Nonetheless, humans take such cultural difference and innovation to extremes, and as a result have diets and food acquisition and production behaviours far removed from even the great apes. In this chapter, we describe the evolution of human diet and food choice. In relation to this, we discuss how the evolution of eating behaviours that favour consumption of foods that are either sweet or fatty have become detrimental to human well-being now, with the advent of industrialized food systems and nutrition transition (Chapter 9).

117

The omnivore's dilemma: risks and rewards
in foraging behaviour

Dietary preferences are developed within cultural frameworks and across life history, and balance conservatism, or safeness, with novelty, or risk. Without the latter, there would have been no transformation of human diet, yet humans and other animals often avoid taking risks. Foraging behaviour serves to minimize risks and maximize gains (Heilbronner *et al.* 2008): finding food and avoiding harmful items are life or death issues, for humans and other animals. Nonetheless, risk may be unavoidable under certain ecological conditions. This is the 'omnivore's dilemma': the need or desire to explore and sample novel foods versus the imperative to prevent consumption of poisonous substances (Addessi *et al.* 2005). Animals also need to balance the chance of obtaining high rewards with the possibility of losing out completely, decisions that those living in food-uncertain environments must make on a daily basis. Risk in foraging behaviour thus encompasses both food novelty and food availability.

Food neophobia (being wary of new foods) is common among humans and primates, and is often mediated by social factors: among capuchin monkeys, new foods are more likely to be eaten if others in the social group are also eating them (Visalberghi and Addessi 2000; Addessi *et al.* 2005). Furthermore, interest in foods eaten by others may be heightened if they are eating novel food items (Visalberghi and Fragaszy 1995). This suggests that the introduction of novel foods among hominins would have spread easily through a population. Studies on captive macaques indicate that new foods are more likely to be consumed if they are high in sugar (Johnson 2007), so immediate palatability is likely to be important to their acceptance. This is logical, since defensive anti-feedants, which can be harmful to health, are often bitter-tasting (Chapter 2). Consuming very small amounts of harmful foods, unless extremely toxic, may not have a fitness disadvantage, as sensory warnings – a burning sensation on the lips, for example – would prevent further ingestion and long-term harm, especially as adverse reactions would be likely to deter consumption among other individuals.

Alongside this, certain groups within a population may be more likely to try new things, including foods, than others. Adolescents, for example, engage in riskier behaviour than mature adults in both human and non-human primates (Barr *et al.* 2004). Among human foragers, children may select and eat different foods from their parents (Bird and Bliege Bird 2000). It is therefore possible that the foraging and consumption patterns of younger hominins were different from those of adults. It is also possible that they were more likely to take risks with food choice; this is supported by the observation that juvenile vervet monkeys are more prepared than adults to explore novel food items (Fairbanks 1993). This is one way in which new foods could have been introduced into the hominin diet.

There is also individual variation in risk-taking in relation to food availability, with physiological differences between individuals contributing to this variation. In macaques, lower serotonin levels decrease aversion to risk when faced with the reward of fruit juice (Long *et al.* 2009). Nutritional status may influence risk-taking. Compared with macaques on diets that contain adequate protein levels, those on low-protein diets go for immediate, secure sources of food, even in low quantities, rather than risk waiting for a larger quantity (Hill *et al.* 1983). Alternatively, in well-nourished animals for which resource unpredictability is the species norm, it may pay to take chances. Although evolutionarily closely related, chimpanzees and bonobos have different ecologies and behaviours, which result in different attitudes to risk (Heilbronner *et al.* 2008). In relation to food rewards for risk-taking, captive chimpanzees are less risk-averse than bonobos (Heilbronner *et al.* 2008). Both species eat ripe fruit, which can be an uncertain resource, but chimpanzees rely less on ubiquitous sources of herbaceous vegetation and may have access to smaller fruiting patches than bonobos, and hence must cope with more foraging risk in the wild (Heilbronner *et al.* 2008). Chimpanzees may also wait longer for rewards, a behavioural strategy (patience) most often associated with humans (Rosati *et al.* 2007), formalized by economists as delayed time preference. As hominins dispersing out of the tropics and into temperate zones (Chapter 4) were very likely to have encountered environments with patchy and uncertain food supplies, both risk-taking and patience are likely to have had significant fitness benefits. Given that risk-taking also varies within individuals (Long *et al.* 2009) and is not generally a fixed behaviour, humans and their ancestors would have been able to shape their responses according to prevailing environmental conditions and food supply.

Humans have taken the strategies of delayed reward and risk to extremes. For example, crop cultivation and animal breeding require calculated risk-taking on future gains (Hayden and Platt 2007). Seeds are sown for future harvests rather than being eaten immediately, while animals are fed in the hope that they will yield enough (or convert enough inedible plants to edible flesh, milk or eggs) to justify the time invested in looking after them. For the earliest farmers, venturing into an unknown food production system would have involved gambling on plant growth outcomes. In contemporary non-subsistence farming economies, gambling on food supplies takes the form of the commodities futures market (Chapter 9). Food suppliers enter into futures contracts with purchasers, giving a guarantee that a certain amount of food will be supplied for a given sum of money. This helps to 'hedge' against fluctuating supply and stabilize food prices. However, many futures contracts are not fulfilled and are traded before their expiration date. Traders speculating in this way have potentially huge rewards for themselves and the companies they work for. However, this may be at the expense of overall public health. Gambling on futures markets may have been a factor, along with high oil prices, increased demand for crops for biofuel, decline in food stockpiles and decreased production, in the large spike in cereal prices in 2008 and the continued volatility in international food markets since then (Food and Agriculture Organization 2010c). In a globalized economy where a large proportion of the population depends on buying rather than growing food, even small price increases cause significant hardships, food insecurity and potentially starvation for those at the lowest income levels. Such people bear disproportionately high risks for little reward in economies they have virtually no control over.

In contemporary industrialized societies, risk is increasingly minimized or removed from most aspects of everyday life, including food production. Despite recent price volatility, food supply in such societies is much more secure than it was even 50 years ago. The risks of eating novel foods are also much reduced, with governmental and industrial regulations on food quality (Chapter 4). Consumers browsing supermarket shelves can select from a wide range of new foods, without being worried about their potential toxicity. When food can be eaten confidently because of the extremely low risk of contamination, prudence can be put to one side. However, as individual or family responsibility for food choice, safety and consumption declines, a new arena of risk opens up. If people no longer need to be concerned about immediate toxicity of novel foodstuffs, they may be less interested in what their food contains, and may be less inclined to take individual responsibility for dietary choices. The vast majority of novel foods in industrialized nations are highly processed, energy-dense transformations of existing foodstuffs. These factors together increase the possibility of abuse of dietary elements, such as fats and sugars, which in small amounts may be safe, but in large amounts become harmful to health (Chapters 10 and 11). Even when people appreciate the detrimental effects of consuming such foods, the human inclination to take risks may shape eating behaviour.

Innovation, dietary niche construction and the development of regional food traditions

Risk and innovation are closely linked. Humans (and probably their recent ancestors, at least) have taken dietary innovation to extremes, leading to huge changes in diet and foraging behaviour over the course of human evolutionary history. Such innovation encompasses the ways in which foods are produced and prepared, along with novelty of foodstuffs themselves. Through chemical processing (including cooking, brewing, preserving and toxin extraction) as well as the sophisticated mechanical processing that started with stone tools and continues today in extensive industrial food factories, humans have transformed what they eat. But they have done so with a very small number of staple foods, many of which are monocot plants. Modern human eating behaviour is a type of 'niche construction' (Chapter 3), in which the dietary environment is shaped and modified from that available in nature.

The earliest hominins, the australopiths, are unlikely to have engaged in significant modification of their dietary environments. Their diets would have been similar to those observed in modern non-human primates, being predominantly plant-based, gathered from the wild and supplemented with wild animal foods (such as insects, eggs, vertebrate meat and honey) (Chapter 2). Use of the earliest stone tools (direct evidence for which appears in the archaeological record around 2.6 million years ago) (Chapter 3) would have increased the efficiency of foraging and hunting, and would have enabled larger carcasses to be processed. This, in combination with the coordinated hunting of herds of animals that probably emerged with *Homo erectus* (Thieme 2005), would have widened the hominin dietary niche to include large game animals. The spread of *Homo* out of Africa and into temperate latitudes by around 1 million years ago would have introduced further novelty into the hominin diet, even if diets more generally may not have been as diverse (Chapter 4). The hominin ability and inclination to innovate would have been essential in adapting behaviourally to environments outside the tropics.

Cooking with heat (discussed further below) is likely to date from at least 800 000 years ago, and was an important transformation in hominin dietary behaviour. Hominins were no longer constrained to eating foods in very similar chemical states to those found in the wild, and started to modify their dietary environments rather than simply responding to prevailing environmental conditions. This would have promoted further differentiation of diets, as different communities would have developed their own ways of preparing foods and creating their dietary niche alongside cultural ones. Agriculture emerged through human niche construction independently in several parts of the world, in the Fertile Crescent in the Near East and New Guinea around 10 000 years ago, and in eastern China, Mesoamerica and South America around 8000 years ago (Chapter 1). This would have helped to establish regional traditions, preferences and eating behaviours. Some early cultivated crops and domesticates, such as squash and maize in Mesoamerica

(Piperno *et al.* 2009), chick peas in the Middle East (Brown *et al.* 2008), rice and pork in south-east Asia (Zong *et al.* 2007) and taro and banana in New Guinea (Sandweiss 2007) remain distinctive elements of the cuisine of these regions to this day.

Once agriculture was established, early forms of trade in foodstuffs emerged, spreading different domesticates from one region to another. One example of this is the spread of chicken as a source of cultivated food from Asia and India to Persia and Greece by 2500 years ago (Toussaint-Samat 2009). Subsequent trade across regions, usually for prestige items (for example, trade of silk and spices from Asia to Europe from around 3000 years ago) also led to the introduction of food animals, particularly cattle, from one place to another (Foltz 1999). Within regions, trade was usually driven by goods and luxury items that were locally unavailable, among them foods. In medieval Europe, these included salted herring, salt, wine, oil and fruit. Globalization and human migration from the fifteenth century onwards led to many new food traditions, including the incorporation of tomato, capsicum and potato into the diets of different European societies after their introductions from Latin America. During global colonization by European nations and subsequent industrialization of European and North American society, new foods were introduced and new food cultures developed (Toussaint-Samat 2009). Mexico developed a distinctive cuisine, which was a hybrid of European and Central American foods from the time of the Spanish Conquest in 1519 (Chapter 10). The Spanish also introduced rice to Mexico (Long-Solis and Vargas 2005). Rice puddings of various kinds are currently seen as traditional to most of Europe, the Middle East and Asia. The one that is traditional to English cuisine was introduced from India in the eighteenth century.

The classic British fast food, fish and chips, is a good example of 'fusion food': a merging of different types of food traditions to create a distinct dish that is now uniquely associated with the United Kingdom. Potato chips (or French fries, as they became known in the United States) were widely consumed among the wealthy in seventeenth century Belgium, and were known among the privileged classes across Europe and North America by the eighteenth century. The practice of fried fish consumption was part of Jewish cuisine across Europe, including England. The novel combination of chips with fish was an urban Jewish economic venture in nineteenth century England, initially as a convenience food on the Sabbath, when cooking at home was not permitted. The diffusion of fish and chips as a commonly consumed dish into the wider British population came with increased industrialization of food production, as the price of fish declined with the invention of trawler fishing in the North Sea during the nineteenth century. The decline in the real price of fish, potato and cooking fat allowed fish and chips to become iconic of working-class cuisine in England by the turn of the twentieth century.

Across the twentieth century and into the twenty-first, widespread globalization of food processing and distribution has taken place, and dishes and cuisines continue to be invented. Immigrant communities who came to Britain in the 1950s and 1960s brought with them new culinary traditions, which were incorporated into mainstream British food. Chicken tikka masala is the iconic example, becoming a 'new' national dish of Britain, as the price of chicken has declined. All present-day industrialized societies have available to them a wide range of cooking and eating traditions, from which cosmopolitan food practices can be constructed, internalized and reinvented as traditional. Such cosmopolitanization is taking place across the world (Chapter 9).

Contemporary humans base their food choices on known cuisines and availability (both physical and economic). They are little different from their hominin ancestors in that they are open to dietary shifts, although the pace of dietary change experienced by contemporary humans and their ancestors over the past few generations has been faster than ever before. For example, the diet of common people in England in the fifteenth century was based largely on cereals (gruels and bread), and to a lesser extent fish, meat and vegetables according to season. This underwent little change for several centuries. Early globalization shifted the traditional English ways of eating. Potato was incorporated into the diet after its introduction to Europe in 1536, and sugar and rice were to follow, along with tea, coffee and chocolate. By the mid-nineteenth century, potatoes had become a traditional staple food. The pace of change over a couple of hundred years was staggering in comparison with other periods in human evolutionary history, such as the adoption of agriculture, which (as described in Chapter 1) took at least 3000 to 4000 years.

Industrialization, which began in earnest during the eighteenth century, added an additional dimension to this rapid change, altering not only the foods that people ate but also the ways in which they sourced and prepared them. As the sphere of economic production shifted from the home and settlement to industrialized towns and cities, people produced less and less food for themselves. This de-coupled economic activity (usually of a physical nature) from food production on a scale never before experienced. The industrialization of food production can be seen as an example of human dietary niche construction, which alongside globalization, has increased food choice among those who can afford it. Industrial methods of processing allowed foods to be preserved and transported great distances. Tinned foods and bakery-produced bread were among the first convenience foods, needing minimal preparation by the consumer. With food available on demand, meal times and patterns of consumption were set by the timetables of industrialized society.

**Increasing dietary quality and evolving food choice:
developing a taste for sugar, animals and fat**

The human digestive tract, with its relatively small, unspecialized teeth at the front end, and a simple gut, indicates, relative to other primates, adaptation to a higher-quality, energy-dense diet, with less bulk and more easily liberated energy per unit of mass consumed (Chapter 2). 'High quality' can be defined in a number of ways, including high energy per unit mass, high protein or micronutrient content, and easily liberated (i.e. digestible) energy. There are enormous variations in human dietary quality and diet components, but few if any human groups under normal conditions choose to eat uncooked mature leaves or other bulky plant materials that are hard for them to digest. Ripe, fleshy fruit, eaten by many primates, is a relatively high-quality food (Chapter 2).

Ripe fruit contains high concentrations of the sugars fructose and glucose (Milton 1999a). Sugary foods are attractive to a range of animals, including bats, birds and primates (Riba-Hernández *et al.* 2003). Unfamiliar foods are more attractive if they are high in sugar (Johnson 2007), and foods containing tannins are more likely to be eaten by some primates if the taste is masked with sugar, indicating that the potential costs of tannin consumption may be outweighed by the benefits of sugar consumption (Remis and Kerr 2002; Chapter 2). The human taste for sugar, discussed further in Chapter 11, is thus linked to an evolutionary heritage of frugivory, particularly the consumption of ripe fruits, and a strong preference for sugary foods.

In the increasingly dry and seasonal environments of the African Pleistocene (Chapter 4), fruit would have been available to tropical hominins but may have been more patchily dispersed in time and space. In drier and more seasonal environments, legumes, plants with less fleshy fruits and seeds and bushes with berries are more abundant (Plummer 2004). These plant foods can be highly nutritious, containing a variety of micronutrients as well as being energy-dense, and were likely to have formed an important part of the *Homo* diet (Chapter 3). Along with nuts and seeds, underground storage organs (USOs) may also have been an increasingly valued element (Wrangham *et al.* 1999). Such plant foods would have been eaten alongside significant quantities of animal products, increasing the quality of hominin and human diets (Plummer 2004). One advantage of being able to eat foods from a number of trophic levels (Chapter 2) is the ability to exploit a wider ecological niche. Eating animals adapted to survive in the drier, open grasslands that emerged in the Pleistocene allowed hominins to inhabit these environments with relative ease (Plummer 2004), despite the comparative paucity of fleshy fruits. Dietary quality would also have been influenced by the ways foodstuffs were prepared: cooking tough, fibrous foods such as USOs, for example, renders them more digestible, as does mechanical processing where husks and seed coatings are removed.

Mechanical and chemical processing

Dietary quality is linked in part to body size. Smaller-bodied animals tend to have a higher-quality diet, as their relative energy needs are greater than those of larger animals. Humans diverge from this trend, as their overall dietary quality and energy density is much higher than that seen in other apes (Milton 1999a). Functionally, the higher quality and higher energy density of the human diet can be ascribed not only to meat-eating, discussed further below, but also to increased reliance on food-processing. Extensive food-processing makes a major contribution to the 'epidemic of obesity' currently observed in many human populations (Chapters 8, 9 and 10). Highly processed food tends to be more energy-dense per unit mass, with less fibre and much less water, the latter resulting in an increase in digestible energy and the former in a reduction of satiety (Milton 1999a). The highly processed foods that form the diet for most people in industrialized nations are 'high-quality' in the sense that they have a high energy content and are easily digested but may be 'low-quality' because they have a relatively poor micronutrient content (Chapter 4).

Food-processing is not unique to modern humans or hominins. Some primates mechanically process food through, for example, removing external seed husks, either by hand or through pounding, making the food easier to digest (Chapter 2). Pleistocene hominins mechanically processed animal carcasses and plants by using tools. Among the hominins, it is likely to have been chemical processing that truly transformed dietary quality. Chemical transformation by the application of heat (cooking) revolutionized human diets, rendering food more digestible by breaking down cell walls and chemical bonds and altering the structure of foods, allowing enzymes to work more effectively (Wrangham *et al.* 1999). Cooking can also modify the secondary compounds produced by plants as defence mechanisms, making them palatable and reducing their toxicity (Chapter 2). Other examples of cooking and processing of food among humans that require only basic technology are drying and detoxification by soaking of starchy tubers such as manioc.

The cooking of food, at least prior to the advent of microwave ovens, requires the controlled use of fire or another heat source. The earliest verified use of fire in a controlled way dates to around 790 000 years ago at the Acheulean site of Gesher Benot Ya'aqov, in Israel (Goren-Inbar *et al.* 2004). Charcoal deposits at earlier sites such as Chesowanja, in Kenya, dated to around 1.4 million years ago, allow for the possibility of an even earlier emergence of controlled fire (Gowlett *et al.* 1981), although similar traces could be left at archaeological sites through naturally-occurring conflagrations. The presence of burnt bones at Swartkrans Member 3, southern Africa, dated to around 1 million years ago, has also been posited as evidence for controlled use of fire (Brain and Sillent 1988), but the deposit contains material from a mixture of sources and ages (Bunn 1999). Although the evidence for controlled use of fire in the earlier part of the Pleistocene is slim and patchy, by the late Middle and Late Pleistocene there are definite and widespread traces of controlled fire at hominin occupation sites (James 1989). Wrangham and colleagues (1999) argue that cooking evolved earlier than suggested by traces of controlled fire in the archaeological record. They attribute the morphological and behavioural 'grade shift' that occurred with the evolution of *H. ergaster/H. erectus* (Wood and Collard 1999), including smaller chewing teeth and increased female body mass, to cooking and its social ramifications (Wrangham *et al.* 1999). It is difficult, however, to see how cooking with heat could have left so few archaeological traces if it was sufficiently widespread and extensively used to cause digestive and social adaptation.

Whether or not cooking with heat resulted in morphological changes to the human digestive system, these same changes could have arisen because of enhanced mechanical and chemical food processing, as well as an increased dependence on vertebrate meat and other fauna. The human gut, although very similar to those of the other apes, has a proportionally smaller large intestine, indicating adaptation to a relatively high-quality and more energy-dense diet (Chapter 2). Since soft tissues are not generally preserved in the fossil record, it is difficult to estimate accurately when the gut proportions seen in modern humans evolved. Based on the shape of the rib cage (which in australopiths is funnel-shaped and in 'true' members of the genus *Homo* is barrel-shaped), it has been suggested that *H. erectus* may have had a reduced gut size (Aiello and Wheeler 1995). This cannot be used to imply that the ancestors of *H. erectus* and early members of the species cooked food by using controlled fire or heat, since chopping food using tools or pulverizing it with hammerstones serves to decrease the particle size of foods, increasing the efficiency of enzyme activity and digestion once consumed (McGrew 1999; Milton 1999a). Extensive mechanical processing prior to ingestion reduces demand on the dentition, and may result in selection for smaller chewing teeth, another feature of *H. erectus* and later hominins.

Eating animals and animal products

Eating insects, animals and their products (eggs, honey, milk) has long been viewed as a crucial component of the higher-quality and more energy-dense human diet, even though many human populations are heavily dependent on plant foods, particularly monocots, especially with the adoption of agriculture (Chapter 2). Faunal resources are also consumed by many other primates. Nonetheless, the inclusion of animal products, primarily from vertebrates, was a major transition in the nutrition of human ancestors in the Pleistocene, and modern human diets include more animal products than do the diets of other primates (Chapter 2). Much of the palaeoanthropological debate about the importance of meat-eating has centred on the consumption of vertebrate flesh, and whether it was first hunted or scavenged. Raymond Dart, the anatomist who discovered the first *A. africanus* specimen, was in no doubt that meat-eating was a fundamental and important aspect of the behaviour of even the earliest hominins. Basing his ideas on finds of bones that may have been used as tools (the 'osteodontokeratic' culture) and traces of carbon-like deposits that he believed indicated controlled fire, Dart (1953 p. 209) argued that

> Man's predecessors . . . seized living quarries by violence, battered them to death, tore apart their broken bodies, dismembered them limb from limb, slaking their ravenous thirst with the hot blood of victims and greedily devouring livid writhing flesh.

Dart's extreme views about flesh-eating in Plio-Pleistocene hominins have few if any advocates now. However, stable isotope studies of the dental apatite of *Australopithecus africanus* and *Paranthropus robustus* indicate that hominins were eclectic feeders that very likely consumed some animal matter (Lee-Thorp *et al.* 1994; Sponheimer and Lee-Thorp 1999). Some of this faunivory might have involved consumption of termites, as suggested by bone 'fishing rods' recovered from the early hominin locality of Swartkrans in southern Africa (Backwell and d'Errico 2001), but there is also the very real possibility that hominins, like modern baboons and chimpanzees, took small animals as prey.

The importance of hominin consumption of larger animals is much more contested. Since the 1970s, palaeoanthropologists have realized that Plio-Pleistocene hominins, living in ecological communities no less complex than the ones that primates exist in today, were not the top predators in their ecosystems. Rather, they were 'the hunted' (Brain 1981) as well as being the hunters, or scavengers. There is good evidence for hominins as prey (Hart and Sussman 2005). The Taung child, the *A. africanus* specimen found by Raymond Dart, bears tell-tale marks of predation by a crowned eagle (Berger 2006), one of the 'big three' predators of primates along with leopards and snakes. There is equally good evidence for early hominins as predators or scavengers, extensive traces being found in the Pleistocene rather than the Pliocene record. Percussion marks, interpreted as hominin butchery, have been identified on large monkeys dated to slightly less than 1 million years ago in east Africa (Shipman *et al.* 1981). Many ungulate bones modified by hominins have been found, such as at Swartkrans Member 3 in southern Africa (Pickering *et al.* 2004). It seems likely that the relative balance of 'hominin as prey' versus 'hominin as predator' shifted during human evolutionary history. Plio-Pleistocene hominins would have functioned as large-bodied apes opportunistically predating on animals while also being subject to significant, systematic predation themselves from carnivores. Later hominins became organized hunters and butchers of much larger animals, as well as occasionally falling victim to predation themselves. Some hominins, exemplified by the Neanderthals, may have taken this to extremes, becoming 'top level' predators (Richards *et al.* 2001).

It is not yet clear whether Plio-Pleistocene hominins gained most of the meat that they ate from actively hunting animals or whether they scavenged from carcasses killed by other animals (Blumenschine *et al.* 2007). It is likely that active pursuit hunting and passive scavenging lay on either ends of a spectrum of meat acquisition possibilities open to all hominins, including early *Homo* and other Plio-Pleistocene species. Bunn (2001) gives a plausible and compelling scenario for hominin meat acquisition, combining 'power scavenging' (active carcass take-over) with hunting. This is based on analogy from observations of contemporary Tanzanian Hadza forager hunting practice alongside detailed examination of cut marks, carcass and element preservation of fossil animal bone assemblages from Plio-Pleistocene localities at Olduvai. For many modern foraging populations as well as primates, meat is an unpredictable resource (Bunn 2001), and the same would have been true for human ancestors. Being alert to opportunities would have been vital to hominin meat procurement, along with within-group cooperation and the ability to process food efficiently by using tools (Plummer 2004) and possibly other technologies such as fire.

Animal products eaten by humans include vertebrate muscle tissue ('meat'), many other animal parts (such as adipose tissue, brain, bone marrow, liver and kidneys), eggs and milk, as well as invertebrates and honey. At least one study of contemporary humans indicates high reliance on animal foods in forager diets (Cordain *et al.* 2000b). Based on data drawn from the *Ethnographic Atlas* (Murdock 1967) on 229 hunter-gatherer societies, a majority (58%) obtained more than two thirds of their subsistence from animal foods (hunted and fished) while only a small number (four per cent) appeared equally reliant on gathered plant foods (Cordain *et al.* 2000a). Consumption of hunted animal foods seemed relatively constant regardless of latitude, while use of plant foods decreased greatly with increasing latitude; at high latitudes (as in the Arctic), the lack of plant food was compensated by increased use of fish and seafood (Cordain *et al.* 2000a).

Although a useful source of data, the *Ethnographic Atlas* (Murdock 1967) must be viewed in context. Modern foraging populations have experienced pressures caused by modernity and their diets may not reflect even the traditional norm for their society, let alone human populations more broadly (Elton 2008a). The *Ethnographic Atlas* (Murdock 1967) does not fulfil the criteria of objectivity and standardization usually required for systematic reviews. In particular, it draws on available ethnographies (rather than representatively sampled populations) that did not necessarily aim to collect data on diet and which may have been biased towards study of a subset of the population, often men (Milton 2000a). Since a less-than-accurate picture of eating and foraging behaviour may therefore emerge (Milton 2000a), precise proportions should be treated with caution. This notwithstanding, cross-cultural and comparative study of human and primate diets, now and in the past, indicates that humans have developed a taste for animal foods that is not seen in other primates, even though there is considerable inter- (and intra-) population variation in modern human meat consumption.

The human taste for animal foods and increase in dietary quality should be viewed as part of an evolving and flexible diet that includes a broad spectrum of plant and animal products. 'Meat-eating' is often used as shorthand for the consumption of animal foods, but a distinction must be made between them. Foraging populations, usually those living at high latitudes with a limited range of plant foods, eat significant quantities of animal matter, but are not confined to consuming meat in the form of muscle tissue (Cordain *et al.* 2000a). Fat and viscera are eaten, and often seen as prized resources. Indeed, they are essential to good health and survival. Reliance on energy intake predominantly from protein obtained from hunted game during winter months, when fat contents (particularly in small animals) are very low, can result in metabolic abnormalities that can lead to death (Speth and Spielman 1983). Early European explorers in the American wilderness experienced such 'rabbit starvation' during the winter months when plant carbohydrate was not available and the small animals consumed were severely fat-depleted (Mann 2000). Symptoms of rabbit starvation, often followed by death, include stomach distension, restlessness and diarrhoea (Steffansson 1944).

Animal consumption by extinct hominins and humans prior to the origins of agriculture is likely to have been different from meat-eating in industrialized societies. Archaeological evidence of percussion marks on bone (Blumenschine 1995) indicates consumption of energy-dense tissue such as the brain, liver and bone marrow. Foods such as offal, marrowbones and sweetbreads were consumed widely prior to the mid-twentieth century in industrialized and industrializing nations but are generally of low status in most of the contemporary industrialized world. Until recently most of these types of tissues ended up in animal feed or as part of highly processed meat products (such as hotdogs) marketed mainly at lower-income groups. Since the spread of bovine spongiform encephalopathy among cattle, the practice of feeding animal waste tissues into ruminant feed products has been made illegal in most economically developed nations. Paradoxically, however, with the increased interest in 'artisanal' and local foods, offal and similar foods have experienced a renaissance in consumption at the higher end of the income spectrum in economically developed nations.

Given the importance of animal sources of energy and nutrients, why did hominins not become exclusive or near-exclusive carnivores? Protein metabolism is the limiting factor. During digestion, protein is broken down into amino acids, which in turn can be converted to their constituent parts, including nitrogen. Such amino acid degradation occurs in the liver, which has a finite ability to produce the enzymes necessary for this process. High levels of protein can thus be toxic because the body cannot catabolize and excrete its breakdown products rapidly enough, leading to nitrogen build-up in tissues in the form of ammonia (Mann 2000). Protein nitrogen is ultimately excreted from the body as urea. In adults, as long as dietary nitrogen intake does not exceed about 65 grams of nitrogen per kilogram of body mass per hour, the body can synthesize sufficient urea for effective excretion of excess nitrogen intake (Rudman *et al.* 1973). Given that protein is 16% nitrogen, the maximum theoretical protein intake for an adult male weighing 80 kg is about 250 g/day (Mann 2000). Even in the countries with among the highest levels of meat intake in the world (Germany, the US and Australia) average protein availability is less than half this value (Food and Agriculture Organization 2010b). To avoid protein intakes exceeding physiological limits, any hominin that obtained more than 55% of its dietary energy from animal foods would have needed to do one or more of the following: consume animals with more than about 10% body fat; selectively butcher animals to maximize their fat intake from brain and organs; and/or maximize their intake of carbohydrates from plant sources (Mann 2000). Since most wild game has very little body fat, hominins would have needed to butcher hunted animals selectively as well as eaten plant carbohydrate to survive.

Along with energy, food provides micronutrients (Chapters 1 and 4) and amino acids vital to health. Humans do not biosynthesize all the nutrients necessary for normal physiological functioning, and rely on food to provide them. Vitamin C is a good example: in common with the majority of other haplorhine primates, humans must have a dietary source of it (Cui *et al.* 2011). This provides strong support for an evolutionary heritage of plant- (especially fruit-) eating, and also reinforces the fact that humans require plant as well as animal foods in their diets. In the taiga and tundra biomes of northerly latitudes where plants edible by humans are relatively scarce, vitamin C is available to foraging populations like the Sami through berries (such as the cloudberry),

Table 5.1 *Amino acid requirements and general availability in proteins*

| Amino acid | Requirements (mg/kg body wt/day) | | Pattern in high-quality proteins (mg/g protein) |
	Infants	Adults	
Phenylalanine	141	16	73
Leucine	135	16	70
Lysine	99	12	51
Valine	92	14	48
Isoleucine	83	12	42
Threonine	68	8	35
Methionine	49	10	26
Histidine	33	—	17
Tryptophan	21	3	11

Adapted from Leibermann 1987

ground-living plants like sorrel, and willow. Given that vitamin C is water-soluble and not stored for long periods in the body (Chapter 4), preservation of such plants (for example, by drying) may have been an important behavioural and cultural adaptation to enable successful exploitation of such extreme environments.

Essential amino acids provide another example of the need to include a range of foodstuffs in the diet. Of the 20 amino acids used in human protein formation, nine are essential to the diet, since humans are unable to synthesize them. Table 5.1 gives the relative requirements for adults and infants of these nine essential amino acids versus the amino acid content in high-quality dietary protein. Although requirements are highest for phenylalanine and leucine, the sulphur-containing amino acid methionine is generally the least abundant in the diet (Geissler and Powers 2006) and limits the production of proteins in the human body. The major food types that supply methionine in significant quantities are meats, poultry, fish and seafood (Table 5.2). As well as providing methionine at high concentrations, meat and seafood provide other amino acids that are comparatively rare in plant sources of protein, as well as high concentrations of iron, zinc and vitamin B_{12} (nutrients that are difficult to obtain in bio-available forms elsewhere).

Not all contemporary human populations have access to, or want to eat, animal products. It is possible to obtain enough protein with an acceptable amino acid balance from a plant-dominated diet, if protein complementarity is achieved. This occurs by combining plant foods containing overlapping and complementary essential amino acids (for example maize, low in lysine, can be combined with legumes such as lentils and chickpeas, which are high in

Table 5.2 *Main dietary sources of methionine*

Food group	Methionine %RDA (200 g food)
Breads/cereals/grains	11
Dairy	30
Fish/seafood	175
Fruits	3
Meat/poultry	130
Nuts/seeds	78
Vegetables	23

Adapted from Leibermann 1987

lysine). The 'founder crops' grown by the earliest farmers in the Fertile Crescent (Brown *et al.* 2008; Chapter 1) contain complementary amino acids (Figure 5.1). In societies that practise vegetarianism, such as some south Asian Hindu groups, dietary diversity ensures that essential amino acid requirements are met. Traditional cuisine will combine, for example, rice and legumes. Many Hindus are also milk consumers ('lacto-vegetarians'), which helps to ensure that all essential amino acids and micronutrients are included in the diet. The need for essential amino acids and other nutrients, such as vitamin C, emphasizes the importance of dietary diversity (Chapter 4): in market-orientated economies, where most food is bought rather than grown and monocultures dominate, balanced nutrition might be difficult to achieve, especially for people on very low incomes (Abdoellah and Marten 1986).

The availability and diversity of fat types are also important for the physical development and health of individuals. Long-chain polyunsaturated fatty acids (LC PUFA) are of particular importance for brain development and function (McCann and Ames 2005). Humans are relatively poor converters of shorter-chain PUFA ($\geq$ 18 carbon atoms), which are found in plants, into LC PUFA ($>$ 18 carbon atoms) (Salem *et al.* 1996), despite being highly encephalized (having a much larger brain relative to body size compared with most other mammals). Since humans need dietary sources of essential fatty acids, the human (and presumably hominin) requirement for LC PUFA has to be met from the diet if brains are to develop and function properly (McCann and Ames 2005). Fatty acids in general are important in building cell membranes as well as being sources of energy. They comprise 'strings' or 'chains' of carbon atoms joined by chemical bonds with a carboxyl group (a cluster of oxygen, carbon and hydrogen atoms) at one end of the string and a methyl group (comprising carbon and hydrogen atoms) at the other (Chapter 10).

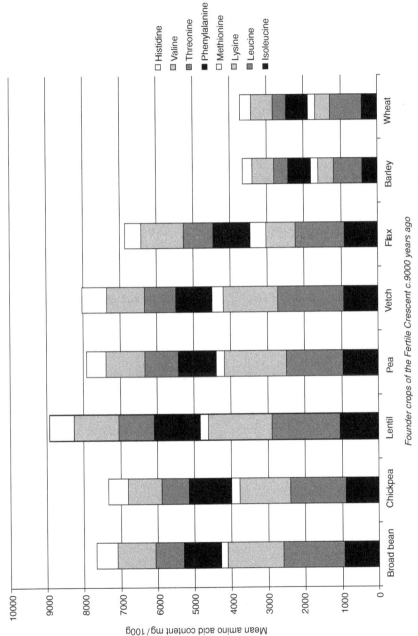

Figure 5.1. Essential amino acid content of founder crops of the Fertile Crescent, eastern Mediterranean.

Fatty acids can be 'saturated', 'monounsaturated' or 'polyunsaturated' depending on how the carbon atoms are joined together. Saturated fatty acids only contain single bonds between the carbon atoms. These are the fatty acids that predominate in foods such as butter, hard vegetable shortenings and fat on red meat. Monounsaturated fatty acids, which are found in avocados, nuts and olives, contain one double bond in the carbon chain. Polyunsaturated fatty acids, found at high concentrations in many seed oils such as sunflower oil, contain more than one double bond in the carbon chain. Double bonds introduce 'kinks' in the carbon chain that help cell membranes to be more flexible, and allow oils made from polyunsaturated fatty acids to be more fluid. Plants do not produce fatty acids longer than an 18 carbon chain, whereas most animals can elongate the length of fatty acids and introduce more double bonds, producing LC PUFA. Thus, although polyunsaturated fatty acids are most commonly associated with plant foods, dietary LC PUFA must come from animal sources. One of the best-known examples is omega 3 (n3) LC PUFA, an essential fatty acid where the first double bond is on the third carbon position from the methyl end. Typically, n3 LC PUFA (such as eicosapentaenoic acid (EPA) and docosahexaenoic acid (DHA) are found in oily fish such as salmon, shellfish, wild game meat and grass-fed red domestic meat, whereas eighteen-carbon n3 PUFA (such as α-linolenic acid) can be found in walnuts, linseed (flax) and green leafy vegetables, as well as in freshwater algae and seaweed. Sunflower oil, in contrast, contains the eighteen carbon omega n6 PUFA, linoleic acid, with the first double bond in the sixth carbon position (Chapter 10).

Increased intake of LC PUFA is likely to have been a key factor in hominin encephalization. Omega-3 (n3) LC PUFA, which supplies material for the neural membrane as well as being vital for neural transmission and reception required for cognitive function, may have particular importance (Chamberlain 1996). Several studies (reviewed in Committee on Animal Nutrition 2003) have indicated the importance of n3 LC PUFA for non-human primate growth and development, particularly of the brain. This requires good maternal nutrition as most brain growth in non-human primates occurs *in utero*. It is likely that most non-human primates get the majority of their essential n3 PUFA from plant sources, as plants dominate their diets, and convert this to LC forms for systemic use. Some primates, baboons and macaques in particular, have been shown to eat shellfish and other types of aquatic/marine resources (Kempf 2009). This behaviour is opportunistic and inconsistent across the ranges of widespread species, due to the presence or absence of marine/aquatic environments (Kempf 2009). Thus it is unlikely that fish and shellfish are significant sources of essential n3 LC PUFA in non-human primates, and there is no reason to expect that those primates without a ready source of such foods have arrested brain growth, development and function.

Plants also provide n3 PUFA in modern human diets. Although low in fatty acids overall, several wild African plants, most commonly used as fall-back foods in contemporary human populations, have high proportions of the essential omega 3 fatty acid α-linolenic acid (Glew *et al.* 2009). Walnuts also contain it, and walnut pollen has been found at the Neanderthal site of Shanidar; although traces of walnuts themselves were not found in the dental calculus of individuals from the site, other plant foods were (Henry *et al.* 2011). Walnut consumption is likely to have been seasonal, however, and an absence of evidence may be due to a lack of recent consumption of walnuts prior to the death of the Neanderthals that much, much later became analytical specimens for contemporary archaeologists. Flax, also rich in the n3 PUFA α-linolenic acid, was one of the founder crops in the Fertile Crescent, with its seeds being used for food (Chapter 1). When the fatty acid content of flax seed is considered in combination with its relatively high essential amino acid content, it can easily be thought of as a Neolithic 'superfood'.

Earlier hominins would have had access to plant foods containing n3 PUFA. In sub-Saharan Africa this may have been in the form of green leafy vegetables prior to the Pleistocene; from the early Pleistocene onwards, n3 PUFA would have been available from more temperate plants such as walnuts and flax to hominins dispersing out of Africa. There is also good archaeological evidence for fish consumption among hominins in and out of Africa (Alperson-Afil *et al.* 2009; Braun *et al.* 2010). Around 1.95 million years ago, Turkana Basin hominins exploited aquatic as well as terrestrial foodstuffs, including catfish, turtles and crocodiles alongside land mammals such as impala and pigs (Braun *et al.* 2010). Analysis of fish assemblages suggests that Plio-Pleistocene hominins may have also consumed them at Olduvai Gorge (Stewart 1994). Catching catfish (one of the most commonly found fish at early archaeological sites) may not require specialized technologies (Steele 2010), especially at lake margins that may dry up seasonally leaving bottom-feeding fish stranded, or when fish are at high densities when spawning (Stewart 1994). Thus, Plio-Pleistocene hominins could have consumed them opportunistically, catching them by hand. They may well have gained essential fatty acids from this source, although the degree to which oily fish and shellfish, which have the highest amounts of n3 LC PUFA, were included in the diet is not known. In addition, just as modern primate consumption of marine and aquatic resources is highly variable (Kempf 2009), there are marked variations in the ways that modern human populations today exploit aquatic or marine resources, so it cannot be expected that hominins in all places and at all times consumed aquatic or marine resources.

The ongoing and unresolved debate about the potential importance of aquatic foods as a source of long-chain fatty acids in promoting hominin brain growth in the Pleistocene (Broadhurst *et al.* 1998; Cunnane 2005) hinges, at least partially, on the evidence for availability and consumption. Isotope and behavioural evidence (Richards 2002; Marean *et al.* 2007) suggest that early modern humans exploited fish and seafood, although there is some evidence for Neanderthal use of marine resources (Stringer *et al.* 2008). Notwithstanding the attractiveness of the view that modern humans dispersed along coastlines (Macaulay *et al.* 2005), such movement was unlikely, not least because of the diverse and often extremely rugged coastal terrain between Africa and south-east Asia (Bailey 2009; Chapter 4). This, in addition to the patchy nature of aquatic and marine environment use (Chapters 3 and 4), implies that widespread use of aquatic resources was not the main resource facilitating the increase in brain size and complexity prior to the origin of modern humans. Since hominins may have needed a non-plant source of essential LC PUFA, it is likely that this came from terrestrial sources. Eaton *et al.* (1998) argued that adequate dietary LC PUFA could have been obtained through scavenging and hunting of terrestrial animal food sources. This is supported by mathematical modelling of fatty acid content of 255 plant and 85 animal foods (including brain tissue) available in African wetland, forest and savannah, which indicates that combined intakes of the three most abundant LC PUFA in human brain tissue (arachidonic acid (AA, 20:4n6), docosatetraenoic acid (DTA, 22:4n6) and DHA (22:6n3) from these sources would have been more than adequate in providing the raw material for encephalization (Eaton *et al.* 1998).

There is evidence beyond the links between encephalization and increased requirement for LC PUFA that suggests a dietary shift among humans and their ancestors. The limited capacity of humans to produce taurine suggests a past in which consumption of animal foods would have reduced both the need and the capacity to synthesize it (Laidlaw *et al.* 1988). True carnivores such as felids totally lack the ability to produce taurine, so must obtain it in their diet by consuming other animals that produce it, or risk developing retinal dysfunction (Hayes and Trautwein 1989). Among contemporary humans, vegans who consume no taurine have been shown to have some tissue levels of taurine, although much lower than omnivores. This suggests some taurine production capability among humans, unlike among true carnivores such as felids. It would also seem that humans can conserve taurine, as its urinary excretion in vegans is only 30% of that of omnivores (Laidlaw *et al.* 1988).

There is preferential absorption of animal haem iron to non-haem iron from plants by the human gut, indicating that humans are likely to be habitual rather than facultative meat eaters (Henneberg *et al.* 1998). Humans are also the near-exclusive hosts of the tapeworms *Taenia saginata* and *Taenia solium*, closely related to those found in canids (Henneberg *et al.* 1998). These gut parasites are transmitted by eating meat (Grove 1990). Since mammal hosts and their parasites undergo close co-evolution (Hafner and Nadler 1998), the evolutionary similarity between the Taeniidae parasitizing humans and those parasitizing dogs suggests that humans may have acquired Taeniidae parasites from dogs at some time point in the past 100 000 years (Henneberg *et al.* 1998).

Several lines of morphological evidence point to an increase in dietary quality with the origins of the human genus, *Homo*, and especially with its first unequivocal member (Wood and Collard 1999), *Homo erectus*. Tooth size decreased (Wood and Collard 1999) and body proportions altered, with the 'barrel-shaped' rib cage indicating a shift to more modern human-like gut proportions (Aiello and Wheeler 1995). This suggests an increase in consumption of higher-quality and more energy-dense foods that were easier to digest and required less mastication. Based on predicted organ mass and tissue energy requirements, the extra energy requirement of the larger brain of modern humans is almost exactly balanced by the lower energy required by their smaller and simpler gut (Aiello and Wheeler 1995) (Table 5.3). In their 'expensive tissue hypothesis', Aiello and Wheeler (1995) point out that the masses of other human organs are close to those predicted for body size, and suggest that a higher-quality diet facilitated both decrease in gut size and increase in brain size, with a feedback loop in which the additional energy liberated from having a smaller gut could be used for brain growth. Dietary change and the associated change in gut size were thus 'prime releasers', making energy available for brain growth. However, when gut areas rather than weights (used by Aiello and Wheeler 1995) are included in similar equations and the comparative primate sample is corrected for the larger-than-average gut sizes of folivores, human gut size is as predicted for a generalized frugivorous primate (Hladik *et al.* 1999). Nonetheless, modern humans do have relatively shorter colons and longer small intestines than other apes, indicating a shift in diet (Milton 1999b), and several authors have pointed out the similarities between the short, simple guts of humans and carnivores (Chivers and Langer 1994; Henneberg *et al.* 1998; Chapter 2).

Morphological changes were accompanied by behavioural shifts. Stone tools first appeared around 2.6 million years ago (Semaw *et al.* 1997), heralding eventual increases in behavioural and foraging complexity (Chapter 3). The appearance and development of stone tool technology indicates the increasing importance of vertebrate foods in the hominin diet (Plummer 2004). Percussion marks on bones indicate that hominins practised marrow extraction (Blumenschine 1995). The manufacture and use of stone tools may have been in synergy with the feedback loop that could have existed between encephalization and the consumption of high-quality foods, including meat and other animal parts (Elton *et al.* 2001). Thus, extractive foraging may have provided an impetus for brain growth and increased cognitive function

Table 5.3 *Observed organ mass of humans compared with their expected mass, on the basis of metabolic size, and the metabolic increments associated with those differences*

	Mass (kg)			
	Observed	Expected	Difference	Metabolic increment (W)
Brain	1.3	0.45	+0.85	+9.5
Gut	1.1	1.88	−0.78	−11.5
Liver	1.4	1.56	−0.16	
Heart	0.3	0.32	−0.02	−0.6
Kidney	0.3	0.24	+0.06	+1.4

Expected metabolic rate is computed for a 65 kg human.
Adapted from Aiello and Wheeler (1995).

(Gibson 1986; Chapter 2). Behavioural shifts, including expansion of the dietary and ecological niches of hominins (Chapter 3) are evident from isotope signals in teeth (Codron *et al.* 2008) as well as dental microwear (Ungar *et al.* 2008). Such evidence, as discussed in Chapter 3, suggests consumption of animal products within eclectic, flexible and variable diets. Niche expansion, including niche construction (Chapter 7), was fundamentally important to the exploitation of the varied and variable environments that hominins encountered when they dispersed out of the tropics into temperate and arctic zones (Chapters 2, 3, 4). Behavioural and dietary shifts were also crucial to the exploitation of the seasonally time-limited environments encountered at higher latitudes (Chapter 4). In such places, some of which were also relatively unproductive in plant foods, the ability to procure enough food during winter months with scarce daylight was essential.

Effective time management among the hominins

Time management is nothing new: humans have always done it, and since industrialization it has become one of the most crucial issues of day-to-day life. Time is precious for humans and their closest relatives the primates. Being a social animal takes a huge amount of time, as superiors need to be challenged, alliances formed and re-formed, and bonds made and maintained. To survive, primates must undertake four key activities: socializing, travelling, resting and foraging (Dunbar 1988). Keeping a group together often requires significant time and effort (Dunbar 1988), which means that, for a given group size, time for other activities such as foraging must be used wisely. This is particularly the case outside the tropics, where summer day length is very long, giving ample time for activities (especially given the greater availability of most foodstuffs) but winter day length is much shorter. The need to manage time effectively has implications for foraging strategy, including prey choice and home and day ranges.

The ability to procure significant quantities of meat may have been an important precursor for hominin dispersal into higher latitudes (Turner 1992). Increased dietary quality and energy density in general, rather than just meat-eating, however, would have significantly improved hominin success at higher latitudes. Humans, like other primates, must balance foraging, resting and travelling with the social interaction (grooming, talking) that is vital to group cohesion (Dunbar 1988). Humans are diurnal, so in societies without extensive artificial light, the vast majority of activity must take place during the day. During winter at higher latitudes, day length is short, placing serious time constraints on foragers, especially those who do not store food. For human ancestors in northern Europe and Asia during the Pleistocene, being able to find and consume maximum calories in minimum time would have been essential for survival. The hominin ability to find and compete for high-quality foods available in most environments (meat, honey, eggs and berries, for example) along with their ability to make food more digestible through processing, may have been an important precursor to life outside the tropics. The preference for energy-dense foods (often dense in protein too, as with meat and fish) would have reinforced their importance in the diet. This has implications for food consumption patterns, obesity and chronic disease in the present day (Chapters 6, 8 and 11).

There are costs and benefits to all foraging strategies, present and past. Optimal foraging theory can help understand the dietary choices made by animals (including humans and their ancestors) as well as the consequences of different strategies, ultimately in terms of fitness (survival and reproductive success). Optimal foraging theory is a form of economic cost/benefit analysis, and various models have been developed to analyse the food procurement strategies of animals and humans (Pyke *et al.* 1997). Two of the best known include the diet breadth or prey choice model (Emlen 1966) and the patch choice model (MacArthur and Pianka 1966). Both can be applied to understand and explain human foraging, including the ways in which ancient humans are likely to have behaved. The diet breadth or prey choice model centres on selection of food to maximize gains (Emlen 1966). Animals forage selectively, and do not necessarily choose to consume everything that is edible. Under the diet breadth model, the animal exploits an optimal set of resources, those foods that offer the best returns for the time and energy expended. The constraints acting on this include the foraging ability of the animal, as well as the ubiquity of 'high-value' foodstuffs in the environment (Alden Smith 1983).

The patch choice model attempts to describe how a given area is exploited for food and how decisions about movement from patch to patch are made, on the assumption that there is an optimal pattern of patch exploitation (MacArthur and Pianka 1966). Underlying this is the compromise inherent in exploiting a number of closely situated but relatively poorly resourced patches. A more sophisticated version of this model, developed by Charnov and Orians (1973, cited in Alden Smith 1983) examines the implications of staying in a patch with decreasing returns as the environment becomes exhausted against the time and energy needed to move to a new patch.

Animal foods are both energy- and protein-rich, with variable levels of fat, and offer high energy returns for relatively low energy expenditure. The larger the animal being hunted, the greater the dietary energy available to the hunter for a given time spent in hunting it. There is good archaeological evidence for hominin hunting from bone assemblages, technology and even tools embedded in bone. Such hunting was probably undertaken by groups of hominins, who would have sought a diversity of medium to large prey species. These would have included reindeer, red deer, ibex, elk, woolly mammoth, woolly rhino, horses, bison and macropods (wallabies and kangaroos), hunted variously by different groups of hominins across the world during the Middle and Late Pleistocene (Boeda *et al.* 1999; Gaudzinski and Roebroeks 2000; Bar-Yosef 2004; Cosgrove and Pike-Tay 2004). Optimality analyses can help to determine how ancient hunters made decisions about what animals to exploit and in what order, including the animal parts to be eaten (Marín Arroyo 2009). They can also help to reveal how far hunters may have travelled in search of prey (Marín Arroyo 2009). Based on optimality models and archaeological assemblages that date to between 10 000 and 14 000 years ago from Spain, Marín Arroyo (2009) argued that the smaller ibex (roughly 50 kg) would only have been hunted in preference to red deer (roughly 90 kg) when their habitat was much nearer the central living base, so that the time saved travelling to the hunting site offset the lower energy returns. Under this model, travelling time would have had to have been very long (over 36 hours) before the complete processing of a carcass (including marrow extraction from bones) afforded gains in dietary energy availability (Marin Arroyo 2009). These results are region-specific, with the model also including landscape features, such as topography, that encourage or preclude the presence of certain species (ibex, for example, inhabit more mountainous localities than do red deer). Thus, in other regions, with different landscapes and prey species, optimal foraging patterns may well have been different.

Plant foods can also give good energy returns for time invested. Some plants, such as palms and nuts, contain high levels of fat, carbohydrate or protein. When these are readily available, they offset the need for animal products. For example, among contemporary hunter-gatherers, the !Kung of the Kalahari Desert have access to mongongo nuts (*Ricinodendron rautaneii*) for eight months of the year (Bentley 1985), reducing their dependency on meat to below 40% of energy intake (Lee 1968). Similarly, in Papua New Guinea, the use of the starch-rich sago palm allows time to forage for less energy-dense but nutrient-rich foods (Ulijaszek and Poraituk 1983; Dwyer and Minnegal 1994), while pre-European hunter-gatherers of California relied heavily on acorns from wild oaks (McCarthy 1993).

Most optimal foraging models of contemporary human behaviour focus on hunting, but several studies based on plant exploitation have shed light on dietary choice and decision-making. For example, optimality models help explain the use of novel, imported foodstuffs in place of more traditional labour- and time-intensive foods, such as the replacement of wild grass seeds by purchased wheat flour in Australian aboriginal communities (O'Connell and Hawkes 1981). Of course, explaining all human or indeed animal food selection on the basis of optimal foraging is reductionist and can be misleading (Alden Smith 1983). Food choice varies by individual taste, for example, and foraging behaviour is also shaped by knowledge and skills. However, whether consuming plants, animals, or most commonly a mix of the two, energy is the limiting factor in ecosystems, and fitness is thus energy-linked (Alden Smith 1983). Appreciating how foraging decisions aid immediate survivorship, health and well-being as well as reproductive success thus requires an understanding of energetics, and knowledge of energetics can, in turn, illuminate eating behaviour.

Eating behaviour

Body size and eating behaviour are intricately linked through body composition, patterns of locomotion characteristic of particular species, and foraging practices and behaviours. The connecting theme is that of energy: for reproduction, physical growth, bodily maintenance, foraging and sociality. Energy balance is a central principle of public health nutrition, with undernutrition and obesity being manifestations of extreme imbalance. From a biological standpoint, individual energy imbalance is an outcome of foraging possibilities and the decisions that surround them. Negative energy balance may be seasonal and balanced across the year, with positive balance at times of year when food is more plentiful (Chapter 4). When food intake or availability is inadequate and/or energy expenditure is high, weight loss occurs and a subsequent recalibration of energy balance results. This recalibration includes a range of powerful physiological and behavioural nutritional adaptations (Ulijaszek

1996) which defend against further energy deficit (Moore 2000), a process which would have had survival advantage among ancestral hominins.

Alternatively, non-seasonal, long-term negative energy balance reflects ecological stress due to a range of factors including climate change and over-foraging in an over-populated resource area. Energy balance may be recovered at a lower body mass, or result in death. Fertility is linked to nutrition in all mammalian species, and negative energy balance switches off or reduces fecundity according to the degree of food shortage, such that fewer offspring are produced. In this way, population can be more balanced in relation to resources. There are two extreme ways in which this can happen. Small-bodied species are more likely to produce many offspring when resources are plentiful, but die in large numbers and produce few offspring when there are food shortages. Rabbits, for example, are well-known for their cycles of population 'boom and bust' (when introduced into plentiful environments with no predators, as in Australia by British settlers, they underwent an extended period of boom). Large-bodied species are more likely to adjust their population sizes to the resources available. They live longer than small-bodied species, and cannot respond rapidly through reproductive effort to changing food resource availability because of their longer reproductive schedules. Apes, hominins and humans, as mammals of medium body size, have (or had) populations usually in reasonable balance with food resources.

Long-term positive energy balance is not usually found in nature, nor is obesity. More dietary resources usually mean more offspring, until the food environment cannot sustain the population. A fat animal in the wild is likely to be slower, less able to obtain food, and more likely to be predated upon than a thinner one. Mammalian feeding regulation involves the interaction of physiology and genotype with environment and food availability in a feedback relationship (Figure 5.2). Non-human animals eat to meet their nutritional requirements, subject to physical constraints such as food availability (Emmans and Oldham 1988). Food intake is regulated through a range of physiological signals that involve cross-talk between endocrine systems of the gut, adipose tissue and the brain (Emmans and Kyriazakis 2001). Human eating behaviour, because of significant neocortical involvement, is more complex and involves personal and psychological factors in addition to food availability. It is an evolved environmental response to food resource availabilities which is plastic. It is regulated by neurophysiological mechanisms both primitive and neocortical, modulated by food preferences that are culture-specific, and can change with life-stage and exposure to novel foods.

Contemporary humans are odd, because they are able to generate food surpluses, and they have developed technological means of uncoupling the act of sexual intercourse from reproduction. Thus while biological fertility in

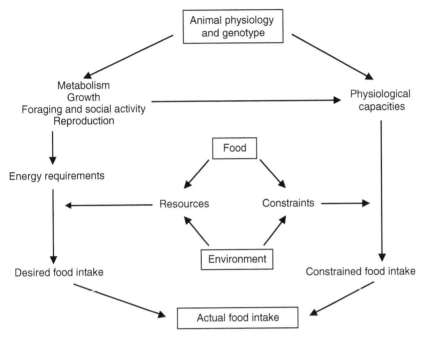

Figure 5.2. Animal feeding to meet requirements subject to constraints (adapted from Emmans and Oldham 1988; Ulijaszek 2002).

industrial society is largely unconstrained by poor nutrition, surplus dietary energy is translated into excess bodily fatness rather than more children. Weight gain is physiologically easy, while seasonal negative energy balance and weight loss are achieved by restricted food intake due to low availability, rather than strong cognitive control (Ulijaszek 2002).

In present-day industrialized society, food availability is limited by price in ways that make high-energy-density foods among the cheapest (Drewnowski and Specter 2004); thus energy intake is regulated less by availability and more by cognitive restraint. In the absence of such restraint, and when dietary energy is plentiful, there are only very weak homeostatic mechanisms to restore energy balance and prevent weight gain. Conscious weight loss can only be achieved through strong cognitive control, as physiological regulation of energy balance is easily overridden by psychological and behavioural factors that urge an individual to eat (Ulijaszek 2002). Appetite is the interface between physiological bodily needs that serve species maintenance, and the local ecology that determines what might be eaten. Physiologically, appetite balances energy intake with metabolic energy demands, including maintenance metabolism, physical activity, physical growth (in the case of physically immature individuals) and reproduction. Industrial and post-industrial humans have subverted the role of appetite in serving maintenance and reproduction, since it is easy to eat for pleasure. Because of the value that the discipline of public health places on balanced body size, function and health, energy balance and weight regulation have become almost universal measures of (or proxies for) human well-being.

Humans are overwhelmingly social feeders, preferring to eat with others than on their own. More generally, many primates forage most efficiently in groups (Dunbar 1988) and this may be the basis of social feeding among humans. But while primate species vary in their extent of social feeding, humans are social in most aspects of their behaviour, including food. Human eating decisions (what, how and when) are very powerfully influenced by social contexts (Mela 1996). When there is no limitation on how much can be eaten, the greater the number of people eating together, the more each person eats (de Castro 1999). In the vast majority of human populations, feeding is structured around meals, even though snacking may occur (Chapter 4). Indeed, among primates and many other mammals, humans are highly unusual in eating food in discrete meals rather than browsing or grazing throughout the day: the only other mammals that tend to feed through 'meals' are large-bodied carnivorans such as lions. Through meals, humans embed feeding in social structures, which are given material expression through kin and household. We usually place special value on eating with our families, above eating with friends, among strangers, or alone. Meals are thus central to social structure and group identity, although they have been challenged in the contemporary industrialized world of the past 60 years or so.

The practice of convenience food consumption has a time depth of several millennia (Chapter 10). Only with the advent of industrial and post-industrial society has social eating been seriously challenged by the rapid and wide-spread adoption of technologies that can lead to social atomization through their use as objects of convenience and novelty, including motor cars, televisions, mobile phones, computers and a range of digital media. Technologies that have some element of social function, among them computers and mobile phones, give only virtual sociality, not the material kind that can involve the physical sharing of food. The list of socially atomizing devices is likely to grow in coming years, rather than contract. The atomization of social eating has been termed 'gastro-anomy' by Fischler and Masson (2008). It is possible that eating in isolation might make people eat more closely to appetite. However, physiological energy balance cues can be missed if people eat out of boredom or when distracted by the novelty generated by media technologies such as television or computers.

Individual eating decisions are shaped by the expectations we have from foods before they are eaten (Mela 1996). For example, you might expect an apple to have a balance of sweet and sour flavours, and a crisp bite. You would be disappointed to varying degrees if some or all of these expectations were not met. Such expectations are created by the interaction of brain, gut and adipose tissue as integrated drivers to start and continue feeding. They include sensory factors such as sight, smell, palatability and memory of previous consumption of foods, balanced against negative feedback signals from learned associations and aversions, and gastrointestinal and adipose signals of satiety (Zheng and Berthoud 2008). Foods have to look, smell and taste good, but also conform to expectations based on previous experiences of eating them. Such expectations are plastic, however, as illustrated by a fashion at the time of writing in many industrialized nations for chocolate flavoured with chilli or sea salt. Palatability influences the amounts of food eaten and involves complex relationships between sensory responses to food as well as conditioned preferences for taste and colour (Mela and Catt 1996). Flavour preferences have a strong relationship with energy content, either as fat or carbohydrate (Booth *et al.* 1982), an adaptive relationship that is likely to have had strong positive survival value among ancestral hominins. In both children (Mela and Catt 1996) and adults (Drewnowski and Greenwood 1983) there is a clear preference for fatty and sweet foods. While all mammals have preferences for particular food sources, these are usually driven by the need to maximize energy intakes. The ability of animals to taste and like sugars probably evolved in response to the emergence of fruit and honey as food sources at the time of angiosperm diversification (Chapter 2).

In general, primates are highly developed selectors of food, using vision, smell and taste to discriminate palatable from less palatable potential food items (Ulijaszek 2002). The energy requirement per unit body weight is lower in primates of large body size (Martin 1993), allowing them to use a wider variety of food sources with lower energy densities than smaller primates. Thus a lowered sensitivity to both sweetness and bitterness in larger primates allows them to find lower energy density foods palatable. Sucrose sensitivity in humans loosely follows the general body size relationship in primates (although higher than would be expected) and would have influenced diversification of food selection among evolving primates (Ulijaszek 2002).

The desire for dietary energy is driven by physiological feed-forward mechanisms from the hypothalamus which are mental responses to food cues in the environment. This is common to all mammals, and makes the finding of food and the feeding response to hunger more immediate, and therefore of evolutionary value. However, humans also have neocortical regulation of appetite and food intake, and in the contemporary industrialized and post-industrial worlds, food cues are abundant. Feed-forward mechanisms therefore dominate in situations where such cues are plentiful, food is easily available (because of low cost and the low amount of effort required to obtain it), palatable, energy-dense and socially enhanced (Berthoud 2006). Neocortical feed-forward mechanisms also operate in creating associative pleasures in food, which humans have in a way that no other species can. While both an adult human and a chimpanzee might enjoy a glass of wine (as Travis the sometime actor–chimpanzee reportedly did), only a human can make the linkages between the smell and taste of that wine and other substances they have previously experienced (including other glasses of wine), and associate their expectations of a wine and previous experiences of drinking it. Without having a large neocortex, humans could not have developed cuisines, not only because cooking can be a complex process involving a range of technologies, but also because the neurophysiology for discerning good foods and appreciating them in an associative manner would not exist.

The physiology of appetite

Placed in the modern world, the mammalian appetite system that humans rely on is like a car built for speed, but with inadequate brakes. Having evolved a reasonably fuel-efficient bodily system, human physiology is unable to become significantly less efficient in the face of constant plenty in the industrialized world. In consequence, much or most surplus dietary energy ends up as bodily fat. The system that controls appetite and food consumption brings together physiological maintenance and growth, bodily storage of energy and reproduction in one controlling neurohormonal mechanism (Ahima and Osei 2001; Jeanrenaud and Rohner-Jeanrenaud 2001; Havel 2004). All mammals share the desire to eat. However, few mammals eat all the time, and humans eat sporadically, although it is easy to eat without feeling hungry, especially if the food is palatable. The desire to eat is generally preceded by a rise in blood insulin followed by a fall in blood glucose, often to levels that are below fasting (Bray 2000). Other appetite-stimulating neuroendocrine signals rise before food is consumed, usually through visual and olfactory stimuli (Bray 2000), and often in anticipation of consumption of particular foods. Hormonal and afferent neural signals from the gut (representing feeding activity) and/or adipose tissues (representing body energy stores) are linked in their control of the expression of neurotransmitters and neuropeptides that regulate eating behaviour.

Neuropeptides that regulate eating behaviour fall into two categories: orexigenic ones that stimulate food intake, decrease activity and promote fat deposition; and anorexigenic ones that inhibit food intake, and increase both activity and subsequent fat loss (Ahima and Osei 2001; Jeanrenaud and Rohner-Jeanrenaud 2001). A major endocrine controller of the balance of orexigenic and anorexigenic neuropeptides is the hormone leptin, which is secreted by the adipose tissue. Through a signalling cascade in the hypothalamus, it down-regulates orexigenic neuropeptides and stimulates anorexigenic ones, reducing appetite and food intake, and increasing both fat oxidation and energy expenditure. Leptin levels do not increase rapidly after overconsumption of dietary energy, indicating that the leptin response system is more tuned to starvation than to overconsumption (Chin-Chance *et al.* 2000). Endocannabinoids are orexigenic mediators that induce appetite and stimulate food intake, opposing the action of leptin to enhance sweet taste (Yoshida *et al.* 2010). Plasma levels of leptin are also lowered by elevated ghrelin production from the gut, inducing a synergistic effect towards over-consumption of food. Ghrelin is known as the 'circulating hunger hormone', its main action being to activate neuropeptide Y (NPY) in the hypothalamus, which in turn stimulates appetite and increases food intake (Dickson and Luckman 1997). This hormone also stimulates appetite in response to exercise and lactation (Ahima and Osei 2001), giving it a central and evolutionarily deep role in appetite regulation. Another such mechanism is the pleasure associated with food consumption, which is stimulated by ghrelin (Jerlhag *et al.* 2006) by amplifying the signalling of the dopamine reward system (Jiang *et al.* 2006; Jerlhag *et al.* 2008).

Taste and smell receptors and peripheral signalling peptides such as insulin, leptin, ghrelin, cholecystokinin and their receptors are under genetic control, as are hypothalamic regulators of energy intake, including neuropeptide-Y, agouti-related protein, cocaine and amphetamine regulated transcript (CART), and factors in the melanocortin pathway (Martin *et al.* 2009). The fat mass and obesity-associated (FTO) major gene is expressed in the brain, and confers risk of obesity through energy intake, rather than expenditure (Cecil *et al.* 2008). Genes expressed elsewhere in the body can also influence appetite (Martin *et al.* 2009).

In general, humans eat to a constant volume or weight (Rolls *et al.* 1998), making it easy to consume too much dietary energy if the foods available are of high energy density. Table 5.4 shows how many calories are consumed if someone eats to a constant weight of intake for a range of foods. The constant weight of intake given in Table 5.4 is 600 g, close to the weight of test lunches used in food psychology studies (Rolls *et al.* 1998). There is a clear divide between convenience foods, with very high energy density, and simple staples, such as boiled rice, lentils and maize, in which energy densities are low. For example, if an individual were to eat 600 g of french fries, they would consume more than four times as much energy than if the same mass of boiled potatoes was eaten.

Table 5.4 *Energy ingested by consuming a standard lunch mass of 600 g of different foods*

Food	Energy (kcal)
French fries	1944
MacDonalds Big Mac	1514
Taco Bell chicken burrito	1458
White bread	1410
Battered fish	1391
Steak, grilled	1308
Boiled rice	852
Spaghetti	624
Lentils	600
Maize	514
Boiled potatoes	432
Apples	282

KFC is omitted because data are presented in a way that does not permit these values to be calculated.
Source: Rolls *et al.* (1998). Nutritional data from Food Standards Agency (2002) and nutrition pages of MacDonalds and Taco Bell websites.

Sugar and fat have sensory properties that act as markers for nutritive energy (Drewnowski 1995); cravings for foods rich in these substances are often given as major reasons for dietary weight loss failure (Drewnowski 1990). Drewnowski (1995) has argued that the combination of fat and sugar produces a potent hedonic synergy, which peaks at eight per cent of the mass of a food as sugar and 20% as fat, values common in many fast foods. The cannabinoid and opioid neuropeptides that respond to pleasure (as well as drug addiction) may be the critical drivers of overconsumption of sugar- and fat-rich foods that exhibit pleasurable taste and textural properties (Levine *et al.* 2003; Cota *et al.* 2006; Olszewski and Levine 2007), especially when they are easily available. The neurological reward response to intense sweetness exceeds that of cocaine, with similar potential for addiction, probably stemming from an inborn hyper-sensitivity to sweetness (Lenoir *et al.* 2007). The over-consumption of fat- and sugar-rich foods goes beyond the hedonic responses to these dietary components. As anyone that adds salt to their food knows, palatability can be enhanced in ways other than sweetness or fatness. Enhancing the flavour of a food encourages greater consumption and therefore greater caloric intake, even when the nutrient composition of the food remains unaltered (Scalafani 2001). The development of cuisine has allowed many different ways in which flavour and texture of foods can be enhanced.

Discussion

Humans can eat almost anything in nature, but usually choose not to. The evolutionarily hard-wired physiological machinery that drives what humans, and all mammals, eat, is the linkage and cross-talk between the brain, gut and adipose tissue, which is primarily sensitive to internal energy balance and external dietary energy availability. Finding enough dietary energy on a regular basis is a principal selective pressure for all primates in the wild, and it is unlikely to have been any different for the hominins. What we, and all mammals, eat is driven by signals of high energy density of foods, notably for sweetness and fat. The system that controls appetite and food consumption brings together physiological maintenance and growth, bodily storage of energy and reproduction in one controlling neurohormonal mechanism. All mammals share the desire to eat when hungry, and overeat when food is plentiful: the latter is a behaviour that allows species to deposit dietary energy on the hoof in times of plenty, if only to remove it again in times of shortage. Many animals eat socially. But as usual, humans are special, with the ability to take overeating and social feeding to levels not seen in any other species. For all mammals, eating behaviour is dependent on qualities internal to foods, such as flavour, smell and texture, and external factors such as the availability and diversity of foodstuffs, and the social context of eating.

Humans and their recent ancestors have taken dietary innovation to extremes, leading to huge changes in diet and foraging behaviour over the course of human evolutionary history. Such innovation encompasses the ways in which foods are produced and prepared, along with novelty of foodstuffs themselves. Humans have shaped their dietary niche through chemical processing (including cooking, brewing, preserving and toxin extraction) as well as the sophisticated mechanical processing that started with stone tools and continued with many different technologies, including industrialization of food production and processing from the late nineteenth century onwards. Humans elaborate on the qualities of food by developing cuisines and through cooking, and by bringing together different food items in combination to make dishes. They also extend social feeding through the consumption of meals together. These elaborations are outcomes of human activity driven by neocortical recruitment to every aspect of feeding. This includes the use of feeding in developing and maintaining social ties, the creation of associative properties to foods, the development of new foods, dishes, meals and meal structures, and the mental expectations any individual has of all of these factors. This should be a marvellous story of how evolved human form and function has been put to good use, in conquering the challenge of food acquisition and developing ways of eating that engage aesthetic sensibilities towards enhancing sociality. At its best, everyday cuisine can really be like this. But in harnessing food production and processing to the industrial model, we have allowed industrial, atomized feeding increasingly to become the norm in many parts of the world. The outcomes of this are most visibly seen in the widespread rise in obesity, and less visibly in the more concerning rise in diabetes prevalence. The social costs of asocial, industrialized feeding might be just as high, if only we had a metric for it.

Part II

A Brave New World

6   *Dietary change and health discordance*

With the emergence of archaic *Homo sapiens* some half a million years ago, the human diet was one of hunting, scavenging, and probably some fishing, as well as the gathering of a broad range of seasonally available wild plant foods (Chapter 3). Although this varied by latitude, climate, geographic locality and ecological niche, a general and broad dietary base was probably exploited at this time, based on available wild plant and animal species. The dietary change that took place in many human societies with the advent of agriculture around 10 000 years ago was a profound departure from ancestral primate foraging and subsistence. This created an environmental change and selective pressures significant enough to cause genetic differentiation between populations, as suggested by global variation in lactase persistence and the salivary amylase *AMY1* gene (Chapter 2). Further, and arguably more dramatically, dietary change with globalization and industrialization (Chapter 9) created the modern dietary habits that feature in industrialized and economically emerging nations, and the discordance between human physiology and metabolism that underpin many chronic diseases (Cordain *et al.* 2005).

Although the diets of humans (and extinct hominins) in non-agricultural populations vary now and varied in the past, they are more similar to each other than either are to the diets of contemporary industrialized populations. Food staples and technologies for processing them, introduced from the origins of agriculture but with most rapid innovation occurring since industrialization, fundamentally altered the nutritional characteristics of the human diet in a wide range of ways (Cordain *et al.* 2005). These include changes in glycaemic load, fatty acid composition, macronutrient balance, micronutrient density, acid–base balance, sodium–potassium ratio, and dietary fibre content. This chapter will examine these changes, and their implications for the nutritional health of contemporary populations.

153

Characteristics and nutrient adequacy of contemporary industrialized diets: implications for health

Macronutrients

Across the world, the contribution of different macronutrients to dietary energy is highly variable, with population means varying between 19% and 35% for protein, 22% and 40% for carbohydrate, and 28% and 58% for fat intake (Cordain *et al.* 2000a). Most diets of contemporary industrialized populations are dominated by carbohydrate from processed grain and sugar-rich products. At the turn of the twenty-first century, a person on the average United States diet received around 52% of their dietary energy from carbohydrate, 15% from protein and 33% from fat. Based on a contemporary hunter-gatherer diet, Eaton *et al.* (1997) estimated the relative macronutrient composition and macronutrient balance of humans prior to the origins of agriculture to be (by energy contribution) 41% from carbohydrate, 37% from protein and 22% from fat, albeit with considerable variation around these values. If the contemporary hunter-gatherer diet is at all analogous to a prehistoric hunter-gatherer diet, then carbohydrate consumption has largely displaced protein intake in contemporary industrial diets (Cordain *et al.* 2005). This has implications for weight control and health, as diets that are high in protein (not necessarily from animal sources alone) but within safe physiological limits (Chapter 5) may help weight control (Skov *et al.* 1999) and have beneficial effects through increasing satiety and suppressing hunger (Johnston *et al.* 2004).

Intensive processing of foods was a major transformation that occurred with industrialization (Chapter 5). Diets rich in processed foods but poor in vegetable matter can predispose to mild but chronic metabolic acidosis (Sebastian *et al.* 2002), an excess of acid in bodily fluids which can exacerbate osteoporosis, kidney stones, hypertension and age-related chronic renal insufficiency (Cordain *et al.* 2005). Foods or dietary components that contribute to a net acid load in the body include meats (by way of sulphur-containing amino acids), seafood, eggs, dairy foods, cereal grains and salt. Although meats, seafood and eggs have very probably always been a part of human and hominin diets, dairy foods, cereals and large amounts of salt have not, and these have added considerably to the acid loads of contemporary human populations. Conversely, the decrease in intake of non-starchy plant foods in contemporary industrial diets has removed sources of alkalinity from the diet (Sebastian *et al.* 2002).

The dominance of processed grain and sugar-rich foods in the modern industrial diet has profound implications for health, as demonstrated by examination of the glycaemic index (GI) and glycaemic load (GL), proxies for carbohydrate intake and load. The GI compares the potential of a given food (for example, bread) to raise blood glucose with a standard amount of readily digested pure glucose (Jenkins *et al.* 1981). Simplistically, the GI describes how readily the carbohydrates in food are metabolized. Many nutritionists divide carbohydrate-based foods into three GI categories, high, medium and low. High-GI foods include sugar, mashed potatoes, white sliced bread and cornflakes; medium-GI foods include digestive biscuits and couscous; low-GI foods include lentils, brown rice and pasta (McMillan-Price *et al.* 2006). The GL takes into account aspects of carbohydrate quality and quantity as they affect postprandial blood glucose concentration (Liu and Willett 2002). The GL is the GI multiplied by the number of grams of carbohydrate consumed, all divided by 100, and is a composite measure of carbohydrate stress.

The contemporary processed-grain- and sugar-dominated diet exposes many people to GLs far in excess of those experienced by populations consuming unrefined wild plant foods (Cordain *et al.* 2005), or indeed unrefined cultivated plant foods. Consumption of high-GL diets results in blood glucose and insulin levels that are elevated when compared with energy-equivalent low GL diets (Jenkins *et al.* 1987). The chronic hyperglycaemia and hyperinsulinaemia that is induced by high-GL diets may result in physiological changes that promote insulin resistance, although this needs further assessment by using intervention studies (O'Sullivan *et al.* 2010). Insulin resistance, as well as being a feature of Type 2 diabetes, is a major component of the metabolic syndrome (Reaven 1995) that also involves a somewhat nebulous combination of centrally distributed obesity, hypertension and dyslipidaemia (Gale 2008), which can be a precursor to cardiovascular disease and Type 2 diabetes.

The amount of fat in the human diet has probably varied considerably over time, with seasonal influences and geographic location. Currently, Western diets are enriched in pro-atherogenic saturated fatty acids predominantly from domesticated animal fats and increasingly from palm oil in processed foods. At the same time there has been an increase in the intake of the even more atherogenic trans-fatty acids generated in foods during processing procedures such as hydrogenation, which solidifies oils for the production of margarine and shortenings (Emken 1984). Both saturated and trans-fats have a direct link with elevated low-density lipoprotein (LDL)–cholesterol levels in humans (Spady *et al.* 1993), which predispose to cardiovascular disease (CVD).

Although analogies between ancient hunter-gatherer diets and contemporary foraging ones are flawed (Chapter 5), they can be an important window on the past. Relatively little is known about the prehistoric and historic diets of Australian aboriginal people, but they were foragers, eating a mix of wild plant and animal foods. Based on modern Australian bushmeat and fish, wild-caught at a number of localities across the continent, the animal foods available to foragers typically contain less than three per cent fat (by mass), with more than 20% of it as polyunsaturated fatty acids (PUFA), of which substantial amounts were health-promoting omega-3 (n-3) PUFA (Naughton *et al.* 1986). This can be used as an illustration of hunter-gatherer fat intakes, although animal fat and its consumption will shift seasonally and also varies between species and geographically. Nonetheless, it is highly likely that the modern industrialized diet contains more fat, and of different types, than traditional diets, both foraging and agrarian. The greatest shift in dietary fat intake among contemporary populations has been one of greatly increased omega-6 (n-6) polyunsaturated fatty acids (PUFA) as a result of increased availability of cultivated grain and seed oils, which are usually n-6 rich but poor in n-3 PUFA. The imbalance in intake of these two types of PUFA has a major impact on cardiovascular health (Chapter 10).

Micronutrients: vitamins and minerals

The transition to diets rich in processed foods, dominated by refined cereals, sugars and vegetable oils, is something that has happened in most industrialized nations, and is underway in economically emerging ones (Chapter 9). Such diets are energy- and often protein-dense, but relatively devoid of many micronutrients. The exception is sodium. Modern processed foods contain relatively high levels of sodium, usually added as salt for its various sensory and preservative properties. Adult sodium consumption in the United States (US) increased markedly between the 1970s and the year 2000, with most recent intake being between 3000 and 4100 milligrams per day (Figure 6.1) (Briefel and Johnson 2004). This level of intake has no precedent in human prehistory or evolution. However, sodium is physiologically essential, and it is unlikely that the earliest humans avoided supplementation with it completely: fruit and vegetables are rich in potassium but poor in sodium, and animals with a plant-based diet may seek out salt licks to redress dietary mineral insufficiencies. This is evident in some monkeys (Rode *et al.* 2003), and also in mountain gorillas living in areas with sodium-depleted soils, who may get over 95% of their sodium from the consumption of decaying wood, a 'food' with very little nutritional value otherwise (Rothman *et al.* 2006). The importance of some salt supplementation to early humans can also be inferred from the prevalence of archaeological remains near 'salines' or mineral deposits at very early

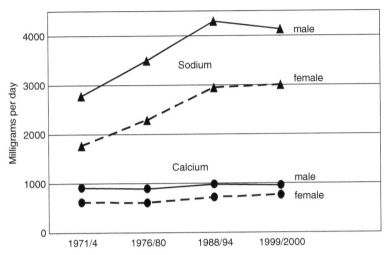

Figure 6.1. Intakes of sodium and calcium by adults (aged 20–74 years) in the United States between 1971 and 2000 (data from Briefel and Johnson 2004).

prehistoric ('palaeo') native American sites (Brown 1980). When presented with salty foods, and in common with other mammals, both chimpanzees (Denton *et al.* 1995) and humans (Young *et al.* 2005) show avidity for salt, a behaviour that may have been adaptive for animals with low sodium ingestion in environments with uncertain access to it (Denton *et al.* 1995). Nonetheless, the potassium intake of hominins and Pleistocene humans was almost certainly higher than among contemporary industrialized humans and simultaneously much lower in sodium content. It has been proposed that this shift has contributed to various chronic diseases in recent times (Cordain *et al.* 2005), including hypertension (Mohan and Campbell 2009), kidney stones (Massey and Whiting 1995), osteoporosis (Frassetto *et al.* 2008) and cancers of the gastrointestinal tract (Sugimura 2000). The links between high sodium consumption and hypertension, a predisposing factor for CVD (Karppanen and Mervaala 2006), have elicited considerable attention in humans and other mammals; one longitudinal study of captive chimpanzees clearly demonstrated the association between relatively high salt intake and high blood pressure, a phenomenon that was reversed when sodium consumption declined (Denton *et al.* 1995).

It is generally accepted that primates (and by inference, foraging hominins) are exposed to greater quantities of dietary micronutrients than humans consuming a less diverse, often monoculture-dominated diet (*sensu* Milton 2003). This is supported by analyses of foods traditionally eaten by Australian aboriginal populations (Brand-Miller and Holt 1998). Among those consuming contemporary industrialized diets, Eaton *et al.* (1997) identified low intakes of thiamine, riboflavin, folate, vitamins A, C and E, iron, zinc and calcium, relative to contemporary hunter-gatherers, but high intakes of sodium. Although it is assumed that unprocessed plant and animal foods provide a complete range and relatively high concentrations of micronutrients (Southgate 1991), a wild, foraged diet does not necessarily provide optimal micronutrition. In a biochemical study of consumed plant parts in Kibale National Park, Uganda, the diets of wild-living monkeys were found to be deficient in iron and sodium, with some also deficient in copper compared with recommended requirements (Rode *et al.* 2003). The same criticisms of recommended intakes apply to both non-human primates and humans (Chapter 4), which may in this case over-estimate the amount of iron needed in the primate diet, but there is likely to be a true physiological deficiency of sodium in the Kibale monkeys, which exhibit non-food consumption behaviours such as mud-puddle- and urine-drinking, probably to increase sodium ingestion (Rode *et al.* 2003). It therefore cannot be straightforwardly assumed that just because early human foraging populations depended on diverse, wild foods, micronutrient deficiency was unknown. Then, as now, micronutrient content of the diet would depend on a great range of factors, including geology, soil quality, plant availability, seasonality and skill in foraging. This notwithstanding, the shift from diets comprising a broad range of animal and plant foods to ones largely based on processed foods rich in refined grains, sugars and oils has very probably led to huge decreases in micronutrient intake among contemporary industrialized societies and economically modernizing populations, as well as some traditional subsistence populations heavily dependent on monocultures (Chapter 4).

Between a quarter and three-quarters of a US sample population consume less than the Recommended Daily Allowance (RDA) for 12 micronutrients (Cordain *et al.* 2005; Figure 6.2). While the RDAs represent safe levels of intake for the vast majority of a population and may not reflect physiological deficiency, it is very likely that when over half of the population has intakes below the RDA, as for vitamins B6 and A, and for magnesium, calcium and zinc, there will be a subset of this group that is physiologically deficient. The implications of such deficiencies, often termed 'hidden hunger' (Chapter 4), for nutritional health include increased risk of infection (vitamins B6 and A, zinc) and osteoporosis (calcium). Similar deficiencies are likely to be found in other populations where micronutrient-rich plant foods and to a lesser extent animal foods have been displaced in the diet by processed products based on milled, micronutrient-poor flour, sugars and oils. Such consumption is likely to cluster among the poor in industrialized nations.

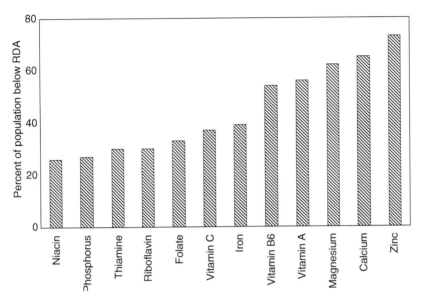

Figure 6.2. Percentage of individuals not meeting recommended daily allowances for selected micronutrients. (United States Department of Agriculture data (1994–1996) for individuals above the age of two years.) Adapted from Cordain *et al.* (2005).

Many countries practise nutrient supplementation of particular processed foods (such as flours, bread, rice, breakfast cereals, margarine, milk and soy-milk) as a public health and risk-management response to food processing systems that strip foods of their nutrient content. Further, the consumption of nutrient supplements in concentrated form constitutes a medicalization of nutrient deficiency. Nonetheless, just as the concept of RDA is far from straightforward (Chapter 4), so is the issue of nutrient supplementation, especially as a means to prevent chronic disease such as cancer and CVD. It has been noted that observational and randomized controlled trial studies may result in contradictory conclusions about the protective effects of antioxidants against such diseases, with the former but not the latter indicating the benefits of supplementation (Lawlor *et al.* 2004). It is highly probable that social and behavioural factors confound many analyses of antioxidant effects on chronic disease, and even when the relevant data are available, time and resource constraints may prevent their inclusion (Lawlor *et al.* 2004). One study found a negative association between plasma concentration of vitamin C and socioeconomic position over the life course, as well as a positive relationship between high-fibre or low-fat diets or daily consumption of alcohol and higher vitamin concentration, independent of socioeconomic status (Lawlor *et al.* 2004). This illustrates the complexity of developing coherent, broadly based

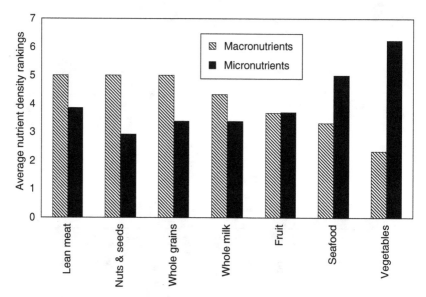

Figure 6.3. Average nutrient density rankings of food groupings based on 100 kcal (418 kJ) samples (7 = highest density for that nutrient, 1 = lowest density). Micronutrient rankings adapted from Cordain *et al.* (2005).

messages in public health, given the wide disparities in social status and behaviour among the populations of most modern nation states. The role of biological variation in response to micronutrient supplementation makes this even more challenging. For example, there is within-population genetic variation in vitamin C transport that influences circulating levels of the vitamin in individuals, with potential implications for health outcomes (Timpson *et al.* 2010).

In sub-pathological states, where the diseases of micronutrient deficiency such as scurvy, xerophthalmia and rickets are not prevalent or even evident, it may be far from straightforward to identify population-level micronutrient deficiencies and their importance. Cordain *et al.* (2005) attempted to identify the extent of micronutrient deficiencies for the contemporary US population by ranking the micronutrient density of different food groups based on 100 kilocalorie samples of a balance of typical US food types in each food grouping. Vegetables and seafood rated highest in nutrient density.

We expand this by performing the same procedure for the macronutrient density of the same food groups (Figure 6.3). To make the macronutrient density comparable with micronutrient density, the sum rank score for each is divided by the total number of nutrients (13 for micronutrients and three for macronutrients) to generate average values. The advent of agriculture and animal husbandry, with the likely displacement of a diverse range of wild plant foods by whole grains and milk, saw a probable decline in dietary micronutrient content. The development of myriad processed foods after the industrial revolution led to further displacement of vegetables, fruits, meats and seafood from the diet. The foods driven out of contemporary industrial diets are the richest in most micronutrients (Cordain *et al.* 2005) (Figure 6.3). Even the unprocessed foods consumed today in industrialized nations are likely to have lower micronutrient densities than the wild plant and animal foods consumed by our foraging ancestors (Eaton and Konner 1985; Brand-Miller and Holt 1998). Vegetables, seafood, meat and fruits rate highest in terms of general micronutrient density (Figure 6.3), while dairy products rate highest as sources of calcium. Whole grains have high macronutrient densities, but are quite low in their micronutrient content. Refined and processed grain products of the sort most commonly consumed in the industrialized world now have higher macronutrient densities than whole grains, and lower micronutrient densities. Various micronutrient deficiencies common in the world now might be related to dietary change following the transition to agriculture, and more recent adoption of industrialized diets. These include deficiencies of iron, iodine and calcium, all of which are associated with pathologies at their extremes (Cordain *et al.* 2005).

Iron deficiency

Well in excess of a billion people currently suffer iron deficiency and its attendant anaemia (Mair and Weiss 2009). Plant sources of iron are very poorly absorbed due to their inorganic form and their binding to anti-nutrient plant components such as oxalates, phytates, tannins and fibre. In some populations, a decline in haem-iron intake (which is more efficiently absorbed than the inorganic iron found in vegetable sources) may have occurred concurrently with new infections that emerged with increased population density and crowding (Mann 2000). However, iron deficiency protects against infectious diseases such as malaria, plague and tuberculosis (Denic and Agarwal 2007). With iron deficiency, epidemic infections would have exerted a selection pressure on human populations under which an iron deficiency phenotype would have survived better (Chapter 7).

Meat-eating and hence haem-iron intake would have varied by season and geographic area in prehistoric times, just as it does in contemporary foragers. For much of human history, at least in agrarian populations, iron intake has been or is limited by economic, cultural and ethical constraints on meat consumption. Nonetheless, in much of the contemporary industrialized world, meat consumption has increased in the past 50 years, as illustrated in

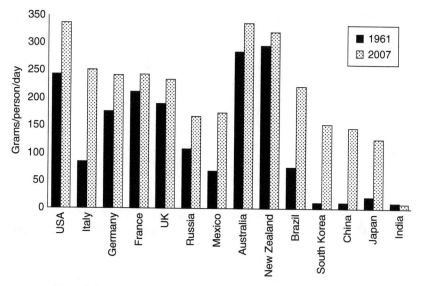

Figure 6.4. Increased availability of meat in national diets (grams/person/day) between 1961 and 2007 (data from Food and Agriculture Organization 2011).

Figure 6.4, which shows meat availability in national diets between 1961 and 2007. This has occurred partly because of increased relative prosperity but also because of the general homogenization – or 'MacDonaldization' – of industrialized diets, where traditional regional variants such as the 'Mediterranean' diet that emphasized fresh fruits and vegetables and starches like pasta and rice are increasingly giving way to plates dominated more by processed foods, fats and often cheap cuts of meat. The exception is India, where religious prohibitions among the vast majority of the population have limited meat consumption. Anaemia rates map loosely onto meat availability across these countries (Figure 6.5).

Iodine deficiency

Disorders of iodine deficiency are well documented (Hetzel 1983). The most profound effects of clinical deficiency are goitre resulting from thyroid gland enlargement, and cretinism (Boyages 1993). The latter emerges from iodine deficiency in the foetus, leading to abnormal brain development. Iodine deficiency is currently the world's leading cause of poor mental development in children. Both thyroid hormones, thyroxine (T4) and tri-iodothyronine (T3), incorporate iodine in their structure. If there is insufficient iodine the thyroid

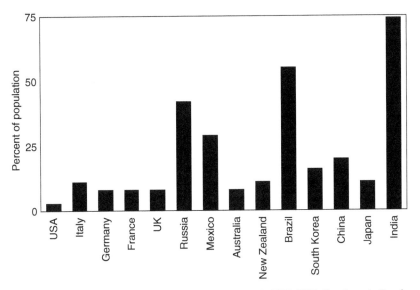

Figure 6.5. Anaemia rates (percent of population), 1993–2005 (data from de Benoist *et al.* 2008).

becomes larger, forming a goitre in the attempt to make adequate T3 and T4. Impairment of thyroid hormones results in slow metabolism, weight gain and fatigue. Although the recommended intake of iodine is low (150 milligrams/ day for Australian adults, 100 milligrams/day for European ones), it is poorly stored in the body and must be obtained regularly. There is considerable iodine deficiency across the world, although this has declined enormously (deBenoist *et al.* 2008). Iodine intake is almost as likely to be insufficient in industrialized countries as developing countries. For example, in Australia, 46% of 1700 students in a nationally-representative sample were shown to be deficient (Li *et al.* 2006). Globally, iodine deficiency is a particular public health problem for pregnant women and young children (deBenoist *et al.* 2004). Even mild iodine deficiency disorder (IDD) in children can lead to increased incidence of attention deficit hyperactivity disorder, poor muscular control, lowered intelligence quotient and hearing problems (McElduff and Beange 2004).

Iodine deficiency in contemporary societies may have arisen as industrialized diets became enriched in goitrogens, from foods such as milk, as well as bacteria and chemical water pollutants (Delange 1994), but perhaps also from various modern cultivated plants, including members of the *Brassica* genus such as broccoli, cabbage and kale. Some individuals may have a higher tolerance for consuming bitter-tasting foods and hence may have greater exposure to toxins, including goitrogens, than those with lower taste thresholds (Wooding *et al.* 2004). The ability to taste phenylthiocarbamide (PTC), which does not arise in nature but is correlated with the ability to taste other bitter substances (such as are found in *Brassica* cultivars), has long been assumed to be genetically determined. Relatively recent work has not only identified the PTC-tasting gene, *TAS2R38* (Kim *et al.* 2003), but also strongly supports the hypothesis of Fisher *et al.* (1939) that balancing natural selection maintains 'taster' and 'non-taster' alleles in populations throughout the world (Wooding *et al.* 2004). Comparative genetic work also indicates that the non-tasting allelic variant in chimpanzees arose independently of the human one (Kim *et al.* 2003; Wooding 2006). Although the tasting distribution is bimodal, it is not straightforwardly so, with some tasters having more sensitivity than others (Wooding 2006). One conundrum is why the genetic polymorphism is maintained through selection, if being a 'non-taster' may be deleterious because of toxin exposure. It may be the case that 'non-tasters' actually have increased sensitivity to other harmful substances, leading to heterozygote advantage, with protection against a wider range of toxins (Wooding *et al.* 2004), often produced by plants as defence mechanisms (Chapter 2).

An alternative (or possibly complementary) explanation for iodine deficiency in modern societies is that the increased carbohydrate intake in contemporary industrial diets (Chapter 11) may have led to increased production by the thyroid gland of the hormone tri-iodothyronine (T3) (Kopp 2004; Cunnane 2005). High-carbohydrate diets are associated with significantly higher T3 levels than low-carbohydrate diets (Azizi 1997), with no reduction in resting oxygen uptake or symptoms of hypothyroidism (Kopp 2004). Increased carbohydrate consumption has increased active T3 levels (without altering thyroid-stimulating hormone levels) and thyroid hormone production, with a concurrent increased demand for iodine (Kopp 2004). The main dietary sources of iodine are seafood, eggs, some vegetables and dairy foods (the latter mainly through contamination with iodine-based sterilizing solutions used in the dairy industry). As the physiological demand for dietary iodine has increased with changing diet, iodine supplies in many parts of the world may be insufficient to meet the human demands for it from unfortified food alone. For example, ocean fish are an ample source of dietary iodine, but there are not enough of them to go around (Chapter 10). The use of iodized salt in many countries, particularly in the baking industry, adds a significant quantity of iodine to the diet. The iodization of salt is a standard public health measure for dealing with iodine deficiency in a population (Li *et al.* 2001). Austria, for example, began salt iodization in 1963 to combat the high prevalence of goitre; by the 1990s goitres were present in less than 5% of the population, and then almost totally in the elderly whose diet had been iodine-deficient for much of their lives

(Lind *et al.* 2002). Since salt use is practically universal and iodizing salt is cheap and easily achieved, it is an ideal target for fortification (de Benoist *et al.* 2008). This strategy does not require increased salt consumption, but given the potentially harmful nature of modern levels of salt intake discussed above, this illustrates one of the many compromises inherent in public health nutrition, with the need to balance iodine requirements, especially for pregnant women and young children, with the potential for development of chronic disease later in life.

Calcium needs and dietary change

Dairy foods are the greatest contributors to dietary calcium intake in contemporary western societies, but diets with a large non-starchy plant component, even if low in dairy foods, may be as high or higher in calcium. Using contemporary forager diets as their comparator, Eaton and Nelson (1991) estimated that the daily calcium intakes of non-dairy eating early foragers would have been the order of 1800 mg per day, far in excess of those of contemporary industrialized populations. For example, in the 1990s Australian adults obtained 846 mg of calcium per day (Australian Bureau of Statistics 1998) while in the 1980s, citizens of the US had intakes between 500 and 800 mg per day (Riggs and Melton 1986). The recommended daily intake (or allowance) (RDA) of calcium for adults is 1000 mg per day in the US, United Kingdom (UK) and Australia. Calcium intakes of adults in the US between 1971 and the year 2000 are shown in Figure 6.1. Averages do not exceed 1000 mg per day at any time across this period. The diets of several foraging populations contain considerable amounts of plant food, with Eaton and Nelson (1991) estimating that early humans consumed around 1.3 kg of plant food per day, with an average calcium concentration of 133 mg of calcium per 100 g of plant material, and a smaller quantity coming from animal foods. Most mammals require around 25 mg of calcium per kilogram of body mass (Heaney *et al.* 1977). If we assume that humans have the same physiological requirement as other mammals, this would make the calcium needs of a 70 kg adult male 1750 mg per day. This is a value that is very close to Eaton and Nelson's (1991) estimate of calcium intakes for early humans. Given that this is nearly twice the US, UK and Australian RDA, it is possible that current recommended calcium levels are set too low. The pattern for lower calcium intake was probably set after the transition to agriculture (Pfeiffer and King 1983). Ulijaszek (1991) modelled dietary change in the Near East at the origins of agriculture, and found that there could have been calcium deficiency, even relative to contemporary norms, among early farmers, especially if they also suffered some degree of energy deficiency, as was very likely (Angel 1984).

Calcium is important for bone growth and maintenance; calcium supplementation, in combination with vitamin D, is often used as a treatment for osteoporosis, a disease of reduced bone density that predisposes to bone fracture and which is a significant public health issue, especially in post-menopausal women (Sambrook and Cooper 2006). The prevalence of osteoporosis in modern industrialized populations is linked not only to diet but also to exercise. In a three-year study of early post-menopausal women, it was observed that those engaged in regular high-intensity exercise maintained their starting bone mass whereas those that did not participate in the regular exercise sessions experienced bone loss (Kemmler *et al.* 2005). This highlights the importance of continued and relatively intense physical activity for bone health. Early hunter-gatherers are likely to have had greater levels of physical activity and mechanical stresses on the skeleton (Eaton and Nelson 1991) than contemporary industrialized humans, but not early agriculturalists (Ulijaszek 1991). It is probable that this activity was maintained throughout life, although there may have been variation in the types of physical activities undertaken by males and females (Larsen 1987). Traditional subsistence archaeological populations also tend to have higher peak bone mass than contemporary humans (Larsen 1987). Smith *et al.* (1984) found that 12 000 year old Near Eastern Natufians had humeral cortical thicknesses on average 17% greater than those of present-day citizens of the United States. It is well known that childhood activity influences adult bone density; randomized controlled trials in children indicate that a combination of calcium supplementation and regular physical exercise such as running, jumping or skipping increases bone mineral content, with calcium apparently mediating bone response to activity (Specker and Binkley 2003).

Calcium content of food is not the only dietary factor influencing bone mineralization and density. Other key nutrients involved in growing and maintaining healthy (and functionally appropriate) bone include vitamin D, phosphorus, magnesium and protein. Based on analogy with modern hunter-gatherers, the diets of early foragers almost certainly contained more magnesium and calcium than contemporary industrialized diets (Eaton *et al.* 1997). The balance between the two nutrients is important for bone mineralization, and there is substantial difference in this balance between hunter-gatherer diets and industrialized ones. Cordain *et al.* (2005) estimated values for the micronutrient content of six food groups that are used to categorize the diet of the United States population (Table 6.1). In the food types consumed by some hunter-gatherers (meats, seafood, vegetables, fruits and nuts/seeds) the calcium to magnesium content is appropriately balanced. However, with

Table 6.1 *Calcium and magnesium content of six basic food groupings, showing the overall Ca:Mg ratio of each* Based on a 100 kcal serving.

Food grouping	Calcium (mg)	Magnesium (mg)	Ca:Mg
Dairy	194	22	8.8:1
Vegetables	117	55	2.1:1
Fruit	43	25	1.7:1
Seafood	43	36	1.2:1
Nuts and seeds	18	36	0.5:1
Meats	6	18	0.3:1

Adapted from Cordain *et al.* (2005).

the addition of dairy foods (particularly when consumed in large quantity), the overall calcium to magnesium balance shifts greatly in favour of calcium (Varo 1974). Counter-intuitively, this high calcium intake may be a major factor in reduced bone mineralization and subsequent reduced bone density because at high calcium intakes, magnesium deficiency is likely (Evans *et al.* 1990). A lifetime's exposure to a diet with a very high calcium to magnesium ratio could compromise intra-cellular magnesium levels, limiting parathyroid hormone secretion and resulting in low calcium levels in the blood, hypo-calcaemia (Rude *et al.* 1976), and possibly impair bone-mineral regulation. Indirect confirmation of this effect comes from study of post-menopausal women taking magnesium supplements, who show gains in bone mineral content when calcium dietary supplementation had no effect (Sojka and Weaver 1995).

Bone health may also be influenced by interactions between the macro- and micronutrient content of the diet. When laboratory-purified proteins are added to basal diets they can induce high levels of calcium in the blood, hypercal-ciuria (Margen *et al.* 1974), although consumption of diets high in meat or other food-based unpurified sources of protein have no such effect (Spencer *et al.* 1983). Potential renal acid load (PRAL) increases with protein intake and leads to greater urinary calcium excretion (Remer and Manz 1995). Since the human kidney cannot excrete urine with a pH value below five, excess urinary acid must be buffered in some way. Calcium derived from the skeleton forms one such buffer (Barzel and Massey 1998). In contemporary industrialized society, most individuals suffer from at least mild metabolic acidosis from time to time, usually as a result of dietary composition (Frassetto *et al.* 2008). Protein, particularly from animal sources (which are rich in sulphur-containing amino acids, including methionine) produce low but significant levels of sulphuric acid *in vivo* and contribute to acidosis. Sebastian *et al.* (2002) have concluded that early hunter-gatherers, although possibly consuming higher levels of animal protein than people do today, had lower net endogenous acid production and thus experienced metabolic alkalosis because of their high intake of vegetable matter, rich in potassium compounds, which are metabolized into endogenous bicarbonates.

Compared with a generalized hunter-gatherer diet with an hypothesized higher meat content, it has been argued that consumption of industrialized diets leads to lower endogenous sulphuric and organic acid production (Sebastian *et al.* 2002). However, the replacement of alkaline base-rich plant foods (such as roots, tubers, leafy green vegetables and fruits) with net acid-producing cereal grains and dairy products (such as cheese) has disproportionately lowered our net base-producing capacity and caused a shift from cellular alkalosis to acidosis, with attendant bone demineralisation and urinary calcium loss. Sebastian *et al.* (2002) estimate that grains alone account for 38% of the acid load that comes from consuming a modern diet. Remmer and Manz (1995) calculated the PRAL of frequently consumed foods in the modern industrialized diet based on renal net acid excretion (NAE), and found that the highest values came from high-protein dairy products such as cheese, while the lowest came from fruits and vegetables. Frassetto *et al.* (1998) used dietary intake data and PRAL values of foods to show that 71% of the variation in NAE (and hence, indirectly, net acid production) could be accounted for by the ratio of protein to potassium content of the diet.

Early hunter-gatherers hypothesized to consume large amounts of meat may have had protein intakes in excess of 35% of total dietary energy intake (Mann 2000; Cordain *et al.* 2000b), which represents between 2.9 and 3.5 grams of protein per kilogram of body mass (Eaton and Nelson 1991). This is well in excess of present-day recommended daily allowances, which stand at 0.8 grams per kilogram of body mass for adults in the US (Bilsborough and Mann 2006). Calcium loss could have been significant but bone mass was higher (Larsen 1987). The large amounts of plant foods consumed were rich in potassium compounds that buffered acid-producing proteins. Thus the diet, although high in protein, had a net alkaline PRAL.

In modern industrialized agrarian populations, in which grains and dairy foods (both net producers of acid) to a large extent displace vegetable matter, the PRAL of the diet has increased, resulting in higher NAE, lower urinary pH, increased urinary calcium loss and potentially greater bone demineralization. The links between a high-plant, high-potassium diet and increased bone density are supported by the observation that dietary supplementation with potassium citrate in post-menopausal women reduces urinary calcium and increases urinary citrate excretion (factors indicating systemic alkalinization) and that such supplementation gives a small but significant increase in bone mineral density and reduced

Table 6.2 *Food types found in western diets generally unavailable to societies prior to the origins of agriculture*

Food or food group	Value (% of energy)
Cereal grains	24
Refined sugars	19
Refined vegetable oils	17
Dairy products	11
Alcohol	1
Total energy	72

Adapted from Cordain *et al.* (2005)

levels of bone mineral resorption markers in urine (Jehle *et al.* 2006). Frassetto *et al.* (1997) similarly showed reduced NAE and lowered blood hydrogen ion concentration in women treated with potassium bicarbonate, while Sebastian *et al.* (1994) showed potassium bicarbonate supplementation to neutralize endogenous acid production, improve calcium balance, reduce bone resorption and increase the rate of bone formation in post-menopausal women.

Contemporary food commodities

Contemporary western diets largely consist of foods that were either unavailable to, or made minimal contribution to the diet of, early human hunter-gatherers. For example, 72% of the energy in the average diet of citizens in the US comes from foods that were unavailable prior to the origins of agriculture (Cordain *et al.* 2005), with many emerging in their familiar form since industrialization (Chapter 5). It would be curious to know what an early hunter-gatherer, or indeed an inhabitant of a Neolithic agricultural settlement such as Çatalhöyük or a medieval European peasant, would make of the bakery products, breakfast cereals, crackers, chips, snack foods, pizza, soft drinks, candy, ice cream, condiments, salad dressings, cookies, cakes and chocolate that have proliferated in the past 50 years or so and which fill the shelves of supermarkets and convenience stores. The largest part of such foods have in common such ingredients as cereal grains, refined sugars and refined vegetable oils (Table 6.2).

Cereals and carbohydrates

Cereals entered the human diet at similar times in the Near East, East Asia and Central America. In the Near East, regular exploitation of cereal grains has been identified in the archaeological record of the Natufian culture around 13 000 years ago (Bar-Yosef 1998). However, more limited use of cereal grains in this region goes back to 40 000 years ago, with finds of stone mortars and bowls associated with the use of wild grass strains (Wright 1991). The seed grains of wild grasses are generally small and detach from the plant easily for wind dispersal, making collection difficult (Brown *et al.* 2009). They are also relatively poor energy sources, since under most circumstances they have high collection and preparation costs but low energy returns (Brown *et al.* 2009). Furthermore, their relatively high fibre, low starch content and coarse outer casing make processing almost essential and cooking preferable, for the sake of digestibility (Cordain *et al.* 2005). It was only with the gradual domestication of the primitive wheat-grasses emmer and einkorn, both of which had larger seeds that stayed attached to the plant stalk longer, that humans developed a reliable staple crop some 10 000 to 11 000 years ago (Salami *et al.* 2003; Brown *et al.* 2009).

Until the industrial revolution, grain-based foods generally contained the complete grain. This included the starch-rich endosperm, germ that is rich in micronutrients (especially in B vitamins, beta carotene, and vitamins A and E) and fibrous bran (Storck and Teague 1952). With the advent of mechanized milling in association with sieving in the nineteenth century, cereal products contained less bran and germ and more starch, often in reduced particulate size and with digestibility in excess of any carbohydrate food consumed by our human and hominin ancestors (Nelson 1985). Not only are the ubiquitous cereal products of today lower in nutrient content and fibre, their physical forms create new biophysical and biochemical challenges for digestion and metabolism, especially in regard to postprandial glycaemic effects (Cordain *et al.* 2005) and gut microbiota (since their composition is influenced by resistant carbohydrates and dietary fibre) (Scott *et al.* 2008). It was not just cereal crops that were increasingly refined in the past couple of centuries: white rice was consumed in Japan by the early nineteenth century, as illustrated in one scene in Hokusai's '36 views of Mount Fuji', which shows a traditional form of rice polishing (Figure 6.6).

Sugar is another carbohydrate that is most commonly found in a highly refined form in contemporary industrialized society. Hominins, like other primates, would have been exposed to natural sugars, primarily through fructose in fruits and glucose in wild honey (Chapter 3). Intake would have varied geographically and seasonally. Evidence from studies of foraging among Australian aboriginal people and the Ache of Paraguay show wild honey consumption of around two kilograms per year or three per cent of averaged daily energy intake (Meehan 1982; Hawkes *et al.* 1982; Brand-Miller and Holt 1998). Prior to colonization of the New World, European sugar intake was also extremely

Figure 6.6. Watermill at Onden (Hokusai, around 1830 (copyright expired)).

limited. However, once processes for its production were industrialized on plantations in the Caribbean, markets for it grew, prices fell, and its place as a privileged consumer product declined (Mintz 1985). The mass market for sugar stimulated and perpetuated the slave trade, and by 1815 the average intake of refined sugar in England was around six to eight kilograms per person per year. Average intake continued to rise steadily until the second half of the twentieth century (Cleave 1974). Not only has there been a vast quantitative increase in sugar intake, but in recent years the US population has made high-fructose corn syrup (HFCS) a significant part of its diet, with attendant risks to health (Chapter 11). The populations of Canada, Mexico, Japan and South Korea also consume HFCS, but to a much lesser extent. The high level of fructose consumption in the US would have been totally unachievable by ancestral hominins (Cordain *et al.* 2005), even on a seasonal basis.

The consumption of refined carbohydrates (including sugar, white flour and rice) was initially the privilege of the higher classes. The class-status of refined foods changed after the industrial revolution. Known and consumed in abundance among the European aristocracy from late medieval times, sugar started to become a poor person's staple in industrializing Britain during the nineteenth century (Mintz 1985). The same happened with respect to white bread in the second half of the twentieth century. The subsequent incorporation into the industrialized diet of greater amounts of sugar-, dairy- and oil-rich products, cheap to produce and with a high energy yield, to the industrialized diet saw further displacement of fibre-rich wholegrains, vegetables and fruits from it.

Fats and oils

Seed oil production has been dated to around 5000 to 6000 years ago. However, apart from some use of olive oil in Mediterranean areas, the oils produced were largely used for lighting and lubrication (O'Keefe 2000). Significant human consumption of vegetable oils only really started in the late 1800s with the advent of mechanical and chemical extraction technologies, but increased dramatically thereafter, especially in the US (Gerrior and Bente 2002). Not only has there been a great increase in the consumption of vegetable oils, but there have also been some fundamental changes in the types of fat consumed, including the introduction of trans-fatty acids to the diets of industrialized populations in the second half of the twentieth century (Emken 1984; Cordain *et al.* 2005), again with attendant health risks (Chapter 10).

Dairy foods

Prior to domestication of milk-giving animals, humans, in common with all other mammals, only consumed milk of their own species during early growth and development and had no exposure to milk or dairy products post-weaning. With the domestication of sheep, goats and cattle in the Near East and elsewhere from around 10 000 years ago (Chapter 1), humans had the potential to consume the milk of their domesticated species. Direct chemical evidence of dairy product use dates back to around 8500 years ago, in Turkey (Evershed *et al.* 2008). With access to milk and milk products of other species, humans were introduced to new types of dietary proteins (among them immunologically active agents), fats and carbohydrates, along with a new source of vitamin D and calcium. Consumption of dairy products has been popularly viewed as detrimental to health. However, several populations, such as the north-west African Fulani and northern Europeans, have adapted genetically to milk consumption, with lactase persistence into adulthood evolving independently in geographically disparate populations (Holden and Mace 2002). Gradients of lactase persistence are evident within regions: in Britain, for example, there is a greater frequency of non-persistence alleles in white women born in the south of England compared with the north (Davey-Smith *et al.* 2009). This example of natural selection (with diet as the probable selective pressure) had profound consequences for human ecology, widening the human ecological niche considerably compared with those of other apes or even the first humans. Herbivores, unlike humans, can exploit environments that are relatively unproductive in plant life directly. Often, these environments are arid, cold or both. Humans can survive on the products of the primary consuming herbivores rather than being primary plant consumers themselves. The Turkana people of East Africa are a good example. Pastoralists that live in an arid environment relatively poor in edible and easily processed plant resources, their exploitation of meat, blood and particularly milk of domesticated animals, primarily cattle, allows them to live in an otherwise ecologically hostile area (Little 1989, 2002). Pastoralism is thus a much more appropriate strategy in that environment than foraging and it is likely that in human history and prehistory, as now, the ability to digest milk sugars into adulthood had significant nutritional and evolutionary fitness benefits in particular regions.

The ecological explanation for lactase persistence and milk consumption, sometimes formalized as the 'culture historical hypothesis' (Simoons 1970), is only one of several postulated reasons for the retention into adulthood of the ability to digest milk. Others include the advantage of lactose consumption in stimulating calcium absorption in higher-latitude regions where exposure to sunlight and thus vitamin D synthesis is restricted (Flatz and Rotthauwe 1973), the negative selective pressure of mortality due to diarrhoeal disease in lactose-intolerant milk consumers (Cook 1978) and the essential water and electrolytes provided by milk in arid regions (Cook 1978). In addition, because lactase deficiency in infants may signal time for weaning, in populations with lactase persistence, where this natural signal does not occur, infants can be weaned earlier, reducing interbirth intervals and hence increasing reproductive fitness (Lieberman and Lieberman 1978). Nonetheless, regardless of the 'prime mover' for lactase persistence, one key to evaluating the costs and benefits of dairy consumption from a public health perspective is awareness of the dietary history of particular populations. In those that have milk-drinking traditions and the consequent ability to synthesize lactase beyond childhood, dairy products can be consumed in moderation as part of a balanced diet.

Meats

Modern agricultural practice in many economically developed societies involves the genetic selection of animals for domestic meat production based on growth rate and fat production. Combined with the feeding of such animals with stored plant fodder and grains, it has not only become possible to avoid seasonal decline in body fat in these animals, but has also become almost universal that weight (and fat) gain is continuous and rapid. Feedlot-fed animals produce 'marbled meat' (Whitaker 1975) with relatively high levels of intramuscular fat, most of which is saturated, with some n-6 PUFA and almost no n-3 PUFA (Mann 2005). Countries that still pasture-feed their domesticated animals largely produce leaner animals with more omega-3 PUFA, because of the greater content of alpha-linolenic acid (18:3n3) in pasture relative to grains (Mann 2005). Such domestic animals are closer in protein-to-fat balance and fatty acid composition to wild animals (Chapter 10) than are grain-fed animals.

Alcohol

The consumption of alcohol is known among primate species, since alcohol signals energy density in foods (Chapter 2). Humans have hijacked this property and made alcohol consumption part of the menu of dietary and narcotic possibilities. The origin of systematically fermented and brewed alcoholic beverages dates to as early as 9000 years ago, in China (McGovern *et al.* 2004). The emergence of distilled alcoholic beverages is less clear, with the first unequivocal evidence for distilling for alcohol destined for consumption (rather than distilling for products such as essential oils) coming from Europe in the twelfth century (Dietler 2006). However, it has been suggested, on the basis of possible pottery stills and Sanskrit texts, that distilled alcohol for consumption was present in south Asia 2500 years ago (Allchin 1979). Moderate (but not heavy) alcohol consumption is associated with lower risk of death due to CVD, while any level of consumption is associated with increased mortality from a range of cancers, including those of the breast, mouth, pharynx, larynx, oesophagus and liver (Thun *et al.* 1997). It is also associated with death due to violence and to cirrhosis of the liver. Before the increased longevity of populations in industrialized societies, most of the negative health effects of alcohol would have been comparatively rare. Violence associated with heavy drinking would have been a major reason for the development of social norms for alcohol consumption in most societies in which it is consumed.

Salt

Hunter-gatherer societies that have been studied in recent times generally do not add salt to foods, although this does not mean that they have diets entirely devoid of sodium. It may be that a diverse and interesting diet sourced from wild-grown foods is sufficiently palatable not to need flavour enhancers such as salt. However, not all foraging diets are or would have been *de facto* diverse and interesting. Based on analogy with modern foragers and primates, it is likely that early humans would be accustomed to a relatively low-sodium diet, and would seek it out, as among other mammals, only when there was a physiological deficit. In other words, even if the diet was bland, they didn't miss what they didn't have. Nonetheless, when salt is available, the physiological need for sodium appears to drive avidity and higher than necessary consumption, with taste buds quickly responding and adjusting to saltier tastes (Denton *et al.* 1995; Young *et al.* 2005). Salt is, after all, one of the fundamental mammalian tastes, with specialized receptors on the tongue. Thus, once use of salt as a condiment was more frequent, its consumption is likely to have been reinforced, as shown by the preference in captive chimpanzees for relatively salty monkey chow biscuits that form the basis of captive, but not wild, diet (Denton *et al.* 1995). This is further supported by the observation that human, chimpanzee and gorilla breast milk is relatively low in sodium, implying a reasonably low baseline need that is then 'primed' by inclusion of salty foods in the weanling or juvenile diet (Denton *et al.* 1995).

Since the Neolithic, salt has been a crucial commodity. The introduction of salt in significant quantities to the human diet is probably linked to two of its properties, its ability to remove moisture from foods, thus increasing their osmotic pressure and making them less likely to spoil, and its ability to increase the palatability of savoury foods. However, the importance of salt goes well beyond its immediate abilities to preserve and flavour food at the level of the individual or household. The first evidence for salt excavation is recorded from around 6000 years ago in China and Europe (Kurlansky 2002; Weller 2002), although it was probably sought on a smaller and less systematic scale earlier (Brown 1980). This may have marked the start of salt production commercially, with demand for salt fuelling trade from salt-rich to salt-poor areas and, as exemplified in China 3000 years ago, promoting social differentiation and bigger and bigger political network formation (Flad *et al.* 2005). It has been argued that salt production facilitated state formation (Flad *et al.* 2005), building on the population increases, urbanization, social and economic stratification and attendant social inequality that emerged after the adoption of agriculture (Chapter 9). The relative scarcity of salt until at least the early modern age kept its value high and trade vital.

Agriculture generates seasonal surpluses of food (Chapter 4), which need to be distributed across the year. Whereas grain and seeds are relatively easily stored once dried, the same is not true for a wide range of vegetables, fish and meat. Salting of such foods is one way of preserving them and ensuring they can be consumed out of season, as well as being able to bring them to urban consumers without wastage. When intensive salt extraction from surface and underground beds made it a more common commodity, trade in and movement of salt-preserved foods became even more widespread, as in medieval Europe. It also created new foods, such as bacon, ham, salted fish and sauerkraut, which remain favoured foods in many places to the present day. Salted foods were among the earliest traded food commodities in Europe and Asia. With colonialism, such foods were introduced to many new places and peoples, helping to reinforce an inbuilt inclination for salt consumption. Most of the salt in the diet of contemporary industrialized populations is found in processed foods, added by manufacturers during production for a range of reasons, including taste enhancement, texture and preservation. Processed foods sell better if they taste better. One aspect of taste that is cheap and easy to provide is saltiness, and the current and unprecedentedly high salt intake in many western diets is thus easy to understand.

Discussion

The shift from diets constituting a broad range of animal and plant foods to ones largely based on processed foods rich in refined grains, sugars and oils has led to huge decreases in micronutrient intake among contemporary industrialized societies and economically modernizing populations. Thus, while energy capture is more efficient than ever before, micronutrient capture is failing. Associated deficiency disorders follow where such dietary deficiencies lead. Well in excess of a billion people currently suffer iron deficiency and its attendant anaemia, while iodine deficiency disorders persist, and osteoporosis (associated with imbalanced intakes of calcium, phosphorus and protein) is widespread. Meat consumption patterns probably changed with the adoption of agriculture and animal husbandry. With this came a probable decline in iron intake; among present-day populations, iron intake is limited by economic, cultural and ethical restraints on meat consumption. As the physiological demand for dietary iodine has increased with increased carbohydrate intake after adopting agricultural lifestyles and diets, environmental iodine supplies in many parts of the contemporary world have become insufficient to meet the body's demand for it. The shift from consumption of a varied animal and wild plant food diet to that of a less diverse diet underpinned by cereal grains and dairy products has reduced human calcium intake and shifted the cellular state from alkalosis to acidosis, resulting in bone demineralization and increased risk of osteoporosis. This might not matter if humans no longer needed strong bones, but out-sourcing physical activity to machines (which industrialized societies have done quite successfully) leads to other health problems such as obesity, Type 2 diabetes and CVD. This profound shift in diet has not finished. New technologies and the demand to feed people are stimulating the development of new foods, whether they be refined carbohydrates or fats. Chapters 9, 10 and 11 will examine different aspects of this issue in more depth.

7 Nutrition and infectious disease, past and present

Introduction

Human populations are extremely plastic with respect to what they can eat (Chapter 2); the intensification of dietary energy capture that came with the adoption of agriculture could not have happened without this behavioural and physiological flexibility. When agriculture emerged in different parts of the world shortly after 10 000 years ago (Chapter 1), infectious disease added new complexity to the ways people lived. Permanent, year-round settlements were a feature of the new agrarian economies, along with increased population size and eventual emergence of social stratification (Chapters 1 and 8). Living together in close proximity allowed existing disease agents to intensify their infection of humans, and also allowed zoonoses (animal-borne diseases) to cross the species barrier into humans, creating new problems of pathogenic infection for them. Niche construction (alterations of the environment in a manner that is expected to increase the chances of survival of the animal that made the alterations) would have intensified natural selection (Laland *et al.* 1999).

Genetic evidence suggests that both malaria and tuberculosis emerged as human diseases before the origins of agriculture, but only became very prevalent after it, with increased transmission rates as population densities grew (Armelagos and Harper 2005). At the origins of agriculture in Africa, forest clearing would have constructed a niche that increased the potential for mosquitoes to increase the spread of malaria (Laland and Kendal 2007). The abnormal red blood cells of individuals with the sickle-cell trait are less easily parasitized by the malaria parasite *Plasmodium falciparum* than are normal red cells, and selection for heterozygosity in the sickle-cell gene would have given a selective advantage among populations exposed to malaria (Allison 1954). With the organization of human populations into the complex societies that followed the origins of agriculture, disease ecology changed such that density-dependent pathogens became more important than sylvatic infections (ones that exist in animals and infect humans directly). Sedentism, clearing land for agriculture and animal husbandry, along with increased human contact with human and animal faeces, provided ideal conditions for the transmission and fixation of novel pathogens in human populations (Cohen 1989). The emergence of towns and cities would have made crowd infections dominant in those places. The nutritional stresses that came after the origins of agriculture would have further facilitated the spread of infectious diseases because of impaired immunological responses and the well-documented synergies between infection and nutrition (Suskind and Tontisirin 2001).

The patterns of infectious disease and undernutrition which emerged after the origins of agriculture are mirrored in present-day less economically developed populations, often as outcomes of poverty, inequality and structural violence (Chapter 1) (Farmer 2004). In this chapter we examine the behavioural and ecological nature of interactions between nutrition and infection, using ideas of developmental plasticity and genetic susceptibility or resistance to infection. We discuss undernutrition–infection interactions in the past, focusing on genetic and dietary adaptations to malaria, the role of iron and haemochromatosis in resistance to infection, and the emergence of tuberculosis as a widespread disease among humans. Undernutrition and infection can influence the course of a pregnancy, affect lactation and the physical growth of children and ultimately survivorship. Thus we also examine ways in which nutrition–infection relationships in pregnancy and early childhood affect reproductive success, and how infant feeding practices operate as adaptive strategies for modifying risk of mortality in environments with high infection risk. The implications of the emergence of undernutrition–infection interactions for present-day public health nutrition are considered, especially in respect of the evolutionary relationships between specific nutrient deficiencies and malaria, tuberculosis and HIV infection. The synergies across these three diseases and nutritional state in the contemporary less economically developed world are also considered.

Infectious disease has been an important driver of natural selection among humans since their modern origin, between around 350 000 and 100 000 years ago, and more recently with the origins of agriculture and the construction of niches that pre-empt and accelerate natural selection against infectious disease. Such natural selection is viewed to have taken place as part of a larger package of adaptation against infectious disease more generally. The disease examples we elaborate on in this chapter interact with nutrition and continue to have enormous impact on the health and well-being of modern human populations, making them objects of global public health concern. They are also examples of the three categories of disorder – haematological (malaria), infectious and immunological (tuberculosis and HIV/AIDS) – against which selection is deemed to have taken place (Amato *et al.* 2009).

Nutrition–infection interactions: some general issues

The pathogenic richness of an environment is related to climate as well as species diversity among birds and mammals (Dunn *et al.* 2010), while susceptibility to infections relies on genetics (Cooke and Hill 2001), environmental factors and nutritional state (Chandra 1988). Young children have the least mature immune systems (Ulijaszek 1998) and aging people experience immunoscenescence (deterioration of the immune response with age) (Franceschi *et al.* 2000). Thus, both age groups have the highest susceptibility to infection. These groups also experience the highest burden of additional immunecompromise caused by inadequate intakes of energy, protein and/or a range of immunologically important micronutrients such as iron, vitamin A and zinc (Tomkins 2002).

Humans have large brains, which have been selected for social and cognitive abilities. Unlike other primates, a significant proportion of human brain growth occurs outside the womb, necessitating slow, prolonged growth and long-term infant and juvenile dependency (which also reflect a need to acquire social and technical skills). The trade-off for the evolution of bipedalism was limited brain growth *in utero* because of restricted pelvic size and its implications for successful delivery of the new-born (Harcourt-Smith and Aiello 2004). Humans require a much longer breastfeeding period than other mammals (Kennedy 2005). By examining the relationships among age at weaning and various life-history variables among non-human primates, Dettwyler (1995) placed the timing of human weaning from breastfeeding, without consideration of customs and beliefs, at between 2.5 and 7 years. In traditional societies that have had little or no exposure to outside forces, breastfeeding duration usually exceeds two years (Sellen 2001). Dietary supplementation of the breastfed infant usually starts when breastfeeding declines in adequacy (around six months of age). According to Kennedy (2005), early weaning (relative to other primates) and dietary supplementation is a strategy that supports a pattern of brain growth which enhances social, extractive and technological skills that serve to enhance the child's reproductive fitness and success if he or she survives to adulthood. With respect to infection, the earliest exposure to pathogens comes at birth, and breastfeeding and hygienic practices are very effective buffers against developing infection.

Generally, breast milk supplies adequate nutrition for the first six months or so of life (Butte *et al.* 2002), although this has recently been questioned by Fewtrell *et al.* (2011), who view exclusive breastfeeding as being associated with higher risk of iron deficiency anaemia, food allergies and coeliac disease. Beyond six months of age, a set of balancing circumstances ensue. Adding solid food to a breastfeeding child's diet adds further nutrition, but may also introduce potential infections if the food is not hygienically prepared. Not adding food leads to progressive undernutrition, impaired immunocompetence and reduced resistance to infection. The problems surrounding the decision of whether or not to supplement an infant's diet has been called the 'weanling's dilemma' (Rowland 1986).

Human juveniles are unusual among mammals in remaining highly dependent on their mothers after weaning, yet being weaned very early relative to crucial life-history variables such as body size, age at first reproduction and emergence of the first molar tooth (Humphrey 2010). Weaning behaviour is likely to have changed over the course of human evolution, with the first major shift towards early weaning and prolonged offspring dependency ('childhood') occurring alongside the substantial ecological and behavioural alterations after the emergence of *Homo erectus* 1.8 million years ago (Humphrey 2010). From the perspective of infection and immunocompetence, the largest risk of weaning is likely to have come from mortality due to infection with diseases such as malaria, with the removal of lactation-conferred immunity. Mortality from food contamination is likely to have been relatively low, as food and liquids would not have been stored. Diarrhoeal disease is unlikely to have been frequent because Pleistocene hominins would not have inhabited permanent settlements. With the advent of agriculture came increased population density, and correspondingly increased rates of infection and mortality risk of early weaning.

As infancy and childhood unfold, undernutrition can emerge when diet becomes inadequate, either because exclusive breastfeeding is no longer adequate to sustain physical growth and function, or because the weaning diet is nutrient-poor. Good food security (that higher social classes both past and present were and are able to command) and the control of infection (by reduced exposure, reduced prevalence, or through treatment) are the principal means by which the cycle of undernutrition and infection can be broken. That this cycle persists among the poor of the less-developed world to the present day testifies to its complexity and power in shaping human nutritional health.

Figure 7.1 is an incomplete illustration of the possible nutrition–infection interactions in early childhood. It is incomplete because time and genotype are absent from it. Time is important because children grow, and immune systems mature and develop memory of previous infections and nutritional deprivations (Murphy *et al.* 2008). Genotype is important because there are many,

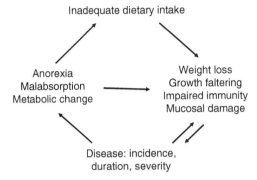

Figure 7.1. Nutrition–infection interactions in early childhood.

often networked resistance and susceptibility alleles to a wide range of pathogens. The cycle can start with inadequate intake, as with prolonged breast-feeding without any dietary supplementation. Across a few months, immune function suffers, and across a longer timeframe physical growth falters. Immunological impairment then makes the child susceptible to infection. Exposure to and development of infectious disease (depending on the nature of the pathogen) then leads to appetite loss, malabsorption, and elevated metabolism of energy and other nutrients. Infections that precipitate diarrhoea and fever facilitate weight loss, loss of appetite, undernutrition and further immunological impairments, which leave a child open to additional subsequent infection. Diarrhoea can cause gut mucosal damage that can lead to increased susceptibility to future infection (Lunn 2000), while fever raises metabolic rate and therefore energy needs. In both cases, a sentinel immune response is mounted by acute phase protein production. Acute phase proteins are produced by the body rapidly during inflammation, and are key players in the initiation of activity in other arms of the immune system. This is vital to mounting an immunological response appropriate to a particular infection, but needs protein to fuel it. Where protein intakes are marginal, there may be bodily loss of protein due to its catabolism for building immunological proteins (Tomkins 2000).

In a pathogen-rich environment, an infant or young child is either buffered from, or exposed to pathogens through caring practices, including those associated with feeding, drinking, touching and being encouraged (or not) to explore their immediate environment. It is also mediated by broader environmental issues like housing and over-crowding. Delayed dietary supplementation of a breastfed child may lead to inhibition of physical growth and undernutrition, leaving the infant more susceptible to infectious diseases, while earlier dietary supplementation may provide adequate nutrient intake, but

Table 7.1 *Infectious disease experience of two Guatemalan children from birth to three years*

Age range (months)	Child 1	2
0–6	Thrush Upper respiratory infection	Thrush Upper respiratory infection Diarrhoea (two episodes) Conjunctivitis
6–12	Upper respiratory infection Diarrhoea Bronchitis	Upper respiratory infection (two episodes) Diarrhoea (three episodes) Measles
12–18	Upper respiratory infection Diarrhoea (two episodes) Bronchitis (three episodes)	Diarrhoea (three episodes) Bronchitis
18–24	Upper respiratory infection (two episodes) Diarrhoea (two episodes) Bronchitis Measles	Upper respiratory infection Diarrhoea (three episodes) Bronchitis (two episodes) Fever
24–30	Upper respiratory infection (two episodes) Diarrhoea (four episodes) Bronchitis (two episodes)	Upper respiratory infection (three episodes) Diarrhoea (four episodes) Bronchitis
30–36	Upper respiratory infection (three episodes) Diarrhoea (two episodes) Bronchitis (two episodes)	Upper respiratory infection (three episodes) Diarrhoea (three episodes) Bronchopneumonia

Where the number of episodes is not stated, it represents one episode.
Source: From Mata (1978).

introduce diarrhoeal pathogens. Once started, the interactions between these two major environmental stressors and the underlying genotype become increasingly complex, with disease ecology (the range of pathogens in a particular environment, their infectivity and pathogenic vigour) influencing the duration and severity of infection.

An example of this complexity comes from Guatemala (Mata 1978) (Table 7.1). Here, a group of 45 children followed from birth until 36 months of age each experienced an average of five episodes of diarrhoea (caused by three different agents) and upper respiratory infection. Although rates of parasitic infections were close to zero at birth, by three years of age, 78% of them were infected with *Ascaris lumbricoides*, 19% with *Giardia lamblia*, over 10% of them with *Entamoeba histolytica*, and 3% with *Trichuris trichiura*. Some children had more intense experiences of infection, with repeated episodes of upper respiratory infections, diarrhoea and bronchitis. Across the 36 month period, one of the children whose data are presented in Table 7.1 experienced 32 episodes of illness, while another experienced 37 episodes.

Repeated exposure to infection influences the development of adaptive immunity, subsequent disease experience, and, if any, the extent of anorexia, fever, and malabsorption during infectious episodes, which impact on nutritional status (Figure 7.1). Specific nutritional deficiencies (of vitamin A and zinc, for example) can also influence immune status and responsiveness, as well as adaptive immunity. Parents and families are faced with constant decisions about the nature and extent of child health care: whether they should seek outside help, whether an illness can be deemed easily recoverable with time, and whether there are known solutions for particular medical problems. Poverty and structural violence (Chapter 1) can deny people access to information, health facilities and medication that influence disease management decisions and sickness behaviour (Farmer 2004). These can make the difference between prolonged or short duration of infection, the severity of infection, and its effects on nutritional status. At the extreme, it can mean the difference between life and death for a child.

Physiological and developmental plasticity are key features of hominin (including human) adaptation (Chapter 4), although early life stresses, especially intra-uterine ones, may have some negative health consequences in later life (Roseboom *et al.* 2001), depending on environmental conditions (Chapters 1 and 9). Epigenetic mechanisms regulate gene expression, can be induced by environmental factors during early fetal life and can be inherited (Bell *et al.* 2010). Thus physiological plasticity may have physiological consequences that can persist across generations. For example, individuals prenatally exposed to famine have been shown to have differentially methylated regions of genes associated with Type 2 diabetes, such methylation influencing the expression of these genes and risk of Type 2 diabetes into future generations (Heijmans *et al.* 2008).

The combined stresses of poor food resources and prolonged, frequent or recurrent infectious disease episodes in childhood result in the inhibition of physical growth. Once begun, growth inhibition may continue for months or years, depending on the severity of the disease environment, food abundance and quality of the nutritional environment. It may also vary according to seasonal patterns of disease and food availability (Chapter 4). Young children are both the most vulnerable to environmental stresses and the most plastic in their response to them. The process of growth inhibition usually ends by the age of two years in most places where such stresses are present. After this age, a shorter child may follow a lower but parallel physical growth trajectory to that of taller children not exposed to such environmental stresses (Eveleth and Tanner 1990), but store up epigenetic effects that may emerge in adult life and across subsequent generations, according to environmental exposure. In more extreme circumstances, inhibition of physical growth can extend into adolescence, although this too may have long-term consequences. Rolland-Cachera *et al.* (1984) have related early adiposity rebound (a greater gain in weight relative to height between the ages of five and seven years) to subsequent development of overweight. Early adiposity rebound is in turn attributable to the consumption of high-protein, low-fat diets by infants at a time of high energy need (Rolland-Cachera *et al.* 2006).

If environments change, so can physical growth patterns. With improved environmental conditions, children that have undergone growth inhibition can not only resume growth rates that are usual for their age, but can show catch-up growth with some or all of the earlier shortfalls being made good, depending on the quality of the improved environment. The most common pattern of growth plasticity is in relation to seasonality of resources and infection (Ulijaszek and Strickland 1993), where physical growth inhibition takes place when there is poor nutrition and/or a high rate of infection, and growth catch-up takes place when food resources are plentiful and/or in absence of infection. If previously growth-inhibited children experience a positive change in their environmental fortunes, catch-up growth can take place at any time across childhood, including adolescence (Golden 1994), although there may be long-term health implications of this which are as yet poorly understood.

The diseases that can influence immunological and nutritional state are varied in their life histories, infectivity and physiology, and include intestinal parasites, tuberculosis, diarrhoeal infections, upper respiratory tract infections, pneumonia, measles, schistosomiasis, malaria, cholera, leprosy, trypanosomiasis and HIV/AIDS (Table 7.2). Adjustment to the pathogenic environment is primarily immunological, but nutrition feeds into this adjustment. It also has varied cost, with ultimate failure to adjust leading to death. Young child mortality, while an undesirable public health outcome, is the primary mechanism of natural selection of resistance to infectious agents.

Undernutrition–infection interactions in the past

Comparisons of the nutritional states of various present-day hunter-gatherer groups with contemporary traditional agriculturalists suggests that the former are usually better off (Jenike 2001), although their state of primitive affluence (Sahlins 1974) is not an affluence that most members of industrialized societies

Table 7.2 *Nutrition–infection processes associated with growth faltering of children, prior to and at the origins of agriculture, and recently*

	Prior to origins of agriculture	At the origins of agriculture	Recently
Diseases and disease states known to affect nutritional status	Intestinal parasites, tuberculosis, malaria	Diarrhoea, upper respiratory tract infections, pneumonia, measles, schistosomiasis	HIV/ AIDS
Diseases and disease categories known to be influenced by nutritional status	Intestinal parasites, tuberculosis, malaria, cholera	Diarrhoea, upper respiratory tract infections, pneumonia, measles, leprosy, trypanosomiasis	
Nutritional deficiencies that inhibit immune system function		Energy, protein, vitamin A, pyridoxine, calcium, zinc	
Diseases known to inhibit immune system function	Malaria	Measles, leprosy	HIV/ AIDS

The table does not take account of new variants or strains of existing diseases.

would recognize. Hunger is usually never completely absent, while the additional nutritional costs of pregnancy and lactation are not usually met in full; women are at particular risk of undernutrition (Jenike 2001), with attendant chances of low birthweight and death in their offspring. However, in the absence of the most common infectious diseases and reduced transmission of others because of low population density, poor nutritional state results in relatively better health and less mortality than among agriculturalists (Jenike 2001).

The palaeopathological evidence for health status at the origins of agriculture is unsurprisingly complex. Some populations appear to have undergone a profound decline in health, whereas in others the evidence is more equivocal. In the eastern Mediterranean, composite data from 14 archaeological sites suggest that the transition from hunting and gathering to agriculture and animal husbandry was associated with a decline in stature, as estimated from long-bone length of relatively small samples (Angel 1984) (Table 7.3). A problem with this analysis is that variation in patterns across the region and among different groups is not fully considered. Elsewhere, it was less the mode of subsistence (foraging versus cultivation, for example) than the external environment more generally that influenced health. Growth perturbations associated with seasonal resource stress have been identified in archaeological populations of North American foragers that had a restricted

Table 7.3 *Mean stature of eastern Mediterranean populations, from the Palaeolithic to the Neolithic periods*

		Stature			
		Males		Females	
Period	Years before present	n	mean	n	Mean
Palaeolithic	32–11 000	35	177	28	167
Mesolithic	11–9 000	61	173	35	160
Early Neolithic	9–7 000	39	170	31	156
Late Neolithic	7–5 000	6	161	13	154

Adapted from Angel (1984).

resource base for at least part of the year (Yesner 1994; Chapter 4), for example. It is not always correct to infer health and nutritional status from a straightforward assessment of subsistence economy (Elton 2008a). Different populations have different ecologies, however subtle the variation. For example, the shift, across many millennia, from hunting and gathering to cultivation and domestication of animals may have resulted in reduced dietary and nutritional diversity (Eaton and Nelson 1991) in many, but not all, places. Stable isotope analyses (Chapter 3) of archaeological populations from Ontario in North America show a decline in dietary heterogeneity with increasing dependence on maize (Schoeninger 2009). In contrast, research on other populations, again using stable isotope methods, indicate that marine food consumption continued across the Palaeolithic to Neolithic transition in Britain and Denmark (Milner *et al.* 2004), with great dietary diversity persisting into the Neolithic in southern Sweden (Liden *et al.* 2004).

Human disease in history and prehistory is closely tied to changing size and density of human populations and the behaviours that promote disease transmission (Cohen 1989). Among prehistoric hunter-gatherer societies, the most important diseases were likely to have been overwhelmingly sylvatic, because low human population density and regular contact with a range of animal species would have given primacy to diseases crossing species barriers and infecting humans. Virtually all animal-derived human pathogens arose from mammals and birds (Dunn *et al.* 2010). Among the mammals, non-human primates represent the most common points of origin of human infections (Wolfe *et al.* 2007). Nearly all major human pathogens are Old World diseases; this might be expected given the common ancestry of humans and Old World primates. Genetic analyses show HIV1 to have evolved from chimpanzee simian immunodeficiency virus found in *Pan troglodytes* in west central Africa

(Gao *et al.* 1999; Keele *et al.* 2006). This has happened at least twice to humans, in one instance resulting in the AIDS pandemic of human immunodeficiency virus (HIV)-1 group M, and in another, infecting a small number of people in Cameroon with the HIV1 group N (van Heuverswyn *et al.* 2006). Human malaria due to *Plasmodium falciparum* originated in gorillas (Liu *et al.* 2010).

The low population densities and mobile lives of humans prior to the origins of agriculture would have limited the extent of human-to-human transmission of infections, the impermanence of settlements keeping exposure to transmissible diseases, airborne and food-borne parasites and faecal pollution to a minimum (Dounias and Froment 2006). If introduced, acute infections with brief and rapid stages of infection would have run their course in susceptible individuals and then died out (Inhorn and Brown 1990), leaving those having succumbed to them either fully recovered, immunologically impaired, or dead.

Natural selection for resistance to infectious disease was under way well before the advent of agricultural society (Cooke and Hill 2001) and it is unlikely that this took place against specific pathogens as we know them now. Rather, genetic adaptations are likely to have emerged in response to sets of pathogenic agents within local ecologies, and the adaptations to disease we see today are relics of the past. Using HapMap project data, Amato *et al.* (2009) carried out a genome-wide scan for signatures of human population differentiation among around four million single nucleotide polymorphisms (SNPs) and related them to biologically functional pathways and diseases. They identified positive selection to have taken place against disorders that can be grouped as being of haematological, infectious and immunological nature, respectively. Positive selection for the development of a diverse immune system took place in deeper evolutionary time, with humans, chimpanzees, orangutans and macaques sharing common evolutionary immunogenetics (Enard *et al.* 2010). Susceptibility and resistance to some infectious diseases observed now may be the result of a small number of common ancestral alleles (Amato *et al.* 2009), although a complex genetic architecture may underpin susceptibility and resistance to many others.

Natural selection for resistance to diarrhoeal disease has been impossible to demonstrate (Gutacker *et al.* 2000), despite its very likely importance as a cause of morbidity and mortality after the origins of agriculture. A great diversity of pathogens can cause diarrhoea, and it is unlikely that genetic resistance to any single pathogen would have conferred overall selective advantage. Genome-wide association studies have successfully identified many common variants linked to a variety of diseases, although studies of infectious diseases have so far been limited in their discovery of new susceptibility variants, partly due to the small sample sizes used in most studies (Thye *et al.* 2010). Genetic resistance to tuberculosis infection has been identified with alleles of the major histocompatibility complex, natural resistance-associated macrophage protein 1 (*SLC11A1*), vitamin D receptor, interferon gamma and nitric oxide synthase (Moller *et al.* 2010), and there are likely to be many more loci identified once larger genome-wide association studies are undertaken (Thye *et al.* 2010).

Natural selection for resistance to malaria is the most easily demonstrated, perhaps because of its intensity of selection and its relative lack of pathogenic diversity. Malaria mortality due to the *P. falciparum* parasite is by far the greatest among the four species of *Plasmodium* that can infect humans. It continues to be a major cause of mortality in the contemporary world. The transition to agriculture led to a decline in the dietary bioavailability of iron alongside the increase in malarial infection in many populations, as the intestinal absorption of haem-bound iron (found in meat and to a much lesser extent, marine foods) is much more efficient than the absorption of inorganic iron typically found in grain foods. The gene mutations responsible for most genetic haemochromatosis (a disorder that causes the body to absorb an excessive amount of iron from the diet) in Europe (*HFE C282Y* and *H63D*) occur in highest frequencies among northern European populations and are thought to have emerged between 6000 and 600 years ago (Distante *et al.* 2004). This may have been an outcome of positive selection for improved iron absorption and storage in an environment of decreased bio-available iron after the transition to agriculture (Naugler, 2008).

It has been argued that natural selection in response to HIV/AIDS is underway, and is of similar amplitude to natural selection due to malaria (Schliekelman *et al.* 2001; Galvani and Novembre 2005). The genes associated with resistance to HIV/AIDS are related in their phenotypic functions, which are immunological (Galvani and Novembre 2005). However, existing genetic variation in susceptibility to HIV/AIDS is not explained by natural selection against it in the present day (Gonzalez *et al.* 2001). For example, a chemokine receptor (*CCR*) genotype that lowers susceptibility to HIV (the *CCR 5 delta 32* AIDS resistance allele) emerged between around 300 and 1900 years ago (Stephens *et al.* 1998). Other genes associated with susceptibility to HIV/AIDS infection, including macrophage inflammatory protein 1-alpha (*MIP-1 alpha*) and che-mokine ligand 5 (*RANTES*), differ greatly in frequency within and between populations (Gonzalez *et al.* 2001). The relationships between diet and genetic adaptations that confer resistance to tuberculosis and malaria (including heredi-tary haemochromatosis (HH)) are discussed in the following subsections.

Diet and malaria

The malaria parasite *Plasmodium falciparum* initially crossed the species barrier from gorillas to humans (Liu *et al.* 2010), making it a new disease for humans well before the origins of agriculture. Genetic analysis of the *P. falciparum* genome sequence and of the speciation of human malaria vectors (Coluzzi 1999; Coluzzi *et al.* 2002) suggests an expansion of this *Plasmodium* species within the past 6000 years from Africa. *Plasmodium vivax*, on the other hand, is thought to have emerged as a primate malaria in Asia between 46 000 and 82 000 years ago, initially colonizing hominoids via a macaque parasite lineage that later became *P. vivax* (Escalante *et al.* 2005), then colonized humans as they migrated out of Africa. Malaria may have infected humans sporadically prior to the origins of agriculture. With the adoption of agriculture, increased population density, planting seasons associated with rainfall, and subsequent irrigation would have brought humans engaged in agricultural work, the *Plasmodium* parasite and its mosquito vector together on a regular if not continuous basis. In urban centres, water storage would have facilitated the breeding of the mosquito vectors of malaria. These conditions would have permitted runaway malarial infection among humans: the rest is prehistory and history. Intense positive selection of malaria-protective genes among populations exposed to this disease took place (Kwiatkowski 2005), with the emergence of a range of malaria-protective genotypes and phenotypes independently in different parts of the world. These are usually heterotic polymorphisms, where the relative fitness of heterozygotes in conferring resistance to malaria is greater than that of either homozygotes, and include glucose-6 phosphate dehydrogenase (G6PD) deficiency, alpha and beta thalassaemias, haemoglobins S and C, and the Duffy blood group antigen. One allele for G6PD underwent positive selection between 2500 and 10 000 years ago (Tishkoff *et al.* 2001; Saunders *et al.* 2002). In any population exposed to malaria, adaptation has involved alleles of multiple genes, often giving rise to multiple resistant traits (for example, G6PD deficiency and alpha thalassaemia sometimes occurring in the same individual) (Sabeti *et al.* 2006).

Both G6PD deficiency and alpha thalassaemia induce low antioxidant capacity in red blood cells, which is protective against malaria. Regular human consumption in the Mediterranean region of fava beans (otherwise known as broad beans, Figure 7.2) (*Vicia fava*), one of the 'founder crops' of the Fertile Crescent (Chapter 1), from around 9000 years ago may have shaped genetic adaptation to malaria after the origins of agriculture (Katz and Schall 1979). In this region, experience and cultural knowledge of food use, including fava beans and other oxidant-rich foods, would have been important in facilitating the emergence of red blood cell G6PD deficiency, maximizing anti-malarial protection and minimizing haemolysis (rupturing of red blood cells, caused in this case by the malarial parasite). Fava beans contain oxidants such as divicine and isouramil. Erythrocytes (red blood cells) that are deficient in G6PD have limited ability to deal with the increased oxidant stress that occurs when such

Figure 7.2. Fava beans (*Vicia fava*).

substances are consumed (Golenser *et al.* 1983; Clark *et al.* 1989). Other oxidants in a variety of food crops may also promote a similar effect in G6PD deficient erythrocytes (Etkin 1986). When G6PD deficient individuals are oxidant-challenged, they experience haemolysis (Greene 1993). Although such haemolysis results in significant morbidity and mortality in some G6PD deficient individuals, increased vulnerability of G6PD-deficient erythrocytes to oxidant stress confers protection against *P. falciparum* infection (Greene 1993), because red blood cells that are G6PD-deficient are fragile and easily ruptured when invaded by malaria parasites. When the threat of malarial infection is high, the benefits of being G6PD-deficient outweigh the costs.

Fava beans continue to be a major part of Middle Eastern diet, being consumed in stews, salads and as pastes with unleavened bread. Oxidant stress only has a selective advantage when malarial infection is a threat to survival. While public health nutrition now might promote the consumption of antioxidant-rich foods to potentially reduce risk of developing atherosclerosis, some cancers, some inflammatory conditions and aging (Young and Woodside 2001), this is potentially harmful in populations with both high rates of G6PD deficiency and malaria. Given that malaria and G6PD deficiency coincide in many of the same populations in sub-Saharan Africa and south and east

Asia, this is far from trivial. With climate change, conditions for malarial transmission may return to the eastern Mediterranean region by the year 2050 (Rogers and Randolph 2000). This could add large numbers of G6DP-deficient individuals to the list of those that would suffer rather than benefit from increased consumption of antioxidant nutrients such as vitamins A (as the pro-vitamin, carotene), C and E, as well as flavonoids (Young and Woodside 2001).

Nutrition and the origins of human tuberculosis

Human tuberculosis is an ancient disease that is important to public health today, and has an impact on nutritional status. Genetic analysis shows the ancestral cells of *Mycobacterium tuberculosis* to be around three million years old (Gutierrez *et al.* 2005). Tuberculosis infection has been identified in one fossil specimen of *Homo erectus* in Turkey (Kappelman *et al.* 2008), indicating that other extinct hominins may also have been exposed to it in one form or another. Genetic studies of the evolution of *M. tuberculosis* suggest that it emerged recently in human prehistory but before the advent of agriculture, and did not cross the species barrier from domesticated cattle (Armelagos and Harper 2005). The earliest modern human tuberculosis palaeopathologies (based on bone assemblages) are for an eastern Mediterranean Neolithic group around 9000 years ago (Hershkovitz *et al.* 2008). There is a contradiction between the estimated origins of the disease prior to the origins of agriculture and its manifestation in human remains after agriculture emerged. It is possible, however, that members of the clonal group that hominins were exposed to may have been less infective and less likely to present as pathology in skeletal tissue, as skeletal lesions appear only with prolonged chronic tuberculosis infection. Among humans, *M. tuberculosis* may have led to far less severe infections prior to the origins of agriculture than after it if undernutrition (known to exacerbate infection) was less prevalent or even absent.

The transition to agriculture saw increased population size and density (Kuijt 2008), and infectious diseases (tuberculosis among them) are a penalty for high-density urban living, in the absence of good public health measures (Dye and Williams 2010). As an illustration of changing population density, Figure 7.3 shows house types across the transition to agriculture in the Near East (adapted from Kuijt 2008), reflecting the move from small-scale settlement and single-room dwellings, to urban form and multi-roomed, multi-storeyed housing. Population densities are estimated to have risen from 10 people per hectare 10 000 years ago to 90 per hectare by 9000 years ago (Kuijt 2008). Regardless of how many people lived in each room of each type

A. 11 700 to 10 500 years before present

B. 10 500 to 9500 years before present

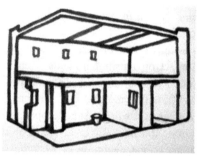

C. 9500 to 8500 years before present

Figure 7.3. House types across the transition to agriculture in the Near East (adapted from Kuijt 2008).

of house, the largest of these would have brought the inhabitants of the equivalent of three or more houses of the earliest period into very close daily proximity, with increased likelihood of transmission of infection.

Of individuals that are newly infected with *M. tuberculosis*, only around one-tenth eventually develop active disease, half of them during the first two years after initial infection (Schmidt 2008). The remaining nine-tenths carry latent infection that is never manifested as active tuberculosis. Since latent tuberculosis often becomes active with the immunological impairment associated with HIV/AIDS, such latency may be a product of immunological inhibition of *M. tuberculosis* by the host (Schmidt 2008). The value of latency may be one of increased survivorship for both the host and the pathogen. Host survivorship is enhanced by long-term inhibition of infection: even if fertility rates are directly influenced, being alive and productive enhances the potential reproductive success of existing offspring. For the pathogen, latency allows it to avoid extinction among small and isolated populations (Corbett *et al.* 2003), such as those prior to the origins of agriculture. The emergence of agriculture may have changed a set of ecological relationships that increased the severity of tuberculosis infection, the most important of which would have been increased nutritional stress. Undernutrition is a major risk factor for

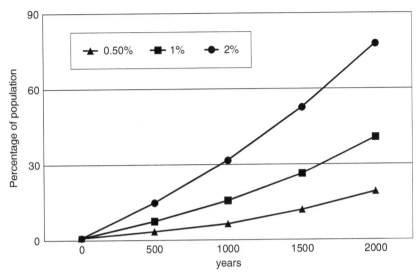

Figure 7.4. The proportion of a population to develop active tuberculosis across the thousand years since the origins of agriculture, if susceptibility to developing the active and infectious form of the disease, due to increased undernutrition, increases by half of one per cent, one per cent and two per cent, respectively.

progression to tuberculosis because of its profound effect on cellular immune function, the key immunological defence against it. In contemporary populations with high rates of latent tuberculosis infection, co-existent malnutrition increases the rate of acquisition of infection and the risk of infection progressing to clinical disease and pathology (Schmidt 2008).

Deficiencies of macro- and micronutrients due to periodic food insecurity and reduced dietary diversity could have impaired immunological function to an extent that latent *M. tuberculosis* was more likely to have become active (Flynn and Chan 2001). Once active, the transmission of *M. tuberculosis* in a population could have been rapid. We explore this possibility by modelling the proportion of a population that needs to overcome latency for active tuberculosis to emerge in human populations (Figure 7.4). Based on a hypothetical population, we estimate how the proportion of active tuberculosis (set at a nominal stable level of one per cent at the origins of agriculture) changes across one thousand years after the origins of agriculture. It is impossible to know the extent of tuberculosis, either latent or active, at the origins of agriculture. However, it is estimated that latent tuberculosis infected around one-third of the world's population toward the end of the twentieth century (Dye *et al.* 1999). This is an extremely high level, reflecting its persistence and spread across the nineteenth and twentieth centuries.

For the purpose of seeing how reduced latency might have facilitated the rapid spread of tuberculosis, the initial level of latency is set at a low level of 11%, one-third of current levels. For active tuberculosis to present itself, both host susceptibility and bacterial infectivity need to be high (de Viedma *et al.* 2005). In the model developed here, variation in infectivity among *M. tuberculosis* strains is held constant, while host susceptibility is reflected in conversion from latent to active tuberculosis by 0.5, 1, and 2% per generation (set at 25 years) of the 11% latent tuberculosis sub-population. It is assumed that the increased conversion from latent to active tuberculosis is due to decline in immunological status caused by impaired nutritional status. Thus if nothing else changed, this model shows the maximum increase in conversion from latent to active tuberculosis across this period.

With increased conversion from latent to active tuberculosis of just 1% per generation, the proportion of active tuberculosis in the general population would have increased from the very modest but nominal 1% (set in the model for the origins of agriculture), to 15% and 40%, 1000 and 2000 years later (Figure 7.4). If the conversion from latent to active tuberculosis were 2%, then 31% and 78% of the general population would have developed active tuberculosis 1000 and 2000 years later, respectively. The proportion of people with latent tuberculosis would have also increased exponentially, such that entire populations could have become infected with either active or latent tuberculosis by around 1500, 700 and 350 years after the origins of agriculture, at conversion rates in excess of stable transmission of 0.5, 1 and 2% respectively. While holding constant various factors that vary in reality, this model shows how quickly the active form of tuberculosis could have become fixed in a population, with just modest increases in individual susceptibility due to declines in nutritional status and increases in population density.

More realistically, other factors would have come into play to hold down the proportion of people with active tuberculosis. One of these would have been increased mortality due to other infections, since tuberculosis itself would have challenged immunocompetence and nutritional state. Another would have been the emergence of genetic resistance to tuberculosis. Resistance to *M. tuberculosis* has been described for several genes and genetic systems (Bellamy 2003), most convincingly for four variants of the gene, *SLC11A1*, that codes for natural resistance-associated macrophage protein 1 (Bellamy *et al.* 1998). What is the likelihood that these may have emerged since the origins of agriculture? One way of examining this is to apply reproductive fitness values from demographic data for populations experiencing high tuberculosis mortality. It is unlikely that this will ever be known for populations at the origins of agriculture, but such data exist for Sweden for the period 1891 to 1900, during the European tuberculosis epidemic (Lipsitch and Sousa 2002).

Survivors of pulmonary tuberculosis in Sweden at that time had between 7% and 15% higher reproductive fitness per generation relative to non-survivors. If the conditions demonstrated for Sweden in the late nineteenth century by Lipsitch and Sousa (2002) were present in prehistory, positive selection for between one and two resistance alleles across a period of 1000 years could have taken place, and for double those estimates across a 2000 year period. In the presence of niche construction at the origins of agriculture, these processes may thus have been very rapid.

Haemochromatosis, iron and infection

Natural selection for nutritionally advantageous traits may have taken place in many ways. With respect to nutrition, the transition to agriculture led to a decline in the dietary bioavailability of iron in many agricultural populations (apart from coastline dwellers which continued their consumption of marine foods (Milner *et al.* 2004)) favouring selection for genes that favour iron storage. Of the 10–20 mg of iron consumed each day in many diets, about one-tenth is absorbed, offsetting the 1–2 mg of iron lost daily from sweat, urine, hair and epithelial cell death (mostly skin and intestinal lining). Vitamin C improves iron absorption by helping convert less absorbable ferric iron to the more easily absorbed ferrous iron. A decline in the diversity of plant foods consumed among populations undergoing the transition to agriculture may have led to a decline in vitamin C intake, thus impeding iron absorption.

In contemporary industrialized societies, the buildup of stored iron as haemosiderin in major organs, joints and glands can lead to tissue damage among those with haemochromatosis (HH), a very common autosomal recessive condition of iron overload (Fleming and Sly 2002). The genetic architecture of HH is likely to be more complex than presently understood, although it is known that the human haemochromatosis protein (HFE) facilitating iron absorption and metabolism is coded by the *HFE* gene. The *HH* mutation of this gene is believed to have first appeared in a central European Celtic population between 2000 and 4000 years ago (Distante *et al.* 2004; Toomajian *et al.* 2003). Individuals who are heterozygous for the recessive mutation *C282Y* on the *HFE* gene show only mild iron accumulation (Bulaj *et al.* 2000), while the 0.3%–0.8% who are homozygous for this mutation (Niederau *et al.* 1994) show high levels of iron storage and tissue damage, and are at high risk of dying if they remain untreated. The *C282Y* mutation explains the majority of all HH cases in European populations (Tomatsu *et al.* 2003), while the *H63D* recessive mutation of the same gene causes a tiny minority of HH, although a compound heterozygote of both recessive mutations *H63D* and *C282Y* is the second most common genetic cause of HH (Walsh *et al.* 2006). The high prevalence of HH among European populations may be adaptive for maximizing iron absorption and storage from diets of low iron bioavailability after the transition to agriculture (Niederau *et al.* 1994). In populations consuming diets that are rich in cereal and dairy foods, even those homozygous for the *C282Y* mutation rarely show iron overload.

Developmental plasticity, nutrition and infection

The inhibition of growth is one way a child can adjust biologically to an unfavourable nutritional and infectious disease environment. However, inhibited growth is usually associated with high rates of morbidity, reduced energy for exploratory behaviour, and compromised intellectual development (Waterlow 1988). It is therefore undesirable from a public health perspective. Viewed intergenerationally, mothers who are small because of poor growth in their own childhood produce small babies (Horta *et al.* 2009; Kramer 1987) that have lower survivorship chances (Hviid and Melbye 2007), another undesirable public health outcome. Should they survive and go on to experience improved circumstances (for example, if their society undergoes nutrition transition (Chapter 9)), their risk of developing many chronic diseases in later life is raised (Barker 1999; Rolland-Cachera *et al.* 2006; Kuzawa and Quinn 2009).

Table 7.2 gives specific nutritional and infective factors associated with growth faltering of children, prior to and at the origins of agriculture, as well as more recently. Although many new variants and strains of existing diseases have emerged in the past 30 years or so (Krause 1998; Morens *et al.* 2004), these are not incorporated, since their relationship with nutrition is likely to be similar to those of older variants. Infections that influence nutritional status and physical growth are either acute and invasive, provoking a systemic response (such as malaria, dysentery, pneumonia and measles), or chronic, affecting the host over a sustained period (including gut helminth infections and tuberculosis). Infections can inhibit physical growth by negatively affecting nutritional status, through decreased food intake, impaired nutrient absorption, direct nutrient losses, increased metabolic requirements, catabolic losses of nutrients, and impaired transport of nutrients to specific tissues. In addition, induction of the acute phase response to infection can contribute to growth faltering because pro-inflammatory cytokines directly inhibit the bone remodelling that is needed for long bones to grow and maintain their integrity (Stephensen 1999). Humans have evolved to withstand energy crises by decreasing their body size, and they are likely to use epigenetic mechanisms that modify the transition into childhood as adaptations to energy deficiency, resulting in short stature (Hochberg and Albertsson-Wikland 2008). Immune responses to infection that influence bodily energy economy through increased metabolic requirements or catabolic loss of macronutrients are likely to use the genetic and epigenetic architecture that evolved prior to the onset of agriculture.

Among the diseases and disease categories associated with either physical growth faltering or poor weight gain are diarrhoea (Moore *et al.* 2001), respiratory tract infections (Liu *et al.* 1999) and malaria (Villamore *et al.* 2002; Friedman *et al.* 2003). Diseases and disease categories that are directly influenced by nutritional status include intestinal parasites, tuberculosis, diarrhoea, cholera, leprosy, upper respiratory tract infections, pneumonia, measles, malaria and trypanosomiasis. Measles, HIV/AIDS, leprosy and malaria each contribute to the nutrition–infection interaction by inhibiting immune system function and increasing susceptibility to other infections. Of the infections shown in Table 7.2, intestinal parasites, malaria, tuberculosis and cholera are likely to have been important prior to the origins of agriculture (Wolfe *et al.* 2007), while crowd epidemic diseases, including measles, diarrhoea, upper respiratory tract infections and pneumonia, are likely to have emerged with changing population size and density after the origins of agriculture (Wolfe *et al.* 2007). HIV/AIDS is a recent contributor to this set of relations. HIV infection delays the onset of puberty (Buchacz *et al.* 2003), while the immunosuppression associated with AIDS leads to increased susceptibility to opportunistic infections such as tuberculosis and diarrhoea (Quinn *et al.* 1986).

The relationships between undernutrition, immunological status and disease are continually evolving, with new strains and variants of agents with the potential to infect humans constantly emerging. For example, a number of diseases that are under surveillance as potential causes of future epidemics and other public health emergencies by the Global Alert and Response System (World Health Organization 2011b) can change relationships among nutritional states and infectious diseases in local ecologies. These diseases include anthrax, influenza, Crimean–Congo, Marburg and dengue haemorrhagic fevers, hepatitis of differing forms, Lassa, Rift Valley and yellow fevers, and severe acute respiratory syndrome (SARS).

Undernutrition, infection and child survivorship

Previous sections have used understandings of present-day undernutrition–infection interactions to examine such relationships in the past. Where natural selection has been considered, this has focused broadly on childhood, and on genetic resistance to infection. In this section, the selective pressures of

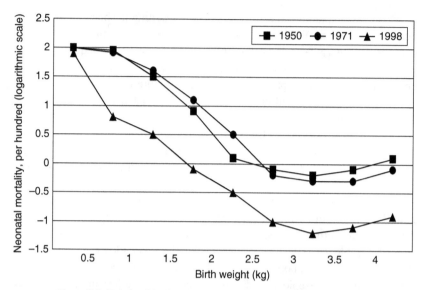

Figure 7.5. Relationships between birth weight and neonatal mortality in the United States, 1950 to 1998 (Lubchenco *et al.* 1972; Wilcox 2001).

undernutrition and infection are examined in relation to differential mortality at three stages of life history: pregnancy, infancy, and childhood after weaning.

The most widely used measures of successful pregnancy are mortality and birth weight. Across societies, infant mortality varies in a J-shaped manner with birth weight, although the exact relationship differs with place and time. Figure 7.5 illustrates the relationship between neonatal mortality and birth weight for the United States population between 1950 and 1998, showing it to be robust even with great mortality declines. However, despite its widespread use, birth weight is not a causal pathway to mortality, but reflects susceptibility to perinatal complications associated with it (Wilcoxon and Russell 1983). Low birth weight may not have a direct relationship with neonatal mortality, but the effects of low birth weight may persist into infancy, and are associated with slow growth, small body size and increased mortality. Figure 7.6 shows relationships between low weight for age and prospective mortality of infants from six traditional societies.

Genetics, maternal body size and nutrition are major components of infant size at birth (Freathy *et al.* 2007; Kramer and Victora 2001; Ladipo 2000). The genetic contribution to birth weight is common to most people, with one of the lead genetic loci associated with it also being associated with Type 2 diabetes in adulthood (Freathy *et al.* 2007). Giving undernourished pregnant women dietary energy and protein supplements can increase birth weight and reduce neonatal mortality slightly, if maternal undernutrition is severe

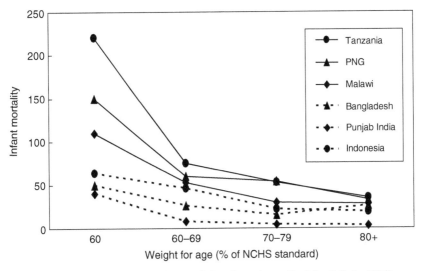

Figure 7.6. Relationships between infant size and mortality (after Pelletier 1994).

(Ceesay *et al.* 1997). Supplementation with a combination of iron, folic acid and multiple micronutrients has been shown to reduce neonatal mortality, attributed to greater gestation length, among poor Chinese women, but not to increase birth weight (Zeng *et al.* 2008). Infectious disease can work in synergy with maternal energy and iron undernutrition on neonatal health through gestation length: malaria increases the risk of preterm delivery and stillbirth through fever and contribution to severe anaemia rather than through parasitaemia per se (Poespoprodjo *et al.* 2008).

Women in traditional societies prior to the availability of public health and primary health care did not usually increase their dietary intakes to meet the energetic needs of pregnancy or lactation (Ulijaszek and Strickland 1993), and it seems unlikely that women in past populations would have done so. Adaptations to low dietary energy availability relative to the energy needs of pregnancy and lactation among women in traditional societies include decreased physical activity, reduced quantity and quality of breast milk after three months of lactation, increased infant mortality with increasing parity, and decreased fertility through maternal depletion (Ulijaszek and Strickland 1993). The origins of agriculture saw reduced diet quality for many populations (Chapter 6); reduced meat consumption (Ulijaszek 1991) alone would have increased the possibility of iron deficiency for women. This could have increased the possibility of unsuccessful pregnancies, as would the increased exposure to malaria in some populations, which would have depleted them of iron.

Breastfeeding has a number of traits that favour infant growth and survivorship, including balanced nutrition and immunological protection. Exclusive breastfeeding can sustain infant health and growth for around the first six months of life (Butte *et al.* 2002), and women in most traditional societies supplement breastfeeding around the age when it declines in adequacy. Breastfeeding, when it continues beyond six months, provides proportionately less dietary energy and other nutrients with increasing age, but plays an important role in inhibiting ovulation and the likelihood of the mother conceiving another child (Ellison 2001).

After the origins of agriculture, the potential for mortality increased, with changes in nutritional and infectious disease ecologies exposing mothers and their children to nutritional stress, pathogenic environments and interactions between the two. It is likely that breastfeeding duration and age at weaning altered across the transition to agriculture, to minimize negative health and mortality outcomes. How it may have changed is far from straightforward, however. On the one hand, in an increasingly pathogenic environment the imperative to continue exclusive breastfeeding would have been high to protect the child from infection caused by foods introduced at weaning and maintain immunological protection. On the other hand, modern studies of traditional agrarian populations indicate that the physical labour of women (in the fields as well as the home) is vital to subsistence. This is also likely to have been the case in ancient agrarian economies, which may have provided the impetus to wean or at least supplement infants earlier, although cross-cultural studies of maternal behaviour highlight that care for young children (under one year of age) has priority over most other activities in many societies (Kramer 2009). In some cases, alloparenting (parenting by people other than parents) may have helped the earliest agriculturalists to balance essential maternal investment with the demands of labour within and outside the home (Kramer 2009). However, such strategies are flexible and highly variable from population to population as well as over time (Valeggia 2009).

Earlier cessation of breastfeeding may have led to decreased interbirth intervals, which is consistent with the population increases and improved reproductive fitness observed with the transition to agriculture (Armelagos *et al.* 1991; Lambert 2009). However, the scenarios presented here cannot be easily verified. Childcare and offspring investment patterns are not preserved in the archaeological record, other than through gross demographic estimates based on burials. In addition, studies of modern populations show considerable inter- and even intra-population variation, indicating that different ancient societies may have altered childcare in a variety of ways according to environmental, economic and social circumstances.

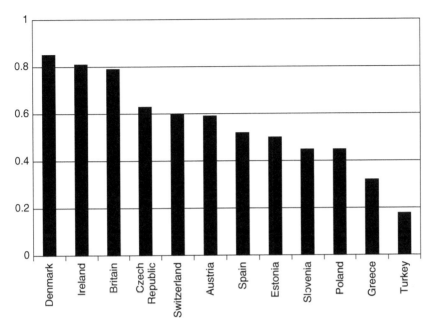

Figure 7.7. Frequency distribution of the lactase persistence allele *LCT*P* in some European populations (adapted from Swallow 2003).

Weaning and dietary supplementation would have been a new vehicle for infection by the newly emergent human gastrointestinal pathogens associated with higher-density living. The ability to digest lactose in milk by the enzyme lactase is high in all human infants, but declines rapidly after weaning in most populations, albeit remaining high throughout life for a smaller number of populations. For many at the origins of agriculture and animal husbandry, continued consumption of milk beyond infancy would have led to malabsorption, diarrhoea, and possibly death. For others, genetically inherited lactase persistence would have been selected for. The lactase persistence allele *LCT*P* arose specifically in humans (and not among ancestral primates) and is most common among populations that are either Northern European or of Northern European origin (Swallow 2003) (Figure 7.7). The mini-chromosome maintenance protein 6 gene (*MCM6*) is upstream of the *LCT* gene and has two regions that regulate its expression. The *C-14010* allele of *MCM6* was positively selected for around 7000 years ago in Africa, around the time that pastoralism was adopted and milk consumption became a principal part of the diet (Tishkoff *et al.* 2006), permitting lactose tolerance beyond infancy among those that had this gene variant.

In the Mediterranean region, the use of wheat, rye and oats as weaning foods at the origins of agriculture could have contributed to higher mortality due to

Table 7.4 *Frequency of the DQ2.5cis isoform of the DR3-DQ2 human leucocyte antigen multigene haplotype associated with highest risk for coeliac disease, in European and North African populations*

Frequency (%)	North Africa	Europe	Middle East
15–25	Suoss (Morocco)(1)	Irish (5)	
10–15	Berber (Morocco)(2) Tunis (Tunisia)(3) Algerian (4)	Spanish (6) Welsh (7) Dutch (8) Swiss (9) Polish (10)	
0–10		French (11) Greek (12) Bulgarian (13) Macedonian (14) Croatian (15)	Arab Israeli (16) Turkish (17) Iranian (18) Non-Ashkenazi Jewish (19)

References: (1) Izaabel *et al.* 1998; (2) Piancatelli *et al.* 2004; (3) Hajjej *et al.* 2006; (4) Arnaiz-Villena *et al.* 1995; (5) Williams *et al.* 2004; (6) Sanchez-Velasco *et al.* 2003; (7) Darke *et al.* 1998; (8) Schipper *et al.* 1996; (9) Grundschober *et al.* 1994; (10) Krokowski *et al.* 1998; (11) Pedron *et al.* 2005; (12) Papassavas *et al.* 2000; (13) Ivanova *et al.* 2002; (14) Hristova-Dimceva *et al.* 2000; (15) Grubić *et al.* 2000; (16) Amar *et al.* 1999; (17) Arnaiz-Villena *et al.* 2001; (18) Farjadian *et al.* 2006; (19) Martinez-Laso *et al.* 1996.

malabsorption of cereals, associated diarrhoea and increased susceptibility to intestinal infections. Early farmers selected grains in order to improve size, ease of harvest and later to increase the 'glueyness' of a dough made from the crushed grain, for bread-making. Such selection was carried out unknowingly by growing and using grains with higher content of the structural protein gluten, which makes dough 'gluey'. But selecting grain crops for their higher gluten content would have increased the potential for malabsorption among susceptible individuals, and perhaps acted as a selection pressure. Evidence that consumption of wheat and other cereals at the origins of agriculture shaped human population genetics comes from HLA haplotype variation associated with risk of coeliac disease among European, Middle Eastern and North African groups. While there are three haplotypes of DR3 HLA associated with coeliac disease (DQ2.2, 2.5 and 8) the DQ2.5cis isoform is the most widely mapped of these among populations, and frequencies of this are shown in Table 7.4. Human populations with little exposure to these agricultural staples, or who engaged their use much more recently (as for example in the British Isles around 6000 years ago, compared with around 10 000 years ago in the eastern Mediterranean region) show greater rates of gluten intolerance, largely because of the lower intensity of natural selection by dietary gluten on human populations in the past (Simopoulos 2004), although overall rates are low in the majority of populations (Elton 2008a).

Implications for the contemporary world

The coevolution of nutrition and infection is an important issue in the contemporary world given the complexity and strength of the relationships of these factors with immunological status, co-morbidity and mortality at different life stages, including pregnancy, infancy and early childhood. These relationships increased in complexity with the origins of agriculture, and continue to do so with each infectious disease to emerge that is new in type or variant. In recent times, the world has begun to face new challenges with emergent diseases such as HIV/AIDS, and resurgence, in new drug-resistant forms and variants, of known diseases and disease categories such as diarrhoea, malaria and tuberculosis, and with the constant threat of zoonoses (Krause 1998). This comes at a time when global levels of chronic disease mortality continue to rise, including in the developing world.

An evolutionary approach to nutrition–infection interactions shows that emerging diseases are nothing new, and predicts that future challenges might take novel forms. Two recent examples of pathogens that have taken advantage of human provisioning behaviour are HIV/AIDS and variant Creutzfeld–Jakob disease (vCJD). The AIDS pandemic emerged from the cross into humans of Simian Immunodeficiency Viruses (SIVcpzPtt) from chimpanzees in West Central Africa (van Heuverswyn *et al.* 2006). Direct evidence that humans can be cross-infected by primate diseases comes from study of occupational exposure to non-human primates and human contraction of Simian Foamy Virus, which infects the majority of captive primates but does not result in disease (Jones-Engel *et al.* 2008). Cross-infection of humans by chimpanzee SIV is most likely to have taken place through the killing of monkeys and trading of monkey (bush) meat for human consumption (van Heuverswyn and Peeters 2007). In this trade, a now covertly culturally prestige food brings hunters and animals into contact with each other, and the handling of blooded meat allows infection of humans. In past populations, the crossing of such a lethal infection might have resulted in the mortality of only small groups. The large sizes, densities and mobilities of human populations since the 1970s have made local infections global, even though (in the case of SIV and HIV) the bushmeat trade may be just the first step and first route of transmission.

The second example, that of variant Creutzfeld–Jakob disease, emerged as a new variant of an established form of dementia in the United Kingdom (UK) in the late 1980s, thought to be caused by prions, non-living, infectious proteins which cause nervous tissue damage and cell death (Dobson 2001). The cause of this emergence is complex, but easily understood. Meat producers in the UK were under pressure to reduce their costs and keep their sale prices low. One response was to increase the economic efficiency of animal feeding practices. Turning waste sheep tissue into cattle feed was an easy industrial synergy which inadvertently allowed a benign prion infection of sheep to cross the species barrier between sheep and cattle, causing bovine spongiform encephalopathy (so-called 'mad cow disease'). While this was a serious enough problem for meat producers, a second species barrier was crossed when humans were infected from the consumption of beef tissue that entered the human food chain, usually in lower-quality meat products that contained significant amounts of nerve tissue. The public health problem this created was vCJD infection among a small number of consumers, who went on to develop early dementia and usually die (Weissmann and Aguzzi 1997).

Discussion

This chapter has shown that diseases such as malaria and tuberculosis were once novel and emergent infections for human populations. Both may have shifted from being of comparatively low prevalence in humans (and possibly hominins) to becoming much more prevalent as subsistence and nutritional ecologies changed at the origins of agriculture. Evolutionary perspectives help us recognize that we live as part of a broader ecology, where we compete with other species, usually defeat and consume them, but are also dominated by them. The environmental niches we construct also allow faster rates of natural selection. In the second half of the twentieth century and into the twenty-first, the sense that food security could be assured among the industrialized nations has lasted less than 50 years; the idea that infectious disease could be largely eradicated in these nations lasted less than 30 years, with the emergence of new zoonoses, most importantly HIV1. An evolutionary perspective shows how tenuous is the human hold over any ecological superiority they might have.

Evolutionary perspectives teach us to think of food, provisioning and nutritional ecology more broadly, in relation to existing, novel and resurgent infectious agents. Human activity changes ecological contexts in which the transmission of infectious agents between species can take place (Chapman *et al.* 2005). Among the most powerful agent of change for the amelioration of infectious disease has been the public health movement. This had its origins in France in the early nineteenth century, when contagious diseases were part of much broader public health concerns, which included maternal and child health, adulteration of foodstuffs, water supply and sewage disposal, hygiene, housing, and social class (Terris 1987). Patterns of health change have been outcomes of powerful economic and political forces across the nineteenth through twenty-first centuries, but they are also contingent upon cultural and ecological processes in history and prehistory. For example, links can be made between food insecurity due to economic inequality and lack of entitlement associated with both the great famine of Ireland (1845–1850) (Fraser 2003), and food supply crises in Zimbabwe in the late twentieth century (Chattopadhyay 2000).

At the time of writing, political hegemony in Zimbabwe was involved in resurgent infection, including widespread outbreaks of cholera between 2008 and 2011, which infected over 100 000 people and resulted in over 4000 deaths. Good food security and health are both outcomes and markers of good governance: politically stable countries are more likely to do better on both counts than unstable ones. Social and economic inequalities (Chapter 8) also structure relationships between nutritional ecology and infection. Farmer (2004) has described the extensive ways in which poverty and social inequality are framed as differential risks for infection with HIV and tuberculosis in developing countries, while Walls and Shingadia (2004) have identified over-crowding, poverty and the HIV epidemic as significant contributors to the resurgence of tuberculosis globally. More generally, Bates and colleagues (2004) have identified poverty, operating at individual, household and community levels, as a key factor in increasing vulnerability to malaria, tuberculosis and HIV infection. Poverty also underpins food insecurity and the nutrition and infection interactions that impact on child growth and survivorship.

The world is more connected than ever before, and human population movement takes place at unprecedented rates. Despite this, humans carry their evolutionary baggage with them wherever they go, in the form of differential genetic resistance to past infections, and dietary and nutritional adaptations. Some evolutionary adaptations influence susceptibility to modern diseases. For example, the CCR5 gene deletion mutation is found in greater proportion in European populations than in African, east Asian or Native American ones, influencing the susceptibility to, and progression of, HIV infection (Sabeti *et al.* 2005), while HIV infection increases susceptibility to tuberculosis among those possessing some HLA haplotypes but not others (Louie *et al.* 2004). Owing to such genetic diversity and its implications for disease susceptibility (understanding of which is still unfolding), public health solutions to nutrition–infection interactions will be of necessity more complex than presently conceived. Until biological variation affecting disease susceptibility and nutritional adaptation can be incorporated into public health nutrition practice, macro-level solutions that result in general environmental improvement are the best political–economic interventions to health problems caused by nutrition–infection interactions. These include malarial vector control, diarrhoeal disease management, and improvement in food security through good food and nutrition policies and reductions in economic inequality (Chapter 8).

8   Inequality and nutritional health

Global inequality in nutritional health in the present day is clear to see, with nearly 800 million people undernourished and around 300 million people obese (Food and Agriculture Organization 2000; World Health Organization 2003). This represents around 13% and 5% of the world's population suffering the extremes of nutritional state. Common sense suggests that greater equality in food availability, or entitlement (Sen 1981), would eradicate over half of the world's nutritional health problems by reducing rates of both undernutrition and obesity. Regrettably, in the contemporary world, food supply, distribution and cost are influenced by global political and economic factors, which have seen increased rather than reduced economic inequality in most countries (Figure 8.1). Patterns of food distribution and consumption have a strong influence on nutritional health and reflect the history of any nation, as well as its social, economic and political structure. Variations in food consumption patterns and nutritional health across nations thus reflect differences in history, ideology and power relationships.

Figure 8.2 shows dietary energy consumption per person in industrialized and developing nations between 1964 and 2003. The daily energy intakes of people in both have risen by around 500 kcal across this period. Highest energy intakes are, and have been, in North America and Europe, and the lowest in south Asia and sub-Saharan Africa (Figure 8.3). Although per capita energy intakes have risen in all regions since the 1960s, the absolute gap between the highest and lowest consumers has not changed, although many nations of east Asia have seen disproportionate increases in intake. The patterns shown in Figures 8.2 and 8.3 are largely reflected in increased inequality across nations, with the economies of wealthier nations generally growing faster than poorer ones, as reflected in a world GINI index (a measure of inequality that ranges from zero to a hundred, and where the former value would be attained in an economically equal world) which has risen from 62.5 in 1988 to 65.5 in 2002 (Milanovic 2005). Similarly, inequality

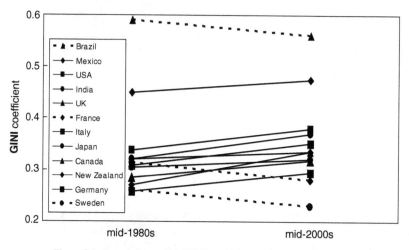

Figure 8.1. Income inequality (GINI coefficients) from the mid-1980s to the mid-2000s in industrialized and economically emerging nations (Organization for Economic Cooperation and Development 2008).

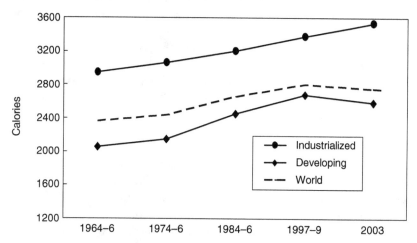

Figure 8.2. Per capita food consumption according to level of economic development, nations merged (data from World Health Organization 2003; Food and Agriculture Organization 2011).

within nations is also large and increasing, with the GINI coefficient (ranging in this case between zero and one) of most nations of the Organization of Economic Cooperation and Development (2008) having increased since the mid-1980s (Figure 8.3). With the exception of the poorest nations (including Bolivia, Botswana, Central African Republic, Sierra Leone, Lesotho and

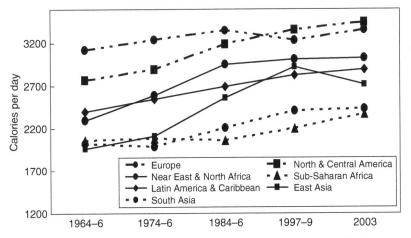

Figure 8.3. Per capita food consumption by global region (data from World Health Organization 2003; Food and Agriculture Organization 2011).

Namibia), within-nation inequality is lower than global inequality when national boundaries are removed from analysis (Milanovic 2005). Such economic inequality is reflected in differences in nutritional health within and between nations (James *et al.* 1997; van de Poel *et al.* 2008). At the household level, inequalities in child malnutrition are greatly influenced by policies made at national and provincial levels (Frongillo *et al.* 1997).

The purpose of this chapter is not to show how social and economic inequalities in nutritional health can be eradicated. This is far too complex a problem to resolve on paper, despite the starkness of the global, regional and national differences in nutritional health that exist. Rather, we try to improve understanding of the problem by adding anthropological and evolutionary ecological perspectives to the interpretations of the emergence of social inequality in humans, and how such differences may structure patterns of nutritional health.

In the present day, socioeconomic factors are major determinants of health and mortality (Townsend and Davidson 1982), and various epidemiological studies have been used to reveal relationships between socioeconomic inequality and health outcomes (Wilkinson 1996; Pickett *et al.* 2005). However, the ways in which measures of both social and economic status are used and interpreted by epidemiologists vary widely (Pearce and Smith 2003) and the mechanisms by which inequality in social and economic status produce inequalities in health are incompletely known (Nguyen and Peschard 2003). While inequality can help manifest ill-health through material means (Kawachi and Kennedy 2002; Townsend and Davidson 1982), non-material inequality can influence health (Marmot 1986). In the Whitehall II cohort study, life expectancy among British civil servants increased with their rank, and could not be accounted for by cultural or class differences in lifestyle (Nguyen and Peschard 2003). Social inequality has been shown to contribute to illness independently of income level (Marmot 2004, 2005; Isaacs *et al.* 2004), indicating that hierarchy has effects that can act across large populations regardless of income level, and not just within discrete groups (Donohoe 2003).

Two forces that oppose social hierarchy in present day complex socially-stratified societies are social cohesion and social capital. Social capital was hypothesized by Hanifan (1916) and Jacobs (1961) as social cohesion through social intercourse of tight-knit groups. Bourdieu (1984) saw social capital as one of three types of symbolic capital, the other two types being economic and cultural. The entry of social capital into health discourse came with observations that individuals placed within a higher density of social networks are more likely to be healthier and live longer than those with fewer social ties (Kawachi *et al.* 1997; Lomas 1998).

With respect to nutritional health, the impacts of poverty and low socio-economic status on undernutrition in both the developing and developed world are well known (Blakely *et al.* 2005; Martorell *et al.* 1988). The same is true for the relationships between low socioeconomic status and obesity in the industrialized world (Sobal and Stunkard 1989; McLaren 2007) and high socioeconomic status and obesity in the economically emerging nations (McLaren 2007). Social and economic inequalities are likely to have conditioned nutritional health from the origins of agriculture to the present day. We argue that social and nutritional inequalities are linked by the attribution of symbolic value to goods and food. Sedentism allowed humans to live in a more material world than ever before. However, this allowed the ascription of value to goods beyond their immediate functional value, and the use of symbolically valued goods to mark social status. Examples of such goods include gold (whose functional value as a metal is limited by its extreme softness), and in the contemporary world designer-labelled clothes, whose functional value is little or no different from that of cheap mass-produced clothes. We argue that food is the most primary of symbolic goods because it is used to mark status in all societies, and could have been used in this way by pre-sedentary populations in the absence of other types of material goods. For example, hunter-gatherer societies place high material and symbolic value on meat, often conferring status on good hunters (Fiddes 1991) and this may have been as true among early hunter-gatherers as contemporary ones. The symbolic coding of food has been elaborated to a high degree across human prehistory and history, a process that continued in the twentieth century at great pace with the development of global food cultures and the diversity of supermarkets and restaurants that deliver them. Social class differences in food preferences and consumption are used to define class differences, and play out in differences in nutritional health. We argue that the strongly socially embedded nature of food as symbol is something that is not lost on food manufacturers, and is essential for public health nutrition to understand, as part of the broader understanding of socioeconomic differences in nutritional health.

Social inequality in evolutionary perspective

Understanding group organization is useful for the understanding of inequalities in diet and nutritional health. Humans can be viewed as being either extremely socially unequal, or equal, depending on the evidence chosen. If your vote is for inequality, look to great ape societies, which are extremely hierarchical, as are many primate societies (Smuts *et al.* 1987). Such hierarchy is usually explained by intense competition for resources (Chapter 2). If your vote is for equality, look to hunter-gatherer societies, which are usually egalitarian and classless and who do not compete with each other for the resources they use (Ingold *et al.* 1997). In his social brain hypothesis, Dunbar (1998) has tried to reconcile these two extremes of sociality in a human evolutionary framework. He argues that the ecological dominance achieved by *Homo erectus* and subsequently *Homo sapiens* during the Pleistocene (1.8 million to 10 000 years ago; Chapter 3) resulted in a shift in the main forces of natural selection, from external environmental ones to competitive interactions within groups. Primate group size is constrained by the information-processing capacity of the brain (and of the neocortex in particular) and its ability to manipulate information about social relationships (Dunbar 1992). The relative advantage of cognitive skills for the management of social relations (through which tasks important for survivorship were and continue to be conducted) would have been selected for among the genus *Homo*, and this would have driven encephalization and increased neocortex size across evolutionary time.

Dunbar (1998) estimated cognitive group size for different primate species by regressing known group size for a species against their average neocortex volume. This holds well for primates, and when extrapolated to humans predicts a cognitive group size of around 150. This number is roughly equivalent to the set of individuals that can maintain personal rather than formal relationships across time (Hill and Dunbar 2003). Human foragers organized at the level of clans have membership of around this number. Below the group size of 150, Zhou *et al.* (2005) have identified a size hierarchy with a scaling ratio close to three, approximating to group sizes of 3–5 (family or support

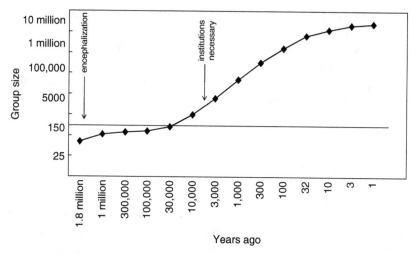

Figure 8.4. Estimates of human and hominin group size across time (speculative hominin estimates from Dunbar 2003), log–log scale.

clique), 12–20 (sympathy group) and 30–50 (bands). Above a group size of around 150 are at least two larger groupings identified in the ethnographic literature: the megaband of around 500 people and the tribe (a linguistic unit) commonly of around 1000–2000 people (Dunbar 1993). In a speculative analysis of hominin social group size based on relative neocortex size, Dunbar (2003) has argued that this may have remained within the broad range for living great apes until well into the *H. erectus* period of between 1.8 and 1 million years ago. From about 1 million years ago, group size is thought to have started to increase at an exponential rate (Figure 8.4). From this time, social complexity is likely to have increased because of the greater complexity of resolving ecological problems when living in larger groups.

In an exploration of the ways in which the social brain could have influenced social organization, Gavrilets *et al.* (2008) found that the hierarchical structure typical of great apes and early hominins would have become disadvantageous with increased pressure to solve problems that came with environmental dominance. By modelling increased within-group competition for a hypothetical resource, they found that alliances of individuals able to overcome the power of alpha-types in a population could have emerged in a phase-transition manner, although the timing of this is uncertain. By incorporating cultural inheritance of social networks developed from such alliances into their model, they found that the political dynamics of intense competition among non-equal individuals for higher social and reproductive success (rather than environmental constraints, social structure, or cultural process) would have resulted in their eventual equality. Furthermore, they found that once alliances start to form, social networks become highly heritable and the emergence of a single alliance of all group members becomes inevitable (Gavrilets *et al.* 2008). Thus, egalitarian alliances may have become the optimal form of human organization in early hunter-gatherer societies, as the survivorship benefits of resolving within-group competition far outweighed those of individualism (Gavrilets *et al.* 2008). It is unlikely that these were maintained painlessly, however. Contemporary hunter-gatherer societies expend significant effort actively maintaining political cohesion (Woodburn 1982) by a range of behaviours, including social control.

Once egalitarianism became the optimal organizational strategy for social-brained humans, a major change in ecological circumstances was needed to oust it. The origin of agriculture may have been the major 'event' (bearing in mind that there was no single rapid shift to this mode of subsistence (Chapter 1)) that saw the re-emergence of social inequality, but the evidence is contradictory. At one extreme, the earliest evidence for social inequality is from the analysis of ornamentation and of traded faunal assemblages associated with Mesolithic burials in France (Vanhaeren and d'Errico 2005). At the other, the absence of elaborated architecture and burials at Çatalhöyük, Anatolia, a centre of high population density at the heart of eastern Mediterranean agricultural origins between 8500 and 7300 years ago (Mellaart 1967; Hodder 2006), suggests an absence of social stratification. Notably, the population of Çatalhöyük did not experience inequality in nutritional health (Angel 1984). Other large prehistoric egalitarian groups include western Anasazi people of the American southwest between the seventh and the thirteenth century, and western Illinois society between 2000 and 1300 years ago; both groups were over a thousand strong (Braun and Plog 1982). The western Illinois are viewed to have maintained identity and purpose by operating as a social network that transmitted materials and information important for societal function through reciprocity and reciprocal roles (although social distance is viewed to have varied among individuals and groups) (Braun and Plog 1982).

The emergence of hierarchy has been associated with intensification of agriculture and its associated technologies (Lenski and Nolan 1984), the decline in importance of coalition size for controlling conflict outcomes, and the increased importance of resource control and use for conflict resolution (Gavrilets *et al.* 2008). Earle (2004) argues that the emergence of hierarchy involved the social incorporation of material media such as landscape constructions (in the form of burial monuments, for example), and elaborate prestige objects such as gold ornaments. Redmond (2008) suggests that the emergence of formal institutions (of religion and law), which facilitate control over people in hierarchical social systems, came with the

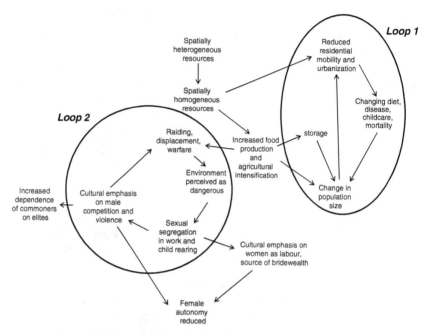

Figure 8.5. A speculative model of the development of inequality among human societies with the adoption and intensification of agriculture (adapted from Kelly *et al.* 2007).

concentration of growing populations into urban centres and of economic surplus in the hands of elites.

Figure 8.5 gives a speculative framework for the development of inequality among human societies, whether at the origins of agriculture or with its intensification, based on Kelly *et al.* (2007) cross-forager society analysis of social inequality. A shift from spatially heterogeneous to homogeneous resources, as would have taken place with the sedentization associated with the adoption of agriculture, would have led to agricultural intensification and increased food production (Lenski and Nolan 1984). Having spatially homogeneous resources allowed intensification of food production, storage and technological development (Lenski and Nolan 1984), which enabled population growth. Growing population size and density could have spurred the formation of urban centres, whose growth could have been fuelled by in-migration from rural areas. It would have also advanced the transmission of infectious diseases (Chapter 7).

The archaeological evidence, however, indicates that urbanization was not immediately successful. Kuijt (2008) estimates population densities at the origins of agriculture in the eastern Mediterranean to have increased dramatically from 10 500 to 10 000 years ago. However, only 500 years later, population densities declined to less than half the peak value of 10 000 years ago. Although the population expansion which came with subsistence intensification resulted in more sedentism and increased birth rate and led to the formation of large villages (Kuijt 2008), many of these only lasted for 300 to 400 years (Eshed *et al.* 2004). This can be explained by two processes. The first is that of a provisioning crisis and new infections caused by the rapid increase in population size (Figure 8.5, Loop 1). While increased food production resolved immediate ecological problems, population growth created new ones, including subsequent food insecurity. The second process is that of migration to existing larger urban centres. While some settlements diminished in population size and disappeared by around 8000 years ago, others persisted and became characterized by high densities of residential architecture (Kuijt 2008). This is exemplified by the town of Çatalhöyük, which by about 8000 years had a population of roughly 5000 people, but despite this large size remained egalitarian (Mellaart 1967; Hodder 2006). Neolithic settlement introduced a new element to human society: the fragmentation of personal social networks. This was good for transmission of novel ideas (and individualism), but bad for social cohesion (and collectivism). The increase in food production that came with agriculture, however, would have facilitated social stratification (Lenski and Nolan 1984), through intergroup competition, crop and animal raiding and warfare (Kelly 1995) (Figure 8.5, Loop 2).

As population sizes continued to increase they would have required increasingly formal institutions whose operation would have set the conditions for elite and hierarchy formation. Using ethnographic data for 907 precolonial societies published in the *Population Atlas of Precolonial Societies* (Mueller *et al.* 1999), Ziltener and Mueller (2007) showed that the size of local communities is significantly related to two measures of social inequality. These are: (1) the number of levels of legal hierarchy beyond the local community prior to colonial rule ($r = 0.33$, $p < 0.01$); and (2) the extent of social stratification ($r = 0.59$, $p < 0.001$). Formation of larger cities could only have been possible with institutional hierarchy and social inequality. Both ancient Athens and Alexandria had populations of between 300 000 and 500 000 people, living in extremes of social and economic inequality. While ancient Greece may lay claims to the origins of democracy in complex society, this was limited to the upper classes; slaves comprised one third of the population of Athens, for example. The maximum size of urban centres has continued to grow to the present day (Figure 8.4). However, the population basis of group social cohesion (and differentiation from others) remains one of overlapping groups, which may also be characterized as networks. The only additional layer of complexity that has been added in the past 300 years or so has been the development of institutional structures representing the domains of education, work, health, law and economics, all of which have become increasingly complex.

Inequality, nutritional health and food symbolism

Inequality in society is reflected in differences of food availability (Sen 1981) and is fundamental to the understanding of the extremes of nutritional ill-health past and present. The relationships between food and nutrition and social and economic inequality are twofold. First, success in the food quest is fundamental to survival and reproduction, and therefore has long term evolutionary pay-offs (Chapter 2). Energetic sufficiency for reproductive success is the driving force for the success of all species, including human beings. Second, food is differentiated by humans according to quality and status and therefore embodies characteristics that can symbolize either success or failure.

Quality is usually considered to be a characteristic feature of food with high nutritional value (Chapter 5), and evolutionary anthropologists often conflate dietary quality with high-protein foods, especially meat. This is because optimal foraging theory teaches that the efficient capture of energy-dense or protein-rich food resources (such as meat) is concordant with good survivorship and reproductive success (Winterhalder 1981). Among most hunter-gatherer groups, meat is of high value in both nutritional and symbolic terms, and good hunters may carry considerable prestige within their society. Quality may also be aesthetic, and high-quality food may be fresh, ripe, well-coloured, well-textured and of good odour, while food of low quality may carry opposite characteristics (Levi-Strauss 1970). Evolutionary biologists have argued that the positive characteristics of correct colour, texture and smell are signals of dietary quality (Simmen and Hladik 1998). However, in some societies, various characteristics associated with quality have become inverted, with for example, the smell of some cheeses denoting positive characteristics to some people but not others (Levi-Strauss 1970). Although cheese emerged as a foodstuff from the need to conserve milk among pastoralists (Ulijaszek and Strickland 1993), it became elaborated and acquired connotations of status only in more recent history. The use of food in the quest for status is universal among all societies, although the notion of what a high-status food comprises can vary greatly among them (Wiessner and Schiefenhovel 1996). As different foods have become symbolic markers of social difference, the extent to which differential consumption is reflected in nutritional health is an important public health issue. We consider this here, using the framework of symbolic capital as elaborated by Bourdieu (1984).

Bourdieu (1984) has argued that as social class groupings are determined by a combination of varying degrees of social, economic and cultural capital, they incorporate symbolic goods, especially those regarded as having the attributes of excellence, as instruments of social distinction. In the contemporary world symbolic goods can include expensive brands of car and clothing, and prestigious residential locations and schools. With respect to food, they can include expensive or exotic food types, and elite restaurants. Luxury foods can be used as prestige objects, which can confer status on their consumers. In unequal societies more generally, excellence is shaped by the dominating class and driven by cultural capital, which marks the differences between classes. Thus, according to Bourdieu, tastes in food, culture and presentation are indicators of class, and trends in food consumption vary according to class. While Bourdieu suggests that such tastes are deep-seated in infant learning, more recent work in psychology shows that physiological taste preferences are in fact plastic (Chapter 2) (Mela 1996) and can therefore be changed by those seeking upward mobility. The tastes of luxury and the tastes of necessity distinguish social classes (Bourdieu 1984), but these can be mimicked. Industrialized systems of production of goods and services (including those of food production and delivery) can serve the aspirations of the upwardly mobile as well as the needs and wants of those who are happy within their class boundaries.

Food is likely to have been the first and most obvious prestige object to act as cultural capital. Humans and other primates often distinguish food according to optimal foraging criteria, but also by cultural preference and symbolic status (Chapter 2). Cultural capital exists in hunter-gatherer society, but it is limited by social mechanisms that control individual differentiation (Woodburn 1982). A very practical reason for this is that nomadic societies have very limited capacities for the accumulation of material objects. One type of prestige object that does not require sedentization for it to operate as cultural capital is food, since it is a disposable good, and can be used in the development and maintenance of social relations through its shared consumption. The high nutritional value of meat, as defined by protein and energy density, and the relative ease with which satiety is reached with its consumption (Berti *et al.* 2008) is a biological reason for the ascription of symbolic value to it among hunter-gatherers. A cultural reason is the capacity of meat to represent most tangibly the power of humans over the natural world (Fiddes 1991).

The sedentization that came with early agriculture allowed accumulation of material goods, including elaborate prestige objects (Earle 2004), which allowed cultural capital to grow beyond that of temporary and immediately consumed symbolic objects. With population growth, the emergence of urban centres and social stratification, class distinction could be perpetuated most simply through the development of cuisine. Differentiation in consumption of food types and in the ways in which they were prepared could have facilitated social differentiation under these conditions, since elaboration and consumption of scarce foods would have been a powerful way of discriminating across social groups. Innovation in food types, for example in the development of bread, yoghurt and cheese, is a response to the need to be able to store food; it can also be considered as a form of production of symbolic goods. And while foods such as bread, yoghurt and cheese came to be consumed by the general population, they may have diffused into generality when their prestige declined as their production became increasingly non-elite, as has happened with a wide range of foods since the seventeenth century in Europe. Among the European aristocracy, a specialized class of practitioners, chefs, emerged as providers of new food-based prestige-objects, in the form of new recipes often involving novel ingredients. Among the benefits of colonialism to European nations was the introduction of new and exotic foodstuffs (Chapters 5 and 11), which were initially incorporated into the cuisine of the elites, and which subsequently became part of everyday diet. Such foods included tomatoes, potatoes, capsicum, turkey, and especially sugar (Mintz 1985).

The earliest restaurants were established to offer restoration and health through food (soup in particular) (Spang 2001). They were reconfigured as locales of more privileged eating in eighteenth century France, as consumption of prestige foods moved from the private to the public sphere (Mennel 1996). Dining at restaurants was quickly appropriated by the emergent middle classes of the time as a practice of distinction. This has been maintained across Europe and has spread across the world. Restaurants exposed the middle classes from the eighteenth century onwards to new foods and recipes, many of which have with time diffused into general consumption of lower social distinction. Cuisine, however, remains a signifier of social class in all contemporary consumer societies. Ethnic cuisine, when rare, may carry cultural capital, which becomes eroded when a particular type of cuisine becomes more common, as for example with Chinese food in Western Europe and North America. The prestige of industrialized fast food has been manipulated by its producers, being set high initially at source (for example with hamburger restaurants in the United States (US)) but declining in status subsequently, while being set high in places of more recent introduction (as for example the same types of hamburger restaurant in Eastern Europe after the collapse of communism in the early 1990s). By taking consumption from the private to the public arena and allowing market forces to dictate the diffusion of cuisine and food types to the general population, the social capital of food has become increasingly linked to economic capital. It continues to be a powerful vehicle for the development and maintenance of social distinction, since the cultural capital gained from it requires economic capital (in the form of both money and leisure time), and allows the building of social capital among those that share prestigious meals.

Food and status

The elemental status of food as a good that carries both material (nutritional) and symbolic value places its manipulation for social distinction central to the production of inequality in food intake, and associated differences in nutritional health. Social class is negatively associated with diet quality, primarily through the mechanism of cost (Darmon and Drewnowski 2008). If lower classes value heartiness and satiety over refinement (Bourdieu 1984), then nutritional state is dominated by economic factors: poor people are the least likely to afford food calories and their food choices will therefore be driven by cost. However, economic factors alone cannot explain variation in nutritional status within communities (Karp 2005) or across nations (Pickett *et al.* 2005), and although food culture has been implicated in influencing nutritional status (Gopalan 1992; Karp 2008), no mechanism has been invoked. We propose that, although income is an important factor influencing food intake, the relationships between dietary intake and nutritional state are also mediated by the symbolic value of food, through the ways in which it influences everyday consumption.

Meat, as discussed above, is well documented as carrying symbolic value in most societies (Fiddes 1991), and is often denied in quantity and quality to lower social classes (Fiddes 1994). Meat consumption has stabilized in the industrialized world and is three times higher than in the less developed world (Rosegrant *et al.* 2001). Under these circumstances, when everyone can afford to eat meat, the higher classes can distinguish themselves by consuming only the most aesthetically desirable types and cuts of meat, or by shunning it altogether and consuming other types of prestige food. In most of the less developed world, meat, of whatever quality, continues to be in great demand. The popular demand for meat is demonstrated by the dramatic increase in its consumption globally, with increasing wealth. Starting from very low levels, per capita consumption of meat in the developing world more than doubled between 1967 and 1997 (Rosegrant *et al.* 2001). Figure 8.6 shows per capita meat availability by global region between 1961 and 2007; although Europe and the Americas have the highest meat consumption, the rising demand for meat in Asia is of the greatest significance, given the far greater population there. While the global demand for meat continues to be unmet, it remains a prestige good that continues to define social distinction and the formation and maintenance of social capital through its consumption.

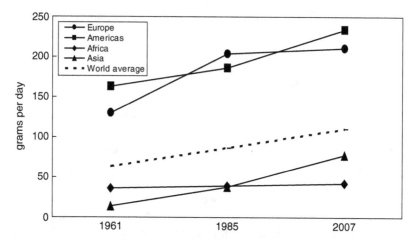

Figure 8.6. Per capita meat availability by global region (data from Food and Agriculture Organization 2011).

The marketing of otherwise low-grade meat and animal tissue into meat products such as burgers and sausages is a practice used throughout the industrialized world and emerging economic nations. This promotes consumption of food of otherwise low symbolic value by raising its symbolic value through branding. This is a practice that permeates all aspects of consumer society (Baudrillard 1970), whether the object of consumption is food, clothing, shelter, comfort or excitement. By attributing high symbolic value to foods of low nutritional quality and pricing them within the reach of economically less well-off people in industrialized nations, major food producers of the present day are able to capitalize on the need to accumulate cultural capital among those not able to do so in ways other than through identification with widely recognized brands.

The symbolic value of different foods varies across societies, but can also change across time. For example, wholegrain breads, fruit and vegetables have more symbolic value among higher classes now than they did in the nineteenth century. Table 8.1 illustrates ways in which the material and symbolic values of foods can vary by class status, and how the latter value can change, using the example of nineteenth and late twentieth century England. Material status is taken to be the nutritional quality of the food, based on energy, protein and micronutrient content. Foods high in energy but of low protein or micronutrient content are considered to be of low quality (Arambepola *et al.* 2008). Cultural values attributed to foods continue to change, and the foods shown in Table 8.1 give an illustrative snapshot.

In the nineteenth century, the poor would have regarded all foods of high energy density as having high symbolic value, with everyday consumption of

Table 8.1 *Material and symbolic qualities of some foods in England*

Nineteenth century, poor		Symbolic value	
		High	Low
Material value	High	Meat, sugar, liver and other organs	Wholegrain bread
	Low	Butter, lard, white bread	
Nineteenth century, wealthy		Symbolic value	
		High	Low
Material value	High	Meat, sugar	Liver, wholegrain bread
	Low	Butter, white bread	Lard
Late twentieth century, lower class		Symbolic value	
		High	Low
Material value	High		Vegetables, baked fish, wholegrain bread
	Low	Branded hamburgers, chips, fried fish, sugar-based products, white bread	
Late twentieth century, higher class		Symbolic value	
		High	Low
Material value	High	Vegetables, baked fish, wholegrain bread, lean meats	
	Low		Branded hamburgers, chips, fried fish, sugar-based products, white bread

bread, potatoes and bacon, the last of which was the major source of animal food (Nelson 2003). The major limitation in obtaining adequate dietary energy would have been income. The wealthy attributed low symbolic value to foods such as liver, lard and wholegrain bread, and high symbolic value to foods of equal material value such as muscle meat, butter and white bread. In the late twentieth century, industrial methods of food production, branding, marketing and a re-conceptualization of status through food and health have changed the symbolic values of a wide range of foods. For example, such value is higher for fried battered fish among lower classes than among higher ones, while steamed or baked fish has higher symbolic value for higher classes. Alternatively, branded hamburgers have higher symbolic value for lower classes than for higher classes. This example reflects a British sensibility, and the class separation of branded burgers may not exist so clearly in other nations such as the US or Australia. The particular foods may differ, but the dissociation of material from symbolic value in the construction of cultural capital through food can be found everywhere. In places where economic factors do not permit overconsumption, obesity is an upper- and middle-class phenomenon. Where overconsumption is possible, foods of low material value are consumed because they are cheap enough to be eaten in quantity, are ascribed high symbolic value, and contribute to obesity.

Symbolic value cannot, however, be transformed into social capital without a social context, whether food is an agent of social connection, is eaten in social context, or simply discussed. Contemporary consumerism has been described as an institutionalized form of status competition, which has been allowed to escalate without limit (Frank and Cook 1995; Easterlin 1995). Food is one vehicle for such competition. Fast-food restaurants mimic the social display of overt consumption of the upper classes, and make such display easy and affordable. Because of this, they become shunned by higher classes, who have their own means of social display through food. Fast food restaurants then become agents of social capital formation among the lower classes. Fast food generally has higher energy density than food prepared in households (Prentice and Jebb 2003), and energy-dense foods undermine innate appetite control systems, thus predisposing to obesity (Jebb 2007). Fast food carries symbolic value which is maintained by large advertising budgets, and is represented in restaurants that are more densely distributed in poorer areas in industrialized nations such as the US and United Kingdom (Blair Lewis *et al.* 2005; Cummins *et al.* 2005).

The embedding of social capital in the symbolic status of food is as old as humanity, and has served the process of social distinction well. It becomes dysfunctional, in public health terms, in consumer societies that pay scant regard to the maintenance of the material quality of food (as opposed to its material safety), although it continues to serve social distinction as powerfully as ever. In this regard, while obesity is more common among lower social classes of most industrialized societies, higher classes perceive that it is better to stay slim, since this ensures their health and longevity as well as their social status.

Social groups, food and nutrition

In the early twenty-first century, few non-industrialized societies are able to resist the problems of undernutrition, while many economically emerging nations are grappling with the dual burden of both undernutrition and over-nutrition. Among industrialized nations, most have significant problems of obesity. In all cases, nutritional problems are stratified socially. Inasmuch as people are connected, so is their health (Granovetter 1973). With respect to nutritional health, both extremes of nutritional state are conditioned by social and economic factors (Hadley 2004; Surkan *et al.* 2007; Feunekes *et al.* 1998), while obesity is linked within social networks (Christakis and Fowler 2007). A social network is a representation of links between individuals and groups, and a society may be represented by networks of varying levels of complexity (Freeman 2004). We use one form of social network, the small world network (Watts and Strogatz 1998), to examine the possible effects of group size and structure on the possibility of egalitarianism and on the rates of undernutrition and obesity in human populations.

Networks, settlement size and egalitarianism

Networks may be structured freely, but above a group size of around 150 people may be influenced by inner-layer typologies. For example, family structure can extend the possible size of non-hierarchical society, if trust between family units can be engendered through mutual acquaintance of individuals in different units. This does not eliminate the possibility of competition between such groups, which might result in hierarchy formation, however. The maximum group size that could possibly function as inner groups (such as nuclear families) linked into a small world network is easily calculated from first principles. Figure 8.7 illustrates the process, giving the maximum number of cognition groups that can exist together in a small world network, if each cognition group is linked to each of the others by one mutual acquaintance (but not necessarily the same one for all groups). If, for example, a cognition group consists of two people (such as husband and wife) (Figure 8.7A), this allows a maximum small world network of three cognition groups, since each cognition group can only link with two others. The size of this hypothetical network, if they lived as a settlement, would be six people. Within the group size hierarchy of Zhou *et al.* (2005), this maps onto the family or support clique (three to five individuals). With cognition groups of four (such as a nuclear family) (Figure 8.7B), the network can accommodate up to five groups, since each cognition group can form a bridge with four others, forming

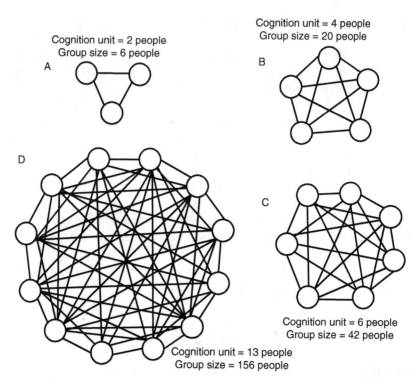

Figure 8.7. Calculating maximum population size in theoretical non-hierarchical settlements organised by cognition groups linked in a small world network, using Watts and Strogatz (1998) systems. Settlements based on cognition groups (represented by circles) of (A) two people; (B) four people; (C) six people; (D) thirteen people. In all cases, each cognition group is linked to each other by one mutual acquaintance (but not necessarily the same one for all groups).

a group of 20 people, equivalent to a sympathy group (12–20 individuals (Zhou *et al.* (2005)). For cognition groups with six members (Figure 8.7C), six bridges between seven groups are possible, leading to a possible population of 42. This is equivalent to Zhou and co-workers' (2005) idea of a band (30–50 people), leading to a hypothetical settlement size of 156 people, equivalent in size to the clan (150 people). The geometric relationship illustrated by Figure 8.7 is formalized in the equation:

Settlement size = (number of ties per cognition group)^2 + (cognition group size)

This condition for linking cognition groups together into a small world network is appropriate for the maintenance of egalitarianism. If some individuals were allowed to bridge more than one cognition group while others were not, the concentration of social relations in one or a small number of people would be permitted, thereby setting the conditions for the control of information and resources among a subset of the population, and the possibility of elite formation.

At a higher level of organization, if a band of 150 people can maintain egalitarian relationships without hierarchy, applying the equation to a cognitive group size of 150 gives a maximum settlement size of 22 650, a number more than four times that estimated by archaeologists for the largest known egalitarian society at Çatalhöyük. This looks odd. However, the individuals within this structure are less likely to be truly individual than linked into kin groupings, or a network within a network. Males and females are more likely to be linked to each other within families, and the cognition units are more likely to have had family-based ties across units. This assumption is probably closer to reality, and if in a perfect demographic world, all Çatalhöyük males were married monogamously to females, and each tie was across family units, each with three children, this would reduce to one fifth the number of ties across cognition groups. It would, in effect, structure the network by its innermost layer, the family group. Applying the equation gives a population value for the small worlds network of 930 families. Given that each family represents five people, this would place the population of Çatalhöyük at 4650. While close to the demographic estimate for Çatalhöyük 8500–7300 years ago, the estimate can be refined by applying estimates for fertility, childhood mortality and survivorship from palaeopathological and palaeodemographic analyses of skeletal assemblages identified there.

Using such a coordinated approach to skeletal finds at Çatalhöyük, Angel (1969) estimated birth rate to have been 5.1 children per woman. With a corresponding death rate of 1.7 children per woman, the average number of surviving children in such a family unit would have been 3.4. With a family unit of 5.4 individuals, application of the equation gives a population value for the network of 921.6 families, which when scaled up by multiplying by family size of 5.4 individuals gives a population of 4977, a value closer to the estimate for Çatalhöyük population at that time. The implication of this observation for the distribution of nutritional ill-health across society is that any trait that travels along gradients of inequality (including undernutrition and obesity as well as tuberculosis and HIV/AIDS) will become unequally distributed once settlement size exceeds this value, unless there are political structures and institutions that are ideologically bound to reduce inequality and/or its consequences.

Small world networks and the clustering of undernutrition and obesity

Starting with the global estimates of 13% and 5% prevalence rates for undernutrition and obesity respectively (Food and Agriculture Organization 2000;

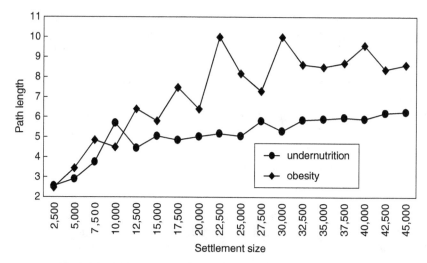

Figure 8.8. Average path length of social transmission of undernutrition and obesity in social brain units of 150 people (average family units of 2 adults and 3 living children) embedded in a small worlds network representing settlement sizes varying from 2500 people to 45 000, using the Watts and Strogatz (1998) algorithm.

World Health Organization 2003), we now model the average path length and clustering coefficients by using the Watts and Strogatz (1998) algorithm for group sizes of 2500–45 000 people organized in small worlds networks comprising cognition groups of 150 people each. The average path length is the measure of network topology that shows the average number of individuals that a trait needs to pass between if that trait is conditioned by social and economic factors (Hadley 2004; Surkan *et al.* 2007; Feunekes *et al.* 1998; Christakis and Fowler 2007). The clustering coefficient varies from zero to one and quantifies how close an individual and their neighbours are to forming a clique or inclusive group. The higher the value, the greater is the degree of clustering. Each family-based cognition unit is modelled to have two adults and three living children.

The average path length of social transmission increases for both undernutrition and obesity as settlement size increases from 2500 to 45 000 people (Figure 8.8). For undernutrition, the most striking increase is between group sizes of 7500 and 10 000 people, while for obesity the average path increases steadily until a population in excess of 25 000 is reached. Figure 8.9 shows the clustering coefficient for both undernutrition and obesity to be fairly similar at settlement sizes below around 10 000 people, the former falling thereafter, such that clustering of undernutrition is greater than of obesity. Published data on social networks and obesity from the Framingham study show the average

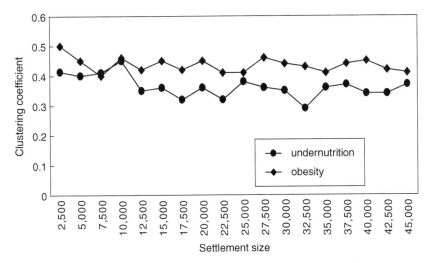

Figure 8.9. Clustering coefficients for social transmission of undernutrition and obesity in social brain units of 150 people (average family units of two adults and three living children) embedded in a small worlds network representing settlement sizes varying from 2500 people to 45 000, using the Watts and Strogatz (1998) algorithm.

clustering coefficient to be 0.66 (Christakis and Fowler 2007). Both our estimates and those of Christakis and Fowler (2007) are consistent with many other observed social networks.

Furthermore, Christakis and Fowler (2007) report their data to six degrees of separation, which represents an average pathway distance of seven. The degree of separation is the social distance between two people as measured by the smallest number of intermediaries between an individual and other members of the network, and is equivalent to the path distance minus one. At the larger population size, we find values a little above this, at between eight and nine.

These differences might be due to a different modelling procedure, although Christakis and Fowler (2007) found that the small world model gave clustering values similar to those of the random model they adopted. Our modelling shows that the clustering of obesity in large settlements is greater than that of undernutrition, stabilizing at nine degrees of separation, compared with six degrees of separation for undernutrition. But below around 15 000 people, the social transmission of both extremes of malnutrition is similar, ranging from two degrees of separation for settlements of 2500 people and increasing to around five degrees of separation at settlement size of 10 000 people. This modelling procedure suggests that in small settlements representative of trad-itional communities, the social separation of both undernutrition and obesity remains small. This may be one explanation for the emergence of the dual burden of undernutrition and obesity within small rural communities of economically emerging nations such as India (Bharati *et al.* 2007). Above around 15 000 people, the likelihood of egalitarianism is small, and the separation of undernutrition and obesity becomes stronger, probably because each type of nutritional state is predominantly carried by different social classes.

The limited extent of social separation of undernutrition and obesity does not explain the emergence of dual-burden malnutrition within households (Doak *et al.* 2005). However, dual-burden households are most commonly found in urban communities (Deleuze Ntandou Bouzitou *et al.* 2005; Doak *et al.* 2005; Khor and Sharif 2003), where much higher levels of social separation are expected. While households are units of kin and economic organization, individual household members in urban society are more likely to be located in different social networks with different access to food and understandings of appropriate embodiment than rural ones. In a small rural community, there may be value placed on being a certain normative body size; in an urban one, there are often sub-groups that value, or normalize, either or both extremes of thinness and fatness. The larger the settlement, the larger the range and number of social networks possible. Culturally variant ideas of appropriate and preferable body image vary with time, society, gender and age group (de Garine and Pollock 1995), although the body size of children broadly reflects parental ideals and control of the household budget (Kenney 2008), at least until adolescence. While there are no network analyses of the clustering of body size ideals across age and sex, within-group analyses suggest their existence. For example, a cross-cultural comparison of appropriate body size in different traditional societies showed plumpness to be favoured as attractive in women, and stature and muscularity to be favoured in men (Brown 1991). Furthermore, differences in age-set ideals of appropriate body size exist, with adolescent females being driven by media-driven perceptions of beauty that are shared by other adolescent females (Niven *et al.* 2009). Adolescent males, on the other hand, favour upper body weight and muscularity (Ata *et al.* 2007) as signalling sexual agency (Schooler *et al.* 2008).

As obesity prevalence has increased in most nations, the socioeconomic stratification of obesity is aided by the social networks that humans are part of (Chapter 1). The probability of becoming obese at different degrees of separation across the emergence of the obesity epidemic (Christakis and Fowler 2007) is illustrated in Figure 8.10. At one degree of separation, the probability of becoming obese remained consistently strong across seven waves of survey between 1973 and 1999. Individuals had similar probabilities of becoming obese at both one and two degrees of separation from an obese person in 1973 and 1981. After 1981, the probability of becoming obese at two degrees of separation from an obese person declined, while that at one degree of

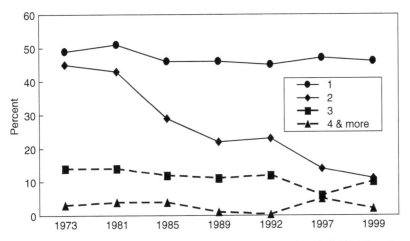

Figure 8.10. Relative probability (percentage) of obesity in an individual if another individual linked to the first by one, two, three and four or more degrees of separation also becomes obese (data from Christakis and Fowler 2007).

separation remained stable. By 1999, the probability of becoming obese at two degrees of separation had become as low as among those with three degrees of separation from an obese person. The 1980s and 1990s saw a dramatic increase in economic inequality in the US (Deaton and Paxson 2004), and it may be that obesity became less socially 'contagious' because of increased economic stratification of US society across this period.

Discussion

Social capital is usually a good thing. It can improve household welfare (Maluccio *et al.* 1999) and nutritional state through the spread of information, promotion of agency and collective action, and promotion of norms of civic behaviour that can buffer people during times of crisis. Its effectiveness has been demonstrated among rural South African communities in smoothing the effects of economic shock (Cross *et al.* 1998), thus buffering against food insecurity. Increasing social capital is seen as a way of promoting health and well-being (Wilkinson 1996). We argue that the potent combination of social capital and food as symbolic good in the formation and maintenance of social class makes this relationship different from other aspects of health. We also argue that group size and relationships matter, and that while inequality may be at the heart of the majority of the world's nutritional health problems, the human social brain, existing in a world of rapid population growth and urbanization, has little option but to continue to live in small worlds networks, and inequality emerges from this. Where population exceeds the ability of small worlds networks to organize everyday life, institutions are needed, and have emerged as humans have moved from hunter-gatherer economic systems to agricultural, industrial and post-industrial ones.

For anthropologists, social and economic inequalities are outcomes of social structures and institutions and the ways they function. Where such structures and institutions deny basic needs such as food security to those of lower status, this becomes a form of structural violence (Farmer 2004), in which under-nutrition everywhere, and obesity in industrialized nations, are the embodied outcomes. Differences in economic inequality across nations (Figure 8.1), while largely associated with globalization, are also due to differences in governmental policies, either in relation to redistribution of wealth or invest-ment in infrastructure that promotes self-reliance (Organization for Economic Cooperation and Development 2008). Recently, it has been shown that indus-trialized nations pursuing market liberal policies have both higher rates of, and rates of increase in, obesity since the 1990s (Offer *et al.* 2010). The implication of these observations for public health nutrition is that inequality matters, and nutritional policies that promote self-reliance are more likely to promote reduction in inequalities in nutritional health than those that don't.

Part III

Once Upon a Time in the West

9 *Nutrition transition*

Human diet reflects human physiological and behavioural flexibility, which is often formalized into food cultures among different societies. Dietary traditions often involve deeply held beliefs about foods and what they represent symbolically, ideologically and socially. Against this, most human populations have undergone dietary change across history and prehistory, whether it be the transition to agriculture (Chapter 6), during industrialization and colonization, or with the most recent globalization of food supply. Nutrition transition theory, formulated by Popkin *et al.* (1993) and Popkin (1994), is a description of changing patterns of diet and nutritional health that have accompanied various types of economic transformation, from hunting and gathering, through agriculture, industrialization and urbanization, to the modern and postmodern world (Chapter 6).

Nutrition transition theory builds on demographic (Thompson 1929; Caldwell 1976) and epidemiological (Omran 1971) transition theory. The former is an explanation for the transformation of nations from having high birth and death rates to low birth and death rates as they develop economically and move from non-industrial to industrial modes of production. The transformation is divided into two processes, fertility transition and mortality transition. Epidemiological transition considers the latter transformation, which involves declines in infectious disease mortality rates in childhood and increases in degenerative disease rates in later life. Historically, two patterns of epidemiological transition are viewed to have taken place. The first involved the emergence of infectious diseases in the economic shift from hunting and gathering to agriculture and animal husbandry (Chapter 7). The second is characterized by the control of infectious disease among the industrializing nations of the nineteenth and twentieth centuries and the rise of biomedicine, leading to a change in disease patterns towards chronic and degenerative diseases. The sequential nature of epidemiological transition has been challenged, for example by Frenk *et al.* (1989), who, basing their argument on data from

Table 9.1 *Ages of nutrition transition*

Pattern	Age	Time	Human organization	Diet
1	Food collecting	Pre-12 000 years ago	Hunter-gatherer	High in complex carbohydrates and fibre; low in fat
2	Famine	Around 12 000 years ago	Origins of agriculture and animal husbandry	Less qualitatively varied; larger variation in seasonal and periodic availability; periods of acute scarcity
3	Receding famine	Eighteenth and nineteenth century	Introduction of agricultural technology, industrial revolution	Increasingly processed; broadly sourced
4	Degenerative diseases	Twentieth century	Urbanization and economic improvement	Major shift to lower nutrient density, higher energy density; excessively high in fat and sugar
5	Behavioural change	Twenty-first century	Postmodern	According to guidelines, to reduce degenerative diseases and prolong health

Modified from Popkin (2002a).

Mexico, proposed a 'protracted–polarized' model of epidemiological change, which incorporates income inequality and widening gaps in health status among social classes and geographical regions. Unlike epidemiological transition theory, protracted–polarized theory attempts to override the rigidity of sequential analyzis and allows for the overlap of patterns.

Since nutrition plays a powerful role in resistance to infection (Chapter 7) and has wide-ranging influence on chronic and degenerative disease, nutrition transition theory can be viewed as the nutritional component of epidemiological transition theory. Nutrition transition theory attempts to explain changes in nutritional health by delineating stages of dietary consumption and physical activity patterns, which are reflected in nutritional outcomes (Table 9.1). Present-day nutritional epidemiology in industrialized and economically emerging nations is explained as an outcome of the shift from a pattern of receding famine and physically demanding labour to the adoption of an industrialized diet that is high in fat, sugar and refined foods and accompanied by sedentary lifestyles.

Scrimshaw (2002) has offered an alternative interpretation of the changes in nutritional health taking place across the world now as involving multiple transitions, with globalization as a dominant factor influencing change. Globalization involves the reduction and removal of between-nation barriers to trade and exchange, and includes the movement of goods, capital, services and people that have gone with them. It also results in the linkage of local and regional economies in worldwide networks of trade. Its earliest forms were colonial, these being replaced by transnational companies and corporations across the late nineteenth and twentieth centuries with the decline of empires and their colonies. In one case study in Accra, Ghana, the framing of disease patterns there as epidemiological transition has been challenged by Agyei-Mensah and Aikins (2010), who see differences and inequalities in disease patterns as following the protracted–polarized model of Frenk *et al.* (1989), with urbanization, poverty and globalization being key factors in their production. These factors, in turn, are shown by them to be shaped by Ghana's colonial history (Agyei-Mensah and de-Graft Aikins 2010).

In this chapter, nutrition transition theory is described and its causation by broader transformative processes discussed, by examining diet and nutrition transition in Mexico since prehistory. Mexico is chosen because there is rich evidence for social, economic and political transformations and their influences on subsistence and diet. Mexico is currently an economically-emerging nation affected by globalization and beset with two types of nutritional health problem: undernutrition among its very poorest people, and overnutrition and obesity among its less-poor and middle-class citizens (Popkin 2009). By placing recent nutrition transition in Mexico in relation to inequality, colonialism and early globalization, an extension to nutrition transition theory is proposed, arguing that prehistories and histories shape the responses of populations to changing nutritional circumstances.

Nutrition transition and social transformation

Nutrition transition theory describes major changes in the nutritional health of human populations which are determined by the interplay of economic, demographic, environmental and cultural change (Popkin 1994, 1998). Within this scheme there are five patterns of nutritional health (Table 9.1) that societies may progress through, starting with formations prior to the emergence of agriculture when hunting and gathering predominated. It proceeds to the origins of agriculture (pattern 2), through the introduction of agricultural and industrial technology (pattern 3), urbanization and economic improvement (pattern 4), and a postindustrial age that has yet to be attained (pattern 5). This stylized synopsis of patterns of change (Popkin 2002a) represents a progressive continuum of anticipated change, based on processes observed in industrialized western nations which are postulated to be occurring with greater rapidity and over a shorter timescale in developing countries at present

(Popkin 2002b, c). Income, price shifts and urbanization are seen as the immediate underlying factors influencing diet and physical activity patterns, with global shifts in the availability and use of technologies that shape mass communication, marketing and food distribution operating more distally (Popkin 2006a, b). Popkin (2002b) stresses that nutrition transition theory is not a singular, rigid construct. Rather, transitions take place unevenly over time and space, with change varying greatly for different geographic and socioeconomic groups.

Nutrition transition theory has been applied at the national level in a way similar to epidemiological transition theory (Omran 1971, 1983) to offer systematic ways in which nutritional change can be identified, and future trends in nutritional health predicted (Caballero and Popkin 2002). The transition from pattern 3 (receding famine) to pattern 4 (non-communicable disease) has acquired particular importance for public health nutrition, to the extent that it is viewed by many as being synonymous with the nutrition transition (Caballero and Popkin 2002). Although Popkin and Gordon-Larsen (2004) frame all patterns as important, they stress the importance of future transition from pattern 4 to pattern 5.

While useful in contextualizing dietary and nutritional change in relation to health, there are various problems with nutrition transition theory. First, it is an ethnocentric imposition of health change processes that took place in industrialized nations onto nations of differing prehistories and histories undergoing industrialization now. In most cases, currently economically emerging nations have experienced varying periods of colonial subservience, and the extent to which this shapes their present-day industrialization and food supply systems remains unanalysed by nutrition transition theorists. A second problem is the extent to which the flexible framework that Popkin (2002b) has proposed has become formalized into a progressive scheme by others. A third problem is a lack of agreement about the fundamental unit of transition, whether it should be the nation state, region, or community, and the level of analysis needed to understand it. Related to this is its limited potential to explain the heterogeneity in nutritional patterns within countries.

While culture and sociality have been identified as being important to nutrition transition (Popkin 1998), this has proved difficult to fit into the existing scheme (B.M. Popkin, personal communication, 2011). Transition from pattern 3 to pattern 4 may vary according to form of social organization, but this is not considered (Bobadilla *et al.* 1993). The transition from pattern 4 to pattern 5 remains contentious, currently applying only to small sectors of society that have adequate financial and social autonomy to make health-related changes in behaviour. Such behavioural change is not possible for most people in most nations, whether economically emerging or industrialized, given global food company dominance and an absence of countervailing forces in most nations. The transnational corporations that control food and beverage production, distribution, marketing and sales are overwhelmingly located in the United States (US) and western Europe, with five corporations dominating the field: Cargill, Kraft and PepsiCo (located in the US), Nestlé (located in Switzerland), and Unilever (the United Kingdom and The Netherlands). The control of global food has intensified in recent decades. In 1991 seven corporations controlled 51% of global food production, while in 2007 four corporations controlled 54% of it. Across this time corporate control of the global food market has expanded more than threefold (Goldman Sachs 2007). Such corporations not only dominate the market for agricultural products, their processing, marketing and delivery to the consumer, they also dominate the market for agrichemicals, seed and animal feed (Lyson and Raymer 2000).

With respect to obesity, the highest-level explanation for its emergence and increase is that of increased food security that has come with prosperity and economic growth (Offer 2006). However, obesity rates are only weakly linked to gross national product among industrialized nations (Pickett *et al.* 2005). In economically developing nations, the relationship is even weaker. Figure 9.1 shows relationships between obesity in adults against per capita gross domestic product (GDP) for 15 economically emerging nations (Brazil, China, India, Iran, Kuwait, Malaysia, Mexico, Morocco, Peru, Philippines, Russia, Saudi Arabia, South Africa, Turkey and Uruguay). While prosperity may influence transition from pattern 3 to pattern 4 in most emerging nations, China and Malaysia have low levels of obesity relative to their GDP, while Mexico and Peru have high levels. There may be greater countervailing forces against the development of obesity in China and Malaysia, and additional contributory factors to obesity in Mexico and Peru. With respect to economic growth, there is no consistent pattern between this and chronic disease rates.

By way of illustration, Figure 9.2 shows growth in GDP of four nations undergoing the nutrition transition, Mexico, China, Brazil and Russia (Popkin and Gordon-Larsen 2004) in relation to global GDP growth between 1977 and 2007, while Figure 9.3 shows chronic disease rates for these four countries. Of these four nations, only China had economic growth consistently in excess of the global average. Brazil has hovered around the global average across this period, while Russia spent much of the twenty years between 1982 and 2002 lurching from economic crisis to deep recession, recovering to well above the global average in the years after 2002. Mexico experienced above-average growth in the 1970s, but subsequently showed economic growth of similar magnitude to that of Brazil. In none of these cases do obesity and chronic disease morbidity and mortality reflect these rates of economic growth in any but the loosest of ways.

It might be expected that China, consistently having had the highest economic growth across this period, would have the highest rates of chronic disease risk,

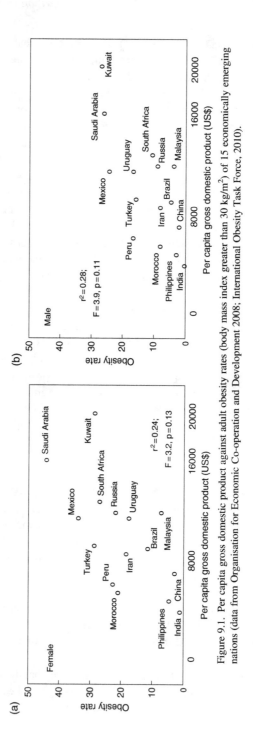

Figure 9.1. Per capita gross domestic product against adult obesity rates (body mass index greater than 30 kg/m^2) of 15 economically emerging nations (data from Organisation for Economic Co-operation and Development 2008; International Obesity Task Force, 2010).

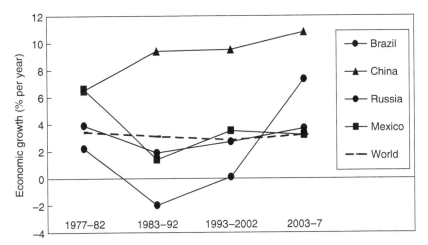

Figure 9.2. Gross domestic product (GDP) growth of nations undergoing the nutrition transition, compared with global GDP growth (Organisation for Economic Co-operation and Development 2008).

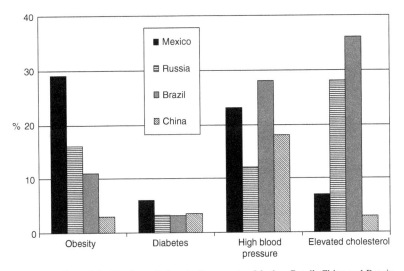

Figure 9.3. Obesity and chronic disease rates, Mexico, Brazil, China and Russia, sexes combined data from World Health Organization 2008; International Obesity Task Force 2010).

but it does not. Rather, it has unexceptional rates of Type 2 diabetes and hypertension but the lowest rates of elevated cholesterol among the four nations represented. Differences in disease rates relative to economic wellbeing may reflect differences in genetic susceptibilities with respect to Type 2 diabetes (Wu *et al.*

2008) but not hypertension (Agarwal *et al.* 2005) among the Chinese populations. Russia, which has experienced the greatest economic trauma of the four nations, has rates for all risk factors within the range for the four nations apart from blood pressure, for which it is the lowest. Low chronic disease rates relative to economic status or growth may reflect local resistance to the global forces promoting these diseases. For example, South Korea, which has low prevalence of obesity compared with other Asian countries with similar or much lower incomes (Kim *et al.* 2000), has not seen increased fat intakes with increased GDP. Rather, the low-fat, rice-based Korean diet has been heavily defended by both the state and individuals.

Differences in disease rates relative to economic wellbeing may also be associated with intra-national inequality. For example, among the world's richer nations, Wilkinson and Pickett (2009) found that life expectancy at birth was lower and obesity rates higher in countries with lower economic equality (the US is the extreme example of this). Among the world's poorest nations, Jones-Smith *et al.* (2011) observed that countries with higher gross domestic product (GDP) and lower income inequality had faster increases in overweight prevalence among poorer groups of women than wealthier ones. This was especially the case for Turkey, Jordan, Egypt, Morocco and Armenia.

There are likely to be other strong contributing forces to increasing obesity rates among the populations where such rates outstrip expectations based on nation-level economic wellbeing, as in the case of Mexico and Peru. In what follows, we examine the diet and nutritional health of the Mexican population using an historical perspective. We argue for an expansion of the nutrition transition framework to include colonialism and current economic relations with other nations, which structure obesogenic environments differently in different countries. Mexico forms the basis of this case study because there is excellent documentation of its colonial food history, its links to past colonizers, and its recent and current relationships with dominant trade partners that influence its food security.

Nutritional health in transition: the case of Mexico

The Mexican population exhibits patterns of chronic disease at levels equivalent to those of much wealthier nations. According to Vargas and Casillas (1990), there have been three periods in the Mexican past during which important changes in diet and nutrition have taken place. The first was the passage from hunting and gathering to intensive agriculture. The second, which these authors consider the most important, was its conquest by Spain, when two different hierarchical societies met. The third was from the 1910 Revolution onwards, when dramatic social and economic transformations led to the formation of contemporary Mexico.

Figure 9.4. Map of contemporary Mexico with settlements key to the development of agriculture in Mesoamerica.

The first change, from hunting and gathering to agriculture, corresponds with Popkin's shift from pattern 1 (food collection) to pattern 2 (famine and the origins of agriculture), and involved the adoption of the cultivation of maize, amaranth, beans, squash, tomatoes and algae, and husbandry of wild fowl. Archaeological evidence places the origins of maize cultivation in the Valley of Tehuacan between 5500 and 3500 years ago (MacNeish 1992) (Figure 9.4), with corn and bean cultivation forming the core of subsistence (Long-Solis and Vargas 2005). The integration of maize cultivation into Mesoamerican subsistence systems led to population growth and the need to increase food production, which encouraged farming populations to expand into new agricultural areas both north and south of Tehuacan (Hill 2001; Bellwood 2001). Little is known of the chronology of the diffusion of maize cultivation in central America, other than that it was widespread by the thirteenth century.

As in the eastern Mediterranean region and elsewhere, urbanization followed the adoption of agriculture. Many city states had been formed in the Valley of Mexico by the thirteenth century (Smith 1984), these having intensive systems of mixed farming and animal husbandry (called chinampa), ensuring the food security of their populations. Chinampa took full advantage of swampland ecology (Popper 2000), the earliest evidence for its use coming from the basin of Mexico by around 2500 years ago (Teotihuacan; Figure 9.4)

Figure 9.5. The lake system in the Valley of Mexico at the time of the Spanish conquest, showing distribution of the chinampas.

and among later Mayan civilizations in Teotihuacan and south-east Mexico. It was practised by the Mexica (or Aztec) populations, extensive areas in the Valley of Mexico (at the site of present-day Mexico City) being devoted to it at the time of Spanish conquest.

Figure 9.5 shows the lake system in the Valley of Mexico at the time of the Spanish conquest, with the distribution of the chinampas. These surround Tenochtitlan (the centre of present-day central Mexico City) and extend across Lake Chalco and Lake Xochimilco, where chinampa agriculture continues as a minority practice to the present day. The chinampa system comprised narrow islands of between six and ten metres in width and between 100 and 200 metres in length, built at lake edges using layers of vegetation and earth. Within them were rectangular fields between two and four metres in width and between 20 and 40 metres in length (Food and Agriculture Organization 2009), surrounded by canals connected to the lake. A mix of agriculture and

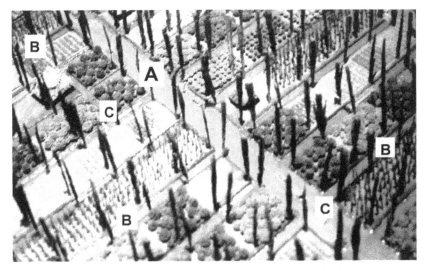

Figure 9.6. A model reconstruction of a chinampa system of mixed agriculture, arboriculture and aquaculture, showing a large (A) and many small (B) water channels, and rafts (C) for mobility around the cultivated mounds (photograph at National Museum of Anthropology, Mexico City, Stanley Ulijaszek).

arboriculture was practised on the fields while aquaculture was practiced in the canals (Figure 9.6). The sides of the fields were reinforced by willow and other trees of economic value. Agricultural crops included corn, beans, squash and chilli planted together, or a combination of cassava, corn and papaya. Vegetables, including green tomato (jitomate), chia, amaranth, chayote and chilacayote, were planted, as were a range of herbs (uauhzontli, quiltonil and quelite cenizo). Aquaculture involved fish, waterfowl and newts (axolotl). Domestic animals (pigs, chickens and ducks) were fed wastes from crops, while animal wastes were captured by the canals. Organic waste from the canals was used to fertilize the fields. The intensity of food production in the few modern chinampas remaining is remarkable: potatoes yield between 3.5 and 8 times more per hectare than on ordinary land, while maize yields between 1.3 and 1.5 times more per hectare (Food and Agriculture Organization 2009).

By the time of the Spanish conquests of Mexico, the city states of Tenochtitlan, Texcoco and Tlacopan (Figure 9.5) formed the Triple Alliance of the Aztec Empire, which through trade and conquest allowed its upper class an elaborate lifestyle (Berdan 2004), of which a very diverse diet was part. Aztec habitual dietary patterns involved the consumption of two or (in the case of labourers) three unelaborated meals per day (Coe 1994). For those with the means, meals involved a main dish and side dishes of a range of possible

Figure 9.7. Aztec woman grinding maize (from the Florentine Codex
(de Sahagun 1540)).

animal- and water-based food sources, vegetables, fruits and herbs. The range
of animal foods available for consumption included turkey, native fowl,
iguana, axolotl, shrimp, fish, insects and larvae (Long-Solis and Vargas
2005). The lower classes, peasants and slaves consumed a maize-based diet,
supplemented with fish and sometimes turkey. Figure 9.7, an illustration from
the Florentine Codex (de Sahagun 1540, p.85), shows a woman grinding maize
to make the flour needed to make the tortillas and atole porridge that were
staples of their diet.

On average, adult Aztec males were shorter than those of the eastern
Mediterranean after the origins of agriculture (Chapter 7), ranging between
156 and 167 cm according to social status (Faulhaber 1964). This suggests
that nutritional status was relatively poor. Post-conquest events were to
diminish nutritional health, through interactions between nutrition and newly
introduced infections. Virgin soil epidemics among the populations of
Mexico followed the Spanish conquest of 1519. These severely depleted

the population and were crucial to Spanish victory over the Atzec Empire. The first of these, in 1520–21, was caused by smallpox, killing between 10% and half of the population of Tenochtitlan, and was decisive in the fall of the city to the Spanish (Fenner *et al.* 1988). A second epidemic of this disease further diminished the population of the Valley of Mexico (Fenner *et al.* 1988). Hunger across this period due to disruption of the agricultural system further contributed to mortality (Vargas and Casillas 1990) and to diminished nutritional state. In the colonial period that followed, the Spanish enslaved the indigenous tribes, destroyed pre-Columbian society and indigenous languages, exploited natural resources, and developed new forms of social privilege and stratification. They introduced European systems of agriculture, along with new plants and animals (including cattle, poultry and pigs, wheat and rice) which competed for land and labour with native foods. Haciendas, or large estates, were granted to Spanish settlers (including the Catholic Church) in Mexico from 1529 onwards. These were usually plantations or large farms, but could also be mining concerns (for silver and gold in particular).

The Spanish conquest resulted in the class system of the indigenous populations being dissolved. With virgin soil epidemics due to the introduction of new infectious agents from Europe and the collapse of systems of trade and agriculture, all indigenous groups, regardless of earlier status, underwent famine, plague and population collapse. The colonizers, of both high and low class at their point of departure from Spain, had greater resistance to the infections they exported as well as privileged access to food and would have experienced much better nutritional health. Indigenous groups, including the once powerful and regionally dominant Aztecs, were distinguished from Spanish people by the colonizers as *naturales*, as opposed to *gente de razon* (rational people) or *gente decente* (decent people) to emphasize the distinction between them (Nutini 1997). Such classification promoted the marginalization and exploitation of indigenous populations by the social elite and gradually the rest of the population. The colonial imposition of the hacienda system amplified this marginality by creating intense social stratification in rural areas.

The dietary consequences of this new type of inequality were significant. The wealthy could re-create the gastronomy of Spain in the New World, including a meal structure based on European patterns of cuisine, with appetizers, side dishes, main courses and puddings, based on both local and introduced ingredients. European styles of food manufacture were also introduced, and from the sixteenth century, cheese and sausage became part of Mexican cuisine. For the upper classes of colonial Mexico, the fusion of local and introduced foods prepared within the structure of high European cuisine became the norm and formed the basis of present-day Mexican cuisine. The poor, reliant on wage labour from hacienda managers for subsistence, struggled to sustain themselves on diets consisting overwhelmingly of maize and beans. Among them, food insecurity was a harsh reality; famine was common across the nineteenth century, largely due to repeated drought. This was exacerbated by rising food prices in response to demand for food (maize prices more than doubled, while those of beans increased six-fold), while the wages of the rural poor remained static (Meyer *et al.* 2002).

The inequalities in nutritional health created by colonialism were maintained across the early period of globalization, when mercantile trade among the colonies (Spanish, Dutch, British, French, Belgian, American, Russian) benefitted the food security of the colonial nations and the new mercantile middle classes and ancestors of the initial colonizers of the colonized nations. At this time a new middle class emerged in Mexican cities and the gap between landless labourers and property-owning upper classes widened. Economic realities in Mexico and all other nations with colonial histories are shaped by national development infrastructures and international trading interdependencies created by the colonizer, be it Spain, Britain, France, Belgium, the US, or any other former colonial nation. The foods available and the cuisines that have developed from their use are therefore framed by the commercial interdependence of the colonizing and colonized nations. The nutrition transition scheme can thus be greatly enhanced by incorporating an age of colonialism after the age of famine. Popkin's (2002a) ages of nutrition transition, modified for the Mexican experience, are shown in Table 9.2, with such an age added as pattern 2a. This incorporates social and economic stratification, which influences dietary availability and nutritional health.

The third age of nutrition transition, that of agricultural and industrial revolution, again benefitted Spain, the colonizing nation, but did nothing to change the unequal set of relations among the populations of colonized Mexico. Production of refrigerated meats, canned vegetables and bottled drinks emerged in Mexico during the industrial boom of the 1890s. The 1910 revolution saw increased urbanization (Meyer *et al.* 2002), accompanied by severe but transitory disruptions in the production and distribution of food between 1910 and 1917. Wheat-based products increased in consumption across the twentieth century, this staple being given higher status and being associated with modernity and social progress. An inclusive national cuisine emerged, with agricultural and industrial modernization resulting in the commodification of both maize and wheat tortillas, transforming the former from a low-status subsistence crop to a market commodity (Pilcher 1998). And while multinational food products entered the Mexican market, national producers

Table 9.2 *Ages of nutrition transition*[a] *according to prehistoric and historical age, modified for the Mexican experience*

Pattern	Age	Time	Class Low	Class High
1	Hunter-gatherer	Pre-5000 years ago	No class; food collecting	No class; food collecting
2	Origins of agriculture and animal husbandry	Around 5000 years ago	Famine	Receding famine
2a	Colonialism and early globalization	1519 until eighteenth century	Famine (both low and high of pre-colonial indigenous population)	Receding famine (new colonizers)
3	Industrial revolution	Nineteenth century	Famine (both low and high of pre-colonial indigenous population)	Receding famine (colonial ancestry and middle classes)
4	Urbanization and economic improvement	Twentieth century	Famine	Degenerative diseases (existing ruling classes and new middle classes)
5	Postmodern	Twenty-first century	Famine and degenerative diseases	Behavioural change

[a] Popkin (2002a).

attempted to adapt them to suit Mexican tastes. Thus Mexican versions of fast foods and snacks followed the incorporation of international food products into established eating patterns.

The food security and nutritional health of Mexicans in the twentieth century has been shaped by the early colonial geography of social and economic stratification and commodization of agriculture, overlaid by Mexican nationalism, and subsequently economic relations with the increasingly dominant US (Morris 1999). In the second half of the twentieth century, the ideology of modernization and the penetration of heavily advertised transnational food products has led to a devaluation of traditional cooking and has encouraged poorer Mexicans to incorporate energy-dense foods rich in fats and refined carbohydrates, which became the cheapest source of calories. Under-nutrition in Mexico has largely been eradicated, through PROGRESA (Programa de Educación, Salud y Alimentación), introduced in 1997 by the federal government of Mexico (Skoufias 2005) and the decline in price of energy-dense foods. In recent decades, urbanization and agricultural decline in Mexico have been matched by increasing food imports from the US, with an increasing proportion of food being sold in supermarkets controlled by a small number of transnational corporations. In Mexico and elsewhere in Latin America, the expansion of retail through supermarkets and large-scale food manufacture have deeply transformed the markets for food (Reardon and Berdegué 2002), local and imported. Increasingly, food products are energy-dense, with high levels of fats and cereal-based refined carbohydrates. A number of transnational fast foods have been localized in Mexico, as elsewhere, such that green chillies can be part of a burger meal, and fizzy cola drinks are made with cane sugar rather than high-fructose corn syrup as in the US (Chapter 11). By adapting to local taste preferences, internationally branded fast foods have become indigenized.

Together with the increasing mechanization of everyday life (Ulijaszek and Lofink 2006), dietary change has left Mexico with an enormous burden of obesity, diabetes and cardiovascular disease. Figure 9.8 shows the rapid increase in chronic disease rates there in the 1980s and 1990s. The most recent dietary trend has been the rise of consumption of caloric beverages, including soft drinks, sweetened tea and coffee, sweetened juice and fruit drinks (Barquera *et al.* 2008, 2010). The final postmodern age of nutrition transition (Table 9.1), that of behavioural change towards improved health through changing lifestyle, is underway only among the middle and ruling classes of Mexico. The poor remain susceptible to degenerative disease.

Since colonial times, processes that have pushed dietary and nutritional change in Mexico have been driven initially by Spain and subsequently by other globally dominant nations of Europe and North America. The nutrition transition model elaborated for Mexico in Table 9.2 echoes Frenk and col-leagues' (1989) 'protracted–polarised' model of epidemiological change in ages 4 and 5 of Popkin's (2002a) scheme, incorporates social and economic inequality into ages 2–5, and adds a further age of colonialism and early globalization. Elsewhere, Raschke and Cheema (2008) have identified the origins of the nutritional transition to have started in East Africa with colonial occupation over 400 years ago. More broadly, Dixon (2009) views nutrition transition to have been underway internationally for over a century, as a product of ever more developed capitalist forms of food production.

Why is the Mexican obesity experience different from those of Brazil, China and Russia? These emerging nations reflect a wide range of colonial histories,

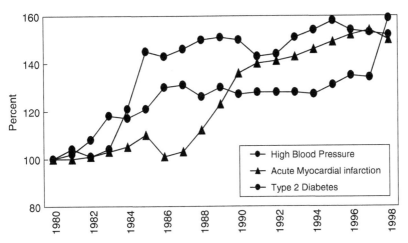

Figure 9.8. Increased age-adjusted mortality rates for diet-related chronic diseases in Mexico, 1980–1998 (1980 set at 100%) (adapted from Rivera *et al.* 2004).

and it may be inappropriate to bunch together nations emerging from communist political and economic systems with those having emerged from colonialism. This separates Russia and China from Mexico and Brazil. Russia was a colonizing nation, and not one that was colonized, while China maintained a large internal economy that failed to industrialize in the eighteenth and nineteenth centuries, and was briefly and partly colonized by the British. Both nations had centralized planned economies under communism in the twentieth century, only adopting the free market system in recent decades, and China only partly. Brazil and Mexico have broadly similar colonial histories, although colonized by different nations. Both have ethnicity-based inequality, which was created by the incoming colonial nation. Both Mexico and Brazil, like most emerging nations, maintain economic and political relationships with more powerful industrialized countries. The difference between these two nations, however, is that the relationship that Mexico has with the globally dominant economic power, the US, is much closer than the one Brazil maintains. Mexican migrants also send much higher remittances home than do Brazilian migrants. Remittances from Mexican emigrants in the US are the highest of any Latin American nation, representing 2.7% of GDP and being mostly used at the family and individual level, overwhelmingly for domestic expenditure, especially food (Carral Cuevas 2005). The flow of funds from relatives in the US has transformed many villages and even some regions in Mexico. Remittances may also promote obesity among the poor that receive them. In the next section, schemes are elaborated for Mexico's colonizer,

Spain, and its more recently dominant colonial cousin, the US, to give a broader description of nutrition transition for Mexico.

An elaboration of the nutrition transition model

The Mexican scheme offered in Table 9.2 remains incomplete without an examination of how it is related to that of its former colonizer, Spain, and its presently dominant neighbour, the US. Since nutrition transition theory alludes to present-day forces of globalization as being important in the shift from pattern 3 to pattern 4 of the nutrition transition, it is useful to see how globalization from an earlier age might have influenced present-day trading relations of Mexico. It is also useful to examine the extent to which the earlier patterns of nutrition transition correspond with Popkin's (2002a) formulation (Table 9.1). To those ends, a nutrition transition model is elaborated for Spain (Table 9.3).

Age 1 for Spain is characterized by prehistoric hunter-gatherers in the Iberian peninsula (of which Spain is a part), who are likely to have had a diet adequate for good nutritional health, as reflected in the tallness of adult males in Europe more generally at that time. At an average of 179 cm, they were comparable in stature to average European males at the end of the twentieth century (Hermanussen 2003). Across Europe, mean stature of adult males had declined to around 166 cm by 7500 years ago, and to below 165 cm after the adoption of agriculture (Piontek and Vancata 2002). The pre-agricultural decline in stature has been attributed by Hermanussen (2003) in part to a shift from large- to small-mammal hunting, as climatic warming reached a maximum between 7500 and 5000 years ago. During this time, cold-adapted large mammals such as reindeer migrated north and east, and were replaced by smaller species (Hermanussen 2003), making hunting less energetically efficient because of reduced frequency of capture. The decline in stature suggests that this transition involved declines in nutritional health and increased mortality.

Agriculture emerged in the Iberian peninsula between 7500 and 6000 years ago (Zapata *et al.* 2004; Pena-Chocarro *et al.* 2005), with the principal adoption of wheat and barley as cereal staples (Zapata *et al.* 2004). The small decline in stature between the trapping phase of hunter-gatherer existence and the origins of agriculture suggests the declines in health and well-being that might have come with agriculture in the eastern Mediterranean were not so pervasive here. However, both beta thalassemia and glucose-6-phosphate dehydrogenase (G6PD) deficiency are prevalent among the contemporary Spanish population (Villegas *et al.* 1998; Rovira *et al.* 1995), indicating that malaria was a strong

Table 9.3 *Ages of nutrition transition[a] according to prehistoric and historical age, modified for the Spanish experience*

Pattern	Age	Time	Class	
			Low	High
1	Hunter-gatherer	Pre-7500–6000 years ago	Hunter-gatherer; no class; food collecting	Hunter-gatherer; no class; food collecting
2	Origins of agriculture and animal husbandry	7500–6000 years ago	Agriculture; emergence of class; no evidence of famine	Agriculture; emergence of class; no evidence of famine
2a	Colonialism	1519	Famine	Strong hierarchy; no evidence of famine
2b	Early globalization	18th century	Famine	No famine
3	Industrial revolution	19th century	Famine	No famine
4	Urbanization and economic improvement	20th century	Receding famine	Degenerative diseases
5	Postmodern	21st century	Degenerative diseases	Behavioural change

[a] Popkin (2002a).

selective force among human populations there. Social inequality emerged from around 3500 years ago, with evidence for local elites being evident at Los Milares (southeastern Spain) from around 3500 years ago (Díaz-del-Rio 2006).

Prior to being a colonizing nation, Spain (and in its earlier form, Iberia) had been colonized in part by Carthage, becoming part of the Carthaginian Republic 2300 years ago, before falling into Roman hands after the second Punic War 2200 years ago. It remained under Roman control for around 600 years, with a respite from colonial control for around 300 years after the decline of the Roman Empire, and around 300 further years of control under the Moorish Empire. Spain's ruling class emerged in medieval times. By the twelfth century, social stratification had amplified to the extent that a feudal system emerged that allowed an aristocracy to flourish (Barton 1997). The Spanish aristocracy of the fifteenth century transformed the Spanish from a colonized to a colonizing people, with the conquest of Mexico being among its earliest colonial adventures. From the sixteenth to the nineteenth century, the Spanish ruling class exported its system of social and economic inequality to much of the Americas and to parts of Africa and Asia, in its pursuit of resources (Kamen 2003). Colonial wars in the eighteenth and nineteenth centuries saw

Spain lose its ascendancy, Mexico being granted independence in 1820. The Spanish–American War of 1898 saw the end of Spanish colonies in the Americas, and the ascendency and subsequent dominance of the US in the regional politics of the Americas.

Spain's nutrition transition into patterns 3, 4 and 5 of Popkin's scheme is unremarkable in relation to other Western European nations. However, Spanish cuisine benefitted from the introduction of the potato, the tomato, the capsicum and other food commodities from the New World. These diffused quickly across Europe, and Spain's colonial food products became those of Europe. In turn, they have become indigenized, and remain part of the everyday diet of most of Europe.

To understand nutrition transition in Mexico, it is important to understand nutrition transition in the US (Table 9.4), because of the great economic and demographic interconnectedness of the two countries, both historically and now. The best evidence for nutritional health of prehistoric North American hunter-gatherers (pattern 1) comes from skeletal and dental measures of stress such as porotic hyperostosis, Harris lines, long bone lengths and widths, and developmental enamel defects (especially linear enamel hypoplasia) (Goodman *et al.* 1984a) among skeletal remains at burial sites at Dickson Mounds, Illinois. Analysis of such material evidence has given the best example of health of indigenous North American gatherers around 1000 years ago, and of their subsequent sedentization and maize-based agriculture by 800 years ago (Goodman *et al.* 1984a). The nutritional health of Lower Mississippian populations at Dickson Mounds prior to the adoption of agriculture was far better than after it (Goodman *et al.* 1984b; Cook 1984), although the patterns more generally in North America are complex (Yesner 1994; Chapter 7). Mortuary finds suggestive of social stratification indicate that inequality emerged soon after the adoption of agriculture (Rothschild 1979).

Prior to European settlement, Upper Mississippian society was flourishing. Figure 9.9 shows Mississippian settlements of the US midwest from 1000 to 500 years ago. Imposed on this map are the locations of the first and second capitals of the State of Illinois, Kaskaskia (entitled so in 1809) and Vandalia (to where it moved in 1820). Table 9.5 gives a chronology of the decline of the indigenous population of Illinois and the settlement and rise of European colonies.

European contact came in 1541 by the Spanish explorer Hernando de Soto (Young and Hoffman 1993; Clayton *et al.* 1993). De Soto's expedition did not lead to Spanish acquisition so far north into America, and the French were the first colonial power to lay claim to this region, over 150 years later. In 1703 a French Jesuit mission was established at the mouth of the Kaskaskia River, after missionary settlement of a group of Middle Mississippian Indians there in

Table 9.4 *Ages of nutrition transition[a] according to prehistoric and historical age, modified for the United States experience*

			Class	
Pattern	Age	Time	Low	High
1	Hunter-gatherer	Pre-5000 years ago	Native American; no class; food collecting	Native American; no class; food collecting
2	Origins of agriculture and animal husbandry	5000–1000 years ago	Native American; Famine	Native American; famine
2a	Colonialism	1620	Famine among Native Americans, both low and high class	Receding famine (new colonizers)
2b	Early globalization	Eighteenth century	Famine among Native American population	Receding famine (colonial ancestry and new migrants)
3	Industrialization	Nineteenth century	Famine among Native American population	Receding famine (colonial ancestry, middle classes and new migrants)
4	Urbanization and economic improvement	Twentieth century	Degenerative diseases among Native American population, poor and new migrants	Degenerative diseases
5	Postmodern (speculative)	Twenty-first century	Degenerative diseases among Native American population and poor	Behavioural change

[a] Popkin (2002a).

1700 (Mooney 1910). While early European settlers coexisted with the Native American population, hostilities erupted over resources by the 1750s, when food insecurity and famine threatened both colonized and colonizer. The French response was to control the indigenous population more formally by introducing a military presence at Kaskaskia in 1759, which was maintained until the territory was ceded to the British in 1763. The French pursued a policy of forced possession of land and dissipation of the local population, which led to their rapid decline. Population decline was assisted by food insecurity and famine (due to land dispossession), and death from new diseases introduced by the colonizers, including malaria. The latter disease was introduced to the Americas by the Spanish colonizers of the fifteenth century, and subsequently by widespread European colonization and the slave trade from

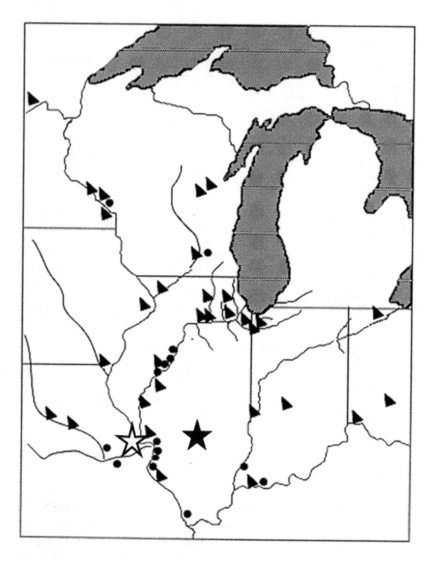

● = Middle Mississippian   ▶ = Upper Mississippian or Caddoan

Figure 9.9. Middle (circle) and Upper (triangle) Mississippian settlements of the
United States midwest, 1000 to 500 years ago, with the first European settlement, Fort
Kaskaskia (then first state capital), represented as an open star, and subsequent capital,
Vandalia, as a black star (modified from Jeske 1996).

Table 9.5 *The European settlement of Illinois*

Year	Act	Effect/purpose
1541	First European contact: Spanish explorer Hernando de Soto	Expedition from Spain in search of resources in North America
1700	Settlement of Native Americans at mouth of Kaskaskia River	Missionization
1703	Jesuit missionary post established at Kaskaskia	Missionization
1759	Fort Kaskaskia established by French settlers	Control and dissipation of indigenous population
1795	Native American groups enter treaty with United States	Deportation of all remaining native peoples to Oklahoma
1809	Illinois Territory created, with Kaskaskia as capital (population around 40 000)	Formal annexation
1814	Illinois attains statehood	State political control
1819	Federal land sold for US $1.23 an acre with a minimum sale of 80 acres	European agricultural settlement
1820	State capital relocated to Vandalia, on the National Road. Steamboat traffic on Illinois River established	Fast connection to Baltimore and St Louis (three weeks between the two), and along Illinois River to Peoria
1832	Black Hawk War	Removal of last organized American Indians
1833	Last remaining Indian lands ceded to government	
1832–4	Cholera epidemic in Illinois	High mortality
1837	Chicago incorporated as a city (population of 4170)	

Africa that followed it. While malaria inhibited development by killing new settlers, it is likely to have killed proportionately more of the indigenous population. The indigenous Kaskaskia population numbered around 2000 at the turn of the eighteenth century. They were reduced to 600 in 1764, and only 210 in 1778 (Mooney 1910). This mirrors similar population declines with colonial contact elsewhere in the world (Ulijaszek 2006).

In 1795, the indigenous population of Illinois entered into treaty relations with the recently formed nation of the US. While hostilities persisted between the European settlers and various indigenous groups in the early 1800s, the Black Hawk War of 1832 completed the process of European domination. This was helped by high mortality from cholera when the second pandemic reached Illinois in 1832, persisting there until 1834. The last remaining indigenously controlled lands were ceded to the government in the following year and the remaining populations deported to reservation life in Oklahoma (Mooney 1910).

Alongside the systematic eradication of the indigenous population in this region came European American development. In 1809, Illinois Territory was created, and Kaskaskia was the first capital, with a population of around 40 000 Europeans. In 1814, the Territory of Illinois was advanced to State-hood. While agricultural settlement of Europeans advanced steadily across the previous 100 years, land which came under Federal control after relocation of the Native American population was sold cheaply and in large quantity, to hasten the agricultural development of the midwest. With such development came the need for faster access to other European population centres, and for trade routes. When the National Road between Baltimore and St Louis was built, the Illinois State capital was relocated to a town on this road, Vandalia, in 1820 (it moved again to Springfield in 1839, where it remains). A steamboat connection was established on the Illinois River in the same year, establishing a transport link between the Great Lakes and the Mississippi River.

With lands freed and hostilities ended, the nineteenth century midwest of the US saw far-reaching change. Developments in agricultural technology and transport brought new ways of food production, processing, distribution and delivery to its consumers (Popkin 2009). The completion of both the Illinois and Michigan Canal and railroad in 1848 linked the sites of grain (wheat and maize) and animal (cattle and swine) production to the Great Lakes and Chicago, which had been incorporated as a city in 1837. The Chicago Board of Trade, established in 1848, was the first modern futures exchange, with the first futures contract being drawn up for the price of maize in 1851. The industrialization that followed included the development of new food tech-nologies that both made food safe and free from contamination, and was used to create new food products and categories. Ready-to-eat breakfast cereals appeared as a new food category in the late 1800s. The food industry that emerged was engaged in the technological transformation of products of midwestern agriculture into food products. Its subsequent development shaped the nature of the US diet. This increasingly influenced diets across the world and has contributed to the shift from pattern 3 to pattern 4 of the nutrition transition in many nations (Table 9.1).

The nutritional health of US citizens was superior to that of Europeans from the mid-1800s into the mid-twentieth century (Komlos and Baur 2004). The American height advantage over western and northern Europeans was between 3 and 9 cm in the mid-nineteenth century (Komlos and Baur 2004). Industri-alization was a response to the need to feed the growing urban populations of the US. Urban populations became reliant on food products based on the midwestern agricultural commodities of maize, wheat and cattle, as well as chicken and pigs. These commodities continue to be the basis of the US diet to the present day (Food and Agriculture Organization 2011), being processed into a dazzling array of food products (Popkin 2011). Many of these food products appeal to a range of senses in addition to appetite, making them easy to overconsume (Chapter 5). By promoting quantity of sales, many of the food manufacturers and retailers of the US have inadvertently facilitated the production of obesogenic environments across the second half of the twentieth century.

Discussion

The nutrition transition framework of Popkin (1998, 2002a) (Table 9.1) is correct in broadest outline. However, we have identified two important omissions from it: (1) social and economic inequality; and (2) colonialism and early globalization. Furthermore, care is needed when applying other parts of this scheme. For example, the age of food collecting is generally associated with better nutritional health than after the origins of agriculture, but it cannot be assumed that all societies prior to the emergence of agriculture had good nutrition. Pre-agricultural populations in the eastern Mediterranean region had better nutritional health than after the origins of agriculture (Chapter 11) but seasonal nutritional stress, as indicated by enamel hypoplasias (Chapter 4) is evident in teeth well before this time. For example, archaic *Homo sapiens* from Iberia have hypoplasias, albeit at lower frequencies than are seen in either prehistoric foragers or early agriculturalists (de Castro and Perez 1995). In the US, the hunter-gatherer populations represented at Dickson Mounds had high rates of palaeopathologies associated with poor nutritional health, although these were two to four times lower than among agriculturalists (Lallo *et al.* 1977; Goodman *et al.* 1980). Within-population variation, including but not confined to social stratification, is likely to have led to different diets (Chapter 5) and it is likely that this would have been associated with differences in nutritional health.

In the nutrition transition framework, the age of agricultural technology and industrial revolution resulted in receding famine. However, the social and material effects of these innovations could not have been multiplied across the European world without colonialism. Of the nations examined in this chapter, Mexico, Spain and the US experienced receding famine with industrialization, with social stratification influencing the extent of this change. Mexico and the US experienced an additional earlier transition, with colonization and early globalization. In these two nations, receding famine after colonization benefitted the new colonizers only. This would have been the case also in places where the indigenous population practised hunting and gathering, as in Australia and Amazonia, except that the local populations were usually dispossessed of their subsistence livelihood and thrown into the lowest of ranks serving the globalizing and globalized political system. In this process, they were forced, by absence of other alternatives, to consume the products of the globalized food supply system. Where it existed prior to colonialism, the social stratification of the societies found and conquered by colonizers was shredded, reducing all native peoples to the lowest status. Industrialization benefitted all colonizers, new migrants and middle classes, but it usually left the indigenous populations socially marginalized and poor. The incorporation of colonialism and early globalization into the analysis of nutrition transition is useful in defining and understanding the commercial and political relationships that continue to influence food trade and price in the present age of emerging degenerative disease among economically emerging nations. While the age of degenerative disease came with urbanization and economic improvement during the twentieth century, this was again mediated by economic and social inequality. The case study of this chapter shows this to be more so in Mexico than in either Spain or the US.

The relationships between the emergence and increase in chronic disease prevalence with twentieth century urbanization and economic improvement are weak, and Mexico is an outlier. While the per capita GDP of Mexico in the mid- 2000s, at US$12 780 per annum, was less than half that of Spain at that time (US$31 312) and less than one third of the US then (US$45 790), its chronic disease profile is not out of step with its richer partners (Figure 9.10), with only the proportion of adults with raised cholesterol being universally lowest among the three. The greater proportion of middle and higher social and economic classes in the US and Spain, and the greater likelihood that they have entered the age of behavioural change, may explain some of these patterns. Behavioural change is viewed by Popkin as involving lifestyle change (personal communication, 2011). While this is usually taken to include diet and physical activity patterns, it can equally involve the incorporation of everyday pharmaceutical interventions to reduce the physiological risk factors associated with chronic and degenerative diseases. This is already widely practised with anti-diabetes, anti-hypertension and anti-hypercholesterolaemia medication in most industrialized countries.

In Mexico, increased prosperity has led to increased birth weight and a reduction in the proportion of infants born at low birth weight. This might modulate the risk of adverse chronic disease outcomes, according to the fetal programming hypothesis (Barker 1992; Lucas *et al.* 1999) (Chapter 1), which suggests that small size at birth is associated with an increased risk of adverse health outcomes in adulthood, including abnormal blood lipid values, diabetes, hypertension, and death from ischaemic heart disease. The probable extent of this change on chronic and degenerative disease rates is unclear, although it can be estimated crudely from known measures of birth weight and chronic disease markers in subsequent life.

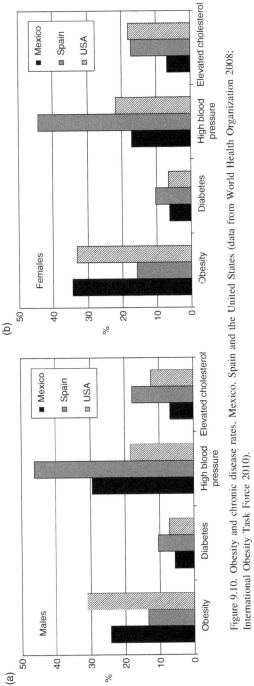

Figure 9.10. Obesity and chronic disease rates, Mexico, Spain and the United States (data from World Health Organization 2008; International Obesity Task Force 2010).

Table 9.6 *Mean values for age, BMI, blood pressure, LDL-cholesterol and fasting blood insulin, adolescents, males and females combined*

		Birth weight quartile		Quartile 1/2
		1	2	
	Birth weight	2.73	3.27	0.83
Values in	Age (years)	14.8	15.0	0.99
adolescence	BMI	23.7	22.3	1.06
	Systolic blood pressure	109.1	107.2	1.02
	Diastolic blood pressure	56.2	56.1	1.00
	LDL-cholesterol	2.3	2.2	1.04
	Fasting insulin (weight-adjusted)	17.2	15.2	1.13

Adapted from Murtaugh *et al.* (2003).

In a large study of birth weight and adult serum cholesterol, Davies *et al.* (2004) found that a 0.5 kg increase in birth weight (from, for example, 2.5 to 3.0 kg) was associated with a decline in cholesterol of 0.035 mmol per litre in males, and no decline in females. In the case of males, such birth weight change would explain at most one per cent of Mexican hypercholesterolaemia in recent times (Figure 9.10), and possibly an additional one per cent increase in this measure, which would have been realized if there had been no increase in birth weight. If it is assumed that the proportion of low birth weight infants declined by eight per cent in Mexico across the period of degenerative disease emergence, this proportion (and potential increase if birth weight had remained unchanged) is reduced to less than 0.1% of the general population.

Data on US adolescents (Murtaugh *et al.* 2003) (Table 9.6) indicate a four per cent difference in serum cholesterol between quartiles one and two of birth weight, which differ in mean birth weight by 0.5 kg. If this can be extrapolated to the general Mexican population, this would explain only 0.3% of the elevated cholesterol there, and possibly an additional 0.3% increase in this measure which would have been realized if there had been no increase in birth weight. With respect to blood pressure, Law *et al.* (2002) found systolic blood pressure of British adults to decline by 0.65 mmHg for every 0.5 kg increase in birth weight. If this can be applied to the Mexican population, low birth weight would explain only 0.5% of the hypertension rate there, with a possibly additional 0.5% increase, which would have been realized if there had been no increase in birth weight. Again, if it is assumed that the proportion of low-birth-weight infants declined by eight per cent in Mexico across the period of degenerative disease emergence, this proportion (and the potential increase if birth weight remained stable) is reduced to 0.04% of the general population.

Data on US adolescents (Murtaugh *et al.* 2003) indicate a two per cent difference in systolic blood pressure between quartiles one and two of birth weight (a difference of 0.5 kg), and no difference in diastolic blood pressure (Table 9.6). If this can be applied to the general Mexican population, then low birth weight would explain a maximum of 0.2% of the overall hypertension rate, and possibly an additional 0.2% increase in hypertension rate which would have been realized if there had been no increase in birth weight.

The greatest proportion of degenerative disease that can be explained by low birth weight is Type 2 diabetes. Following the same procedure shows low birth weight to contribute a very small amount to overall Type 2 diabetes rates. British data (Barker 1992) show the risk of developing impaired glucose tolerance or diabetes in adult life to increase by 18% with a 0.5 kg decline in birth weight. If low birth weight declined by eight per cent across the period of chronic disease emergence, then this would explain 1.4% of the Type 2 diabetes rate in the general population, and possibly an additional 1.4% increase in this rate, which would have been realized if there had been no increase in birth weight. The US adolescents (Table 9.6) of quartile one have a mean fasting insulin value 13% greater than that of adolescents in quartile two. By applying this again to the general Mexican population, this would explain one per cent of the overall diabetes rate observed there, and possibly an additional 1.4% increase in this rate which would have been realized if there had been no increase in birth weight. Thus the fetal programming hypothesis carries very little weight in trying to understand the changing chronic disease patterns in Mexico across recent decades. Indeed, the effects of changing birth weight patterns are trivial compared to the larger environmental, political, social and economic forces that promote these chronic diseases in Mexico. However, the transgenerational epigenetic consequences of fetal stress (Chapters 4 and 7) are unknown but may be significant.

Inequality is another factor that could explain the high levels of chronic disease risk in Mexico, although social and economic mobility as a factor operating through increased birth weight can be discounted as a dominant explanation. Pickett *et al.* (2005) have identified income inequality to be positively associated with adult obesity, diabetes and daily energy intake among industrialized nations. In this chapter (and in Chapter 8) we have shown how inequality has pervaded all the societies examined, from the origins of agriculture to the present day. Low social status has psychosocial effects that contribute to poor health by way of anxiety, stress and inability to control everyday life events and future possibilities (Marmot 2004). Is it possible that deep-seated inequality, such as that experienced by many indigenous Mexicans and poorer US citizens, has deeper and more pervasive impacts on health than inequality of more recent origin?

Institutional marginalization and structural violence of the type Farmer (2004) describes for much of the contemporary developing world usually reflects deep-seated inequality. Illness may be a result of neither culture nor pure individual will, but of historically given (and often economically driven) processes and forces that constrain individual agency or the capacity of humans to make choices and impose them on the world. Some of these processes and forces have been described earlier in this chapter, and in Chapter 4. Mexico underwent transformation when one set of colonial forces descended upon it in the sixteenth century. By the nineteenth century, its entire indigenous population had been marginalized. Then it came under the influence of a second dominant power, the US, a nation that had asserted hegemonic power upon its indigenous population early during its formation as a state. The emergence of degenerative disease among the Mexican poor can therefore be seen as an outcome of structural violence. Most recently this has involved national and multinational corporations extending commercial food products into every corner of Mexican society. And while the Mexican economy grew enormously between the 1940s and 1980s with unprecedented industrialization and urbanization, this came with predominantly US investment and has resulted in increasing dependence on this northern neighbour.

The industrialized food system is perhaps an unwitting accomplice of nutritional structural violence, while its achievements have transformed human quality of life by delivering predictable, safe and clean food to the billions of people on earth that do not engage in subsistence agriculture. However, its central ethos of profit maximization promotes consumption among many, often in ways that do not promote health. As an agent of dietary change, the history of the industrialized food system is an important part of the nutrition transition narrative, although one that is not generally incorporated. We have shown how European settlers in the US adopted maize agriculture practised by the indigenous populations, incorporated wheat cultivation and animal husbandry, and set up systems of agricultural production and trade, food processing and distribution that shaped the world food system and continued into the twentieth and twenty-first centuries. The food commodities system, first formalized in Chicago, traded maize, wheat, cattle and pigs initially. These few species (along with a very small number of others) have become the staples of fast- and convenience-foods that form the majority of the dietary energy intake of people in the US. The financial and corporate support that helped Mexico develop economically across the twentieth century also allowed the US food system to penetrate its markets.

The added layers of inequality, colonialism and early globalization also help to frame nutritional health and the recent emergence of degenerative disease among indigenous populations as nutrition transition. One question not answered by the extended nutrition transition framework offered here is why social and economic class differences in nutritional health persist. One argument might be that, apart from income, human agency (the ability of individuals to make decisions and to impose them on the world) is one of the most important factors influencing health. Indigenous groups have had agency systematically stripped away from them since contact with dominant, often colonially expanding groups. Lower social classes, where prospects for upward mobility are limited, also lack control and agency. Self-control and self-determination are prerequisites to making a transition to Popkin's (1998, 2002a) age of behavioural change; at present, such qualities are concentrated among higher social classes. Among these classes, self-control and self-determination are concentrated among those with an historically grounded sense of status and entitlement. Popkin's stage of behavioural change is not a given, in any society. And it can be argued that attainment of this age requires deeper examination of inequality and its impacts on nutritional health (Chapter 8).

10 *Fats in the global balance*

Introduction

Fats are common in nature in diverse forms, and when eaten, represent a more concentrated form of energy than either protein or carbohydrate. For this reason, they were probably sought out by human ancestors, since their consumption enabled dietary energy budgets to be met more easily. Fats have been good sources of dietary energy across prehistory and history, either when food supplies were limited or when work schedules were energetically demanding. Only in recent decades in industrialized societies has food security improved and the energetic demands of physical work declined to very low levels, making positive energy balance difficult to resist for many. Consumption of large amounts of fat can be problematic from a public health perspective because of its potential to increase weight gain. While there is no direct evidence that total fat intake influences rates of cardiovascular disease (CVD) or cancers (Food and Agriculture Organization 2008), excess bodily fatness (to which fat consumption contributes) has a direct relationship with increased rates of CVD and Type 2 diabetes.

Figure 10.1 gives dietary fat availability per head in 1961 and 2007 for a range of industrialized and economically emerging nations. While availability of animal fat has increased dramatically in France and Italy and declined in the United States (US), United Kingdom (UK), Australia and New Zealand, availability of vegetable fats has increased greatly in all the nations represented in this figure. And fats from both animal and vegetable sources have increased in availability in all nations apart from the UK and New Zealand. In these two countries, declines in animal fat availability have been largely, but not totally, displaced by increased availability of vegetable fats. Industrialized nations of Asia, such as Japan and South Korea, and emerging nations, such as Mexico, Brazil, China and India, generally have low levels of animal fat availability. Most dietary sources of saturated fats have been animal products, whether

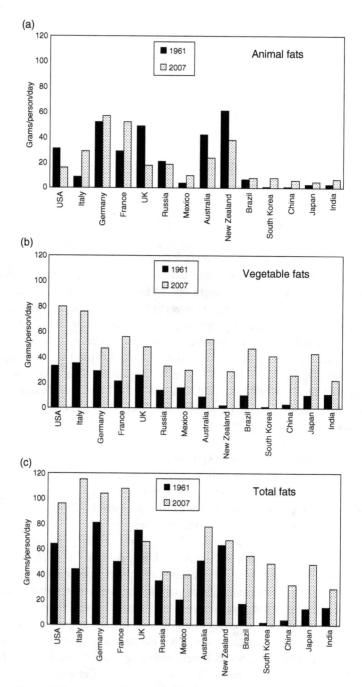

Figure 10.1. Fat availability in national diets (grams/person/day) in 1961 and 2007 (data from Food and Agriculture Organization 2011).

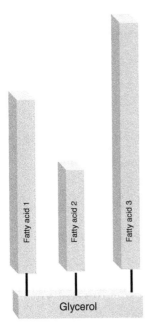

Figure 10.2. Triacylglycerol molecule: the typical molecular form of dietary fat or oil. Three fatty acids (generally different) are attached to a three-carbon glycerol molecule. The fatty acids can be of varying carbon chain length and have differing numbers of double bonds (0 = saturated, 1 = monounsaturated [MUFA], ≥2 = polyunsaturated [PUFA]).

meat, organs or dairy, although palm oil use in the food industry is displacing the predominance of animal-derived saturated fats in the diets of some countries.

Fats and oils in the human diet are predominantly in the form of triacylglycerols, which consist of three fatty acids linked to a glycerol (Figure 10.2). These fatty acids can vary in carbon chain length, but are generally between 8 and 30 carbons long and can have variable numbers of double bonds between carbon atoms to form three classes of fatty acids. These are saturated (zero double bonds); monounsaturated fatty acids (MUFA; one double bond); and polyunsaturated fatty acids (PUFA, two or more double bonds) (Figure 10.3).

There are two main classes of PUFA, omega-3 (n-3) and omega-6 (n-6) (Figure 10.4; Chapter 5). While n-6 PUFA are found mostly in cereals and vegetable oils, they also occur in smaller amounts in poultry, eggs and nuts, whereas n-3 PUFA are found mostly in fish, meat (from pasture-fed animals) and some seeds, nuts and eggs. Although both plant and animal foods contain PUFA, the plant forms never exceed 18 carbons in chain length, while animal

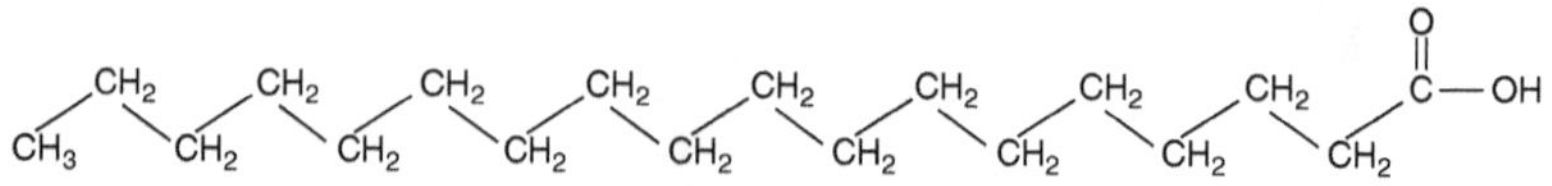

A saturated fatty acid: Stearic acid 18:0 (Octadecanoic acid)

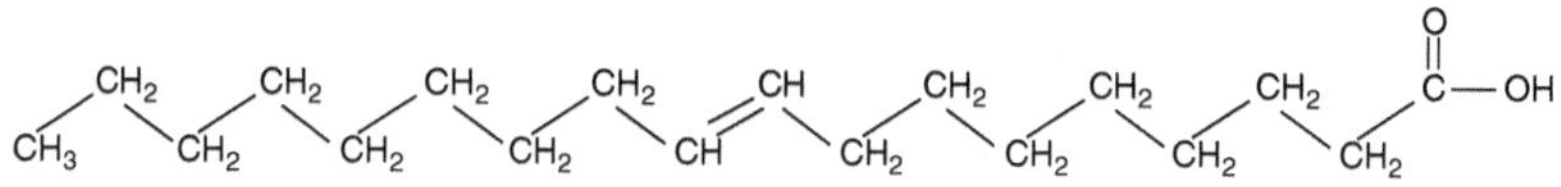

A monounsaturated fatty acid: Oleic acid 18:1 (cis-9-Octadecenoic acid)

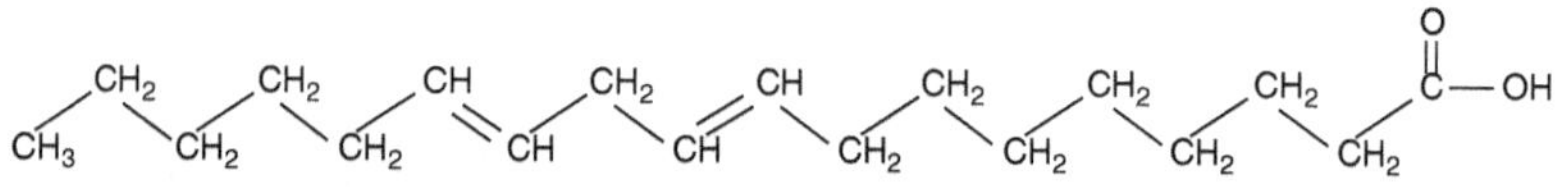

An omega-6 Polyunsaturated fatty acid: Linoleic acid 18:2n6 (cis, cis-9,12-octadecadienoic acid)

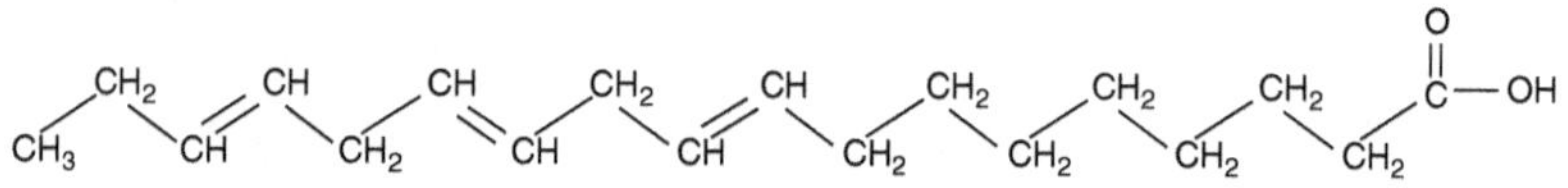

An omega-3 Polyunsaturated fatty acid: alpha-Linolenic acid 18:3n3 (cis,cis,cis-9,12,15-Octadecatrienoic acid)

Figure 10.3. Illustration of a saturated fatty acid (stearic acid), a monounsaturated fatty acid (oleic acid) and the two 18-carbon PUFA, alpha linolenic acid (ALA, 18:3n-3) and linoleic acid (LA, 18:2n-6) which represent the precursors of the omega-6 and omega-3 families respectively. Mammalian metabolism allows insertion of extra double bonds between the first double bond and acid end, but not extra double bonds between the first double bond and the methyl end. In this way the closest double bond to the terminal methyl group (omega end of the molecule) to the left is always at position 3 or 6, hence the name of the series.

tissues can contain longer forms, termed long chain PUFA (LCPUFA, more than 18 carbons in length). Industrial food processing has also created the trans-fatty acids, which are now prevalent in diets in the form of margarines and shortenings (the fats used in cakes, biscuits and cookies). Most contemporary western diets are generally high in saturated and trans-fats and n-6 PUFA, but low in n-3 PUFA. In contrast to usual diets in economically developed nations, and based on data from Australian foragers, hunter-gatherers tend to consume foods relatively low in saturated, trans-fats and n-6 PUFA, but higher in n-3 PUFA (O'Dea 1991a). This is also the case for some diets of the health-conscious in industrialized and post-industrial countries today.

Cardiovascular disease and coronary heart disease (CHD) are major causes of death in industrialized societies and have been linked in part to

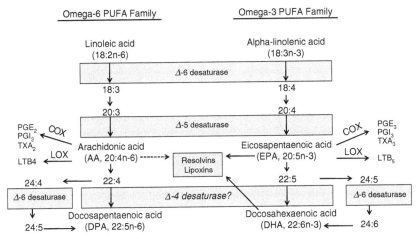

Figure 10.4. Pathways of chain elongation and desaturation steps (double bond addition) of the omega-6 and omega-3 PUFA families, leading from the mainly plant-based 18-carbon forms to the long-chain fatty acids AA, EPA and DHA (adapted from Russo 2009). COX, cyclo-oxygenase; LOX, lipoxygenase. Note: (i) Mammals lack any enzymatic processes for inter-converting between these two families of PUFA. (ii) The final Δ-4 desaturase step is in doubt and conversion of 22:4n6 & 22:5n3 to 22:5n6 and DHA, respectively, is more likely to involve a chain elongation followed by a further Δ-6 desaturase step and finally a chain reduction step (Sprecher 1992; D'Andrea *et al.* 2002).

high blood pressure, hyperlipidaemia (elevated serum total and low density lipoprotein (LDL)-cholesterol and triacylglycerol (TG)) and Type 2 diabetes. These aspects of metabolism can be altered by changing diet, including amounts and types of fat consumed. The fatty acids eaten in the diet vary in their digestibility, absorption, metabolism, and their influence on health and well-being. The total amount of fat in the diet is less important in the direct causation of CVD than the relative amounts of specific fatty acids (Gardner and Kraemer 1995; Nelson *et al.* 1995; Connor and Connor 1997). In contemporary western societies, consumption of high-fat, domesticated animal foods has been linked to mortality from CVD (Barnard *et al.* 1995), while high intakes of lean red meat (with all visible fat trimmed off) have been associated with lowered plasma lipids (O'Dea *et al.* 1990). The cholesterol-lowering effect of lean meat is rapidly reversed by the addition of animal fat to the diet (O'Dea *et al.* 1990), but not by the addition of the monounsaturated fatty acids (MUFA) such as those found in olive oil, for example, or PUFA (Morgan *et al.* 1993). Similarly, total and LDL-cholesterol levels do not vary with overall fat intake when saturated fat intakes are kept constant (Nelson *et al.* 1995).

In this chapter we explore the nature of fats in the diet, how they have changed across evolutionary and recent times, and how they influence disease patterns.

Dietary fat and disease risk

Relationships between fat intake and blood cholesterol levels are well known, as is the knowledge that not all fats are equal in this regard. The most hypercholesterolaemic fatty acids are the saturated fatty acids, which vary in carbon chain length from 8 to 18 (Grundy 1997a,b). Both MUFA (Gardner and Kraemer 1995) and PUFA (Grundy 1997a) have mild hypocholaesterolaemic properties. Equations have been developed to predict the relative effect of fat type on serum cholesterol levels (Yu *et al.* 1995; Müller *et al.* 2001). Generally the change in serum total cholesterol and change in LDL-cholesterol is expressed in mmol/l and the change in intake of fatty acids is expressed as percentage of energy intake. Müller *et al.* (2001) refined earlier equations developed by Yu *et al.* (1995) and included the hypercholesterolaemic effects of trans-fats, but removed stearic acid (18:0) from the algorithm as this fatty acid has no appreciable effect on serum cholesterol (Yu *et al.* 1995) (Table 10.1).

High-fat diets can be consumed without detrimental effects on blood lipids and CVD risk as long as the saturated and trans-fatty acid contents are low (Mensink and Katan 1992; Gardner and Kraemer 1995; Nelson *et al.* 1995). This may have been the case among hunter-gatherers with a traditional diet, where often high fat intakes, usually from wild game animals, have been associated with low blood concentrations of LDL-cholesterol and TG (Corcoran and Rabinowitch 1937; Bang and Dyerberg 1980; Connor 2001), both associated with low CVD risk. Bang and Dyerberg (1980) showed that, despite having a dietary fat intake similar to or higher than the Danish population of the time, Greenland Inuit had significantly lower blood lipid levels and a near-absence of CVD, unlike the general Danish population. Inuit fat intakes came mainly from marine animals, were high in MUFA and PUFA (particularly n-3), and low in saturated fat. This was in contrast to the Danish population, whose fat intake was rich in saturated fat from dairy, domesticated meat and processed foods (Table 10.2). Application of the equation of Müller *et al.* (2001) (Table 10.1) shows that the total serum cholesterol level of the Inuit population would be 14% higher if their fatty acid intake profile was the same as that of the general Danish population. This is close to the 17% difference in this measure between the Inuit and Danish populations of Bang and Dyerberg's (1980) study.

Table 10.1 *Percentage change in total serum cholesterol and low-density lipoprotein (LDL) cholesterol levels due to specific fatty acids when 100 kcal or more of dietary intake comes from a specific fatty acid*

Fatty acid	Lauric	Myristic	Palmitic	Trans fatty acids	Oleic	Linoleic and alpha linolenic
Type	12:0	14:0	16:0		18:1	18:2 and 18:3
Change in total serum cholesterol	+1	+12	+6	+4	−0.04	−1.7
Change in LDL cholesterol	+1	+7	+5	+4	−0.04	−1.7

Equations:
Change in total serum cholesterol mmol/L = 0.01 (change in lauric acid) + 0.12 (change in myristic acid) + 0.057 (change in palmitic acid) + 0.039 (change in trans fats from soy oil) + 0.031 (change in trans fats from fish oil) − 0.0044 (change in oleic acid) − 0.017 (change in linoleic and alpha linolenic acids)
Change in LDL cholesterol mmol/L = 0.01 (change in lauric acid) + 0.071 (change in myristic acid) + 0.047 (change in palmitic acid) + 0.043 (change in trans fats from soy oil) + 0.025 (change in trans fats from fish oil) − 0.0044 (change in oleic acid) − 0.017 (change in linoleic and alpha linolenic acids)
All changes, in mmol/L have been converted into percentages.
From Muller *et al.* (2001).

Table 10.2 *Comparison of dietary fat intake and blood lipid levels between Danes and Greenland Inuit*

Variable	Greenland Inuit	Danes
Dietary intake		
Fat (% energy)	37	42
Saturated fat (% of total fat)	23	53
MUFA (% of total fat)	57	35
PUFA (% of total fat)	19	12
n-6 PUFA (g)	5	10
n-3 PUFA (g)	14	3
Blood lipids		
Total cholesterol (mmol/L)	5.3	6.2
Triacylglycerols (mmol/L)	0.6	1.3

Adapted from Bang and Dyerberg (1980) and Cordain *et al.* (2002a).

With respect to dietary fat intake and CHD risk, the type of fat consumed is more important than total fat intake (Hu *et al.* 2001). Adducing evidence from randomized controlled trials, Skeaff and Miller (2009) found CHD mortality to be positively associated with trans-fatty acid intake and negatively associated with long chain (LC) n-3 PUFA. They also showed that consumption of low-fat diets did not reduce CHD mortality, although fat intakes with high polyunsaturated to saturated fat ratios reduced the risk of total CHD events. Consumption of LC n-3 PUFA also reduced the risk of coronary events. At present, however, recommended intakes of n-3 LC PUFA set by agencies (for example, the European Food Safety Authority Panel on Dietetic Products, Nutrition and Allergies, 2010) are much lower than levels determined as beneficial in trials.

Atherosclerotic development and progression (the process of thickening and hardening of the arteries) and the thrombosis of CVD may be consequences of both excessive intake of saturated fat and PUFA imbalance. With the increased consumption of domesticated animal fats and seed oils containing n-6 PUFA in the diets of many industrialized nations across the past 50 years or so, tissue arachidonic acid (AA, 20:4n-6) levels have risen at the expense of LC n-3 PUFA (Simopoulos 1999; Kris-Etherton *et al.* 2000). The predominance of n-6 PUFA in contemporary industrialized diets has also led to substantially higher physiological production of eicosanoids derived from the n-6 PUFA, AA (Figure 10.5), relative to those derived from the corresponding n-3 PUFA, eicosapentaenoic acid (EPA, 20:5n-3) (Simopoulos 1999; James *et al.* 2000). This disrupts the balance of actions of these compounds, creating an internal environment dominated by AA-derived prostaglandins and leukotrienes that favour vaso-constriction, hyper platelet-aggregability, hypertension, throm-bosis and inflammatory processes (Kinsella *et al.* 1990a). In contrast to the possible consequences of elevated tissue AA levels, diets containing fish or fish oil (which are rich in LC n-3 PUFA) may lead to a reduction in plasma AA and down-regulation of AA metabolism to its eicosanoid hormones (Kinsella *et al.* 1990a), lowering the risk of hypertension and pro-inflammatory states, including ones that may predispose to CVD.

There is continued debate about a possible cardioprotective role of n-6 PUFA consumption. It may be that what n-6 PUFA consumption replaces in the diet is as important as the corresponding quantity of n-3 PUFA con-sumed. In a meta-analysis of randomized controlled trials of n-6, n-3 and combined n-6 + n-3 PUFA supplementation, Ramsden *et al.* (2010) found that supplementation with both PUFA types combined was associated with 22% lower myocardial infarction and CHD mortality, while supplementation with n-3 PUFA alone was associated with 13% lower mortality. These authors argue that dietary advice to increase n-6 PUFA intake, if based on

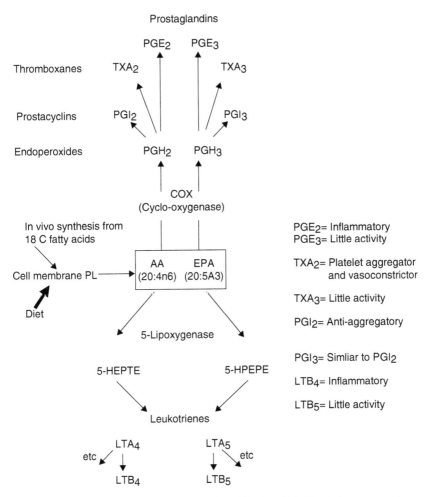

Figure 10.5. Oxidative metabolism of arachidonic acid (n-6) and eicosapentaenoic acid (n-3) by the cyclo-oxygenase and 5-lipoxygenase pathway, showing the relative shift from a pro-inflammatory, pro-thrombotic environment with AA dietary dominance, by inclusion of omega-3 PUFA (adapted from Simopoulos 2004).

results from mixed n-3/n-6 data, could be misguided. In a subsequent article, they suggest that reductions in CHD mortality previously attributed to n-6 PUFA or total PUFA may be due to substantial simultaneous increases in n-3 PUFA intakes in general and of EPA and DHA in particular, and that the accompanying increases in n-6 PUFA may attenuate this effect (Ramsden *et al.* 2011).

The extent to which fats predispose to deposition of body fat varies according to other aspects of the diet. For example, a study using a mouse model has shown n-6 PUFA to be pro-adipogenic when it is part of a diet that is high in carbohydrate but anti-adipogenic when part of a diet low in carbohydrate but high in protein (Madsen *et al.* 2008). The mechanism promoting or inhibiting fat deposition involves cyclic adenosine mononucleotide phosphate (cAMP) signalling, which controls the production of anti-adipogenic prostaglandins (PGE$_2$ and PGF$_{2\alpha}$) derived from AA. The glucagon to insulin ratio is higher on a high-protein diet, leading to increased cAMP-induced signalling and cyclo-oxygenase (COX)-mediated prostaglandin synthesis, and less fat mass deposition. A lower glucagon to insulin ratio on a high-carbohydrate diet leads to lower protein-kinase-mediated induction of COX and subsequent increased fat mass deposition. Madsen *et al.* (2008) also observed that mice on a high-protein/n-6 PUFA diet had increased production of hepatic PGC$_{1\alpha}$ (which regulates hepatic gluconeogenesis) and greater expression of genes involved in energy-demanding processes such as urea synthesis and gluconeogenesis. They concluded that the decreased adipogenic action of n-6 PUFA was not from increased energy dissipation by uncoupled respiration reactions, but reflected the energy demand of increased gluconeogenesis and urea production.

Trans-fatty acids and disease

Prior to the advent of food processing techniques involving catalytic hydrogenation of polyunsaturated vegetable oils, the human diet contained only traces of trans-fatty acids. These came from vacenic acid (18:1 *trans* 11) and conjugated linoleic acid in meat and dairy products from ruminant animals. Trans-fats appeared in the human diet in significant quantities soon after 1909, when this new technique was industrialized, first in the UK and in the US two years later (Gunstone 2002). By partially hydrogenating PUFA in vegetable oils, the melting point of the oil can be raised to a point where it becomes a soft solid, able to be spread as margarine, or used as a shortening in baking (King and White 1999). Partial hydrogenation may also alter the remaining double bonds from cis- to trans- configuration (Figure 10.6). The former are found in the fats of most foods of natural origin, while the latter are now mainly products of human-driven chemical manipulation; human metabolism thus has little experience of dealing with trans-fats (Ascherio and Willet 1997). Consumption of trans-fatty acids raises serum LDL-cholesterol and lipoprotein (a) levels and lowers high density lipoprotein (HDL)-cholesterol levels. It also increases the ratio of total cholesterol to

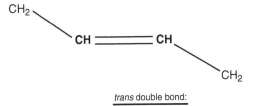

trans double bond:

Unusual fatty acid form in nature, but appears in partially hydrogenated fatty acids, leads to fatty acids
with a straight structure

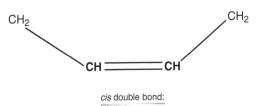

cis double bond:

Normal fatty acid form in nature, leads to fatty acids with a bent structure

Figure 10.6. Cis- and trans- double bond orientations in fatty acids.

HDL-cholesterol more than two-fold relative to the consumption of the equivalent amount of saturated fat (Ascherio and Willet 1997). Trans-fatty acids increase the risk of CVD more than any other macronutrient, even at low intake levels; up to 100 000 CVD deaths per year in the US might be attributed to their consumption (Mozaffarian *et al.* 2006). Trans-fatty acids may contribute to CVD because of the inability of digestive enzymes, lipid transport systems and cellular metabolism to handle them effectively. Poor ester cleavage of trans-fatty acids from lipid molecules may leave high concentrations of them in blood vessels for extended periods of time, permitting them to be incorporated in arterial plaque. Trans-fatty acids are able to disrupt the hepatic Δ6-desaturase enzyme involved in the conversion of shorter-chain PUFA in the diet into the longer-chain, more unsaturated ones, such as the desirable LC n-3 PUFA eicosapentaenoic (EPA; 20:5n-3) and docosahexaenoic (DHA; 22:6n-3) acids.

Animal foods and dietary fat

The wild game animals available to hominins would have had considerably less total and saturated fat than modern-day domesticated animals (Naughton

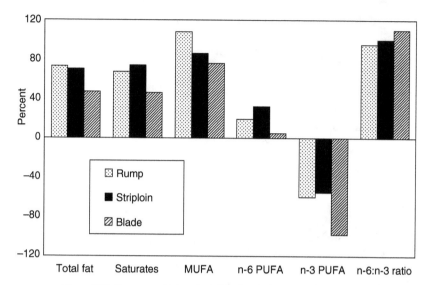

Figure 10.7. Extent to which grain-fed beef cattle exceed grass-fed cattle in their muscle fat types and fatty acid ratio (percentage). Muscle fat analyses of Australian pasture-fed and grain-fed (150–200 days) beef cattle (mg/100 g muscle tissue) (adapted from Ponnampalam *et al.* (2006)). Analyses are means of 18 samples of each cut from different animals. In each case the grain-fed animals had less than half the EPA+DHA content of those grass-fed.

et al. 1986; Cordain *et al.* 2002a), with little intramuscular fat and only small seasonal fat deposits around internal organs (O'Dea 1991a). In a study of the fat content of Australian beef cattle, Ponnampalam *et al.* (2006) showed grain-fed animals to have significantly more total fat, saturated fat and n-6 PUFA than grass-fed animals (Figure 10.7). This is an outcome of feeding animals on n-6 PUFA-rich grain-based diets, which are used to fatten animals quickly for the meat market, rather than feeding them on n-3-rich pasture forage. Muscle tissue fat levels of Australian wild game animals generally consumed by Aboriginal hunter-gatherers seldom exceeded 2.6% (Naughton *et al.* 1986), with 30 to 50% of this being PUFA from the phospholipids of cell membranes (Mann 2000). The n-6 to n-3 ratio of muscle tissue of such animals is around 3:1 (Sinclair and O'Dea 1990). With selective butchering and maximization of fat (and energy) intake from brain and other organs, ancestral hominins may have obtained an even lower ratio of n-6 to n-3 intake (Naughton *et al.* 1986).

In the present day, it is difficult to avoid consumption of fat in meat in industrialized and post-industrial nations. One reason is the extent to which animals that are bred for meat are grain-fed. Cordain *et al.* (2002d) analysed

Table 10.3 *Muscle fat composition of North American elk, deer and antelope compared with grain- and pasture-fed cattle (mg/100 g tissue)*
Predicted percentage change in total serum cholesterol and LDL cholesterol from consuming 100 g tissue from each of these animals, calculated by using the equation of Müller *et al.* (2001)

Fatty acid class	Elk	Deer	Antelope	Pasture-fed cattle	Grain-fed cattle
Saturates	610	989	895	910	1909
Monounsaturates	507	612	610	793	1856
Polyunsaturates	625	746	754	262	341
n-3 PUFA	178	225	216	61	46
n-6 PUFA	448	524	536	138	243
LC PUFA	281	295	331	152	175
n-6:n-3 ratio	2.5	2.3	2.4	2.2	5.3
Predicted increase in:					
Total serum cholesterol (%)	0.3	0.5	0.4	0.6	1.2
LDL cholesterol (%)	0.3	0.4	0.3	0.4	0.9

(Adapted from Cordain *et al.* 2002d).

various tissue samples from North American elk, deer and antelope and compared these with grain-fed and pasture-fed cattle (Table 10.3). The common grain-fed cattle in the US have substantially higher total fat and saturated fat levels in muscle tissue than wild game animals and pasture-fed cattle. They also have lower absolute levels of n-3 PUFA and a substantially higher n-6:n-3 ratio due to the abundance of n-6 PUFA and lack of n-3 PUFA in grain used as feed. In contrast, pasture-fed domesticated meat animals have lipid profiles closer to those of wild game animals because of the relatively high n-3 PUFA and low n-6 PUFA levels in grasses they consume, and the overall lower energy density of grasses compared with grain. Predicting the percentage change in total serum cholesterol and low-density lipoprotein (LDL) cholesterol levels when 100 kilocalories of dietary intake comes from muscle tissue of each of these animals (using the equation of Müller *et al.* 2001) shows the increases to be slight for all apart from grain-fed cattle. These changes are based on meat cuts trimmed of excess fat. Using the same procedure to predict the changes in total serum cholesterol and LDL cholesterol with consumption of fatty meats relative to lean meat shows much larger increases. For example, consuming a burger that contains 32 g of fat, of which 26 g is saturated and 6 g is polyunsaturated, would elevate total serum cholesterol by 14% and LDL cholesterol by 11%, respectively.

Total fat intake of hunter-gatherers is likely to have been generally low but quite variable (Kinsella *et al.* 1990b; Cordain 2000b; Eaton *et al.* 1997; O'Dea 1991a). Eaton *et al.* (1997) made a rough estimate of total fat intake of prehistoric hunter-gatherers, suggesting that it might have been around 22% of total energy intake. Cordain *et al.* (2000a) have suggested that fat intakes of up to 58% of dietary energy intake would have been occasionally possible. Both Eaton *et al.* (1997) and Cordain *et al.* (2000a) estimate that prehistoric hunter-gatherer diets would usually have been low in saturated fat. Patterns of dietary fat intake are likely to have changed dramatically since the time of early hunter-gatherers, with the adoption of agriculture and animal husbandry, the industrial revolution, and contemporary food processing technologies each having different effects. Total fat intake generally now accounts for over 30% of total energy intake in most industrialized countries, and intakes of saturated fat and n-6 PUFA have increased, while those of n-3 PUFA have fallen. In most industrialized countries the ratio of n-6 to n-3 PUFA in the diet exceeds 12:1 (Sinclair and O'Dea 1990), far in excess of the 1:1 ratio usual among hunter-gatherer groups (Simopoulos 2006) that are not dependent on monocot staples.

Physiological needs for fatty acids, and human diet

Linoleic acid (LA, 18:2n-6) and alpha-linolenic acid (ALA, 18:3n-3) are 18-carbon PUFA that are essential to humans (Figure 10.3), and are precursor fatty acids for the n-6 and n-3 PUFA series, respectively (Figure 10.4). The long-chain (greater than 18 carbons) members of these two series of fatty acids are formed in animal metabolism by alternating chain elongation and desaturation (double bond addition) steps, and usually accumulate in the phospholipid (PL) fraction of cell membranes, where they exert various effects on cell function and indirectly affect vascular function. The first step in each pathway of fatty acid synthesis is the rate-limiting Δ6-desaturation although the Δ6-desaturase step is not the rate-limiting one (Sardesai 1992). As the desaturation – chain elongation ladder is descended, the net formation of products from the 18-carbon chain length precursors becomes increasingly inefficient (Hassam *et al.* 1975). In the case of n-3 PUFA, where consumption of ALA (the 18-carbon precursor) is not high, it is out-competed for the desaturase enzyme by the n-6 PUFA, LA. Availability of LA is very high in most modern western diets (Emken *et al.* 1994). Hence EPA and DHA are incorporated most efficiently by ingestion of marine animals, whose flesh and oils are rich in these PUFA, and/or terrestrial animals rich with some DPA and

EPA, including red meat from pasture-fed animals (Kifer and Miller 1969; Crawford *et al.* 1976; Mann 2005).

Both EPA and DHA have a number of important physiological functions, including the mediation of immunological and inflammatory processes. Disruption of their synthesis can lead to impaired health outcomes related to n-3:n-6 balance through their respective eicosanoids (Mahfouz 1981). These negative health outcomes might include CVD, arthritis, various allergies, possibly also depression (Su *et al.* 2003) and anxiety disorders (Yehuda *et al.* 2005).

The relative health value of consumption of ALA compared with EPA and DHA continues to be debated. Increased intakes of ALA result in increased tissue levels of ALA and EPA but lead to virtually no change in DHA levels (Li *et al.* 1999; Burdge and Calder 2005). The overall conversion efficiency of ALA into EPA and DHA is 0.2% and 0.05%, respectively (Pawlosky *et al.* 2001), and elevated tissue levels of EPA and DHA occur only when these fatty acids are consumed directly from dietary sources or fish oil supplements. Sinclair *et al.* (2007) predicted that substantial decreases in the absolute quantities of LA and increases in ALA, as well as a decrease in the LA:ALA dietary intake ratio, are needed to enhance *in vivo* EPA and DHA synthesis. The current consumption of LA in western societies is more than 10 times greater than ALA, and a drastic reduction in LA intake would likely ensure greater bodily conversion of ALA to EPA and DHA (Lands 2008).

The PUFA profiles of adipose tissue and plasma of subjects in contemporary industrialized societies is likely to mirror the high intake of LA from cereals and seed oils, with n-6 PUFA intakes far exceeding those of n-3 PUFA. This is especially so in the phospholipid fatty acid pools, from which AA (n-6) and EPA (n-3) are obtained for conversion to a number of vaso-active steroid-hormone like compounds, including the eicosanoid categories of prostaglandins and leukotrienes. Most mammals are able to synthesize longer-chain PUFA from LA and ALA (Mead *et al.* 1986). As neither LA nor ALA can be synthesized *de novo* by terrestrial mammals (Brenner 1987), the diet of these animals must supply these two fatty acids, usually from plant sources, although carnivores may obtain LC desaturation–elongation products from the flesh of other animals (Crawford and Sinclair 1972). Cell membrane fluidity, which influences hormone–receptor binding, is enhanced by consumption of long-chain PUFA. Insulin resistance may be due to rigid membrane structure limiting the number of insulin receptors, caused by incorporation of less LC PUFA (Russo 2009). The LC PUFA with greatest potential for increasing membrane fluidity are AA, followed by EPA, then DHA (Yang *et al.* 2011).

Omega-3 intakes, eicosanoid production and chronic disease

There are many eicosanoid metabolites of the 20-carbon fatty acids AA and EPA (Corey *et al.* 1980) including prostaglandins (PG), thromboxanes (TXA), leukotrienes, lipoxins, resolvins, docosatrienes and protectins (Bergstrom *et al.* 1964; Curtis-Prior 1988; Serhan 2005), epoxides and other derivatives of the cyclo-oxygenase, lipoxygenase and cytochrome P450 pathways. Their roles are extensive and include the control of vascular tone, blood clotting and the inflammatory response. They appear to act as local hormones, being rapidly inactivated. The cyclo-oxygenase products (PGs, prostacyclin (PGI) and TXA) have potent vaso-active properties. Prostacyclin is produced mainly by the endothelial cells lining the blood vessels and is a powerful inhibitor of platelet aggregation and a smooth muscle cell relaxant. Thromboxane (Hamberg *et al.* 1975) is produced mainly in the platelets, is a powerful platelet-aggregating agent and strongly constricts smooth muscle cells (FitzGerald *et al.* 1987). Like PGI, it is formed from 20 carbon PUFA following their release from membrane bound phospholipids by the action of phospholipases. The control of vascular tone is achieved to a large extent by the balance of these two eicosanoids.

Figure 10.5 illustrates the oxidative metabolism of n-6 AA and n-3 EPA by cyclo-oxygenase and 5-lipoxygenase pathways. Because n-6 PUFA are predominant in most western diets (Crawford *et al.* 1986; Sinclair and Mann 1996; Mann *et al.* 2006), AA is the predominant substrate for TXA and PGI, rather than EPA. Thus TXA_2 (Hamberg and Samuelsson 1974) and PGI_2 (Whittaker *et al.* 1976) are formed at the expense of TXA_3 and PGI_3 (Simopoulos 2004), forming a pro-inflammatory, pro-thrombotic physiological environment. High levels of tissue AA can lead to the loss of eicosanoid homeostasis (Kinsella *et al.* 1990b) and decreased PGI_2/TXA_2 ratios, predisposing to atherosclerosis and thrombosis. In general, consumption of LC n-3 PUFA inhibits TXA_2 production while a small amount of inactive TXA_3 is formed (Needleman *et al.* 1979; Fischer and Weber 1984). Atherogenicity is further reduced with the consumption of LC n-3 PUFA, because of reduced production of platelet-activating factor (PAF) (Sperling *et al.* 1987) and increased formation of nitric oxide, which is another vasodilator.

The administration of EPA or fish oils has been shown to reduce atherogenicity in other ways. For example, Hashimoto *et al.* (1984) and Skeaff and Holub (1988) found decreased aggregation and TXB_2 in platelets provided with EPA, the decrease in TXB_2 production being mediated both by a decrease in the absolute amount of AA and the inhibitory effect of EPA on AA-metabolism via the cyclo-oxygenase pathway (Goodnight *et al.* 1981). The excretion of TXA_2 metabolites is elevated in atherosclerotic patients but falls with fish oil feeding, with both TXA_3 and PGI_3 metabolites (from EPA) being formed (Knapp *et al.* 1986). Dietary DHA can also be retro-converted rapidly to EPA (Schlenk *et al.* 1969), which is metabolized to PGI_3, as is the dietary EPA itself, with no effect on AA metabolism in the endothelium; this improves vascular function and limits platelet aggregation. Hamazaki *et al.* (1989) found an increase in PGI_3-M excretion on the day of fish consumption among members of a Japanese fishing village, but no relationship between the excretion of the urinary metabolite PGI_2-M with either LA or AA intake. This suggests that the AA pool is large and not quickly influenced by diet, even when large amounts of AA are consumed, whereas LC n-3 PUFA pools are smaller and require constant dietary intake to maintain their levels.

The ratio of n-6 to n-3 PUFA in membranes can be modified by dietary change, especially by n-3 LC PUFA intake. The n-3 LC PUFAs can also modify physiological function by mediating AA metabolism to its eicosanoids, and as direct competitive precursors for oxygenated metabolites (Sprecher 1986). Among Inuit, there are lower levels of eicosanoid-related diseases such as asthma, atherosclerosis, breast and colon cancer, thrombosis and psoriasis (Lands 1986a,b) among those living traditional subsistence lives than among Europeans (Dyerberg 1986). Some of these differences are due to greater consumption of foods rich in n-3 PUFA among Inuit (Dyerberg *et al.* 1975). Any increase in intake of LC n-3 PUFA leads to rapid incorporation into phospholipids (von Schacky and Weber 1985; Hodge *et al.* 1993) at the expense of AA. Once incorporated into cellular membranes, EPA can be released (Fischer and Weber 1984), reducing AA availability for eicosanoid production, not only by displacing AA from cell PL, but by competing with AA for cyclo-oxygenase and lipoxygenase access. This effect is easily reversed if n-3 PUFA consumption declines, because of rapid depletion of n-3 PUFA in tissue phospholipid (Hodge *et al.* 1993). Weber *et al.* (1986) found that biochemical changes to platelet function were completely reversed in humans four weeks after discontinuing fish oil ingestion. In humans, ALA can be desaturated and elongated to EPA, but it cannot accumulate to any great extent until dietary ALA is present at high levels, because of the competition with LA for desaturase enzymes (Lands *et al.* 1990). Only by consuming preformed LC n-3 PUFA can EPA and DHA accumulate, especially in the brain, retina and reproductive organs (Mathias and Dupont 1989).

Omega-6 and omega-3 fatty acids, inflammation and disease

The likely role of dietary n-3 PUFA in suppression of inflammatory conditions was first identified by Kromann and Green (1980) in Greenland Inuits. Subsequently, various studies have shown inverse relationships between n-3 PUFA intake (generally from fish and marine mammals) and rates of autoimmune and inflammatory disorders such as asthma, psoriasis, CVD and hypertension (Simopoulos 2004, 2006). The proposed mechanism for the reduced rates of these disorders centres on alterations in eicosanoid production (Figure 10.5), whereby leukotriene (LTB_5) and prostaglandin (PGE_3), both of which are derived from EPA and have weak or no inflammatory potential, displace or compete with AA-derived LTB_4 (a potent inducer of leukocyte chemotaxis and adherence) and PGE_2 (which is pro-inflammatory) (Goldman *et al.* 1983). High n-3 PUFA intake also results in replacement of some TXA_2 (which is pro-thrombotic) with the inert TXA_3, without affecting the anti-aggregatory and vascular dilation properties of prostacyclin (Figure 10.5) (Simopoulos 2004). The n-3 PUFA are also used to synthesize resolvins and protectins (Ariel and Serhan 2007) which are anti-inflammatory. Pro-inflammatory cytokines, such as tumor necrosis factor alpha interleukins 1 alpha, 2 and 6, predominantly derived from monocytes and macrophages (Simopoulos 2004; Calder 2008), are reduced by ingestion of n-3 PUFA (Endres *et al.* 1989; von Schacky 2007). Such cytokines generally help combat infections, but when produced in excess or when poorly modulated, result in over-activation of both T and B lymphocytes and cause excessive inflammation. Inflammation is one component of the immune response to many infections. However, excessive inflammation due to over-expression of TNFα has been invoked as a mechanism of fever induction in malaria due to *Plasmodium falciparum* infection (McGuire *et al.* 1994) and to a range of other infectious diseases (Knight and Kwiatkowski 1999).

There is evidence that genetic polymorphisms exist among individuals controlling cytokine production, with possible differing frequencies in different population as shown by Interleukin-6 promoter polymorphism differences between northern and southern European groups (Kelberman *et al.* 2004). The understanding of the production and activity of IL-6 is gaining much attention, and research is expanding into associations between genetic polymorphisms for IL-6, inflammation, obesity, dietary interactions and insulin resistance. IL-6 is produced by a wide range of cells, including adipocytes, and levels in the body generally parallel fat levels and body mass index (BMI) (Woods *et al.* 2000). Yudkin *et al.* (1999) have suggested that IL-6 may be a link between obesity, insulin resistance and inflammation, leading to CVD, although Festa *et al.* (2000) have suggested that C-reactive protein (CRP) may play the same role. Nystrom (2007) has suggested that CRP, IL-6 and interleukin 1 (IL-1) are all part of the inflammatory milieu of CVD that predisposes to Type 2 diabetes.

Omega-3 PUFA and lipoprotein metabolism

Most dietary fat is consumed as triacylglycerols (TG), which vary greatly in fatty acid composition and positional distribution on the glycerol backbone

(Figure 10.2); both of these factors influence their biological properties (Kinsella *et al.* 1990b). Following digestive breakdown and absorption, fatty acids that have chain lengths that are greater than 12 carbon atoms are formed into TG in the mucosal cells of the digestive tract, assembled into lipoprotein particles (chylomicrons) and enter the blood via the lymphatic system (Mead *et al.* 1986). Shorter-chain fatty acids undergo rapid transportation to the liver by the hepatic portal vein as water-soluble protein complexes. Lipoprotein lipase (LPL) hydrolyses the circulating chylomicron-TG, releasing fatty acids, principally as an energy source in muscle tissue, but also for storage in adipose tissue. As the TG component of the chylomicrons decreases, the remnant lipoproteins become smaller and are taken up by the liver, by specific apoE binding receptors (Betteridge 1989). Subsequently in the liver, fatty acids and cholesterol are incorporated into very low-density lipoproteins (VLDL) which are secreted into the blood circulation, gradually depleted of TG and converted first to intermediate-density lipoprotein (IDL) and then to low-density lipoproteins (LDL), which comprise largely cholesterol esters (CE) in the core and apoB on the outer surface (Betteridge 1989). High-density lipoproteins (HDL) accumulate excess cholesterol from cells and play a central role in 'reverse cholesterol transport' by returning cholesterol from the periphery to the liver directly or through IDL and LDL (O'Dea 1991b).

In general, n-3 PUFA are associated with modest but important changes in blood lipids (Russo 2009). Animal studies show dietary EPA to decrease hepatic TG formation (Rustan *et al.* 1988a) and hepatic cholesterol ester synthesis (Rustan *et al.* 1988b). Thus, VLDL secretion may be reduced by direct inhibition of the two enzymes that are essential for the production of VLDL core lipids (Harris 1990). Fish oil feeding generally reduces postprandial lipaemia (very high levels of lipids in the blood), although chylomicron clearance is not increased, which suggests that n-3 PUFA is instrumental in reducing either chylomicron production or secretion (Harris and Munzio 1990). A study in which African green monkeys were fed fish oils resulted in decreased plasma LDL and HDL cholesterol, and apoA-1 (Parks and Rudel 1990). Their LDL particles were smaller and contained less cholesterol as a result of such feeding, while hepatic secretions of cholesterol and TG were reduced. In addition, atherosclerosis in the coronary arteries and aorta were lower in the fish-oil-fed monkeys than in controls (Parks and Rudel 1990). Russo (2009) reports that epidemiological and interventional approaches show a 30%–50% reduction in CVD related mortality in those consuming 30–35 g/day of fish or EPA and DHA supplements of up to 665 mg/day. Observed reductions in CVD mortality due to n-3 PUFA consumption may be more related to their anti-arrhythmic effects, however (Russo 2009).

When dietary fat intake is high (more than around 40% of total energy intake), exogenous and endogenous cholesterol and saturated fatty acids interact to increase plasma LDL-cholesterol levels (Kinsella *et al.* 1990a) by impairing hepatic uptake of LDL particles (Spady and Dietschy 1988) and increasing cholesterol synthesis rate (Sanders 1990). Mensink and Katan (1992) assessed the effect of changes in carbohydrate and fatty acid intake on serum lipids and lipoprotein levels by multiple regression analysis of 27 controlled trials. By developing a set of equations relating isocaloric substitution of carbohydrate by different types of fat, they found that the replacement of carbohydrate by fat lowered serum TG regardless of the nature of the fat, while replacement of saturated with polyunsaturated fats raised the HDL to LDL cholesterol ratio, both reducing the risk of CVD. Replacement of saturated fats by carbohydrates had no effect on the HDL to LDL ratio.

The diet of US citizens changed greatly between the 1960s and the 1990s, a time that also saw a steady decline in CHD mortality due to dietary change and smoking decline (Sprafka *et al.* 1990). Consumption of refined carbohydrates increased (Gross *et al.* 2004) (Chapter 11) while fat consumption patterns changed, with smaller amounts of saturated and monounsaturated fats and greater amounts of polyunsaturated fats being eaten (Stephen and Wald 1990). The extent to which changing patterns of carbohydrate and fat consumption may have contributed to the decline in CHD mortality can be modelled using equations of Mensink and Katan (1992) for change in total serum cholesterol and HDL/LDL ratio per percentage point of energy replaced (Table 10.4) across the period in question. Entering known changes in patterns of carbohydrate and fat intakes into these equations gives a decline in total serum cholesterol of 3% and an increase in the HDL/LDL ratio of 2%. This represents around a third of the total observed decline in serum cholesterol and about a quarter of the increase in HDL/LDL cholesterol ratio across this period (Johnson *et al.* 1993). Other factors that may have contributed to changing serum lipid profiles in the US include increases in both fat and carbohydrate intakes, and changing ratios of fat types consumed.

Dietary omega-3 PUFA and the brain

Happiness and sadness, along with fear, are among the most basic of emotions, and there is a high likelihood that they have been influenced by natural selection (Nesse 1989). The mediation of mood by social factors suggests that this is an important contributor to behaviour and its plasticity. Brain cell membranes have high requirements for both AA (n-6) and DHA (n-3) which

Table 10.4 *Equations for change in per cent total serum cholesterol, TG and HDL/LDL ratio per per cent of energy replaced*

Change in total serum cholesterol per percent of energy replaced =	0.039 (carbohydrate to saturated fat)
	− 0.003 (carbohydrate to monounsaturated fat)
	− 0.015 (carbohydrate to polyunsaturated fat)
Change in HDL/LDL ratio per percent of energy replaced =	0.000 (carbohydrate to saturated fat) + 0.003 (carbohydrate to monounsaturated fat)
	+ 0.005 (carbohydrate to polyunsaturated fat)

Adapted from Mensink and Katan (1992).

are important for membrane fluidity, and whose absence can affect cerebral development (Colin *et al.* 2003). Pawles and Volterrani (2008) have suggested an association between n-3 PUFA deficiency and mood disorders, while Levant *et al.* (2008), using a rat model, found relationships between decreased brain DHA levels and increased corticosterone stress response, as well as decreased serotonin content and turnover in the frontal cortex. These changes are consistent with the physiology of depression. DHA reduces neurological dysfunction through anti-apoptotic and neurotrophic pathways in the brain (Orr and Bazinet 2008), these neurotrophic pathways supporting the survival of existing neurons and encouraging the growth and differentiation of new neurons. DHA was important for encephalization during hominin evolution (Carlson and Kingston 2007), and may be part of the natural milieu for optimal human brain function now. Dietary change with the onset of agriculture (which led to an increased ratio of n-6 to n-3 PUFA intake) may have led to the greater possibility of depression in human populations. Depression may have been a useful attribute for the establishment of status hierarchies after the origins of agriculture (Chapter 9), because social hierarchies are in part outcomes of past conflicts, and submissive behaviour is a successful way for subordinates to survive a defeat (Gilbert 2000). Other primate species have dominance hierarchies that result in stress to the point where reproduction is inhibited (Sapolsky 2005). With mental depression, humans have a mechanism that inhibits social contestation but permits reproduction within established social bounds, such as class and caste systems.

In animal models, depression due to chronic stress (Mahieu *et al.* 2008) and increased susceptibility to bipolar disorder (Rao *et al.* 2007) are outcomes of consuming diets that are restricted in n-3 PUFA. The combination of n-3 PUFA dietary restriction with psychosocial stress in rats has been linked to overeating (Mahieu *et al.* 2008), and the human situation may mirror this. Unhappiness is associated with overeating (Whybrow 2005), while those of lowest socioeconomic status (who are more prone to overeating and obesity in industrialized societies) are most likely to be depressed, have low self-esteem, or see little purpose or meaning to life (Marmot *et al.* 1997). Those of lowest socioeconomic position in industrialized nations also usually have the poorest dietary quality (in terms of nutrient density, but not energy density) and lowest intakes of fish and n-3 PUFA (Darmon and Drwenowski 2008). Hibbeln (2009) suggests that the very low intake of n-3 PUFA in combination with high intakes of n-6 PUFA of most industrialized populations has a profound effect on mental health. For example, there is a 65-fold higher risk of major depression in the countries with the lowest levels of seafood consumption compared with countries with the highest levels of intake (Hibbeln 1998), and a 30-fold higher risk for bipolar disease among those consuming very low or negligible amounts of seafood (Noaghuil and Hibbeln 2003). Speculatively, it can be argued that socioeconomic differences in diet quality might contribute to the maintenance of social inequality, via inequalities in n-3 PUFA consumption and their effects on mental health, at least in nations that have limited access to fish and seafood. The qualities that mental illness offers society are those of subordination; if more mental illness is found among lower classes and they cannot afford to consume foods high in n-3 PUFA, this may become instrumental in further social and economic stratification.

Discussion

Dietary fat is important because it provides greater energy density than any other macronutrient. From an evolutionary perspective, its consumption very probably enabled dietary energy budgets of hominins and early humans to be met more easily, and allowed greater dietary breadth and plasticity in diet and foraging behaviour (Chapter 4). Only in recent times in industrialized societies, where food availability has been secured and physical work schedules have declined to very low levels, has its importance been questioned, with CVD, diabetes and obesity emerging in the second half of the twentieth century as significant public health problems.

Fat is not just fat: there are many types of fat, which vary with their carbon chain-length, numbers and types of double bonds. Their structures influence their roles in human physiology beyond the provision of dietary energy, and of health outcomes. Fatty acids are so varied that it is difficult to ascribe labels of goodness and badness upon them unequivocally. The goodness or badness of a fatty acid depends on how much is eaten, with which other fatty acids, and with what other components of the diet. Thus their virtue is context-dependent, much like the vast majority of people.

Early hunter-gatherers would have been hard-pushed to consume large amounts of saturated fats, as would early agriculturalists. The increase in saturated fat consumption and the introduction of trans-fatty acids into the diets of most industrialized nations during the twentieth century have had significant impacts on blood lipids and arguably on rates of CVD (smoking decline is the other major change that has influenced CVD rates). One band of fatty acids that emerges with a positive reputation is the long chain n-3 PUFAs, although most contemporary industrialized populations struggle to obtain sufficient quantities of them. They are protective against the many chronic diseases that are now significant public health problems, and were probably consumed in greater proportion relative to other fats prior to the advent of agriculture than they are today.

With the origins of agriculture came the widespread consumption of grain-based n-6 PUFAs, which although not generally harmful when obtained in grain foods alone, became so when the dietary quantity increased dramatically through extraction as oils from seeds and used broadly for cooking and processed food formulation, from the twentieth century. Most recently, the shift in balance towards the consumption of fats high in n-6 PUFA in recent decades has been adopted in most economically emerging nations, and is a contributing factor to the nutrition transition (Chapter 9). It is unlikely that the consumption of n-6 PUFA will drop substantially into the future, and even more unlikely that consumption of n-3 PUFAs will increase greatly.

11 *Feed the world with carbohydrates*

Introduction

Populations around the world obtain around 56% of their daily energy intake from carbohydrate, with intake from sugar being just over 8% of total energy availability (Food and Agriculture Organization 2010a). Total energy availability increased globally per head by 27% between 1961 and 2007, with availability of carbohydrate increasing by 22% overall. The availability of refined sugar has increased by nearly 50%. Not only do people eat more carbohydrate per head now than at any time in the historic and prehistoric past, they eat types of carbohydrate different from those available in the past, especially in industrialized societies. These include processed grain foods like bread and pastries, sugary confectionery foods and drinks, potatoes and most types of white rice. Consumption of such foods, we argue, has profound implications for human health and well-being, since humans are poorly adapted to deal with large quantities of refined carbohydrate. As rates of obesity in most countries have increased (International Obesity Task Force 2010), so has the prevalence of Type 2 diabetes, and other disorders such as gout, acne and myopia (Cordain *et al.* 2005; Doherty 2009; Collier *et al.* 2008; Saw 2003) in different age groups. All of these may involve hyperinsulinaemia (excessive levels of insulin circulating in the blood), brought about by consumption of high intakes of refined carbohydrates superimposed on a physiology of insulin resistance.

Sugar consumption exceeds an average of 75 g per person per day in most developed and emerging nations (Figure 11.1), as well as in the island nations of the Caribbean that have a colonial history of plantation sugar production (including Cuba, Barbados, Dominica, the Dominican Republic, Grenada, Jamaica, Saint Vincent and the Grenadines, and Trinidad and Tobago). The consumption of sweeteners has increased in most of the industrialized world, reflecting an insatiable appetite and demand for sweetness in human society

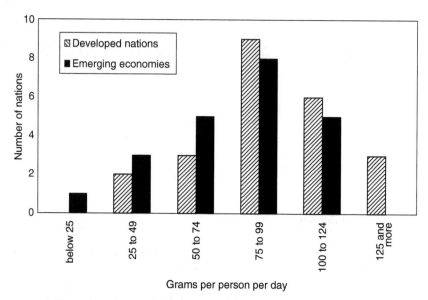

Figure 11.1. Sugar availability in developed and emerging economies, 2007 (data from Food and Agriculture Organization 2011).

(Chapters 5 and 6). This category of substances includes artificial sweeteners such as aspartame, but is dominated by high-fructose corn syrup (HFCS) in the US, Mexico, South Korea and Japan.

Refined sugar was largely absent from human diets prior to around 1700 years ago (Mintz 1985). The technology for refining sugar from the monocot plant sugarcane was developed in India during the Gupta dynasty in the fourth century (Adas 2001), and sugar was traded across Asia for consumption by privileged classes soon after. Its popularity, and the technologies for its production, spread across Mesopotamia and Asia, and were brought to Europe with the spread of the Arab empire into Iberia by the eighth century. It entered north Europe in the thirteenth century, when returning crusaders brought it with them from the Middle East. Sugar production has never looked back. Refined grain foods (such as white bread, white rice and pastries and breakfast cereals made from white wheat flour) have a more recent history, but have become equally popular as technologies for processing grains and making food products from them have allowed the development of affordable markets for them. This may have helped the process of nutrition transition, as elaborated by Popkin (1998, 2002b) and discussed in Chapter 9.

Figure 11.2 shows the proportion of total dietary energy available from fat, total carbohydrate and refined sugar in different nations, according to total daily energy available per head (Food and Agriculture Organization 2011).

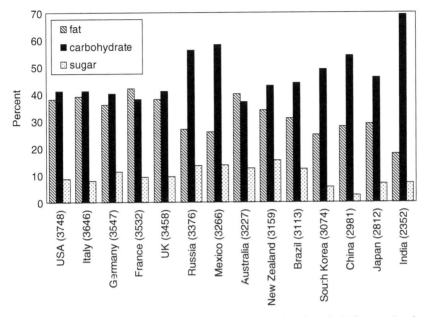

Figure 11.2. Proportion of national diets from fat, carbohydrate (including sugar) and sugar alone, according to daily dietary energy availability (in brackets) (data from World Health Organization 2010; Food and Agriculture Organization 2011).

There is a slight gradient toward greater total fat and sugar availability, but lower total carbohydrate, with increasing national per capita availability of dietary energy. Across all nations, carbohydrate available for consumption is between 37 and 69% of total dietary energy available. While the highest value, for India, represents significant availability for consumption of both refined and unrefined carbohydrates, the lowest value, for Australia, represents carbohydrate consumption overwhelmingly from processed cereal grain foods. Dietary availability of refined sugar varies from 3% of total dietary energy available in China to 16% in New Zealand.

While extremely palatable, refined carbohydrates and sugar come with considerable health-related baggage. Refined carbohydrates (starch) and glucose-containing sugar are rapidly digested and assimilated after consumption, and lead to postprandial increases in blood glucose and subsequently insulin, the latter of which has long-term consequences for the development of insulin resistance (IR) and Type 2 diabetes (Chapter 6). Refined carbohydrate consumption also increases sympathetic nervous system (SNS) activity, while neither fat nor protein do so to any appreciable extent (Kopp 2009). The SNS maintains bodily homeostasis under usual circumstances and increases in activity when under stress, mobilizing bodily resources to counter it. In traditional societies, raised SNS activity would usually be in response to threat or physical stress. In industrialized societies, raising SNS activity due to consumption of refined carbohydrate is a kind of false mobilization, causing increased blood pressure and blood biochemical changes. If this takes place repeatedly as a consequence of habitually high intakes of refined carbohydrate, this can lead to a range of cardiovascular disease (CVD)-related pathologies, including atherosclerosis, heart failure and ventricular arrhythmia (abnormal heart rate or rhythm) (Kopp 2009).

Consumption of refined carbohydrates is associated with vascular inflammation, plaque formation and CVD (Kopp 2006). These operate by a range of interrelated mechanisms, including insulin-mediated activation of the renin–angiotensin system (RAS), growth factors, cytokines, SNS and acute phase (C-reactive) protein, causing dyslipidaemia and atherosclerosis, which can lead to coronary failure, and ultimately death. Other maladaptive responses to consumption of refined carbohydrates include the mood disorder syndromes of carbohydrate craving obesity (CCO), premenstrual syndrome (PMS) and seasonal affective disorder (SAD), which have been linked with episodic bouts of carbohydrate consumption and depressed mood via abnormal regulation of the neurotransmitter serotonin in the hypothalamic region of the brain (Wurtman 1990; Wurtman and Wurtman 1995).

While the health problems associated with eating refined carbohydrates are well known, their consumption is unlikely to decline in the near future. This is because cereals form the major component of dietary energy across the world's populations, despite disproportionate increases in production of oil crops, fruit, vegetables and meat since 1961 (Figure 11.3). In this chapter we examine the changing nature of dietary carbohydrate availability and consumption in the past 50 years or so in much of the industrialized world and more recently in economically emerging nations, as nutrition transition (Chapter 9) is underway. We examine the role of consumption of refined starchy foods and HFCS in the production of diseases of civilization (Trowell and Burkitt 1981) including Type 2 diabetes, cardiovascular disease, and the predisposing conditions of obesity and insulin resistance. We also examine links between the consumption of refined carbohydrates and the less deadly but still common disorders of gout, acne and myopia.

We argue for a model of carbohydrate transition disorders which links these three conditions by the consumption of refined carbohydrates, especially HFCS. We examine the possibility that a subset of nutrition transition theory (Chapter 9) can be set aside for understanding the emergence of diseases associated with the consumption of refined carbohydrates. We call this a carbohydrate transition, which is most advanced in the US. But we begin with

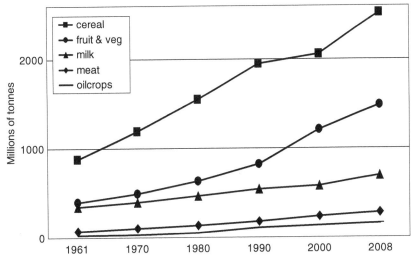

Figure 11.3. World food production 1961–2008 (Food and Agriculture Organization 2011).

a description of changing carbohydrate consumption patterns in the world and the extent to which changes in the US have influenced patterns elsewhere.

Carbohydrate transition

Nutrition transition theory (Chapter 9) (Popkin 1998, 2002a) attempts to explain changes in nutritional health of human populations produced by modifications in both dietary intake and energy expenditure patterns, which are in turn outcomes of the interplay of changing economic, demographic, environmental and cultural factors. Components of dietary change in nutrition transition include increased consumption of fats and oils, sugar and other refined carbohydrates. Evidence for what we describe as carbohydrate transition comes primarily from the US (Gross *et al.* 2004). Figure 11.4 shows changing patterns for carbohydrate consumption in that nation between 1909 and 1997. Between 1909 and 1963, total dietary carbohydrate consumption declined by 34%, while dietary fibre consumption declined by nearly 40% (Gross *et al.* 2004). Between 1909 and 1980, consumption of whole grain cereal based foods nearly halved, but from the 1960s, there was a dramatic increase in the consumption of HFCS. This trend has paralleled the upward trend in Type 2 diabetes in the US (Gross *et al.* 2004), although the relationship is likely to be indirect.

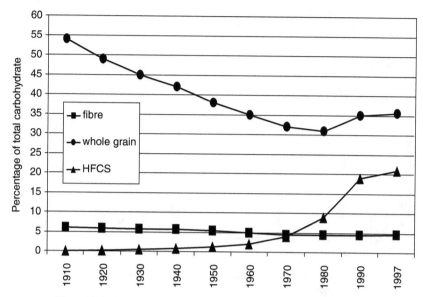

Figure 11.4. Carbohydrate transition in the United States, 1909–1997 (adapted from Gross *et al.* 2004).

Diets in most countries in Asia, Latin America, northern Africa and the Middle East increased in their content of fat and refined carbohydrate across the 1980s and 1990s (Popkin 2001), although the fat and refined carbohydrate content of diets in Latin America and North Africa have since stopped increasing (Food and Agriculture Organization 2011). The increases described by Popkin (2001) are reflected in the data on per capita sugar and sweetener availability in a range of industrialized and emerging economies (Figure 11.5). Most of these countries have seen increased per capita availability of both between 1962 and 2007. The United Kingdom and Australia have seen overall declines in sugar availability from 1962 to 2007, although both countries had among the highest levels of consumption in the world in the 1960s. The US has seen a decline in sugar availability, but this has been more than compensated for by increased availability of sweeteners, most importantly HFCS. The great increase in sweetener availability in the 1980s in South Korea and Japan is due to increased consumption of HFCS (White 2008). India and China have seen little change in their availability of sweeteners, although per capita sugar availability has increased greatly, from very low levels in 1962.

Much of the increased consumption of these products has been in the form of industrially produced food products, where sugar and sweeteners are often

(a)

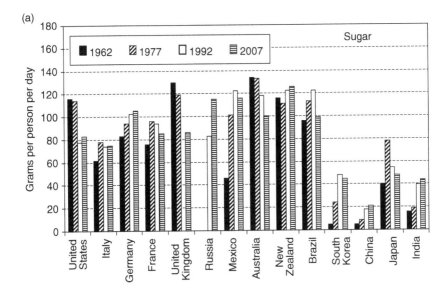

(b)

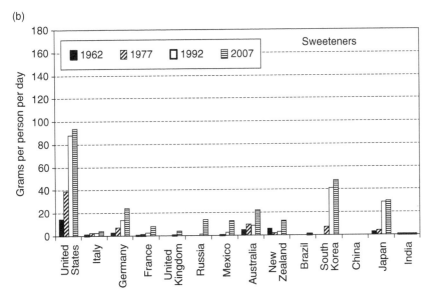

Figure 11.5. Per capita availability of sugar and sweeteners in industrialized and emerging nations, 1962 to 2007 (Food and Agriculture Organization 2011).

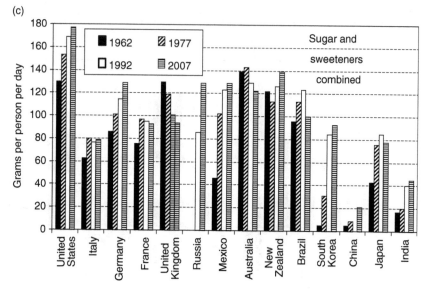

Figure 11.5. (*cont.*)

used to increase the palatability and preservation of foods, even savoury ones. Food technology has been used both to respond to existing markets for products, and to create new market niches. This may involve the production of existing ingredients more cheaply, completely new ingredients, new food types with existing ingredients, existing food types with proportions of new ingredients, and new food types with new ingredients. Because food products are placed in a competitive marketplace in most countries, they must maximize some combination of novelty, status, price and palatability that will ensure their economic success. The cheaper raw ingredients are overwhelmingly cereal-based commodities and fats (Chapters 9 and 10), and it is unsurprising that the majority of food products on the market involve some palatable combination of these ingredients.

The drive to create new food products to develop and maintain market share by transnational companies has profound effects on human eating behaviour and health. The processing of agricultural raw materials by the food industry has produced a huge range of food products with reduced micronutrient content and high energy density. It has also resulted in the production of foods with altered physical matrices and new combinations of ingredients that make them more pleasurable to eat. And where palatability leads, increased consumption follows.

Not all new ingredients are entirely compatible with good health, as with HFCS consumption and Type 2 diabetes risk. High-fructose corn syrup is a liquid of variable fructose to glucose ratio, manufactured by enzymatic breakdown of white crystalline cornstarch to glucose, then isomerization of much of the glucose to fructose. Called HFCS42, it is a mixture containing 52% glucose, 42% fructose, and some sugar byproducts, and is used in most industrially produced baked goods and many processed foods in the US (Bray *et al.* 2004). Further treatment of HFCS42 by liquid chromatography results in a mixture containing up to 90% fructose, called HFCS90. This is blended with HFCS42 to give a mixture containing 55% fructose (HFCS55), which is very widely used in commercial beverages in the US. HFCS42 has been estimated to be 1.16 times as sweet as sucrose (Bray *et al.* 2004), although its balance of fructose and glucose would suggest no difference. For reasons of economy, the food industry in the US adopted this product with enthusiasm: sugar from either cane or beet costs more and is less sweet.

The manufacturing process for HFCS was developed in the 1920s (Marshalle and Kooi 1957) and refined in Japan during the 1960s. It became a major part of the US diet from the 1970s onwards, when its production enabled an alternative use for US-grown corn at a time when its role as a source of vegetable oil was usurped by the now cheaper soy bean. The US Agricultural Adjustment Act of 1938 was the first act of national government to make price-support mandatory for the production of corn, wheat and cotton. While corn was used as food aid to the developing world from 1949 onwards (when the Agricultural Act of that year made such use possible) the surpluses far exceeded global demand, even as food aid. Alternatives were sought to mop up this surplus. Since limits to corn production were politically difficult (farmers' quotas were not up for negotiation), HFCS production became the instrument for dealing with surplus. As a consequence, HFCS entered the US food system in great quantity; at that time the US was a net importer of sugar, and the introduction of import tariffs on this commodity helped the internal market for HFCS to develop.

The US is the world's largest producer of corn, and the surpluses diverted into HFCS production were heroic. By the late 1990s, HFCS made up 40% of all caloric sweeteners sold in the US (Putnam and Allshouse 1999) and was the predominant caloric sweetener in soft drinks. Much as its entry into the US food market was driven politically and economically, the place of HFCS in the human food chain outside the US has come under political–economic scrutiny. For example, in 2002 Mexico taxed imports of HFCS from the US to protect its sugar industry, after a petition against the dumping of HFCS by the US to Mexico was rejected by the World Trade Organization in 2001. This product has penetrated food markets in Canada and Mexico, political attempts to stem its flow into Mexico having largely

Table 11.1 *Per capita high-fructose corn syrup availability (grams per day) in the United States and Mexico, 1992–2010*

Year	United States	Mexico
1992	74	1
1995	84	2
2000	90	5
2005	83	4
2008	78	15
2010	77	33

(Data from United States Department of Agriculture 2011, and United Nations Demographic Yearbook 2001: http://www.ers.usda.gov/briefing/sugar/data. htm#yearbook; http://unstats.un.org/unsd/demographic/products/dyb/dybcens.htm)

failed. In 2007, the European Union introduced quotas on its importation to protect sugar producers within the Union. However, as demand for sugar and sweeteners has risen, quotas were relaxed in 2011. Table 11.1 shows HFCS availability per person in the US and Mexico between 1992 and 2010. By 2008 it constituted 19% of total sugar and sweetener availability per head in the US. While HFCS availability in Mexico was low until 2005, in 2008 it ceased to impose duties on HFCS imports from the US, in return for the removal of restrictions on sugar exports to the US. In 2010, per capita availability had more than doubled since 2008, to 33 g per day.

Between 1994 and 1998, the intake of HFCS by US citizens above the age of two years was 318 calories per day, or one sixth of all energy and one third of all carbohydrate intake (Nielsen *et al.* 2002; Bray *et al.* 2004), a value that has changed little since (Table 11.1). Availability in the European Union remains low, at below 2 g per person per day, although it varies enormously across countries. The highest availability is in Hungary, while there is a total absence of it in eight countries including the Czech Republic, Ireland, Denmark and Austria (Michael Goran, personal communication). The ubiquity of HFCS in the US in soft drinks and fruit juices and many processed foods, including jams, confectionery, cakes, biscuits, dairy desserts, flavoured yoghurts, canned fruits, ice cream, ketchup, breads, cookies, and many other baked goods (Bray *et al.* 2004) is an extreme manifestation of carbohydrate transition. The other major one is the increased availability of sugar and other refined carbohydrates across most of the industrialized and economically emerging world. Foods made with such refined carbohydrates are a long way from nature, and it is highly likely that other novel carbohydrates with market-dominating potential will emerge in the future.

Refined carbohydrates and health

Refined carbohydrate-based foods and most refined sugar products elicit a rapid rise in blood glucose after consumption because of their high glucose content and easy digestibility. This has implications for insulin response, sensitivity and resistance. The simplest measure of the potential of a food to elicit a postprandial increase in blood glucose is the glycaemic index (GI) (Jenkins *et al.* 1981). Glycaemic index (GI) and glycaemic load (GL) (Chapter 6) for many foods are available (Foster-Powell *et al.* 2002). Depending on the strain of plant grown, nutrient composition and method of processing, many foods, including cakes, muffins, breads, breakfast cereals, ice cream, crackers, cookies, rice, corn and corn-products vary across categories of GI, from low to high. Minimally processed foods that have a long heritage of consumption by humans, including most fruit and vegetables (even though most have undergone modification through plant selection, breeding and sometimes genetic modification) have low GIs. Most refined cereal foods and sugar-based drinks have high GIs, a notable exception being most forms of pasta. Most fruits, legumes and vegetables generally have low GIs.

Health benefits of consuming foods of low GI are clear. The decreased glycaemic and insulinaemic responses to the carbohydrate content and composition of such foods include reduced insulin demand, improved blood glucose control and reduced blood lipid levels (Augustin *et al.* 2002). The higher the GI and GL of a diet, the more likely it is that obesity (Ludwig *et al.* 1999), Type 2 diabetes (Salmeron *et al.* 1997), CVD (Liu *et al.* 2000) and cancers of the colon and breast (Augustin *et al.* 2002) will develop. The major risk factors for insulin resistance (IR) are the same as those for the major chronic diseases of diabetes and metabolic syndrome: genetics, obesity and lack of physical activity. With high intakes of refined carbohydrates in contemporary industrialized diets, hyperinsulinaemia is a common outcome, and a factor that links human behaviour to disease outcomes (McKeown-Eyssen 1994). The way in which potential foods are chosen, grown, prepared, processed and/or cooked influences their potential for this condition, especially through their effects on GI.

The main properties of any food that determine its GI are its carbohydrate content and type, and the nature of food processing it has been subjected to. These effects are summarized in Table 11.2. The balance of monomer units that make up a carbohydrate, be they glucose, fructose or otherwise, influences the glycaemic response. The greater the proportion of monomers other than glucose a carbohydrate contains, the lower is the glycaemic response. Starches that are made up of many monomer units are called polysaccharides, and their molecular structure governs the rate of digestion and absorption. For example,

Table 11.2 *Factors that influence the glycaemic response and the glycaemic index*

Factors that affect GI	Factors that decrease GI	Factors that increase GI
Nature of starch	▲ Amylose/amylopectin	▼ Amylose/amylopectin
Nature of monosaccharide	Fructose	Glucose
Alpha-amylase inhibitors	▲ Lectin	▼ Lectin
	▲ Phytates	▼ Phytates
Ripeness and food storage	Unripeness cooling	Ripeness
Particle size	Large particles	Grinding (small particles)
Cooking/food processing	Parboiling	Flaking, popping
	Cold extrusion	
Viscous fibre	▲ Guar	▼ Guar
Nutrient–starch interactions	▲ Protein	▼ Protein
	▲ Fat	▼ Fat

Adapted from Augustin *et al.* (2002).

the polysaccharide amylopectin (which forms most of the starch in rice, potatoes and maize) has a branched chain structure which allows it to be more rapidly digested than more linear forms of starch, such as amylose, which is found in lower proportion in rice and potatoes. Processing procedures such as flaking, extrusion, grinding, storing and cooking affect the starch particle size and the integrity of both the starch granules and plant cell walls, making carbohydrate molecules more available to digestive enzymes in the gut (Augustin *et al.* 2002).

While the factors that influence the GI of a food are multiple, there are a number of general principles. For fruits that are eaten raw, those with the highest levels of fructose and highest fructose to glucose ratios, including apples and pears, have the lowest GI. All fruits with a fructose to glucose ratio of less than 1.5 have a medium to high GI. Most vegetables, whether raw or cooked, fall into the low and medium GI categories. In general, beans and pulses have very low levels of fructose and glucose. (Rao and Belavady 1978); pulses generally have low GIs. The degree of ripeness of a fruit or vegetable influences its GI: when an item is less ripe it contains a greater proportion of resistant starch, called such because it resists digestion in the human gut (although it may be less resistant in primate guts (Chapter 2)). As a food ripens, such starches are converted to less resistant starches, including sugars. Some foods, especially pulses and root crops such as taro and yam, have alpha-amylase inhibitors, which inhibit the digestion of starches. Lectins are sugars with a high affinity for proteins; when eaten, they can impair digestion and digestibility of carbohydrate (Rea *et al.* 1985). Most of them are denatured by cooking, rendering them inactive or less active, depending on the extent and type of cooking. Unprocessed cereals and pulses have the highest amounts of lectins, and their processing increases energy availability from these food types. Phytates are found in the hulls of nuts, grains and seeds, and have strong binding affinity to the micronutrients calcium, iron and zinc, as well as lowering the GI of starches (Kumar *et al.* 2010).

Food preparation changes the GI of foods. For example, the grinding of foods to small particle size increases GI. The manual grinding of plant substances has been commonplace across traditional societies, whether to increase the efficacy of medicinal plants, increase the digestibility of food plants, or reduce the toxicity of a potential plant by subsequent soaking and leaching, as with manioc cultivators in South America (Dufour 1989). Milling is an extension of this; fermentation and cooking are further extensions. Bread could not exist as a food without these three processes. The longer and more thorough the cooking of a food is, the higher its GI. Pasta that is cooked for a shorter period of time and is firm (*al dente*) has a lower GI than pasta that is cooked until it is soft. Allowing rice or potato to cool before consumption lowers their GIs because a proportion of their digestible starch retrogrades to forms of starch of lower digestibility.

Industrialization of food manufacture saw the technologies of grinding, milling and cooking made more efficient, as well as reducing the toxicity of foods to extremely low levels (Chapter 5). Industrialization also saw increased outsourcing of food preparation from the home into the commercial sphere. This led to the commercial production of convenience foods such as, for example, pies and bread in the UK. In more recent decades, industrial food production has been able to turn food commodities into a range of forms that can be used to generate novel foods. Such technologies extend beyond those of scorching, roasting, baking and boiling available to traditional societies, and include those of parboiling and cold extrusion, which can lower the GI of a food, and popping and flaking, which can increase it.

Physiological studies of hunter-gatherer societies with recent incorporation of industrially processed foods high in refined carbohydrates into their diets show them to have increased levels of obesity, insulin resistance and Type 2 diabetes (O'Dea *et al.* 1987; Lillioja *et al.* 1991). This is no surprise given the difference in GIs between introduced foods such as rice and bread, and more traditional foods such as acacia seeds and yam (in the case of Australian Aboriginal people). Industrial food production has become increasingly complex, and substances that enhance shelf-life, palatability and the aesthetics of food products are incorporated as a matter of course. Some of these can influence GI, for example, guar gum (Wood *et al.* 1990).

This is a derivative of the guar bean, which is rarely eaten by humans in its natural state. Guar gum forms a gel when mixed with water, and is used to increase the viscosity of foods including ice cream and yoghurt, and to give more gel-like qualities to low-quality cheese and cold meat products. It also lowers the GIs of the foods to which it is added.

Across recent decades, food companies have developed a seemingly endless and inventive range of food products made with refined cereal grains, fats and sugars for public consumption with almost no regulatory health commentary. The rise of refined carbohydrate consumption is worrying with respect to the high prevalence of both CVD and Type 2 diabetes. The idea that insulin resistance (IR) was a causative factor in the pathogenesis of several chronic diseases was first put forward in the 1980s (Reaven 1988). Since then, relationships between Type 2 diabetes and CVD have been identified extensively by epidemiological study and clinical observation (Liu 1998). Insulin interacts with apolipoprotein E in increasing CVD risk (Orchard *et al.* 1994), by making low-density lipoprotein (LDL) more sensitive to oxidation (Sobal *et al.* 2000). Oxidized LDL is involved in the pathogenesis of atherosclerotic lesions (Beaudeux *et al.* 1995). Conversely, insulin sensitivity and basal nitric oxide production are linked (Petrie *et al.* 1996).

Liu (1998) postulated a mechanism by which diet influenced CVD risk through insulin resistance and hyperinsulinaemia (Figure 11.6). This involves the development of hyperglycaemia and/or hyperinsulinaemia by way of long-term consumption of a high GL diet, leading to hypertension, dyslipidaemia (elevated very low-density lipoprotein, decreased high-density lipoprotein), impaired fibrinolysis and greater potential for thrombosis. Insulin resistance has a genetic component but is also significantly influenced by weight gain and a high GL diet, which also affects weight gain. The resulting hyperinsulinaemia has a range of metabolic effects relating to development of CVD, including dyslipidaemia, upregulated thrombosis, hypertension, and impaired fibrinolysis (the process by which the body prevents naturally occurring blood clots from growing).

Results from the US Nurses' Health Study (which started in 1976 and continues to the present day) validate the model of Liu (1998); risk of CVD morbidity among those in the highest quintile for dietary GL was 1.9 times greater than those in the lowest quintile (Liu *et al.* 2000). However, the consumption of a high GI diet increased the risk of CVD morbidity twofold in women with BMI greater than 23 kg/m^2, but not in lean women, indicating that IR strongly interacts with dietary GL in influencing CVD outcome (Liu 1998). The links between insulin resistance, lipotoxicity, Type 2 diabetes and CVD are now well-known (deFronzo 2010). Lipotoxicity represents the deleterious effect of excessive fat tissue accumulation on glucose metabolism

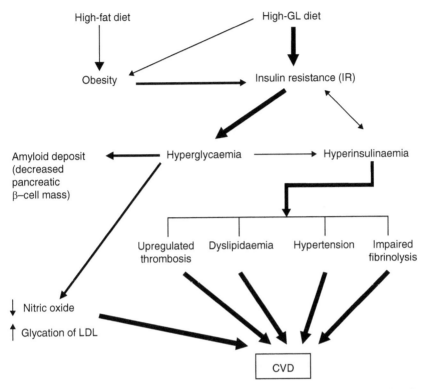

Figure 11.6. The central role of insulin resistance in the pathogenesis of CVD. Adapted from Liu (1998).

(Unger 2003), and is seen as key to both the development of insulin resistance and the progression to CVD (DeFronzo 2010). Contemporary industrialized diets that are high in refined carbohydrates promote both glucose toxicity and lipotoxicity through hepatic triacylglycerol production and cellular lipid deposition.

Traditional means of processing, such as grinding and cooking, would have raised the energy availability and GI of starchy foods in a way that would have increased the availability of digestible energy. However, these processes were not as effective in reducing foods to fine particles as industrial processes from the late nineteenth century onwards have been. While colonialism and early globalization led to many new foods being introduced to different populations, new industrial technologies for food processing opened possibilities for new foods from the middle of the nineteenth century onwards. Agricultural development and industrial food processing have allowed large urban populations to be fed cheaply and safely. Without this, industrial and post-industrial society could not flourish. However, many of the foods developed by food processing industries cannot be considered to be natural: think of the variety of snack-foods available in any supermarket, and how far from nature they are. Industrial processes do not mimic nature, and if foods can be engineered to be palatable and impervious to spoilage, it should be possible to engineer them with low GI. A major obstacle to this is the 'arms race' between competing food companies to sell more products: palatability is a major component of the saleability of food.

Carbohydrates in an evolutionary context

Frugivory is a fundamental primate dietary adaptation (Chapter 2) and humans have evolved from frugivorous ancestors. Since fruits are not homogeneous in their seasonality, type and ripeness when used, they represent a variety of sources of carbohydrate to which humans are adapted in some way. Brain and reproductive tissues have evolved specific requirements for glucose as a fuel source (Sokoloff 1977; Frienkel 1980), perhaps as a consequence of a long prehistory of angiosperm consumption and frugivory (Chapter 2). It is possible that insulin resistance (IR) evolved in prehistoric hunter-gatherers and ancestral, possibly scavenging, hominins across the past two million years or so as a response to diets that were high in animal foods and lower in carbohydrates (Brand-Miller and Colagiuri 1994). The emergence of significant meat-eating and extra-somatic food processing among hominins from around two million years ago led to increased energy density of the diet. Among early *Homo sapiens*, hunting (Lee and De Vore 1968; Garn and Leonard 1989) and the lower availability of edible plant foods for some hominin populations may have shifted the macronutrient balance of the diet towards higher protein and lower carbohydrate intakes, with varying levels of fat availability according to location and season.

Among some contemporary hunter-gatherer populations, foods rich in protein can form a significant part of the diet, although the proportion of animal products in the diet can vary from 31% to 68% of total intake by weight (Jenike 2001). Among Australian hunter-gatherers, 54% of their dietary energy comes from protein sources, mostly meat, with 33% from carbohydrate and 13% from fat (O'Dea *et al.* 1988; O'Dea 1991a). Higher protein intakes have been reported for Inuit and native Canadians living as foragers (Mann *et al.* 1962; Szathmary *et al.* 1987). However, these assumptions, as discussed in Chapter 5, must be treated with caution, as they are based on a sample of only a small proportion of foraging populations that may not be accurate representations of foraging populations in the past. Plant foods may have formed a much more important part of the ancestral human diet than archaeological and other dietary evidence indicates, with 'absence of evidence' not necessarily equating to 'evidence of absence' (Chapters 3 and 5).

This notwithstanding, Brand-Miller and Colagiuri (1994) argue that the consumption of low-carbohydrate diets in our evolutionary past resulted in selection for IR among females, with metabolic conservation of glucose for fetal survival and breast milk production. In pregnancy, the fetus and placenta use glucose almost exclusively as an energy source, as well as for synthesis of glycoproteins and glycolipids, while in lactation there is a high demand for glucose for lactose production (Brand-Miller and Colagiuri 1994). There is a progressive increase in peripheral IR during pregnancy in humans (Buchanan *et al*. 1990), with increased IR in the muscles and increased insulin sensitivity in the mammary tissue during lactation (Burnol *et al*. 1990). More generally, the demand of bodily tissues (especially of the reproductive system and brain) for glucose as a primary energy source would have been a liability in environments that could not supply adequate quantities of carbohydrate to meet that demand. Brand-Miller and Colagiuri (1994) suggest that variation in predisposition of different populations to Type 2 diabetes can be explained by differences in exposure to carbohydrates across the past 12 000 years or so (Chapter 1). They argue that IR may have been a normal state among humans prior to the consumption of high-carbohydrate diets based on grain use after the advent of agriculture (Eaton and Konner 1985; Garn and Leonard 1989). In populations with longer exposure to agriculture and high-carbohydrate diets the selection pressure for IR was relaxed, whereas in societies never, or only recently, exposed to agriculture, selection for IR continued, predisposing individuals within these groups to greater risk of Type 2 diabetes, as among Native Americans, Australian Aboriginal people, New Zealand Maori and Pacific Islands populations. In Australia, the diabetes rates of Aboriginal people exceed those of the total non-indigenous population by a factor of 3.7, while in the US, the rates among Native Americans are 2.3 times higher than among the non-indigenous population. The New Zealand population of this comparison is slightly younger than those of the US and Australia, but Type 2 diabetes rates among Maori are 2.6 times greater than among the European population, while those of migrant Pacific Islanders are 3.5 times greater.

Among Native Americans, observations of Type 2 diabetes rates may point to a thrifty genotype effect, since Pima females in Arizona consume less sugar, and less carbohydrate overall, than the general US population, while consuming the same number of calories overall (Reid *et al*. 1971), although any claims for 'thrifty genotype' must also be viewed in the context of intergenerational nutritional environments (Pollard 2008; Chapter 4). It is difficult to tell whether the high rates of Type 2 diabetes in Australian aboriginal people, Maori and Pacific Islanders reflects a thrifty genotype effect, since they eat more sugar, starch and carbohydrate, as well as more dietary energy overall, than their European counterparts (Lee *et al.* 1994; Sluyter *et al.* 2010).

The thrifty genotype hypothesis (Neel 1962, 1992) postulates that ancestral exposure to cycles of feast and famine underlies the development of IR as a coping mechanism, by selecting for individuals with better mechanisms for increasing the deposition of food energy as body fat in times of plenty for later use in times of food restriction. Starvation can lead to both increased gluco-neogenesis and peripheral IR (de Fronzo *et al.* 1978; Newman and Brodows 1983). Following from this, Reaven (1998) argued that natural selection did not confer metabolic efficiency by way of high IR on populations undergoing starvation, but favoured muscle protein conservation during periods of starvation by reduced gluconeogenesis from amino acids. However, human metabolism can adjust to chronic high-protein, low-carbohydrate diets by either increasing hepatic glucose production via gluconeogenesis (which involves the breakdown of protein) and/or decreasing peripheral glucose utilization (Phinney *et al.* 1983), which can be arguably described as IR.

Both Reaven's (1998) and Neel's (1992) arguments contain plausible elements, since the nutritional stresses that would have led to selection for thrifty genotypes are likely to have varied from population to population. Arguments for and against prehistoric hunter-gatherer starvation must consider variation across groups in nutritional ecology and seasonality of food availability (Chapter 4). For example, four groups of contemporary hunter-gatherers, the Ache of Paraguay, the Hiwi of Venezuela, the Efe of the Democratic Republic of Congo, and the Hadza of Tanzania, show seasonally low intakes of dietary energy of between 74% and 49% of their high season values (Jenike 2001). The outcome of an analysis of seasonal energy balance of these four hunter-gatherer groups is given in Figure 11.7, which shows the daily energy intake of adult men and women combined, at seasons of high and low intake, as a proportion of their daily energy requirement. Daily energy requirement is calculated by first predicting basal metabolic rate from mean body weight and height using equations for adults aged 18 to 30 years (Food and Agriculture Organization/World Health Organization/United Nations University 1985), and multiplying this by 1.78, the composite value for physical activity level for forager societies, as estimated by Jenike (2001). The Ache and Efe achieve positive energy balance in both high and low seasons, while the Hadza achieve positive balance across the year, with negative balance during the low food availability season. The Hiwi, however, achieve a small positive energy balance in the high food availability season, and a very large negative balance in the low season.

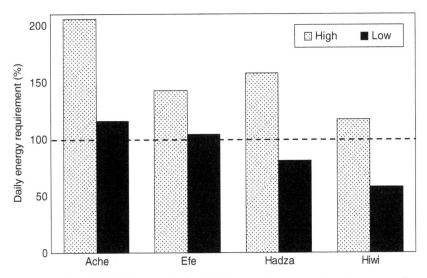

Figure 11.7. Daily energy intake of adult men and women combined, at seasons of high and low intake, as a proportion of daily energy requirement.

While the mean body mass index of all four groups is in the normal range for good health (mean values range between 20.8 and 23.2 kg/m^2), one of them, the Hiwi, are likely to experience seasonal starvation. If it can be assumed that the seasonal energy capture of these groups as represented here was also representative of their evolutionary past, then selection for thrifty energy metabolism due to starvation might have taken place among the Hiwi but not the other groups, even though all of them occupy (and have occupied) tropical ecosystems. Despite the lack of evidence that prehistoric hunter-gatherers suffered periodic starvation (Cordain *et al.* 1999), seasonal starvation among some groups cannot be excluded, particularly among those that have learned to live at higher latitudes (Jenike 2001). Since there are many genes that contribute to diabetes (at the time of writing, 38 Type 2 diabetes loci have been identified (Voight *et al.* 2010)), there are many ways in which such selection could have taken place, and the genetic basis for even one phenotype, such as IR, can also vary.

While there appears to be an epidemic of Type 2 diabetes across the world (Wild *et al.* 2004), its prevalence is higher among non-European populations (Zimmet *et al.* 2001) and highest among indigenous populations in nations that have been colonized by Europeans. While there is value in calling upon a thrifty genotype as an explanation for these patterns, this concept should not be reified as if it were based on only one or just a few gene systems (Keighley *et al.* 2007). Any putative thrifty genotype is most likely to be a complex genetic mechanism distributed across several loci that regulate energy intake, extraction, expenditure and storage (Snyder *et al.* 2004). Known gene loci for both Type 2 diabetes and obesity are plentiful, and are likely to increase as more genome-wide investigations take place (Voight *et al.* 2010; Higgins *et al.* 2010). The identities of the genetic variants mediating the effects at most of the diabetes loci are not yet known, and those that are known contribute less than 10% of the estimated genetic contribution to Type 2 diabetes (Voight *et al.* 2010). Similarly, the contributions to obesity rates of genes known to be associated with obesity, whether monogenic or polygenic, is well below 10%. Since obesity is intricately linked with Type 2 diabetes, there are interactions between genes associated with this condition and obesity, as well as between genes and environments (Higgins *et al.* 2010). The functional mechanisms of different thrifty genotypes therefore remain idealizations rather than realities, because of these complexities.

Glycaemic load, fructose and modern diseases

Industrial food technologies have created many high-GI, refined carbohydrate-based foods that require very little digestive work, releasing glucose into the blood rapidly (Cordain *et al.* 2005). The long-term consumption of foods of high GI and diets of high GL affect both metabolism and health (Liu and Willett 2002; Ludwig 2002), primarily owing to the hyperglycaemia and hyperinsulinaemia they induce, which result in a range of hormonal and physiological changes, many of which are associated with the development of IR (Cordain *et al.* 2005). Obesity, Type 2 diabetes, CVD and dyslipidaemia are connected through IR, and the clustering of these conditions is termed 'metabolic syndrome' or Syndrome X (Reaven 1995; Chapter 6). High IR and diets with high GL also play major parts in other less severe disorders including acne (Cordain *et al.* 2002c; Cordain 2005; Smith *et al.* 2007a, b), gout (Reaven 1995; Cordain 2005) and myopia (Cordain *et al.* 2003). These are either rare or non-existent in societies that consume minimally processed and low-GL diets (Eaton *et al.* 1988; Cordain *et al.* 2002a, 2005).

Gout involves a build up of monosodium urate crystals in the joints (the big toe being the most commonly affected area), swelling and subsequent pain. The crystal build up is due to high plasma levels of uric acid (hyperuricaemia), which reflects the balance of its hepatic production and urinary excretion. Cordain (2006) has observed that contemporary hunter-gatherers eating traditional diets almost never suffer from gout (Roberts-Thomson and Roberts-Thomson 1999). Historical accounts show it to be a disorder of the wealthy (Johnson and Rideout 2004) which has become more common across western society in recent times (Fam 2005). While it has been blamed on high levels of consumption of meat and seafood, Cordain (2006) finds it odd that such diets should cause a crippling disease in present-day populations, when humans and their ancestral hominins have had more than two million years to adapt to diets high in meat. It has been demonstrated that consumption of a diet low in both alcohol and carbohydrate but high in protein can reduce both blood uric acid levels and gout severity among those suffering from this condition (Dessein *et al.* 2000), suggesting that meat consumption may not be the principal factor in the causation of gout. An alternative explanation put forward by Fam (2002) links gout to IR and the metabolic syndrome through the consumption of diets with high GLs and fructose, respectively.

Acne is a disorder of the pilosebaceous unit of the skin, which comprises the hair shaft, follicle and sebaceous gland. Most commonly, it results in inflamed spots and blotches on the face. It is thought to arise from the interplay of four factors: (1) increased growth and abnormal differentiation of follicular cells, which obstruct the follicular opening; (2) increased sebum production in response to androgen hormone stimulation; (3) infection by the bacterium *Propionibacterium acnes*; (4) an immune response to these bacteria, involving inflammation (Smith *et al.* 2007a, b). Acne is common among adolescents in western societies (Kilkenny *et al.* 1997; Dreno and Poli 2003), but is rarely found in other societies (Cordain 2005). It may develop in genetically predisposed individuals in response to environmental triggers (Taylor *et al.* 2002) of which diet may be a key feature. The consumption of a diet with a high GL has been associated with hyperinsulinaemia and acne among urbanized Inuit (Bendiner 1974).

Simple myopia, or short-sightedness, is due to eye length that is excessive relative to the corneal power of the eye. Myopia is largely absent in wild animals (Curtin 1985), and it is easy to see how myopia would have been selected against among pre-agricultural societies (Mak *et al.* 2006). If an individual cannot scan or read the environment clearly, they are disadvantaged in obtaining food, especially in competitive circumstances, and are less likely to identify predators. The prevalence of myopia has risen in recent decades, Saw (2003) identifying such increases in Asia to be far greater in urban than in rural populations. Dayan *et al.* (2005) found that the general increase in myopia among a nationally representative sample of Israeli males between the ages of 16 and 22 years was greatest among those with the greatest number of years of schooling. Studies of related urban and isolated individuals with similar levels of childhood schooling have shown higher levels of myopia among the former (Garner *et al.* 1999; Lewallen *et al.* 1995). Furthermore, while young Australian aboriginal adults suffered far less myopia than their European counterparts in 1977, by the year 2000, rates had increased sevenfold (Taylor *et al.* 2003) to levels comparable to the majority European population. Common myopia has been attributed to genetic and environmental factors, although modern education and sedentary work patterns have received most attention (Saw 2003). Hyperinsulinaemia as a consequence of consuming high-GL diets has also been invoked as one explanation for the recent increase in rates of myopia (Cordain *et al.* 2002d).

While seemingly unconnected, these three modern disorders can be linked through the consumption of industrialized diets, especially the consumption of processed starches and sugars including HFCS (Figure 11.8). The hyperinsulinaemia that results from consumption of high-GI carbohydrate foods and insulin resistance has a number of effects on subsequent metabolism. These include elevating insulin-like growth factor-1 (IGF-1) levels and decreasing the binding proteins for IGF-1 (insulin-like growth factors 1 and 3), which further elevate IGF-1 levels. This leads to cell growth in the eye and sebaceous glands and to overproduction of sebum in the sebaceous glands, resulting in myopia and acne, respectively. The high prevalence of acne in adolescents might be explained by the transitory insulin resistance and increased insulin secretion encountered during puberty (Caprio *et al.* 1989). In a longitudinal study of pubertal insulin resistance, Goran and Gower (2001) found a 32% reduction in insulin sensitivity between Tanner stages I and III with a subsequent increase in fasting glucose and insulin.

Fructose consumption increases hepatic uric acid production directly and via lactic acid formation, while alcohol has a similar effect through lactic acid, leading to increased plasma uric acid levels and gout. Purine-rich foods such as meats and seafood have a small positive effect on uric acid production but a much stronger effect on kidney excretion of uric acid, lowering plasma levels. However, this protective effect is blocked by high levels of insulin (high GI foods) and lactic acid (alcohol and fructose). Cordain (2006) initially identified the combination of a high-GL diet, alcohol consumption and high intakes of fructose from sugar and HFCS to be associated with gout. High levels of meat and seafood consumption are insufficient explanations, since contemporary hunter-gatherers consuming diets high in animal protein and low in carbohydrates do not experience gout (Cordain *et al.* 2000a). Furthermore, elimination of high-purine foods that would reduce uric acid production does not ameliorate symptoms among gout sufferers (Griebsch and Zollner 1974; Clifford *et al.* 1976). Fructose also increases hepatic uric acid production (Raivio *et al.* 1975); similarly, sucrose (a disaccharide with units of both glucose and fructose), but not glucose alone, increases plasma uric acid levels (Fox *et al.* 1985). Fructose enters glycolysis after the key rate-limiting phosphofructokinase (PFK) step, and high intakes of it result in unregulated phosphorylation of fructose to fructose phosphate, and depletion of adenosine

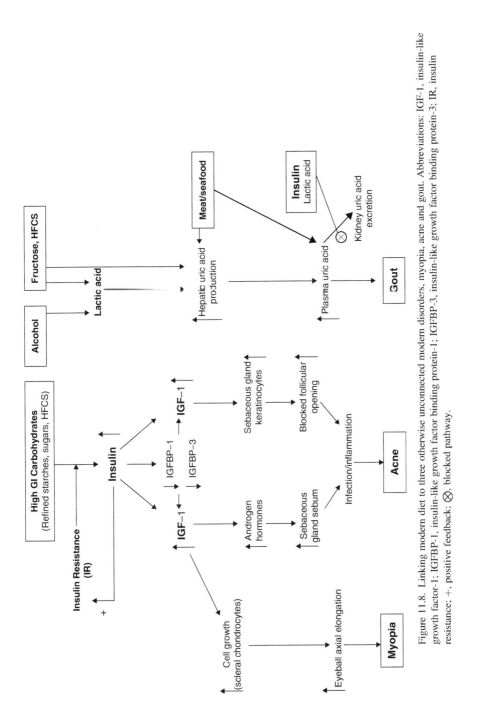

Figure 11.8. Linking modern diet to three otherwise unconnected modern disorders, myopia, acne and gout. Abbreviations: IGF-1, insulin-like growth factor-1; IGFBP-1, insulin-like growth factor binding protein-1; IGFBP-3, insulin-like growth factor binding protein-3; IR, insulin resistance; +, positive feedback; ⊗, blocked pathway.

triphosphate (ATP) and the inorganic phosphate needed for synthesis of both ATP and fructose phosphate. Decreased levels of inorganic phosphate in the liver increase the rate of conversion of the purines guanosine and adenosine monophosphates (GMP and AMP) respectively to uric acid, which then enters the circulating blood. Increased fructose phosphorylation also leads to increased lactic acid in the blood which inhibits urinary excretion of uric acid (Yamamoto *et al.* 1993). Similarly, high insulin levels (which occur as a result of consuming a high-GL diet) also inhibit urinary excretion of uric acid (Facchini *et al.* 1991). Alcohol both promotes synthesis of uric acid and inhibits its excretion, through lactic acid production.

Acne is almost a rite of passage for adolescents in western countries. While clearly an adolescent phenomenon, the role of GL in the causation of acne was put forward by Cordain *et al.* (2002c) when they observed that among Ache hunter-gatherers of Paraguay, and Kitavan subsistence horticulturalists of Papua New Guinea, adolescents rarely experienced acne when their usual diets were consumed, but it was common when they consumed processed carbohy-drate-rich commodities. The hyperinsulinaemia that accompanies consumption of high-GI foods, coupled with the transient insulin resistance observed during puberty (Caprio *et al.* 1989; Moran *et al.* 1999; Goran and Gower 2001), give rise to hyperglycaemia in this age group. A link between sex hormones, acne and IR has been shown in women with polycystic ovary syndrome (PCOS), where IR is virtually universal, and acne, associated with hyperinsulinaemia and hyperandrogenism, is extremely common (Falsetti *et al.* 2002). Treatments that address hyperinsulinaemia directly, such as insulin-sensitizing drugs (Harborne *et al.* 2003) or indirectly through slowed carbohydrate digestion, such as alpha-glucosidase inhibitors (Ciotta *et al.* 2001) also reduce symptoms of PCOS and acne.

The mediator between puberty, consumption of a high-GL diet, induced hyperinsulinaemia and acne is insulin-like growth factor-1 (IGF-1), which is known to stimulate cell proliferation and inhibit apoptosis (Kaaks *et al.* 2000), with keratinocytes of the sebaceous gland being particularly affected. Growth hormone, insulin and high caloric intake all increase production of IGF-1, while elevated postprandial insulin levels inhibit hepatic production of the binding protein for IGF-1, insulin-like growth factor binding protein 1 (IGFBP-1) (Powell *et al.* 1991). This allows more IGF-1 to circulate freely and initiate cell proliferation. Among the cell types that undergo proliferation are those of the keratinocytes of the pilosebaceous unit. This leads to blocking of the follicular opening, increased sebum production and accumulation in the blocked follicular duct. This provides an excellent environment for the prolif-eration of *Propionibacterium acnes,* which lives on fatty acids in sebum. It is one of hundreds of species of usually non-pathogenic bacteria that live on skin.

High levels of sebum production arise from increased production of andro-gen hormones during puberty and reduction in hepatic production of sex hormone binding globulin (SHBG), which controls androgenic activity. Inhibition of SHBG production has been linked to IR and hyperinsulinaemia (Franks 2003) and elevated free IGF-1 levels (Singh *et al.* 1990). In a dietary intervention study involving adolescent males with mild to severe acne, Smith *et al.* (2007a, b) showed subjects placed on a low-GL diet for 12 weeks had less acne, lower fasting insulin and higher levels of SHBG and IGFBP-1 (indicating less free/active androgens and IGF-1), relative to controls.

Acne, gout and myopia may be linked by the consumption of refined carbohydrates, especially HFCS (Figure 11.8). The three are largely separated by life-stage, and rarely cluster in the same individuals, however. The most common timing of onset of simple myopia is in mid-childhood through adolescence (Saw 2003), while acne is most abundant in puberty. Gout is uncommon in children and adolescents. Separate contributors of seafood and alcohol consumption are additionally important in the causation of gout, while pubertal endocrinology is additionally important in the causation of acne. Removal of one or more contributors will reduce the prevalence of one or more of these conditions. Acne is much less common outside of puberty, while gout is much less common among those that do not regularly consume fructose and/or high GI foods. Most importantly, among those consuming diets of low GL, acne, gout and myopia are all much less common, as are Type 2 diabetes and CVD. In the US, a significant contributor to the carbohydrate load in the diet, particularly raising the fructose intake, is a very un-natural food, HFCS. In the next section we examine ways in which its consumption can be linked to chronic disease.

Fructose consumption and health

The most common form in which fructose is consumed in industrialized society is sugar, which is composed of both glucose and fructose. The most common natural sources are ripe fruits, especially apples and pears, and honey (in which 60% of the sugar is fructose). In the US, the most common form of fructose consumed is as high-fructose corn syrup (HFCS). It is usually difficult to ingest enough fructose for it to be harmful through the consumption of fruit, and while consuming harmful amounts of honey is possible, it is usually too expensive for people in industrialized societies to buy regularly in large quantities. Sugar, and in the US HFCS, are cheap and can be eaten on a daily basis without challenging an individual's monetary food budget. Even though ancestral hominin and human diets

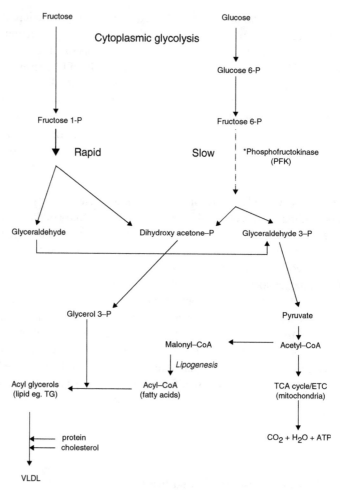

Figure 11.9. Simplified hepatic pathway for fructose and glucose metabolism. Adapted from Mayes (1993).

could contain honey, which could be consumed in great quantity, this was available only seasonally (Chapter 4), as was fruit in many regions of the world. During seasonal highs of consumption, fructose intakes could have exceeded current levels of consumption in industrialized societies. An extreme example is that of the Mbuti hunter-gatherers, who during the honey season (June to August) could attain as much as 70% of their food by weight in honey (Ichikawa 1981). This is around 270 g of fructose per day, on a very good day, compared with the average citizen of the US in the 1990s, who consumed around 40 g of fructose per day, with the top decile of the population consuming up to 70 g per day. More usually, hunter-gatherer fructose intakes would probably be at least an order of magnitude below contemporary US levels (Bray 2007).

While both sugar and HFCS can be harmful to health when consumed in excess, HFCS may carry the greater risk. This is because it is processed differently to sucrose by the body. At the absorption level, the intestinal enzyme sucrase is required for digestion of sucrose, while for HFCS, the fructose and glucose are unlinked, and are absorbed rapidly in the small intestine because there is no need for enzymatic breakdown in the gut. As the body controls the rate of sucrase production, it is possible that the rate of sucrose digestion and absorption is slowed, although minutely, compared with HFCS. At a metabolic level, fructose feeding has been found in studies to be involved directly with hypertriglyceridaemia, aberrant leptin signalling of energy balance regulation, and hyperinsulinaemia with reduced glycaemic control (Basciano *et al.* 2005). Fructose feeding has also been shown to promote obesity in mice (Jürgens *et al.* 2005), while high fructose intake in humans has been shown to stimulate triacylglycerol production in the liver and induce insulin resistance (Faeh *et al.* 2005). Rats fed a high-fructose diet experience a large increase in blood leptin levels, suggesting that fructose is associated with the development of leptin resistance, although it is not yet clear whether this is through direct action of fructose or through fat gain following fructose feeding. Leptin is involved in the regulation of energy balance, and leptin resistance can lead to obesity because its regulatory signals are not recognized by the hypothalamus. The same rats, when switched to a high-fat diet, gained more weight, mostly as fat (Shapiro *et al.* 2008). Rats fed a fructose-rich diet for five weeks almost doubled their serum homocysteine levels (Oron-Herman *et al.* 2003); serum homocysteine levels correlate well with coronary artery disease in humans, also being highly elevated in diabetic patients (Okada *et al.* 1999).

Fructose intake is also associated with more atherogenic LDL particle size in overweight school children (Aeberli *et al.* 2007), while adults consuming between 20% and 25% of their total daily energy intake from fructose over a four to six week period have increased fasting triglyceride (TG) and LDL cholesterol levels (Schaefer *et al.* 2009), both of which are associated with increased CVD risk. High fructose intakes inhibit the breakdown of fat in the adipose tissue and increase the production of lactic acid in the liver, giving rapid increases in levels of pyruvic and lactic acids, resulting in increased production of very low density lipoproteins (VLDL) (Abdel-Sayed *et al.* 2008), which is associated with CVD risk.

Within limits, fructose is a good source of dietary energy. It is an intermediary in the glycolysis pathway of glucose metabolism to pyruvate in the liver.

Although it has been thought of as a fuel for sperm motility, this has recently been challenged (Lahnsteiner *et al.* 2010). Outside reasonable limits, fructose consumption is problematic. Most human cells cannot take up fructose from the bloodstream since they lack the transporter that allows this to happen (Bray 2007). Almost all fructose is taken up by liver cells and metabolized there, initially via phosphorylation, bypassing the phosphofructokinase (PFK) rate-limiting step in glycolysis (Havel 2005) (Figure 11.9). With glucose metabolism, this step leads to a controlled molecular flow of glucose through to acetyl-CoA and hence energy release as ATP in the mitochondria, or as fatty acid (acyl-CoA) synthesis via malonyl-CoA and subsequent attachment to glycerol to yield storage fats in the form of acyl glycerols such as triacylglycerols (TG). Packaging of TG with hepatic cholesterol and proteins leads to production of Very Low Density Lipoproteins (VLDL). As fructose metabolism bypasses the rate limited PFK step, high levels of intake can lead to uncontrolled lipid production, and increased levels of circulating lipids (Havel 2005), at least among subjects on acute feeding trials.

A number of other factors differentiate the digestion, absorption and metabolism of fructose and glucose. Fructose is absorbed differently and to a lesser extent than glucose in the small intestine. The glut-5 transporter essential for the movement of fructose across cell membranes is lacking in pancreatic beta-cells; this may be why fructose does not stimulate insulin release from the pancreas (Sato *et al.* 1996). Unlike glucose, fructose cannot enter brain tissue because the brain lacks the glut-5 transporter. This means that it is unlikely to induce a satiety signal from the hypothalamus, and it can be eaten freely without assuaging hunger (Bray *et al.* 2004). Consumption of highly fructose-sweetened beverages has been shown to increase subjective hunger ratings and *ad libitum* fat intake the following day (Elliott *et al.* 2002). Recent studies of functional magnetic resonance imaging (fMRI) of the brain have shown differences in cortical response to glucose and fructose infusions, although neither seemed to affect hypothalamic response (Purnell *et al.* 2011). The blood oxygenation level-dependent responses (BOLD) measured by fMRI are indicators of regional blood flow and are used as a surrogate measure of neuronal activity. Such BOLD signals have been shown to increase during glucose infusion but decrease during fructose infusion. This has been interpreted by Purnell *et al.* (2011) as evidence for a neurological basis for fructose consumption to promote weight gain.

Relationships between diabetes prevalence and intakes of fat, carbohydrate, HFCS and total energy have been identified for the US population (Gross *et al.* 2004). When adjusted for total energy intake, HFCS intake remains positively associated with Type 2 diabetes prevalence, while fat and protein intake do not. In a study of the effects of dietary fructose, carbohydrates and glycaemic load on IR, Wu *et al.* (2004) found that subjects in the highest quintile of fructose intake had 14% higher insulin secretion than those in the lowest quintile. Cantena *et al.* (2003) showed that insulin receptor numbers and insulin receptor mRNA falls dramatically during high fructose intake in rats, suggesting increased insulin resistance, as well as increases in blood pressure and plasma TG levels. Furthermore, Taghibiglou *et al.* (2000) found that high fructose feeding in hamsters resulted in elevated glucose and insulin levels and an almost halving in insulin sensitivity.

The 'hexosamine hypothesis' was put forward by McClain (2002) to explain how chronic overconsumption of fructose may lead to Type 2 diabetes. Hexosamine flux regulates glucose and satiety signalling pathways. The rate-limiting enzyme in the synthesis of hexosamine is glutamine:fructose-6-phosphate aminotransferase. Overexpression of this enzyme due to elevated fructose presence leads to hepatic lipogenesis (Rumberger *et al.* 2003) followed by insulin resistance (Hawkins *et al.* 1997) in skeletal muscles and hyperinsu-linaemia, increased potential for greater fat storage, and increased risk of obesity and Type 2 diabetes (Basciano *et al.* 2005). Teo *et al.* (2010) have identified excess flux through the hexosamine biosynthetic pathway in adipocytes as a fundamental cause of 'glucose toxicity' and the development of insulin resistance. Whether this is directly or indirectly related to fructose availability is not clear, however, as adipocytes have limited capacity to take up fructose.

It is easy to hypothesize how this mechanism for preferential fat storage could have evolved under conditions of seasonal variation in fruit and honey availability. However, this hypothesis would be wrong, since analysis of modular co-evolution of networks of genes found in *Homo sapiens* indicates that the genetic machinery for amino sugar metabolism evolved with the protists (Zhao *et al.* 2007), perhaps over a billion years ago. This makes sense, in that this system is a workhorse for the interchangeability of metabolic substances in the creation of cellular structure. Consuming foods high in one particular substrate, fructose, could have been recruited by ancestral frugivores for the efficient deposition of energy. From an evolutionary perspective fructose consumption, whether from seasonally available fruit or honey, is preferable to consumption of other forms of sugar, including glucose, because it facilitates fat gain in times of plenty. Its negative role emerged when times of plenty became perpetual, as in present-day industrialized societies. These negatives are related to CVD, Type 2 diabetes, obesity, and the metabolic syndrome.

Rats fed HFCS have been shown to develop some of the metabolic changes associated with the metabolic syndrome, even in the absence of increased body weight (Ferder *et al.* 2010), confirming that its effects are not limited to obesity-related pathways. One example of a non-obesity-related pathway is the decline in insulin-stimulated autophosphorylation, a necessary step for insulin action, demonstrated in rats fed a high-fructose diet (Ueno *et al.* 2000). This is an effect that results in increased polyol formation and advanced glycation end products, compounds that contribute to the complications and premature atherosclerosis accompanying diabetes (Basciano *et al.* 2005). Perez-Pozo *et al.* (2010) induced many of the physiological components of metabolic syndrome in just two weeks of feeding 200 g of fructose per day to human adults. They found increased levels of plasma triglyceride and insulin levels, and lower levels of HDL cholesterol. They also found that subjects consuming fructose had raised blood pressure, insulin resistance and increased body fatness. In addition, fructose consumption increased plasma uric acid levels. While this level of intake is double the average per capita for HFCS consumption in the US, it is within the physiological range of intake, since the top quintile of US adults consume more than 110 g of it per day (Duffey and Popkin 2008). This shows how quickly high fructose consumption can change the metabolic profile of an individual towards the metabolic syndrome, and gout. Whether such changes are sustained during long-term high-level fructose consumption is likely but yet to be clearly shown.

Discussion

Human diet has come a very long way from its ancestral state, no more so than with the entry of foods high in refined carbohydrates. Human control of food has also come a long way, with cooking revolutionizing the way that humans live, and putting food processing central to feeding behaviour (Chapter 5). Whether this happened around two million years ago (Wrangham 2009) or more recently, the effect was to increase the energy availability of foods already consumed, and increase the range of items that could be consumed as food. Humans have developed a wealth of food processing possibilities that can be practised at low levels of technology. These include initial selection of potential foods, processing before cooking, modes of cooking (including roasting, baking and boiling), and preparation for storage (including pickling and fermentation). By increasing the digestibility and reducing the toxicity of foods, processing results in the out-sourcing of some elements of physiological digestion. Around two million years ago, guts reduced in size as hominins underwent encephalization and began to consume a higher quality diet (Aiello and Wheeler 1995). We now have digestive systems that are able to deal with a great diversity of diet, but are not worked anywhere near to capacity when highly processed foods are consumed. This is nowhere more evident than among populations in economically developed and emerging nations, where diets are dominated by refined carbohydrates.

While the nature and extent of nutrition transition (Popkin 2002a) can be debated (Chapter 9), human populations generally consume more dietary energy, fats, oils and sugar the more prosperous they become. In this chapter we suggest that a carbohydrate transition, an increased consumption of refined carbohydrates including sugars, is underway, with additional health consequences to the ones elaborated by Popkin (2002a). This transition is most advanced in the US, where HFCS has become a major source of dietary carbohydrate and sweetness for the population. Refined carbohydrates are easy to overeat relative to needs, so they promote overweight and obesity. And the sugars among them promote glucose toxicity while obesity promotes lipotoxicity, and both promote insulin resistance, Type 2 diabetes and CVD. When found in the same person, this chronic disease jackpot is called metabolic syndrome, which is now found in populations across the world (Grundy 2008). We have a lot of evolutionary baggage that is useful for enhancing survivorship through improving fat deposition from the consumption of sugars, especially fructose. Much of this baggage has very deep ancestry, and has been recruited for new tasks, as with the hexosamine metabolic pathway and fructose metabolism. This mechanism should not be manipulated without care, since it sits at the crossroads of many key metabolic processes. But contemporary high carbohydrate diets do manipulate it, with clear negative outcomes.

The world's population is currently experiencing an epidemic of Type 2 diabetes (Wild *et al.* 2004), and this disease is currently the fifth most common cause of death in the world (Roglic *et al.* 2005). Predictions are that rates will carry on increasing. Meanwhile the food industry continues to produce foods that contribute to an excess mortality of 2.9 million people per year due to this disease alone. This is above the upper range of mortality estimates for the ten most deadly wars during the decade of the 1990s, where estimates range from 0.8 million to 2.9 million deaths in Rwanda, Angola, Somalia, Bosnia, Liberia, Burundi, Chechnya, Tajikistan, Algeria and the Gulf war combined (Murray *et al.* 2002). This makes Type 2 diabetes at least ten times more deadly than warfare. And it makes the producers of refined carbohydrates, such as HFCS, more potentially complicit in deaths due to this disease than arms manufacturers are in deaths in wars.

12 *Postscript*

Humans are innovators and explorers. As a result, our species has always lived in a world that is rapidly changing, owing to the movement of people or because of technological, cultural and behavioural developments. Human diets are and always have been varied and variable, yet the pace of change in the ways in which foods are produced, processed, distributed and consumed is far greater now, after industrialization, than ever before. Even though humans are highly plastic and resilient to change, we have aimed to show in this book that these shifts in diet and nutrition have profound implications for public health now, as well as in the future. This is not to say that all changes, especially in the rich, developed world, have necessarily been for the worse. People living in affluent industrialized nations, particularly those in the higher socioeconomic classes, enjoy immense food security, experience safer childbirth, and have low rates of infection, accidents and premature mortality, at least for the moment. Indeed, some of the rise in chronic disease in rich nations can be attributed to an aging population: since so few people die prematurely because of childbirth, infection or accident in these countries, they are living long enough to develop diseases such as Type 2 diabetes, cancer and coronary heart disease (CHD). It is clear, however, that the rapid shifts in human diet are not overwhelmingly positive. People are experiencing chronic disease at younger and younger ages, and levels of obesity are rising rapidly in children as well as adults. Many developing nations face the multiple burdens of infectious disease, chronic disease, undernutrition and food insecurity. Even at the level of the household there can be a dual burden of underweight and obesity in countries undergoing nutrition transition (Doak *et al.* 2005).

Across the world, it is the poor (in both absolute and relative terms) that are challenged the most in a rapidly changing nutritional world. Inequality is at the heart of the majority of the world's nutritional health problems. Despite large global population size and densities in the contemporary world, humans are evolutionarily hard-wired to live and function in small groups or networks.

Increases in population size thus require the formation of institutions and division of labour. This results in social and economic inequality. Where this leads to denial of basic needs such as food security, it becomes a form of structural violence (Farmer 2004), of which undernutrition everywhere and obesity in industrialized nations are the embodied outcomes. Simplistic narratives of obesity reduction in developed economies promote eating less and exercising more. However, this supposes that all members of those societies have more or less equal access to resources, and this is not the case. Diets appropriate for living better lives, both socially and in terms of health, can be constructed in many ways but can also be undermined by a lack of economic entitlement (Sen 1981) or inequality, such that foods rich in nutrients beyond energy and/or protein are difficult to obtain for many. Industrialization has created an obesogenic environment where calories from fats and refined carbohydrates such as sugar are incredibly cheap and ubiquitous, especially in energy-dense processed foods. However, foods such as fruit, vegetables and wholegrains are more expensive and not necessarily readily available to the poorest populations. Thus, although most (but not all) people in industrialized nations have access to far more calories than they need, the forms that these calories take may differ between social classes, with those on lower incomes tending to have better access to and preferentially choosing energy-dense foods compared with those that are more micronutrient- and fibre-rich.

Inequality matters for public health nutrition. Nutritional policies that promote self-reliance are more likely to lead to reduction in nutritional health inequalities than those that do not. This has long been recognized by development agencies (Administrative Committee on Coordination Sub-Committee on Nutrition 2000), and the importance of self-reliance has been stressed within a broader context of disease control, environmental health, education and health promotion (World Health Organization 2000). The narrative of nutrition transition, while correct in broadest outline, can benefit from incorporating observations about social and economic inequality in the present, and colonialism and early globalization in the past. Self-determination and an individual's ability to control significant aspects of their own and their family's life are prerequisites to making a transition to healthy behavioural change. At present, such qualities are concentrated among higher social classes, and among these classes, self-control and determination are concentrated among those with a historically grounded sense of status and entitlement.

Public health nutrition aims to benefit human form and function, but nutritional health is as much an outcome of social action and political and economic processes as of personal and familial choice. Social and economic inequalities in nutritional health reflect social and political realities. However, the frameworks whereby nutritional health norms are measured and determined are themselves underpinned by social, economic and political factors. For example, recommended daily allowances (RDA) locate food provisioning within daily practice (usually regularized for industrialized practice) and a weekly schedule. But human beings did not evolve to be bound by industrial schedules. Rather, seasonal practice, whether as hunter-gatherers, agriculturalists or pastoralists, would result in dietary and nutrient intakes that would have balanced across periods of days, weeks, months, or even years. Human physiological plasticity evolved under such circumstances, and while the desire to minimize day-to-day and seasonal nutritional stress may be natural, RDAs are not. In the contemporary industrialized world, we are buffered against all kinds of environmental dietary variation. This is not necessarily bad: few people, in both subsistence and non-subsistence economies, would choose to go hungry. However, the current disconnect between human biology and industrial diets in most of the economically developed world, an outcome of historical, political and economic forces that have shaped the world food system, has swung too far in the opposite direction and has reinforced inequitable distribution of resources. Food security has turned into health insecurity in developed nations, and in developing and less developed countries, globalized markets and the demand for fresh produce year-round has led to productive agricultural land being used for big business rather than supplying local economies.

One of the things that industrial and subsequently post-industrial society has done in many places (especially the United State (US)) has been the displacement of foods with food products, food markets with supermarkets, and dining with feeding. In the US, which has the most industrialized food production system in the world, the emergence of high-fructose corn syrup demonstrates how political pressures can shape the contents of foods and ultimately the health of a population. Alongside economic and political pressures on time, food production and the act of eating, the appearance of new technologies and the demand to feed people is stimulating the development of new foods. Although applying such solutions to global food production and supply problems could be enormously beneficial, public health nutrition must be alert to the fact that the technological shaping of human diets has not finished. Lessons from recent history suggest that health and well-being will not be top of the industrial food production agenda.

Industrialization allows great efficiencies of food production, allowing large (and increasing) urban populations to be sustained on cheap food products. This has meant a grade shift, in many places, away from what any natural human diet might be toward the consumption of a wide range of food products that are manufactured from a very limited range of plant and animal species, but which appeal to the human (and primate) desire for novelty and palatability. The shift from diets constituted by a broad range of animal and plant foods to ones largely based on processed foods rich in refined grains, sugars and oils has led to huge decreases in micronutrient intake among contemporary industrialized societies and economically developing populations. It has also created a different physiological environment that predisposes to, among other things, insulin resistance, in addition to the risks that emerge from obesity itself.

The industrialization of food has joined the increasing demand for time efficiency with the desire for food security and the human taste for food novelty. This has caused mass consumption of types of food that may not be particularly healthy and created health problems for many. Economists might see rationality in mass consumption, since consumers logically seek to maximize their welfare. However, actively seeking to be obese is uncommon, and it is unlikely that anyone chooses to develop Type 2 diabetes from overconsumption of refined carbohydrates. The reason for this contradiction between desire and reality is not only availability but time-inconsistency: people diverge from formal economic rationality by wanting different things at different times. For example, we might want pizza now and a slim body later. So we go for the pizza. And when later becomes now, pizza wins out again (Offer *et al.* 2012).

In the face of plenty (as in the contemporary industrialized world), humans must exert considerable control to avoid overeating, especially when energy-dense foods are the cheapest. Such control is not easy, and goes against evolutionary principles, common to mammals as a whole, of maximizing intakes during times of high food abundance to protect ourselves against times of shortfall. Finding enough dietary energy on a regular basis is a selective pressure on all primates in the wild, and is unlikely to have been any different for the hominins and modern humans. What we (and all mammals) eat is driven by signals of high energy density of foods, notably sweetness and fat. Industrialized food systems are extremely adept at creating foods that appeal to the senses from a very limited range of food commodities and chemicals. Humans respond positively to such foods, often more so than to foods that are dense in nutrients beyond energy. Markets provide many kinds of convenience for consumers, and increased convenience is a potential contributor to population obesity, especially when the foods that are convenient are energy-dense (Ulijaszek 2007). At present, when food is made more convenient, unhealthy choices are more easily made. It might be hoped for the future that the demand for healthy foods might stimulate the successful development, marketing and sale of functional foods (Charalampopoulos *et al.* 2002) at a large enough extent and low enough price to have broad public health impacts.

Improving nutritional health is not simply about taking measures to address food production, distribution and demand, although these are hugely important areas. People and populations vary biologically and ecologically, factors that inevitably impact upon nutrition. Genetic differences between individuals can have important effects on food consumption, for example (Timpson *et al.* 2008). Although public health is concerned largely with population-based measures, it is individuals that make up populations. Knowledge of variation within and between populations will help to refine public health messages and interventions. Human genetic diversity has implications for disease suscepti-bility also, so public health solutions to problems that involve interactions between nutrition and infection will need to be more complex than at present. Until genetic variation affecting disease susceptibility and nutritional adapta-tion can be incorporated into public health nutrition practice, macro-level solutions that result in general environmental improvement are the best polit-ical economic interventions to health problems caused by nutrition–infection interactions. These include malarial vector control, diarrhoeal disease manage-ment, and improvement in food security (through policies that promote diet quality beyond energy content and/or reduce economic inequality).

Just as biology varies, so do behaviour and culture. Humans imitate and adopt as well as innovate, and this is as true for diets as any other areas of life. Although there are well-established dietary and food traditions across the world's populations, these are changeable and changing. For example, pasta was not always a significant part of the Italian diet but became increasingly so in early medieval times (Serventi and Sabban 2002). It became a universal staple only with the industrialization of its production in the mid-nineteenth century. There is great time-depth to the movement of foods across the world, and to the cosmopolitanization of diets. Sets of relationships among human groups within regions, often later formalized as nation states, were often established centuries ago and persist to the present day in framing food relationships between those nations and their diets. Indeed, the world food system, which shapes what and how people eat almost everywhere in the present day, emerged with the commodification of food crops and the indus-trialization of diet from the nineteenth century onwards.

Although the desire of humans to imitate and adopt as well as innovate is unlikely to change, the global commercial landscape is very different now from that of even 50 years ago. A very small number of multinational corpor-ations control much of the world's food supply, and one way in which to promote the consumption of healthier food would be to address the homogen-ization and globalization of processed, often fast, food cultures. A healthy diet did not stop with Mesolithic hunter-gatherers, and even in developed nations there are many so-called traditional diets that are associated with good nutri-tional health, whether embedded within Italian, French, Japanese, Korean or other national cuisines. This suggests that even if the social and cultural underpinnings are vastly different, there are many ways of arriving at the same (positive) place, nutritionally.

Transformations of human societies have been big and small. In this book we have focused on the big ones, simply because in the deeper past these are usually the only types of changes for which there is evidence. However, social change is likely to continue, and alongside it, diet and nutritional health. Nutritionists promoting change for improved health are engaged in the process of transforming the everyday when seeking to change people's diets. Mostly, people are capable of transforming themselves if they have good reason to do so. So it is important for nutritionists to provide reasons for the consumption of healthy diets that have individual, social and cultural resonance for the people they wish to influence. Public health messages to combat obesity, for example, usually focus on long-term risks of chronic disease. Despite this, obesity rates remain high and in some cases continue to rise. From an evolutionary perspective, the implications of obesity for mate choice might be a more compelling focus than the risks of developing disease later in life (Dunbar 2012), since both men and women judge both sexes as being less attractive the more they diverge from the optimum body shape (Perilloux *et al.* 2010). This is an extreme example, and is itself fraught with a plethora of other potentially negative issues such as body image and dysfunctional eating behaviour. However, given that humans are adept at uncoupling immediate gratification from long-term health outcomes, it may be that future health and longevity is the wrong utility function for public health to use. Greater impact may be made by focusing on more immediate benefits, rather than future costs.

Evolutionary nutrition is a growing area (Elton and O'Higgins 2008; Lindeberg 2010), and this book is not an end-point. We hope to have extended the discussion of how dietary choices have shaped our form and function across evolutionary time, and how in turn, our form and function continues to shape our nutritional health as biocultural animals, influenced by cultural processes and structures as well as biological ones. Political, economic and social factors are especially important in structuring what is possible for us to eat, and diet is implicated in susceptibilities to both infectious and chronic disease. Rather than taking a classic Darwinian or selectionist approach to an evolutionary issue in health and medicine, we have chosen to adopt an evolutionary ecology perspective that emphasizes variation and variability. We hope to have argued successfully that far from being adapted to a Stone Age diet and maladapted to post-agricultural subsistence, humans are suited to consuming a vast range of foodstuffs (Elton 2008a). Thus, an important message for public health nutrition that emerges from studying the evolution of human diets is that there is not, nor has there ever been, a 'set' human diet. But being able to eat anything doesn't mean that humans should eat everything. Critical engagement with the evolutionary underpinning of everyday practice and the political, economic, social and cultural factors that influence it by public health nutritionists should help to create better practitioners. We hope that this book has offered a few insights into evolutionary and social processes that influence what we eat, and how and when. We also hope that we have helped further the understanding of some of the functionally negative outcomes of diets and eating behaviours that are far removed nutritionally and socially from those of even our very recent ancestors. Most importantly, we hope that this book leads to more critical thinking about human diet.

References

Abdel-Sayed, A., Binnert, C., Lê, K. A. *et al.* (2008). A high-fructose diet impairs basal and stress-mediated lipid metabolism in healthy male subjects. *British Journal of Nutrition*, **100**: 393–9.

Abdoellah, O. S. & Marten, G. G. (1986). The complementary roles of homegardens, upland fields, and rice fields for meeting nutritional needs in West Java. In: *Traditional Agriculture in South East Asia: A Human Ecology Perspective*, ed. G. G. Marten, pp. 293–325. Boulder, CO: Westview Press.

Ackermann, R. R. & Cheverud, J. M. (2004). Detecting genetic drift versus selection in human evolution. *Proceedings of the National Academy of Sciences*, **101**: 17946–51.

Adas, M. (2001). *Agricultural and Pastoral Societies in Ancient and Classical History*. Philadelphia, PA: Temple University Press.

Addessi, E., Galloway, A. T., Visalberghi, E. & Birch, L. L. (2005). Specific social influences on the acceptance of novel foods in 2–5-year-old children. *Appetite*, **45**: 264–71.

Administrative Committee on Coordination Sub-Committee on Nutrition (2000). *4th Report on the World Nutrition Situation – Nutrition Throughout the Life Cycle*. Geneva: World Health Organization.

Aeberli, I., Zimmermann, M. B., Molinari, L. *et al.* (2007). Fructose intake is a predictor of LDL particle size in overweight school children. *American Journal of Clinical Nutrition*, **86**: 1174–8.

Agarwal, A., Williams, G. H. & Fisher, N. D. L. (2005). Genetics of human hypertension. *Trends in Endocrinology and Metabolism*, **16**(3): 127–33.

Agyei-Mensah, S. & Aikins, A. d-G. (2010). Epidemiological transition and the double burden of disease in Accra, Ghana. *Journal of Urban Health*, **87**: 879–97.

Ahima, R. S. & Osei, S. Y. (2001). Molecular regulation of eating behavior: new insights and prospects for therapeutic strategies. *Trends in Molecular Medicine*, **7**: 205–13.

Aiello, L. C. & Wheeler, P. (1995). The expensive tissue hypothesis: the brain and the digestive system in human and primate evolution. *Current Anthropology*, **36**: 199–221.

Aiello, L. C., Collard, M. & Thackeray, J. F. (2000). Assessing exact randomization-based methods for determining the taxonomic significance of variability in the human fossil record. *South African Journal of Science*, **96**: 179–83.

Alba, D. M., Fortuny, J. & Moya-Sola, S. (2010). Enamel thickness in the Middle Miocene great apes *Anoiapithecus*, *Pierolapithecus* and *Dryopithecus*. *Proceedings of the Royal Society B: Biological Sciences*, **277**: 2237–45.

Alden Smith, E. (1983). Anthropological applications of optimal foraging theory: a critical review. *Current Anthropology*, **24**: 626–51.

Alexander, R. M. (1993). The relative merits of foregut and hindgut fermentation. *Journal of Zoology*, **231**: 391–401.

Allchin, F. R. (1979). India: the ancient home of distillation? *Man*, **14**: 55–63.

Allison, A. C. (1954). Protection afforded by sickle cell trait against subtertian malarial infection. *British Medical Journal*, **1**: 290–4.

Alperson-Afil, N., Sharon, G., Kislev, M. *et al.* (2009). Spatial organization of Hominin activities at Gesher Benot Ya'aqov, Israel. *Science*, **326**: 1677–80.

Altmann, J., Schoeller, D., Altmann, S. A., Muruthi, P. & Sapolsky, R. M. (1993). Body size and fatness of free-living baboons reflect food availability and activity levels. *American Journal of Primatology*, **30**: 149–61.

Altmann, S. A. (1998). *Foraging for Survival: Yearling Baboons in Africa*. Chicago, IL: Chicago University Press.

Amar, A., Kwon, O., Motro, U. *et al.* (1999). Molecular analysis of HLA class II polymorphisms among different ethnic groups in Israel. *Human Immunology*, **60**: 723–30.

Amato, R., Pinelli, M., Miele, G. & Cocozza, S. (2009). Genome-wide scan for signatures of human population differentiation and their relationship with natural selection, functional pathways and diseases. *PLoS One*, **7531**: 1–8.

Ambrose, S. H. (1993). Isotopic analysis of palaeodiets: methodological and interpretive consideration. In: *Investigations of Ancient Human Tissue*, ed. M. K. Sandford, pp. 59–130. Langhorne: Gordon and Breach.

Andrews, P. (1981). Species diversity and diet in monkeys and apes during the Miocene. In: *Aspects of Human Evolution*, ed. C. B. Stringer, pp. 25–61. London: Taylor and Francis.

Andrews, P. & Harrison, T. (2005). The last common ancestor of apes and humans. In: *Interpreting the Past*, ed. D. E. Lieberman, R. J. Smith & J. Kelley, pp. 103–121. Boston, MA: Brill Academic Publishers.

Andrews, P. & Humphrey, L. (1999). *African Miocene Environments and the Transition to Early Hominines*. New York: Oxford University Press.

Angel, J. L. (1969). The bases of paleodemography. *American Journal of Physical Anthropology*, **30**: 427–38.

Angel, L. (1984). Health as a crucial factor in the changes from hunting to developed farming in the Eastern Mediterranean. In: *Paleopathology at the Origins of Agriculture*, ed. M. N. Cohen & G. Armelagos, pp. 51–73. New York: Academic Press.

Arambepola, C., Scarborough, P. & Rayner, M. (2008). Validating a nutrient profile model. *Public Health Nutrition*, **11**: 371–8.

Ariel, A. & Serhan, C. N. (2007). Resolvins and protectins in the termination of acute inflammation. *Trends in Immunology*, **28**: 176–83.

Arim, M. & Marquet, P. A. (2004). Intraguild predation: a widespread interaction related to species biology. *Ecology Letters*, **7**: 557–64.

Armelagos, G. H., Goodman, A. H. & Jacobs, K. H. (1991). The origins of agriculture: population growth during a period of declining health. *Population and Environment*, **13**(1): 9–22.

Armelagos, G. J. & Harper, K. N. (2005). Genomics at the origins of agriculture, part two. *Evolutionary Anthropology*, **14**: 109–121.

Arnaiz-Villena, A., Benmamar, D., Alvarez, M. *et al.* (1995). HLA allele and haplotype frequencies in Algerians. Relatedness to Spaniards and Basques. *Human Immunology*, **43**: 259–68.

Arnaiz-Villena, A., Karin, M., Bendikuze, N. *et al.* (2001). HLA alleles and haplotypes in the Turkish population: relatedness to Kurds, Armenians and other Mediterraneans. *Tissue Antigens*, **57**: 308–17.

Ascherio, A. & Willet, W. C. (1997). Health effects of trans fatty acids. *The American Journal of Clinical Nutrition*, **66**(4): S1000–S1010.

Ata, R. N., Ludden, A. B. & Lally, M. M. (2007). The effects of gender and family, friend, and media influences on eating behaviors and body image during adolescence. *Journal of Youth and Adolescence*, **36**: 1024–37.

Augustin, L. S., Franceschi, S., Jenkins, D. J. A., Kendall, C. W. C. & La Vecchia, C. (2002). Glycemic index in chronic disease: a review. *European Journal of Nutrition*, **56**: 1049–71.

Australian Bureau of Statistics (1998). *National Nutrition Survey Nutrient Intakes and Physical Measurements Australia 1995*. Canberra: AGPS.

Azizi, F. (1997). Effect of dietary composition on fasting-induced changes in serum thyroid hormones and thyrotropin. *Metabolism*, **27**: 935–42.

Backhed, F., Ley, R. E., Sonnenburg, J. L., Peterson, D. A. & Gordon, J. I. (2005). Host-bacterial mutualism in the human intestine. *Science*, **307**: 1915–20.

Backwell, L. R. & d'Errico, F. (2001). Evidence of termite foraging by Swartkrans early hominids. *Proceedings of the National Academy of Sciences*, **98**: 1358–63.

Bailey, G. N. (1975). The role of molluscs in coastal economies: the results of midden analysis in Australia. *Journal of Archaeological Science*, **2**: 45–62.

(2009). The Red Sea, coastal landscapes, and hominin dispersals. In: *The Evolution of Human Populations in Arabia*, ed. M. Petraglia & J. Rose, pp. 15–37. Dordrecht: Springer.

Balaresque, P., Bowden, G. R., Adams, S. M. *et al.* (2010). A predominantly Neolithic origin for European paternal lineages. *Public Library of Science Biology*, **8**: 1–9.

Bang, H. O. & Dyerberg, J. (1980). The bleeding tendency in Greenland Eskimos. *Danish Medical Bulletin*, **27**(4): 202–5.

Barker, D. J. P. (ed.) (1992). *Fetal and Infant Origins of Adult Disease*. London: British Medical Journal Publishing.

(1999). The fetal origins of coronary heart disease and stroke: evolutionary implications. In: *Evolution in Health and Disease*, ed. S. C. Stearns, pp. 246–50. Oxford: Oxford University Press.

Barker, D. J. P., Eriksson, J. G., Forsen, T. & Osmond, C. (2002). Fetal origins of adult disease: strength of effects and biological basis. *International Journal of Epidemiology* **31**: 1235–9.

Barker, D. J. P., Godfrey, K. M., Osmond, C. & Bull, A. (1992). The relation of fetal length, ponderal index and head circumference to blood pressure and the risk of hypertension in adult life. *Paediatric and Perinatal Epidemiology*, **6**: 35–44.

Barnard, N. D., Nicholson, A. & Howard, J. L. (1995). The medical costs attributable to meat consumption. *Preventive Medicine*, **24**(6): 646–55.

Baro, M. & Deubel, T. F. (2006). Persistent hunger: perspectives on vulnerability, famine, and food security in Sub-Saharan Africa. *Annual Review of Anthropology*, **35**: 521–38.

Barquera, S., Hernandez-Barrera, L., Tolentino-Mayo, M. L. *et al.* (2008). Dynamics of adolescent and adult beverage intake patterns in Mexico. *FASEB Journal*, **22**: 461.

Barquera, S., Campirano, F., Bonvecchio, A. *et al.* (2010). Caloric beverage consumption patterns in Mexican children. *Nutrition Journal*, **9**: 47.

Barr, C. S., Schwandt, M. L., Newman, T. K. & Highley, J. D. (2004). The use of adolescent non human primates to model human alcohol intake. *Annals of the New York Academy of Sciences*, **1021**: 221–33.

Barton, R. A., Whiten, A., Byrne, R. W. & English, M. (1993). Chemical composition of baboon plant foods: implications for the interpretation of intra- and interspecific differences in diet. *Folia Primatologica*, **61**: 1–20.

Barton, R. A., Whiten, A., Strum, S. C., Byrne, R. W. & Simpson, A. J. (1992). Habitat use and resource availability in baboons. *Animal Behaviour*, **43**: 831–44.

Barton, S. (1997). *The Aristocracy in Twelfth-Century León and Castile*. Cambridge: Cambridge University Press.

Bar-Yosef, O. (1998). The Natufian culture in the Levant, threshold to the origins of agriculture. *Evolutionary Anthropology*, **6**: 159–77.

(2004). Eat what is there: hunting and gathering in the world of neanderthals and their neighbors. *International Journal of Osteoarchaeology*, **14**: 333–42.

Barzel, U. S. & Massey, L. K. (1998). Excess dietary protein can adversely affect bone. *Journal of Nutrition*, **128**: 1051–3.

Basciano, H., Federico, L. & Adeli, K. (2005). Fructose, insulin resistance, and metabolic dyslipidaemia. *Nutrition and Metabolism*, **2**(1): 5–6.

Bates, I., Fenton, C., Gruber, J. *et al.* (2004). Vulnerability to malaria, tuberculosis, and HIV/AIDS infection and disease. Part I: determinants operating at individual and household level. *Lancet Infectious Disease*, **4**: 267–77.

Baudrillard, J. (1970). *The Consumer Society: Myths and Structures*. Paris: Gallimard.

Beaudeux, J. L., Guillausseau, P. J., Peynet, J. *et al.* (1995). Enhanced susceptibility of low-density lipoprotein to in vitro oxidation in Type 1 and Type 2 diabetic patients. *Clinica Chimica Acta*, **239**: 131–41.

Beck, U. (1992). *Risk Society: Towards a New Modernity*. London: Sage.

Behrman, J. R. (1988). Nutrition, health, birth order and seasonality: intrahousehold allocation among children in rural India. *Journal of Development Economics*, **28**: 43–62.

Belfer-Cohen, A. & Goring-Morris, N. (2009). For the first time. *Current Anthropology*, **50**(5): 669–72.

Bell, C. G., Finer, S., Lindgren, C. M. *et al.* (2010). Integrated genetic and epigenetic analysis identifies haplotype-specific methylation in the FTO Type 2 diabetes and obesity susceptibility locus. *PLoS ONE*, **5**: e14040.

Bell, R. H. V. (1971). A grazing ecosystem in the Serengeti. *Scientific American*, **225**: 86–93.

Bellamy, R. (2003). Susceptibility to mycobacterial infections: the importance of host genetics. *Genes and Immunity*, **4**: 4–11.

Bellamy, R., Ruwende, C., Corrah, T. *et al.* (1998). Variations in the NRAMP1 gene and susceptibility to tuberculosis in West Africa. *New England Journal of Medicine*, **338**: 640–4.

Bellwood, P. (2001). Early agricultural population diasporas? Farming, languages, and genes. *Annual Review of Anthropology*, **30**: 181–207.

Bendiner, E. (1974). Disastrous trade-off: Eskimo health for white civilization. *Hospital Practice*, **9**: 156–89.

Bentley, G. R. (1985). Hunter-gatherer energetics and fertility: a reassessment of the !Kung San. *Human Ecology*, **13**: 79–109.

Bentley, G. R. *et al.* (1999). Women's strategies to alleviate nutritional stress in a rural African society. *Social Science and Medicine*, **48**: 149–62.

Berdan, F. (2004). *The Aztecs of Central Mexico: An Imperial Society*, 2nd edn. Belmont: Thomson-Wadsworth.

Berger, L. R. (2006). Brief communication: predatory bird damage to the Taung type-skull of *Australopithecus africanus* Dart 1925. *American Journal of Physical Anthropology*, **131**: 166–8.

Berger, L. R., de Ruiter, D. J., Churchill, S. E. *et al.* (2010) *Australopithecus sediba*: a new species of *Homo*-like australopith from South Africa. *Science*, **328**: 195–204.

Bergstrom, S., Danielsson, H. & Samuelsson, B. (1964). The enzymatic formation of prostaglandin E2 from arachidonic acid. *Biochimica et Biophysica Acta*, **90**: 207–212.

Berlin, B. & Berlin, E. A. (1977). Ethnobiology, subsistence, and nutrition in a tropical forest society: the Aguaruna Jivaro. *Studies in Aguaruna Jivaro Ethnobiology*, Report No. 1. Berkeley, CA: University of California.

Berthoud, H.-R. (2006). Homeostatic and non-homeostatic pathways involved in the control of food intake and energy balance. *Obesity*, **14**: S197–S200.

Berti, C., Riso, P. & Porrini, M. (2008). Satiating properties of meat preparations: role of protein content and energy density. *Journal of the American College of Nutrition*, **27**: 244–52.

Betteridge, D. J. (1989). Lipids, diabetes and vascular disease: the time to act. *Diabetic Medicine*, **6**: 195–218.

Beyin, A. (2011). Upper Pleistocene human dispersals out of Africa. A review of the current state of the debate. *International Journal of Evolutionary Biology* vol. **2011**, Article ID 615094, 17 pages, doi:10.4061/2011/615094.

Bharati, S., Pal, M., Battacharya, B. N. & Bharati, P. (2007). Prevalence and causes of chronic energy deficiency and obesity in Indian women. *Human Biology*, **79**: 395–412.

Bilsborough, S. & Mann, N. (2006). A review of issues of dietary protein intake in humans. *International Journal of Sport Nutrition and Exercise Metabolism*, **16**: 129–52.

Binford, L. R. (1968). Post-Pleistocene adaptations. In: *New Perspectives in Archaeology*, ed. S. R. Binford & L. R. Binford, pp. 313–41. Chicago, IL: Aldine.

Bird, D. W. & Bliege Bird, R. (2000). The ethnoarchaeology of juvenile foragers: shellfishing strategies among Meriam children. *Journal of Anthropological Archaeology*, **19**: 461–76.

Blair Lewis, L., Sloane, D., Miller Nascimento, L. *et al.* (2005). African Americans' access to healthy food options in south Los Angeles restaurants. *American Journal of Public Health*, **95**: 668–73.

Blakely, T., Hales, S., Kieft, C., Wilson, N. & Woodward, A. (2005). The global distribution of risk factors by poverty level. *Bulletin of the World Health Organization*, **83**: 118–26.

Blumenschine, R. J. (1991). Hominid carnivory and foraging strategies, and the socio-economic function of early archeological sites. *Philosophical Transations of the Royal Society of London*, **34**: 211–19.

Blumenschine, R. J. (1995). Percussion marks, tooth marks, and experimental determinations of the timing of hominid and carnivore access to long bones at FLK Zinjanthropus, Olduvai Gorge, Tanzania. *Journal of Human Evolution*, **29**: 21–51.

Blumenschine, R. J., Prassack, K. A., Kreger, C. D. & Pante, M. C. (2007). Carnivore tooth-marks, microbial bioerosion, and the invalidation of test of Oldowan hominin scavenging behavior. *Journal of Human Evolution*, **53**: 420–26.

Boaretto, E., Wu, X., Yuan, J. *et al.* (2009). Radiocarbon dating of charcoal and bone collagen associated with early pottery at Yuchanyan Cave, Hunan Province, China. *Proceedings of the National Academy of Sciences*, **106**(24): 9595–600.

Bobadilla, J.-L., Frenk, J., Frejka, T., Lozano, R. & Stern, C. (1993). The epidemiological transition and health priorities. In: *Disease Control Priorities in Developing Countries*, ed. D. T. Jamison, W. H. Mosley, A. R. Measham & J.-L. Bobadilla, Chapter 3. New York: Oxford University Press for World Bank.

Bodmer, R. E. (1989). Frugivory in Amazonian Artiodactyla: evidence for the evolution of the ruminant stomach. *Journal of Zoology (London)*, **219**: 457–67.

Boeda, E., Geneste, J. M., Griggio, C. *et al.* (1999). A Levallois point embedded in the vertebra of a wild ass (*Equus africanus*): hafting, projectiles and Mousterian hunting weapons. *Antiquity*, **73**: 394–402.

Booth, D., Mather, P., Fuller, J. (1982). Starch content of ordinary foods associatively conditions human appetite and satiation, indexed by intake and eating pleasantness of starch-paired flavours. *Journal for Intake Research*, **3**: 163–84.

Boriskovskii, P. I. (1968). Vietnam in primeval times. *Soviet Anthropology and Archaeology*, **7**: 14–32.

Bourdieu, P. (1984). *Distinction: A Social Critique of the Judgment of Taste* (R. Nice, translator). Cambridge, MA: Harvard University Press.

Boyages, S. (1993). Clinical review 49: iodine deficiency disorders. *Journal of Clinical Endocrinology and Metabolism*, **77**: 587–591.

Brain, C. K. (1981). *The Hunters or the Hunted? An Introduction to African Cave Taphonomy*. Chicago, IL: University of Chicago Press.

Brain, C. K. & Sillent, A. (1988). Evidence from the Swartkrans cave for the earliest use of fire. *Nature*, **336**: 464–6.

Brand-Miller, J. C. & Colagiuri, S. (1994). The carnivore connection: dietary carbohydrate in the evolution of NIDDM. *Diabetologia*, **37**: 1280–6.

Brand-Miller, J. C. & Holt, S. H. (1998). Australian aboriginal plant foods: a consideration of their nutritional composition and health implications. *Nutrition Research Reviews*, **11**: 5–23.

Braun, D., & Plog, S. (1982). Evolution of "tribal" social networks: theory and prehistoric North American evidence. *American Antiquity*, **47**: 504–25.

Braun, D. R., Harris, J. W. K., Levin, N. E. *et al.* (2010). Early hominin diet included diverse terrestrial and aquatic animals 1.95 Ma in East Turkana, Kenya. *Proceedings of the National Academy of Sciences*, **107**: 10002–7.

Bray, G. A. (2000). Afferent signals regulating food intake. *Proceedings of the Nutrition Society*, **59**(3): 373–84.

(2007). How bad is fructose? *American Journal of Clinical Nutrition*, **86**: 895–6.

Bray, G. A., Nielsen, S. J. & Popkin, B. M. (2004). Consumption of high-fructose corn syrup in beverages may play a role in the epidemic of obesity. *American Journal of Clinical Nutrition*, **79**: 537–43.

Brenner, R. R. (1987). Biosynthesis and interconversion of the essential fatty acids. In: *Handbook of Eicosanoids: Prostaglandins and Related Lipids, Vol I: Chemical and Biochemical Aspects,* Part A, ed. A. L. Willis, pp. 99–117. Boca Raton, FL: CRC Press.

Briefel, R. R. & Johnson, C. L. (2004). Secular trends in dietary intake in the United States. *Annual Review of Nutrition*, **24**: 401–31.

Broadhurst, C. L., Cunnane, S. C. & Crawford, M. A. (1998). Rift Valley lake fish and shellfish provided brain-specific nutrition for early *Homo*. *British Journal of Nutrition*, **79**: 3–21.

Brosnan, S. F. & de Waal, F. B. M. (2003). Monkeys reject unequal pay. *Nature*, **425**: 297–9.

Brown, I. W. (1980). Salt and the eastern North American Indian: an archaeological study. *Lower Mississippi Survey Bulletin* Number 6. Peabody Museum, Harvard University.

Brown, P. J. (1991). Culture and the evolution of obesity. *Human Nature*, **2**: 31–57.

Brown, T. A., Jones, M. K., Powell, W. & Allaby, R. G. (2009). The complex origins of domesticated crops in the Fertile Crescent. *Trends in Ecology and Evolution*, **24**: 103–9.

Brunet, M., Beauvilain, A., Coppens, Y. *et al.* (1995). The first australopithecine 2,500 kilometres west of the Rift Valley (Chad). *Nature*, **378**: 273–5.

Brunet, M., Guy, F., Pilbeam, D. *et al.* (2002). A new hominid from the Upper Miocene of Chad, Central Africa. *Nature*, **418**: 145–51.

(2005). New material of the earliest hominid from the Upper Miocene of Chad. *Nature*, **434**: 752–5.

Bruorton, M. R., Davis, C. L. & Perrin, M. R. (1991). Gut microflora of vervet and samango monkeys in relation to diet. *Applied and Environmental Microbiology*, **57**: 573–8.

Buchacz, K., Royol, A. D., Lindsey, J. C. *et al.* (2003). Delayed onset of pubertal development in children and adolescents with perinatally acquired HIV. *Journal of Acquired Immune Deficiency Syndromes*, **33**(1): 56–65.

Buchanan, T. A., Metzger, B. E., Frienkel, N. & Bergman, R. N. (1990). Insulin sensitivity and B-cell responsiveness to glucose during the pregnancy in lean and moderately obese women with normal glucose tolerance and mild gestational diabetes. *American Journal of Obstetrics and Gynecology*, **162**: 1008–14.

Bulaj, Z. J., Ajioka, R. S., Phillips, J. D. *et al.* (2000). Disease-related conditions in relatives of patients with hemochromatosis. *New England Journal of Medicine*, **343**: 1529–35.

Bunn, H. (1999). Comment on Wrangham *et al.*: the raw and the stolen. *Current Anthropology*, **40**: 567–94.

Bunn, H. T. (2001). Hunting, power scavenging and butchering by Hadza foragers and by Plio-Pleistocene *Homo*. In: *Meat Eating and Human Evolution*, ed. C. Stanford & H. T. Bunn, pp. 199–218. Oxford: Oxford University Press.

Bunn, H. T. & Kroll, E. M. (1986). Systematic butchery by Plio/Pleistocene hominids at Olduvai Gorge, Tanzania. *Current Anthropology*, **27**: 431–52.

Burdge, G. C. & Calder, P. C. (2005). Conversion of alpha-linolenic acid to longer chain polyunsaturated fatty acids in human adults. *Reproduction Nutrition Development*, **45**: 581–97.

Burnol, A. F., Loizeau, M. & Girard, J. (1990). Insulin receptor activity and insulin sensitivity in mammary gland of lactating rats. *American Journal of Physiology*, **259**: E828-E834.

Butte, N. F., Lopez-Alarcon, M. G. & Garza, C. (2002). *Nutrient Adequacy of Exclusive Breastfeeding for the Term Infant During the First Six Months of Life*. Geneva: World Health Organization.

Caballero, B. & Popkin, B. M. (eds.) (2002). *The Nutrition Transition: Diet and Disease in the Developing World*. New York: Academic Press.

Calder, P. C. (2008). Polyunsaturated fatty acids, inflammatory processes and inflammatory bowel diseases. *Molecular Nutrition and Food Research*, **52**: 885–97.

Caldwell, J. C. (1976). Toward a restatement of demographic transition theory. *Population and Development Review*, **2**: 321–66.

Cantena, C., Giacchetti, G., Novello, M. *et al.* (2003). Cellular mechanisms of insulin resistance in rats with fructose-induced hypertension. *American Journal of Hypertension*, **16**: 973–8.

Caprio, S., Plewe, G., Diamond, M. P. *et al.* (1989). Increased insulin secretion in puberty: a compensatory response to reductions in insulin sensitivity. *Journal of Pediatrics*, **114**: 963–7.

Carlson, B. A. & Kingston, J. D. (2007). Docosahexaenoic acid, the aquatic diet, and homin in encephalization: difficulties in establishing evolutionary links. *American Journal of Human Biology*, **19**: 132–41.

Carral Cuevas, M. (2005). *Integration, Migration and Cooperation: The Mexican Case*. Washington, D.C.: Inter-American Development Bank.

Cecil, J. E., Tavendale, R., Watt, P., Hetherington, M. M. & Palmer, C. N. A. (2008). An obesity-associated FTO gene variant and increased energy intake in children. *New England Journal of Medicine*, **359**(24): 2558–66.

Ceesay, S. M., Prentice, A. M., Cole, T. J. *et al.* (1997). Effects on birth weight and perinatal mortality of maternal dietary supplements in rural Gambia: 5 year randomised controlled trial. *British Medical Journal*, **315**: 786–90.

Cerling, T. E. *et al.* (2011). Diet of *Paranthropus boisei* in the early Pleistocene of East Africa. *Proceedings of the National Academy of Sciences*, **108**: 9337–41.

(2006). Stable isotopes in elephant hair documents migration patterns and diet changes. *Proceedings of the National Academy of Sciences*, **103**: 371–3.

Chamberlain, J. G. (1996). The possible role of long-chain, omega-3 fatty acids in human brain phylogeny. *Perspectives in Biology and Medicine*, **39**: 436–45.

Chandra, R. K. (1988). Nutritional regulation of immunity: an introduction. In: *Nutrition and Immunology*, ed. R. K. Chandra, pp. 1–8. New York: Alan R. Liss.

Chapman, C. A. (1995). Primate seed dispersal: coevolution and conservation implications. *Evolutionary Anthropology*, **4**: 74–82.

Chapman, C., Gillespie, T. & Goldberg, T. (2005). Primates and the ecology of their infectious diseases: how will anthropogenic change affect host-parasite interactions? *Evolutionary Anthropology*, **14**: 134–44.

Charalampopoulos, D., Wang, R., Pandiella, S. S. & Webb, C. (2002). Application of cereals and cereal components in functional foods: a review. *International Journal of Food Microbiology*, **79**: 131–41.

Charnov, E. L. & Orians, G. H. (1973). Optimal foraging: some theoretical explorations. Dissertation. Department of Biology University of Utah.

Chattopadhyay, R. (2000). Zimbabwe: structural adjustment, destitution and food insecurity. *Review of African Political Economy*, **84**: 307–16.

Childe, V. G. (1936). *Man Makes Himself.* London: Watts and Co.

Chin-Chance, C., Polonsky, K. & Schoeller, D. (2000). Twenty-four-hour leptin levels respond to cumulative short-term energy imbalance and predict subsequent intake. *Journal of Clinical Endocrinology and Metabolism*, **85**: 2685–91.

Chisholm, B. S., Nelson, D. E. & Schwarcz, H. P. (1982). Stable-carbon isotope ratios as a measure of marine versus terrestrial protein in ancient diets. *Science*, **216**: 1131–2.

Chivers, D. J. (1992) Diets and guts. In: *The Cambridge Encyclopaedia of Human Evolution*, ed. J. S. Jones, R. D. Martin & D. R. Pilbeam, pp. 60–64. Cambridge: Cambridge University Press.

Chivers, D. J. (1994). Functional anatomy of the gastrointestinal tract. In: *Colobine Monkeys: Their Ecology, Behaviour and Evolution*, ed. A. G. Davis & J. F. Oates, pp. 205–28. Cambridge: Cambridge University Press.

Chivers, D. J. & Hladik, C. M. (1980). Morphology of the gastrointestinal tract in primates: comparisons with other mammals in relation to diet. *Journal of Morphology*, **116**: 337–86.

Chivers, D. J. & Langer, P. (1994). Gut form and function: variations and terminology. In: *The Digestive System in Mammals*, ed. D. J. Chivers & P. Langer, pp. 3–8. Cambridge: Cambridge University Press.

Christakis, N. A. & Fowler, J. H. (2007). The spread of obesity in a large social network over 32 years. *New England Journal of Medicine*, **357**: 370–9.

Ciotta, L., Calogera, A. E., Farina, M. *et al.* (2001). Clinical, endocrine and metabolic effects of acarbose, a glucosidase inhibitor; in PCOS patients with increased insulin response and normal glucose tolerance. *Human Reproduction*, **16**: 2066–72.

Clark, I. A., Chaudhri, G. & Cowden, W. B. (1989). Some roles of free radicals in malaria. *Free Radicals in Biological Medicine*, **6**: 315–21.

Clayton, A., Knight, V. R., Jr. & Moore, E. C. (1993). *The De Soto Chronicles*. Tuscaloosa, AL: University of Alabama Press.

Cleave, T. L. (1974). *The Saccharine Disease*. Bristol: John Wright & Sons, Ltd.

Clifford, A. J., Riumallo, J. A., Young, V. R. & Scrimshaw, N. S. (1976). Effect of oral purines on serum and urinary uric acid of normal, hyperuricemic and gouty humans. *The Journal of Nutrition*, **106**: 428–34.

Clutton-Brock, T. H. & Harvey, P. H. (1980). Primates, brains and ecology. *Journal of Zoology*, **190**: 309–23.

Cobb, S. N. (2008). The facial skeleton of the chimpanzee-human last common ancestor. *Journal of Anatomy*, **212**: 469–85.

Codron, D., Lee-Thorp, J. A., Sponheimer, M., de Ruiter, D. & Codron, J. (2006). Inter- and intrahabitat dietary variability of chacma baboons (*Papio ursinus*) in South African savannas based on fecal 13C, 15N, and %N. *American Journal of Physical Anthropology*, **129**: 204–14.

Codron, D., Lee-Thorp, J., Sponheimer, M., de Ruiter, D. & Codron, J. (2008). What insights can baboon feeding ecology provide for early hominin niche differentiation? *International Journal of Primatology*, **29**: 757–72.

Codron, D., Luyt, J., Lee-Thorp, J. A. *et al.* (2005). Utilization of savanna-based resources by Plio-Pleistocene baboons. *South African Journal of Science*, **101**: 245–8.

Coe, S. D. (1994). *America's First Cuisines*. Austin, TX: University of Texas Press.

Cohen, M. N. (1989). *Health and the Rise of Civilisation*. New Haven, CT: Yale University Press.

Colin, A., Reggers, J., Castronovo, V. & Ansseau, M. (2003). Lipids, depression and suicide. *Encephale*, **29**: 49–58.

Collier, C. N., Harper, J. C., Cnatrell, W. C. *et al.* (2008). The prevalence of acne in adults 20 years and older. *Journal of the American Academy of Dermatology*, **58**: 56–9.

Coluzzi, M. (1999). Malaria genetics. The clay feet of the malaria giant and its African roots: hypotheses and inferences about origin, spread and control of *Plasmodium falciparum*. *Parasitologia*, **41**: 277–83.

Coluzzi, M., Sabatini, A., delle Torre, A., di Deco, M. A. & Petrarca, V. (2002). A polytene chromosome analysis of the *Anopheles gambiae* species complex. *Science*, **298**: 1415–18.

Committee on Animal Nutrition (2003). *Nutrient Requirements of Non-Human Primates*, 2nd edn. Washington, D.C.: The National Academies Press.

Connor, W. E. (2001). N-3 fatty acids from fish and fish oil: panacea or nostrum? *American Journal of Clinical Nutrition*, **74**: 415–16.

Connor, W. E. & Connor, S. L. (1997). Should a low-fat, high-carbohydrate diet be recommended for everyone? The case for a low-fat, high-carbohydrate diet. *New England Journal of Medicine*, **337**(8): 562–3.

Cook, D. C. (1984). Subsistence and health in the Lower Illinois Valley: osteological evidence. In: *Paleopathology and the Origins of Agriculture*, ed. M. N. Cohen & G. J. Armelagos, pp. 237–69. London: Academic Press.

Cook, G. C. (1978). Did persistence of intestinal lactase into adult life originate on the Arabian Peninsula? *Man*, **13**: 418–27.

Cooke, G. S. & Hill, A. V. S. (2001). Genetics of susceptibility to human infectious disease. *Nature Reviews Genetics*, **2**: 967–77.

Corbett, E. L., Watt, C. J., Walker, N. *et al.* (2003). The growing burden of tuberculosis – global trends and interactions with the HIV epidemic. *Archives of Internal Medicine*, **163**: 1009–21.

Corcoran, A. C. & Rabinowitch, I. R. (1937). A study of the blood lipoids and blood protein in Canadian Eastern Arctic Eskimos. *Biochemistry Journal*, **31**(3): 343–8.

Cordain, L. (2005). Implications for the role of diet in acne. *Seminars in Cutaneous Medicine and Surgery*, **24**(2): 84–91.

(2006). Gout. *The Paleo Diet Newsletter*, **2**(4): 1–7.

Cordain, L., Brand-Miller, J. & Mann, N. (1999). Scant evidence of periodic starvation among hunter-gatherers. *Diabetologia*, **42**: 383–4.

Cordain, L., Brand-Miller, J., Eaton, S. B. *et al.* (2000a). Plant-animal subsistence ratios and macronutrient energy estimations in worldwide hunter-gatherer diets. *American Journal of Clinical Nutrition*, **71**: 682–92.

(2000b). Macronutrient estimations in hunter-gatherer diets. *American Journal of Clinical Nutrition*, **72**(6): 1589–92.

Cordain, L., Eaton, S. B., Miller, J. B. and Hill, K. (2002a). The paradoxical nature of hunter-gatherer diets: meat-based, yet non-atherogenic. *European Journal of Clinical Nutrition*, **56**: S42–S52.

(2002b). Fatty acid analysis of wild ruminant tissues: evolutionary implications for reducing diet-related chronic disease. *European Journal of Clinical Nutrition*, **56**(3): 181–91.

Cordain, L., Lindeberg, S., Hurtado, M. *et al.* (2002c). Acne vulgaris: a disease of Western civilization. *Archives of Dermatology*, **138**(12): 1584–90.

(2002d). An evolutionary analysis of the aetiology and pathogenesis of juvenile-onset myopia. *Acta Ophthalmologica Scandinavica*, **80**: 125–35.

Cordain, L., Eades, M. R. & Eades, M. D. (2003). Hyperinsulinemic diseases of civilization: more than just syndrome X. *Comparative Biochemistry and Physiology Part A*, **136**: 95–112.

Cordain, L., Eaton, B. E., Sebastian, A. *et al.* (2005). Origins and evolution of Western diet: health implications for the 21st century. *American Journal of Clinical Nutrition*, **81**: 341–54.

Corey, E. J., Niwa, H., Flack, J. R. *et al.* (1980). Recent studies on the chemical synthesis of eicosanoids. In: *Advances in Prostaglandin and Thromboxane Research*, vol. **6**, ed. B. Samuelsson, P. W. Ramwell, R. Paoletti, pp. 19–25. New York: Raven Press.

Cosgrove, R. & Pike-Tay, A. (2004). The Middle Palaeolithic and late Pleistocene Tasmania hunting behaviour: A reconsideration of the attributes of modern human behaviour. *International Journal of Osteoarchaeology*, **14**: 321–32.

Cota, D., Tschop, M. H., Horvath, T. L. & Levine, A. S. (2006). Cannabinoids, opioids and eating behavior: the molecular face of hedonism? *Brain Research Reviews*, **51**: 85–107.

Cotton, C. M. (1996). *Ethnobotany: Principles and Applications*. Chichester: John Wiley and Sons.

Covert, H. H. (2003). The earliest fossil primates and the evolution of prosimians. In: *The Primate Fossil Record*, ed. W. C. Hartwig, pp. 13–20. Cambridge: Cambridge University Press.

Cowlishaw, G. U. Y. (1997). Trade-offs between foraging and predation risk determine habitat use in a desert baboon population. *Animal Behaviour*, **53**: 667–86.

Crawford, M. A. & Sinclair, A. J. (1972). Nutritional influences in the evolution of mammalian brain. In *CIBA Foundation Symposium on Lipids, Malnutrition and the Developing Brain*, ed. K. Elliot & J. Knight, pp. 267–87. Amsterdam: Associated Scientific Publishers.

Crawford, M. A., Casperd, N. M. & Sinclair, A. J. (1976). The long chain metabolites of linoleic acid in liver and linolenic acid in liver and brain in herbivores and carnivores. *Comparative Biochemistry and Physiology*, **54B**: 395–401.

Crawford, M. A., Doyle, W., Craft, I. L. and Laurance, B. M. (1986). A comparison of food intake during pregnancy and birthweight in high and low socioeconomic groups. *Progress in Lipid Research*, **25**: 249–54.

Creel, S., Winnie, J. A. & Christianson, D. (2009). Glucocorticoid stress hormones and the effect of predation risk on elk reproduction. *Proceedings of the National Academy of Sciences*, **106**: 12388–93.

Cross, C., Mngadi, T. & Mbhele, T. (1998). *Poverty at ground zero: social capital and household shock events in KwaZulu Natal*. Discussion Document. Washington: International Food Policy Research Institute.

Cui, J., Pan, Y. H., Zhang, Y., Jones, G. & Zhang, S. (2011). Progressive pseudogenization: Vitamin C synthesis and its loss in bats. *Molecular Biology and Evolution*, **28**(2): 1025–31.

Cummins, S., McKay, L. & Macintyre, S. (2005). McDonald's restaurants and neighbourhood deprivation in Scotland and England. *American Journal of Preventive Medicine*, **29**: 308–10.

Cunnane, S. C. (2005). *Survival of the Fattest: The Key to Human Brain Evolution*. Hackensack, NJ: World Scientific.

Curtin, B. J. (1985). *The Myopias*. Philadelphia, PA: Harper & Row.

Curtis-Prior, P. B. (1988). *Prostaglandins: Biology and Chemistry of Prostaglandins and Related Eicosanoids*. New York: Curtis Livingstone.

D'Andrea, S. *et al.* (2002) The same rat D6-desaturase not only acts on 18 but also 24-carbon fatty acids in very long chain polyunsaturated fatty acid biosynthesis. *Biochemical Journal*, **364**: 49–55.

Damuth, J. & McFadden, B. J. (1990). *Body Size in Mammalian Paleobiology: Estimation and Biological Implications*. New York: Cambridge University Press.

Darke, C., Guttridge, M., Thompson, J. *et al.* (1998). HLA class I (A, B) and II (DR, DQ) gene and haplotype frequencies in blood donors from Wales. *Experimental Clinical Immunogenetics*, **15**: 69–83.

Darmon, N. & Drewnowski, A. (2008). Does social class predict diet quality? *American Journal of Clinical Nutrition*, **87**: 1107–17.

Dart, R. A. (1953). The predatory transition from ape to man. *International Anthropological and Linguistic Review*, **1**: 201–19.

Davey-Smith, G., Lawlor, D. A., Timpson, N. J. *et al.* (2009). Lactase persistence related genetic variant: population substructure and health outcomes. *European Journal of Human Genetics*, **17**: 357–67.

Davies, A. A., Davey-Smith, G., Ben-Shlomo, Y. & Litchfield, P. (2004). Low birth weight is associated with higher adult total cholesterol concentration in men: findings from an occupational cohort of 25,843 employees. *Circulation*, **110**: 1258–62.

Day, R. L., Laland, K. N. & Odling-Smee, J. (2003). Rethinking adaptation: the niche-construction perspective. *Perspectives in Biology and Medicine*, **46**: 80–95.

Dayan, Y. B., Levin, A., Morad, Y. *et al.* (2005). The changing prevalence of myopia in young adults: a 13-year series of population-based prevalence surveys. *Investigative Ophthalmology and Visual Science*, **46**(8): 2760–5.

de Benoist, B., Andersson, M., Egli, I., Takkouche, B. & Allen, H. (eds). (2004). *Iodine Status Worldwide: WHO Global Database on Iodine Deficiency*. Geneva: World Health Organization.

de Benoist, B., McLean, E., Andersson, M. & Rogers, L. (2008). Iodine deficiency in 2007: global progress since 2003. *Food and Nutrition Bulletin*, **29**: 195–202.

de Castro, J. M. (1999). What are the major correlates of macronutrient selection in Western populations? *The Proceedings of the Nutrition Society*, **58**: 755–763.

de Castro, J. M. B. & Pérez, P. J. (1995). Enamel hypoplasia in the middle pleistocene hominids from Atapuerca (Spain). *American Journal of Physical Anthropology*, **96**: 301–14.

de Foliart, G. (1992). Insects as human food. *Crop Protection*, **11**: 395–9.

de Fronzo, R. A. (2010). Insulin resistance, lipotoxicity, type 2 diabetes and atherosclerosis: the missing links. The Claude Bernard Lecture 2009. *Diabetologia*, **53**: 1270–87.

de Fronzo, R. A., Soman, V., Sherwin, R. T., Hendler, R. & Felig, P. (1978). Insulin binding to monocytes and insulin action in human obesity, starvation and refeeding. *Journal of Clinical Investigation*, **62**: 204–13.

de Garine, I. & Pollock, N. J. (1995). *Social Aspects of Obesity*. Amsterdam: Gordon and Breach.

de Heinzelin, J., Clark, J. D., White, T. *et al.* (1999). Environment and behavior of 2.5-million-year-old Bouri hominids. *Science*, **284**: 625–9.

de Menocal, P. B. (1995). Plio-Pleistocene African Climate. *Science*, **270**: 53–9.

(2004). African climate change and faunal evolution during the Plio-Pleistocene. *Earth and Planetary Science Letters*, **220**: 3–24.

de Sahagun, B. (1540–85). *Florentine Codex*. Florence: Biblioteca Medicea-Laurenziana.

de Viedma, D. G., Lorenzo, G. M., Cardona, P.-J. *et al.* (2005). Association between the infectivity of Mycobacterium tuberculosis strains and their efficiency for extrarespiratory infection. *Journal of Infectious Diseases*, **192**: 2059–65.

Deaton, A. & Paxson, C. (2004). Mortality, income, and income inequality over time in Britain and the United States. In: *Perspectives on the Economics of Aging*, ed. D. A. Wise, pp. 205–46. Chicago, IL: University of Chicago Press.

Delange, F. (1994). The disorders induced by iodine deficiency. *Thyroid*, **4**: 107–28.

Deleuze Ntandou Bouzitou, G., Fayomi, B. & Delisle, H. (2005). Child malnutrition and maternal overweight in same households in poor urban areas of Benin. *Sante*, **15**: 263–70.

Delwiche, C. C., Zinke, P., Johnson, C. M. & Virginia, R. A. (1979). Nitrogen isotope distribution as a presumptive indicator of N2-fixation. *Botanical Gazette*, **140**: 564–9.

Denic, S. & Agarwal, M. M. (2007). Nutritional iron deficiency: an evolutionary perspective. *Nutrition*, **23**: 603–14.

Dennell, R. (2003). Dispersal and colonisation, long and short chronologies: how continuous is the Early Pleistocene record for hominids outside East Africa? *Journal of Human Evolution*, **45**: 421–40.

Densmore, F. (1974). *How Indians use Wild Plants for Food, Medicine, and Crafts*. New York: Dover.

Denton, D., Weisinger, R., Mundy, N. I., Wickings, E. J. & Dixson, A. (1995). The effect of increased salt intake on blood pressure of chimpanzees. *Nature Medicine*, **1**: 1009–16.

Department for International Development (DFID) (2004). *The Impact of Climate Change on Pro-Poor Growth*. London: Department for International Development.

Dessein, P. H., Shipton, E. A., Stanwix, A. E., Joffe, B. I. & Ramokgadi, J. (2000). Beneficial effects of weight loss associated with moderate calorie/carbohydrate restriction, and increased proportional intake of protein and unsaturated fat on serum urate and lipoprotein levels in gout: a pilot study. *Annals of the Rheumatuc Diseases*, **59**: 539–43.

Dettwyler, K. A. (1995). A time to wean: the hominid blueprint for the natural age of weaning in modern human populations. In: *Breastfeeding: Biocultural Perspectives*, ed. P. Stuart-Macadam & K. A. Dettwyler, pp. 39–74. New York: Aldine de Gruyter.

Deurenberg, P., Weststrate, J. A. & Seidell, J. C. (1991). Body mass index as a measure of body fatness: age and sex specific prediction formulas. *British Journal of Nutrition*, **65**: 105–14.

Díaz-del-Rio, P. (2006). An appraisal of social inequalities in Central Iberia (c. 5300–1600 CAL BC). In: *Social Inequality in Iberian Late Prehistory*, ed. P. Díaz-del-Rio & L. G. Sanjuán, PP. 67–79. Oxford: Archaeopress.

Dickson, S. L. & Luckman, S. M. (1997). Induction of c-fos messenger ribonucleic acid in neuropeptide Y and growth hormone (GH)-releasing factor neurons in the rat arcuate nucleus following systemic injection of the GH secretagogue, GH-releasing peptide-6. *Endocrinology*, **138**: 771–7.

Dietler, M. (2006). Alcohol: anthropological/archaeological perspectives. *Annual Reviews of Anthropology*, **35**: 229–49.

Dillehay, T. D., Ramirez, C., Pino, M. *et al.* (2008). Monte Verde: seaweed, food, medicine, and the peopling of South America. *Science*, **320**: 784–6.

Distante, S., Robson, K. J. H., Graham-Campbell, J. *et al.* (2004). The origin and spread of the HFE-C282Y haemochromatosis mutation. *Human Genetics*, **115**: 269–79.

Dixon, J. (2009). From the imperial to the empty calorie: how nutrition relations underpin food regime transitions. *Agriculture and Human Values*, **26**: 321–33.

Doak, C. M., Adair, L. S., Bentley, M., Monteiro, C. & Popkin, B. M. (2005). The dual burden household and the nutrition transition paradox. *International Journal of Obesity*, **29**: 129–36.

Dobney, K. & Larson, G. (2006). Genetics and animal domestication: new windows on an elusive process. *Journal of Zoology*, **269**: 261–71.

Dobson, C. M. (2001). The structural basis of protein folding and its links with human disease. *Philosophical Transactions of the Royal Society of London*, B, **356**: 133–45.

Doherty, M. (2009). New insights into the epidemiology of gout. *Rheumatology*, **48** (suppl. 2): ii2–ii8.

Dominguez-Rodrigo, M., Serrallonga, J., Juan-Tresserras, J., Alcala, L. & Luque, L. (2001). Woodworking activities by early humans: a plant residue analysis on Acheulian stone tools from Peninj (Tanzania). *Journal of Human Evolution*, **40**: 289–99.

Donnelly, J. (2002). *The Great Irish Potato Famine*. Stroud: Sutton Publishing.

Donohoe, M. (2003). Causes and health consequences of environmental degradation and social injustice. *Social Science and Medicine*, **56**: 573–87.

Douglas, M. (1978). *Culture*. New York: Russell Sage Foundation.

Dounias, E. & Froment, A. (2006). When forest-based hunter-gatherers become sedentary: consequences for diet and health. *Forests and Human Health*, **224**: 26–33.

Dounias, E., Selzner, A., Koizumi, M. & Levang, P. (2007). From sago to rice, from forest to town: the consequences of sedentarization for the nutritional ecology of Punan former hunter-gatherers of Borneo. *Food and Nutrition Bulletin*, **28**: 294–302.

Dowdeswell, J. A. & White, J. W. C. (1995). Greenland ice core records and rapid climate change. *Philosophical Transactions of the Royal Society of London*, A, **352**: 359–71.

Dreno, B. & Poli, F. (2003). Epidemiology of acne. *Dermatology*, **206**: 7–10.

Drewnowski, A. (1990). Taste and food preferences in human obesity. In: *Taste, Experience and Feeding*, ed. E. D. Capaldi & T. L. Powley, pp. 227–40. Washington DC: American Psychological Association.

(1995). Energy intake and sensory properties of food. *American Journal of Clinical Nutrition*, **62**: S1081–S1085.

Drewnowski, A. & Greenwood, M. R. C. (1983). Cream and sugar: human preferences for high fat foods. *Physiology and Behaviour*, **30**: 629–33.

Drewnowski, A. & Specter, S. E. (2004). Poverty and obesity: the role of energy density and energy costs. *American Journal of Clinical Nutrition*, **79**: 6–16.

Dudley, R. (2004). Ethanol, fruit ripening and the historical origins of human alcoholism in primate frugivory. *Integrative and Comparative Biology*, **44**: 315–23.

Duffey, K. J. & Popkin, B. M. (2008). High-fructose corn syrup: is this what's for dinner? *American Journal of Clinical Nutrition*, **88**: 1722S–1732S.

Dufour, D. L. (1989). The bitter is sweet: a case study of bitter cassava (*Manihot esculenta*) use in Amazonia. In: *Tropical Forests, People and Food: Biocultural Interactions and Applications to Development*, ed. C. M. Hladik *et al.*, pp. 575–588. Paris: The Parthenon Publishing Group.

Dunbar, R. I. M. (1983). Theropithecines and hominids: contrasting solutions to the same ecological problem. *Journal of Human Evolution*, **12**: 647–58.

(1988). *Primate Social Systems*. London: Croom Helm.

(1992). Neocortex size as a constraint on group size in primates. *Journal of Human Evolution*, **22**: 469–93.

(1993). Coevolution of neocortical size, group size and language in humans. *Behavioral and Brain Sciences*, **11**: 681–735.

(1998). The Social Brain Hypothesis. *Evolutionary Anthropology*, **6**: 178–90.

(2003). The social brain: mind, language and society in evolutionary perspective. *Annual Reviews of Anthropology*, **32**: 163–81.

(2012). Obesity: an evolutionary perspective. In: *Insecurity, Inequality and Obesity*, ed. A. Offer, R. Pechey & S. Ulijaszek, pp. 55–68. Oxford: Oxford University Press.

Dunn, F. L. (1968). Epidemiological factors: health and disease in hunter-gatherers. In: *Man the Hunter*, ed. R. B. Lee & T. DeVore, pp. 221–8. Chicago, IL: Aldine.

Dunn, R. R., Davies, T. J., Harris, N. C. & Gavin, M. C. (2010). Global drivers of human pathogen richness and prevalence. *Proceedings of the Royal Society, B*, **277**: 2587–95.

Dwyer, P. & Minnegal, M. (1994). Sago gardens and variable garden yields: a case study from Papua New Guinea. *Man and Culture in Oceania*, **10**: 81–102.

Dye, C. & Williams, B. G. (2010). The population dynamics and control of tuberculosis. *Science*, **328**: 856–61.

Dye, C., Scheele, S., Dolin, R., Pathania, G. & Raviglione, M. (1999). Consensus statement. Global burden of tuberculosis: estimated incidence, prevalence, and mortality by country. WHO Global Surveillance and Monitoring Project. *Journal of The American Medical Association*, **282**: 677–86.

Dyerberg, J. (1986). Linolenate-derived polyunsaturated fatty acids and prevention of atherosclerosis. *Nutrition Reviews*, **44**: 125–34.

Dyerberg, J., Bang, H. O. & Hjorne, N. (1975). Fatty acid composition of the plasma lipids in Greenland Eskimos. *American Journal of Clinical Nutrition*, **28**: 958–66.

Dyson, T. (1991). On the demography of South Asian famines, Part I. *Population Studies*, **45**: 5–25.

Earle, T. (2004). Culture matters in the Neolithic transition and emergence of hierarchy in Thy, Denmark. *American Anthropologist*, **106**: 111–25.

Easterlin, R. A. (1995). Will raising the incomes of all increase the happiness of all? *Journal of Economic Behavior and Organization*, **27**: 35–47.

Eaton, S. B. & Eaton, S. B. III. (1999). The evolutionary context of chronic degenerative diseases. In: *Evolution in Health and Disease*, ed. S. C. Stearns, pp. 251–9. Oxford: Oxford University Press.

Eaton, S. B. & Konner, M. (1985). Paleolithic nutrition. A consideration of its nature and current implications. *New England Journal of Medicine*, **312**: 283–9.

Eaton, S. B. & Nelson, D. A. (1991). Calcium in evolutionary perspective. *American Journal of Clinical Nutrition*, **54**: 281S–287S.

Eaton, S. B. *et al.* (1998). Dietary intake of long-chain polyunsaturated fatty acids during the Paleolithic. In: *The Return of ω3 Fatty Acids into the Food Supply*, vol. **I**: *Land-Based Animal Food Products and Their Health Effects*, ed. A. P. Simpoulos, pp. 12–23. Basel: Karger.

Eaton, S. B., Cordain, L. & Lindeberg, S. (2002). Evolutionary health promotion: a consideration of common counter arguments. *Preventive Medicine*, **34**: 119–23.

Eaton, S. B., Eaton, S. B. III. & Konner, M. J. (1997). Paleolithic nutrition revisited: a twelve-year retrospective on its nature and implications. *European Journal of Clinical Nutrition*, **51**(4): 207–16.

Eaton, S. B., Eaton, S. B. III. & Konner, M. J. (1999). Palaeolithic nutrition revisited. In: *Evolutionary Medicine*, ed. W. R. Trevathan, E. O. Smith & J. J. McKenna, pp. 313–332. Oxford: Oxford University Press.

Eaton, S. B., Konner, M. & Shostak, M. (1988). Stone agers in the fast lane: chronic degenerative diseases in evolutionary perspective. *American Journal of Medicine*, **84**: 739–49.

Edmundson, W. C. & Edmundson, S. A. (1988). Food intake and work allocation of male and female farmers in an impoverished Indian village. *British Journal of Nutrition*, **60**: 433–9.

Eertmans, A., Baeyens, F. & Van den Bergh, O. (2001). Food likes and their relative importance in human eating behavior: review and preliminary suggestions for health promotion. *Health Education Research*, **16**(4): 443–56.

Efremov, I. A. (1940). Taphonomy: a new branch of paleontology. *Pan-American Geologist*, **74**: 81–93.

Ellen, R. (1991). Foraging, starch extraction and the sedentary lifestyle in the lowland rainforest of central Seram. In: *Hunters and Gatherers*, vol. **I**: *History, Evolution and Social Change*, ed. T. Ingold, D. Riches & J. Woodburn, pp. 117–34. Oxford: Berg.

Elliott, S. S., Keim, N. L., Stern, J. S., Teff, K. & Havel, P. J. (2002). Fructose, weight gain and insulin resistance syndrome. *American Journal of Clinical Nutrition*, **76**: 911–22.

Ellison, P. T. (2001). *On Fertile Ground: A Natural History of Human Reproduction.* Cambridge, MA: Harvard University Press.

Elton, S. (2006). Forty years on and still going strong: the use of the hominin-cercopithecid comparison in palaeoanthropology. *Journal of the Royal Anthropological Institute*, **12**: 19–38.

(2008a). Environments, adaptation, and evolutionary medicine: should we be eating a stone age diet? In: *Medicine and Evolution: Current Applications, Future Prospects*, ed. S. Elton and P. O'Higgins, pp. 9–33. Boca Raton, FL: CRC Press.

(2008b). The environmental context of human evolutionary history in Eurasia and Africa. *Journal of Anatomy*, **212**: 377–93.

Elton, S. & O'Higgins, P. (2008). *Medicine and Evolution: Current Applications, Future Prospects*. Boca Raton, FL: Taylor & Francis.

Elton, S., Bishop, L. C. & Wood, B. (2001). Comparative context of Plio-Pleistocene hominin brain evolution. *Journal of Human Evolution*, **41**: 1–27.

el-Zaatari, S. (2007). Ecogeographic variation in Neandertal dietary habits: evidence from microwear texture analysis. PhD dissertation, State University of New York at Stony Brook.

Emken, E. A. (1984). Nutrition and biochemistry of trans and positional fatty acid isomers in hydrogenated oils. *Annual Review of Nutrition*, **4**: 339–76.

Emken, E. A., Adlot, R. O. & Gulley, R. M. (1994). Dietary linoleic acid influences desaturation and acylation of deuterium labelled linoleic and linolenic acid in young adult males. *Biochimica et Biophysica Acta*, **1213**: 277–88.

Emlen, J. M. (1966). The role of time and energy in food preferences. *American Naturalist*, **100**: 611–17.

Emmans, G. & Kyriazakis, I. (2001). Consequences of genetic change in farm animals on food intake and feeding behaviour. *Proceedings of the Nutrition Society*, **60**: 115–25.

Emmans, G. C. & Oldham, J. D. (1988). Modelling of growth and nutrition in different species. In: *Modelling of Livestock Production Systems*, ed. S. Korver & J. A. M. van Arendonk, pp. 13–21. Dordrecht: Kluwer Academic Press.

Enard, D., Depaulis, F. & Crollius, H. R. (2010). Human and non-human primate genomes share hotspots of positive selection. *PLoS Genetics*, **6**(2): e1000840– e1000852.

Endres, S. *et al.* (1989). The effect of dietary supplementation with n–3 polyunsaturated fatty acids on the synthesis of interleukin-1 and tumor necrosis factor by mononuclear cells. *New England Journal of Medicine*, **320**: 265–71.

Escalante, A. A., Cornejo, O. E., Freeland, D. E. *et al.* (2005). A monkey's tale: the origin of *Plasmodium vivax* as a human malaria parasite. *Proceedings of the National Academy of Sciences*, **102**(6): 1980–5.

Eshed, V., Gopher, A., Gage, T. & Hershkovitz, I. (2004). Has the transition to agriculture reshaped the demographic structure of prehistoric populations? New evidence from the Levant. *American Journal of Physical Anthropology*, **124**: 315–29.

Esteller, M. (2008). Epigenetics in cancer. *New England Journal of Medicine*, **358**(11): 1148–59.

Etkin, N. L. (1986). Multidisciplinary perspectives in the interpretation of plants used in indigenous medicine and diet. In: *Plants in Indigenous Medicine and Diet*, ed. N. Etkin, pp. 2–29. Bedford Hills: Redgrave Press.

European Food Safety Authority Panel on Dietetic Products, Nutrition and Allergies. (2010). *Nutrition*. http://www.efsa.europa.eu/en/panels/nda.htm. Accessed 3 November, 2010.

Evans, G. H. *et al.* (1990). Association of magnesium deficiency with the blood pressure-lowering effects of calcium. *Journal of Hypertension*, **8**: 327–37.

Eveleth, P. B. & Tanner, J. M. (1990). *Worldwide Variation in Human Growth*, 2nd edn. Cambridge: Cambridge University Press.

Evershed, R. P., Payne, S., Sherratt, A. *et al.* (2008). Earliest date for milk use in the Near East and southeastern Europe linked to cattle herding. *Nature*, **455**: 528–31.

Facchini, F., Chen, Y. D., Hollenbeck, C. B. & Reaven, G. M. (1991). Relationship between resistance to insulin-mediated glucose uptake, urinary uric acid clearance and plasma uric acid concentration. *Journal of the American Medical Association*, **266**(21): 3008–11.

Faeh, D., Minehira, K., Schwarz, J. M. *et al.* (2005). Effect of fructose overfeeding and fish oil administration on hepatic de novo lipogenesis and insulin sensitivity in healthy men. *Diabetes*, **54**: 1907–13.

Fairbanks, L. (1993). Risk taking by juvenile vervet monkeys. *Behaviour*, **124**: 57–72.

Falsetti, L., Gambera, A., Adrico, S. & Sartori, E. (2002). Acne and hirsutism in polycystic ovary syndrome: clinical, endocrine-metabolic and ultrasonographic differences. *Gynecological Endocrinology*, **16**: 275–84.

Fam, A. G. (2002). Gout, diet, and the insulin resistance syndrome. *The Journal of Rheumatology*, **29**(7): 1350–5.

(2005). Gout: excess calories, purines and alcohol intake and beyond. Response to a urate lowering diet. *Journal of Rheumatology*, **32**(5): 773–7.

Farjadian, S., Moqadam, F. & Ghaderi, A. (2006). HLA class II gene polymorphism in Parsees and Zoroastrians of Iran. *International Journal of Immunogenetics* **33**, 185–91.

Farmer, P. (2004). Sidney W. Mintz Lecture for 2001: an anthropology of structural violence. *Current Anthropology*, **45**: 305–25.

Faulhaber, H. (1964). La distribucion de la estatura y del indice cefálico en Mesomerica. *Actas y Memorias del 35 Congreso Internacional de Americanistas*, **3**: 99–108.

Fedigan, L. & Fedigan, L. M. (1988). *Cercopithecus aethiops*: a review of field studies. In: *A Primate Radiation: Evolutionary Biology of the African Guenons*, ed A. Gautier-Hion, F. Bourliere, J. P. Gautier & J. Kingdon, pp. 389–411. Cambridge: Cambridge University Press.

Fenner, F., Henderson, D. A., Arita, I., JeZek, I. & Ladnyi, D. (1988). *Smallpox and its Eradication*. History of International Public Health, No. 6. Geneva: World Health Organization.

Ferder, L., Ferder, M. D. & Inserra, F. (2010). The role of high-fructose corn syrup in metabolic syndrome and hypertension. *Current Hypertension Reports*, **12**(2): 105–12.

Ferro-Luzzi, A. & Branca, F. (1993). Nutritional seasonality: the dimensions of the problem. In: *Seasonality and Human Ecology*, ed. S. J. Ulijaszek & S. S. Strickland, pp. 149–65. Cambridge: Cambridge University Press.

Ferro-Luzzi, A. *et al.* (2001). *Seasonal Undernutrition in Rural Ethiopia: Magnitude, Correlates and Functional Significance* (International Food Policy Research Institute Research Report 118). Washington, D.C.: International Food Policy Research Institute.

Ferro-Luzzi, A., Branca, F. & Pastore, G. (1994). Body mass index defines the risk of seasonal energy stress in the third world. *European Journal of Clinical Nutrition*, **48**: S165–S178.

Festa, A. *et al.* (2000). Chronic subclinical inflammation as part of the insulin resistance syndrome: the insulin resistance atherosclerosis study (Iras). *Circulation*, **102**: 42–7.

Feunekes, G. I. J., de Graaf, C., Meyboom, S. & van Staveren, W. A. (1998). Food choice and fat intake of adolescents and adults: associations of intakes within social networks. *Preventive Medicine*, **27**: 645–56.

Fewtrell, M., Wilson, D. C., Booth, I. & Lucas, A. (2011). Six months of exclusive breast feeding: how good is the evidence? *British Medical Journal*, **342**: C5955.

Fiddes, N. (1991). *Meat: A Natural Symbol.* London: Routledge.

(1994). Social aspects of meat eating. *Proceedings of the Nutrition Society,* **53**: 271–80.

Finch, C. E. & Stanford, C. B. (2004). Meat-adaptive genes and the evolution of slower aging in humans. *Quarterly Review of Biology,* **79**(1): 4–50.

Finlayson, C. (2004). *Neanderthals and Modern Humans: An Ecological and Evolutionary Perspective.* Cambridge: Cambridge University Press.

Fiorenza, L., Kullmer, O., Bacso, S. & Schrenk, F. (2008). Function and wear pattern analysis in Neanderthals and early *Homo sapiens* dentitions. *American Journal of Physical Anthropology,* **135**: 96.

Fischer, S. & Weber, P. C. (1984). Prostaglandin I3 is formed in vivo in man after dietary eicosapentaenoic acid. *Nature,* **307**: 165–8.

Fischer, S., Vischer, A., Preac-Mursic, V. & Weber, P. C. (1987). Dietary docosahexaenoic acid is retroconverted in man to eicosapentaenoic acid, which can be quickly transformed to prostaglandin I3. *Prostaglandins,* **34**, 367–75.

Fischler, C. & Masson, E. (2008). *Manger: Français, Européens Et Américains Face À l'Alimentation.* Paris: Odile Jacob.

Fisher, R. A., Ford, E. B. & Huxley, J. (1939). Taste-testing the anthropoid apes. *Nature,* **144**: 750.

Fitch, C. E. & Stanford, C. B. (2004). Meat-adaptive genes and the evolution of slower aging in humans. *Quarterly Review of Biology,* **79**: 3–50.

FitzGerald, G. A., Healy, C. & Daugherty, J. (1987). Thromboxane biosynthesis in human disease. *Federation Proceedings,* **46**: 154–9.

Fitzhugh, W. W. (1997). Biogeographical archaeology in the eastern North American arctic. *Human Ecology,* **25**: 385–418.

Flad, R., Zhu, J., Wang, C. *et al.* (2005). Archaeological and chemical evidence for early salt production in China. *Proceedings of the National Academy of Sciences,* **102**: 12618–22.

Flatz, G. & Rotthauwe, H. W. (1973). Lactose nutrition and natural selection. *Lancet,* **7820**: 76–7.

Fleagle, J. G. (1999). *Primate Adaptation and Evolution.* San Diego, CA: Academic Press.

Fleming, R. E. & Sly, W. S. (2002). Mechanisms of iron accumulation in hereditary hemochromatosis. *Annual Reviews in Physiology,* **64**: 663–80.

Flynn, J. L. & Chan, J. (2001). Tuberculosis: latency and reactivation. *Infection and Immunity,* **69**(7): 4195–201.

Foley, R. A. (1993). The influence of seasonality on hominid evolution. In: *Seasonality and Human Ecology,* ed. S. J. Ulijaszek & S. S. Strickland, pp. 17–37. Cambridge: Cambridge University Press.

(1995). The adaptive legacy of human evolution: a search for the environment of evolutionary adaptedness. *Evolutionary Anthropology,* **4**: 194–203.

Foley, R. & Elton, S. (1998). Time and energy: the ecological context for the evolution of bipedalism. In: *Primate Locomotion: Recent Advances,* ed. E. Strasser, J. Fleagle, A. Rosenberger & H. McHenry, pp. 419–33. New York: Plenum Press.

Foltz, R. (1999). *Religions of the Silk Road: Overland Trade and Cultural Exchange from Antiquity to the Fifteenth Century.* London: Macmillan.

Food and Agriculture Organization (2000). *The State of Food Insecurity in the World.* Rome: Food and Agriculture Organization.

(2008). *Fats and fatty acids in human nutrition: report of an expert consultation. FAO Food and Nutrition Paper 91.* Rome: Food and Agriculture Organization.

(2009). Globally important agricultural heritage systems: Chinampa agricultural system (Mexico). www.fao.org [accessed 21 March, 2009].

(2010a). *The State of Food Insecurity in the World.* Rome: Food and Agriculture Organization.

(2010b). *Crop Prospects and Food Situation in the Global Information and Early Warning System on Food and Agriculture.* Geneva: Food and Agriculture Organization.

(2010c). Price surges in food markets: how should organised futures markets be regulated? Economic and Social Perspectives – Policy Brief No 9. Rome: Food and Agriculture Organization.

(2011). Food consumption. www.faostat.org [accessed 22 June 2011].

Food and Agriculture Organization, World Health Organization & United Nations University (1985). *Energy and Protein Requirements. World Health Organization Technical Report Series.* Gevena: World Health Organization.

Food Standards Agency (2002). *McCance and Widdowson's The Composition of Foods, Sixth Summary Edition.* Cambridge: Royal Society of Chemistry.

Foster-Powell, K., Holt, S. H. A. & Brand-Miller, J. C. (2002). International table of glycemic index and glycemic load values: 2002. *American Journal of Clinical Nutrition*, **76**: 5–56.

Fox, E. B. A., van Schaik, C. P., Sitompul, A. & Wright, D. N. (2004). Intra- and interpopulational differences in orangutan (*Pongo pygmaeus*) activity and diet: implications for the invention of tool use. *American Journal of Physical Anthropology*, **125**: 162–74.

Fox, I. H., John, D., DeBruyne, S., Dwosh, I. & Marliss, E. B. (1985). Hyperuricemia and hypertriglyceridemia: metabolic basis for the association. *Metabolism*, **34**(8): 741–46.

Franceschi, C., Bonafè, M., Valensin, S. *et al.* (2000). Inflammaging: an evolutionary perspective on immunosenescence. *Annals of the New York Academy of Science*, **908**: 244–54.

Frank, R. H. & Cook, P. J. (1995). *The Winner-Takes-All Society.* New York: Free Press.

Franks, S. (2003). Polycystic ovary syndrome. *New England Journal of Medicine*, **13**: 853–61.

Fraser, E. D. G. (2003). Social vulnerability and ecological fragility: building bridges between social and natural sciences using the Irish Potato Famine as a case study. *Conservation Ecology*, **7**: 9.

Frassetto, L. A., Todd, K. M., Morris, R.C. Jr. & Sebastian, A. (1998). Estimation of net endogenous noncarbonic acid production in humans from diet potassium and protein contents. *American Journal of Clinical Nutrition*, **68**: 576–83.

Frassetto, L. A., Morris, R.C. Jr., Sellmeyer, D. E. & Sebastian, A. (2008). Adverse effects of sodium chloride on bone in the aging human population resulting from habitual consumption of typical American diets. *Journal of Nutrition*, **38**(2): S419–S422.

Frassetto, L., Morris, R. C. Jr. & Sebastian, A. (1997). Potassium bicarbonate reduces urinary nitrogen excretion in postmenopausal women. *Journal of Clinical Endocrinology and Metabolism*, **82**: 254–9.

Freathy, R. M., Weedon, M. N., Bennett, A. *et al.* (2007). Type 2 Diabetes TCF7L2 risk genotypes alter birth weight: a study of 24,053 individuals. *American Journal of Human Genetics*, **80**: 1150–61.

Freeman, L. C. (2004). *The Development of Social Network Analysis: A Study in the Sociology of Science.* Vancouver: Empirical Press.

Frenk, J., Bobadilla, J. L., Sepúlveda, J. & López-Cervantes, M. (1989). Health transition in middle-income countries: new challenges for health care. *Health Policy and Planning*, **4**(1): 29–39.

Friedman, J. F., Kurtis, J. D., Mtalib, R. *et al.* (2003). Malaria is related to decreased nutritional status among male adolescents and adults in the setting of intense perennial transmission. *Journal of Infectious Disease*, **188**: 449–57.

Frienkel, N. (1980). Of pregnancy and progeny. *Diabetes*, **29**: 1023–34.

Friis, E. M., Pedersen, K. R. & Crane, P. R. (2010). Diversity in obscurity: fossil flowers and the early history of angiosperms. *Philosophical Transactions of the Royal Society, B,* **365**: 369–82.

Frisancho, A. R. (1993). *Human Adaptation and Accommodation.* Ann Arbor, MI: University of Michigan Press.

Friso, S. & Choi, S. W. (2002). Gene–nutrient interactions and DNA methylation. *Journal of Nutrition*, **132**: 2382S–2387S.

Frongillo, E. A., de Onis, M. & Hanson, K. M. P. (1997). Socioeconomic and demographic factors are associated with worldwide patterns of stunting and wasting of children. *Journal of Nutrition*, **127**: 2302–9.

Fullerton, S. M., Clark, A. G., Weiss, K. M. *et al.* (2000). Apolipoprotein E variation at the sequence haplotype level: implications for the origin and maintenance of a major human polymorphism. *American Journal of Human Genetics*, **67**: 881–900.

Gabunia, L., Vekua, A., Lordkipanidze, D. *et al.* (2000). Earliest Pleistocene hominid cranial remains from Dmanisi, Republic of Georgia: taxonomy, geological setting, and age. *Science*, **288**: 1019–25.

Gabunia, L., Anton, S. C., Lordipanidze, D., Vekua, A., Justus, A. & Swisher, C. C. (2001). Dmanisi and dispersal. *Evolutionary Anthropology*, **10**: 158–70.

Gage, T. B. & DeWitte, S. (2009). What do we know about the agricultural demographic transition? *Current Anthropology*, **50**: 649–55.

Gale, E. A. M. (2008). Head to Head. Should we dump the metabolic syndrome? Yes. *British Medical Journal*, **336**: 640.

Gallou-Kabani, C. & Junien, C. (2005). Nutritional epigenomics of metabolic syndrome: new perspective against the epidemic. *Diabetes*, **54**: 1899–906.

Galvani, A. P. & Novembre, J. (2005). The evolutionary history of the CCR5-Δ32 HIV-resistance mutation. *Microbes and Infection*, **7**: 302–9.

Gao, F., Bailes, E., Robertson, D. L. *et al.* (1999). Origin of HIV-1 in *Pan troglodytes troglodytes. Nature*, **397**: 436–41.

Gardner, C. D. & Kraemer, H. C. (1995). Monounsaturated versus polyunsaturated dietary fat and serum lipids. A meta-analysis. *Arteriosclerosis, Thrombosis, and Vascular Biology*, **15**(11): 1917–27.

Garn, S. M. & Leonard, W. R. (1989). What did our ancestors eat? *Nutrition Reviews*, **47**: 337–45.

Garner, L. F., Owens, H., Kinnear, R. F. & Frith, M. J. (1999). Prevalence of myopia in Sherpa and Tibetan children in Nepal. *Optometry and Vision Science*, **76**: 282–5.

Gaudzinski, S. & Roebroeks, W. (2000). Adults only: reindeer hunting at the Middle Palaeolithic site Salzgitter Lebenstedt, Northern Germany. *Journal of Human Evolution*, **38**: 497–521.

Gaulin, S. J. C. (1979). A Jarman/Bell model of primate feeding niches. *Human Ecology*, **7**: 1–20.

Gavrilets, S., Duenez-Guzman, E-A, Vose, M. D. & Svensson, E. I. (2008). Dynamics of alliance formation and the egalitarian revolution. *PLoS ONE*, **3**, DOI: 10.1371/journal.pone.0003293.

Geissler, C. & Powers, C. (2006). *Human Nutrition*. Edinburgh: Elsevier/Churchill Livingstone.

Gerrior, S. & Bente, L. (2002). Nutrient content of the US food supply, 1909–99: a summary report. Home Economics report No. 55. Washington, D.C.: US Department of Agriculture, Centre for Nutrition Policy and Promotion.

Gianfrancesco, F. & Musameci, S. (2004). The evolutionary conservation of the human chitotriosidase gene in rodents and primates. *Cytogenetic and Genome Research*, **105**: 54–6.

Gibbons, A. (2009). Of tools and tubers. *Science*, **324**: 588–9.

Gibson, K. R. (1986). Cognition, brain size and the extraction of embedded food resources. In: *Primate Ontogeny, Cognition and Social Behaviour*, ed. J. G. Else & P. C. Lee, pp. 93–105. Cambridge: Cambridge University Press.

Gilbert, P. (2000). Varieties of submissive behaviour as forms of social defense: their evolution and role in depression. In: *Subordination and Defeat: An Evolutionary Approach to Mood Disorders and their Therapy*, ed. L. Sloman & P. Gilbert, pp. 3–45. Mahwah: Lawrence Erlbaum Associates.

Glander, K. E. (1982). The impact of plant secondary compounds on primate feeding behaviour. *Yearbook of Physical Anthropology*, **25**: 1–18.

Glew, R. S., Amoako-Atta, B., Ankar-Brewoo, G. *et al.* (2009). Non-cultivated plant foods in West Africa: nutritional analysis of the leaves of three indigenous leafy vegetables in Ghana. *Food*, **3**: 39–42.

Goebel, T. (1999). Pleistocene human colonization of Siberia and peopling of the Americas: an ecological approach. *Evolutionary Anthropology*, **8**: 208–27.

Golden, M. H. (1994). Is complete catch-up possible for stunted malnourished children? *European Journal of Clinical Nutrition*, **48**: S58-S71.

Goldman Sachs (2007). *Global: Food & Beverages Integrative ESG*. Global Investment Research Report February 8. London: The Goldman Sachs Group, Inc.

Goldman, D. W., Pickett, W. C. & Goetzl, E. J. (1983). Human neutraphil chemotatic and degranulating activities of leukotriene B5 (LTB5) derived from eicosapentaenoic acid. *Biochemical and Biophysical Research Communications*, **117**: 282–8.

Golenser, J., Miller, J., Spira, D. T., Navok, T. & Chevion, M. (1983) Inhibitory effect of a fava bean component in the in vitro development of *Plasmodium falciparum* in normal and glucose-6-phosphate deficient erythrocytes. *Blood*, **61**: 507–10.

Gomes, C. M. & Boesch, C. (2009). Wild chimpanzees exchange meat for sex on a long-term basis. *PLoS ONE*, **4**: e5116.

Gommes, R., Guerny, J. D., Nachtergaele, F. & Brinkman, R. (1998). *Potential Impacts of Sea Level Rise on Populations and Agriculture*. Rome: Food and Agriculture Organization.

Gonzalez, E., Dhanda, R., Bamshad, M. *et al.* (2001). Global survey of genetic variation in CCR5, Rantes, and MIP-1: impact on the epidemiology of the HIV-1 pandemic. *Proceedings of the National Academy of Sciences, USA* **98**(9): 5199–204.

Goodman, A. H., Armelagos, G. J. & Rose, J. C. (1984a). The chronological distribution of enamel hypoplasias from prehistoric Dickson Mounds populations. *American Journal of Physical Anthropology*, **65**: 259–66.

   (1980). Enamel hypoplasias as indicators of stress in three prehistoric populations from Illinois. *Human Biology*, **52**: 515–28.

Goodman, A. H., Lallo, J., Armelagos, G. J. & Rose, J. C. (1984b). Health changes at Dickson Mounds (A.D. 950–1300). In: *Paleopathology at the Origins of Agriculture*, ed. M. N. Cohen & G. J. Armelagos, pp. 271–306. London: Academic Press.

Goodnight, S. H., Harris, W. S. & Connor, W. E. (1981). Effect of dietary w-3 fatty acids on platelet composition and function in man. A prospective study. *Blood*, **58**: 881–5.

Gopalan, C. (1992). Undernutrition: measurement and implication. In: *Nutrition and Poverty*, ed. S. R. Osmani, pp. 17–48. New York: Oxford University Press.

Goran, M. I. & Gower, B. A. (2001). Longitudinal study on pubertal insulin resistance. (2001). *Diabetes*, **50**(11): 2444–50.

Goren-Inbar, N., Alperson, N., Kislev, M. E. *et al.* (2004). Evidence of hominin control of fire at Gesher Benot Ya`aqov, Israel. *Science*, **304**: 725–7.

Gotthard, K. & Nylin, S. (1995). Adaptive plasticity and plasticity as an adaptation: a selective review of plasticity in animal morphology and life history. *Oikos*, **74**: 3–17.

Gowlett, J. A. J., Harris, J. W. K., Walton, D. & Wood, B. A. (1981). Early archaeological sites, hominid remains and traces of fire from Chesowanja, Kenya. *Nature*, **294**: 125–9.

Granovetter, M. S. (1973). The strength of weak ties. *American Journal of Sociology*, **78**: 1360–80.

Greene, L. S. (1993). G6PD deficiency as protection against *Falciparum* malaria: an epidemiologic critique of population and experimental studies. *Yearbook of Physical Anthropology*, **36**: 153–78.

Greenow, K., Pearce, N. J. & Ramji, D. P. (2005). The key role of apolipoprotein E in atherosclerosis. *Journal of Molecular Medicine*, **83**: 329–42.

Griebsch, A. & Zollner, N. (1974). Effect of ribomononucleotides given orally on uric acid production in man. *Advances in Experimental Medicine and Biology*, **41**: 443–9.

Grine, F. E., Judex, S., Daegling, D. J. *et al.* (2010). Craniofacial biomechanics and functional and dietary inferences in hominin paleontology. *Journal of Human Evolution*, **58**: 293–308.

Grine, F. E., Ungar, P. S. & Teaford, M. F. (2006). Was the Early Pliocene hominin '*Australopithecus*' *anamensis* a hard object feeder? *South African Journal of Science*, **102**: 301–10.

Gross, L. S., Li, L., Ford, E. S. & Liu, S. (2004). Increased consumption of refined carbohydrates and the epidemic of type 2 diabetes in the United States: an ecologic assessment. *American Journal of Clinical Nutrition*, **79**: 774–9.

Grove, D. I. (1990). *A History of Human Helminthology*. Wallingford: CAB International.

Grubić, Z., Zunec, R., Cecuk-Jelicić, E., Kerhin-Brkljacić, V. & Kastelan, A. (2000). Polymorphism of HLA-A, -B, -DRB1, -DQA1 and -DQB1 haplotypes in a Croatian population. *European Journal of Immunogenetics*, **27**: 47–51.

Grundschober, C., Sanchez-Mazas, A., Excoffier, L. *et al.* (1994). HLA-DPB1 DNA polymorphism in the Swiss population: linkage disequilibrium with other HLA loci and population genetic affinities. *European Journal of Immunogenetics*, **21**: 143–57.

Grundy, S. M. (1997a). What is the desirable ratio of saturated, polyunsaturated, and monounsaturated fatty acids in the diet? *American Journal of Clinical Nutrition*, **66**(4): S988-S990.

(1997b). Cholesterol and coronary heart disease. The 21st century. *Archives of Internal Medicine*, **157**(11): 1177–84.

(2008). Metabolic syndrome pandemic. *Arteriosclerosis, Thrombosis, and Vascular Biology*, **28**: 629–36.

Gunstone, F. D. (ed) (2002). *Vegetable Oils in Food Technology – Composition, Properties, and Uses*. Oxford: Blackwell Publishing.

Gutacker, M., Valsangiacomo, C. & Piffaretti, J. C. (2000). Identification of two genetic groups in *Bacteroides fragilis* by multilocus enzyme electrophoresis: distribution of antibiotic resistance (*cfiA, cepA*) and enterotoxin (*bft*) encoding genes. *Microbiology*, **146**: 1241–54.

Gutierrez, M. C., Brisse, S., Brosch, R. *et al.* (2005). Ancient origin and gene mosaicism of the progenitor of *Mycobacterium tuberculosis*. *PLoS Pathog*, **1**: e5. doi: 10. 1371/journal.ppat.0010005.

Hadley, C. (2004). The costs and benefits of kin – kin networks and children's health among the Pimbwe of Tanzania. *Human Nature*, **15**: 377–95.

Hadley, C. & Patil, C. L. (2008). Seasonal changes in household food insecurity and symptoms of anxiety and depression. *American Journal of Physical Anthropology*, **135**, 225–32.

Hafner, M. S. & Nadler, S. A. (1998). Phylogenetic trees support the coevolution of parasites and their hosts. *Nature*, **332**: 258–9.

Haile-Selassie, Y. (2001). Late Miocene hominids from the Middle Awash, Ethiopia. *Nature*, **412**: 178–81.

Hajjej, A., Kâabi, H., Sellami, M. *et al.* (2006). The contribution of HLA class I and II alleles and haplotypes to the investigation of the evolutionary history of Tunisians. *Tissue Antigens*, **68**: 153–62.

Hales, C. N. & Barker, D. J. P. (1992). The thrifty phenotype hypothesis. *British Medical Bulletin*, **60**: 5–20.

Halperin, R. H. (1980). Ecology and mode of production: seasonal variation and the division of labor by sex among hunter-gatherers. *Journal of Anthropological Research*, **36**: 379–99.

Hamazaki, T., Fischer, S., Urakaze, M., Sawazaki, S., Yano, S. & Kuwamori, T. (1989). Urinary excretion of PGI2/3-M and recent n-6/3 fatty acid intake. *Prostaglandins*, **37**: 417–42.

Hamberg, M. & Samuelsson, B. (1974). Prostaglandin endoperoxides: novel transformations of arachidonic acid in human platelets. *Proceedings of the National Academy of Sciences, USA*, **71**: 3400–4.

Hamberg, M., Svensson, J. & Samuelsson, B. (1975). Thromboxanes. A new group of biologically active compounds derived from prostaglandin endoperoxides. *Proceedings of the National Academy of Sciences, USA*, **72**: 2994–8.

Handley, L. L., Austin, A. T., Robinson, D. *et al.* (1999). The N-15 natural abundance of ecosystem samples reflect measures of water availability. *Australian Journal of Plant Physiology*, **26**: 185–99.

Hanekamp, J. C. & Bast, A. (2007). Food supplements and European regulation within a precautionary context: a critique and implications for nutritional, toxicological and regulatory consistency. *Critical Reviews in Food Science and Nutrition*, **47**: 267–85.
  (2008). Why RDAs and ULs are incompatible standards in the U-shape micronutrient model: a philosophically orientated analysis of micronutrients' standardizations. *Risk Analysis*, **28**: 1639–52.

Hanifan, L. J. (1916). The rural school community center. *Annals of the American Academy of Political and Social Science*, **67**: 130–8.

Hanlon, C. S. & Rubinsztein, D. C. (1995). Arginine residues at codons 112 and 158 in the apolipoprotein E gene correspond to the ancestral state in humans. *Atherosclerosis*, **112**: 85–90.

Hanya, G., Noma, N. & Agetsuma, N. (2003). Altitudinal and seasonal variations in the diet of Japanese macaques in Yakushima. *Primates*, **44**: 51–59.

Harborne, L., Fleming, R., Lyall, H., Sattar, N. & Norman, J. (2003). Metformin or antiandrogen in the treatment of hirsutism in polycystic ovary syndrome. *Journal of Clinical Endocrinology and Metabolism*, **88**: 4116–23.

Harcourt, A. H. & Stewart, K. J. (2007). *Gorilla Society: Conflict, Compromise, and Cooperation Between the Sexes*. Chicago, IL: University of Chicago Press.

Harcourt, W. E. H. & Aiello, L. C. (2004). Fossils, feet and the evolution of human bipedal locomotion. *Journal of Anatomy*, **204**: 403–16.

Hardy, B. L. (2010). Climatic variability and plant food distribution in Pleistocene Europe: implications for Neanderthal diet and subsistence. *Quaternary Science Reviews*, **29**: 662–79.

Harpending, H. C., Batzer, M. A., Gurven, M., Jorde, L. B., Rogers, A. R. & Sherry, S. T. (1998). Genetic traces of ancient demography. *Proceedings of the National Academy of Sciences, USA*, **95**: 1961–7.

Harris, W. S. & Munzio, F. (1990). Fish oil reduced postprandial triglyceride concentrations without accelerating lipid emulsion removal rates. *American Journal of Clinical Nutrition*, **58**: 68–74.

Harris, W. S. (1990). Omega-3 fatty acids: effects on lipid metabolism. *Current Opinion in Lipidology*, **1**: 5–11.

Hart, D. & Sussman, R. W. (2005). *Man the Hunted: Primates, Predators and Human Evolution*. Cambridge, MA: Westview Press.

Hashimoto, Y., Naito, C., Kawamura, M. & Oka, H. (1984). Effects of the ratio of exogenous eicosapentaenoic acid to arachidonic acid on platelet aggregation and serotonin release. *Thrombosis Research*, **34**: 439–46.

Hassam, A. G., Sinclair, A. J. & Crawford, M. A. (1975). The incorporation of orally fed radioactive γ-linolenic acid and linoleic acid into the liver and brain lipids of suckling rats. *Lipids*, **10**: 417–20.

Havel, P. J. (2004). Update on adipocyte hormones: regulation of energy balance and carbohydrate/lipid metabolism. *Diabetes*, **53**(1): S143-S151.

(2005). Dietary fructose: implications for dysregulation of energy homeostasis and lipid/carbohydrate metabolism. *Nutrition Reviews*, **63**(5): 133–57.

Hawkes, K., Hill, K. & O'Connell, J. F. (1982). Why hunters gather: optimal foraging and the Ache of eastern Paraguay. *American Ethnologist*, **9**: 379–98.

Hawkins, M., Barzilai, N., Liu, R. *et al.* (1997). Role of the glucosamine pathway in fat-induced insulin resistance. *Journal of Clinical Investigation*, **99**(9): 2173–82.

Hayden, B. (2009). The proof is in the pudding: feasting and the origins of domestication. *Current Anthropology*, **50**: 597–601.

Hayden, B. Y. & Platt, M. L. (2007). Animal cognition: great apes wait for grapes. *Current Biology*, **17**: R922–R923.

Hayes, K. C. & Trautwein, E. A. (1989). Taurine deficiency syndrome in cats. *The Veterinary Clinics of North America: Small Animal Practice*, **19**(3): 403–13.

Heaney, R. P., Recker, R. R. & Saville, P. D. (1977). Calcium balance and calcium requirements in middle-aged women. *American Journal of Clinical Nutrition*, **30**: 1603–11.

Heaton, T. H. E. (1999). Spatial, species, and temporal variations in the 13C/12C ratios of C3 plants: implications for palaeodiet studies. *Journal of Archaeological Science*, **26**: 637–49.

Heijmans, B. T., Tobi, E. W., Stein, A. D. *et al.* (2008). Persistent epigenetic differences associated with prenatal exposure to famine in humans. *Proceedings of the National Academy of Sciences, USA*, **105**: 17046–9.

Heilbronner, S. R., Rosati, A. G., Stevens, J. R., Hare, B. & Hauser, M. D. (2008). A fruit in the hand or two in the bush? Divergent risk preferences in chimpanzees and bonobos. *Biology Letters*, **4**: 246–9.

Heinzelin, J. D. *et al.* (1999). Environment and behavior of 2.5-million-year-old Bouri hominids. *Science*, **284**: 625–9.

Helle, S. & Helama, S. (2007). Climatic variability and the population dynamics of historical hunter-gatherers: the case of Sami of Northern Finland. *American Journal of Human Biology*, **19**: 844–53.

Henneberg, M., Sarafis, V. & Mathers, K. (1998). Human adaptations to meat eating. *Human Evolution*, **13**: 229–34.

Henry, A. G., Brooks, A. S. & Piperno, D. R. (2011). Microfossils in calculus demonstrate consumption of plants and cooked foods in Neanderthal diets (Shanidar III, Iraq, Spy I and II, Belgium). *Proceedings of the National Academy of Sciences, USA*, **108**: 486–91.

Hermanussen, M. (2003). Stature of early Europeans. *Hormones*, **2**: 175–8.

Herrera, C. M. & Pellmyr, O. (eds.) (2002). *Plant-Animal Interactions: An Evolutionary Approach*. Oxford: Blackwell Science.

Hershkovitz, I., Donoghue, H. D., Minnikin, D. E. *et al.* (2008). Detection and molecular characterization of 9000-year-old *Mycobacterium tuberculosis* from a Neolithic settlement in the Eastern Mediterranean. *PLoS One*, **3**: e3426.

Hetzel, B. S. (1983). Iodine deficiency disorders (IDD) and their eradication. *Lancet*, **2**: 1126–9.

Hibbeln, J. R. (1998). Fish consumption and major depression. *Lancet*, **351**: 1213.

   (2009). Depression, suicide and deficiencies of omega-3 essential fatty acids in modern diets. In: *Omega-3 Fatty Acids, the Brain and Retina: World Review of Nutrition and Dietetics*, Vol. **99**, eds. A. P. Simopoulos & N. G. Bazan, pp. 17–30. Basel: Karger.

Higgins, P., Voruganti, V. S. & Cornuzzie, A. G. (2010). Genetics of body weight and obesity. In: *Human Variation: From the Laboratory to the Field*, ed. C. G. N. Mascie-Taylor, A. Yasukouchi, S. Ulijaszek, pp. 17–32. Boca Raton, FL: CRC Press.

Hill, A. V. S. (1999). Genetics and genomics of infectious disease susceptibility. *British Medical Bulletin*, **55**: 401–13.

Hill, C. W., Riopelle, A. J. & King, A. R. (1983). Protein deprivation and food-related risk-taking preferences of rhesus monkeys. *Animal Learning and Behavior*, **11**: 116–18.

Hill, D. A. (1997). Seasonal variation in feeding behavior and diet of wild Japanese macaques (*Macaca fuscata yakui*) in lowland forest of Yakushima. *American Journal of Primatology*, **43**: 305–22.

Hill, J. H. (2001). Proto-Uto-Aztecan: a community of cultivators in central Mexico? *American Anthropologist*, **103**: 913–34.

Hill, K. A. & Hurtado, A. M. (1996). *Ache Life History: The Ecology and Demography of a Foraging People*. New York: Aldine de Gruyter.

Hill, K., Hawkes, K., Hurtado, M. & Kaplan, H. (1984). Seasonal variance in the diet of Ache hunter-gatherers in Eastern Paraguay. *Human Ecology*, **12**: 101–35.

Hill, R. A. & Dunbar, R. I. M. (1998). An evaluation of the roles of predation rate and predation risk as selective pressures on primate grouping behaviour. *Behaviour*, **135**: 411–30.

   (2002). Climatic determinants of diet and foraging behaviour in baboons. *Evolutionary Ecology*, **16**: 579–93.

Hill, R. A. & Dunbar, R. I. M. (2003). Social network size in humans. *Human Nature*, **14**: 53–72.

Hill, R. A., Barrett, L., Gaynor, D. *et al.* (2003). Day length, latitude and behavioural (in)flexibility in baboons. *Behavioral Ecology and Sociobiology*, **53**: 278–86.

Hladik, C. M. (1978). Adaptive strategies of primates in relation to leaf-eating. In: *The Ecology of Arboreal Folivores*, ed. G. G. Montgomery, pp. 373–95. Washington, D.C.: Smithsonian Institution Press.

Hladik, C. M., Chivers, D. J. & Pasquet, P. (1999). On diet and gut size in non-human primates and humans: is there a relationship to brain size? *Current Anthropology*, **40**: 695–7.

Hobson, K. & Clark, R. (1992). Assessing avian diets using stable isotopes II: Factors influencing diet-tissue fractionation. *Condor*, **94**: 189–97.

Hochberg, Z. & Albertson-Wikland, K. (2008). Evo-devo of infantile and childhood growth. *Pediatric Research*, **64**: 2–7.

Hodder, I. (2006). *The Leopard's Tale: Revealing the Mysteries of Çatalhöyük*. London: Thames and Hudson.

Hoddinott, J. & Yohannes, Y. (2002). *Dietary Diversity as a Household Food Security Indicator*. Washington, DC: Food and Nutrition Technical Assistance Project, Academy for Educational Development.

Hodge, J., Sanders, K. & Sinclair, A. J. (1993). Different utilization of eicosapentaenoic acid and docosahexaenoic acid human plasma. *Lipids*, **28**: 525–31.

Hoffman, S. M. (1999). After Atlas shrugs: cultural change or persistence after a disaster. In: *The Angry Earth: Disaster in Anthropological Perspective*, ed. A. Oliver-Smith & S. M. Hoffman, pp. 302–25. New York: Routledge.

Holden, C. & Mace, R. (1997). Phylogenetic analysis of the evolution of lactose digestion in adults. *Human Biology*, **69**: 605–28.

(2002). Pastoralism and the evolution of lactase persistence. In: *Human Biology of Pastoral Populations*, ed. W. R. Leonard & M. H. Crawford, pp. 280–307. Cambridge: Cambridge University Press.

Holmes, J. A., Atkinson, T. Darbyshire, D. P. F. *et al.* (2010). Middle Pleistocene climate and hydrological environment at the Boxgrove hominin site (West Sussex, UK) from ostracod records. *Quaternary Science Reviews*, **29**: 1515–27.

Hong, R. (2007). Effect of economic inequality on chronic childhood undernutrition in Ghana. *Public Health Nutrition*, **10**: 371–8.

Horta, B. L., Gigante, B. L., Osmond, C., Barros, F. C. & Victora, C. G. (2009). Intergenerational effect of weight gain in childhood on offspring birthweight. *International Journal of Epidemiology*, **38**: 724–32.

Hristova-Dimceva, A., Verduijn, W., Schipper, R. & Schreuder, G. (2000). HLA-DRB and -DQB1 polymorphism in the Macedonian population. *Tissue Antigens*, **55**: 53–6.

Hu, F. B., Manson, J. E. & Willett, W. C. (2001). Types of dietary fat and risk of coronary heart disease: a critical review. *Journal of the American College of Nutrition*, **20**: 5–19.

Humphrey, L. T. (2010). Weaning behaviour in human evolution. *Seminars in Cell & Developmental Biology*, **21**: 453–61.

Hviid, A. & Melbye, M. (2007). The impact of birth weight on infectious disease hospitalization in childhood. *American Journal of Epidemiology*, **165**(7): 756–61.

Hyndman, D. C. (1979). *Wopkaimin Subsistence: Cultural Ecology in the New Guinea Highland Fringe*. PhD Thesis, University of Queensland, Australia.

    (1982). Biotope gradient in a diversified New Guinea subsistence system. *Human Ecology*, **10**(2): 219–59.

Ichikawa, M. (1981). Ecological and sociological importance of honey to the Mbuti net hunters, eastern Zaire. *African Study Monographs*, **1**: 55–68.

Ingold, T. (1982). Comment on Testart 1982 The significance of food storage among hunter-gatherers: residence patterns, population densities, and social inequalities. *Current Anthropology*, **23**: 523–37.

Ingold, T. & Vergunst, J. (eds) (2007). *Ways of Walking. Ethnography and Practice on Foot. Anthropological Studies of Creativity and Perception*. Aldershot: Ashgate.

Ingold, T., Riches, D. & Woodburn, J. (1997). *Hunters and Gatherers*, Vol **II**: *Property, Power and Ideology*. Oxford: Berg.

Inhorn, M. C. & Brown, P. J. (1990). The anthropology of infectious disease. *Annual Review of Anthropology*, **19**: 89–117.

Institute of Medicine of the National Academies (2002). Dietary fats: total fat and fatty acids. In: *Dietary Reference Intakes for Energy, Carbohydrate, Fiber, Fatty acids, Cholesterol, Protein and Amino Acids (Macronutrients)*, pp. 335–432. Washington, D.C.: The National Academy Press.

International Obesity Task Force (2010). Obesity prevalence data. www.iotf.org. Accessed 5 March 2010.

Isaac, G. L. (1983). Bones in contentions: competing explanations for the juxtaposition of early Pleistocene artifacts and faunal remains. In: *Animals and Archaeology: Hunters and Their Prey*, ed. J. A. Clutton-Brock & C. Grigson, pp. 64–85. Oxford: British Archaeological Reports International Series.

Isaacs, J. D., Stephen, L. & Schroeder, S. A. (2004). Class – the ignored determinant of the nation's health. *New England Journal of Medicine*, **351**: 1137–42.

Isbell, L. A. (1994). Predation on primates: ecological patterns and evolutionary consequences. *Evolutionary Anthropology*, **3**: 61–71.

Isbell, L. A., Pruetz, J. D., Lewis, M. & Young, T. P. (1998). Locomotor activity differences between sympatric patas monkeys (*Erythrocebus patas*) and vervet monkeys (*Cercopithecus aethiops*): implications for the evolution of long hind-limb length in *Homo*. *American Journal of Physical Anthropology*, **105**: 199–207.

Ivanova, M., Rozemuller, E., Tyufekchiev, N. *et al.* (2002). HLA polymorphism in Bulgarians defined by high-resolution typing methods in comparison with other populations. *Tissue Antigens*, **60**: 496–504.

Izaabel, H., Garchon, H., Caillat-Zucman, S. *et al.* (1998). HLA class II DNA polymorphism in a Moroccan population from the Souss, Agadir area. *Tissue Antigens*, **51**: 106–10.

Jablonski, N. G. (2002). Fossil Old World monkeys. In: *The Primate Fossil Record*, ed. W. C. Hartwig, pp. 255–99. Cambridge: Cambridge University Press.

Jackson, F. L. C. (1991). Secondary compounds in plants (allelochemicals) as promotors of human biological variability. *Reviews in Anthropology*, **20**: 505–46.

Jacobs, J. (1961). *The Death and Life of Great American Cities*. New York: Random House.

James, M. J., Gibson, R. A. & Cleland, L. G. (2000). Dietary polyunsaturated PUFAs and inflammatory mediator production. *American Journal of Clinical Nutrition*, **71**: 343S–348S.

James, S. R. (1989). Hominid use of fire in the Lower and Middle Pleistocene: a review of the evidence. *Current Anthropology*, **30**: 1–26.

James, W. P. T., Nelson, M., Ralph, A. & Leather, S. (1997). Socioeconomic determinants of health: the contribution of nutrition to inequalities in health. *British Medical Journal*, **314**: 1545.

Janmaat, K. R. L., Byrne, R. W. & Zuberbuehler, K. (2006). Primates take weather into account when searching for fruits. *Current Biology*, **16**: 1232–7.

Janson, C. J. (1992). Evolutionary ecology of primate social structure. In: *Evolutionary Ecology and Human Behaviour*, ed. B. Winterhalder & E. A. Smith, pp. 95–130. New York: Aldine.

Jarman, P. J. (1974). The social organization of antelope in relation to their ecology. *Behaviour*, **58**: 215–67.

Jeanrenaud, B. & Rohner-Jeanrenaud, F. (2001). Effects of neuropeptides and leptin on nutrient partitioning: dysregulations in obesity. *Annual Review of Medicine*, **52**: 339–51.

Jebb, S. A. (2007). Dietary determinants of obesity. *Obesity Reviews*, **8**(1): S93–S97.

Jehle, S., Zanetti, A., Muser, J., Hulter, H. N. & Krapf, R. (2006). Partial neutralization of the acidogenic western diet with potassium citrate increases bone mass in postmenopausal women with osteopenia. *Journal of the American Society of Nephrology*, **17**: 3213–22.

Jenike, M. (2001). Nutritional ecology: diet, physical activity and body size. In: *Hunter-Gatherers: An Interdisciplinary Perspective*, ed. C. Panter-Brick, R. H. Layton, P. Rowley-Conwy, pp. 205–38. Cambridge: Cambridge University Press.

Jenike, M. R. (1996). Activity reduction as an adaptive response to seasonal hunger. *American Journal of Human Biology*, **8**: 517–34.

Jenkins, D. J. A., Wolever, T. M., Taylor, R. H. *et al.* (1981). Glycemic index of foods: a physiological basis for carbohydrate exchange. *American Journal of Clinical Nutrition*, **34**: 362–6.

Jenkins, D. J., Wolever, T. M. & Collier, C. N. (1987). Metabolic effects of a low-glycaemic diet. *American Journal of Clinical Nutrition*, **46**: 968–75.

Jenkins, S. G., Partridge, S. T., Stephenson, T. R., Farley, S. D. & Robbins, C. T. (2001). Nitrogen and carbon isotope fractionation between mothers, neonates and nursing offspring. *Oecologia*, **129**: 336–341.

Jerlhag, E., Egecioglu, E., Dickson, S. L. *et al.* (2006). Ghrelin stimulates locomotor activity and accumbal dopamine-overflow via central cholinergic systems in mice: implications for its involvement in brain reward. *Addiction Biology*, **11**: 45–54.

Jerlhag, E., Egecioglu, E., Dickson, S. L., Svensson, L. & Engel, J. A. (2008). Alpha-conotoxin MII-sensitive nicotinic acetylcholine receptors are involved in mediating the ghrelin-induced locomotor stimulation and dopamine overflow in nucleus accumbens. *European Neuropsychopharmacology*, **18**: 508–18.

Jeske, R. J. (1996). World systems theory, core periphery interactions and elite economic exchange in Mississippian societies. *Journal of World-Systems Research* 2, Number 10.

Jiang, H., Betancourt, L. & Smith, R. G. (2006). Ghrelin amplifies dopamine signaling by cross talk involving formation of growth hormone secretagogue receptor/dopamine receptor subtype 1 heterodimers. *Molecular Endocrinology*, **20**(8): 1772–85.

Johns, T. (1999). The chemical ecology of human ingestive behaviours. *Annual Reviews of Anthropology*, **28**: 27–50.

Johnson, C. L. *et al.* (1993). Declining serum total cholesterol levels among US adults: the National Health and Nutrition Examination Surveys. *Journal of the American Medical Association*, **269**: 3002–8.

Johnson, E. C. (2007). Rhesus macaques (*Macaca mulatta*) are not neophobic toward novel food with a high sugar content. *American Journal of Primatology*, **69**: 591–6.

Johnson, R. J. & Rideout, B. A. (2004). Uric acid and diet: insights into the epidemic of cardiovascular disease. *New England Journal of Medicine*, **350**: 1071–3.

Johnston, C. S., Tjonn, S. L. & Swan, P. D. (2004). High protein, low fat diets are effective for weight loss and favourably alter biomarkers in healthy adults. *Journal of Nutrition*, **134**: 586–91.

Jolly, C. J. (1970). The seed-eaters: a new model of hominid differentiation based on a baboon analogy. *Man*, **5**: 5–26.

(2001). A proper study for mankind: analogies from the Papionin monkeys and their implications for human evolution. *Yearbook of Physical Anthropology*, **44**: 177–204.

Jones-Engel, L., May, C. C., Engel, G. A. *et al.* (2008). Diverse contexts of zoonotic transmission of Simian Foamy Viruses in Asia. *Emerging Infectious Diseases*, **14**: 1200–8.

Jones-Smith, J., Gordon-Larsen, P., Siddiqi, A. & Popkin, B. M. (2011). Cross-national comparisons of time trends in overweight inequality by socioeconomic status among women using repeated cross-sectional surveys from 37 developing countries, 1989–2007. *American Journal of Epidemiology*, **173**: 667–75.

Jürgens, H., Haass, W., Castañeda, T. R. *et al.* (2005). Consuming fructose-sweetened beverages increases body adiposity in mice. *Obesity Research*, **13**: 1146–56.

Kaaks, R., Toniolo, P., Akhmedkhanov, A. *et al.* (2000). Serum C-peptide, insulin-like growth factor (IGF)-I, IGF-binding proteins, and colorectal cancer risk in women. *Journal of the National Cancer Institute*, **92**: 1592–600.

Kamen, H. (2003). *Empire: How Spain Became a World Power, 1492–1763*. New York: Harper Collins.

Kaplan, H., Hill, K., Lancaster, J. & Hurtado, A. M. (2000). A theory of human life history evolution: diet, intelligence, and longevity. *Evolutionary Anthropology*, **9**: 156–85.

Kappelman, J., Cihat Alçiçek, M., Kazanci, N. *et al.* (2008). Brief communication: First *Homo erectus* from Turkey and implications for migrations into temperate Eurasia. *American Journal of Physical Anthropology*, **135**(1): 110–16.

Karp, R. J. (2005). Malnutrition among children in the United States. The impact of poverty. In: *Modern Nutrition in Health and Disease,* 10th edn, ed. M. E. Shils, M. Shike, A. C. Ross, B. Caballero & R. J. Cousins, pp. 860–74. Baltimore, MD: Williams Wilkins Lippincott.

   (2008). Social class and diet quality. *American Journal of Clinical Nutrition,* **88**: 1177–8.

Karppanen, H. & Mervaala, E. (2006). Sodium intake and hypertension. *Progress in Cardiovascular Diseases,* **49**: 59–75.

Katz, S. H. & Schall, J. (1979). Fava bean consumption and biocultural evolution. *Medical Anthropology,* **3**: 459–76.

Kawachi, I. & Kennedy, B. P. (2002). *The Health of Nations: Why Inequality is Harmful to Your Health.* New York: The New Press.

Kawachi, I., Kennedy, B. P., Lochner, K. & Prothrow-Stith, D. (1997). Social capital, income inequality, and mortality. *American Journal of Public Health,* **87**: 1491–8.

Kay, R. F. (1975). The functional adaptations of primate molar teeth. *American Journal of Physical Anthropology,* **43**: 195–216.

   (1984). On the use of anatomical features to infer foraging behavior in extinct primates. In: *Adaptations for Foraging in Nonhuman Primates,* ed. P. S. Rodman & J. G. H. Cant, pp. 21–53. New York: Columbia University Press.

Kay, R. F. & Sheine, W. S. (1979). On the relationship between chitin particle size and digestibility in the primate *Galago senegalensis. American Journal of Physical Anthropology,* **50**: 301–8.

Keele, B. F., van Heuverswyn, F., Li, Y. *et al.* (2006). Chimpanzee reservoirs of pandemic and nonpandemic HIV-1. *Science,* **313**: 523–6.

Keighley, E. D., McGarvey, S. T., Quested, C. *et al.* (2007). Nutrition and health in modernizing Samoans: temporal trends and adaptive perspectives. In: *Health Change in the Asia-Pacific Region,* ed. R. Ohtsuka and S. Ulijaszek, pp. 147–91. Cambridge: Cambridge University Press.

Kelberman, D., Hawe, E., Luong, L. A. *et al.* (2004). Effect of Interleukin-6 promoter polymorphisms in survivors of myocardial infarction and matched controls in the North and South of Europe. The HIFMECH Study. *Thrombosis and Haemostasis,* **92**(5): 1122–8.

Kelly, M. P., Morgan, A., Bonnefoy, J. *et al.* (2007). *The social determinants of health: developing an evidence base for political action.* Report to WHO by the Measurement and Evidence Knowledge Network. Geneva: World Health Organization.

Kelly, R. L. (1995). *The Foraging Spectrum: Diversity in Hunter-Gatherer Lifeways.* Washington, D.C.: Smithsonian Institution Press.

Kemmler, W., von Stengel, S., Weineck, J., Lauber, D., Kalender, W. & Engelke, K. (2005). Exercise effects on menopausal risk factors of early postmenopausal women: 3-yr EFOPS results. *Medicine and Science in sports and Exercise,* **37**: 194–203.

Kempf, E. (2009). Patterns of water use in primates. *Folia Primatologica,* **80**: 275–94.

Kennedy, E. & Meyers, L. (2005). Dietary Reference Intakes: development and uses for assessment of micronutrient status of women – a global perspective. *American Journal of Clinical Nutrition,* **81**: S1194–S1197.

Kennedy, E., Mannar, V. & Iyengar, V. (2003). Alleviating hidden hunger: approaches that work. *International Atomic Energy Bulletin*, **45**: 54–60.

Kennedy, G. E. (2005). From the ape's dilemma to the weanling's dilemma: early weaning and its evolutionary context. *Journal of Human Evolution*, **48**: 123–45.

Kenney, C. T. (2008). Father doesn't know best? Parents' control of money and children's food insecurity. *Journal of Marriage and the Family*, **70**: 654–9.

Khor, G. L. & Sharif, Z. M. (2003). Dual forms of malnutrition in the same households in Malaysia – a case study among Malay rural households. *Asia Pacific Journal of Clinical Nutrition*, **12**: 427–37.

Kifer, R. R. & Miller, D. (1969). Fish oils – fatty acid composition energy values, metabolism and vitamin content. *Fish Industries*, **5**: 25–6.

Kigutha, H. N., van Staveren, W. A. & Hautvast, J. G. A. J. (1998). Elderly under nutritional stress: a seasonal study on food consumption and nutritional status in Kenya. *International Journal of Food Sciences and Nutrition*, **49**: 423–33.

Kilkenny, M., Strathakis, V., Hibbert, M. *et al.* (1997). Acne in Victorian adolescents: associations with age, gender, puberty and psychiatric symptoms. *Journal of Paediatrics and Child Health*, **33**: 430–4.

Kim, S., Soojae, M. & Popkin, B. M. (2000). The nutrition transition in South Korea. *American Journal of Clinical Nutrition*, **71**: 44–53.

Kim, U. K., Jorgensen, E., Coon, H. *et al.* (2003). Positional cloning of the human quantitative trait locus underlying taste sensitivity to phenylthiocarbamide. *Science*, **299**: 1221–5.

King, J. M. & White, P. J. (1999). Impact of processing on formation of trans fatty acids. *Advances in Experimental Medicine and Biology*, **459**: 51–65.

Kinsella, J. E., Broughton, K. D. S. & Whelan, J. W. (1990a). Dietary unsaturated fatty acids: interactions and possible needs in relation to eicosanoid synthesis. *The Journal of Nutritional Biochemistry*, **1**: 123–40.

Kinsella, J. E., Lokesh, B. & Stone, R. A. (1990b). Dietary n-3 polyunsaturated fatty acids and amelioration of cardiovascular disease: possible mechanisms. *American Journal of Clinical Nutrition*, **52**: 1–28.

Kleiber, M. (1961). *The Fire of Life: An Introduction to Animal Energetics.* New York: Wiley.

Knapp, H. R., Reilly, I. A., Alessandrini, P. & FitzGerald, G. A. (1986). In vivo indexes of platelet and vascular function during fish-oil administration in patients with atherosclerosis. *New England Journal of Medicine*, **314**: 937–42.

Knight, J. C. & Kwiatkowski, D. (1999). Inherited variability of tumor necrosis factor production and susceptibility to infectious disease. *Proceedings for the Association of American Physicians*, **111**: 290–8.

Knott, C. D. (2005). Energetic responses to food availability in the great apes: implications for hominin evolution. In: *Primate Seasonality: Implications for Human Evolution*, ed. D. K. Brockman & C. P. Schaik, pp. 351–78. Cambridge: Cambridge University Press.

Komlos, J. & Baur, M. (2004). From the tallest to (one of) the fattest: the enigmatic fate of the size of the American population in the twentieth century. *Economics and Human Biology*, **2**: 57–74.

Kopp, W. (2004). Nutrition, evolution and thyroid hormone levels – a link to iodine deficiency disorder? *Medical Hypotheses*, **62**: 871–5.

(2006). The atherogenic potential of dietary carbohydrate. *Preventive Medicine*, **42**(5): 336–42.

(2009). Chronically increased activity of the sympathetic nervous system: our diet-related "evolutionary" inheritance. *Journal of Nutritional Health and Aging*, **13**(1): 27–9.

Korstjens, A. H. & Dunbar, R. I. M. (2007). Time constraints limit group sizes and distribution in red and black-and-white colobus monkeys. *International Journal of Primatology*, **28**: 551–75.

Kramer, K. (2009). Does it take a family to raise a child? Cooperative breeding and the contributions of Maya siblings, parents and older adults in raising children. In: *Substitute Parents: Biological and Social Perspectives on Alloparenting in Human Societies*, ed. G. Bentley & R. Mace, pp. 77–99. Oxford: Berghan Books.

Kramer, M. & Victora, C. (2001). *Low Birth Weight and Perinatal Mortality: Nutrition and Health in Developing Countries*. Clifton: Humana Press.

Kramer, M. S. (1987). Determinants of low birth weight: methodological assessment and meta-analysis. *Bulletin of the World Health Organization*, **65**(5): 663–737.

Krause, R. M. (ed.) (1998). *Emerging Infections*. New York: Academic Press.

Krauss, R. M. (2001). Dietary and genetic effects on low density lipoprotein heterogeneity. *Annual Review of Nutrition*, **21**: 283–95.

Kris-Etherton, P. M., Taylor, D. S., Yu-Peth, S. *et al.* (2000). Polyunsaturated PUFAs in the food chain in the USA. *American Journal of Clinical Nutrition*, **71**: 179S–188S.

Krokowski, M., Bodalski, J., Bratek, A., Boitard, C. & Caillat-Zucman, S. (1998). HLA class II allele and haplotype distribution in a population from central Poland. *European Journal of Immunogenetics*, **25**: 5–9.

Kromann, N. & Green, A. (1980). Epidemiological studies in the Upernavik district, Greenland: incidence of some chronic diseases 1950–1974. *Acta Medica Scandinavica*, **208**: 401–6.

Kuijt, I. (2008). Demography and storage systems during the Southern Levantine Neolithic demographic transition. In: *The Neolithic Demographic Transition and its Consequences*, eds. J. P. Bocquet-Appel & O. Bar-Yosef, pp. 257–313. Berlin: Springer.

Kullmer, O., Sandrock, O., Abel, R. *et al.* (1999). The first *Paranthropus* from the Malawi Rift. *Journal of Human Evolution*, **37**: 121–7.

Kuman, K. & Clarke, R. J. (2000). Stratigraphy, artefact industries and hominid associations for Sterkfontein, Member 5. *Journal of Human Evolution*, **38**: 827–47.

Kumar, V., Sinha, A. K., Makkar, P. S. & Becker, K. (2010). Dietary roles of phytate and phytase in human nutrition: a review. *Food Chemistry*, **120**: 945–59.

Kupczik, K. (2008). Virtual biomechanics: basic concepts and technical aspects of finite element analysis in vertebrate morphology. *Journal of Anthropological Sciences*, **86**: 193–8.

Kurlansky, M. (2002). *Salt: A World History*. New York: Walker and Company.

Kuzawa, C. W. (2007). Developmental origins of life history: growth, productivity, and reproduction. *American Journal of Human Biology*, **19**: 654–61.

Kuzawa, C. W. & Quinn, E. A. (2009). Developmental origins of adult function and health: evolutionary hypotheses. *Annual Review of Anthropology*, **38**: 131–47.

Kuzmin, Y. V. (2006). Chronology of the earliest pottery in East Asia: progress and pitfalls. *Antiquity*, **80**: 362–71.

Kwiatkowski, D. P. (2005). How malaria has affected the human genome and what human genetics can teach us about malaria. *American Journal of Human Genetics*, **77**: 171–92.

Laden, G. & Wrangham, R. (2005). The rise of the hominids as an adaptive shift in fallback foods: plant underground storage organs (USOs) and australopith origins. *Journal of Human Evolution*, **49**: 482–98.

Ladio, A. H. & Lozada, M. (2009). Human ecology, ethnobotany and traditional practices in rural populations inhabiting the Monte region: resilience and ecological knowledge. *Journal of Arid Environments*, **73**: 222–7.

Ladipo, O. A. (2000). Nutrition in pregnancy: mineral and vitamin supplements. *American Journal of Clinical Nutrition*, **72**(1): S280–S290.

Lahnsteiner, F., Mansour, N. & Caberlotto, S. (2010). Composition and metabolism of carbohydrates and lipids in *Sparus autata* semen and its relation to viability expressed as sperm motility when activated. *Comparative Biochemistry and Physiology B*, **157**(1): 39–45.

Laidlaw, S. A., Shultz, T. D., Cecchino, J. T. & Kopple, J. D. (1988). Plasma and urine taurine levels in vegans. *American Journal of Clinical Nutrition*, **47**: 660–3.

Laland, K. N. & Kendal, B. (2007). The niche construction perspective. *Journal of Evolutionary Psychology*, **5**: 51–66.

Laland, K. N., Odling-Smee, F. J. & Feldman, M. W. (1999). Evolutionary consequences of niche construction and their implications for ecology. *Proceedings of the National Academy of Sciences, USA*, **96**: 10242–7.

Lallo, J., Armelagos, G. J. & Mensforth, R. (1977). The role of diet, disease and physiology in the origins of porotic hyperostosis. *Human Biology*, **49**: 471–83.

Lambert, J. E. (1997). *Digestive Strategies, Fruit Processing, and Seed Dispersal in the Chimpanzees (Pan troglodytes) and Redtail Monkeys (Cercopithecus ascanius) of Kibale National Park, Uganda*. PhD Dissertation, University of Illinois, Urbana-Champaign.

   (1998). Primate digestion: interactions among anatomy, physiology, and feeding ecology. *Evolutionary Anthropology*, **7**: 8–20.

   (2002). Digestive retention times in forest guenons (*Cercopithecus* spp.) with reference to chimpanzees (*Pan troglodytes*). *International Journal of Primatology*, **23**: 1169–85.

   (2005). Competition, predation and the evolutionary significance of the cercopithecine cheek pouch: the case of *Cercopithecus* and *Lophocebus*. *American Journal of Physical Anthropology*, **126**: 183–92.

Lambert, J. E., Chapman, C. A., Wrangham, R. W. & Conklin-Brittain, N. L. (2004). Hardness of cercopithecine foods: implications for the critical function of enamel thickness in exploiting fallback foods. *American Journal of Physical Anthropology*, **125**: 363–8.

Lambert, P. M. (2009). Health versus fitness: competing themes in the origins and spread of agriculture? *Current Anthropology*, **50**(5): 603–8.

Lands, B. (2008). A critique of paradoxes in current advice on dietary lipids. *Progress in Lipid Research*, **47**: 77–106.

Lands, W. E. M. (1986a). *Fish and Human Health*. Orlando, FL: Academic Press. (1986b). Renewed questions about polyunsaturated fatty acids. *Nutrition Reviews*, **44**: 189–94.

Lands, W. E., Morris, A. & Libelt, B. (1990). Quantitative effects of dietary polyunsaturated fats on the composition of fatty acids in rat tissues. *Lipids*, **25**: 505–16.

Larsen, C. S. (1987). Bioarchaeological interpretations of subsistence economy and behavior from human skeletal remains. *Advances in Archaeological Methods and Theory*, **10**: 339–445.

Latour, B. (2003). The promises of constructivism. In: *Chasing Technoscience: Matrix for Materiality*, ed. D. Ihde, pp. 27–46. Indiana: Indiana University Press.

Law, C. M., Shiell, A. W., Newsome, C. W. *et al.* (2002). Fetal, infant, and childhood growth and adult blood pressure: a longitudinal study. Study from birth to 22 years of age. *Circulation*, **105**: 1088–92.

Lawlor, D. A., Davey-Smith, G., Kundu, D., Bruckdorfer, K. R. & Ebrahim, S. (2004). Those confounded vitamins: what can we learn from the differences between observational versus randomised trial evidence? *Lancet*, **363**: 1724–7.

Le Gros Clark, W. E. (1959). *The Antecedents of Man. An Introduction to the Evolution of the Primates*. Edinburgh: Edinburgh University Press.

Leakey, L. S. B. (1960). The newest link in human evolution: the discovery by L. S. B. Leakey of *Zinjanthropus boisei*. *Current Anthropology*, **1**: 76–7.

Lee, A. J., O'Dea, K. & Mathews, J. D. (1994). Apparent dietary intake in remote aboriginal communities. *Australian Journal of Public Health*, **18**(2): 190–7.

Lee, R. B. (1968). What hunters do for a living, or, how to make out on scarce resources. In: *Man the Hunter*, ed. R. B. Lee & I. DeVore, pp. 30–48. Chicago, IL: Aldine.

Lee, R. B. & De Vore, I. (1968). *Man the Hunter*. Chicago, IL: Aldine.

Lee-Thorp, J. A. (2011). The demise of Nutcracker Man. *Proceedings of the National Academy of Sciences, USA*, **108**(24): 9319–20.

Lee-Thorp, J. A. & Van der Merwe, N. J. (1987). Carbon isotope analysis of fossil bone apatite. *South African Journal of Science*, **83**: 712–13.

Lee-Thorp, J. A., Sponheimer, M., Van der Merwe, N. J. (2003). What do stable isotopes tell us about hominid dietary and ecological niches in the Pliocene? *International Journal of Osteoarchaeology*, **13**: 104–13.

Lee-Thorp, J. A., Van der Merwe, N. J. & Brain, C. K. (1989). Isotopic evidence for dietary differences between two extinct baboon species from Swartkrans. *Journal of Human Evolution*, **18**: 183–90.

Lee-Thorp, J. A., Van der Merwe, N. J. & Brain, C. K. (1994). Diet of *Australopithecus robustus* at Swartkrans from stable carbon isotopic analysis. *Journal of Human Evolution*, **27**: 361–72.

Leibermann, L. S. (1987). Biocultural consequences of animals versus plants as sources of fats, protein and other nutrients. In: *Diet and Human Evolution*, ed. M. Harris & E. B. Ross, pp. 225–60. Philadelphia, PA: Temple University Press.

Lenoir, M., Serre, F., Cantin, L. & Ahmed, S. H. (2007). Intense sweetness surpasses cocaine reward. *PLoS ONE*, **2**(8): e698–e707.

Lenski, G. and Nolan, P. D. (1984). Trajectories of development: a test of ecological evolutionary theory. *Social Forces*, **63**: 1–23.

Leonard, W. R. (1991). Age and sex differences in the impact of seasonal energy stress among Andean agriculturalists. *Human Ecology*, **19**: 351–68.

Levant, B., Ozias, M. K., Davis, P. F. *et al.* (2008). Decreased brain docosahexaenoic acid content produces neurobiological effects associated with depression: interactions with reproductive status in female rats. *Psychoneuroendocrinology*, **33**: 1279–92.

Levine, A. S., Kotz, C. M. & Gosnell, B. A. (2003). Sugars and fats: the neurobiology of preference. *Journal of Nutrition*, **133**(3): S831–S834.

Levi-Strauss, C. (1970). *The Raw and the Cooked*. London: Cape.

Lewallen, S., Lowdon, R., Courtright, P & Mehl, G. L. (1995). A population-based survey of the prevalence of refractive error in Malawi. *Ophthalmic Epidemiology*, **2**: 145–9.

Ley, R. E. *et al.* (2005). Obesity alters gut microbial ecology. *Proceedings of the National Academy of Sciences, USA*, **102**(31): 11070–5.

Li, D., Sinclair, A., Wilson, A. *et al.* (1999). Effect of dietary alpha-linolenic acid on thrombotic risk factors in vegetarian men. *American Journal of Clinical Nutrition*, **69**: 872–82.

Li, M., Eastman, C. J., Waite, K. V. *et al.* (2006). Are Australian children iodine deficient? Results of the Australian National Nutritional Iodine Nutrition Study. *Medical Journal of Australia*, **184**: 165–9.

Li, M., Ma, G., Boyages, S. C. & Eastman, C. J. (2001). Re-emergence of iodine deficiency in Australia. *Asia Pacific Journal of Clinical Nutrition*, **10**: 200–3.

Lidén, K., Eriksson, G., Nordquist, B., Gotherstrom, A. & Bendixen, F. (2004). 'The Wet and the Wild followed by the Dry and the Tame' – or did they occur at the same time? Diet in Mesolithic – Neolithic Southern Sweden. *Antiquity*, **78**: 23–33.

Lieberman, D. E. (1993). The rise and fall of seasonal mobility among hunter-gatherers: the case of the Southern Levant. *Current Anthropology*, **34**: 599–631.

(2009). Palaeoanthropology: *Homo floresiensis* from head to toe. *Nature*, **459**: 41–2.

Lieberman, M. & Lieberman, D. (1978). Lactase deficiency: a genetic mechanism which regulates the time of weaning. *American Naturalist*, **985**: 625–7.

Lillioja, S., Nyomba, B. L., Saad, M. F. *et al.* (1991). Exaggerated early insulin release and insulin resistance in a diabetes-prone population: a metabolic comparison of Pima Indians and Caucasians. *Journal of Clinical Endocrinology and Metabolism*, **73**: 866–76.

Lind, P., Kuming, G., Heinisch, M. *et al.* (2002). Iodine supplementation in Australia: methods and results. *Thyroid*, **12**: 903–7.

Lindeberg, S. (2010). *Food and Western Disease: Health and Nutrition from an Evolutionary Perspective*. Oxford: Wiley-Blackwell.

Lindstedt, S. L. & Boyce, M. S. (1985). Seasonality, fasting endurance, and body size in mammals. *American Naturalist*, **125**: 873.

Lipsitch, M. & Sousa, A. O. (2002). Historical intensity of natural selection for resistance to tuberculosis. *Genetics*, **161**: 1599–607.

Little, M. A. (1989). Human biology of pastoralist populations. *Yearbook of Physical Anthropology*, **32**: 215–47.

(2002). Human biology, health and ecology of nomadic Turkana Pastoralists. In: *Human Biology of Pastoral Populations*, ed. W. R. Leonard and M. H. Crawford, pp. 151–82. Cambridge: Cambridge University Press.

Liu, S. (1998). Insulin resistance, hyperglycemia and risk of major chronic diseases: a dietary perspective. *Proceedings of the Nutrition Society of Australia*, pp. 140–67.

Liu, S. & Willett, W. C. (2002). Dietary glycaemic load and atherothrombotic risk. *Current Atherosclerosis Reports*, **4**: 454–61.

Liu, S., Willett, W. C., Stampfer, M. J. *et al.* (2000). A prospective study of dietary glycaemic load, carbohydrate intake, and risk of coronary heart disease in US women. *American Journal of Clinical Nutrition*, **71**: 1455–61.

Liu, W., Li, Y., Learn, G. H. *et al.* (2010). Origin of the human malaria parasite *Plasmodium falciparum* in gorillas. *Nature*, **467**: 420–5.

Liu, Y. X., Li, H. Q., Yang, X. Q. & Karlberg, J. (1999). Early linear growth retardation in Chongqing, China. *Journal of Paediatric Child Health*, **35**: 272–7.

Lomas, J. (1998). Social capital and health: implications for public health and epidemiology. *Social Science and Medicine*, **47**: 1181–8.

Long, A. B., Kuhn, C. M. & Platt, M. L. (2009). Serotonin shapes risky decision making in monkeys. *Social Cognitive and Affective Neuroscience,* **4**: 346–56.

Longhurst, R. (1986). Seasonality and poverty: implications for policy and research. *Institute of Development Studies Bulletin*, **17**(3): 67–71.

Long-Solís, J. & Vargas, L. A. (2005). *Food Culture in Mexico*. London: Greenwood Press.

Louie, L. G., Hartogensis, W. E., Jackman, R. P. *et al.* (2004). Mycobacterium tuberculosis/HIV-1 coinfection and disease: role of human leukocyte antigen variation. *Journal of Infectious Diseases*, **189**: 1084–91.

Lubchenco, L. O., Searls, D. T. & Brazie, J. V. (1972). Neonatal mortality rate: relationship to birth weight and gestational age. *Journal of Pediatrics*, **81**: 814–22.

Lucas, A., Fewtrell, M. S. & Cole, T. J. (1999). Fetal origins of adult disease – the hypothesis revisited. *British Medical Journal*, **319**: 245–9.

Lucas, P. W. (2004). *Dental Functional Morphology: How Teeth Work*. New York: Cambridge University Press.

Ludwig, D. S. (2002). The glycemic index: pathophysiological mechanisms relating obesity, diabetes, and cardiovascular disease. *Journal of the American Medical Association*, **287**: 2414–23.

Ludwig, D. S., Majzoub, J. A., Al-Zahrani, A. *et al.* (1999). High glycaemic index foods, overeating, and obesity. *Paediatrics*, **103**: E26.

Lunn, P. G. (2000). The impact of infection and nutrition on gut function and growth in childhood. *Proceedings of the Nutrition Society*, **59**: 147–54.

Lyson, T. A. & Raymer, A. L. (2000). Stalking the wily multinational: power and control in the US food system. *Agriculture and Human Values*, **17**: 199–208.

Macarthur, R. & Pianka, E. R. (1966). On optimal use of a patchy environment. *American Naturalist*, **100**: 603–9.

Macaulay, V., Hill, C. & Achilli, A. (2005). Single, rapid coastal settlement of Asia revealed by analysis of complete mitochondrial genomes. *Science*, **308**: 1034–6.

Macchiarelli, R., Bondioli, L., Falk, D. *et al.* (2004). Early Pliocene hominid tooth from Galili, Somali Region, Ethiopia. *Collegium Antropologicum*, **28**: 65–76.

Macho, G. A. & Shimizu, D. (2010). Kinematic parameters inferred from enamel microstructure: new insights into the diet of *Australopithecus anamensis*. *Journal of Human Evolution*, **58**: 23–32.

Macho, G. A., Shimizu, D., Jiang, Y. & Spears, I. R. (2005). *Australopithecus anamensis*: a finite-element approach to studying the functional adaptations of extinct hominins. *The Anatomical Record Part A: Discoveries in Molecular, Cellular, and Evolutionary Biology*, **283A**(2): 310–18.

Macho, G. *et al.* (1996). Climatic effects on dental development of Theropithecus oswaldi from Koobi Fora and Olorgesailie. *Journal of Human Evolution*, **30**: 57–70.

MacNeish, R. S. (1992). *The Origins of Agriculture and Settled Life*. Norman, OK: University of Oklahoma Press.

Madsen, L., Pedersen, L. M., Laiset, B. *et al.* (2008). cAMP-dependent signaling regulates the adipogenic effect of n-6 polyunsaturated fatty acids. *Journal of Biological Chemistry*, **283**(11): 7196–205.

Magallón, S. (2010). Using fossils to break long branches in molecular dating: a comparison of relaxed clocks applied to the origin of angiosperms. *Systematic Biology*, **59**(4): 384–99.

Mahfouz, M. (1981). Effect of dietary trans fatty acids on the delta 5, delta 6 and delta 9 desaturases of rat liver in microsomes in vivo. *Acta Biologica et Medica Germanica*, **40**: 1699–705.

Mair, S. M. & Weiss, G. (2009). New pharmacological concepts for the treatment of iron overload disorders. *Current Medicinal Chemistry*, **16**(5): 576–90.

Mak, W., Kwan, M. W. M., Cheng, T. S. *et al.* (2006). Myopia as a latent phenotype of a pleiotropic gene positively selected for facilitating neurocognitive development, and the effects of environmental factors in its expression. *Medical Hypotheses*, **66**: 1209–15.

Maluccio, J., Haddad, L. & May, J. (1999). *Social capital and income generation in South Africa, 1993–98*. Discussion Paper No. 71. Washington, D.C.: International Food Policy Research Institute.

Mann, G. V., Scott, E. M., Hursch, L. M. *et al.* (1962). The health and nutritional status of Alaskan Eskimos. A survey of the Interdepartmental Committee on Nutrition for National Defence, 1958. *American Journal of Clinical Nutrition*, **11**: 31–9.

Mann, N. J. (2000). Dietary lean red meat and human evolution. *European Journal of Nutrition*, **39**: 71–9.

   (2005). Omega-3 fatty acids from red meat in the Australian diet. *Lipid Technology*, **17**: 79–82.

Mann, N. J., Pirotta, Y., O'Connell, S. *et al.* (2006). Fatty acid composition of habitual omnivore and vegetarian diets. *Lipids*, **41**: 637–46.

Marean, C. W., Bar-Matthews, M., Bernatchez, J. *et al.* (2007). Early human use of marine resources and pigment in South Africa during the Middle Pleistocene. *Nature*, **449**: 905–8.

Margen, S., Chu, J. Y., Kaufmann, N. A. & Calloway, D. H. (1974). Studies in calcium metabolism. 1: The calciuretic effect of dietary protein. *American Journal of Clinical Nutrition*, **27**: 584–9.

Marín Arroyo, A. B. (2009). Assessing what lies beneath the spatial distribution of a zooarchaeological record. The use of GIS and spatial correlations at El Mirón Cave (Spain). *Archaeometry* doi: 10.1111/j.1475–4754.2008.00411.

Marlowe, F. W. (2002). Why the Hadza are still hunter-gatherers. In: *Ethnicity, Hunter Gatherers and the 'Other'*, ed. S. Kent, pp. 247–75. Washington, D.C.: Smithsonian Institution Press.

Marlowe, F. W. & Berbesque, J. C. (2009). Tubers as fallback foods and their impact on Hadza hunter-gatherers. *American Journal of Physical Anthropology*, **140**: 751–8.

Marmot, M. (1986). Social inequalities in mortality. In: *Class and Health: Research and Longitudinal Data*, ed. R. G. Wilkinson, pp. 21–34. London: Tavistock Press.

(2004). *Status Syndrome – How Your Social Standing Directly Affects Your Health and Life Expectancy*. London: Bloomsbury Press.

(2005). Social determinants of health inequalities. *Lancet*, **365**: 1099–104.

Marmot, M., Ryff, C. D., Bumpass, L. L., Shipley, M. & Marks, N. F. (1997). Social inequalities in health: next questions and converging evidence. *Social Science and Medicine*, **44**(6): 901–10.

Marshall, A. & Wrangham, R. (2007). Evolutionary consequences of fallback foods. *International Journal of Primatology*, **28**: 1219–35.

Marshall, A. J., Boyko, C. M., Feilen, K. L., Boyko, R. H. & Leighton, M. (2009). Defining fallback foods and assessing their importance in primate ecology and evolution. *American Journal of Physical Anthropology*, **140**: 603–14.

Marshalle, R. O. & Kooi, E. R. (1957). Enzymatic conversion of D-glucose to D-fructose. *Science*, **125**(3249): 648–9.

Martin, B., Maudsley, S., White, C. M. & Egan, J. M. (2009). Hormones in the naso-oropharynx: endocrine modulation of taste and smell. *Trends in Endocrinology and Metabolism*, **20**: 163–70.

Martin, F. P. J., Dumas, M. E., Wang, Y. *et al.* (2007). A top-down systems biology view of microbiome-mammalian metabolic interactions in a mouse model. *Molecular Systems Biology*, **3**: 1–16.

Martin, J. F., Johnston, C. S., Han, C.-T. *et al.* (2000). Nutritional origins of insulin resistance: a rat model for diabetes-prone human populations. *Journal of Nutrition*, **130**: 741–4.

Martin, R. D. (1993). Scaling. In: *The Cambridge Encyclopedia of Human Evolution*, ed. S. Jones, R. Martin & D. Pilbeam, p. 42. Cambridge: Cambridge University Press.

(1996). Scaling of the mammalian brain: the maternal energy hypothesis. *News in Physiological Sciences*, **11**: 149–56.

Martinez-Laso, J., Gazit, E., Gomez-Casado, E. *et al.* (1996). HLA DR and DQ polymorphism in Ashkenazi and non-Ashkenazi Jews: comparison with other Mediterraneans. *Tissue Antigens*, **47**: 63–71.

Martorell, R., Mendoza, F. & Castillo, R. (1988). Poverty and stature in children. In: *Linear Growth Retardation in Less Developed Countries*, ed. J. C. Waterlow, pp. 57–70. New York: Raven Press.

Massey, L. K. & Whiting, S. J. (1995). Dietary salt, urinary calcium and kidney stone risk. *Nutrition Review*, **53**: 131–9.

Masterson, T. J. (1997). Sexual dimorphism and interspecific cranial form in two capuchin species: *Cebus albifrons* and *C. apella*. *American Journal of Physical Anthropology*, **104**: 487–511.

Mata, L. J. (1978). *The Children of Santa Maria Cauque: A Prospective Field Study of Health and Growth*. Cambridge, MA: MIT Press.

Mathias, M. M. & Dupont, J. (1989). Effects of dietary fat on eicosanoid production in normal tissues. In: *Carcinogenesis and Dietary Fat*, ed. S. Abraham, pp. 29–52. Boston, MA: Kluwer Academic Publishers.

Mathieu, G., Denis, S., Lavialle, M. & Vancassel, S. (2008). Synergistic effects of stress and omega-3 fatty acid deprivation on emotional response and brain lipid composition in adult rats. *Prostaglandins, Leukotrienes, and Essential Fatty Acids*, **78**: 391–401.

Mayes, P. A. (1993). Intermediary metabolism of fructose. *American Journal of Clinical Nutrition*, **58**: 754S–765S.

McCann, J. C. & Ames, B. N. (2005). Is docosahexaenoic acid, an n–3 long-chain polyunsaturated fatty acid, required for development of normal brain function? An overview of evidence from cognitive and behavioral tests in humans and animals. *American Journal of Clinical Nutrition*, **82**: 281–95.

McCarthy, H. (1993). Managing oaks and the acorn crop. In: *Before the Wilderness: Environmental Management by Native Californians*, ed. T. C. Blackburn & K. Anderson, pp. 213–38. Menlo Park, CA: Ballena Press.

McClain, D. A. (2002). Hexosamines as mediators of nutrient sensing and regulating in diabetes. *Journal of Diabetes Complications*, **16**: 72–80.

McCorriston, J. & Hole, F. (1991). The ecology of seasonal stress and the origins of agriculture in the Near East. *American Anthropologist*, **93**: 46–69.

McElduff, A. & Beange, H. (2004). Iodine deficiency in Australia: be alarmed. Opinions and perspectives. *Journal of Intellectual and Developmental Disability*, **29**: 85–7.

McGovern, P. E., Zhang, J., Tang, J. *et al.* (2004). Fermented beverages of pre- and proto-historic China. *Proceedings of the National Academy of Sciences, USA*, **101**: 17593–8.

McGrew, W. (1999). Comment on Wrangham *et al.* 1999: The raw and the stolen. *Current Anthropology*, **40**: 567–94.

McGuire, W. *et al.* (1994). Variation in the TNF-alpha promoter region associated with susceptibility to cerebral malaria. *Nature*, **371**: 508–10.

McKenna, P., Hoffmann, C., Minkah, N. *et al.* (2008). The macaque gut microbiome in health, lentiviral infection, and chronic enterocolitis. *PLoS Pathog*, **4**(2): e20. doi:10.1371/journal.ppat.0040020.

McKeown-Eyssen, G. (1994). Epidemiology of colorectal cancer revisited: are serum triglycerides and/or plasma glucose associated with risk? *Cancer Epidemiology, Biomarkers and Prevention*, **3**: 687–95.

McLaren, L. (2007). Socioeconomic status and obesity. *Epidemiologic Reviews*, doi:10.1093/epirev/mxm001.

McMichael, A. & Githeko, A. (2001). Human health. In: *Climate Change 2001: Impacts, Adaptation, and Vulnerability*, ed. J. J. McCarthy *et al.* pp. 451–86. Cambridge: Cambridge University Press.

McMillan-Price, J., Petocz, P. & Atkinson, F. (2006). Comparison of 4 diets of varying glycemic load on weight loss and cardiovascular risk reduction in overweight and obese young adults: a randomized controlled trial. *Archives of Internal Medicine*, **166**: 1466–75.

McPherron, S. P., Alemseged, Z., Marean, C. W. *et al.* (2010). Evidence for stone-tool-assisted consumption of animal tissues before 3.39 million years ago at Dikika, Ethiopia. *Nature*, **466**: 857–60.

Mead, J. F., Alfin-Slater, R. B., Howton, D. R. & Popják, G. (1986). *Lipids: Chemistry, Biochemistry and Nutrition*. New York: Plenum Press.

Meehan, B. (1982). *Shell Bed to Shell Midden*. Canberra, Australia: Australian Institute of Aboriginal Studies.

Mela, D. (1996). Eating behaviour, food preferences and dietary intake in relation to obesity and body-weight status. *Proceedings of the Nutrition Society*, **55**: 803–16.

Mela, D. J. & Catt, S. (1996). Ontogeny of human taste and smell preferences and their implications for food selection. In: *Long-Term Consequences of Early Environment: Growth, Development and the Lifespan Development Perspective*, ed. C. J. K. Henry & S. J. Ulijazek, pp. 139–54. Cambridge: Cambridge University Press.

Mellaart, J. (1967). *Catal Huyuk: A Neolithic Town in Anatolia*. London: Thames and Hudson.

Mennel, S. (1996). *All Manners of Food: Eating and Taste in England and France from the Middle Ages to the Present*, 2nd edn. Chicago, IL: University of Illinois Press.

Mensink, R. P. & Katan, M. B. (1992). Effect of dietary fatty acids on serum lipids and lipoproteins. *Arteriosclerosis and Thrombosis*, **12**: 911–19.

Mercader, J., Bennett, T. & Raja, M. (2008). Middle Stone Age starch acquisition in the Niassa Rift, Mozambique. *Quaternary Research*, **70**: 283–300.

Mery, F. & Burns, J. (2010). Behavioural plasticity: an interaction between evolution and experience. *Evolutionary Ecology*, **24**: 571–83.

Meyer, M. C., Sherman, W. L. & Deeds, S. M. (2002). *The Course of Mexican History*, 7th edn. Oxford: Oxford University Press.

Milanovic, B. (2005). *Worlds Apart. Measuring International and Global Inequality*. Princeton, NJ: Princeton University Press.

Mills, A. & Milewski, A. (2007). Geophagy and nutrient supplementation in the Ngorongoro Conservation Area, Tanzania, with particular reference to selenium, cobalt and molybdenum. *Journal of Zoology*, **271**: 110–18.

Milner, N., Craig, O. E., Bailey, G. N., Pedersen, K. & Andersen, S. H. (2004). Something fishy in the Neolithic? A re-evaluation of stable isotope analysis of mesolithic and neolithic coastal populations. *Antiquity*, **78**: 9–22.

Milton, K. (1984). The role of food processing factors in primate food choice. In: *Adaptations for Foraging in Non-Human Primates: Contributions to an*

Organismal Biology of Prosimians, Monkeys and Apes, ed. P. S. Rodman & J. G. H. Cant, pp. 249–79. New York: Columbia University Press.

(1987). Primate diets and gut morphology: implications for human evolution. In: *Food and Evolution: Toward a Theory of Human Food Habits*, ed. M. Harris & E. B. Ross, pp. 93–116. Philadelphia, PA: Temple University Press.

(1988). Foraging behaviour and the evolution of primate intelligence. In *Machiavellian Intelligence*, ed. R. W. Byrne & A. Whiten, pp. 285–305. Oxford: Clarendon Press.

(1999a). Nutritional characteristics of wild primate foods: do the diets of our closest living relatives have lessons for us? *Nutrition*, **15**: 488–98.

(1999b). A hypothesis to explain the role of meat-eating in human evolution. *Evolutionary Anthropology*, **8**: 11–21.

(2000a). Hunter-gatherer diets – a different perspective. *American Journal of Clinical Nutrition*, **71**: 665–7.

(2000b). Back to basics: why foods of wild primates have relevance for modern human health. *Nutrition*, **16**: 480–3.

(2003). The critical role played by animal source foods in human (*Homo*) evolution. *Journal of Nutrition*, **133**: S3886–S3892.

(2004). Ferment in the family tree: does a frugivorous dietary heritage influence contemporary patterns of human ethanol use? *Integrative and Comparative Biology*, **44**: 304–14.

Minnegal, M. & Dwyer, P. D. (2007). Foragers, farmers and fishers: responses to environmental perturbation. *Journal of Political Ecology*, **14**: 34–57.

Mintz, S. W. (1985). *Sweetness and Power: Place of Sugar in Modern History*. London: Penguin.

Mitchikpe, C. E. S., Dossa, R. A. M., Ategbo, E. A. D., Van Raaij, J. M. A. & Kok, F. J. (2009). Seasonal variation in food pattern but not in energy and nutrient intakes of rural Beninese school-aged children. *Public Health Nutrition*, **12**: 414–22.

Mohan, S. & Campbell, N. R. (2009). Salt and high blood pressure. *Clinical Science*, **117**(1): 1–11.

Moller, M., de Wit, E. & Hoal, E. G. (2010). Past, present and future directions in human genetic susceptibility to tuberculosis. *FEMS Immunology and Medical Microbiology*, **58**: 3–26.

Molloy, A. M. (2004). Genetic variation and nutritional requirements. *World Review of Nutrition and Dietetics*, **93**: 153–63.

Moodley, Y., Linz, B., Yamaoka, Y. *et al.* (2009). The peopling of the Pacific from a bacterial perspective. *Science*, **323**: 527–30.

Mooney, J. (1910). Kaskaskia Indians. In: *The Catholic Encyclopedia*, ed. C. G. Herbermann *et al.* New York: The Robert Appleton Company. Retrieved March 26, 2012 from New Advent: http//www.newadvent.org/cathen/086086.htm.

Moore, M. S. (2000). Interactions between physical activity and diet in the regulation of body weight. *Proceedings of the Nutrition Society*, **59**: 193–8.

Moore, S. R., Lima, A. A. M., Conaway, M. R. *et al.* (2001). Early childhood diarrhoea and helminthiases associate with long-term linear growth faltering. *International Journal of Epidemiology*, **30**: 1457–64.

Moran, A., Jacobs, D. J., Steinberger, J. *et al.* (1999). Insulin resistance during puberty: results from clamp studies in 357 children. *Diabetes*, **48**: 2039–44.

Morens, D. M., Folkers, G. K. & Fauci, A. S. (2004). The challenge of emerging and re-emerging infectious diseases. *Nature*, **430**: 242–9.

Morgan, D. & Sanz, C. (2006). Chimpanzee feeding ecology and comparison with sympatric gorillas in the Goualougo Triangle, Republic of Congo. In: *Feeding Ecology in Apes and Other Primates*, ed. G. Hohmann, M. M. Robbins & C. Boesch, pp. 97–122. Cambridge: Cambridge University Press.

Morgan, S. A., Sinclair, A. J. & O'Dea, K. (1993). Effect on serum lipids of addition of safflower oil or olive oil to very-low-fat diets rich in lean beef. *Journal of the American Dietetic Association*, **93**: 644–8.

Morris, S. D. (1999). Reforming the nation: Mexican nationalism in context. *Journal of Latin American Studies*, **31**: 363–97.

Mozaffararian, D., Katan, M. B., Ascherio, A., Stampfer, M. J. & Willet, W. C. (2006). Trans fatty acids and cardiovascular disease. *New England Journal of Medicine*, **354**: 1601–13.

Muccioli, G. G., Naslain, D., Backhed, F. *et al.* (2010). The endocannabinoid system links gut microbiota to adipogenesis. *Molecular Systems Biology*, **6**: 392.

Mueller, H. P., Kock, C., Seiler, E. & Arpagaus, B. (1999). *Atlas vorkolonialer Gesellschaften. Sozialstrukturen und kulturelles Erbe der Staaten Afrikas, Asiens und Melanesiens*. Berlin: Reimer.

Müller, H., Kirkhus, B. & Pedersen, J. I. (2001). Serum cholesterol predictive equations with special emphasis on trans and saturated fatty acids: an analysis from designed controlled studies. *Lipids*, **36**(8): 783–91.

Murdock, G. P. (1967). Ethnographic atlas: a summary. *Ethnology*, **6**: 109–236.

Murphy, K. P., Traver, P. & Walport, M. *et al.* (2008). *Janeway's Immunobiology*. Abingdon, UK: Garland Science.

Murray, C. J. L., King, G., Lopez, A. D., Tomijima, N. & Krug, E. G. (2002). Armed conflict as public health problem. *British Medical Journal*, **324**: 346–9.

Murtaugh, M. A., Jacobs, D. R., Moran, A., Steinberger, J. & Sinaiko, A. R. (2003). Relation of birth weight to fasting insulin, insulin resistance, and body size in adolescence. *Diabetes Care*, **26**: 187–91.

Nakagawa, N. (2008). Despotic wild patas monkeys (*Erythrocebus patas*) in Kala Maloue, Cameroon. *American Journal of Primatology*, **70**: 238–46.

Napier, J. R. & Napier, P. H. (1967). *The Natural History of the Primates*. Cambridge, MA: MIT Press.

Nash, L. T. (1986). Dietary, behavioral and morphological aspects of gummivory in primates. *Yearbook of Physical Anthropology*, **29**: 113–37.

Naughton, J. M., O'Dea, K. & Sinclair, A. J. (1986). Animal foods in traditional Australian Aboriginal diets: polyunsaturated and low in fat. *Lipids*, **21**: 684–90.

Naugler, C. (2008). Hemochromatosis: a Neolithic adaptation to cereal grain diets. *Medical Hypothesis*, **70**: 691–2.

Needleman, P., Raz, A., Minkes, M. S., Ferrendelli, J. A. & Sprecher, H. (1979). Trienic prostaglandins, prostacyclin and thromboxane biosynthesis and unique biological properties. *Proceedings of the National Academy of Sciences, USA*, **76**: 944–8.

Neel, J. V. (1962). Diabetes mellitus: a 'thrifty' genotype rendered detrimental by 'progress'? *American Journal of Human Genetics*, **14**: 353–62.

(1992). The thrifty gene revisited. In: *The Genetics of Diabetes Mellitus*, ed. J. Kobberlong & R. Tattersall, pp. 283–93. London: Academic Press.

Nelson, G. J., Schmidt, P. C. & Kelley, D. S. (1995). Low-fat diets do not lower plasma cholesterol levels in healthy men compared to high-fat diets with similar fatty acid composition at constant caloric intake. *Lipids*, **30**(11): 969–76.

Nelson, J. H. (1985). Wheat: its processing and utilization. *American Journal of Clinical Nutrition*, **41**: 1070–6.

Nelson, M. (2003). Social-class trends in British diet, 1860–1980. In: *Food, Diet and Economic Change Past and Present*, ed. C. Geissler & D. J. Oddy, pp. 101–20. Leicester: Leicester University Press.

Nelson, S. V. (2007). Isotopic reconstructions of habitat change surrounding the extinction of *Sivapithecus*, a Miocene hominoid, in the Siwalik Group of Pakistan. *Palaeogeography, Palaeoclimatology, Palaeoecology*, **243**: 204–22.

Nesse, R. (2008). Foreword. In: *Medicine and Evolution: Current Applications, Future Prospects*, ed. S. Elton & P. O'Higgins, pp. xi–xii. Boca Raton, FL: Taylor & Francis.

Nesse, R. M. (1989). Evolutionary explanations of emotions. *Human Nature*, **1**(3): 261–89.

Nestle, M. (2002). *Food Politics*. Berkeley, CA: University of California Press.

Newman, W. P. & Brodows, R. G. (1983). Insulin action during fasting and refeeding in rat determined by euglycemic clamp. *American Journal of Physiology*, **249**: E514–E518.

Nguyen, V. K. & Peschard, K. (2003). Anthropology, inequality and disease. *Annual Reviews in Anthropology*, **32**: 447–74.

Nicholls, R. J. & Leatherman, S. P. (1995). Global sea-level rise. In: *As Climate Changes: International Impacts and Implications*, ed. K. M. Strzepek & J. B. Smith, pp. 92–123. Cambridge: Cambridge University Press.

Niederau, C., Strohmeyer, G. & Stremmel, W. (1994). Epidemiology, clinical spectrum and prognosis of hemochromatosis. *Advances in Experimental Medicine and Biology*, **356**: 293–302.

Nielsen, S. J., Siega-Riz, A. M. & Popkin, B. M. (2002). Trends in energy intake in USA between 1977 and 1996: similar shifts seen across age groups. *Obesity Research*, **10**: 370–8.

Niven, A., Fawkner, S., Knowles, A. M., Henretty, J. & Stephenson, C. (2009). Social physique anxiety and physical activity in early adolescent girls: the influence of maturation and physical activity motives. *Journal of Sports Sciences*, **27**: 299–305.

Noaghuil, S. & Hibbeln, J. R. (2003). Cross-national comparisons of seafood consumption and rates of bipolar disorders. *American Journal of Psychiatry*, **160**: 2222–7.

Norgan, N. G. (1997). The beneficial effects of body fat and adipose tissue in humans. *International Journal of Obesity*, **21**: 738–46.

Nutini, H. (1997). Class and ethnicity in Mexico: somatic and racial considerations. *Ethnology*, **36**: 227–38.

Nystrom, T. (2007). C-reactive protein: a marker or a player? *Clinical Science*, **113**: 79–81.

O'Connell, T. C. & Hedges, R. E. M. (1999). Isotopic comparison of hair and bone: archaeological analyses. *Journal of Archaeological Science*, **26**: 661–5.

O'Connell, J. F. & Hawkes, K. (1981). Alyawara plant use and optimal foraging theory. In: *Hunter-gatherer Foraging Strategies: Ethnographic and Archeological Analyses*, ed. B. Winterhaldes & E. A. Smith, pp. 99–125. Chicago, IL: University of Chicago Press.

O'Dea, K. (1991a). Traditional diet and food preferences of Australian Aboriginal hunter-gatherers. *Philosophical Transactions of the Royal Society of London, B*, **334**: 233–41.

(1991b). *Dietary Regulation of Plasma Lipid Levels*. Report to the Australian Pork Corporation.

et al. (1990). Cholesterol-lowering effect of a low-fat diet containing lean beef is reversed by the addition of beef fat. *American Journal of Clinical Nutrition*, **52**(3): 491–4.

O'Dea, K., Naughton, J. M., Sinclair, A. J., Rabuco, L. & Smith, R. M. (1987). Lifestyle change and nutritional status in Kimberley Aborigines. *Australian Aboriginal Studies*, **1**: 46–51.

O'Dea, K., White, N. G. & Sinclair, A. J. (1988). An investigation of nutrition related risk factors in an isolated Aboriginal community in northern Australia: advantages of a traditionally orientated lifestyle. *Medical Journal of Australia*, **148**: 177–80.

O'Keefe, S. F. (2000). An overview of oils and fats, with special emphasis on olive oil. In: *The Cambridge World History of Food,* Vol. 1, ed. K. F. Kiple & K. C. Ornelas, pp. 375–97. Cambridge: Cambridge University Press.

O'Leary, M. H. (1988). Carbon isotopes in photosynthesis. *BioScience*, **38**: 328–36.

O'Regan, H. J., Chenery, C., Lamb, A. *et al.* (2008). Diets of modern macaques assessed using stable isotope analysis of hair, bone and tooth enamel. *Journal of Human Evolution*, **55**: 617–26.

O'Regan, H. J. & Kitchener, A. C. (2005). The effects of captivity on the morphology of captive, domesticated and feral mammals. *Mammal Review*, **35**: 215–30.

O'Sullivan, T. A., Bremner, A. P., O'Neill, S. & Lyons-Wall, P. (2010). Comparison of multiple and novel measures of dietary glycemic carbohydrate with insulin resistant status in older women. *Nutrition and Metabolism*, **7**: 25. doi: 10.1186/1743-7075-7-25.

Oates, J. F. (1977). The guereza and its food. In: *Primate Ecology*, ed. T. H. Clutton-Brock, pp. 276–321. New York: Academic Press.

Offer, A. (2006). *The Challenge of Affluence. Self-Control and Well-Being in the US and Britain since 1950*. Oxford: Oxford University Press.

Offer, A., Pechey, R. & Ulijaszek, S. (2012). *Insecurity, Inequality and Obesity in Affluent Societies*. Oxford: Oxford University Press.

Offer, A., Pechey, R. & Ulijaszek, S. J. (2010). Obesity under affluence varies by welfare regimes: the effect of fast food, insecurity, and inequality. *Economics and Human Biology*, **8**: 297–308.

Okada, E., Oida, K., Tada, H. *et al.* (1999). Hyperhomocysteinemia is a risk factor for coronary arteriosclerosis in Japanese patients with type 2 diabetes. *Diabetes Care*, **22**: 484–90.

Olejniczak, A. J., Smith, T. M., Skinner, M. M. *et al.* (2008). Three-dimensional molar enamel distribution and thickness in Australopithecus and Paranthropus. *Biology Letters*, **4**: 406–10.

Olszewski, P. K. & Levine, A. S. (2007). Central opioids and consumption of sweet tastants: when reward outweighs homeostasis. *Physiology and Behavior*, **91**: 506–12.

Omori, K. & Greksa, L. P. (2002). Seasonal variation in the dietary adequacy of highland Pwo and Sgaw Karen (Thailand). *American Journal of Human Biology*, **14**: 519–31.

Omran, A. R. (1971). The epidemiologic transition: a theory of the epidemiology of population change. *Milbank Memorial Fund Quarterly*, **49**: 509–37.

   (1983). The epidemiological transition theory. A preliminary update. *Journal of Tropical Paediatrics*, **29**: 305–16.

Oppenheimer, S. (2009). The great arc of dispersal of modern humans: Africa to Australia. *Quatenary International*, **202**: 2–13.

Orchard, T., Eichner, J., Kuller, L. *et al.* (1994). Insulin as a predictor of CHD: interaction with apoE phenotype: a report from MRFIT. *Annals of Epidemiology*, **4**: 40–5.

Organization for Economic Co-operation and Development (2008). *Growing Unequal? Income Distribution and Poverty in OECD Countries.* Paris: Organization for Economic Co-operation and Development.

Oron-Herman, M., Rosenthal, T. & Sela, B. A. (2003). Hyperhomocysteinemia as a component of syndrome X. *Metabolism*, **52**: 1491–5.

Orr, S. K. & Bazinet, R. P. (2008). The emerging role of docosahexaenoic acid in neuroinflammation. *Current Opinion in Investigational Drugs*, **9**: 735–43.

Osborne, A. H., Vance, D., Rohling, E. J. *et al.* (2008). A humid corridor across the Sahara for the migration of early modern humans out of Africa 120,000 years ago. *Proceedings of the National Academy of Sciences, USA*, **105**: 16444–7.

Panagiotou, G. & Nielsen, J. (2009). Nutritional systems biology: definitions and approaches. *Annual Reviews of Nutrition*, **29**: 329–39.

Panter-Brick, C. (1996). Physical activity, energy stores, and seasonal energy balance among men and women in Nepali households. *American Journal of Human Biology*, **8**: 263–74.

Papassavas, E., Spyropoulou-Vlachou, M., Papassavas, A. *et al.* (2000). MHC class I and class II phenotype, gene, and haplotype frequencies in Greeks using molecular typing data. *Human Immunology*, **61**: 615–23.

Parfitt, S. A., Barendregt, R. W., Breda, M. *et al.* (2005). The earliest record of human activity in northern Europe. *Nature*, **438**: 1008–12.

Parkington, J. (2001). Presidential address: mobility, seasonality and Southern African hunter-gatherers. *The South African Archaeological Bulletin*, **56**: 1–7.

Parks, J. S. & Rudel, L. L. (1990). Effect of fish oil in atherosclerosis and lipoprotein metabolism. *Atherosclerosis*, **84**: 83–94.

Passmore, R., Nicol, B. M., Narayana Rao, M., Beaton, G. H. & Demayer, E. M. (1974). *Handbook on Human Nutritional Requirements*. World Health Organization Monograph Series, No. 61. Geneva: Food and Agriculture Organization/ World Health Organization.

Patterson, N., Richter, D. J., Gnerre, S., Lander, E. S. & Reich, D. (2006). Genetic evidence for complex speciation of humans and chimpanzees. *Nature*, **441**: 1103–8.

Pawles, E. K. & Volterrani, D. (2008). Fatty acid facts, Part I. Essential fatty acids as treatment for depression, or food for mood? *Drug News and Perspectives*, **21**: 446–51.

Pawlosky, R. J. *et al.* (2001). Physiological compartmental analysis of alpha-linolenic acid metabolism in adult humans. *Journal of Lipid Research*, **42**: 1257–65.

Payne, T. S. (2002). Harvest and storage management of wheat. In: *Bread Wheat: Improvement and Production*. FAO Plant Production and Protection Series, No. **30**, ed. B. C. Curtis, S. Rajaram & H. G. Macpherson, pp. 567–75. Rome: FAO.

Pearce, N. & Smith, D. G. (2003). Is social capital the key to inequalities in health? *American Journal of Public Health*, **93**: 122–9.

Pearsall, D. M. (2009). Investigating the transistion to agriculture. *Current Anthropology*, **50**: 609–13.

Pedron, B., Yakouben, K., Adjaoud, D. *et al.* (2005). Listing of common HLA alleles and haplotypes based on the study of 356 families residing in the Paris, France, area: implications for unrelated hematopoietic stem cell donor selection. *Human Immunology*, **66**: 721–31.

Pelletier, D. L. (1994). The relationship between child anthropometry and mortality in developing countries: implications for policy, programs and future research. *Journal of Nutrition* **124**, 2047S–2081S.

Pena-Chocarro, L. *et al.* (2005). The spread of agriculture in northern Iberia: new archaeobotanical data from El Mirón cave (Cantabria) and the open-air site of Los Cascajos (Navarra). *Vegetation History and Archaeobotany*, **14**: 268–78.

Pennington, J. A. T. & Hubbard, V. S. (1997). Derivation of Daily Values used for nutrition labeling. *Journal of the American Dietetic Association*, **97**: 1407–12.

Pennycuick, C. J. (1979). Energy cost of locomotion and the concept of "foraging radius". In: *Serengeti: Dynamics of an Ecosystem*, ed. A. R. E. Sinclair & M. Norton-Griffiths, pp. 164–84. Chicago, IL: Chicago University Press.

Perez-Perez, A. *et al.* (2003). Non-occlusal dental microwear variability in a sample of Middle and Late Pleistocene human populations from Europe and the Near East. *Journal of Human Evolution*, **44**: 497–513.

Perez-Pozo, S. E., Schold, J., Nakagawa, T. *et al.* (2010). Excessive fructose intake induces the features of metabolic syndrome in healthy adult men: role of uric acid in the hypertensive response. *International Journal of Obesity*, **34**: 454–61.

Perilloux, H. P., Webster, G. D. & Gaulin, S. J. C. (2010). Signals of genetic quality and maternal investment capacity: the dynamic effects of fluctuating asymmetry and waist-to-hip ratio on men's ratings of women's attractiveness. *Social, Psychological and Personality Science*, **1**: 34–42.

Perry, G. H., Dominy, N. J., Claw, K. G. *et al.* (2007). Diet and the evolution of human amylase copy number variation. *Nature Genetics*, **39**: 1256–60.

Peters, C. R. & O'Brien, E. M. (1994). Potential hominid plant foods from woody species in semi-arid versus sub-humid sub-tropical Africa. In: *The Digestive System in Mammals: Food, Form and Function*, ed. D. J. Chivers & P. Langer, pp. 166–90. Cambridge: Cambridge University Press.

Peters, C. R. & Vogel, J. C. (2005). Africa's wild C4 plant foods and possible early hominid diets. *Journal of Human Evolution*, **48**: 219–36.

Peters, C. R., O'Brien, E. M. & Drummond, R. B. (1992). *Edible Wild Plants of Sub-Saharan Africa: An Annotated Checklist Emphasizing the Woodland and Savanna Floras of Eastern and Southern Africa, Including the Plants Utilized for Food by Chimpanzees and Baboons*. Kew: Royal Botanic Gardens.

Petrie, J. R., Ueda, S., Webb, D. J., Elliott, H. L. & Connell, J. M. C. (1996). Endothelial nitric oxide production and insulin sensitivity: a physiological link with implications for pathogenesis CVD. *Circulation*, **93**: 1331–3.

Pfeiffer, S. & King, P. (1983). Cortical bone formation and diet among protohistoric Iroquoians. *American Journal of Physical Anthropology*, **60**: 23–8.

Phinney, S. D., Bistrian, B. R., Wolfe, R. R. & Blackburn, G. L. (1983). The human metabolic response to chronic ketosis without caloric restriction: physical and biochemical adaptation. *Metabolism*, **32**: 757–68.

Piancatelli, D., Canossi, A., Aureli, A. *et al.* (2004). Human leukocyte antigen-A, -B, and-Cw polymorphism in a Berber population from North Morocco using sequence-based typing. *Tissue Antigens*, **63**: 158–72.

Pickering, T. R., Dominguez-Rodrigo, M., Egeland, C. P. & Brain, C. K. (2004). Beyond leopards: tooth marks and the contribution of multiple carnivore taxa to the accumulation of the Swartkrans Member 3 fossil assemblage. *Journal of Human Evolution*, **46**: 595–604.

Pickett, K. E., Kelly, S., Brunner, E., Lobstein, T. & Wilkinson, R. G. (2005). Wider income gaps, wider waistbands? An ecological study of obesity and income inequality. *Journal of Epidemiology and Community Health*, **59**: 670–4.

Pilcher, J. (1998). *Que Vivan Los Tamales! Food and the Making of Mexican Identity*. Albequerque, NM: University of New Mexico Press.

Pimm, S. L. & Lawton, J. H. (1978). On feeding on more than one trophic level. *Nature*, **275**: 542–4.

Pinhasi, R., Fort, J. & Ammerman, A. J. (2005). Tracing the origin and spread of agriculture in Europe. *Public Library of Science Biology*, **3**(12): 2220–8.

Piontek, J. & Vancata, V. (2002). Transition to agriculture in Europe: evolutionary trends in body size and body shape. In: *Ecological Aspects of Past Human Settlements in Europe*, ed. P. Bennike, E. Bodzsar & C. Susanne, pp. 61–92. Budapest: Eötvös University Press.

Piperno, D. R., Ranere, A. J., Holst, I., Iriarte, J. & Dickau, R. (2009). Starch grain and phytolith evidence for early ninth millennium B.P. maize from the Central Balsas River Valley, Mexico. *Proceedings of the National Academy of Sciences, USA*, **106**(13): 5019–24.

Pitulko, V. V., Nikolsky, P. A. & Girya, E. Y. (2004). The Yana RHS Site: humans in the Arctic before the last glacial maximum. *Science*, **303**: 52–6.

Plavcan, J. M. (2000). Inferring social behavior from sexual dimorphism in the fossil record. *Journal of Human Evolution*, **39**: 327–44.

Plavcan, J. M. & Carel, P. S. (1997). Intrasexual competition and body weight dimorphism in anthropoid primates. *American Journal of Physical Anthropology*, **103**: 37–68.

Plavcan, J. M. & van Schaik, C. P. (1997). Intrasexual competition and body weight dimorphism in anthropoid primates. *American Journal of Physical Anthropology*, **103**: 37–68.

Plummer, T. (2004). Flaked stones and old bones: biological and cultural evolution at the dawn of technology. *American Journal of Physical Anthropology*, **125**: 118–64.

Plummer, T. W., Ditchfield, P. W., Bishop, L. C. *et al.* (2009). Oldest evidence of toolmaking hominins in a grassland-dominated ecosystem. *PLoS ONE*, **4**, e7199.

Poespoprodjo, J. R., Fobia, W., Kenangalem, E. *et al.* (2008). Adverse pregnancy outcomes in an area where multidrug-resistant *Plasmodium vivax* and *Plasmodium falciparum* infections are endemic. *Clinical Infectious Diseases*, **46**: 1374–81.

Pollard, T. M. (2008). *Western Diseases: An Evolutionary Perspective*. Cambridge: Cambridge University Press.

Ponnampalam, E. N., Mann, N. J. & Sinclair, A. J. (2006). Effect of feeding systems on omega-3 fatty acids, conjugated linoleic acid and trans fatty acids in Australian beef cuts: potential impact on human health. *Asia Pacific Journal of Clinical Nutrition*, **15**(1): 21–9.

Popkin, B. M. (2009). *The World is Fat. The Fads, Trends, Policies, and Products that are Fattening the Human Race*. New York: Avery.

(2011). Agricultural policies, food and public health. *EMBO Reports*, **12**: 11–18.

(1994). The nutrition transition in low-income countries: an emerging crisis. *Nutrition Review*, **52**(9): 285–98.

(1998). The nutrition transition and its health implications in lower income countries. *Public Health Nutrition*, **1**: 5–21.

(2001). The nutrition transition and obesity in the developing world. *Journal of Nutrition*, **131**: S871–S873.

(2002a). An overview on the nutrition transition and its health implications: the Bellagio meeting. *Public Health Nutrition*, **5**: 93–103.

(2002b). The dynamics of the dietary transition in the developing world. In: *The Nutrition Transition: Diet and Disease in the Developing World*, ed. B. Caballero & B. M. Popkin, pp. 111–28. New York: Academic Press.

(2002c). What is unique about the experience in lower- and middle-income less-industrialized countries compared with the very-high-income industrialized countries? The shift in stages of the nutrition transition in the developing world differs from past experiences! *Public Health Nutrition*, **5**: 205–14.

(2006a). Technology, transport, globalization and the nutrition transition. *Food Policy*, **31**: 554–69.

(2006b). Global nutrition dynamics: the world is shifting rapidly toward a diet linked with noncommunicable diseases. *American Journal of Clinical Nutrition*, **84**(2): 289–98.

Popkin, B. M. & Gordon-Larsen, P. (2004). The nutrition transition: worldwide obesity dynamics and their determinants. *International Journal of Obesity*, **28**: S2–S9.

Popkin, B. M., Keyou, G., Zhai, F. *et al.* (1993). The nutrition transition in China: a cross-sectional analysis. *European Journal of Clinical Nutrition*, **47**(3): 333–46.

Popper, V. (2000). *Investigating Chinampa Farming. Cotsen Institute of Archaeology, University of California*. Los Angeles, CA: Blackdirt.

Potts, R. (1998). Variability selection in hominid evolution. *Evolutionary Anthropology: Issues, News, and Reviews*, **7**: 81–96.

Powell, D., Suwanichkul, A., Cubbage, M. *et al.* (1991). Insulin inhibits transcription of the human gene for insulin-like growth factor-binding protein-1. *The Journal of Biological Chemistry*, **266**: 18868–76.

Powers, W. R. & Jordan, R. H. (1990). Human biogeography and climate change in Siberia and arctic North America in the fourth and fifth millennia BP. *Philosophical Transactions of the Royal Society of London, B*, **330**: 665–70.

Prentice, A. M. & Jebb, S. A. (2003). Fast foods, energy density and obesity: a possible mechanistic link. *Obesity Reviews*, **4**: 187–94.

Preutz, J. D. & Bertolani, P. (2007). Savanna chimpanzees, *Pan troglodytes verus*, hunt with tools. *Current Biology*, **17**: 412–17.

Price, D. T. (2009). Ancient farming in eastern North America. *Proceedings of the National Academy of Sciences, USA*, **106**(16): 6427–8.

Proches, S., Wilson, J. R. U., Vamosi, J. C. & Richardson, D. M. (2008). Plant diversity in the human diet: weak phylogenetic signal indicates breadth. *BioScience*, **58**: 151–9.

Purnell, J. Q., Klopfenstein, B. A., Stevens, A. A. *et al.* (2011). Brain functional magnetic resonance imaging response to glucose and fructose infusions in humans. *Diabetes, Obesity and Metabolism*, **13**: 229–34.

Putnam, J. J. & Allshouse, J. E. (1999). *Food consumption, prices and expenditures, 1970–97*. US Department of Agriculture Economic Research Service Statistical Bulletin No. 965, April 1999. Washington, D.C.: US Government Printing Office.

Pyke, G. H., Pulliam, H. R. & Charnow, E. L. (1997). Optimal foraging: a selective review of theory and tests. *Quarterly Review of Biology*, **52**: 137–54.

Quinn, T., Mann, J. M., Curran, J. W. & Piot, P. (1986). AIDS in Africa: an epidemiologic paradigm. *Science*, **234**: 955–63.

Rahmstorf, S. (2010). A new view on sea-level rise. *Nature Reports Climate Change*, **1004**: 44–5.

Raivio, K. O., Becker, A., Meyer, L. J. *et al.* (1975). Stimulation of human purine synthesis de novo by fructose infusion. *Metabolism*, **24**: 861–9.

Ramsden, C. E., Hibbeln, J. R. & Majchrzak-Hong, S. F. (2011). Letter to the Editors: Don't disregard the essential distinction between PUFA species. *British Journal of Nutrition*, **106**: 953–7.

Ramsden, C. E., Hibbeln, J. R., Majchrzak, S. F. & Davis, J. M. (2010). N-6 fatty acid specific and mixed polyunsaturated dietary interventions have different effects on

CHD risk: a meta-analysis of randomised controlled trials. *British Journal of Nutrition*, **104**(11): 1586–600.

Rao, A. & Casimir, M. J. (1988). How non-food producing nomads obtain their food: peripatetic strategies in Afghanistan. In: *Coping with Uncertainty in Food Supply*, ed. I. de Garine & G. A. Harrison, pp. 360–78. Oxford: Oxford University Press.

Rao, J. S., Ertley, R. N., De Mar, J. C. Jr. *et al.* (2007). Dietary n-3 PUFA deprivation alters expression of enzymes of the arachidonic and docosahexaenoic acid cascades in rat frontal cortex. *Molecular Psychiatry*, **12**: 151–7.

Rao, P. U. & Belavady, B. (1978). Oligosaccharides in pulses: varietal differences and effects of cooking and germination. *Journal of Agricultural and Food Chemistry*, **26**(2): 316–19.

Raschke, V. & Cheema, B. (2008). Colonization, the new world order, and the eradication of traditional food habits in East Africa: historical perspective on the nutrition transition. *Public Health Nutrition*, **11**(7): 662–74.

Rasmussen, D. T. (2003). The origin of primates. In: *The Primate Fossil Record*, ed. W. C. Hartwig, pp. 5–10. Cambridge: Cambridge University Press.

Ravosa, M. J., Kunwar, R., Stock, S. R. & Stack, M. S. (2007). Pushing the limit: masticatory stress and adaptive plasticity in mammalian craniomandibular joints. *Journal of Experimental Biology*, **210**: 628–41.

Rea, R. L., Thompson, L. U. & Jenkins, D. J. A. (1985). Lectins in foods and their relation to starch digestibility. *Nutrition Research*, **5**: 919–29.

Reardon, T. & Berdegué, J. (2002). The rapid rise of supermarkets in Latin America: challenges and opportunities for development. *Development Policy Review*, **20**: 371–88.

Reaven, G. M. (1988). Role of insulin resistance in human disease. *Diabetes*, **37**: 1595–607.

(1995). Pathophysiology of insulin resistance in human disease. *Physiological Review*, **75**: 473–86.

(1998). Hypothesis: muscle insulin resistance is the ("not-so") thrifty genotype. *Diabetologia*, **41**: 482–4.

Reddy, G. P. (1994). Hunter-gatherers and the politics of environment and development in India. In: *Key Issues in Hunter-Gatherer Research*, ed. E. S. Burch & L. J. Ellanna, pp. 357–76. Oxford: Berg.

Redmond, W. H. (2008). Formal institutions in historical perspective. *Journal of Economic Issues*, **42**: 569–76.

Reed, K. E. (1997). Early hominid evolution and ecological change through the African Plio-Pleistocene. *Journal of Human Evolution*, **32**: 289–322.

Reid, J. M., Fullmer, S. D., Pettigrew, K. D. *et al.* (1971). Nutrient intake of Pima Indian women: relationships to diabetes mellitus and gallbladder disease. *American Journal of Clinical Nutrition*, **24**: 1281–9.

Remer, T. & Manz, F. (1995). Potential renal acid load of foods and its influence on urine pH. *Journal of the American Dietetic Association*, **95**: 791–7.

Remis, M. J. & Kerr, M. E. (2002). Taste responses to fructose and tannic acid among gorillas (*Gorilla gorilla gorilla*). *International Journal of Primatology*, **23**: 251–61.

Riba-Hernández, P., Stoner, K. E. & Lucas, P. W. (2003). The sugar composition of fruits in the diet of spider monkeys (*Ateles geoffroyi*) in tropical humid forest in Costa Rica. *Journal of Tropical Ecology*, **19**: 709–16.

Richards, M. P. (2002). A brief review of the archeological evidence for Paleolithic and Neolithic subsistence. *European Journal of Clinical Nutrition*, **56**: 1262–78.

Richards, M. P. & Trinkaus, E. (2009). Isotopic evidence for the diets of European Neanderthals and early modern humans. *Proceedings of the National Academy of Sciences, USA*, **106**: 16034–9.

Richards, M. P., Pettitt, P. B., Stiner, M. C. & Trinkaus, E. (2001). Stable isotope evidence for increasing dietary breadth in the European mid-Upper Paleolithic. *Proceedings of the National Academy of Sciences, USA*, **98**: 6528–32.

Riggs, B. L. & Melton, L. J. (1986). Involutional osteoporosis. *New England Journal of Medicine*, **314**: 1676–84.

Rightmire, G. P. (2009). Middle and later Pleistocene hominins in Africa and Southwest Asia. *Proceedings of the National Academy of Sciences, USA*, **106**: 16046–50.

Rivera, J. A., Barquera, S., Gonzalez-Cossio, T., Olaiz, G. & Sepulveda, J. (2004). Nutrition transition in Mexico and in other Latin American countries. *Nutrition Reviews*, **62**: S149–S157.

Roberts, R. G., Jones, R., Spooner, N. A. *et al.* (1994). The human colonisation of Australia: optical dates of 53,000 and 60,000 years bracket human arrival at Deaf Adder Gorge, Northern Territory. *Quaternary Science Reviews*, **13**: 575–83.

Roberts-Thomson, R. A. & Roberts-Thomson, P. J. (1999). Rheumatic disease and the Australian aborigine. *Annals of Rheumatic Diseases*, **58**(5): 266–70.

Robinson, L. E., Buchholz, A. C. & Mazurak, V. C. (2007). Inflammation, obesity, and fatty acid metabolism: influence of n-3 polyunsaturated fatty acids on factors contributing to metabolic syndrome. *Applied Physiology, Nutrition, and Metabolism*, **32**: 1008–24.

Robson, S. L. & Wood, B. (2008). Hominin life history: reconstruction and evolution. *Journal of Anatomy*, **212**: 394–425.

Rode, K. D., Chapman, C. A., Chapman, L. J. & McDowell, L. R. (2003). Mineral resource availability and consumption by colobus monkeys in Kibale National Park, Uganda. *International Journal of Primatology*, **24**: 541–73.

Rodman, P. S. & McHenry, H. M. (1980). Bioenergetics and the origin of hominid bipedalism. *American Journal of Physical Anthropology*, **52**: 103–6.

Rogers, D. J. & Randolph, S. E. (2000). The global spread of malaria in a future, warmer world. *Science*, **289**: 1763–6.

Rogers, M. E., Maisels, F., Williamson, E. A., Fernandez, M. & Tutin, C. E. G. (1990). Gorilla diet in the Lopé Reserve, Gabon: a nutritional analysis. *Oecologica*, **84**: 326–39.

Roglic, G., Unwin, N., Bennett, P. H. *et al.* (2005). The burden of mortality attributable to diabetes: realistic estimates for the year 2000. *Diabetes Care*, **28** (9): 2130–5.

Rolland-Cachera, M. F., Deheeger, M., Bellisle, F. *et al.* (1984). Adiposity rebound in children: a simple indicator for predicting obesity. *American Journal of Clinical Nutrition*, **39**: 129–35.

Rolland-Cachera, M. F., Deheeger, M., Maillot, M. & Bellisle, F. (2006). Early adiposity rebound: causes and consequences for obesity in children and adults. *International Journal of Obesity*, **30**: S11–S17.

Rolls, B. J., Castellanos, V. H., Halford, J. C. *et al.* (1998). Volume of food consumed affects satiety in men. *American Journal of Clinical Nutrition*, **67**: 1170–7.

Rosati, A. G., Stevens, J. R., Hare, B. & Hauser, M. D. (2007). The evolutionary origins of human patience: temporal preferences in chimpanzees, bonobos and adult humans. *Current Biology*, **17**: 1663–8.

Roseboom, T. J., van der Meulen, J. H. P., Ravelli, A. C. J. *et al.* (2001). Effects of prenatal exposure to the Dutch famine on adult disease in later life: an overview. *Molecular and Cellular Endocrinology*, **185**: 93–8.

Rosegrant, M. W., Paisner, M. S., Meijer, S. & Witcover, J. (2001). *2020 Global Food Outlook, Trends, Alternatives, and Choices. A 2020 Vision for Food, Agriculture, and the Environment Initiative*. Washington, D.C.: International Food Policy Research Institute.

Rothman, J. M., Van Soest, P. J. & Pell, A. N. (2006). Decaying wood is a sodium source for mountain gorillas. *Biology Letters*, **2**: 321–4.

Rothschild, N. A. (1979). Mortuary behavior and social organization at Indian Knoll and Dickson Mounds. *American Antiquity*, **44**: 658–75.

Rovira, A., Vulliamy, T., Pujades, M. A., Luzzatto, L. & Corrons, J. L. V. (1995). Molecular genetics of glucose-6-phosphate dehydrogenase (G6PD) deficiency in Spain: identification of two new point mutations in the G6PD gene. *British Journal of Haematology*, **91**: 66–71.

Rowland, M. G. (1986). The weanling's dilemma: are we making progress? *Acta Paediatrica Scandinavica*, **323**: S33–S42.

Rowley-Conwy, P. (1982). Comment on Testart 1982 The significance of food storage among hunter-gatherers: residence patterns, population densities, and social inequalities. *Current Anthropology*, **23**: 523–37.

(1983). Sedentary hunters: the Ertebolle example. In: *Hunter-Gatherer Economy in Prehistory: A European Perspective*, ed. G. Bailey, pp. 111–26. Cambridge: Cambridge University Press.

(1984). The laziness of the short-distance hunter: the origins of agriculture in western Denmark. *Journal of Anthropological Archaeology*, **3**: 300–24.

Rude, R. K., Oldham, S. B. & Singer, F. R. (1976). Functional hypoparathyroidism and parathyroid hormone end-organ resistance in human magnesium deficiency. *Clinical Endocrinology*, **5**: 209–24.

Rudman, D., DiFulco, T. J., Galambos, J. T. *et al.* (1973). Maximal rates of excretion and synthesis of urea in normal and cirrhotic subjects. *Journal of Clinical Investigation*, **52**: 2241–9.

Rumberger, J. M., Wu, T., Hering, M. A. & Marshall, S. (2003). Role of hexosamine biosynthesis in glucose-mediated up-regulation of lipogenic enzyme mRNA levels. *Journal of Biological Chemistry*, **278**(31): 28547–52.

Russo, G. L. (2009). Dietary n-6 and n-3 PUFA: from biochemistry to clinical implications in cardiovascular prevention. *Biochemical Pharmacology*, **77**(6): 937–46.

Rustan, A. C., Nossen, J. O., Christiansen, E. N. & Drevon, C. A. (1988a). Eicosapen-taenoic acid reduces hepatic synthesis and secretion of triacylglycerol by decreasing the activity of acyl-coenzyme. *American Journal of Lipid Research*, **29**: 1417–26.

Rustan, A. C., Nossen, J. O., Osmundsen, H. & Drevon, C. A. (1988b). Eicosapentaenoic acid inhibits cholesterol esterification in cultured parenchymal cells and isolated microsomes from rat liver. *Journal of Biological Chemistry*, **263**: 8126–32.

Sabeti, P. C., Schaffner, S. F., Fry, B. *et al.* (2006). Positive natural selection in the human lineage. *Science*, **312**: 1614–20.

Sabeti, P. C., Walsh, E., Schaffner, S. F. *et al.* (2005). The case for selection at Ccr5-Delta32. *PLoS Biology*, **3**(11): 1963.

Sahlins, M. (1974). *Stone Age Economics*. London: Routledge.

Salami, F., Ozkan, H., Brandolini, A., Schafer-Pregl, R. & Martin, W. (2003). Genetics and geography of wild cereal domestication in the near east. *Nature Reviews Genetics*, **3**: 429–41.

Salem, N. Jr., Wegner, B., Mena, P. & Uauy, R. (1996). Arachidonic and docosahex-aenoic acids are biosynthesized from their 18-carbon precursors in human infants. *Proceedings of the National Academy of Sciences, USA*, **93**: 49–54.

Salmerón, J., Ascherio, A., Rimm, E. B. *et al.* (1997). Dietary fibre, glycaemic load, and the risk of NIDDM in men. *Diabetes Care*, **20**: 545–50.

Sambrook, P. & Cooper, C. (2006). Osteoporosis. *Lancet*, **367**: 2010–18.

Sanchez-Velasco, P., Gomez-Casado, E., Martinez-Laso, J. *et al.* (2003). HLA alleles in isolated populations from North Spain: origin of the Basques and the ancient Iberians. *Tissue Antigens*, **61**: 384–92.

Sanders, T. A. B. (1990). Dietary fatty acids: effects on lipid metabolism. *Current Opinion in Lipidology*, **1**: 12–17.

Sandholzer, C., Delport, R., Vermaak, H. & Utermann, G. (1995). High frequency of the apo E4 allele in Khoi San from South Africa. *Human Genetics*, **95**: 46–8.

Sandweiss, D. H. (2007). Small is big: the microfossil perspective on human-plant interaction. *Proceedings of the National Academy of Sciences, USA*, **104**: 3021–2.

Sapolsky, R. M. (2005). The influence of social hierarchy on primate health. *Science*, **308**: 648–52.

Sardesai, V. M. (1992). Nutritional role of polyunsaturated fatty acids. *Journal of Nutritional Biochemistry*, **3**: 154–66.

Saris, W. H. M. (2001). Very-low-calorie diets and sustained weight loss. *Obesity*, **9**: S295–S301.

Sarkinen, E., Korhonen, M., Erkkila, A. *et al.* (1998). Effect of apo E polymorphism on serum lipid responses to the separate modification of dietary fat and dietary cholesterol. *American Journal of Clinical Nutrition*, **68**: 1215–22.

Sato, Y., Ito, T., Udaka, N. *et al.* (1996). Immunohistochemical localization of facilitated-diffusion glucose transporters in rat pancreatic islets. *Tissue Cell*, **28**: 637–43.

Saunders, M. A., Hammer, M. F. & Nachman, M. W. (2002). Nucleotide variability at G6PD and the signature of malarial selection in humans. *Genetics*, **162**(2): 1849–61.

Savy, M., Martin-Prevel, Y., Traissac, P., Eymard-Duvernay, S. & Delpeuch, F. (2006). Dietary diversity scores and nutritional status of women change during the seasonal food shortage in rural Burkina Faso. *Journal of Nutrition*, **136**: 2625–32.

Saw, S. M. (2003). A synopsis of the prevalence rates and environmental risk factors for myopia. *Clinical and Experimental Optometry*, **86**(5): 289–94.

Scalafani, A. (2001). Psychobiology of food preferences. *International Journal of Obesity*, **25**(5): S13–S16.

Schaefer, E. J., Gleason, J. A. & Dansinger, M. L. (2009). Dietary fructose and glucose differentially affect lipid and glucose homeostasis. *Journal of Nutrition*, **139**(6): S1257–S1262.

Schipper, R., Schreuder, G., D'Amaro, J. & Oudshoorn, M. (1996). HLA gene and haplotype frequencies in Dutch blood donors. *Tissue Antigens*, **48**: 562–74.

Schlenk, H., Sand, D. M. & Gellerman, J. L. (1969). Retroconversion of docosahexaenoic acid in rat. *Biochimica et Biophysica Acta*, **187**: 201–7.

Schliekelman, P., Garner, C. & Slatkin, M. (2001). Natural selection and resistance to HIV. *Nature*, **411**: 545–6.

Schmeda-Hirschmann, G. (1994). Plant resources of the Paraguayan Chaco. *Economic Botany*, **48**: 252–8.

Schmider, B. (1982). The Magdalenian culture of the Paris river-basin and its relationship with the Nordic cultures of the late Old Stone Age. *World Archaeology*, **14**: 259–69.

Schmidt, C. W. (2008). Linking TB and the environment. *Environmental Health Perspectives*, **116**: 479–85.

Schmidt-Nielsen, K. (1997). *Animal Physiology: Adaptation and Environment*. Cambridge: Cambridge University Press.

Schoeninger, M. J. (2009). Stable isotope evidence for the adoption of maize agriculture. *Current Anthropology*, **50**: 633–40.

Schoeninger, M. J. & DeNiro, M. J. (1984). Nitrogen and carbon isotopic composition of bone collagen from marine and terrestrial animals. *Geochimica et Cosmochimica Acta*, **48**: 625–39.

Schooler, D., Impett, E. A., Hirschman, C. & Bonem, L. (2008). A mixed-method exploration of body image and sexual health among adolescent boys. *American Journal of Men's Health*, **2**: 322–39.

Scott, K. P., Duncan, S. H. & Flint, H. J. (2008). Dietary fibre and the gut microbiota. *British Nutritional Foundation Nutrition Bulletin*, **33**: 201–11.

Scott, R. S., Ungar, P. S., Bergstrom, T. S. *et al.* (2005). Dental microwear texture analysis shows within-species diet variability in fossil hominins. *Nature*, **436**: 693–5.

Scrimshaw, N. S. (2002). Foreword. In: *The Nutrition Transition: Diet and Disease in the Developing World*, ed. B. Caballero & B. M. Popkin, pp. ix–xii. New York: Academic Press.

Sebastian, A., Frassetto, L. A., Sellmeyer, D. E., Merriam, R. L. & Morris, R.C. Jr. (2002). Estimation of the net acid load of the diet of ancestral preagricultural *Homo sapiens* and their hominid ancestors. *American Journal of Clinical Nutrition*, **76**: 1308–16.

Sebastian, A., Harris, S. T., Ottaway, J. H., Todd, K. M. & Morris, R. C. (1994). Improved mineral balance and skeletal metabolism in postmenopausal women treated with potassium bicarbonate. *New England Journal of Medicine*, **330**: 1776–81.

Sellen, D. W. (2000). Seasonal ecology and nutritional status of women and children in a Tanzanian pastoral community. *American Journal of Human Biology*, **12**: 758–81.

Sellen, D. W. (2001). Comparison of infant feeding patterns reported for nonindustrial populations with current recommendations. *Journal of Nutrition*, **131**: 2707–15.

Semaw, S., Renne, P., Harris, J. W. K. *et al.* (1997). 2.5-million-year-old stone tools from Gona, Ethiopia. *Nature*, **385**: 333–6.

Sen, A. (1981). *Poverty and Famines: An Essay on Entitlement and Deprivation.* Oxford: Clarendon Press.

Senut, B., Pickford, M., Gommery, D. *et al.* (2001). First hominid from the Miocene (Lukeino Formation, Kenya). *Earth and Planetary Science*, **332**: 137–44.

Serhan, C. N. (2005). Novel eicosanoid and docosanoid mediators: resolvins, docosatrienes, and neuroprotectins. *Current Opinion in Clinical Nutrition and Metabolic Care*, **8**(2): 115–21.

Serventi, S. & Sabban, F. (2002). *Pasta: The Story of a Universal Food.* Transl. A. Shugaar. New York: Columbia University Press.

Shackleton, N. J. & Pisias, N. G. (1985). Atmospheric carbon dioxide, orbital forcing, and climate. In: *The Carbon Cycle and Atmospheric CO_2: Natural Variations Archean to Present,* ed. E. T. Sundquist & W. S. Broeker. *Geophysical Monograph,* **32**: 412–17.

Shackleton, N. J., Berger, A. & Peltier, W. R. (1990). An alternative astronomical calibration of the lower Pleistocene timescale based on ODP Site 677. *Transactions of the Royal Society, Edinburgh, Earth Sciences*, **81**: 251–61.

Shackleton, N. J., Crowhurst, S., Hagelberg, T., Pisias, N. G. & Schneider, D. A. (1995a). A new Late Neogene time scale: application to Leg 138 Sites. In: *Proceedings of the Ocean Drilling Program, Scientific Results,* ed. N. G. Pisias, L. A. Janacek, A. Palmer-Julson & T. H. Van Andel, **138**: 73–101.

Shackleton, N. J., Hall, M. A. & Pate, D. (1995b). Pliocene stable isotope stratigraphy of Site 846. In: *Proceedings of the Ocean Drilling Program, Scientific Results,* ed. N. G. Pisias, L. A. Janacek, A. Palmer-Julson & T. H. Van Andel, **138**: 337–55.

Shapiro, A., Mu, W., Roncal, C. A. *et al.* (2008). Fructose induced leptin resistance exacerbates weight gain in response to subsequent high-fat feeding. *American Journal of Physiology, Regulatory, Integrative and Comparative Physiology*, **295**: R1370–R1375.

Shintani, T. T., Hughes, C. K., Beckham, S. & O'Connor, H. K. (1991). Obesity and cardiovascular risk intervention through the ad libitum feeding of traditional Hawaiian diet. *American Journal of Clinical Nutrition*, **53**: S1647–S1651.

Shipman, P., Bosler, W. & Davis, K. L. (1981). Butchering of giant geladas at an Acheulian site. *Current Anthropology*, **22**: 257.

Simmen, B. & Hladik, C. M. (1998). Sweet and bitter taste discrimination in primates: scaling effects across species. *Folia Primatologica*, **69**: 129–38.

Simondon, K. B., Ndiaye, T., Dia, M. *et al.* (2008). Seasonal variations and trends in weight and arm circumference of non-pregnant rural Senegalese women, 1990–1997. *European Journal of Clinical Nutrition*, **62**: 997–1004.

Simoons, F. J. (1970). Primary adult lactose intolerance and the milking habit: a problem in biological and cultural interrelations. II. A culture historical hypothesis. *American Journal of Digestive Diseases*, **15**: 695–710.

Simopoulos, A. P. (1999). Essential fatty acids in health and chronic disease. *American Journal of Clinical Nutrition*, **70**: 560S–569S.

(2004). Genetic variation: nutritional implications. In: *Nutrigenetics and Nutrigenomics: World Review of Nutrition and Dietetics,* vol. 93, ed. A. P. Simopoulos & J. M. Ordovas, pp. 1–28. Basel: Karger.

(2006). Evolutionary aspects of diet, the omega-6/omega-3 ratio and genetic variation: nutritional implications for chronic diseases. *Biomedicine and Pharmacotherapy*, **60**: 502–7.

Sims, L. S. (1996). Uses of the recommended dietary allowances: a commentary. *Journal of the American Dietetic Association*, **96**: 659–62.

Sinclair, A. J. & Mann, N. J. (1996). Short term diets rich in arachidonic acid influence plasma phospholipid PUFA levels and prostacyclin and thromboxane production in humans. *Journal of Nutrition*, **126**: S1110–S1114.

Sinclair, A. J. & O'Dea, K. (1990). Fats in human diets through history: is the Western diet out of step in reducing fat in meat animals? In: *Reducing Fat in Meat Animals*, ed. G. Wood & G. Fisher, pp. 1–47. New York: Elsevier.

Sinclair, A. J., Begg, D., Matthai, M. & Weisinger, R. S. (2007). Omega 3 fatty acids and the brain: review of studies in depression. *Asia Pacific Journal of Clinical Nutrition*, **16**: S391–S397.

Singh, A., Hailton-Fairley, D., Seppala, M. *et al.* (1990). Effect of insulin-like growth factor type 1 (IGF-I) and insulin on the secretion of sex hormone binding globulin and IGF-I binding protein (IBP-I) by human hepatoma cells. *Journal of Endocrinology*, **124**: R1–R3.

Skeaff, C. M. & Holub, B. J. (1988). The effect of fish oil composition on platelet aggregation responses in washed human platelet suspensions. *Thrombosis Research*, **51**: 105–15.

Skeaff, C. M. & Miller, J. (2009). Dietary fat and coronary heart disease: summary of evidence from prospective cohort and randomised controlled trials. *Annals of Nutrition and Metabolism*, **55**(1–3): 173–201.

Skoufias, E. (2005). *PROGRESA and its Impacts on the Welfare of Rural Households in Mexico. Research Report 139.* Washington, D.C.: International Food Policy Research Institute.

Skov, A. R., Toubro, S., Ronn, B., Holm, L. & Astrup, A. (1999). Randomised trial on protein vs carbohydrate in ad libitum fat reduced diet for the treatment of obesity. *International Journal of Obesity-Related Metabolic Disorders*, **23**: 528–36.

Sluyter, J. D., Schaaf, D., Metcalf, P. A. & Scragg, R. K. R. (2010). Dietary intakes of Pacific, Māori, Asian and European adolescents: the Auckland High School Heart Survey. *Australian and New Zealand Journal of Public Health*, **34**: 32–7.

Smith, K. S., Berridge, K. C. & Aldridge, J. W. (2011). Disentangling pleasure from incentive salience and learning signals in brain reward circuitry. *Proceedings of The National Academy of Sciences, USA*, **108**: 255–64.

Smith, M. E. (1984). The Aztlan migrations of the Nahuatl chronicles: myth or history? *Ethnohistory*, **31**: 153–86.

Smith, P., Bloom, R. A. & Berkowitz, J. (1984). Diachronic trends in humeral cortical thickness of Near Eastern populations. *Journal of Human Evolution*, **13**: 603–11.

Smith, R. J. & Jungers, W. L. (1997). Body mass in comparative primatology. *Journal of Human Evolution*, **32**: 523–59.

Smith, R. N., Mann, N. J., Braue, A., Mäkeläinen, H. & Varigos, G. A. (2007a). A low-glycemic-load diet improves symptoms in acne vulgaris patients: a randomized controlled trial. *American Journal of Clinical Nutrition*, **86**(1): 107–15.

(2007b). The effect of a high-protein, low glycemic-load diet versus a conventional, high glycemic-load diet on biochemical parameters associated with acne vulgaris: a randomized, investigator-masked, controlled trial. *Journal of the American Academy of Dermatology*, **57**(2): 247–56.

Smolkova, B., Dusinska, M., Raslova, K. *et al.* (2004). Seasonal changes in markers of oxidative damage to lipids and DNA; correlations with seasonal variation in diet. *Mutation Research/Fundamental and Molecular Mechanisms of Mutagenesis*, **551**: 135–44.

Smuts, B., Cheney, D. L., Seyfarth, R. M., Wrangham, R. W. & Struhsaker, T. T. (1987). *Primate Societies*. Chicago, IL: University of Chicago Press.

Snyder, E. E., Walts, B., Perusse, L. *et al.* (2004). The human obesity gene map: the 2003 update. *Obesity Research*, **12**: 369–410.

Sobal, G., Menzel, J. & Sinzinger, H. (2000). Why is glycated LDL more sensitive to oxidation than native LDL? A comparative study. *Prostaglandins, Leukotrienes and Essential Fatty Acids*, **63**(4): 177–86.

Sobal, J. & Stunkard, A. J. (1989). Socioeconomic status and obesity: a review of the literature. *Psychological Bulletin*, **105**: 260–75.

Sockol, M. D., Raichlen, D. A. & Pontzer, H. (2007). Chimpanzee locomotor energetics and the origin of human bipedalism. *Proceedings of the National Academy of Sciences, USA*, **104**: 12265–9.

Sojka, J. E. & Weaver, C. M. (1995). Magnesium supplementation and osteoporosis. *Nutrition Reviews*, **53**: 71–4.

Sokoloff, L. (1977). Relation between physiological function and energy metabolism in the central nervous system. *Journal of Neurochemistry*, **29**: 13–26.

Somel, M., Creely, H., Franz, H. *et al.* (2008). Human and chimpanzee gene expression differences replicated in mice fed different diets. *PLoS ONE*, **3**: e1504.

Southgate, D. A. (1991). Nature and variability of human food consumption. *Philosophical Transactions of the Royal Society of London, B*, **334**: 281–8.

Spady, D. K. & Dietschy, J. M. (1988). Interaction of dietary cholesterol and triglycerides in the regulation of hepatic low density lipoprotein transport in hamsters. *Journal of Clinical Investigation*, **81**: 300–9.

Spady, D. K., Woollett, L. A. & Dietschy, J. M. (1993). Regulation of plasma LDL-cholesterol levels by dietary cholesterol and fatty acids. *Annual Review of Nutrition*, **13**: 355–81.

Spang, R. L. (2001). *The Invention of the Restaurant*, 2nd edn. Cambridge, MA: Harvard University Press.

Specker, B. & Binkley, T. (2003). Randomized trial of physical activity and calcium supplementation on bone mineral content in 3- to 5-year-old children. *Journal of Bone and Mineral Research*, **18**: 885–92.

Spencer, H., Kramer, L., DeBartolo, M., Norris, C. & Osis, D. (1983). Further studies of the effect of a high protein diet as meat on calcium metabolism. *American Journal of Clinical Nutrition*, **37**: 924–9.

Sperling, R. I., Robin, J. L., Kylander, K. A. *et al.* (1987). The effects of n-3 polyunsaturated fatty acids on the generation of platelet-activating factor – acether by human monocytes. *Journal of Immunology*, **139**: 4186–4191.

Speth, J. D. & Spielman, K. A. (1983). Energy source, protein metabolism, and hunter-gatherer subsistence strategies. *Journal of Anthropology and Archeology*, **2**: 1–31.

Sponheimer, M. & Lee-Thorp, J. A. (1999). Isotopic evidence for the diet of an early hominid, *Australopithecus africanus*. *Science*, **283**: 368–70.

(2003). Using carbon isotope data of fossil bovid communities for palaeoenvironmental reconstruction. *South African Journal of Science*, **99**: 273–5.

Sponheimer, M., Lee-Thorp, J., deRuiter, D. J. *et al.* (2003a). Diets of Southern African Bovidae: the stable isotope evidence. *Journal of Mammalogy*, **84**: 471–9.

Sponheimer, M., Loudon, J. E., Codron, D. *et al.* (2006a). Do "Savanna" chimpanzees consume C4 resources? *Journal of Human Evolution*, **51**: 128–33.

Sponheimer, M., Passey, B. H., de Ruiter, D. J. *et al.* (2006b). Isotopic evidence for dietary variability in the early hominin *Paranthropus robustus*. *Science*, **314**: 980–2.

Sponheimer, M., Robinson, D., Ayliffe, L. K. *et al.* (2003b). Nitrogen isotopes in mammalian herbivores: hair delta 15N values from a controlled feeding study. *International Journal of Osteoarchaeology*, **13**: 80–7.

Sprafka, J. *et al.* (1990). Continued decline in cardiovascular disease risk factors: results of the Minnesota Heart Survey, 1980–1982 and 1985–1987. *American Journal of Epidemiology*, **132**(3): 489–500.

Sprecher, H. (1986). The metabolism of n-3 and n-6 fatty acids and their oxygenation by platelet cyclooxygenase and lipoxygenase. *Progress in Lipid Research*, **25**: 19–28.

Stanford, C. B. (1995). The influence of chimpanzee predation on group size and anti-predator behaviour in red colobus monkeys. *Animal Behaviour*, **49**: 577–87.

(1998). *Chimpanzee and Red Colobus: The Ecology of Predator and Prey*. Cambridge, MA: Harvard University Press.

Steele, T. E. (2010). A unique hominin menu dated to 1.95 million years ago. *Proceedings of the National Academy of Sciences, USA*, **107**: 10771–2.

Steffansson, V. (1944). *Arctic Manual*. New York: Macmillan.

Steiper, M. E. & Young, N. M. (2006). Primate molecular divergence dates. *Molecular Phylogenetics and Evolution*, **41**: 384–94.

Stephen, A. M. & Wald, N. J. (1990). Trends in individual consumption of dietary fat in the United States, 1920–1984. *American Journal of Clinical Nutrition*, **52**: 457–69.

Stephens, J. C., Reich, D. E., Goldstein, D. B. *et al.* (1998). Dating the origin of the CCR5-Delta32 AIDS-resistance allele by the coalescence of haplotypes. *American Journal of Human Genetics*, **62**: 1507–15.

Stephensen, C. B. (1999). Burden of infection on growth failure. *Journal of Nutrition*, **129**: 534–8.

Steward, J. H. (1955). *Theory of Culture Change: The Methodology of Multilinear Evolution.* Urbana, IL: University of Illinois Press.

Stewart, K. M. (1994). Early hominid utilisation of fish resources and implications for seasonality and behaviour. *Journal of Human Evolution*, **27**: 229–45.

Stoger, R. (2008). The thrifty epigenotype: an acquired and heritable predisposition for obesity and diabetes? *BioEssays*, **30**: 156–66.

Storck, J. & Teague, W. D. (1952). *Flour for Man's Bread, A History of Milling.* Minneapolis, MN: University of Minnesota Press.

Stover, P. J. & Caudill, M. A. (2008). Genetic and epigenetic contributions to human nutrition and health: managing genome-diet interactions. *Journal of the American Dietetic Association*, **108**: 1480–7.

Strait, D. S., Weber, G. W., Neubauer, S. *et al.* (2009). The feeding biomechanics and dietary ecology of *Australopithecus africanus*. *Proceedings of the National Academy of Sciences, USA*, **106**: 2124–9.

Strassmann, B. & Dunbar, R. I. M. (1998). Human evolution and disease: putting the Stone Age in perspective. In: *Evolution in Health and Disease*, ed. S. C. Stearns, pp. 91–101. Oxford: Oxford University Press.

Strier, K. B. (2000). *Primate Behavioral Ecology.* Needham: Allyn & Bacon.

Stringer, C., Finlayson, J. C., Barton, R. N. E. *et al.* (2008). Neanderthal exploitation of marine mammals in Gibraltar. *Proceedings of the National Academy of Sciences, USA*, **105**: 14319–24.

Struhsaker, T. T. (2010). *The Red Colobus Monkeys: Variation in Demography, Behavior, and Ecology of Endangered Species.* Oxford: Oxford University Press.

Su, K.-P., Huang, S. Y., Chiu, C. C. & Shen, W. W. (2003). Omega-3 fatty acids in major depressive disorder: a preliminary double-blind, placebo-controlled trial. *European Neuropsychopharmacology*, **13**(4): 267–71.

Sugimura, T. (2000). Nutrition and dietary carcinogens. *Carcinogenesis*, **21**(3): 387–95.

Surkan, P. J., Ryan, L. M., Vieira, L. M. C., Berkman, L. F. & Peterson, K. E. (2007). Maternal social and psychological conditions and physical growth in low-income children in Piaui, Northeast Brazil. *Social Science and Medicine*, **64**: 375–88.

Suskind, R. M. & Tontisirin, K. (2001). *Nutrition, Immunity and Infection in Infants and Children.* Philadelphia, PA: Lippincott Williams and Wilkinson.

Susman, R. L. (1994). Fossil evidence for early hominid tool use. *Science*, **265**: 1570–3.

Sussmann, R. W. (1991). Primate origins and the evolution of the angiosperms. *American Journal of Primatology*, **23**: 209–23.

Suwa, G., Asfaw, B., Beyene, Y. *et al.* (1997). The first skull of *Australopithecus boisei. Nature,* **389**: 489–92.

Suwa, G., Kono, R. T., Simpson, S. W., Asfaw, B., Lovejoy, C. O. & White, T. D. (2009). Paleobiological implications of the *Ardipithecus ramidus* dentition. *Science,* **326**: 69–99.

Swallow, D. M. (2003). Genetics of lactase persistence and lactose intolerance. *Annual Review of Genetics,* **37**: 197–219.

Szalay, F. S. & Delson, E. (1979). *Evolutionary History of the Primates.* New York: Academic Press.

Szathmary, E. J. E., Ritenbaugh, C. & Goodby, C. M. (1987). Dietary change and plasma glucose levels in an Amerindian population undergoing cultural transition. *Social Science and Medicine,* **24**: 791–804.

Taghibiglou, C., Carpentier, A., Van Iderstine, S. C. *et al.* (2000). Mechanisms of hepatic very low density lipoprotein overproduction in insulin resistance: evidence for enhanced lipoprotein assembly, reduced intracellular ApoB degradation, and increased microsomal triglyceride transfer protein in a fructose-fed hamster model. *Journal of Biological Chemistry,* **275**: 8416–25.

Tavaré, S., Marshall, C. R., Will, O., Soligo, C. & Martin, R. D. (2002). Using the fossil record to estimate the age of the last common ancestor of extant primates. *Nature,* **416**: 726–9.

Taylor, A. B. (2002). Masticatory form and function in the African apes. *American Journal of Physical Anthropology,* **117**: 133–56.

(2006). Feeding behavior, diet, and the functional consequences of jaw form in orangutans, with implications for the evolution of *Pongo. Journal of Human Evolution,* **50**: 377–93.

Taylor, H. R., Robin, T. A., Lansingh, V. C., Weih, L. M. & Keeffe, J. E. (2003). A myopic shift in Australian Aboriginals: 1977–2000. *Transactions of the American Ophthalmological Society,* **101**: 107–12.

Taylor, S., Cook-Bolden, F., Rahman, Z. & Strachan, D. (2002). Acne vulgaris in skin of colour. *Journal of the American Academy of Dermatology,* **46**: S98–S106.

Teaford, M. F. & Oyen, O. J. (1989). Differences in the rate of molar wear between monkeys raised on different diets. *Journal of Dental Research,* **68**: 1513–18.

Teaford, M. F. & Ungar, P. S. (2000). Diet and the evolution of the earliest human ancestors. *Proceedings of the National Academy of Sciences, USA,* **97**: 13506–11.

Teaford, M. F. & Walker, A. (1984). Quantitative differences in dental microwear between primate species with different diets and a comment on the presumed diet of *Sivapithecus. American Journal of Physical Anthropology,* **64**: 191–200.

Teel, R. W. & Huynh, H. (1998). Modulation by phytochemicals of cytochrome P450-linked enzyme activity. *Cancer Letters,* **133**: 135–41.

Teo, C. F., Wollaston-Hayden, E. E. & Wells, L. (2010). Hexosamine flux, the O-Glcnac modification, and the development of insulin resistance in adipocytes. *Molecular and Cellular Endocrinology,* **318**: 44–53.

Terris, M. (1987). Epidemiology and the public health movement. *Journal of Public Health Policy,* **8**(3): 315–29.

Testart, A. (1982). The significance of food storage among hunter-gatherers: residence patterns, population densities, and social inequalities. *Current Anthropology*, **23**: 523–37.

The Angiosperm Phylogeny Group (2009). An update of the Angiosperm Phylogeny Group classification for the orders and families of flowering plants: APG III. *Botanical Journal of the Linnean Society*, **161**: 105–21.

Thieme, H. (2005). The Lower Palaeolithic art of hunting: the case of Schöningen 13 II-4, Lower Saxony, Germany. In: *The Individual Hominid in Context: Archaeological Investigations of Lower and Middle Palaeolithic Landscapes, Locales and Artefacts*, ed. C. Gamble & M. Porr, pp. 115–132. London: Routledge.

Thompson, W. (1929). Danger spots in world population. *American Journal of Sociology*, **34**: 959–75.

Thorpe, S. K. S., Holder, R. L. & Crompton, R. H. (2007). Origin of human bipedalism as an adaptation for locomotion on flexible branches. *Science*, **316**: 1328–31.

Thun, M. J., Peto, R., Lopez, A. D. *et al.* (1997). Alcohol consumption and mortality among middle-aged and elderly U.S. adults. *New England Journal of Medicine*, **337**: 1705–14.

Thye, T., Vannberg, F. O., Wong, S. H. *et al.* (2010). Genome-wide association analyses identifies a susceptibility locus for tuberculosis on chromosome 18q11.2. *Nature Genetics*, **42**: 739–41.

Tikkanen, M. J., Huttunen, J. K., Ehnholm, C. & Pietinen, P. (1990). Apolipoprotein E4 homozygosity predisposes to serum cholesterol elevation during high-fat diet. *Arteriosclerosis*, **10**: 285–8.

Timpson, N. J., Emmett, P. M., Frayling, T. M. *et al.* (2008). The fat mass- and obesity-associated locus and dietary intake in children. *American Journal of Clinical Nutrition*, **88**: 971–8.

Timpson, N. J., Forouhi, N. G., Brion, M.-J. *et al.* (2010). Genetic variation at the SLC23A1 locus is associated with circulating concentrations of L-ascorbic acid (vitamin C): evidence from 5 independent studies with >15,000 participants. *American Journal of Clinical Nutrition* doi: 10.3945/ajcn.2010.29438.

Tishkoff, S. A., Reed, F. A., Ranciaro, A. *et al.* (2006). Convergent adaptation of human lactase persistence in Africa and Europe. *Nature Genetics*, **39**: 31–40.

Tishkoff, S. A., Varkonyi, R., Cahinhinan, N. *et al.* (2001). Haplotype diversity and linkage disequilibrium at human G6PD: recent origin of alleles that confer malarial resistance. *Science*, **293**: 455–62.

Tomatsu, S., Orii, K. O., Fleming, R. E. *et al.* (2003). Contribution of the H63d mutation in Hfe to murine hereditary hemochromatosis. *Proceedings of the National Academy of Sciences, USA*, **100**(26): 15788–93.

Tomkins, A. (2000). Malnutrition, morbidity and mortality in children and their mothers. *Proceedings of the Nutrition Society*, **59**: 135–46.

(2002). Nutrition, infection and immunity: public health implications. In: *Nutrition and Immune Function*, ed. P. C. Calder, C. J. Field & H. S. Gill, pp. 375–412. Wallingford: CABI Publishing.

Tontisirin, K., Nantel, G. & Bhattacharjee, L. (2002). Food-based strategies to meet the challenges of micronutrient malnutrition in the developing world. *Proceedings of the Nutrition Society*, **61**: 243–50.

Toomajian, C., Ajioka, R. S., Jorde, L. B., Kushner, J. P. & Kreitman, M. (2003). A method for detecting recent selection in the human genome from allele age estimates. *Genetics*, **165**: 287–97.

Toussaint-Samat, M. (1994). *A History of Food*. Cambridge: Wiley-Blackwell.

(2009). *A History of Food*. Chichester: John Wiley and Sons.

Townsend, P. & Davidson, N. (eds.) (1982). *Inequalities in Health: The Black Report*. London: Penguin Books.

Trowell, H. C. & Burkitt, D. P. (1981). *Western Diseases: Their Emergence and Prevention*. London: Edward Arnold.

Turner, A. (1992). Large carnivores and earliest European hominids: changing determinants of resource availability during the Lower and Middle Pleistocene. *Journal of Human Evolution*, **22**: 109–26.

Turner, T. R., Anapol, F. & Jolly, C. J. (1997). Growth, development, and sexual dimorphism in vervet monkeys (*Cercopithecus aethiops*) at four sites in Kenya. *American Journal of Physical Anthropology*, **103**: 19–35.

Tylleskär, T., Howlett, W. P., Rwiza, II. T. *et al.* (1993). Konzo: a distinct disease entity with selective upper motor neuron damage. *Journal of Neurology, Neurosurgery and Psychiatry*, **56**: 638–43.

Ueno, M., Bezerra, R. M., Silva, M. S. *et al.* (2000). A high-fructose diet induces changes in pp185 phosphorylation in muscle and liver of rats. *Brazilian Journal of Medical and Biological Research*, **33**: 1421–7.

Ulijaszek, S. J. (1991). Human dietary change. *Philosophical Transactions of the Royal Society of London, B*, **334**: 271–9.

(1993). Seasonality of reproductive performance in rural Gambia. In: *Seasonality and Human Ecology*, ed. S. J. Ulijaszek & S. S. Strickland, pp. 76–88. Cambridge: Cambridge University Press.

(1996). Energetics, adaptation, and adaptability. *American Journal of Human Biology*, **8**: 169–82.

(1998). Immunocompetence. In: *Cambridge Encyclopaedia of Human Growth and Development*, ed. S. J. Ulijaszek, F. E. Johnston & M. A. Preece, p. 340. Cambridge: Cambridge University Press.

(2002). Human eating behaviour in an evolutionary ecological context. *Proceedings of the Nutrition Society*, **61**: 517–26.

(ed.) (2006). *Population, Reproduction and Fertility in Melanesia*. Oxford: Berghahn Books.

(2007). Obesity: a disorder of convenience. *Obesity Reviews*, **8** (suppl. 1): 183–7.

Ulijaszek, S. J. & Lofink, H. (2006). Obesity in biocultural perspective. *Annual Reviews of Anthropology*, **35**: 337–60.

Ulijaszek, S. J. & Strickland, S. S. (1993). *Nutritional Anthropology: Prospects and Perspectives in Human Nutrition*. London: Smith-Gordan and Company Ltd.

Ulijaszek, S. J. & Poraituk, S. P. (1983). Subsistence patterns and sago cultivation in the Purari delta. In: *The Purari – Tropical Environment of a High Rainfall River Basin*, ed. T. Petr, pp. 577–88. The Hague: Dr. W. Junk.

Ulrich, C. M. (2005). Nutrigenetics in cancer research: folate metabolism and colorectal cancer. *Journal of Nutrition*, **135**: 2698–702.

Ungar, P. S. (2010). *Mammal Teeth: Origin, Evolution and Diversity*. Baltimore, MD: The Johns Hopkins University Press.

Ungar, P. S., Grine, F. E. & Teaford, M. F. (2006). Diet in early *Homo*: a review of the evidence and a new model of adaptive versatility. *Annual Review of Anthropology*, **35**: 209–28.

  (2008). Dental microwear and diet of the Plio-Pleistocene hominin *Paranthropus boisei*. *PLoS ONE*, **3**: e2044.

Unger, R. H. (2003). Lipid overload and overflow: metabolic trauma and the metabolic syndrome. *Trends in Endocrinology and Metabolism*, **14**(9): 398–403.

United Nations Demographic Yearbook (2011). http://unstats.un.org/unsd/demographic/products/dyb/dybcens.htm.

United States Department of Agriculture (2011). http://www.ers.usda.gov/briefing/sugar/data.htm#yearbook.

Valeggia, C. R. (2009). Flexible caretakers: responses of Toba families in transition. In: *Substitute Parents: Biological and Social Perspectives on Alloparenting in Human Societies*, ed. G. Bentley & R. Mace, pp. 100–14. Oxford: Berghan Books.

Van de Poel, E., Hosseinpoor, A. R., Speybroeck, N., van Ourti, T. & Vega, J. (2008). Socioeconomic inequality in malnutrition in developing countries. *Bulletin of the World Health Organization*, **86**: 241–320.

Van Heuverswyn, F. & Peeters, M. (2007). The origins of HIV and implications for the global epidemic. *Current Infectious Disease Reports*, **9**: 338–46.

Van Heuverswyn, F., Li, Y., Neel, C. *et al.* (2006). Human immunodeficiency viruses: SIV infection in wild gorillas. *Nature*, **444**(7116): 164.

Vanhaeren, M. & d'Errico, F. (2005). Grave goods from the Saint-Germain-la-Riviere burial: evidence for social inequality in the Upper Palaeolithic. *Journal of Anthropological Archaeology*, **24**: 117–34.

Vargas, L. A. & Casillas, L. (1990). La alimentacion en Mexico durante los primeros anos de la colonia. In: *Historia General de la Medicina en Mexico: Medicina Novohispania*, vol. **XVI**, ed. F. M. Cortes, pp. 85–111. Mexico City: Academia Nacional de Medicina – Facultad de Medicina de la Universidad Nacional Autonoma de Mexico.

Varo, P. (1974). Mineral element balance and coronary heart disease. *International Journal of Vitamin Research*, **44**: 267–73.

Villamore, E., Msamanga, G., Spiegelman, D. *et al.* (2002). Effect of multivitamin and vitamin A supplements on weight gain during pregnancy among HIV-1-infected women. *American Journal of Clinical Nutrition*, **76**: 1082–90.

Villegas, A., Ropero, P., Ataulfo Gonzalez, F. *et al.* (1998). High incidence of the CD8/9 (+G) beta 0-thalassemia mutation in Spain. *Haematologica*, **83**: 1066–8.

Visalberghi, E. & Addessi, E. (2000). Seeing group members eating a familiar food enhances the acceptance of novel foods in capuchin monkeys. *Animal Behaviour*, **60**: 69–76.

Visalberghi, E. & Fragaszy, D. (1995). The behaviour of capuchin monkeys, *Cebus apella*, with novel food: the role of social context. *Animal Behaviour*, **49**: 1089–95.

Voelker, A. H. L., Rodrigues, T., Billups, K. *et al.* (2010). Variations in mid-latitude North Atlantic surface water properties during the mid-Brunhes (MIS 9–14) and their implications for the thermohaline circulation. *Climate of the Past*, **6**: 531–52.

Voight, B. F., Scott, L. J., Steinthorsdottir, V. *et al.* (2010). Twelve type 2 diabetes susceptibility loci identified through large-scale association analysis. *Nature Genetics*, **42**: 579–89.

von Schacky, C. (2007). n-3 PUFA in CVD: influence of cytokine polymorphism. *Proceedings of the Nutrition Society*, **66**: 166–70.

von Schacky, C. & Weber, P. C. (1985). Metabolism and effects on platelet function of the purified eicosapentaenoic and docosahexaenoic acids in humans. *Journal of Clinical Investigation*, **76**: 2446–50.

Vrba, E. S. (1980). Evolution, species and fossils: how does life evolve? *South African Journal of Science*, **76**: 61–84.

  (1994). An hypothesis of heterochrony in response to climatic cooling and its relevance to early hominid evolution. In: *Integrative Paths to the Past: Palaeoanthropological Advances in Honour of F. Clark Howell*, ed. R. S. Corruccini & R. L. Ciochon, pp. 345–74. New Jersey: Prentice Hall.

Walls, T. & Shingadia, D. (2004). Global epidemiology of paediatric tuberculosis. *Journal of Infection*, **48**: 13–22.

Walsh, A., Dixon, J. L., Ramm, G. A. *et al.* (2006). The clinical relevance of compound heterozygosity for the C282y and H63d substitutions in hemochromatosis. *Clinical Gastroenterology and Hepatology*, **4**: 1403–10.

Wandel, M. & Holmboe-Ottesen, G. (1992). Food availability and nutrition in a seasonal perspective: a study from the Rukwa region in Tanzania. *Human Ecology*, **20**: 89–107.

Waterland, R. A. (2009). Is epigenetics an important link between early life events and adult disease? *Hormone Research*, **71** (suppl. 1): 13–16.

Waterlow, J. C. (1988). Observations on the natural history of stunting. In: *Linear Growth Retardation in Less Developed Countries*, ed. J. C. Waterlow, pp. 1–12. New York: Raven Press.

Watson, P. E. & McDonald, B. W. (2007). Seasonal variation of nutrient intake in pregnancy: effects on infant measures and possible influence on diseases related to season of birth. *European Journal of Clinical Nutrition*, **61**: 1271–80.

Watts, D. J. & Strogatz, S. H. (1998). Collective dynamics of small world networks. *Nature*, **393**: 440–2.

Weaver, M. E. & Ingram, D. L. (1969). Morphological changes in swine associated with environmental temperature. *Ecology*, **50**: 710–13.

Weber, P. C., Fischer, S., von Schacky, C., Lorenz, R. & Strasser, T. (1986). Dietary omega-3 polyunsaturated fatty acids and eicosanoid formation in man. In: *Health*

Effects of Polyunsaturated Fatty Acids in Seafoods, ed. A. P. Simopoulos, R. R. Kifer & R. E. Martin, pp. 49–60. Orlando, FL: Academic Press.

Weissmann, C. & Aguzzi, A. (1997). Bovine spongiform encephalopathy and early onset variant Creutzfeldt–Jakob disease. *Current Opinion in Neurobiology*, **7**: 695–700.

Weller, O. (2002). The earliest salt exploitation in Europe: a salt mountain in the Spanish Neolithic. *Antiquity*, **76**: 317–18.

Wells, J. C. K. (2010). *The Evolutionary Biology of Human Body Fatness: Thrift and Control*. Cambridge: Cambridge University Press.

Weniger, G.-C. (1989). The Magdalenian in Western Central Europe: settlement pattern and regionality. *Journal of World Prehistory*, **3**: 323–72.

West, J. A. & Louys, J. (2007). Differentiating bamboo from stone tool cut marks in the zooarchaeological record, with a discussion on the use of bamboo knives. *Journal of Archaeological Science*, **34**: 512–18.

Weston, E. M., Friday, A. E., Johnstone, R. A. & Schrenk, F. (2004). Wide faces or large canines? The attractive versus the aggressive primate. *Proceedings of the Royal Society of London, B*, **271**: 416S–419S.

Wheatley, B. P. (1987). The evolution of large body size in orangutans: a model for hominoid divergence. *American Journal of Primatology*, **13**: 313–24.

Whitaker, J. W. (1975). *Feedlot Empire: Beef Cattle Feeding in Illinois and Iowa, 1840–1900*. Ames, IA: The Iowa State University Press.

White, J. S. (2008). Straight talk about high-fructose corn syrup: what it is and what it ain't. *American Journal of Clinical Nutrition*, **88**: S1716–S1721.

White, T., Suwa, G. & Asfaw, B. (1994). Australopithecus ramidus, a new species of early hominid from Aramis, Ethiopia. *Nature*, **371**: 306–12.

White, T. D., Ambrose, S. H., Suwa, G. *et al.* (2009a). Macrovertebrate paleontology and the Pliocene habitat of *Ardipithecus ramidus*. *Science*, **326**: 67–93.

White, T. D., Asfaw, B., Beyene, Y. *et al.* (2009b). *Ardipithecus ramidus* and the paleobiology of early hominids. *Science*, **326**: 64–86.

White, T. D., Wolde Gabriel, G., Asfaw, B. *et al.* (2006). Asa Issie, Aramis and the origin of *Australopithecus*. *Nature*, **440**: 883–9.

Whiten, A., Spiteri, A., Horner, V. *et al.* (2007). Transmission of multiple traditions within and between chimpanzee groups. *Current Biology* (2007), doi:10.1016/j.cub.2007.05.031.

Whittaker, N., Morton, D. R., Kinner, J. H. *et al.* (1976). The hemiacetal structure of Prostaglandin X (prostacyclin). *Prostaglandins*, **12**: 915–29.

Whybrow, P. C. (2005). *American Mania: When More Is Not Enough*. New York: W. W. Norton & Company.

Wiessner, P. & Schiefenhovel, W. (eds.) (1996). *Food and the Status Quest*. Oxford: Berghahn.

Wilcox, A. J. (2001). On the importance—and the unimportance—of birthweight. *International Journal of Epidemiology*, **30**: 1233–41.

Wilcoxon, A. J. & Russell, I. T. (1983). Birthweight and perinatal mortality: II. On weight-specific mortality. *International Journal of Epidemiology*, **12**: 319–25.

Wild, S., Roglic, G., Green, A., Sicree, R. & King, H. (2004). Global prevalence of diabetes. *Diabetes Care*, **27**(5): 1047–53.

Wilkinson, R. (1996). *Unhealthy Societies: The Afflictions of Inequality*. London: Routledge.

Wilkinson, R. & Pickett, K. (2009). *The Spirit Level: Why More Equal Societies Almost Always Do Better*. London: The Penguin Group.

Willems, E. P. & Hill, R. A. (2009). Predator-specific landscapes of fear and resource distribution: effects on spatial range use. *Ecology*, **90**: 546–55.

Williams, F., Meenagh, A., Single, R. *et al.* (2004). High resolution HLA-DRB1 identification of a Caucasian population. *Human Immunology*, **65**: 66–77.

Williams, R. J. & Martinez, N. D. (2004). Limits to trophic levels and omnivory in complex food webs: theory and data. *American Naturalist*, **163**: 458–68.

Winterhalder, B. (1981). Optimal foraging strategies and hunter-gatherer research in anthropology: theory and models. In: *Hunter-Gatherer Foraging Strategies: Ethnographic and Archeological Analyses*, ed. B. Winterhalder & E. A. Smith, pp. 218–31. Chicago, IL: University of Chicago Press.

Winterhalder, B. & Kennett, D. J. (2009). Four neglected concepts with a roleplay in explaining the origins of agriculture. *Current Anthropology*, **50**(5): 645–8.

Wireman, J. *et al.* (2006). Quantitative, longitudinal profiling of the primate fecal microbiota reveals idiosyncratic, dynamic communities. *Environmental Microbiology*, **8**(3): 490–503.

Wolfe, N. D., Dunavan, C. P. & Diamond, J. (2007). Origins of major human infectious diseases. *Nature*, **447**: 279–83.

Wood, B. (2002). Hominid revelations from Chad. *Nature*, **418**: 133–5.

Wood, B. & Collard, M. (1999). The human genus. *Science*, **284**: 65–71.

Wood, B. & Richmond, B. G. (2000). Human evolution: taxonomy and paleobiology. *Journal of Anatomy*, **196**: 19–60.

Wood, B. & Strait, D. (2004). Patterns of resource use in early *Homo* and *Paranthropus*. *Journal of Human Evolution*, **46**: 119–62.

Wood, P. J., Braaten, J. T., Scott, F. W., Riedel, D. & Poste, L. M. (1990). Comparisons of viscous properties of oat and guar gum and the effects of these and oat bran on glycemic index. *Journal of Agricultural and Food Chemistry*, **38**: 753–7.

Woodburn, J. (1982). Egalitarian Societies. *Man*, **17**: 431–51.

Wooding, S. (2006). Phenylthiocarbamide: a 75-year adventure in genetics and natural selection. *Genetics*, **172**: 2015–23.

Wooding, S., Kim, U. K., Bamshad, M. J. *et al.* (2004). Natural selection and molecular evolution in PTC, a bitter-taste receptor gene. *American Journal of Human Genetics*, **74**: 637–46.

Woods, A., Brull, D. J., Humphries, S. E. & Montgomery, M. E. (2000). Genetics of inflammation and risk of coronary artery disease: the central role of interleukin-6. *European Heart Journal*, **21**: 1574–83.

World Health Organization (2000). *Turning the Tide of Malnutrition: Responding to the Challenge of the 21st Century*. Geneva: World Health Organization.

(2003). *Diet, Nutrition and the Prevention of Chronic Diseases.* Technical Report Series 916. Geneva: World Health Organization.

(2008). *World Health Statistics 2008.* Geneva: WHO Press.

(2011a). WHO Global Infobase. Apps.who.int/infobase. Accessed 22 June 2011.

(2011b). Global Alert and Response. www.who.int. Accessed 23 July 2011.

Wrangham, R. (2009). *Catching Fire: How Cooking Made Us Human.* Basic Books.

Wrangham, R. W., Conklin, N. L., Chapman, C. A. & Hunt, K. D. (1991). The significance of fibrous foods for Kibale Forest Chimpanzees. *Philosophical Transactions of the Royal Society, B,* **334**(1270): 171–8.

Wrangham, R. W., Jones, J. H., Laden, G., Pilbeam, D. & Conklin-Brittain, N. (1999). The raw and the stolen – cooking and the ecology of human origins. *Current Anthropology,* **40**: 567–94.

Wright, K. (1991). The origins and development of ground stone assemblages in Late Pleistocene Southwest Asia. *Paleorient,* **17**: 19–45.

Wu, T., Giovannucci, E., Pichon, T. *et al.* (2004). Fructose, glycemic load, and quantity and quality of carbohydrate in relation to plasma C-peptide concentrations in US women. *American Journal of Clinical Nutrition,* **80**: 1043–9.

Wu, Y., Li, H., Loos, R. J. F. *et al.* (2008). Common variants in Cdkal1, Cdkn2a/B, Igf2bp2, Slc30a8, and Hhex/Ide genes are associated with type 2 diabetes and impaired fasting glucose in a Chinese Han population. *Diabetes,* **57**: 2834–42.

Wurtman, J. J. (1990). Carbohydrate craving. Relationship between carbohydrate intake and disorders of mood. *Drugs,* **39**(3): S49–S52.

Wurtman, R. J. & Wurtman, J. J. (1995). Brain serotonin, carbohydrate-craving, obesity and depression. *Obesity Research,* **3**(4): S477–S480.

Wynne-Edwards, K. E. (2001). Evolutionary biology of plant defences against herbivory and their predictive implications for endocrine disruptor susceptibility in vertebrates. *Environmental Health Perspectives,* **109**: 443–8.

Yajnik, C. S. & Deshmukh, U. S. (2008). Maternal nutrition, intrauterine programming and consequential risks in the offspring. *Reviews in Endocrine and Metabolic Disorders,* **9**: 203–11.

Yajnik, C. S., Lubree, H. G., Rege, S. S. *et al.* (2002). Adiposity and hyperinsulinaemia in Indians are present at birth. *Journal of Clinical Endocrinology and Metabolism,* **87**: 5575–80.

Yamamoto, T., Moriwaki, Y., Takahashi, S., Nasako, Y. & Higashino, K. (1993). Effect of lactate infusion on renal transport of purine bases and oxypurinol. *Nephron,* **65**(1): 73–6.

Yang, X., Sheng, W., Sun, G. Y. & Lee, J. C.-M. (2011). Effects of fatty acid unsaturation numbers on membrane fluidity and α-secretase-dependent amyloid precursor protein processing. *Neurochemistry International,* **58**: 321–9.

Yates, A. A. (2006). Which dietary reference intake is best suited to serve as the basis for nutrition labeling for daily values? *Journal of Nutrition,* **136**: 2457–62.

Yehuda, S., Rabinovitz, S. & Mostofsky, D. I. (2005). Mixture of essential fatty acids lowers test anxiety. *Nutritional Neuroscience,* **8**(4): 265–7.

Yesner, D. R. (1994). Seasonality and 'resource stress' among hunter-gatherers: archaeological signatures. In: *Key Issues in Hunter-Gatherer Research*, ed. E. S. Burch & L. J. Ellanna, pp. 151–68. Oxford: Berg.

Yoshida, R., Ohkuri, T., Jyotaki, M. *et al.* (2010). Endocannabinoids selectively enhance sweet taste. *Proceedings of the National Academy of Sciences, USA*, **107**: 935–9.

Young, G. & Hoffman, M. (eds.) (1993). *The Expedition of Hernando de Soto West of the Mississippi, 1541–1543.* Fayetteville, AF: Arkansas University Press.

Young, I. S. & Woodside, J. V. (2001). Antioxidants in health and disease. *Journal of Clinical Pathology*, **54**: 176–86.

Young, J. H., Chang, Y.-P.C., Kim, J.D.-O. *et al.* (2005). Differential susceptibility to hypertension is due to selection during the Out-of-Africa Expansion. *PLoS Genetics*, **1**(6): e82.

Yu, S. S., Derr, J., Etherton, T. D. & Kris-Etherton, P. M. (1995). Plasma cholesterol-predictive equations demonstrate that stearic acid is neutral and monounsaturated fatty acids are hypocholesterolemic. *American Journal of Clinical Nutrition*, **61** (5): 1129–39.

Yudkin, J. S., Stehouwer, C. D., Emeis, J. J. & Coppack, S. W. (1999). C-reactive protein in healthy subjects: associations with obesity, insulin resistance, and endothelial dysfunction. A potential role for cytokines originating from adipose tissue? *Arteriosclerosis, Thrombosis, and Vascular Biology*, **19**: 972–8.

Zapata, L., Pena-Chocarro, P. & Stika, H. P. (2004). Difusion de la agricultura en la Peninsula Iberica. In: *Actas del III Congreso del Neolítico en la Península Ibérica*, ed. R. O. Peredo, C. G-M. Piñeiro, P. A. Cabal, pp. 103–14. Santander: Servicio Publicaciones Universidad de Cantabria Santander.

Zeng, L., Dang, S., Dibley, M. J., Chang, S. & Kong, L. (2008). Impact of micronutrient supplementation during pregnancy on birth weight, duration of gestation, and perinatal mortality in rural western China: double blind cluster randomised controlled trial. *British Medical Journal*, **337**: a2001.

Zhao, J., Ding, G. H., Tao, L. *et al.* (2007). Modular co-evolution of metabolic networks. *BMC Bioinformatics*, **8**: 311–22.

Zheng, H. & Berthoud, H. R. (2008). Neural systems controlling the drive to eat: mind versus metabolism. *Physiology*, **23**: 75–83.

Zhou, W.-X., Sornette, D., Hill, R. A. & Dunbar, R. I. M. (2005). Discrete hierarchical organization of social group sizes. *Proceedings of the Royal Society of London*, **272**: 439–44.

Zhu, R. X., Hoffman, K. A., Potts, R. *et al.* (2001). Earliest presence of humans in northeast Asia. *Nature*, **413**: 413–17.

Zihlman, A. L. & McFarland, R. K. (2000). Body mass in lowland gorillas: a quantitative analysis. *American Journal of Physical Anthropology*, **113**: 61–78.

Ziltener, P. & Mueller, H.-P. (2007). The weight of the past traditional agriculture, socio-political differentiation and modern development in Africa and Asia: a cross-national analysis. *International Journal of Comparative Sociology*, **48**: 371–415.

Zimmet, P., Alberti, K. & Shaw, J. (2001). Global and societal implications of the diabetes epidemic. *Nature*, **414**: 782–7.

Zong, Y., Chen, Z., Innes, J. B. *et al.* (2007). Fire and flood management of coastal swamp enabled first rice paddy cultivation in east China. *Nature*, **449**: 459–63.

Index

CPSIA information can be obtained
at www.ICGtesting.com
Printed in the USA
FSHW022313090920
73654FS